MISCARRIAGES OF JUSTICE IN CAN

Causes, Responses, Remedies

Innocent people are regularly convicted of crimes they did not commit. A number of systemic factors have been found to contribute to wrongful convictions, including eyewitness misidentification, false confessions, informant testimony, official misconduct, and faulty forensic evidence.

In *Miscarriages of Justice in Canada*, Kathryn M. Campbell offers an extensive overview of wrongful convictions, bringing together current sociological, criminological, and legal research, as well as current case-law examples. For the first time, information on all known and suspected cases of wrongful conviction in Canada is included and interspersed with discussions of how wrongful convictions happen, how existing remedies to rectify them are inadequate, and how those who have been victimized by these errors are rarely compensated. Campbell reveals that the causes of wrongful convictions are, in fact, avoidable, and that those in the criminal justice system must exercise greater vigilance and openness to the possibility of error if the problem of wrongful conviction is to be resolved.

KATHRYN M. CAMPBELL is an associate professor in the Department of Criminology at the University of Ottawa. She is also the faculty director of Innocence Ottawa, a pro-bono, student-run innocence project that assists individuals who have been wrongly convicted.

Miscarriages of Justice in Canada

Causes, Responses, Remedies

KATHRYN M. CAMPBELL

Dear Maggie, Keep up the good fight for the wrongly convicted! Best, Kathryn

UNIVERSITY OF TORONTO PRESS
Toronto Buffalo London

© University of Toronto Press 2018
Toronto Buffalo London
utorontopress.com
Printed in the U.S.A.

ISBN 978-0-8020-9124-6 (cloth)   ISBN 978-0-8020-9406-3 (paper)

 Printed on acid-free, 100% post-consumer recycled paper with vegetable-based inks.

Library and Archives Canada Cataloguing in Publication

Campbell, Kathryn M. (Kathryn Maria), 1960–, author
Miscarriages of justice in Canada : causes, responses, remedies / Kathryn
M. Campbell.

Includes bibliographical references and index.
ISBN 978-0-8020-9124-6 (hardcover). – ISBN 978-0-8020-9406-3 (softcover)

1. Judicial error – Canada.   2. False imprisonment – Canada.   I. Title.

KE9440.C36 2018   347.71′012   C2017-906749-4
KF9756.C36 2018

This book has been published with the help of a grant from the Federation for the
Humanities and Social Sciences, through the Awards to Scholarly Publications Program,
using funds provided by the Social Sciences and Humanities Research Council of Canada.

University of Toronto Press acknowledges the financial assistance to its publishing
program of the Canada Council for the Arts and the Ontario Arts Council, an agency of
the Government of Ontario.

 Canada Council
for the Arts
Conseil des Arts
du Canada

ONTARIO ARTS COUNCIL
CONSEIL DES ARTS DE L'ONTARIO
an Ontario government agency
un organisme du gouvernement de l'Ontario

Funded by the
Government
of Canada
Financé par le
gouvernement
du Canada
 Canadä

In memory of my parents, Mary Kathryn and Sandy Campbell, with love and gratitude.

Contents

Tables

Foreword

Steven Truscott was fourteen years old when he was convicted for the murder of twelve-year-old Lynne Harper in 1959 in Goderich, Ontario. Truscott was the last person to be seen with Harper on 9 June 1959 before her body was found in a wooded area near her home two days later; she had been strangled and sexually assaulted. Truscott was initially sentenced to death, but his sentence was later commuted to life imprisonment, and public outcry about his case in part led to a moratorium on capital punishment in Canada in 1967. During that time Truscott appealed against his conviction to the Ontario Court of Appeal and the Supreme Court of Canada, but was refused by both courts (*Re Truscott*). After serving ten years in prison on his life sentence, Truscott lived a life of relative obscurity under another name to avoid unwanted attention.

Decades passed and in 2001 Truscott attempted to have his conviction reviewed, and two years later his file made its way to my desk. Interestingly enough, I myself was a teenager when Truscott, as a teenager, was accused of the rape and murder of Lynne Harper; as a law student I had studied his case but only as a capital punishment issue and certainly not as a wrongful conviction case. Then in 2004 as a minister of justice, the case was referred to me given my responsibility to make determinations about miscarriages of justice. Accordingly, I am aware of how our justice system is capable of mistakes, but also how mechanisms exist to rectify them.

The process of conviction review takes place in Canada only when a convicted person has exhausted all of their appeals and there is new and significant information about the case that, if it had been heard at trial, may have altered the outcome. Given that conviction review is an extraordinary measure and does not represent a fourth level of appeal, the convicted person must demonstrate that a miscarriage of justice likely occurred. In this case, there were some questions raised regarding the timing of Lynne Harper's death, based on stomach contents evidence, which at trial had demonstrated that Truscott was the only individual capable of murdering her within that time frame. New evidence proffered at this juncture pointed to the flaws in reasoning made regarding the forensic evidence, questions raised around the alleged scientific "certainty" of earlier evidence around the time of death and the possibility of exonerating Mr Truscott.

In most cases the capable lawyers involved with the Criminal Conviction Review Group assess the merits of applications for conviction review; however, given the sensitive nature of this case and its historical significance, a former justice of the Quebec Court of Appeal, the Honourable Justice Fred Kaufman, was appointed to review the case. His excellent and thorough assessment of the factors involved in Mr Truscott's conviction, and my ongoing discussions with him and sustained examination of the file, resulted in my determination that "there was a reasonable basis to conclude that a miscarriage of justice had likely occurred" in this case. That determination, however, did not resolve the issue of remedy. In effect once a determination that a miscarriage of justice has occurred is made, the minister of justice can either quash the conviction and order a new trial or refer the matter to the appellate court in the jurisdiction for a fresh hearing on the merits. After agonizing review I decided to refer the matter to the Ontario Court of Appeal, as I appreciated that if I quashed the conviction the Ontario attorney general would stay the proceedings and therefore a "justice" determination would not be had.

When I announced my decision it was seriously criticized by, among others, Mrs Truscott, who felt that I should have quashed the conviction and which would have established her husband's innocence. The problem was that quashing the conviction was not a stand-alone remedy. It still required the ordering of a new trial, which was not in my hands, and which would not have taken place. Accordingly, so that Mr Truscott could finally have justice rendered in his case, I referred it to the Ontario Court of Appeal, which, upon review of the evidence, determined in August 2007, "Mr. Truscott's conviction was a miscarriage of justice and must be quashed" (*R. v. Truscott* [2007] ONCA No. 575).

This case is an example of the system correcting its own errors, albeit many decades after the fact. In this book, Kathryn Campbell has demonstrated that conviction review comes at the end of a long process for convicted persons, and for many it is inaccessible due to high costs and evidentiary burdens. She further argues, and it is a position that I share, that Canada is in need of a commission that is independent from government, similar to the English Criminal Cases Review Commission, and that the minister of justice may not be in the best position to make decisions around conviction review, nor may the resources be available for that purpose. As Justice MacCallum (in the Commission of Inquiry into the Wrongful Conviction of David Milgaard, 2006, on p. 411 of the inquiry and p. 290 of this book) put it:

> The federal Minister of Justice should not be the gatekeeper to determine whether an alleged wrongful conviction should be returned to the Court for further review. The involvement of a federal politician in the review of individual cases of alleged wrongful conviction invites public advocacy and accusations of political influence … As long as responsibility for conviction review remains with the federal Minister of Justice, there will be the potential for political pressure and public advocacy to play a role in the decision making process, or, at the very least, for the perception to exist that the decision can be so influenced. The conviction review process must not only be truly independent, it must be seen to be independent.

In this book Professor Campbell presents an overview of an impressive number of issues related to miscarriages of justice, incorporating research, case law, and legal analyses to shed light on not only how wrongful convictions happen in Canada, but also how they can be rectified and prevented in future. This is the first book-length academic study and analysis of wrongful convictions in Canada, and it is unique in that it attempts to situate the study of miscarriages of justice within the context of discussions around theory, justice, criminal law, and due process. While a rather ambitious goal, Professor Campbell manages to capture the nature and extent of the problem of wrongful convictions in Canada and reveal how this problem has emerged, how it is addressed, and how it can be prevented. She outlines how wrongful convictions occur when innocent people are mistakenly identified as perpetrators of crimes, how they sometimes confess to things they have not done, how they may be unfairly targeted by police and prosecution, and how jailhouse informants may lie to implicate the innocent for their own benefit. Further, Professor Campbell illustrates how the means to rectify wrongful convictions through the systems of appeal, conviction review, and compensation are inadequate to address the needs of the wrongly convicted. Finally, her examination of restorative justice practices, the need for an independent commission for conviction review, and a statutory scheme for compensation of the wrongly convicted all represent important remedies to the problem, remedies that are tenable and do not require significant fiscal burdens to cash-strapped provincial and federal governments.

What is especially compelling about this book is the significant contribution that Professor Campbell makes to the literature and to understanding miscarriages of justice. In particular, appendix A of this book is comprised of an impressive overview of all known cases of wrongful conviction, as well as data on the prevalence of the contributing factors for each case. This wealth of data can be used as a source for future analyses related to policy affecting the wrongly convicted, as well as for comparisons with other jurisdictions.

As well, tables 8, 9, and 13 represent important compilations of data that advance our knowledge about wrongful convictions. Table 8 in chapter 8 ("Forensic Evidence and Expert Testimony") illustrates the problematic cases involving the former Dr Charles Smith and demonstrates what can arise when expert testimony is accepted without question and afforded too much weight by the courts. Table 9 in chapter 9 illustrates wrongful conviction cases on appeal ("Conventional Remedies through the Courts and Conviction Review"), and reveals a great deal about the error-correction function of these courts. Finally, Table 13 in chapter 11 ("Compensation: The Obstacle Course") outlines the cases of thirty-three Canadians who have received compensation for being wrongly convicted and imprisoned and illustrates the long wait-times, provincial variation, and arbitrary nature of the process. Other contributions to the literature include chapter 12 ("The Impact of Public Lobbying on Wrongful Convictions: The Role of the Media, Lobby Groups, and Innocence Projects"), which illustrates how wrongful convictions have now become a mainstream phenomenon, and how coverage of specific cases has often had the effect of forcing governments to revisit them and at times have resulted in exonerations. Of particular note is chapter 13 on comparative law ("Lessons from Other Jurisdictions") where Professor Campbell illustrates how other jurisdictions address wrongful convictions and may provide lessons for Canada.

Miscarriages of Justice in Canada: Causes, Responses, Remedies adds its powerful and scholarly voice to the burgeoning field of innocence scholarship. This book will be indispensable not only for law students and legal scholars, but to others in the humanities and the social sciences who may be interested in miscarriages of justice. As Professor Campbell notes in the introduction to her book, "through an examination of the many contributing factors within the context of current conceptions of justice, criminality, fairness, and due process, it is hoped that the nature of miscarriages of justice in Canada will be revealed." Professor Campbell has done this exceptionally well, and even more so has provided a compendium on miscarriages of justice in Canada that will serve as a model for future study of this intractable problem and as a source book for those working to free the wrongly convicted.

Professor Irwin Cotler
Emeritus Professor of Law at McGill University
Former Minister of Justice and Attorney General of Canada
Chair, Raoul Wallenberg Centre for Human Rights

Acknowledgments

The genesis for this book really began many years ago when I first viewed the film *Hurricane*, which details the wrongful conviction of Rubin Carter for a triple homicide in the state of New Jersey in 1966. During the scene where he is found guilty, I recall feeling an overwhelming sense of dread as to what that experience must have actually been like, to be accused and then convicted of a horrific crime, and at the same time be completely innocent. That sense of great injustice over wrongful convictions continues to motivate my research today and hence the desire to produce a Canadian edition that brings together research, case law, and commentary about this significant issue.

The idea for the book itself began over fourteen years ago, following a conference I co-chaired with Myriam Denov at the University of Ottawa in 2002 which examined wrongful convictions in Canada, bringing together lawyers, policy analysts, academics, researchers, and the wrongly convicted themselves. A special edition of the *Canadian Journal of Criminology and Criminal Justice* in 2004 that followed the conference was one of the first contributions to the literature examining the issue of wrongful convictions from within a Canadian context. At that time, I was struck at the dearth of Canadian content in academic literature around wrongful convictions and innocence scholarship; this book is thus an attempt to add to what is now a growing body of scholarship. While a rather ambitious goal, I do hope that this volume provides a basis for further study of this intractable problem.

I want to thank a number of people who willingly gave of their time in helping me put together this volume. Each contributed in their own unique fashion and I am grateful to them all, in no particular order of importance.

I wish to thank Alexander Campbell, who was invaluable in the overall editing of the final draft of this book and who helped to put together the appendix of cases.

I am especially grateful to Professor Chris Bruckert, who was invaluable for her great patience in helping me to grasp the nuances of sociological theory.

I am grateful to Professor Dominique Robert, who helped in clarifying Quebec criminal justice policy on the use of informants by the courts.

I also want to thank Mihael Cole, who assisted me in better understanding the role of the Crown attorney in the criminal trial process.

I am thankful to Laura Sciascia, who in her capacity as a bio-chemist helped to clarify the complexity of DNA science.

A number of people provided guidance around criminal case law, and I am especially grateful to Justice Lori-Renée Weitzman and also Justice Patrick Healy for pointing me in the direction of a number of significant cases relevant to the study of wrongful convictions.

Many thanks, too, to Professor Marcel Merette, who in his capacity as (then) vice-dean/research of the Faculty of Social Sciences (now dean of the Faculty of Social Sciences), University of Ottawa, generously provided funding for a number of research assistants.

I am extremely grateful to several research assistants, who have provided invaluable support in researching the minutiae of this book, including David D'Intino, Marshneil Vaz, Randie Greco, Erica Giulione, and Megan Mitchell. I must also underscore the excellent work of four extraordinary assistants, Amy Conroy, Michael Lait, Laura Case, and Pam Zbarsky, without whose help this book would never have been written, let alone finished.

I would like to especially thank the three anonymous reviewers who provided important suggestions and insights into the final draft of this manuscript.

Finally, there are a number of people who provided support and overall encouragement in the writing of this volume, and they include Calvin Finn, Mary Martha Campbell, Patricia Campbell, Myriam Denov, Peter McCarthy, Janet Rhodes, Arleen Rotchin, Tara Santini, Kerry Scullion, Cheryl Webster, Loretta Kucic, Jody Markow, and Win Wahrer. Last, but certainly not least, I want to thank Craig Norman, whose love and faith in me is always the greatest source of encouragement.

While I am indebted to these people and others for their assistance, any and all errors contained in this text are solely my own.

MISCARRIAGES OF JUSTICE IN CANADA

Causes, Responses, Remedies

Chapter One

Introduction

Thomas D'Arcy McGee came to Canada in 1857 by way of Ireland and the United States. In his early career, D'Arcy McGee was a newspaper man, editor of the *Boston Pilot*, parliamentary correspondent for the Dublin *Freeman*, one of the leaders of the Young Ireland movement, and part of an unsuccessful uprising against the Crown (Kirwin, 1981). A champion of the rights and welfare of the poor, both in rural Irish communities and American Irish urban ghettos, he began a newspaper in Montreal in 1857 and was elected to the Legislative Assembly in 1858. Historically speaking, McGee is considered a poet, a statesman, and a peacemaker and was one of the founding Fathers of the Confederation of Canada. At that time, however, he was also considered a young radical, a traitor, and a fomenter of discord and conflict. These drastically different views of one of Canada's founding fathers are also apparent in the ongoing debate as to who was responsible for his death – he was killed by a single bullet to the head on Sparks Street in Ottawa on 7 April 1868. Police efforts quickly focused on one suspect – Patrick Whelan – and evidence soon began to mount pointing to Whelan as the killer. Following a brief trial, Whelan was found guilty and hanged, in front of a crowd of five thousand, on 11 February 1869.

Similar to modern-day miscarriages of justice, many factors appeared to co-occur that resulted in what has been described as one of Canada's earliest wrongful convictions.[1] D'Arcy McGee was a politician and a radical; his assassination was a high-profile one and received much attention in the press. The murder was called "an act of moon-struck madness" and the Montreal *Herald* ran the following headline: "NO DOUBT WHELAN GUILTY."[2] The police were under great pressure to solve the murder quickly and the government offered a $2,000 reward for capture of the assassin. Eyewitnesses described a man resembling Whelan within the vicinity of the murder, but most evidence against him was circumstantial. It was Whelan's political leanings as a Fenian[3] sympathizer that worked against him. Yet he proclaimed his innocence until the very end, stating, "They've got to find me guilty yet."

What is interesting to note about this case, over 140 years later, is that the factors that influenced this alleged wrongful conviction and execution continue to contribute to miscarriages of justice today. The D'Arcy McGee murder was a prominent case that played out in the media, the victim was a politician, police were under great pressure to solve the crime, and the bulk of the evidence against the only suspect was, as noted, highly circumstantial. The objective of this book is to provide an accounting of how these issues continue to plague our modern-day criminal justice system. Through an examination of the many contributing factors, within the context of current conceptions of justice, criminality, fairness, and due process, it is hoped that the nature of miscarriages of justice in Canada will be revealed. A further focus of the book, and perhaps unique to Canada, are policy responses to this problem, as evidenced through conviction review, commissions of inquiry, and compensation. The purpose of the analysis here is to bring together current sociological, criminological, and legal research and thinking, as well as innocence scholarship and current case-law examples, in situating the issue of miscarriages of justice within the Canadian context.

This introductory chapter provides some insights into the ongoing debates in the literature regarding how this problem has been defined, measured, and studied. The concepts of wrongful convictions or miscarriages of justice are constructs weighted with further ambiguous notions of justice, due process, and questions of innocence. In order to begin a book examining such issues, it is important that these terms be investigated, and to an extent clarified, to provide a framework for understanding what is to follow. This, of course, leads to further questions about the extent of the problem given the difficulty as to how to define these concepts, an issue that is the subject of dissension within legal and criminological circles, it is not surprising that the extent of the problem is also considered immeasurable.

This chapter offers some considerations on the concept of miscarriage of justice as a human-rights violation as well as within the context of social harm. It also offers reflections on how the problem has been studied in the past, as well as providing an overview of the limitations of this current project. Finally, the chapter ends with a brief summary of the book's different sections.

Definitions

Miscarriages of Justice

One oft-used definition of a miscarriage of justice is when an individual who is in fact innocent of the crime is accused, convicted, or imprisoned; however, this definition is insufficient to cover all of the possible miscarriages of justice that can occur. In his introduction to *Miscarriages of Justice: A Review of Justice in Error*, Walker (1999a) underlines the difficulty in defining the term. He points out that our conception of justice itself is fraught with ambiguity, innuendo, and confusion, which makes defining what it is not equally if not more problematic. Walker adopts an individualistic rights-based approach to defining miscarriages of justice, which can occur

> ... whenever suspects or defendants or convicts are treated by the State in breach of their rights, whether because of, first, deficient processes or, second, the laws which are applied to them or, third, because there is no factual justification for the applied treatment or punishment; fourth whenever suspects or defendants or convicts are treated adversely by the State to a disproportionate extent in comparison with the need to protect the rights of others; fifth, whenever the rights of others are not effectively or proportionately protected or vindicated by State action against wrongdoers or, sixth, by State law itself. (Walker, 1999a, 33)

Another category of the wrongly convicted, for Walker, constitutes those who are factually innocent, although he does not always qualify those as miscarriages of justice per se, since, according to him, the appeals process itself may rectify the system's own errors. This logic would thus dictate that a miscarriage of justice in this latter sense would include only those cases that failed on appeal and were heard by the Criminal Cases Review Commission (CCRC), a body that adjudicates miscarriage-of-justice cases that have gone through the court system in the United Kingdom.

Similar to this perspective, Greer focuses on human-rights issues that accompany miscarriages of justice, and while his definition recognizes the conviction of a factually innocent person as constitutive of a miscarriage of justice, he also recognizes other categorizations (1994). They include those cases characterized as representing "unjustified avoidance of conviction" (due to defects in criminal law or procedure, decisions not to charge or prosecute, or unjustified acquittals) and those termed "unjustified convictions" (due to criminalization of conduct that should be lawful, plea, charge, and sentence bargaining, convictions through anti-terrorist processes, convictions stemming from impropriety, and mistaken convictions) (1994, 63–73). Naughton's conception of what constitutes a miscarriage of justice is likely the broadest comprising a number of competing perspectives. This includes a lay perspective (gleaned from media and government sources) that focuses on the wrongful conviction of the factually innocent or the wrongful acquittal of the factually guilty (2013, 16) and a criminal justice perspective that seeks to "determine whether there is a sufficiency of admissible evidence to find defendants guilty or not guilty of the specific criminal offences that they are charged with"; here he is referring to "legal" innocence (20). His definition also includes consideration of the due-process perspective, as exemplified by Walker's rights-based approach, although Naughton believes this conceptualization is flawed from a sociological point of view. He outlines how the term miscarriage of justice is too limiting to cover all the types of errors, malpractice, and misconduct that occur in these cases, and proposes an alternative – "abortions of justice" – which are thought to "occur when actors either internal or external to the workings of the criminal justice process knowingly and intentionally cause wrongful convictions" (29). Furthermore, Naughton also divides miscarriages of justice into types: "exceptional," "routine," and "mundane" (2007). For him, the exceptional cases are those that the Criminal Cases Review Commission refers back to the Court of Appeal, the routine cases are those quashed by the Court of Appeal on first appeal, and the mundane cases are those quashed by the Crown Court after appeal from Magistrates Court on first appeal. Naughton also points out that the media focus on mainly exceptional, high-profile cases results in a distortion of the true scale of the problem and serves to downplay the harms that occur in the less serious cases (2007).

Wrongful Convictions and Innocence: Actual, Factual, Procedural

The term miscarriage of justice is often used interchangeably with wrongful conviction. Huff, Rattner, and Sagarin (1996, xxii), some of the first American innocence scholars, restrict their definition to wrongful convictions and focus on "cases in which the convicted persons did not commit the crimes alleged – in other words, they are behaviourally innocent of the crimes." Humphrey and Westervelt (2001) define wrongful convictions in two ways: "(1) the defendant is found guilty at trial but, in fact, is innocent; and/or (2) the adjudicatory process is significantly compromised by prejudicial and other potentially reversible errors, regardless of the accused's guilt or innocence" (7).

Other authors have focused more attention on defining the concept of innocence per se.[4] Medwed (2008) has in fact coined the term "innocentrism" to describe the growing innocence movement comprised of the proliferation of innocence projects, legislative developments that facilitate DNA forensic analysis, and policy changes to address known factors that contribute to wrongful conviction. He argues that this term, while not a panacea, provides a focus that can complement an emphasis on substantive and procedural rights at the core of criminal law. The debate itself surrounds the conceptual of factual/actual innocence versus that of procedural innocence. Givelber differentiates the two terms: "Actual innocence means what it says – the defendant did not commit the crime of which he has been convicted. Wrongfully-convicted defendants may or may not be actually innocent; their defining characteristic is that their convictions were secured as a result of a material legal error" (1997, 1317n.92).

Similarly, Siegel (2005) argues that wrongful convictions are not restricted to those cases of "factual innocence" but rather include "any conviction achieved in part through the violation of constitutional rights or through the use of systems and procedures that render the proceedings fundamentally unfair" (1219n.1). This latter category essentially represents procedural innocence. Burnett (2002) also recognizes the difficulty with the term innocence; the popular public connotation is that of a blameless individual; however, the legal system has only the discrete categories of guilty/not guilty. Findley argues that in fact there are many standards of innocence, depending on whether the term is being identified for research or litigation purposes, given the jurisdiction and nature of proceedings (2011). He also warns of the danger of too narrow a construction of innocence to only "wrong-person" cases since that fails to accommodate the majority of innocent people in the criminal justice system. Moreover, Garrett, in his study of the first 250 American, post-conviction DNA exonerees, found that courts in the United States are reticent to recognize innocence and often deny relief by finding harmless error to account for the appellant's guilt (2008a, 2011) and that the U.S. constitution holds no claim of innocence.

Roach and Trotter (2005) have situated the concept of miscarriage of justice within the context of the so-called War on Terror. Similar to Walker's earlier arguments about the unjust application of laws against Irish terrorist suspects in the United Kingdom in the 1970s and 1980s, Roach and Trotter illustrate how the rights of individuals continue to be breached in the current War on Terror – and in many ways, much more so than in the past. They argue that measures taken since 11 September 2001 to address the threat of terrorism in both North America and parts of Europe have resulted in miscarriages of justice for those designated as enemy combatants or inadmissible aliens. A by-product of excessive and forceful governmental reactions to real and alleged terrorist activity is insufficient recognition and treatment of the rights of individuals to whom they are applied. The emergent discourse regarding miscarriage of justice within the context of terrorism amply illustrates the dangers involved when governments circumvent the fetters of criminal prosecutions and use immigration and military law to detain and deport individuals suspected of terrorist activity.[5] For Roach and Trotter, a narrower definition of miscarriage of justice or wrongful conviction "should be triggered whenever a person is detained in a manner that does not provide sufficient safeguards for the determination of whether the criteria for detention accurately apply to that person. In other words, our focus is on factual innocence as defined by the relevant law whether that be the law of war, immigration law or criminal trials" (1037).

Innocence in Canadian Criminal Law

Recent scholarship has underscored the limitations of Canadian law in establishing innocence (Roach, 2008; Sherrin, 2010). From a Canadian perspective, Roach (2010) has described "actual innocence" as an American export and as much of a construct, legally, socially, and politically, as connotations of guilt. Given that the legal system is limited to findings for either guilt or acquittal, there is little room for establishing a finding of factual innocence. A recent pronouncement in the Ontario Court of Appeal provided some clarity as to that court's position on innocence. William Mullins Johnson was wrongly convicted in his niece's death and sought a finding of factual innocence from the court (cf. Campbell 2012). While the court entered an acquittal, it refused his request and stated that it had "no jurisdiction to make a formal legal declaration of factual innocence."[6] It went on to say that "there are important policy reasons for not, in effect, recognizing a third verdict, other than 'guilty' or 'not guilty,' of 'factually innocent.' The most compelling, and, in our view, conclusive reason is the impact it would have on other persons found not guilty by criminal courts."[7] Moreover, the Lamer Commission of Inquiry,[8] which, under the chairmanship of Justice Antonio Lamer, examined three wrongful convictions in Newfoundland and Labrador in the 1990s, found that "a criminal trial does not address 'factual innocence.' The criminal trial is to determine whether the Crown has proven its case beyond a reasonable doubt. If so, the accused is guilty. If not, the accused is not guilty. There is no finding of factual innocence since it would not fall within the ambit or purpose of the criminal law" (2006, 320).

On account of the myriad influences that affect how the concept is defined, and for the purposes of this book, the term miscarriage of justice will borrow from Walker's individual rights-based definition. Thus, a miscarriage of justice is understood to have occurred in cases where deficient processes resulted in a person being convicted of a crime who is in fact innocent of the charge and whose wrongful conviction is not detected through ordinary courts. This is similar to most standardized definitions of innocence, and one that is used by many innocence projects, where innocence is described as situations where individuals have been accused of crimes of which they did not commit or where a crime was never actually committed.[9] This working definition does not deny that other forms of miscarriage of justice occur; rather, it is a means of limiting the focus of the multitudinous research and case law to be examined. While recognizing that the definition is somewhat narrow, it is necessary to have a starting point that is manageable; thus, process-related types of miscarriages of justice will be the focus of this book.

Incidence: Measuring the Immeasurable

Attempts to measure the extent of wrongful conviction have been described as a "positivistic fallacy."[10] In essence, any actual number estimate is likely inaccurate, given the difficulties inherent in establishing what exactly constitutes a wrongful conviction, and, in turn, how frequently it may occur. The debates surround whether the problem is "epidemic or episodic" (Simon, 2006) or in other words an "aberration or systemic problem" (Uphoff, 2006). At extreme ends of the continuum are estimates that cases of wrongful convictions range from tens of thousands annually, including all routine cases of successful appeals against criminal convictions,[11] to Justice Antonin Scalia's pronouncement that American convictions have "an error rate of .027 percent – or to put it another way, a success rate of 99.973 percent,"[12] or Judge Learned Hand's oft-quoted maxim that "our [criminal] procedure has always been haunted by the ghost of the innocent man convicted. It is an unreal dream."[13] Another extreme opinion regarding the incident of the wrongly convicted comes from Hoffman (2007), who describes what he terms the "myth" of factual innocence, or rather the fallacy that wrongful conviction is a regular occurrence.[14] Hoffman justifies his argument by asserting that, while there may have been approximately 500 known wrongfully convicted rape and homicide defendants over the previous two decades,[15] at the same time there were altogether 40 million felony cases filed that were not overturned by the courts (2007, 671), which, according to him, is not a bad error rate. Taken further, however, Hoffman's argument falls apart, since there is an implicit assumption that, absent evidence to the contrary, all of these other unchallenged convictions are "rightful." This type of thinking neglects the consideration that many plea bargains are pleas of convenience to end the expense and inconvenience of a trial, particularly for summary or misdemeanour offences, regardless of actual guilt or innocence.[16]

Consequently, it is not uncommon to find very wide ranges and estimates of the incidence of wrongful conviction in the literature, the bulk of it emanating from the United States. For many years, Huff, Ratner, and Sagarin's early study of wrongful conviction held sway, with its estimate that .5 per cent (or half of 1 per cent) of all convictions occurring in the United States were possibly in error (Huff, Rattner, and Sagarin, 1986). This would translate to approximately 5,000–10,000 cases of wrongful conviction annually; however, that number should be treated cautiously, because their study took place in only one jurisdiction.[17] A later survey of justice officials in another state confirmed this earlier figure of at least 0.5 per cent as plausible (Zalman et al., 2008), and a study that indicated a 2.3 per cent error rate for death-penalty cases, while not directly comparable,[18] lends some support for the lower figure (Gross and O'Brien, 2008).

In their deconstruction of exonerations of false convictions in the United States from 1989 to 2003, Gross et al., (2005) believe that any guess at the number of wrongful convictions in that country would be in the tens of thousands (551). At the same time, Forst (2004) cautions against taking estimates at their face value and believes that the "speculative nature of these estimates cannot be overemphasized"

(5n.10). He argues that 10,000 is both too high and too low; too high in that some wrongful convictions are due to procedural errors in cases with "true" offenders, and too low in that the rate of erroneous convictions is higher for felonies than for capital crimes.

In a later study Gross (2008) makes a compelling argument that, beyond murder and sexual-assault cases (where DNA evidence, when present, can effectively exonerate individuals), very little is, and can be, known about any other aspects of false convictions. He states that over 95 per cent of the known exonerations in the United States are either murder or rape cases but these in fact account for only a small fraction (2 per cent) of all felony convictions, and very little is known about the frequency of false convictions for the vast majority of other crimes.

Innocence scholarship in the United States indicates that the accepted "estimate," now shorthand for a "general felony wrongful conviction rate of between ½ of 1% and 1% … is a subjective judgment based on an assessment of the present overall condition of the criminal justice system in the United States" (Zalman, 2012, 230). The debates about incidence in that country continue and reflect less a question of mathematical precision than the divisiveness characteristic of the political culture. Those leaning towards the higher end of the spectrum endorse a position that wrongful conviction is a widespread problem, with damaging repercussions demanding immediate action, while those on the other end speak of it as an irregularity, troublesome but hardly worth the attention it has garnered and unwittingly bringing the entire criminal justice system into disrepute. Zalman recognizes that, whatever estimate is ultimately used, it is no more than a hypothesis, and his position is that regardless of whether the estimate is .5 per cent, 1 per cent, or 3 per cent, it should be used to support innocence reform activity (2012). The frequently updated American National Registry of Exonerations[19] currently lists its number of exonerations at 2,143 (from 1989 to 2017), and although this number is not contextualized within all criminal convictions for a given year, it provides some evidence as to the number of cases ultimately "caught" by the system.

Early rates in the United Kingdom indicate that, until 1991, the Home Office[20] received 700–800 petitions per year from individuals who believed they were victims of miscarriages of justice.[21] Moreover, evidence presented at the Runciman Commission, a royal commission on criminal justice held during the early 1990s, found in a survey of Crown Court cases that "problematic" convictions occurred at a rate of 2 per cent (250 cases per annum) in the view of judges and 17 per cent (about 2,000 annually) in the view of defence lawyers (Zander and Henderson, 1993). A study for the National Association of Parole Officers in Britain at Long Lartin prison in 1992 revealed that up to 6 per cent of inmates may have been wrongly convicted (Carvel, 1992). More recent statistics for the Scottish Criminal Cases Review Commission (SCCRC) further reflect small percentages: with an annual application rate of 100 cases (which is approximately 0.002 per cent of the Scottish population or 0.1 per cent of convicted persons annually), it refers only 4.5 per cent of those cases back to the Court of Appeal (Leverick et al., 2017). While not reflective of the percentage of wrongful convictions in Scotland per se, these estimates reveal that only a small number of felony convictions ever make it to the SCCRC for review and even smaller percentages are found to be unsafe and referred back to the Court of Appeal, Criminal Division.

In Canada, while there is a growing body of innocence scholarship, there has been only one attempt to date to estimate the number of wrongful convictions statistically; McLellan (2012a) proffers a Canadian rate of wrongful convictions based on the American "estimate." His figures indicate that, of the 403,340 criminal cases decided by Canadian courts in 2010, 262,616 resulted in findings of guilt and 87,214 received custodial dispositions. According to McLellan (2012a, 6), that total, when based on the high end of the American estimate of 1 per cent, translates into 872 wrongful convictions in Canada for that year.[22] Not surprisingly, this estimate is substantially less than the American one, based in a large measure on the fact that there are fewer annual felony convictions (or convictions for indictable offences) in Canada and thus fewer individuals serving a term of incarceration.

The cases listed in appendix A and in Table 1 below provide a snapshot of what is publicly known about several recent criminal cases in Canada which have come before the courts and media and in which a miscarriage of justice likely occurred. Considering the difficulty in establishing a reliable estimate of wrongful convictions in Canada at any given time, the information on these cases at best simply reflects current information about these cases alone and should not be taken as a definitive picture of the reality of miscarriages of justice in Canada. The information contained in the appendix was derived from media sources, reported cases, government publications, and lobby-group websites and is thus limited in scope; yet, though these approximations are at best rough, they do provide some insights into the problem. In some instances the individuals have had their cases revisited by the courts as a result of a conviction review (twenty cases), others have also been compensated for their ordeal (thirty-two), and the majority have had their cases overturned by the courts through the ordinary process of appeal (fifty).[23] What was also revealed was that few women are wrongfully convicted in Canada (six women versus sixty-four men, confirmed; two women versus eleven men, suspected), which likely reflects the existing gender disparity found in criminal convictions overall. Moreover, the cases involving women were more likely for crimes against children (seven of eight cases), again reflecting the reality that woman are often more involved with the raising of children and thus are more likely to be involved in crimes against them.

The information in Table 1 demonstrates the great provincial variation in the numbers of cases, with Ontario evincing the greatest numbers (thirty-one) and virtually none found in Yukon or Nunavut. While the absence of cases in these territories and the low numbers from the Northwest Territories (two) may lead to the conclusion that few wrongful convictions actually occur there, the limited data preclude the drawing of any firm conclusions. At the same time, the gross overrepresentation of Indigenous prisoners in the criminal justice statistics of the territories may be indicative of other, racially based difficulties with these territorial justice systems.[24]

These 83 cases also provide some information, albeit limited, as to the role of a number of well-known contributing factors in wrongful convictions. As will be discussed in greater detail in later chapters, a great deal of wrongful-conviction research and innocence scholarship has pointed to the presence of several well-established factors that have repeatedly contributed to miscarriages of justice. They include eyewitness misidentification (chapter 2), police misconduct (chapter 3), ineffective counsel and prosecutorial misconduct (chapter 4), false or unreliable

Table 1. Provincial variation in Canadian wrongful-conviction cases

Province/Territory	Number of Wrongful Convictions	Number of Suspected Wrongful Convictions
Alberta	8	2
British Columbia	4	1
Manitoba	4	1
New Brunswick	2	2
Newfoundland and Labrador	4	0
Northwest Territories	2	0
Nova Scotia	3	1
Nunavut	0	0
Ontario	31	2
Prince Edward Island	2	0
Quebec	9	3
Saskatchewan	1	1
Yukon	0	0
Total	**70**	**13**

confessions (chapter 5), jailhouse informants/co-accused testimony (chapter 6), and mistaken or problematic expert testimony or evidence (chapter 7). Table 2 reflects the numbers and overall percentage of these factors in the seventy confirmed cases contained in appendix A.[25]

What this small survey reveals is that the most common contributing factor to wrongful convictions is eyewitness misidentification (44 per cent), followed by problematic police investigation (39 per cent), police/Crown failure to disclose evidence (30 per cent), mistaken or problematic forensic/expert testimony/evidence (27 per cent), fabricated complainant testimony (27 per cent), unreliable jailhouse informant/co-accused testimony (21 per cent), erroneous judicial instructions (19 per cent), false confessions (10 per cent), racial prejudice (10 per cent), overzealous prosecution (10 per cent), and, finally, poor legal representation (3 per cent). Significantly, most cases demonstrated evidence of one or more of the contributing factors; it was rare that only a single factor had an impact on the conviction in error. As noted, these numbers must be treated cautiously since they are neither exclusive nor reflective of the complete picture on wrongful convictions in Canada; what they do indicate is that the factors that appear to contribute to wrongful convictions in these cases are similar to those found in other jurisdictions. Moreover, for these Canadian cases, the majority of the wrongful convictions came to light only after many years of lobbying and legal intervention. Similarly, very few of the individuals in these cases have actually received compensation: only 32 of the 70 cases, or 46 per cent. The numbers and percentages likely reflect only a small portion of the actual cases, given the myriad difficulties inherent to detection, the loss of cases through attrition, and the fact that many cases never come to light at all.

Comparison with figures from two American sources is informative. Percentages found from the National Registry of Exonerations are contained in Table 3 and the Innocence Project in Table 4. The Registry, a project of the University of California Irvine Newkirk Center for Science and Society, the University of Michigan Law School, and Michigan State University College of Law, provides a comprehensive overview of factors relating to the number of known exonerations of

Table 2. Evidentiary and procedural issues in Canadian wrongful-conviction cases

Evidentiary / Procedural Issue	Evidence of Casual or Contributing Factor	Percentages of Wrongful Conviction Cases
Fabricated, erroneous, or unreliable eyewitness identification	31	44.28%
Problematic police investigation or police misconduct	27	38.57%
Police/Crown failure to disclose evidence	21	30%
Mistaken or problematic forensic or expert evidence	19	27.14%
Fabricated or problematic witness or complainant testimony	19	27.14%
Unreliable co-accused testimony or jailhouse informant testimony	15	21.43%
Erroneous judicial instructions	13	18.57%
False confessions	7	10%
Racial prejudice	7	10%
Overzealous or malicious prosecution	6	8.57%
Poor legal representation	2	2.85%

Table 3. Data from the National Registry of Exonerations

Contributing Factor	National Registry of Exonerations
Mistaken eyewitness testimony	32%
Official misconduct	47%
False or misleading forensic evidence	23%
Jailhouse informants	7%
Perjury or false accusation	55%
False confessions	13%
Inadequate legal defence	23%

Table 4. Data from the Innocence Project

Contributing Factor	Innocence Project Data
Mistaken eyewitness testimony	72%
Government misconduct	No statistics available
Invalidated or improper forensics	47%
Jailhouse informants	15%
Perjury or false accusation	Not specifically addressed
False confessions	27%
Inadequate legal defence	No statistics available

wrongly convicted persons in the United States since 1989[26] and contains detailed information on 1,991 cases.[27] Moreover, it provides information about each case, including geographic and demographic details as well as information on whether or not DNA played a role in the exoneration and on which factors contributed to the wrongful conviction. The information contained in the Registry comes from publicly available documents and the criteria for classifying cases as exonerations are based on official actions by courts and other government agencies.

The percentages contained in the data from the National Registry reflect evidence of the following contributing factors, by order of significance: perjury or false accusation (55 per cent),[28] official misconduct (47 per cent), mistaken witness identification (32 per cent), false or misleading forensic evidence (23 per cent), inadequate legal defence (23 per cent), and false confessions (13 per cent). Under another heading of "tags," information is also contained regarding whether or not jailhouse informants played a role in the conviction (7 per cent).[29]

The Innocence Project, established in 1992 at the Benjamin N. Cardozo School of Law at Yeshiva University in New York City, was the first project to facilitate the exoneration of the wrongly convicted. It describes itself as "a national litigation and public policy organization dedicated to exonerating wrongfully convicted individuals through DNA testing and reforming the criminal justice system to prevent future injustice."[30] The Innocence Project works on 300 files on a given day and to date has facilitated exonerations in over 350 cases with the use of forensic DNA analysis. Its website contains information on the causes of wrongful convictions as revealed through the project's casework, as well as information on policy-reform efforts.

Not surprisingly, the Innocence Project found evidence for many of the same contributing factors as noted in the National Registry: mistaken eyewitness testimony (72 per cent), invalidated or improper forensics (47 per cent), jailhouse informants (15 per cent), and false confessions (27 per cent). The Innocence Project data do not contain information specifically on complainant testimony or perjury/false accusations; it is possible that this information is subsumed under government misconduct, which is acknowledged as a contributing factor (as is inadequate legal defence), but no statistics or percentages are available for these terms. The data contained on the Innocence Project website come from the over 330 cases in which it has obtained exonerations to date; however, the project investigates only those cases where DNA evidence is available to facilitate exoneration.

It is important to note that none of these data sets are exhaustive and each has its limitations. It is likely that the Innocence Project data are the most complete since they represent the cases that the project lawyers have worked on directly, sometimes for years, and thus their access to information on each case is greater and knowledge of the files first-hand. At the same time, given that they restrict their work to solely DNA-based cases, this limits the applicability of their findings to other wrongful convictions where there is no bodily-fluid evidence and where exonerations may be questioned. The data from the Registry, however, contain information on a greater number of cases. Yet the data are derived from publicly available documents, which have their own limitations, and in recognition of the possibility of error the Registry itself contains sections that ask the public for information to "tell us about an exoneration that we missed" as well as for information to "correct an error or add information about an exoneration on our list."[31]

What these differing data sets illustrate is that miscarriages of justice in a given jurisdiction, regardless of the actual incidence, are a recurring problem for the criminal justice system that begs a solution. This is true whether it is considered from a resource or a justice perspective; the fiscal costs to the criminal justice system in overturning a conviction are enormous, and the costs to public confidence in the system more generally are incalculable. At the same time, and not to overstate an obvious point, wrongful convictions often result in guilty individuals remaining untried and unpunished; a wrongful conviction (in most cases) equates to the absence of a rightful conviction.[32] Consequently, the importance of wrongful convictions from a law-enforcement perspective is particularly significant. While these estimates have often been used to justify criminal justice reform in many jurisdictions, they can also serve a further purpose in that they demonstrate the need for continual vigilance around criminal justice processing that goes beyond progressive efforts to change.

The Study of Miscarriages of Justice: Atheoretical?

Among the literature on miscarriages of justice, mention of theory is mostly absent; while this may reflect the fact that such scholarship is atheoretical in nature, it may also speak to the impossibility of conceptualizing wrongful conviction from a single theoretical perspective. As Leo (2005) suggests, there have been only a few attempts to understand aspects of this issue through a theoretical lens, and with limited success. As an example, he cites Huff, Rattner, and Sagarin's seminal book *Convicted but Innocent: Wrongful Conviction and Public Policy* (1996), where they suggest that Packer's (1968) two competing models – one focused on crime control, the other on due process – are appropriate for understanding the study of wrongful convictions. The first model emphasizes the enhancement of crime-control strategies of the police and prosecutors, while the second is concerned with due-process rights and procedural protections for defendants. The argument is that a greater focus on crime control will increase the rates of wrongful conviction, while a focus on the latter will reduce them. These two divergent models stress the conflict between, on the one hand, society's interest in convicting the guilty, and, on the other, the rights of criminal defendants. At the same time, Leo demonstrates that Packer's structural framework is just that – a framework – and not a theoretical construct[33] per se, and does little more than explain ideal types that help to understand some contradictions in criminal procedure (Leo, 2005). Moreover, recent scholarship suggests that these concepts are not conceptually incongruent; Findley (2009), for example, finds an intersection between the crime-control and due-process models. He introduces what he terms as the reliability model, based upon best practices and the truth-seeking values shared by both models of justice.

Leo's second example of theory, more theory than model, describes the work of Lofquist (2001), who draws on theories of organizational wrongdoing (understood though two different frameworks of rational choice/agency theories or organizational process/structural theories), particularly from within the context of the study of white-collar crime, to situate wrongful convictions.[34] From an agency viewpoint, a wrongful conviction proceeds in a linear fashion, through an orderly sequence of events whereby decision makers at the various stages of criminal justice processing pursue a wrongful course of action. From an organization-process or structural-theory approach, wrongful convictions result from premature commitment to the wrong suspect, a disregard of alternative possibilities, and the overall structure of the criminal justice system itself, which is oriented towards convictions. While this theoretical perspective shows some promise, Leo points out that criminologists need to reach further, to move beyond legal categories and "look at the micro level and macro level forces, contexts, and structures that underlie the normal processes and production of perception, belief, and error in American criminal justice" (2005, 216).

Other sociological theories[35] may shed light on aspects of the problem of miscarriage of justice. Early subculture theory, generally understood, is informative regarding the phenomenon of tunnel vision,[36] the tendency of police and prosecutors to concentrate on a single suspect or theory of the crime while ignoring exculpatory evidence. This juxtapositioning, so evident in the "us" (actors in the criminal justice system) versus "them" (criminals, writ large) perspective, and revealed through policy and practice, encourages the targeting of *one* so-called suspect rather early in an investigation, which often works to the detriment of finding the *right* suspect. Similarly, structural-stigma theory (Hannem, 2012) examines how stigmatic assumptions are embedded in laws and policies that affect those considered to be a risk. This theory offers some insights into how those marginalized by race, poverty, or mental illness possess less power and influence and are more often targeted by the criminal justice system through a wrongful conviction.

Critical race theory is also informative in this regard, demonstrating that racism is an endemic part of North American life for racialized groups, ingrained in historical consciousness and current legal discourses (Parker and Lynn, 2002). While overall racial discrimination in prison populations is self-evident in the excessive numbers of African American prisoners in the United States, a recent study done by the National Registry of Exonerations demonstrates similar discrimination among the wrongly convicted. Despite the fact that African Americans represent only 13 per cent of the U.S. population, they constituted a majority of innocent defendants wrongfully convicted of crimes and later exonerated; 47 per cent of the more than 1,900 exonerations listed in the National Registry of Exoneration were African Americans and this was true for all major crime categories.[37]

In Canada, there is no shortage of Indigenous prisoners in penitentiaries, particularly in the western part of the country. In fact, while Indigenous peoples make up 3.1 per cent of the adult Canadian population, on average 18.5 per cent of federally sentenced prisoners are of First Nations, Métis, and Inuit ancestry (Perreault, 2009). This overrepresentation has a long history based within the framework of colonization and the resultant assimilationist efforts of the federal government, which have been likened to cultural genocide.[38] Facets of this systemic discrimination continue today and an historic example of such a wrongful conviction is that of Donald Marshall, Jr, a member of the Mi'kmaq First Nation, in Nova Scotia, in 1971. The commission of inquiry that examined the errors in this case identified racism as a contributing factor to his wrongful conviction, and noted that Marshall "was convicted and sent to prison, in part at least, because he was a Native person" (Royal Commission on the Donald Marshall, Jr Prosecution, 1989a, 17). Moreover, if the estimates of the wrongly convicted discussed earlier are correct (or closer approximations to the truth), there are likely also large numbers of Indigenous prisoners currently in Canadian jails and prisons whose convictions are in error.

Men's gendered over-representation in criminal statistics is paralleled by an equal over-representation in the numbers of wrongly convicted; it is predominantly men who are victims of miscarriages of justice and the numbers of women are relatively negligible. Given that gendered power is central to understanding why men commit more crimes than women do, it is likely that the same processes are also operating behind why more men are wrongly convicted for crimes they did not commit than are women (Messerschmidt, 1993, 84). At the same time, this theory is limited with respect to miscarriages of justice, since the wrongly convicted (male or female) are in fact not guilty of the crimes of which have been convicted. Thus, a greater comprehension of the construction of masculinities, in particular hegemonic masculinity, does little to further an overall understanding of the processes that explain a gender imbalance in this instance.

One recent, and apposite, attempt to understand miscarriages of justice theoretically is seen in McLellan's appropriation of the theory of risk (McLellan, 2012a). Essentially, risk theory (as proffered by, inter alia, Beck, 1992, Cohen, 1986, Feeley and Simon, 1992, 1994, Garland, 2001, and O'Malley, 2005) focuses on the fact that global fears of increasing rates of crime – perceptions of "crime as risk" – have fostered a response that is far in excess of the perceived threat; in turn, new forms of risk-based control have been developed to rein in those perceived to present a risk of future crime, through prediction and opportunity reduction. Put simply, the tenets of risk theory involve actuarial categorizations of individual members of targeted groups that in turn further targets them for surveillance, categorization, and control; a rationality of risk has converted Foucault's notion of the "delinquent" subject into the concept of "actuarial man" (Robinson, 2002). Thus, crime-control policies are increasingly more likely to be aimed at managing selected risk groups and efficient system management rather than to be based on older notions of retributive justice, normalization, or even rehabilitation (Feeley and Simon, 1992). McLellan points out that this increased emphasis on public protection from an alleged greater risk of crime victimization has resulted in a diminishment of due-process rights of accused persons, including the presumption of innocence (2012a).[39] For those wrongly accused and wrongly convicted, the implications of a risk-based society are harsh: caught up in a system aimed at targeting specific groups who are thought to pose a greater risk owing to some misleading form of classification, these individuals are doubly victimized through their wrongful conviction. Not only is the apparent risk they pose managed by a false conviction, but the arbitrariness within which individuals become targeted by authorities further exemplifies the egregiously intrusive character of the empowered state. In fact, a tangible "risk" involved in wrongful convictions, as an example of error, is a risk to the credibility of the criminal justice system.

Nobles and Schiff (2000) situate miscarriages of justice within the perspective of autopoietic systems theory as it applies to law, a theory initially established by Niklas Luhmann (1995, 2004). A complex construct, linked to systems theory, sociology, and philosophy, as well as to the nature of language itself, autopoiesis views the legal system as a closed system of communication, where new legal communications can emerge only from existing ones (Teubner, Nobles, and Schiff, 2003). From this perspective, law is viewed as a system constantly regenerating itself from its own elements; a miscarriage of justice is thus seen as an example of law generating a critique of its own errors. From this perspective, media and political communications on law and its failings are able to produce change. An example is the legislative and procedural changes that occurred in the United Kingdom during the 1990s that could be described as the legal system's response to media and justice campaigns around high-profile miscarriages of justice (Nobles and Schiff, 2000).

Naughton considers Foucault's theory of subjugated discourses as relevant to discussions of wrongful convictions. For him, Foucault's (1980) conception of power and the importance of "giving a voice to subjugated discourses" or "unearthing anti-discourses" provides for a more critical exploration and acknowledgment of previously unrecognized cases of wrongful conviction (in his view, those successful appeals and acquittals that he includes in his definition of miscarriages of justice). This perspective views the dominant, or rather "exceptionalist," understanding of wrongful criminal convictions as far too limited in terms of the scale of the problem and the scale of the victims. What is interesting is that Naughton suggests a parallel argument to that of the historically dominant discourses regarding the prison and/or the asylum that were challenged by counter-discourses or anti-discourses of those realities. Naughton believes that in the same way "there is a corresponding necessity for the elevation of disqualified discourses that accompany routine and/or mundane miscarriages of justice" (2007, 36). While this may be a compelling argument, such an admission would likely prove too threatening to conservative establishments, for whom such "routine" cases are not wrongful convictions per se but merely examples of the system correcting its own errors (Hickman, 2004).

On its face, none of these theories is adequate to "make sense" of miscarriages of justice. Perhaps there is a simple reason – a miscarriage of justice is a complex, nuanced issue with legal, social, and philosophical elements; it does not occur solely on one level but rather on numerous ones – individual, institutional, bureaucratic, and structural. In this context there can be no "grand" theory or narrative that neatly explains why these errors occur; conceivably, it is more productive to rely on an eclectic assortment of theories that collectively constitute a multidisciplinary perspective drawing from criminology, sociology, and legal studies. Moreover, a growing body of literature has demonstrated that the logic of a conviction can fall apart at different points along the way. The simplistic legal rendering whereby a guilty person is found guilty beyond a reasonable doubt, based on evidence that was collected and presented in a straightforward manner, is a rare occurrence. A wrongful conviction can be likened to a perfect storm, defined by Merriam Webster as "a critical or disastrous situation created by a powerful concurrence of factors."[40] In the case of a miscarriage of justice, errors can occur prior to a suspect being targeted and then again at the various levels of investigation, interrogation, trial, and conviction, resulting in a conviction in error; this is further compounded by the many existing roadblocks to exoneration, including time limits on appeal, barriers regarding access to evidence, and the impossible levels of evidentiary proof required. To add insult to injury, certainly in the Canadian context, compensation rarely follows exoneration. While the analogy of the perfect storm may be hackneyed, it seems apt in this situation.

The normative assumption behind this book is that the criminal justice system is deeply flawed. At times, guilty individuals are convicted for the crimes they commit, but at others innocent persons are found guilty for things they did not do. A common, and questionable, assumption at the root of this thinking is that the system itself can administer justice. Existing laws and evidentiary procedures are presumed to be in place to protect everyone, yet, regardless, errors frequently occur throughout the criminal justice process, from investigation, arrest, and trial all the way through to sentencing. It is a highly imperfect system. By deconstructing and examining what the errors in the system are, and how, when, why, and where they occur (and to whom), this book may provide a better understanding of how to prevent them from reoccurring and move towards approximations of the ever-elusive, indefinable ideal of justice.

Miscarriages of Justice – Rights Violations and Social Harm

Walker (1999a), whose definition of miscarriage of justice is individualistic and rights-based, notes that a number of rights are affected by the operation of the criminal justice system, including the following: humane treatment, liberty, privacy, family life, and existence itself (this latter one in jurisdictions with capital punishment).[41] He underlines the centrality of rights within the criminal justice process; all citizens deserve rights protection by the state, and accused persons' rights should be safeguarded by procedural and evidentiary rules. Two other researchers have examined the problem of wrongful convictions from a rights perspective, Sherrin (2008) in his extensive overview of possible Canadian Charter[42] protections from wrongful convictions and Naughton (2005a; 2007) in his discussion of protections from the social harm of a wrongful conviction and of human-rights with respect to subjugated discourses.

Sherrin examines the extent to which protections afforded under the Charter have provided safeguards against wrongful convictions in Canada and finds that "the *Charter* seems to have been largely irrelevant" (400). While he argues that the Charter may have enhanced some procedural protections with respect to the admission of evidence (specifically its accumulation, presentation, and use), its overall impact has been somewhat limited with respect to rights protections. The only "substantial" gains attributable to the Charter in this context, he concludes, are in the area of disclosure and the law relating to reverse onuses. And, with respect to the law of disclosure, while an accused person now has the right of disclosure to view all relevant evidence held by the prosecution, this issue was largely decided in the courts through common law[43] and not constitutional protections per se. The Charter has also allowed for courts to affirm the long-standing principle of the "beyond a reasonable doubt" burden of proof in criminal cases; while case law had already affirmed this principle, its inclusion in section 11(d)[44] of the Charter has further entrenched this right.

Sherrin points out that other rights protections are only minimal with respect to the following areas: the right to make full answer and defence, the right to exclude prejudicial evidence, the right to silence, the right against self-incrimination, the right against unlawful search and seizure, the right against arbitrary detention, the right to be informed of the reasons for detention, the right to counsel, the right to trial within a reasonable time, the right to challenge prospective jurors for cause, limited exclusions on the right to bail, and the overall right to exclude incriminating evidence (381–99). At the same time, Sherrin does draw tenuous connections between the possibility of Charter protections and their impact on some documented causes of wrongful conviction, such as problems with eyewitness identification and jailhouse-informant testimony, erroneous use of forensic sciences, prosecutorial misconduct, and witness perjury. No case law has as of yet confirmed this theory, and when courts do intervene in these instances, they appear to use their common law rather than their constitutional jurisdiction (Sherrin, 2007, 402).

Consistent with a larger movement that abandons traditional conceptions of crime and criminology in favour of an alternative discipline of social harm (Hillyard et al., 2004), Naughton situates the problem of wrongful conviction within a social-harm perspective (2004; 2007). His early expansive definition of wrongful convictions, which included all successful appeals against criminal conviction in the United Kingdom, described the many deprivations that result from a wrongful conviction as forms of social harm: physical, emotional, psychological, and financial. This larger definition of miscarriage of justice to include all successful appeals is meant to provide a more adequate depiction of the number of wrongful convictions and the harms that they engender, including the effects on family members and the overall costs of this problem (Naughton, 2004, 104). Naughton's thinking in this area appears to have evolved to the degree that, while he continues to acknowledge the social harms associated with a wrongful conviction, he also acknowledges the difficulties inherent in articulating what exactly constitutes a miscarriage of justice (2013).

While statutory protections exist against unfair treatment by state agents, the difficulty lies in their enforcement, as rights-based arguments regarding miscarriages of justice underscore. In spite of the Charter and common law fetters that restrain police in Canada with respect to how suspects are arrested and questioned, and the fact that Crown attorneys must share all relevant evidence with defendants, wrongful convictions can and do still occur. Moreover, harm-based arguments do little to further an understanding of miscarriages of justice, save for reinforcing the fact that perhaps many more people suffer the deprivations of a wrongful conviction than were previously believed. What these types of arguments also highlight is the fact that criminal law reform is a blunt tool for addressing the larger systemic issues that contribute to miscarriages of justice in the first instance, namely the targeting of already marginalized persons, an inadequate system of legal aid that may deny competent representation by counsel, and the presence of tunnel-vision thinking that causes police and Crown attorneys to focus inadvertently on the wrong suspect. The influence of these larger systemic issues will be addressed throughout this book.

Sections of the Book

Leo (2005) maintains that much wrongful-conviction scholarship in the United States has resulted in an "intellectual dead end" by reinventing the wheel each time, a pattern that involves reiterating well-known causes and then recommending possible policy responses. Similarly, Gross (2008) finds that a large portion of wrongful-conviction scholarship discusses the oft-quoted "canonical list of factors" which has been found to contribute to miscarriages of justice. A simple focus on individual causes, without placing them within a larger context, fails to consider the systems and frameworks within which miscarriages of justice occur and also ignores other interactive effects. As Leo points out, "one must go beyond the study of individual sources of error to understand how social forces, institutional logics, and erroneous human judgments and decisions come together to produce wrongful convictions" (Leo, 2005, 211). With these caveats in mind, the purpose of this volume is to transcend a simple reiteration of the existing literature by providing a broader overview of the many factors that may contribute to a miscarriage of justice, and at the same time present a larger, systemic context for understanding how such miscarriages continue to occur. This will be done from a comparative position, by offering insights not only into how wrongful convictions can and do occur within Canada but also into how the Canadian experience compares to what has occurred in other jurisdictions, from both a policy and practical perspective. Essentially, by viewing wrongful convictions as coherent examples of criminal justice policy failures, this volume also attempts to bring together lessons from Canadian scholarship and Canadian cases, with regard to responding to and remedying miscarriages of justice more generally.

The book is divided into three parts, with the first, "Factors Contributing to Miscarriages of Justice," divided into five separate chapters. Chapter 2 focuses on eyewitness identification and misidentification, which is now recognized as the leading contributing factor to wrongful convictions. A great deal of psychological research on human memory demonstrates its frailties and the harms that can occur when placing too much emphasis on the reliability of eyewitness testimony. Research has indicated that memory-recall errors should be classified as either under the control of the system itself or inherent to the witness. Results emerging from this research have now influenced policy reform affecting the use of eyewitness testimony in a number of jurisdictions. Case examples illustrate that convincing witnesses are highly believable, regardless of whether or not they are correct, and that courts at times need guidance from experts on how to understand the problems with this type of evidence. Chapter 3 presents an overview of the role that police officers may play in contributing to miscarriages of justice. Police officers, as the first point of entry into the criminal justice system, must make critical initial decisions about questioning, arrest, and charge. They may become caught up in political pressures to solve high-profile cases quickly and there are a number of wrongful-conviction cases where police have been guilty of tunnel vision by narrowly focusing on a particular suspect while ignoring any evidence to the contrary. Chapter 4 focuses on other legal professionals and how they may be involved in miscarriages of justice, including prosecutors, defence counsel, and the judiciary. Prosecutors have also been found to contribute to miscarriages of justice through misconduct, including tunnel vision, inadequate charge screening, failing to disclose evidence, and suppressing evidence. While remedies exist in tort to address various forms of malicious prosecution, they are notoriously difficult to pursue. Defence attorneys may also play a role in miscarriages of justice, in particular through ineffective assistance at trial. As with the conduct of police and prosecutors, claims of ineffective assistance of counsel are difficult to prove and the standard of competence is rather low. Finally, judges as legal professionals and arbiters in criminal cases may serve to produce or prevent miscarriages of justice through decisions regarding the admissibility of evidence, jury charges, and screening mechanisms. What will be demonstrated is that all actors in the criminal justice system bear some responsibility for error and, ultimately, error correction.

Chapter 5 examines the role of false confessions in contributing to miscarriages of justice. While confessing to something one has not done defies logic, highly stylized police-interrogation practices have been found to induce false confessions in a number of high-profile wrongful convictions. While the common law confessions rule provides some protection against allowing coerced confessions into evidence, as do Charter protections against self-incrimination, particular psychological vulnerabilities may nonetheless dispose individuals to confess falsely. The role that jailhouse informants play in contributing to miscarriages of justice will be discussed in chapter 6. While these individuals have proved indispensible to the police with respect to bringing charges forward against many, the incentives to provide information are so great that the provision of false information has become routine. As a consequence, many wrongful convictions have resulted in part owing to false or misleading information provided by jailhouse informants. Many Canadian provinces have reacted by developing policies that greatly circumscribe the use of such information.

The next section of the book, "Evidentiary Detection Methods: Missteps and Innovations," contains two chapters that focus on the refinement of emergent technologies and the role that they have played in both facilitating and preventing miscarriages of justice. In chapter 7 the role of DNA forensic identification in the exoneration of the wrongly convicted will be discussed. For law enforcement, DNA has proved to be an invaluable tool, not only in solving crimes where biological materials are present, but also in facilitating the elimination of suspects, the latter a major step in diminishing wrongful convictions. The legal framework for such evidence as an investigative tool in Canada, the DNA Identification Act, and the role of the DNA Data Bank will be critically examined as well as how Canadian jurisprudence has now clarified the limits of DNA evidence under the Charter. Chapter 8 examines the role of experts and expert evidence in criminal trials, as well as the increasing use of forensic evidence at trial. A brief overview of some forms of forensic evidence will be provided as well as a discussion of forensic pathology more generally. Given that experts play an important role for both the prosecution and defence counsel, the role of experts in promoting and/or discrediting various forms of evidence will be discussed. Case examples will be used to illustrate where errors in the reliability of forensic evidence contributed to wrongful convictions.

The final section of the book, "Responses to Miscarriages of Justice," considers remedies to address miscarriages of justice, with specific reference to the Canadian context. Chapter 9 focuses on the role of court remedies such as appeal of a criminal conviction, tort or civil action, and challenging an alleged Charter violation as a means to overturn what may be considered to be a conviction in error. A further emphasis in this chapter is on the particular Canadian remedy of conviction review, through sections 696.1–.6 of the Criminal Code,[45] permitted only when all sources of appeal have been exhausted and when new matters or "fresh evidence" arises capable of questioning the earlier conviction. The focus in chapter 10 is on the lessons learned through a number of commissions of inquiry called to outline the circumstances that contributed to particular cases of miscarriage of justice and provide policy recommendations for change. The inquiries examined the following cases: Donald Marshall, Jr, Guy Paul Morin, Thomas Sophonow, Gregory Parsons, Ronald Dalton, Randy Druken, James Driskell, and David Milgaard. What these inquiries demonstrate is a particular commitment to the correct administration of justice and an effort to dissect known errors; at the same time, they are a costly and arduous means to hold the criminal justice system, as well as actors within it, accountable. Chapter 11 focuses on the issue of compensating the wrongly convicted. Canada has a number of obligations, nationally and internationally, towards compensating the wrongly convicted and federal/provincial/territorial guidelines exist that direct how and when such compensation should occur. In reality, however, compensation happens in a rather piecemeal fashion and the dated guidelines are in need of an overhaul.

Chapter 12 studies the impact of external pressure on wrongful convictions, in particular the role of the media, lobby groups, and innocence projects. What has become evident is that there are a number of mechanisms that play a critical role in exposing miscarriages of justice. Media reporting on particular injustices can help to sensitize the public as well as force political and judicial action. Lobby groups targeting specific cases have also fostered greater attention to this issue. Finally, innocence projects have proliferated over the last three decades, partly in response to perceived inadequacies in the criminal justice system in addressing miscarriages of justice. Chapter 13 provides an overview of how other jurisdictions have addressed the problem of miscarriages of justice, both within and outside the criminal justice system. Various forms of review boards, innocence commissions, commissions of inquiry, and a number of other initiatives have been developed to revisit questionable convictions. Lessons can be learned from the successes and failures of these other bodies. Finally, chapter 14 will examine the role of prevention and other remedies with respect to future miscarriages of justice.

Conclusions

Some argue that wrongful convictions as a form of miscarriage of justice are entirely preventable. Several post-mortem analyses support this contention that, in some specific cases of miscarriage of justice, the reasons for why they had occurred have become quite clear. Martin (2001b) contends that wrongful convictions are neither inevitable nor impossible to eliminate. Rather, wrongful convictions appear to occur in cases where specific factors are at play: in high-profile cases (often involving children or women) where there is great pressure to convict in a charged and politicized environment and when there is a willingness to prosecute and convict without real scrutiny of the evidence, owing in part to stereotypes and biases that become part of investigations (Martin, 2001b, 520). This book will endeavour to expose how these specific factors interact and co-occur and cause some individuals, who are in fact innocent of the crime at hand, to be found guilty of a crime they did not commit.

PART ONE

Factors Contributing to Miscarriages of Justice

Chapter Two

Eyewitness Identification and Misidentification

"It (memory) is a complex process of perception, storage and recall, vulnerable at every stage to suggestion, distortion and omission."[1] (J.M. Doyle [2005])

Introduction

Errors that occur in the identification of suspects by witnesses have long been recognized as the leading cause of wrongful convictions (Huff, Rattner, and Sagarin, 1986; Innocence Project, n.d.). Errors can occur at many stages in the process of witness identification, from initial description to police line-up and testimony at trial. The aim of this chapter is to consider the nature of this type of error. It offers a discussion of the psychology of memory, an examination of the different types of variables that affect the misidentification of suspects, an overview of procedural issues related to the use of eyewitness testimony in the adversarial system, and examples of wrongful-conviction cases where such errors have occurred. In addition, the chapter studies policy reforms in both the United States and Canada, where these reforms have emerged largely as a result of lessons learned from eyewitness errors that led to wrongful convictions. Finally, the role of expert witnesses testifying as to the frailties of eyewitness-identification evidence is explored.

Eyewitness Identification and Memory

"I was certain, but I was wrong."[2]

Those words are the headline of an article in the *New York Times* written by Jennifer Thompson, a survivor of a sexual assault that occurred in 1984. At that time, an intruder raped Jennifer, a college student, at knifepoint in her apartment. In her terror, she focused on aspects of the assailant's face so that, in the event she survived the attack, she would be able to identify her attacker to the police. After consulting mug shots and creating a composite sketch, Jennifer identified Ronald Cotton as her attacker and was completely confident in her choice. At trial, Cotton was convicted of one count of rape and one count of burglary and was sentenced to life in prison plus fifty-four years, in part as a result of Thompson's compelling testimony. Eleven years later, through the use of DNA forensic analysis, another individual, Bobby Poole, was proven to be the actual assailant and Ronald Cotton was exonerated. Jennifer Thompson now speaks publicly about her experience, the impact it has had on her life, and the anguish she feels about sending an innocent man to jail for eleven years.[3] Her experience, one among many other cases of convictions in error resulting from mistaken eyewitness identification, clearly illustrates the frailties of human memory; it also reveals that certainty in testimony does not necessarily always translate into accuracy.[4]

Erroneous eyewitness identification and testimony has long been acknowledged as a leading contributing factor to wrongful convictions. Indeed, earlier studies indicated that it was *the* most significant factor. Huff et al. (1986) concluded in their seminal study that misidentification influenced the outcome of 60 per cent of the reported cases of wrongful convictions they reviewed in 1986. Further, Scheck, Neufeld, and Dwyer (2000) found that, in the 52 cases they had studied where DNA exonerations had occurred, all the defendants had been convicted in part through incorrect eyewitness identification. Of the more than 350 DNA exonerations facilitated by the work of the Innocence Project at the Benjamin N. Cardozo School of Law at Yeshiva University, over 72 per cent of them have involved mistaken identity.[5] In their summary of a number of studies examining the reliability of eyewitness identification, Cutler and Penrod (1995, 12) found that correct identifications occurred in only 41.8 per cent of the cases, whereas false identification occurred in 35.8 per cent. Gross and Shaffer's 2012[6] study of the first 873 exonerations reported in the National Registry of Exonerations revealed that, in 43 per cent of the exonerations, eyewitnesses were mistaken; the numbers were highest for sexual-assault (80 per cent) and robbery (81 per cent) cases (2012, 40). Garrett's in-depth examination of the first 250 exonerations since DNA testing became available in the 1980s in the United States concludes that in 190 cases (76 per cent) the suspects were wrongly identified (Garrett, 2011, 9).[7] Finally, the data in appendix A indicate that, for these Canadian cases, eyewitness error was a contributing factor in 31 of the known 70 cases of miscarriage of justice, or 44 per cent. It is impossible to provide anywhere near an exact figure of how many convictions in error occur as a result of mistaken eyewitness identification, but these numbers underline the significance of the issue regarding the safety of a conviction.

Given that tens of thousands of prosecutions occur annually in the United States and Canada and rely heavily on eyewitness testimony, the potential magnitude of this type of error cannot be overstated. Estimates in Canada indicate that there are approximately 8,000 identification tests each year, and even a "99 percent rate of correct decisions would mean 80 mis- and failed identifications each year" (Read, 2006, 524). The manner in which this type of evidence is collected, understood, and used by the courts is highly problematic. In particular, while some argue that eyewitness testimony is inherently fallible, juries are nonetheless receptive to it in spite of that fact (Baxter, 2007). Moreover, juries tend to believe eyewitnesses, despite attempts by counsel to discredit this type of evidence and in the face of cautionary instructions by judges (Clements, 2007, 284).

Psychological Research on Memory

The study of the psychology of human behaviour has long existed outside the purview of the domain of law, with little convergence of the two disciplines.

Psychological research has focused on understanding human behaviour more generally. It has only been in recent years that jurists and researchers in law and criminal justice have begun to recognize that certain aspects of psychological research may have particular relevance to legal matters, inter alia, jury behaviour and evidentiary issues. More specifically, a plethora of research over the past thirty years has shed some light on the inherent frailties of human memory and the impact of this on witness identification during line-ups and at trial (cf. Cutler, 2011; Cutler and Penrod, 1995).

Psychological research from as far back as the 1970s has demonstrated problems with eyewitness identification; however, it was not until the 1990s that criminal justice personnel began to take note of these findings (Wells and Olson, 2003, 278). This change was due in part to the advent of DNA forensic analysis, which provided a more precise, scientific form of certainty with respect to suspect involvement when physical evidence was present at a crime scene. Those working in the criminal justice system were confronted with many individuals convicted on the basis of eyewitness testimony who were subsequently exonerated through DNA evidence during the 1990s. Accordingly, the legal community had little choice but to acknowledge what psychologists had long known to be true: eyewitnesses are often wrong.

A significant factor when examining eyewitness evidence is the problem encountered with human memory and its fallibility. When an event is observed, human memories encode various aspects of that event that are salient to the observer, for a variety of reasons, based on age, condition, experiences, and perceptions. At the same time, what is observed is encoded in a number of ways, since there are different types of memory: episodic, semantic, script, and procedural. When the event is later recalled, different types of memories are relied upon. Episodic memory represents a storehouse of actual experiences that are available for conscious recall and also includes memory of past events or personal experiences in a particular time and place (Schacter, 2001, 27). It is a higher-order memory in that it allows the event to be recalled as well as the circumstances and feelings associated with it. In contrast, semantic memory is based on facts and general knowledge and can be intellectually recalled; events stored semantically, however, require more effort to recall. A third type of memory is script memory. It represents more abstract, generalizable information and is not of single episodes or events. Finally, the least complex type of memory is procedural, where memories are stored without conscious recall; procedural memory involves the storage of skills and knowledge involved in human motor performance – for example, riding a bike – and is at times difficult to verbalize. It is likely that eyewitnesses must rely on episodic or semantic memory when recalling aspects of crimes they have witnessed. These types of memory make up declarative memory (Tulving, 1984). This is often subject to forgetting over time, which can in turn cause problematic, but inadvertent, errors on the part of eyewitnesses.

The earliest psychological study of eyewitness error in the courtroom was Munsterberg's treatise "On the Witness Stand," published in 1908. One of the first psychology professors at Harvard in an emergent field, Munsterberg conducted several experiments and concluded that eyewitness errors were a normal part of human memory and that witness sincerity or certainty did not equate with accuracy. His findings challenged the legal community to examine its reliance on eyewitness testimony (cf. Memom et al., 2008). However, the challenge was quickly silenced by a renowned legal scholar of the period, John Henry Wigmore, who disputed the new "science" on the basis that it lacked credibility and that such findings had not as yet been replicated (Doyle, 2005). Seventy years later, this type of psychological research has garnered a warmer reception in legal circles. Studies undertaken by Buckhout, Loftus, Wells, Kassin, Culter, and Penrod have demonstrated the fallibility of eyewitness memory and the significance of error for criminal trials.[8] At the same time, this path has not been without problems and there are still many detractors. In particular, critics note that most of this research has been undertaken in controlled experiments or through staged crimes, and not in real-life crime situations, thus rendering its applicability outside the psychology laboratory somewhat questionable.

Elizabeth Loftus was one of the first researchers to demonstrate not only the fallibility of human memory but also the impact that post-event information can have on altering witness memory.[9] Essentially, while the bulk of Loftus's work focused on repressed memory, she also found that witnesses and their testimony could be greatly influenced and their memory of an event greatly altered by what occurred following the incident they witnessed. Something as simple as being told by a police officer, "Good job, you picked the right guy," has a huge impact on witness confidence, even in cases where the suspect is innocent. In turn, this can affect the outcome at trial as confident witnesses appear more believable, even if they are incorrect. Also, Loftus was able to demonstrate that witnesses may exercise "unconscious transference" – which involves viewing a suspect for the first time in one context, such as a photo-pack array, and then recognizing that individual in another context, an actual line-up (Castelle and Loftus, 2001). Thus, a suspect will be "remembered," but the original context will be lost. In such a case, a witness may be confident that they recognize a particular suspect, but their memory of that individual is not from the actual crime scene.

What was compelling about Loftus's work was its scientific rigour, which led the legal community to acknowledge for the first time that the science of psychology might have something to offer. Loftus was in demand at many criminal trials, where she testified about individual witness inaccuracy in identification. Latterly, it was the work of Gary Wells, which followed on Loftus's original research, that truly expanded the role of experimental cognitive psychology in eyewitness-identification research.[10] Wells's work essentially developed the notion of what are now commonly referred to as estimator and system variables, and how these affect eyewitness identification and can be altered to improve witness accuracy. Given their prominence and explanatory power, they will be discussed in greater detail below.

Eyewitness Identification: Variables and Procedural Issues

Research has now established that there are a number of consistent factors that are thought to influence the accuracy of eyewitness identification. One means of categorizing these variables is to determine whether they are system variables or estimator variables (Wells and Olson, 2003, 279). System variables are those variables under the control of the system, which can be affected and manipulated by those who are interviewing eyewitnesses, including methods used by police to retrieve and record witness statements. A number of system variables that greatly affect the identification process include the type of line-up, the selection of "fillers" (or members of a line-up or photo array who are not the actual suspect), blind administration, instructions to witnesses before identification procedures, the manner of administration of line-ups or photo arrays, and instruction to or communication with the witness during the procedure.[11] Moreover, system variables can and have been manipulated in a variety of real-life and experimental settings to understand more about the process of identification. By contrast, estimator variables are those characteristics inherent to the witness, the perpetrator, the event, or the conditions surrounding the event that have an impact on the reliability and accuracy of identifications. They include such things as race, conditions during the original identification, witness confidence, presence of a weapon, emotional state of the witness, and so on. Both types of variables, under differing circumstances, can influence the process and outcome of witness identification of suspects in criminal investigations, with far-reaching consequences.

System Variables

Police Line-ups

One significant factor under the control of actors in the criminal justice system that has a considerable impact on eyewitness identification is the line-up; police line-ups are a standard tool in criminal justice investigations. They have long been used as a means of allowing eyewitnesses to choose a suspect from an array of similar-looking individuals. A great deal of psychological research has been undertaken in recent years examining various aspects of line-ups, including composition, presentation, and instructions given to witnesses (cf. Clark et al., 2009; Douglass et al., 2010; Gronlund et al., 2009; Meissner and Brigham, 2001; and Pickel, 2009). Line-ups can be either live or comprised of photographs. They involve placing a criminal suspect (or his or her photo) among other people (or photos) in front of an eyewitness so as to ascertain whether the witness will identify the suspect as the perpetrator of the crime (Wells and Olson, 2003, 279). Fillers or "foils" are generally other individuals in the line-up, who may or may not resemble the suspect in some way, and who are not suspected of the crime in question.[12] A double-blind line-up is one where the police officer administering the line-up is unaware of who the fillers are and who is the actual suspect, allowing for less potential influence of the witness.

Line-up Presentation Method

Police line-ups or photo spreads of suspects can be conducted in one of two ways. The witness can be shown all of the suspects or photos either simultaneously or separately or sequentially. In the simultaneous line-up, the witness will examine all suspects or photos at the same time and, through a comparative process, may choose one of the suspects as the alleged perpetrator. A relative judgment is made, whereby a person is likely to select the person in the line-up who looks most like the offender, *relative* to the others in the line-up (Wells, 1984). Conversely, sequential viewing involves an examination of suspects or photos of suspects separately and one at a time, whereby the witness must make a decision on each suspect or photo before viewing the next one. In this instance, witnesses must rely more on their actual memory of the suspect instead of comparing him or her to other, similar-looking individuals. This type of memory processing involves absolute judgments rather than comparative or relative judgments (Leippe, 1995). The research around the most accurate or best method of line-up presentation appears inconclusive at best (Gronlund et al., 2009).[13]

Witness Instructions

Once a witness is presented with a line-up of prospective suspects for identification purposes, the police officer administering the line-up will provide particular instructions about how to proceed. It is here that the potential exists for contamination or influence of witness evidence during identification, so this process can be fraught with difficulty. In other words, the manner in which the individuals in the line-up are presented to the witness may affect the outcome; the police officer may inadvertently influence the witness selection through verbal and non-verbal cues. In fact, Clark, Marshall, and Rosenthal (2009) have classified two types of influence, which result in different patterns of identification results. One has been described as subtle influence, comprised of making cautionary statements to witnesses, whereas the other is similarity influence, which involves prompting the witness to identify the person most similar to the perpetrator in the line-up. Moreover, it has been found that the more choices an individual is presented with, the greater likelihood that the wrong person will be chosen (Ainsworth, 1998).

Given the difficulties involved in recalling salient details following a traumatic event, witnesses may be susceptible to these subtle forms of encouragement (cf. Innocence Project, 2009a). Whereas lawyers are forbidden to use leading questioning during trial, leading questions by police officers are not unacceptable during the suspect-identification phase. The effect could well be that an individual, traumatized by the event itself and not completely convinced of which suspect is the "right" one, is easily swayed by subtle police pressure to choose someone and end their ordeal. Whether it is the "actual" perpetrator becomes almost irrelevant. Since *United States v. Wade*,[14] defendants in that country have the right to have a lawyer present during a live line-up, in part owing to the fact that "the Sixth Amendment guarantees an accused the right to counsel not only at his trial but at any critical confrontation by the prosecution at pretrial proceedings where the results might well determine his fate and where the absence of counsel might derogate from his right to a fair trial."[15] In Canada, *R. v. Ross*[16] established a right to counsel during line-ups, and violation of this right has resulted in the exclusion of evidence. Furthermore, the Royal Canadian Mounted Police (RCMP) allow a lawyer to be present during the line-up procedure, if requested by the accused (RCMP, Operation Manual 25.6, Physical lineups, # 2.5). Regardless of the absence or presence of counsel, the line-up proceedings and any resulting identification could likely have a great impact on an individual's right to a fair trial.

Other system variables that may have an impact on eyewitness identification include composite sketches, mugshots, and show-ups. An inherent difficulty with the inaccuracy of composite sketches of perpetrators has to do with the lapse of time between viewing the suspect and making the actual sketch. In addition, when a witness is asked to recall parts of an individual's face to comprise such a sketch – eye colour, size of nose, ears, and so on – he or she may find it difficult to recall features as separate entities, so the accuracy of these types of sketches is very low (Frowd et al., 2005). In addition, just as with other types of confirmation biases, Wells notes that when a witness constructs a composite, that image can start to replace the memory of the actual face the person saw.[17] Research has found some support for the verbal-overshadowing effect, which is the phenomenon whereby describing a previously seen face impairs the later recognition of that face (Dodson and Schooler, 1997). Clearly, this effect may have some impact on memory when a witness helps to compile a composite sketch and examines mugshots. Overall, however, the research in this area is inconsistent since it has also been found that viewing mugshots had no effect on subsequent identifications in line-ups (Lindsay et al., 1994).

Show-up identifications normally occur pre-trial and involve presenting the witness with a single suspect, and then asking if this person is the perpetrator of the crime. This can occur in a police car, in the area where the crime allegedly occurred, or even in a courtroom. If positively identified, a suspect can then be charged, and possibly convicted, based on this rather faulty form of identification evidence. It has been argued that show-ups are the least reliable of all identification procedures and accused persons have few protections when subjected to them (Cicchini and Easton, 2010). Obviously, the circumstances surrounding the show-up identification serve to bias the witness towards choosing the suspect: he/she may be in handcuffs or under arrest, and the identification often takes place in the rather charged aftermath shortly following the commission of a crime. As with other forms of eyewitness identification, show-ups are inherently problematic and can even occur when a suspect refuses to partake in a line-up procedure.[18]

Estimator Variables

Essentially, estimator variables are those factors that have an impact on eyewitness identification but whose effect can be assessed only after the fact (Wells and Olson, 2003). To date, there has been a great deal of applied psychological research examining the impact of these variables on eyewitness behaviour,[19] research that provides guidance to the practice of police-eyewitness identification procedures. These variables can be loosely characterized as falling into a number of categories, such as witness characteristics, event characteristics, and testimony characteristics. Witness characteristics include such things as age, race, and personality traits (e.g., suggestibility). Event characteristics include natural and intentional appearance changes of the suspect, the time and amount of attention paid to the event, and the presence of a weapon. Finally, testimony characteristics include witness confidence and certainty-accuracy relationships, which may be affected by repeated viewing, confirming feedback, and speed of identification.

Witness Characteristics

The age of an eyewitness could likely influence their ability to accurately recall sali-ent features of a crime scene. At both ends of the spectrum, children and older adults may have problems in providing accurate eyewitness identifications, but for dif-fering reasons. It seems that while children's recollections of details of an event are somewhat shorter and less complete than those of adults, they are no less accurate (Goodman and Reed, 1986). Children can accurately recall crime details in ways that are comparable to adults, but when suggestive interviewing techniques are used, children become more inaccurate (Pozzulo et al., 2009). On the other hand, older adults have lower levels of episodic recall than do younger adults, and presumably younger children (Zacks and Hasher, 2006); at the same time, older adults often use compensatory strategies to increase their recall, such as taking more time and effort to remember (Dixon et al., 2001). Thus, age is an important consideration in deter-mining whether or not an eyewitness can accurately recall the circumstances of a crime scene and/or details about the perpetrator. Other factors that may influence the suggestibility of eyewitnesses, and in turn affect the ability to recall information accurately, include cognitive capacity, intellectual deficiency, intoxication through alcohol or psychotropic drugs, and levels of alertness.

A further factor affecting eyewitness-identification accuracy is the cross-race effect, also known as other-race effect or own-race bias, which basically means that individuals recognize and identify those from their own racial or ethnic background more accurately than they do people from other races or ethnic back-grounds (Meissner and Brigham, 2001). Research has demonstrated this effect across a number of racial and ethnic groups, as well as in laboratory settings with a number of different experimental conditions and also in real-life criminal cases involving eyewitness identification (Marcon et al., 2010). Thus, if one is more inclined to correctly identify perpetrators who share similar racial or ethnic fea-tures, eyewitnesses who are dissimilar to alleged perpetrators in this regard have an increased chance of erring when making cross-racial identifications. In fact, Gross et al. (2005) found in their study of American exonerations that, over a four-teen-year period, cross-racial misidentification was a significant issue, particularly with black defendants and white victims. This could prove problematic in a trial situation, given that jurors are in the position of judging the credibility of these identifications but may not be aware of the complex issues surrounding them (Johnson, 1984). Even prosecutors appear unaware of the existence of this bias; one study demonstrated that 84 per cent believed that eyewitness identifications are "probably correct" 90 per cent of the time (Rutledge, 2001). Ignorance about this effect has likely contributed to cross-racial misidentifications going unchallenged.

The substantial over-representation and mass incarceration of African Ameri-cans in the United States criminal justice system has been well documented (cf. Alexander, 2010; Londono, 2013). Historic and systemic racism has contributed to this situation, but errors in cross-racial eyewitness identification may also have played some small part. In Canada, where the racial divide leans more towards over-representation of Indigenous people in all facets of criminal justice process-ing, the possibility that non-Indigenous eyewitnesses may err when identifying alleged perpetrators who may be of Indigenous origin is a risk.[20] At the same time, it would be wrong to equate the Canadian experience in this regard with that of the United States, since minority over-representation of African Americans in the American criminal justice system is considerably larger.

Event Characteristics

The presence of a weapon at a crime scene likely enhances the arousal of the individual viewing that scene. The "weapon focus effect," the subject of much experimental research on eyewitness accuracy, indicates that witnesses and crime victims tend to focus their attention on the weapon when the perpetrator is armed and their consequent memory for peripheral features of the perpetrator become less accurate as a result (Steblay, 1992). Apparently, the presence of a weapon increases fear and the level of threat, and being unusual in most settings, it attracts greater attention. As a result, common sense would dictate that, in a highly charged situation when a crime is taking place, the presence of a weapon would attract greater attention and less consideration would then be paid to the individual carrying the weapon. A wide variety of studies have examined the so-called weapon effect as it pertains to the gender of the perpetrator (Pickel, 2009), whether the weapon was consistent with the activated schema (Pickel et al., 2008), and situations of high or low arousal (Kramer et al., 1990), to name a few.

Given that a much of the research on this phenomenon has occurred in controlled laboratory settings, it is unclear whether the same results can be found within real-life crime situations. Despite the fact that negative emotional events, such as the presence of a weapon, can have an impact on the recollection of other details in a controlled setting, field studies have not always yielded similar results. In fact, Wagstaff et al. (2003) found quite different results in their study of actual crime victims' accuracy of recall. While things such as hair colour and hair length were accurately recalled, they found no significant effects for weapon presence or for age. They also point to the difficulty of controlling for all variables in these settings and the fact that real-life witnesses may be more cautious, given the gravity of error, as opposed to witness/subjects in laboratory settings, who may be more influenced by a desire to please the researcher. Moreover, the amount of time a witness is exposed to an event has been found to have an impact on later recollection of that event. It is common sense that the longer amount of time one has to view someone or something, the greater likelihood of accurate recall, and there have been experimental studies demonstrating this phenomenon. Yet Read et al. (1990) indicate that the direct positive relationship between exposure duration and accuracy may not be as straightforward as previously thought. It would seem that similarity between photo and earlier-face presentation is important for more accurate recall, that retrieval conditions are significant too, and that, despite changes to appearance, recognition of a face will be more accurate if a subject already has some familiarity with it (880–1).

Testimony Characteristics

In a courtroom setting, witness confidence in identification, whether accurate or not, can greatly influence juries.This variable has attracted research attention over the years, much of which has indicated that, at best, witness confidence is a very weak predictor of accuracy and, at worst, means absolutely nothing and could have some bearing on a false identification (Leippe and Eisenstadt, 2007). The research has shown that witness confidence in line-up identifications has more to do with events occurring outside of the identification situation, such as feedback from questioning officers, information from other witnesses, and questioning that occurs following the event (Shaw 1996; Skagerberg, 2007; Wells and Bradfield, 1998). A number of studies have demonstrated that witness confidence in the accuracy of their identification of suspects can be falsely inflated by repeated questioning (Shaw and McClure, 1996), particularly when being told that another witness has identified the same subject (Luus and Wells, 1994), and also by confirming interviewer feedback (Bradfield et al., 2002). Moreover, a recent study by Douglass et al. (2010) concluded that post-identification feedback can in fact change witnesses' judgments, even in cases where witness evaluators were given instructions to ignore or disregard the feedback. In particular, witness suggestibility, described as particular cognitive, social, and developmental factors that may have an impact on an individual's ability to restore and recall information about a stressful event (Ceci and Bruck, 1993), can likely be altered by misleading information obtained following that event (Loftus, 2005).

American Case Law

Case law around eyewitness testimony in the United States has evolved in the past four decades, to the point where courts now acknowledge the fallibility of human memory and the importance of standardizing line-up procedures. The first contemporary case to address problems associated with eyewitness testimony was *Stovall v. Denno*,[21] where the court found that procedures containing an "element of suggestion"[22] that the suspect was the perpetrator were unconstitutional. The 1967 case of *United States v. Wade*[23] also established the requirements in that country for police powers and was aimed directly at police procedure during line-ups that could result in mistaken identification; it permitted defence lawyers to be present during line-ups (a Sixth Amendment right) and allowed judges to exclude evidence obtained through unlawful procedures during line-ups (Doyle, 2005, 72). Further, in both *Neils v. Biggers*[24] and *Manson v. Braithwaite*,[25] courts set additional parameters for police-identification practice in the United States, focusing more on the issue of "reliability" than on "suggestiveness."[26]

The test for reliability of an eyewitness identification was first established in *Biggers* and affirmed in *Braithwaite*. It required that judges weigh the following factors:

1. Witness's opportunity to view the criminal;
2. Witness's degree of attention;
3. Accuracy of prior description given by the witness;
4. Witness's level of subjective certainty about the identification; and
5. Time lapse between the crime and the identification.[27]

A great deal of research in recent years has not been able to show consistently that any of these factors is particularly instructive with respect to accuracy of recall

(Clements, 2007, 280–4). The only exception is the fifth directive, since it has been demonstrated that the amount of time that has passed before a witness or victim identifies the perpetrator is significant with respect to identification reliability (ibid., 283). As discussed, it is common sense that memory will fade following an incident and that, the closer to the confrontation that identification is made, the more accurate it likely is.

Canadian Case Law

In Canadian jurisdictions, judges will warn juries about the dangers of convicting when the identification of the accused is at issue. A trial judge must instruct the jury to be cautious in dealing with eyewitness testimony where the Crown's case relies substantially upon the accuracy of such evidence.[28] A specific warning should also be issued to members of the jury when an accused is at risk of being convicted based on uncorroborated eyewitness identification, though what is required to displace the risk of the jury's overreliance on such testimony is not well defined and will depend on the facts of each case (*R. v. Tebo*).[29] Furthermore, this duty to warn is important when the identification was made under poor viewing conditions, when unprofessional or improper identification procedures were used, or when improper influences were applied (Paciocco and Stuesser, 2015, 572–3). Canadian jurisprudence has dictated the need for a warning to be given to juries when such problems arise with identification evidence. Clearly, warnings given to the jury by a presiding judge must be sufficiently strong that the jury understands that the witness evidence is not "science" per se. The Supreme Court of Canada in *R. v. Burke* emphasized the need to ensure that the trier of fact remains aware of the "inherent frailties of identification evidence arising from the psychological fact of the unreliability of human observation and recollection."[30]

In specific cases when the initial warnings given to juries about eyewitness fallibility have been found to be insufficient, the verdict can be set aside. In the case of *R. v. Hibbert*,[31] a woman was brutally beaten and the circumstantial case against the accused rested in part on her in-dock identification[32] of him. The victim did not identify the accused through a photo line-up, and she thought she might "have had a conversation with him,"[33] but not necessarily on the day of the attack. However, the victim did see the accused on television news footage and identified him later at the preliminary hearing and during trial. The defence argued that such evidence had little probative value since it had been contaminated by the news broadcast and because it was generally unreliable.[34] Clearly, a strong warning was needed in this case, since the conditions under which the eyewitnesses first identified the suspect were questionable and occurred *following* his arrest. In this instance, the appeal was allowed and a new trial ordered, in part because the trial judge should have "cautioned the jury more strongly that the identification of the accused in court … was highly problematic as direct reliable identification of the perpetrator of the offence."[35] Moreover, the court also noted that it is important to warn the jury about the very weak link between the "confidence level of a witness and the accuracy of that witness."[36]

In *R. v. McIntosh*,[37] the Crown's case relied heavily on eyewitness testimony. The issues revolved around evidence regarding an armed-robbery suspect presented by three eyewitnesses. On appeal the question was whether the trial judge erred in refusing to admit expert evidence on the issue of eyewitness identification. In dismissing the appeal, on the grounds that expert-evidence testimony in this case was considered to be within the normal experience of the jury, Justice George Duncan Finlayson observed: "For this reason alone, expert testimony on matters which are covered by the jury instruction has less appeal. Our judges are not only encouraged to comment on the evidence, there are some cases in which they are obliged to do so."[38] In fact, judges are required to advise juries about the frailties of eyewitness identification and the weak probative value of identification evidence when there is dissimilarity between the initial description the witness provided and the suspect who is identified.[39]

Thomas Sophonow's case is particularly illustrative with respect to the devastating effects of erroneous eyewitness identification.[40] Sophonow's long ordeal began in 1982 when he was accused of murdering Barbara Stoppel, who had been killed in a Winnipeg donut shop in 1981. Sophonow's first trial ended in a mistrial; he was later convicted at a second and subsequent third trial. The Manitoba Court of Appeal overturned the guilty verdict of the third trial and acquitted Sophonow in 1985. By that time, Sophonow had served forty-five months in prison; he was finally exonerated in 2000 when the attorney general of Manitoba apologized to him for his ordeal and instituted a commission of inquiry to investigate his case.[41] The commission, chaired by former Supreme Court of Canada justice Peter Cory, outlined a number of problematic aspects of this case, one in particular being the misidentification of Thomas Sophonow as a suspect by several witnesses.[42]

John Doerksen was a witness who claimed to have seen a tall man in the donut shop around the time of the murder. Doerksen pursued this man on foot after he left the shop, a small altercation ensued, and then the man disappeared. Doerksen gave a description of the man to the police that evening. In the weeks following the murder, on a number of occasions, Doerksen identified other persons as suspects, who were all later eliminated by the police. Moreover, three months following the murder, Doerksen attended a police line-up. While Thomas Sophonow was part of that line-up and stood out as the tallest individual, Doerksen failed to identify him. Two days later, Doerksen came face to face with Sophonow at the Remand Centre; at that time Thomas Sophonow's picture had been widely circulated in the press. Approximately a week later, Doerksen returned to the police station and advised them that he was now "90% sure" that Thomas Sophonow was the man he saw on the night of the murder. Furthermore, a number of other issues raised questions during the inquiry that further indicated the unreliability of Doerksen's identification of Sophonow. Despite not being able to identify Sophonow during the line-up parade, Doerksen was adamant in the following three trials that Sophonow was the killer; it was later revealed that Doerksen had eyesight problems and had trouble with night vision; and, finally, Doerksen had befriended the victim's family, which could have ultimately affected the certainty of the identification. Doerksen likely suffered from unconscious transference (Castelle and Loftus, 2001), whereby his repeated exposure to Sophonow, at the Remand Centre and through the media, affected his "memory" of where he had originally seen him.

Another witness in this case, Norman Janower, claimed to have viewed the alleged killer in the donut shop that evening over a period of seven to ten seconds. He made a tentative identification of Sophonow from both a photo-pack line-up and a live line-up three months following the murder. By the time of the first trial, Janower's identification was certain; this certainty also remained even following Sophonow's exoneration. This was likely because the police had confirmed that he had, in fact, picked out the suspect following the identification parade.[43] When both of these witnesses (and two others) went from tentative to certain identifications, they were no doubt influenced by the police, other witnesses, and repeated exposure to Sophonow in line-ups and through media. These several mistaken identifications contributed significantly to Sophonow's wrongful conviction.

A lesser-known, historical case of blatantly improper identification procedures resulting in a wrongful conviction is that of Réjean Hinse of Quebec. Hinse was arrested in 1961 and convicted of armed robbery in 1964. He received a fifteen-year sentence and was released on parole after serving five years in Saint-Vincent de Paul Penitentiary, a turn-of-the-century prison with deplorable conditions that finally closed in 1989. It was through a chance encounter that Hinse became involved in this case at all. He was in Mont Laurier, Quebec, to deliver a car that he had sold to someone when the victims identified him as one of five armed perpetrators who had robbed their home. In the subsequent line-up, not only was Hinse the sole suspect (the fillers were other police officers), but he was also the only one wearing a hat; the witnesses had declared the suspect had been wearing a hat at the time of the robbery. In 1994 the Quebec Court of Appeal allowed his appeal and set aside his conviction based on fresh evidence; the court then entered a stay of proceedings for abuse of process. Not satisfied with this outcome and believing that he had been denied a clear pronouncement of innocence, Hinse sought leave to appeal the legality and constitutionality of the stay to the Supreme Court. The first request was denied, but in January 1997 Hinse was finally acquitted of the robbery by the Supreme Court of Canada, some thirty-six years after the crime.[44]

Jason Hill is a more recent victim of the perils of faulty eyewitness identification.[45] Hill was a suspect in ten robberies and was targeted early on as his photo was released to the media prior to his arrest. The evidence against him was largely based on two eyewitnesses who worked at a bank and who were interviewed together by the police while Hill's picture was placed on the desk in front of them. That, in addition to the police failure to reinvestigate adequately the robberies when new exculpatory evidence emerged, contributed to his wrongful conviction. It was the photo-pack lineup used to identify Hill that was the most problematic, since Hill was the only Indigenous person in the line-up. While he was ultimately convicted for one of the robberies and served over twenty months in jail, Hill was in due course successful on appeal.

Policy Reform: Canada and the United States

In Canada, there are no specific or uniform guidelines for composing and administering line-ups; rather, police colleges provide "best practices" guides for police forces to establish their own procedures (Conway, 2006). In recent years the federal police force, the RCMP, have attempted to introduce policies addressing the shortcomings in traditional identification processes. This initiative was largely influenced by the 2001 Sophonow report (published by the commission of inquiry examining the circumstances around Thomas Sophonow's wrongful conviction), which contained a number of recommendations for police, Crown attorneys, and judges regarding the procurement and use of eyewitness testimony in criminal cases.[46] The RCMP policy,[47] which affects detachments throughout Canada, changed the administration of both live and photo line-ups; the latter are now to be used only when it is impractical to do a physical line-up. For live or physical line-ups, the procedures are straightforward. The accused cannot be compelled to participate and must give his/her consent; otherwise the accused can be viewed only in a cellblock or courtroom. Other restrictions include the requirement that a photo of the suspect cannot be shown to the witness before viewing and that the viewing can be either secret or open. The line-up must include a minimum of six people in addition to the suspect who are similar in age, physical appearance, and dress, and preferably should not include other police officers as fillers. The police officer in charge of the line-up is not permitted to see the line-up beforehand; however, defence counsel are permitted to attend if requested. Given that the suspect is permitted to select his/her place in the line-up, the RCMP uses a simultaneous procedure rather than the sequential one, which appears controversial in the literature. Participants are instructed to remain silent while viewing, and once they have identified someone, the name is recorded as well as the suspect's position in the line-up and a photograph is taken of that person. Following each witness viewing, suspects/accused persons can change their places.

For photo line-ups, RCMP policy requires that the photographs used (either computer-generated or standard photographs) be presented sequentially, rather than simultaneously. Further, when there is more than one witness, photo line-ups should be administered separately. The Identification of Criminals Act[48] dictates the conditions under which photographs and fingerprints may be taken in order to identify persons and this legislation also applies to the photographs used in the photograph-pack arrangements created by the RCMP. A number of conditions apply that protect the rights of individuals whose photographs are taken and subsequently used. In assembling the photograph pack, the policy dictates that only one suspect/accused be contained in each similar-sized photograph pack, and that all photographs "closely" resemble the description of the accused/suspect. Finally, in presentation of the photograph pack, the policy dictates that the pack is to be shown in a different order for each witness and should involve a double-blind presentation.[49] In cases where the officer may be aware of who the suspect is, the policy requires that the officer have no knowledge of where the photograph of the suspect is in the line-up and avoid any hints, reactions, confirmations, or denials of whether the suspect was selected. The policy assures that witnesses have sufficient time with each photograph, and once an identification has been made, the officer must ask the witness why they recognize that person. Given that this policy is relatively new, it is unclear as to the extent to which it has been implemented nationally.

In addition, similar guidelines for police and prosecutors were contained in the 2005 Report on the Prevention of Miscarriages of Justice, compiled by the federal/provincial/territorial heads of the Prosecution Committee Working Group, comprised of police and prosecutors from the federal Department of Justice.[50] Their second report, released in 2011, contained a survey of nine police forces regarding the implementation of the 2005 recommendations with respect to eyewitness identification. All these forces confirmed that photo-packs were then being viewed sequentially and not as a package; moreover, all noted that comments and statements made by witnesses were being recorded in writing or by video and audio where possible (Department of Justice, 2011, 63). In addition, all but one of the police forces reported that a police officer independent of the investigation conducts the identification parade.

In the United States, a series of guidelines were produced in 1999, at the behest of then attorney general, Janet Reno, following her discovery of a number of wrongful convictions on the basis of mistaken eyewitness identification (National Institute for Justice, 1999). The guidelines expressed a clear preference for cognitive interviewing techniques (to be discussed below) for pre-line-up instructions to witnesses (informing them that the suspect may or may not be present); such techniques, it was believed, offered an immediate measure of eyewitness confidence (Doyle, 2005, 187). While these guidelines provided important direction for police forces across that country, they have not been uniformly implemented.

Likewise, much American research over the previous decade has endorsed the adoption of a number of procedures to address eyewitness misidentification, including:

1. Blind line-up administration: where the police officer administering the line-up is unaware of who the suspect is;
2. Line-up composition: fillers in the line-up should resemble the description of the perpetrator and the suspect should not be made to stand out in anyway; in photo line-ups, photographs of the suspect should be contemporary;
3. Witness instruction: the witness is informed that the suspect may or may not be present in the line-up and that the investigation will continue regardless of the line-up result;
4. Confidence statements: immediately following the identification, the witness provides an assessment of how confident they are in their identification; and
5. Recording of identification procedures: videotaping of the procedure is recommended.[51]

Fourteen states have implemented these reforms through laws, court actions, and policy directions, and at the same time a number of jurisdictions have made such reform procedures part of their standard practice.[52]

With debates continuing in the scientific community regarding research in this area, the National Academy of Sciences convened a committee of experts in 2014 to examine and evaluate the current scientific research on eyewitness identification.[53] The experts included academic researchers as well as senior members of the judiciary, government, and law enforcement. While it acknowledged that "the accuracy of eyewitness identification is improving and evolving" (NAS, 2014, 103), and despite great strides made in research and practice, the committee recognized that both police and courts continue to need guidance in understanding best practices. In terms of law enforcement, it stated that, while law-enforcement practices have considerably improved, "these efforts ... have not been uniform and often fall short as a result of insufficient training, the absence of standard operating procedures, and the continuing presence of actions and statements at the crime scene and elsewhere that may intentionally or unintentionally influence eyewitness' identifications" (103). It further recommended a number of steps to improve law-enforcement practices in this area, including:

1. Provide all law enforcement agents with ongoing "training on vision and memory and the variables that affect them, on practices for minimizing contamination, and on effective eyewitness identification protocols" (104).
2. Implement double-blind line-up and photo-array procedures (104), as well as "the adoption of clear, written policies and training on photo array and live lineup administration" (105).
3. Develop and use standardized witness instructions, including instructing the witness "that the perpetrator may or may not be in the photo array or lineup and that the criminal investigation will continue regardless of whether the witness selects a suspect."
4. Document witness confidence judgments specifically at the time when a suspect is first identified (108), and provide no feedback to the witness by the person administering the line-up.
5. Videotape the witness identification process (108).

Furthermore, the committee recommended a number of practices aimed at increasing the value of eyewitness-identification evidence in court proceedings, including:

1. Conduct pre-trial judicial inquiries, where "judges should make basic inquiries when eyewitness identification evidence is offered," in particular regarding line-ups, asking what information had been given to the eyewitness before the line-up, what instructions had been given to the eyewitness in connection with administering the line-up, and whether the line-up had been administered "blindly" (110).
2. Make juries aware of prior identifications, "including the procedures used and the confidence expressed by the witness at that time" (111).
3. Make use of scientific-framework expert testimony; this involves having experts "[describe] what factors may influence a witness's visual experience of an event and the resolution and fidelity of that experience, as well as factors that underlie and influence subsequent encoding, storage, and recall of memories of an event," since this "can inform the fact-finder in a criminal case" (111).
4. Use jury instructions as an alternative means to convey information (112).[54]

Finally, given the existing flux in the field, the committee provided recommendations aimed at improving the scientific foundations of eyewitness-identification research, including:

1. Establish a national research initiative on eyewitness identification, involving "the academic research community, law enforcement community, the federal

government, and philanthropic organizations" (113). This initiative should encompass:

a. a practice- and data-informed research agenda;
b. protocols and policies for the collection, preservation, and exchange of field data (114);
c. guidelines for the conduct and reporting of applied scientific research (114);
d. rigorous standards for systematic reviews and meta-analytic studies (115); and
e. basic instruction for police, prosecutors, defence counsel, and judges on aspects of the scientific method relevant to eyewitness identifications procedures (115).

2. Conduct additional research on system and estimator variables (117). [What is interesting is that] "at this time the committee does not recommend one lineup procedure over another (i.e., the sequential versus simultaneous debate); however, it encourages more research in this specific area, taking discriminability and likelihood of guilt as evaluation criteria into consideration" (117).

While Canadian reform efforts have advocated retaining the sequential line-up procedure, the National Academy of Sciences has not, because, in its view, "the relative superiority of competing identification procedures (i.e., simultaneous versus sequential lineups) is unresolved and there is no consensus among law enforcement officials as to the superiority of one over the other" (NAS, 2014, 3, 24).[55]

Jury Instructions

A further means of attempting to counter the difficulties with eyewitness testimony allows judges to caution juries about the dangers of relying on eyewitness-identification evidence. In fact, in Canada judges are required to caution the jury on this very matter and warn them about specific weaknesses of eyewitness testimony.[56] At the same time, there is no consensus in the literature that these types of instructions are effectual or even comprehensible to juries (Cutler and Penrod, 1995; Wise, Dauphinais, and Safer, 2007). Dufraimont (2008a, 2008b) argues that juries often do not understand the complex legal arguments presented to them by judges, since jury members are essentially laypersons entrusted with sorting through what are often difficult legal questions and arguments. Most juries would be neither conversant with the frailties of this type of testimony nor aware of the bulk of psychological research that warns against its uncritical acceptance. One argument in support of judges providing jury instructions on the frailties of eyewitness evidence is that ultimately a judge is not advocating for one side or the other but sits in a position of impartiality, and is simply providing a framework for understanding (Schermbrucker, 2004). Moreover, in Canada, judges not only instruct the jury on the applicable law but go further to apply the law to evidence (Stuesser, 2006, 28).

Justice Cory's recommendations in the commission of inquiry examining the wrongful conviction of Thomas Sophonow endorsed the idea that judges give a number of particular charges to juries about the admission of eyewitness evidence. First, judges should instruct juries that confidence in witness identification is not related to the accuracy of the identification. Second, judges should make juries aware of occasions where witnesses have gone from feeling tentatively about an identification to becoming more certain about it, and the reasons for this change. Finally, he emphasized the need for judges to stress to juries that mistaken eyewitnesses have significantly contributed to wrongful convictions in Canada and the United States.

An example of Model Jury Instructions put forward by the Canadian Judicial Council, National Judicial Institute of Canada, reflects a comprehensive understanding of the factors that affect the reliability of eyewitness evidence and are found in appendix D.[57] To a degree, these instructions reflect Justice Cory's recommendations and are to be given when the Crown's case depends entirely or largely on eyewitness-identification evidence that is challenged by the defence. When it is the defence submitting the evidence, the instruction would be worded differently, in particular, the special warning regarding wrongful conviction does not apply to this evidence. At the same time, the jury should consider the same factors to assess the eyewitness-identification evidence, but the instruction must be related to the standard of reasonable doubt.[58] The instructions underline how wrongful convictions have occurred in the past when too much unquestioned reliance is placed on this evidence, emphasize that confidence is not a predictor of reliability, and stress the importance of specific factors relevant to the particular case. These latter include the reliability of the eyewitness (including questions about eyesight, memory, etc.), the circumstances of the identification (length of time, visibility, lighting, etc.) eyewitness description (specificity, differences, certainty, etc.), and the procedure following identification (line-up, photos, confirmation, etc.). There are also procedures in place in cases of in-dock identification, if the witness failed to identify the suspect previously and when cross-racial identification is at issue.

Cognitive Interview

One development in the field of cognitive psychology that holds promise with respect to improving the accuracy of eyewitness identification is the cognitive interview (Schacter, 2001). Emerging from psychological studies on memory (Beatty and Willis, 2007), cognitive interviewing appears to mitigate some of the difficulties associated with memory recall. The cognitive interview was developed over twenty-five years ago to increase the amount of information retrieved through interviewing by providing a means of obtaining a detailed retrieval of the original event (Memon et al., 2010). In fact, this technique was specifically developed to assist police and legal professionals in conducting witness interviews (Geiselman et al., 1986). When first introduced, it was proffered as an alternative to the standard police interview and entailed unique methods for assisting eyewitnesses in recalling suspects and other details of crimes. The idea was that, by using a graduated means of open-ended questions, it would facilitate the recollection of events by both actual victims and witnesses of crimes (Fisher et al., 1989).

The steps are simple and witnesses are slowly taken through each one:

1. Context reinstatement: witnesses are asked to reinstate mentally the environmental and personal context that existed at the time of the crime, including other people, objects, the weather, etc.;

2. Comprehensive reporting: witnesses are asked to report everything, even partial information, regardless of the perceived importance of the information;
3. Variety of perspectives: witnesses are asked to recount the event in a variety of orders, including reverse order, or starting with the event that impressed the witness the most and then going backward and forward; and
4. Recounting the event from a variety of perspectives: witnesses are asked to report the event from the perspectives of other persons who were also present, explain how they would have seen it, etc. (Geiselman et al., 1986, 386, 390–1).

In addition, there are five specific techniques that can be used by an investigator to elicit specific information following the narrative of the event. They include:

1. Physical appearance: witnesses are asked if there was anything unusual about the suspect, or if he/she reminded them of someone, and why, etc.;
2. Names spoken: witnesses are asked to recall any names spoken during the incident or any initials of possible names;
3. Speech characteristics: witnesses are asked if the voice of the person reminded them of someone, or if there was anything strange about the speech pattern, such as an accent;
4. Conversation: witnesses are asked if there were any unusual words spoken or phrases used; and
5. Numbers: witnesses are asked to recall if there were any numbers or letters spoken (Geiselman et al., 1986, 391).

Moreover, interviewers are discouraged from interrupting the witness, are instructed to allow the witness to control the flow of information, and to engage in active listening (Memon et al., 2010, 342). A more enhanced version of the cognitive interview provides a detailed framework for communicating with the witness and building rapport, and involves instructing witnesses not to fabricate information but to state if they are uncertain (Fisher and Geiselman, 1992).

Early research indicated that cognitive interviewing, in experimental settings, enhanced the completeness and accuracy of eyewitness reports, and in comparison to the standard interviewing technique, it did not require greater time or more questions and its overall effect seemed to be specific to generating correct information (Geiselman et al., 1986, 399). In fact, this model of interviewing is currently used by a number of police forces in England and Wales. More recent assessments of its efficacy are equivocal. Some research points to the therapeutic value of these interviewing techniques for victims and witnesses, heightening their sense of control and restoring some power lost through victimization as well as increasing memory-recall and the amount of information obtained (Fisher and Geiselman, 2010). But other research indicates that its effects are compromised when not applied properly (Dando et al., 2009) and that it is too cumbersome, complicated, and time-consuming to use on a regular basis. Moreover, not everyone has the same cognitive capacity or level of abstract thinking required to be able to respond effectively to this type of questioning (Brown and Geiselman, 1990).

It could be argued that a method of questioning that forces witnesses to provide several versions of the same story (from a number of perspectives), versions that will, in all likelihood, either support or refute the original story, can serve only to increase the accuracy of their identifications. The use of open-ended questions and focusing on reporting everything seen or heard in context will allow witnesses to create their own version of events, detached from the official police version. At the same time, such a method requires a qualitatively different police questioning strategy and approach to interrogation, one difficult to implement within a law-enforcement culture that prizes expeditious closure of often highly charged investigations. Furthermore, without the necessary fiscal support and proper training of police officers in implementing such techniques, they are unlikely to be applied in anything other than a cursory manner.

Expert Testimony regarding the Frailties of Eyewitness Identification Evidence

Increasingly, both defence counsel and prosecutors rely on expert witnesses in criminal and civil trials to assist judges and triers of fact in deciding upon the merits of particular evidentiary questions. In fact, in one study that examined what prosecutors and defence attorneys themselves know and understand about eyewitness identification, prosecutors were deemed to be "significantly less knowledgeable than the defence attorneys on almost every issue including the weak relationship between eyewitness confidence and accuracy at trial, jurors' inability to distinguish between accurate and inaccurate eyewitnesses and the benefits of sequential lineups" (Wise et al., 2009, 1266). Lawyers in both Canada and the United States have felt the need to draw on expert testimony at trial that would underline the dangers of accepting this type of evidence; however, the manner in which the courts have treated these types of requests differs in the two countries. While initially reticent to admitting eyewitness expert testimony, since the mid-1980s appellate courts in the United States have become more receptive to it. Reasons cited for this change include: shifts in criteria for admitting expert testimony; widespread acceptance that errors in eyewitness testimony are a major factor in wrongful convictions; and general agreement among psychologists concerning the problems inherent in this type of evidence (Pedzek, 2007). One reason frequently cited as to why judges do not allow experts to testify about eyewitness testimony is that this issue is considered to be a matter of common sense (Cutler, 2004). Nevertheless, this appears to contradict a growing body of psychological research that raises a number of questions regarding so-called common-sense intuitions about eyewitness identification (Roach, 2007, 216). There continues to be debate about the importance of expert testimony to help explain the dangers surrounding witness identification. Testimony generally presented in these cases involves experts speaking to hypothetical scenarios with respect to questions about the conditions under which the eyewitness claims to have seen the perpetrator, including questions about both system and estimator variables. These experts cannot speak directly to the behaviour of specific eyewitness evidence in a particular case; rather, they can refer to psychological factors that may have had an impact on the case and attempt to dispel any misconceptions about memory-recall (Pedzek, 2007, 104).

In the United States, while it is now more common to introduce expert testimony about individual memory and its fallibility, there is little agreement as to under what conditions such testimony is admissible (Headley, 2002, 692). The *Neil v. Biggers*[59] case, discussed earlier, sets out the particular criteria necessary for jurors to evaluate the reliability of eyewitness-identification evidence. This includes the accuracy of the witness's prior description of the defendant, the opportunity to view the defendant at the time of the crime, the level of certainty demonstrated, the witness's degree of attention, and the time between the crime and the confrontation.[60] In Canadian courts, expert evidence around the fallibility of eyewitness identification is generally not admissible; more often it is judges who retain the discretion to warn the jury about problems of convicting when identity is at issue. Yet, while rarely allowing expert testimony on eyewitness evidence, the courts have left the door open for its use in the future.[61]

In Canada, *Hibbert* specifically examined the potential weakness of in-court identification and established the need for a strong warning to the jury about the difficulties with eyewitness identification. In that case the conditions under which the eyewitnesses first identified the suspect were questionable and occurred *following* his arrest. Speaking for the majority, Justice Louise Arbour found that, as stated by Justice Cory in the Sophonow Inquiry, in this case "it would have been prudent to emphasize for the benefit of the jury the very weak link between the confidence level of a witness and the accuracy of that witness."[62] In addition, in the case of *McIntosh*, the Ontario Court of Appeal upheld the lower-court judgment to exclude expert testimony from a psychologist about the fallibility of eyewitness testimony. The case was based on testimony from three eyewitness and Justice Finlayson found that testimony from a psychologist about the frailties of this evidence was not "outside the normal experience of the trier of fact"[63] and therefore not necessary since it did not meet the criteria established in *R. v. Mohan.*[64]

More recently, in a pre-trial motion in the lower-court decision of *R. v. Henderson*,[65] a Manitoba judge allowed expert testimony on the shortcomings of eyewitness identification. In that case, Justice Sinclair noted:

> Generally Canadian courts have been reluctant to admit expert testimony on eyewitness identification where the proposed testimony merely reminds jurors of what they already know. Where the proposed evidence can be shown to be outside of the common every day experience of lay persons or provides evidence to overcome myths or provides scientifically sound information that is counter-intuitive, then such evidence would, in my view, be necessary for the jury to be able to properly assess and weigh the evidence of the eyewitnesses ... It seems ironic to me, however, given the inherent frailties of eyewitness evidence, and its acknowledged overwhelming impact on a jury, that an accused should be denied a valid tool on which to challenge it. This is all the more so, considering the fact that research has shown that erroneous eyewitness evidence has occurred more than it should in the criminal justice system and wrongful convictions have directly resulted.[66]

In that instance, such testimony was permitted but was nonetheless severely circumscribed and limited to very specific areas. Shortly thereafter, another decision emerged from the Manitoba Court of Appeal regarding the use of experts to provide testimony regarding the fallacies of eyewitnesses that moved in the complete opposite direction. In *R. v. Woodward*,[67] a murder trial where there were nine eyewitnesses, the trial judge refused to admit expert evidence regarding eyewitness identification since he did not consider it necessary to assist the trier of fact. On appeal, Justice Richard J.F. Chartier justified this refusal on the grounds that "educating the jury on the frailties of eyewitness identification is generally best left with the trial judge through strong jury instructions."[68] This flip-flopping of the courts in Manitoba reflects the tensions inherent in the admission of expert testimony and is likely indicative of a future tendency towards non-admissibility.[69]

Judges sitting alone, without juries, are in a unique position regarding their consideration of eyewitnesses, since they must instruct *themselves* as to the difficulties surrounding this evidence. Justice Patrick Healy underscored the importance of judges' vigilance around eyewitnesses in a case of dangerous driving where identification of the driver was at issue. In *R. v. Touchette*,[70] a police officer saw the accused for fifteen seconds, when his car and the accused's car were stopped at a red light, from a distance of approximately five to six feet. There were no other witnesses. The police officer claimed to recognize the accused, previously known to him, with 100 per cent certainty. Justice Healy emphasized the need for caution in the face of eyewitnesses who may be sincere, credible, and acting in good faith but may also be mistaken. Moreover, he noted the importance of considering all of the circumstances where the identification is made, as well as the strength and weaknesses of the proof. When judges themselves emphasize the problems with eyewitness testimony, they are, in essence, confirming how this awareness factors into decision making.

These cautions appear consistent with the guidelines found in *R. v. Bigsky*,[71] where Justice Georgina Jackson of the Saskatchewan Court of Appeal provided a number of factors for judges to consider in eyewitness cases when sitting without a jury. In her summary of case law in this area, she established that whether courts of appeal will intervene in judge-alone cases depends on:

> (i) whether the trial judge can be taken to have instructed himself or herself regarding the frailties of eyewitness testimony and the need to test its reliability; (ii) the extent to which the trial judge has reviewed the evidence with such an instruction in mind; (iii) the extent to which proof of the Crown's case depends on the eyewitness's testimony or, in other words, the presence or absence of other evidence that can be considered in determining whether a court of appeal should intervene; (iv) the nature of the eyewitness observation including such matters as whether the eyewitness had previously known the accused and the length and quality of the observation; and (v) whether there is other evidence which may tend to make the evidence unreliable, i.e., the witness's evidence has been strengthened by inappropriate police or other procedures between the time of the eyewitness observation and the time of testimony.[72]

Legal scholars in Canada are of mixed opinion regarding the efficacy of presenting expert testimony on the frailties of eyewitness identification. Stuesser strongly argues against using experts on eyewitness testimony at trials where identification issues are being argued; he finds that "the traditional safeguards of cross-examination, counsel submissions and jury instructions adequately inform juries as to the problems with eyewitness identification" (2006, 544). In fact, he argues that it is better to use expert opinion outside the courtroom, more specifically for evidence-gathering practices, given that much of what is provided by experts is inherently intuitive. This attitude is also shared by the drafters of the Report on the Prevention of Miscarriages of Justice, compiled by the federal/provincial/territorial heads of the Prosecution Committee Working Group.[73] In their recommendations regarding eyewitness evidence, they do not advocate for expert evidence in this regard. The report states that expert-witness testimony in this matter "is redundant and usurps the function and role of the trier of fact. This is not information that is outside the regular knowledge of the jury and has the potential to distort the fact-finding process. The dangers inherent in eyewitness identification are well-documented and can be best dealt with by a proper caution by the court."[74]

The report does recommend ongoing training for police and prosecutors to inform them of the problems with this type of evidence. Yet it seems contradictory to advocate "ongoing" training for actors in the criminal justice system as to problems associated with this evidence and, at the same time, not to allow laypersons (as jurors), who possess much less knowledge about these practices, the same opportunity to inform themselves through expert testimony. In fact, a large Norwegian study on knowledge and beliefs about eyewitness testimony has demonstrated that all groups (judges, jurors, and the general public) had limited knowledge of the perils of eyewitness testimony (Magnussen et al., 2010).

As chair of the Sophonow Inquiry, Justice Cory recommended that, in cases involving eyewitnesses, trial judges should admit "properly qualified" expert evidence about eyewitness identification, while also informing the jury about studies in this field, the consequences of mistaken identity, and the frailties of memory. He argues that it is not junk science and that rigorous scholarship has demonstrated the frailties of human memory and its impact on witness identification. As stated in the inquiry's report, the "tragic consequences of mistaken eyewitness identification in cases have been chronicled and jurors and trial judges should have the benefit of expert evidence on this important subject. The expert witness can explain the process of memory and its frailties and dispel myths, such as that which assesses the accuracy of identification by the certainty of a witness. The testimony of an expert in this field would be helpful to the triers of fact and assist in providing a fair trial." Perhaps because he was confronted with the appalling details of a specific case where erroneous testimony by a number of witnesses served to wrongly convict Sophonow, Justice Cory was better able to appreciate the important role that experts could play in preventing future miscarriages based on the same types of mistakes. Moreover, Roach makes cogent arguments for an increased exercise of judicial discretion to exclude unreliable evidence, in general, and unreliable identification evidence, specifically (Roach, 2007).

Exclusion of Eyewitness Evidence

Given the difficulties encountered in the use of this type of evidence, there are some who advocate for its overall exclusion, except for cases where the witness is familiar with the suspect (Clements, 2007, 272; Douglas, 2009). Baxter believes that many of the proffered solutions to the problem do not go far enough and that a more effective solution would be for judges to exercise greater discretion in determining whether to allow this evidence to get to the jury at all (2007, 176).

Judges will often exclude eyewitness evidence if its prejudicial effect outweighs its probative value, consistent with the practice of excluding other types of prejudicial evidence (cf. *R. v. Corbett* on hearsay evidence, *R. v. Khelawon* on evidence of an earlier conviction, and *R. v. Seaboyer* on the so-called rape-shield protections).[75] One inherent difficulty with this process is the risk of the judge usurping the role of the jury by making decisions about the value and weight of evidence in their place. Canadian courts have shown a preference to warn the jury about the potential weaknesses of identification evidence instead of excluding the evidence entirely (*R. v. Mezzo*).[76] Nevertheless, if judges were to exercise this type of discretion more frequently, it might result in less questionable eyewitness evidence ever getting to the jury (Baxter, 2007). Canadian courts have attempted to address the risks of eyewitness testimony in other ways, including by confirming a right to counsel when a physical line-up takes place, though this is an extremely limited response given that police often use photo line-ups to secure such evidence (cf. *R. v. Ross*).[77]

While recognizing that the exclusion of unreliable evidence under section 7 of the Charter is not a principle of fundamental justice per se, Roach endorses the position that there is room for the common law practice of exclusion when the prejudicial effect of this evidence outweighs its probative value. He believes that jurisprudence will likely continue to develop in such a way that the courts' treatment of this issue will be reflected more in the common law tradition of the exclusion of identification evidence based on a weighing of probative value and prejudicial effect than in a larger recognition of a broad constitutional right to the exclusion of unreliable evidence (Roach, 2007, 225). The conservative nature of many Canadian courts would likely be more comfortable with the former approach than with the latter.

Conclusions

Eyewitness error is rarely, if ever, intentional. In a great majority of cases what is occurring are mistakes in the "normal operation of human memory" (Doyle, 2005, 6). Nonetheless, the consequences of this form of error are far-reaching and can result in wrongful convictions. As discussed, both police and courts are attempting to mitigate the effects or occurrence of these types of errors by reforming policy and practice, informed by many decades of psychological and legal research; however, reform efforts in this area have proven to be challenging (cf. Findley, 2016; Kahn-Fogel, 2015). In Canada, RCMP policy on eyewitness-identification processes is structured in such a way that the influence of administering officers on witness's choices is greatly reduced and the presentation of suspects (particularly when using photo-packs) limits the chances of relative judgments being made about potential perpetrators. Similarly, case law has evolved to the point where judges are now required to provide detailed instructions to juries regarding the fallibility of eyewitness testimony and other factors that relate to identification processes for each particular case. While these steps are encouraging, the RCMP policy functions solely as a guideline for other provincial and municipal police forces and does not force them to adhere to the same principles in undertaking eyewitness investigations. Likewise, while judges must provide jury instructions regarding the fallibility of eyewitness identifications, Canadian courts are still loath to allow expert testimony about this type of evidence. The field of research on this topic is such that the "average" person's understanding of the complexities of human memory and recall is limited and that it would hardly be usurping their role for judges to begin to allow testimony from experts in this regard. The bottom line with respect to this evidence is that it is reliant on, and a product of, human memory, forever malleable to outside influences and subject to erosion over time. Given these rather serious and inevitable limitations, criminal prosecutions that rely solely on eyewitness identification should be scrutinized and more concerted efforts should be made to alleviate the damaging effects that emerge from this form of testimony.

Chapter Three

The Role of Legal Professionals in Contributing to Wrongful Convictions: Police

"The seeds of almost all miscarriages of justice are sown within a few days, sometimes hours of a suspect's arrest." (Mullin, 1991)

Introduction

A number of legal professionals, acting within the parameters of their designated roles during criminal proceedings, have the opportunity to affect the outcome of an investigation and trial. These professionals, including police, prosecuting attorneys, defence counsel, and the judiciary, have varying levels of influence at varying stages in the arrest, trial, conviction, and sentencing processes; each in turn can have an impact on the safety of a conviction.

This chapter examines the role of police and how, as gatekeepers to the criminal justice system, they make the first decisions about arrest, detention, and charge. At the same time, given that police are also part of a "crime control" culture, on occasion they may be swept up in the pressure to find and prosecute a suspect. Two significant factors to be discussed, which have been shown to contribute to miscarriages of justice on the part of the police, are "noble cause" corruption and tunnel vision. Moreover, this chapter discusses both criminal-law and tort-law remedies as means of holding police accountable for their investigative procedures. It also examines recent structural and systemic reforms designed to train police officers to avoid making errors that can result in wrongful convictions in the first instance.

Police: Misconduct through Noble Cause Corruption

The police play a significant role in criminal prosecutions and as such they must make decisions under extremely stressful and at times threatening situations, decisions that may have major ramifications for themselves and the public at large. As agents of the state, the police function to uphold the law and are entrusted with that power by virtue of their training, their membership in a force, and their adherence to the "noble cause" of policing. The noble cause that the police are meant to uphold in their work has been described as a moral commitment to finding and arresting those guilty of criminal actions (Caldero and Crank, 2004). Put simply, most reactive police work begins with the notification of a criminal act, followed by an investigation, collection of evidence, arrest of suspects, and testimony at trial to support a conviction. Yet, in practice, it is far from simple and police are susceptible to public pressure to arrest and convict suspects, particularly in high-profile cases or where children have been victimized. It is in those circumstances where the police may fall victim to noble cause corruption, which has been described as the justification of improper professional practices in order to achieve the perceived "correct" result (Lamer, 2006, 71).

Much of the literature on noble cause corruption in policing defines it rather simplistically. It has been characterized as "a moral commitment to make the world a safer place" (Caldero and Crank, 2004, 29), or "corruption committed in the name of good ends ... corruption of police powers when officers do bad things because they believe that the outcomes will be good" (Caldero and Crank, 2000). MacFarlane defines it as "an ends-based police and prosecutorial culture that masks misconduct as legitimate on the basis that the guilty must be brought successfully to justice" (2008). He prefers the term "noble cause distortion" since the investigators themselves are not corrupt per se but instead believe they are pursuing justice through methods that are inappropriate and sometimes unconstitutional or criminal.

This "commitment" to the noble cause may manifest itself in myriad ways, including losing evidence, ignoring a suspect's Charter right to counsel or to silence, focusing solely on inculpatory evidence and ignoring exculpatory evidence regarding a particular suspect, coercion and threatening of suspects to achieve a confession, and so on. Other examples of this behaviour include testimonial deception, fabricating material evidence, false claims regarding how evidence was obtained, selective presentation of evidence, and improper collusion in the presentation of evidence (Kleinig, 2002, 290). One consequence that can occur is that a case is made for arresting and trying the wrong suspect which may then result in a wrongful conviction.

Such behaviour is often motivated by public pressure to solve crimes quickly, a strongly held conviction in police culture that the ends justify the means, and a sincere belief in the moral authority of the police to solve crime. The notion of noble cause corruption emerged from Klockars's (1980) earlier work regarding what he termed the "Dirty Harry problem,"[1] which raised the question as to what extent it was justifiable for police to commit "dirty" or illegal acts to achieve a desired end. Given that few disincentives exist to deter unlawful behaviour in pursuit of a suspect when solving crime, it is not particularly surprising that this means-ends thinking exists. Further, Klockars (1980) argued early on that this form of policing stems from the operative assumption that most, if not all, suspects are guilty. More recently, Klockars (2005) continues to posit that the Dirty Harry problem is "an ineluctable part of police work" and that "it is insoluble" (581). Some believe that noble cause corruption can also be characterized by moral ambiguity (Kleinig, 2002). This form of corruption is thought to differ greatly from other forms of corruption motivated by material gain; noble cause corruption is not self-serving but is rather directed towards the public good, ensuring public safety, promoting justice, and obtaining the conviction of the guilty. Where this behaviour falls down is when rights are abrogated in the pursuit of "justice" or when the wrong persons are targeted.

Two aspects of noble cause corruption that have received further research attention and serve similar functions are confirmation bias and tunnel vision.

Confirmation bias occurs through the actions of police when investigating a crime and has been described as "the seeking or interpreting of evidence in ways that are partial to existing beliefs, expectations, or a hypothesis in hand" (Nickerson, 1998, 175). Thus consistent with a given hypothesis about a particular suspect, confirmation bias occurs as police seek information that inculpates a given suspect and effectively ignores exculpatory information (Hill et al., 2008). On the other hand, tunnel vision encompasses confirmation bias, is far more insidious, and is practised by various actors in the criminal justice system.

Police: Misconduct through Tunnel Vision

"The police found their suspect and then proceeded to search for the facts to fit him." (Former U.S. attorney general Homer Cummings, referred to in *Frank* [1957, 66])

Through investigating criminal cases, police officers are in a unique position to affect evidence, witnesses, and ultimately the outcome of criminal proceedings; their conduct can contribute to miscarriages of justice, particularly as a result of tunnel vision (Martin, 2001a). Justice Fred Kaufman, in the report of the Commission on the Proceedings involving Guy Paul Morin, describes tunnel vision as "the single-minded and overly narrow focus on a particular investigative or prosecutorial theory, so as to unreasonably colour the evaluation of information received and one's conduct in response to that information" (Kaufman, 1134). The result is that all other theories or plausible explanations are often ignored and exculpatory evidence that could eliminate an individual is disregarded. Kaufman recognizes that tunnel vision can occur on the part of both investigators and prosecutors, is systemic and structural in nature, and can have an impact in shaping the testimony of witnesses (MacFarlane, 2008, 32).

In MacFarlane's overview of tunnel vision, he points out that it signifies a type of wilful blindness on the part of both police and prosecutors; at the same time, it does not mean that people are acting dishonestly, but rather that intense public pressure to solve a serious crime forces them to find a suspect quickly (2008, 31). Essential elements of tunnel vision are thought to include an overly narrow focus on a particular investigative or prosecutorial theory, which influences how information is evaluated and acted upon and results in unconscious filtering of evidence that "builds a case" against a particular suspect while ignoring exculpatory evidence (MacFarlane, 2008, 34). Furthermore, Findley and Scott (2006, 307) aptly demonstrate that tunnel vision results from a number of cognitive distortions that are part of our psychological make-up; extensive research by experimental psychologists over the past few decades has supported the existence and persistence of these distortions. The biases that are inherent to tunnel vision serve to unconsciously distort our perceptions and our interpretations of them and include confirmation bias, hindsight bias, and outcome bias. As discussed, confirmation bias involves seeking out, interpreting, or recalling evidence or information that supports existing beliefs; hindsight bias is a means of projecting new knowledge, or outcomes, into the past whereby the early stages of the process connect causally to the end; and outcome bias reflects hindsight judgments about whether a decision was a good or bad one, a correct or incorrect one (Findley and Scott, 2006, 309–20). What these biases demonstrate is that, once an individual has been targeted as a suspect, then, for whatever reason, particular cognitive processes operate, often unconsciously, to reinforce initial suspicions. The strength of these beliefs is such that, when other evidence is discovered that may contradict earlier presuppositions, it is often minimized, discounted, or ignored. What Findley and Scott underline is that, in the vast majority of cases, tunnel vision is not due to conscious efforts on the part of police, prosecutors, and the judiciary to bow to institutional pressures and pursue the wrong suspect at the expense of the truth; rather, it is an inevitable part of human nature when data is accessed and interpreted.

Tunnel vision is also thought to result from a number of institutional pressures on both police and prosecutors. This includes the often sensational nature of the case, which forces an expeditious outcome; resource constraints that limit the numbers of officers and hours that are allocated to cases; emotional attachment to victims and to obtaining justice; and the emergent victims-rights movements which place greater pressure on police. Moreover, prosecutors also share the pressure to convict in these high-profile cases, and in doing their job most believe in the guilt of the accused. Their close working relationship with the police and their unidimensional view of the case (absent information on other eliminated suspects) fosters a type of tunnel vision on their part as well (MacFarlane, 2008, 45–55). In order to avoid being "trapped in the tunnel," MacFarlane argues in favour of pre-screening of suspects files more carefully and exploring all leads at the early stages, through sending police files to the Crown prior to charge and to utilizing case conferences more often, which allow for greater scrutiny of evidence prior to charging (2008, 43). At the same time, instances of tunnel vision and noble cause corruption on the part of both the police and the prosecution are evident in other aspects of police work, outside of high-profile cases.

As Justice Lamer notes in the report of the commission of inquiry examining the wrongful conviction of three individuals, tunnel vision can create a vicious circle: "Tunnel vision is rarely the result of malice on the part of individuals. Rather it is generated by a police and prosecutorial culture that allows the subconscious mind to rationalize a biased approach to the evidence. Moreover, it is mutually reinforcing amongst police officers, amongst prosecutors and in the interaction between these groups of professionals. It may even affect judges."[2] A number of other commissions of inquiry[3] that have taken place in recent years in Canada and elsewhere have also underlined the impact of tunnel vision on miscarriages of justice. Not surprisingly, focusing in the early stages of an investigation on one individual, while ignoring other exculpatory evidence, has had a significant impact on wrongful convictions. This was emphasized first in the Kaufman Inquiry into the wrongful conviction of Guy Paul Morin. In this instance, Justice Kaufman pointed out that tunnel vision so coloured the investigator's treatment of Morin's alibi evidence that it became apparent that the investigator's intention was clearly to disprove the alibi rather than consider it in an open-minded way. In fact, in his testimony at the inquiry, Inspector John Shepherd, an investigating officer on the case, admitted to differential treatment of evidence that supported Morin's guilt and evidence that supported his innocence – a classic example of tunnel vision.[4] In the inquiry investigating the wrongful conviction of Thomas Sophonow, tunnel vision was clearly operating as the police quickly focused on him as a suspect and ignored evidence or explanations contrary to their theory of the crime. Justice Cory pointed out that this narrow focus on Sophonow by the police likely allowed another more plausible suspect to slip through the cracks of the investigation. Even though the evidence regarding the timing of the murder made it "theoretically possible, although practically difficult and unlikely" for Sophonow to have arrived at the donut shop and committed the murder, he nonetheless became the prime suspect.[5]

The Lamer Commission of Inquiry pertaining to the cases of Ronald Dalton, Gregory Parsons, and Randy Druken found much confusion, disorganization, and incompetence in the investigations undertaken by the police, particularly with respect to Parsons and Druken.[6] In Gregory Parsons's case, the police lacked training, experience, and leadership; tunnel vision contributed to the acceptance of hearsay statements as truthful, the pressuring of some witnesses to change their statements to be consistent with the police version of events, an exaggeration of worthless and trivial evidence, and ignoring contradictory evidence.[7] For Randy Druken, tunnel vision on the part of the police led to the early conclusion that he was guilty and contributed to a number of questionable police practices, including attempts to influence key witnesses to change their stories; reliance and unwarranted reliability on, and misuse of, the polygraph results of the defendant and key witnesses; ignoring or discounting scientific/forensic evidence; witness and media contamination of the evidence of potential witnesses; and a lack of analysis of surveillance information.[8]

Despite evidence of tunnel vision in a number of known wrongful-conviction cases in Canada in recent years, Justice Edward P. MacCallum, who chaired the inquiry investigating the wrongful conviction of David Milgaard, found no evidence of tunnel vision – or simple incompetence – in that case. He stated that the investigation by the Saskatoon police and the RCMP was conducted in good faith and complied with the standards of policing of the day; "tunnel vision, negligence and misconduct have been alleged, but not shown."[9] MacCallum argued that neither tunnel vision nor incompetence on the part of the police was evident in this case since they investigated more than two hundred other suspects, followed other leads, and held an honest but reasonable belief that Milgaard was responsible for the murder.[10] These findings appear to contradict the strong evidence of tunnel vision that did in fact occur in this case: the police quickly focused on Milgaard as a suspect, they ignored evidence about the "real" killer provided by his own wife, and evidence that a serial rapist was at large in the same neighbourhood was also disregarded. Furthermore, two key witnesses, who had initially provided Milgaard with an alibi by stating that they had been with him on the morning of the murder, later changed their stories after much police interviewing and pressure. Even after DNA conclusively demonstrated Milgaard's innocence and pointed to another suspect, the Saskatoon police had difficulty believing the evidence.[11]

Holding Police Accountable: Criminal Law

The possibilities of pursuing the police through legal action when they either fail to do their duty or act with impunity are somewhat limited. Non-criminal acts may be addressed through disciplinary actions of the police force, whereas the Criminal Code allows for criminal charges to be brought against police for actions prohibited therein. Yet charging and convicting police officers, even for the most reprehensible of offences (i.e., murder), is very difficult[12] and the circumstances under which the Crown might pursue police officers through criminal law are rarer still. There would need to be overwhelming evidence of misconduct in addition to some evidence of bodily harm. Moreover, the chances of succeeding in such actions are slim, primarily because the Criminal Code does not allow citizens to defend themselves against lawful arrest (hence the resisting-arrest provision).

The recent case of *R. v. Nasogaluak*[13] in the province of Alberta is particularly noteworthy since it allowed for the reduction in sentencing, below the mandatory minimums dictated by the Criminal Code, in cases of particularly egregious misconduct on the part of the police. Following a high-speed chase by the RCMP on a suspicion he was drinking and driving, police ordered Mr Nasogaluak to exit his car; he refused. He was removed from his car and punched in the head three times by one officer and another punched him twice in the back to free his arms for handcuffs. At the station, while there were no visible signs of injury, Nasogaluak complained of pain and an inability to breathe; he was refused medical attention. Upon admission to the hospital following his release, it was determined he had two broken ribs and a collapsed lung that needed emergency surgery. While he initially pleaded guilty for impaired driving, at sentencing Nasogaluak moved for a stay of proceedings based on police conduct in breach of his rights under sections 7, 11(d), and 12 of the Charter.

The trial judge found that the RCMP had used excessive force and violated Nasogaluak's section 7 rights. While the typical sentence should have been six to eighteen months for impaired driving and evading police, as a remedy for the Charter breach, he was given a one-year conditional discharge and one-year driving prohibition. Allowing the appeal, the Alberta Court of Appeal upheld the lower court's finding that excessive force had been used, that the accused's setion 7 rights were violated under the Charter, and that the sentence could be reduced. While the Supreme Court did not find resort to reduction below a mandatory minimum to be always applicable in cases of Charter breaches, it left the door open for that possibility in exceptional cases where there has been egregious misconduct by police or other state actors. More generally, it underlined that sentencing discretion must be exercised within the confines of the Criminal Code. What this case illustrates is a greater openness to hold the police accountable when they violate suspect rights, while also establishing a very high bar for ascertaining when those rights have actually been violated.

Holding Police Accountable: Tort Law

The private law of civil wrongs, or tort law, provides individuals who feel they have been unjustly accused, arrested, or convicted the opportunity to seek redress through restitution from the police in civil law. Tort actions in this regard include malicious prosecution, abuse of process, false imprisonment, and misfeasance in public office; each of these civil-law remedies is slow, expensive, and with uncertain outcome. In addition, those already mistrustful of a system that has failed them are unlikely to rely on that same justice system for recourse. In sum, tort law does not appear to be an ideal forum for pursuing complaints about wrongful accusation and wrongful conviction (Chamberlain, 2008). Nonetheless, the courts have recently recognized the tort of negligent investigation, which may provide another avenue for the wrongly accused and convicted to pursue the police for negligence in their duty.

Negligence law is based on the idea that, when a relationship exists between two persons that is said to give rise to a duty of care, then reasonable care must be taken by one person to avoid harm or injury to the other. In other words, this "neighbour" principle requires persons "to avoid acts or omissions which you can reasonably foresee would be likely to injure your neighbor."[14] And, in cases where insufficient care has been taken, a tort in negligence law can be pursed. The courts have established that a prima facie duty of care exists between individuals when there is sufficient foreseeability of harm, as well as a direct relationship of proximity between the individuals.[15] Finally, there must also be no overriding policy reasons that would negate the establishment of a duty of care.[16] The courts have applied this analysis to find a duty of care between solicitors and clients, and doctors and patients, among others.

There seems to be a new openness on the part of the courts to holding police and prosecutors accountable in this way. In 2007 the Supreme Court of Canada recognized the tort of negligent investigation and was the first common law country to do so (Fraser, 2007), allowing citizens to sue the police if it can be proved that they acted negligently in pursuing them in a criminal action. The tort was established in the case of *Hill v. Hamilton-Wentworth Regional Police Service Board*,[17] where the courts found that the police owed a duty of care to suspects during an investigation; however, the tort was not made out on the facts of Hill's case. Hill was a suspect in ten robberies that had occurred in the Hamilton area over a three-week period in 1994–5. The suspect in these crimes had used the same modus operandi and eyewitnesses had given similar descriptions of him to the police.

Hill became a suspect early on in the investigation and his photo was released to the media, potentially tainting any later identifications. The evidence against him included a Crime Stoppers tip (anonymous tip to the police), identification by the police through a surveillance photo, several eyewitness identifications, a potential sighting of Hill near the scene of one of the robberies, eyewitness evidence that the robber appeared to be Indigenous (Hill was), and a police belief that all the robberies were committed by the same individual (Sutherland, 2007). Hill was subsequently arrested and his picture became part of a photo line-up. While the other eleven fillers[18] physically resembled Hill, a fundamental problem with the composition of the line-up was that he was the only Indigenous person. As pointed out by the Aboriginal Legal Services of Toronto (ALST)[19] (2007), having one Indigenous person in a police line-up established in pursuit of an Indigenous suspect is inherently racist. It perpetuates an attitude commonly taken towards racialized groups by dominant majorities, consistent with the mentality of "they all look the same." Given the extreme overrepresentation of Indigenous peoples in the criminal justice system, this was a substantial oversight on the part of the police. It is also possible that the "cross-race effect," as discussed in chapter 2, had an effect on the outcome of the case, given that Hill was the only Indigenous person in the line-up. As submitted by the ALST, "police officers in this case should have considered the fairness of the photo line-up in light of the propensity of people to view Aboriginal persons as criminals" (2007, 35). Moreover, there had been a number of witnesses who described the robber as "Hispanic" and having no Hispanic foils in the line-up rendered it inherently unfair (ALST, 2007).

Following Hill's arrest, a great deal of exculpatory evidence[20] surfaced and the ten original charges against him were reduced to one. Hill was ultimately convicted for this robbery charge and served over twenty months in jail; he was acquitted on appeal and brought a civil suit[21] against the police and Crown attorney's office. The Supreme Court considered the claims of negligence brought forward, which included: suspect identification based on the fact that the two tellers were interviewed together with Hill's picture in front of them; witness interview methods; photo line-up methods (as discussed above); and police failure to reinvestigate the robberies adequately when new exculpatory evidence emerged. The court found that "police are not immune from liability under the Canadian law of negligence, that the police owe a duty of care in negligence to suspects being investigated, and that their conduct during the course of an investigation should be measured against the standard of how a reasonable officer in like circumstances would have acted … The law of negligence does not demand a perfect investigation. It requires only that police conducting an investigation act reasonably."[22] Chief Justice Beverley McLachlin further recognized that the police do play a role in miscarriages of justice: "The record shows that wrongful convictions traceable to faulty police investigations occur ... Police conduct that is not malicious, not deliberate, but merely fails to comply with standards of reasonableness can be a significant cause of wrongful convictions."[23] At the same time, McLachlin supported the idea that this tort will "assist in responding to failures of the justice system, such as wrongful convictions or institutional racism."[24] By creating the possibility of pursuing the police through this tort action, the Court considered it as a further protection for the wrongly convicted: "The existing remedies for wrongful prosecution and conviction are incomplete and may leave a victim of negligent investigation without legal recourse. The torts of false arrest, false imprisonment and malicious prosecution do not provide an adequate remedy for negligent acts …To deny a remedy in tort is, quite literally, to deny justice."[25]

Some speculate that this may well be a rather ambitious objective for the tort of negligent investigation and perhaps it will be undercut by the Court's articulation of the applicable standard of care – that of a "reasonable police officer" – since this is tempered by the Court's deference to the practices at the time when the arrest occurred (Sutherland, 2007). In spite of the fact that the racist police practice evident in the composition of the line-up in Hill may not have been considered by the courts to be good practice for police officers more generally, it still found that this was consistent with how police operated in 1995. Indeed, though there have been recent victories for claimants in this area, the majority of cases decided since Hill indicate that the courts will defer to the discretionary decisions of police officers in many cases. Claims may be more likely to succeed where there is obvious negligence on the part of police, including where tunnel vision has clearly contributed to the wrongful conviction, where police ignore relevant evidence of an accused's innocence, where charges were laid without adequate inquiry or justification, and where the actions leading to the wrongful conviction are well documented and publicized (Chamberlain, 2012).

Even where the facts may be conducive to a claim for negligent investigation however, holding only one individual – a police officer – liable in negligence for a wrongful conviction may not be the best approach for a problem that is clearly systemic in nature. Freund posits that the remedy should be left to government compensation schemes where factual innocence must be established (2008). It has also been argued, by the dissent in *Hill*, that this tort could open the door to situations where factually guilty individuals, able to prove negligent investigation, could be exonerated. Police services across Canada share this concern that the tort could open a flood of litigation against the police if and when their investigations have not resulted in convictions (Chamberlain, 2008, 3). In reality, this fear is partially unfounded, given that "the Hill decision is ... perhaps best viewed as only a partial loss for law enforcement agencies in Canada. While the case does confirm the existence of a tort of negligent investigation, it also adopts a standard of care that requires consideration of historical circumstances and, as a result, likely has the effect of shielding investigating officers from liability in many cases" (Nicholson, 2009, 2–4).

The Hill decision underscores the fact that policing in and of itself is a profession that adheres to a proscribed set of standards, consisting of rules and procedures that have not yet been delineated by Parliament (Roach, cited in Nicholson, 2009, 2). Following *Hill*, it is now up to police services to "make every effort to remain attuned and in step with advances in policing techniques and standards, as well as with more general changes in society at large, in order to avoid challenges to the manner in which they carry out investigations" (Nicholson, 2009, 4). The fear of floodgates of litigation following the *Hill* decision has yet to be realized and seems highly unlikely given the many roadblocks that exist in establishing negligence claims more generally.

Structural and Systemic Reforms

While legal reforms may occur following a wrongful conviction and are welcome in the legal community, such reforms are essentially reactive in nature. Consequently, their reach may be somewhat limited and the extent to which reforms that occur through the courts and through jurisprudence actually affect police practices remains questionable. What may be of greater value are proactive efforts, those that prevent wrongful convictions from occurring in the first instance. Given the spate of wrongful convictions that have occurred in Canada over the previous three decades, police forces throughout the country have attempted to address the factors that contribute to them through a number of structural and systemic reforms. Often the main focus of such reforms has been to enhance educational opportunities that focus on increasing police training around the factors that contribute to wrongful convictions as well as reinforcing proper investigative techniques.[26] The majority of this training appears to be in the area of Major Case Management (MCM) – which provides a means for police services to organize and prioritize the vast amounts of information that often accompany serious crimes, notably homicide, sexual assault, and abductions.[27]

Police services in the province of Ontario, for example, use MCM in major crimes to compile information through specialized software, to keep track of all investigative materials, to streamline investigations, and to identify common links between crimes committed in different locations.[28] The impetus for this training occurred as a result of the Bernardo Investigation Review,[29] chaired by Justice Archie Campbell, that examined, inter alia, the role of the police regarding the investigation and arrest of Paul Bernardo in 1995. What appeared problematic in this investigation was a lack of coordinated effort and little cooperation and communication between police and other actors in the criminal justice system, which allowed Bernardo to remain at large and continue to commit serial rape and murder for a period of time, despite the police's best efforts. A key recommendation of Justice Campbell was the need for an automated management system for police services in Ontario when investigating serious crimes; what emerged was the current Major Case Management system.[30]

On the national level, the Canadian Police College in Ottawa provides courses in MCM, serious-crime investigation, and sensitization to wrongful convictions, to which police agencies may send officers for specific training. Most provinces provide training in MCM, file coordination, and serious-crime investigations of varying degrees and levels, training that is offered to municipal police, provincial police, and the RCMP.[31] Notably, the findings from a number of commissions of inquiry examining wrongful convictions serve to inform pedagogy for these courses, allowing police to learn from the errors of other police officers as well as providing lessons on how to prevent wrongful convictions in the first place by recognizing the contributing factors when they occur. The advantages to this type of training are that police become sensitized not only to the need for the sharing of information in investigations but also to the need for vigilance around tunnel vision and the importance of proceeding with caution, particularly early on in an investigation. When police become more aware of the significance of their investigative practices in contributing to wrongful convictions, then the greater the likelihood of finding the true perpetrator of a given crime. Training in and the use of MCM strategies serve a preventive function in avoiding wrongful convictions, but greater overall vigilance in this regard could lead to larger changes on a systemic level, whereby police routinely question their own assumptions and practices in major crime investigations.

Conclusions

Wrongful convictions tend to erode public confidence in the role of police and, as noted by Goldsmith, "without public trust in police, 'policing by consent' is difficult or impossible and public safety suffers" (Goldsmith, 2005, 443). It is impossible to ascertain whether police officers in Canada have become more accountable to the public regarding their investigative actions following the decision in *Hill*. Perhaps the courts are limited in their ability to hold the police accountable, and it is really the public at large that holds this power. With the advent of the introduction of body-worn cameras, increasingly used to enhance police accountability and improve police-citizen relations, it would appear that police have less opportunity to deny misconduct in those cases when it does occur.[32] Similarly, citizens armed with cameras have the right to film police carrying out their public functions, so long as they do not interfere with police work.[33] Many recent cases where footage of police misconduct has "gone viral" have resulted in a number of criminal prosecutions against police officers. At the same time, one unintended result of this increased public vigilance regarding police behaviour may be that police officers will find other, underground, means of dealing with suspects outside of the norms of expected conduct. Regardless, increased vigilance alone is unable to address adequately the institutional pressures that result in tunnel vision, which in turn causes police to focus on the wrong suspect and influences how the evidence collected is evaluated and acted upon. As discussed, tunnel vision greatly contributes to wrongful convictions perpetrated by the police. Human nature is such that these kinds of errors are likely to continue to occur and what are needed are not only continual vigilance but also ongoing police training and greater overall accountability.

The Role of Legal Professionals in Contributing to Wrongful Convictions: Prosecutors, Defence Counsel, and the Judiciary

Introduction

Other actors working within the criminal justice system also play a role not only in contributing to miscarriages of justice but also in preventing them. For their part, prosecutors are guardians of the public interest and their role is to ensure a fair process so that the outcome of a trial rests on its factual basis. Nonetheless, they are sometimes guilty of overzealousness in their fight to "win" cases, and given their close alignment with the police services in criminal cases, they may also be guilty of tunnel vision. Defence attorneys, on the other hand, have a complex role in providing both information and support to their clients regarding their rights, clarity about criminal trial processes, and the consequences of pleadings. At the same time, not all defence counsel have the same ability and knowledge of the law and jurisprudence, nor are they able to serve their clients to the same degree. Finally, judges also have a part to play with respect to addressing miscarriages of justice, in particular at the preliminary inquiry stage, with their charge to juries and in their power to hand down a directed verdict when warranted. The focus of this chapter is on outlining the roles and responsibilities of each of these legal professionals with respect to miscarriages of justice.

The Role of the Prosecution

"A delicate balance is required between the dual responsibilities of being an advocate in an adversarial process yet never 'winning or losing.'" (Lamer, 2006, 279)

Prosecutors or Crown attorneys function as guardians of the public interest and are also bound by certain professional obligations, which are meant to ensure that criminal prosecutions are carried out fairly, objectively, and with integrity.[1] This principle is reiterated in the rules of professional conduct, where it is emphasized that "when engaged as a prosecutor, the lawyer's primary duty is not to seek to convict but to see that justice is done through a fair trial on the merits." The prosecutor's role is to represent the state, on behalf of the victim of an alleged crime, and present evidence and witnesses to bolster the state's argument that the accused did, in fact, commit the crime. It is the responsibility of the prosecution to convince the judge or jury of that fact, beyond a reasonable doubt. While the accused may present evidence of his or her innocence, it is the responsibility of the prosecution to prove guilt. The role of the Crown attorney is a difficult one, and earlier case law explains the dilemmas faced by the Crown's office:

> It cannot be overemphasized that the purpose of a criminal prosecution is not to obtain a conviction; it is to lay before a jury what the Crown considers to be credible evidence relevant to what is alleged to be a crime. Counsel have a duty to see that all available legal proof of the facts is presented: it should be done firmly and pressed to its legitimate strength, but it must also be done fairly. The role of the prosecutor excludes any notion of winning or losing; his function is a matter of public duty than which in civil life there can be none charged with greater personal responsibility. It is to be efficiently performed with an ingrained sense of the dignity, the seriousness and the justness of judicial proceedings. (*Boucher v. The Queen* [1954], 110 C.C.C. 263 [S.C.C.] at 270)

In addition to the rules of professional conduct set out by the provincial law society to which the lawyer belongs, Crown prosecutors serve a public function and are therefore expected to act in the public interest at all times. When a prosecutor fails to meet the relevant standards of professional conduct, the breach may be dealt with by the provincial law society under which the prosecutor holds membership, though this review process is limited to acts that are dishonest or taken in bad faith and will not interfere with the wide latitude given to actions taken under prosecutorial discretion save for instances of "flagrant impropriety."[2] Jurisprudence has thus emphasized the importance of public duty, fairness, and discretion with respect to the role and function of the Crown. While laudable goals, these are difficult ideals to live up to at times, given the pressurized atmosphere that often surrounds high-profile cases and the public demand that they be solved quickly.

Whereas the idea of "winning and losing" cases on behalf of the prosecution runs counter to Justice Ivan Cleveland Rand's oft-cited pronouncement above in *Boucher*, MacFarlane points out that the very nature of our adversarial system forces participants to adopt that very mindset (2008, 45). This in turn means, unfortunately, that miscarriages of justice can occur. Green (2005) argues that a Crown culture does indeed exist in the Canadian context, one that "places paramount value on winning, that confuses its functions with those of the police, and that stubbornly resists the prospect of factual error" (264). Acts of deliberate malfeasance or nonfeasance on the part of the Crown's office are relatively uncommon; also, wilfully unlawful acts, acts of illegal conduct, or failure to meet legal obligations occur infrequently too. More common are acts of omission, particularly when evidence or information is withheld from the defence since it is thought not to be "relevant," or what Green describes as an abandonment of "the obligation to positively protect innocence ... [which] ... is left exclusively to 'the defence'" (2005, 267).

Prosecutorial Misconduct

While relatively rare, instances of prosecutorial misconduct do occur. Similar to the police, Crown attorneys are under pressure to "solve" high-profile cases, with expedient trials and, ultimately, convictions. The role of a prosecutor is inherently contradictory: they are "expected to be neutral, independent ministers of justice" and yet also face intense pressure to obtain convictions (Bandes, 2005–6, 483). As public servants, prosecutors have abundant resources at their disposal, but at the same time they are answerable to the government and to the public. Joy (2006) believes there are a number of incentives for prosecutors to engage in misconduct: "Prosecutorial misconduct is largely the result of three institutional conditions: vague ethics rules that provide ambiguous guidance to prosecutors; vast discretionary authority with little or no transparency; and inadequate remedies for prosecutorial misconduct, which create perverse incentives for prosecutors to engage in, rather than refrain from, prosecutorial misconduct" (400).

Prosecutorial misconduct is comprised of a wide range of things, including, inter alia, actions occurring pre-trial (such as omissions in investigative work and in determining charges, and in preparing cases based on inadequate information) and decisions after conviction in the face of evidence that someone else perpetrated the crime (sometimes lying, deliberately withholding evidence, and other bad-faith behaviour) (Bandes, 2005–6, 479). The most prevalent forms of prosecutorial "misbehaviour" have been described as inflammatory jury addresses and improper cross-examinations (Frater, 2002, 209). Moreover, problems may arise when prosecutors seek to lay charges based on what has been termed the "moral worth of criminal defendants," rather than the facts of the case or the probability of a conviction (Wright and Miller, 2008). It has been argued that this factor alone contributes greatly to wrongful convictions. A further characterization is that of prosecutors as agents of trust, and misconduct in that context becomes construed as a violation of that trust (Schoenfeld, 2005). A final recurring theme is a tendency for the prosecution to "develop a fierce loyalty to a particular version of events: the guilt of a particular suspect or group of suspects" (Bandes, 2005–6, 479). Such an outlook often persists in the face of contrary evidence and is accompanied by a refusal to consider other possible stories, even in the aftermath of exoneration, "at the expense of concern for larger questions of justice" (Bandes, 2005–6, 488).

Medwed (2004) argues that, for many prosecutors, an institutional culture exists that makes them resistant to claims of innocence following a conviction. This intransigence, aside from larger questions about the administration of justice, allows the "real" killer to roam free and represents a misdirection of public resources. A refusal to consider other possibilities regarding innocence translates into stubbornness at other stages as well: refusal to contemplate other suspects or refusal to examine other additional evidence. Medwed blames this mainly on the "organization conviction psychology, where convictions are prized above all else" (2004, 137). Moreover, acknowledging the possibility of innocence in past convictions involves acknowledging error and opens up Crown actions for further scrutiny.

In the United States, the prosecutor's office is under different pressures than in Canada. First of all, district attorneys are elected officials, and consequently they must appease the populations they serve; and, second, given the fact that they are elected, a determining factor in their remaining elected is the number of convictions they procure. In fact, research has indicated that American prosecutors are motivated by conviction rates and these rates ultimately serve as a measure of their efficacy (Medwed, 2004); external pressures from victims' advocacy groups also influence prosecutorial discretion (Fisher, 1988), as does the race of the defendant (Davis, 1998).

The joint case of Rolando Cruz and Alejandro Hernandez, two Illinois men who spent ten years on death row, illustrates the impact of prosecutorial intransigence. Cruz and Hernandez were sentenced to death for the kidnapping, sexual assault, and murder of a ten-year-old girl in 1985. Shortly after their sentencing, another man who had a history of similar crimes confessed to this killing, but his testimony was downplayed and not followed up. Cruz and Hernandez had alibis for the time of the crime and there was no physical evidence linking them to the crime scene; the only evidence against them came from jailhouse informants who benefited from their testimony and an alleged confession to a police officer that was later recanted. A *Chicago Tribune* newspaper series on their cases indicated that political machinations were at play: the state's attorney had in fact indicted Cruz and Hernandez only two weeks before his bid for re-election.[3] These types of "partisan trials" are also not uncommon in the United Kingdom, particularly in terrorism cases[4] and those "involving political matters … [they] are inherently unfair proceedings for which governments have essentially predetermined that a conviction will be obtained" (Lutz et al., 2002, 113).

While unusual, there have been some instances in Canada where prosecutors have influenced the outcome of a case that later resulted in a wrongful conviction. In Manitoba, George Dangerfield, a Crown prosecutor working for the attorney general's office in the 1980s and 1990s, has been implicated in four convictions that were based on evidence that was later found to be questionable. The murder convictions of Thomas Sophonow, Kyle Unger, and James Driskell were all prosecuted by Dangerfield and were all in error; what occurred in those cases has since been subjected to review through commissions of inquiry. Among other issues, in Driskell's case it was found that Dangerfield knew a Crown witness lied on the stand but allowed the testimony nonetheless; in Sophonow's case, the Crown attorneys involved (including Dangerfield) failed to disclose evidence that would have raised questions about the credibility of Crown witnesses; and in Unger's case a jailhouse informant who testified against Unger was given consideration on outstanding charges of his own, and his testimony was later found to be false. A further man, Frank Ostrowski, who was prosecuted by Dangerfield is currently having his appeal heard by the Manitoba Court of Appeal; he was released in 2009 on appeal after serving twenty-three years in jail for a murder he may well not have committed.[5] There are also calls for still other cases prosecuted by Dangerfield to be examined further.[6] While the complete results of the investigation into Dangerfield's other cases has yet to be tabled, all four cases mentioned above have similarities: "failure to disclose exculpatory evidence, secret deals to drop charges in return for testimony, and reliance on unsavoury witnesses" (MacDonald, 2009). All of these convictions occurred prior to the availability of DNA identification evidence and prior to the advent of stricter common law rules regarding disclosure of Crown evidence. It seems possible that Dangerfield worked in conjunction with a police force that was determined to achieve convictions at all costs, allowing this type of flawed evidence to stand without question.

As a final example, prosecutorial misconduct was one of the many factors that contributed to the wrongful conviction of Donald Marshall, Jr. Over the course of

Marshall's case, Crown prosecutor Donald C. MacNeil failed to discharge his professional obligations by neglecting to properly interview witnesses who had given contradictory statements and by not disclosing that inconsistencies existed in the witness statements relied upon in the prosecution. A royal commission of inquiry examining Marshall's prosecution determined that these professional failures contributed to the wrongful conviction in this case.[7]

Malicious Prosecution

As in instances of police misconduct, the private law of civil wrongs can offer possible remedies when Crown attorneys have acted beyond the dictates of their job. But, again, the remedies of tort law are slow and expensive and have uncertain outcomes. One remedy, malicious prosecution, can be brought against the Crown's office but requires that the plaintiff prove the defendant acted without reasonable and probable cause and with a purpose other than carrying the law into effect (Fleming, 1977, 598).[8] While rarely successful in the courts, given the difficulty of proving the existence of the subjective fault requirement of malice,[9] recent decisions may indicate a new openness of the courts to holding police and prosecutors accountable in this way. The Supreme Court in *R. v. Nelles* established four criteria (from Fleming, 1977) for a charge of malicious prosecution:

1. The proceedings must have been initiated by the defendant;
2. The proceedings must have terminated in favour of the plaintiff;
3. The plaintiff must show that the proceedings were instituted in the absence of reasonable and probable cause; and
4. The plaintiff must show that the defendant was motivated by malice or a primary purpose other than that of carrying the law into effect (para. 42).

Malicious prosecution cases are notoriously difficult to win; as of 2009, there were only three reported cases in which the Crown was found liable for malicious prosecution.[10] For example, in 2002 Jason Dix[11] was successful in a civil action of malicious prosecution and false imprisonment against the federal and provincial attorneys general, the Alberta Crown, and the RCMP. Dix was incarcerated for twenty-three months awaiting trial for a double homicide that he did not commit. He became a suspect as the result of a police sting[12] operation and was subjected to a number of other unethical police actions: he experienced eleven hours of interrogation, without anything to eat or drink; he was forced to drive to the crime scene; and evidence against him was procured through jailhouse informants who benefited from their testimony. In addition, the police induced an informant to fabricate a letter framing Dix and implicating him in a hired killing; the prosecutor in this case, Arnold Piragoff, was aware the letter was false but nonetheless used it at bail hearings to bolster arguments that Dix was dangerous.[13] The case against Dix was ultimately dismissed owing to a lack of evidence; in 2003 he was awarded $764,863[14] in compensation for malicious prosecution and false imprisonment. The judge in the case was highly critical of Piragoff for having misled the court and for having charged Dix with the crime despite a lack of probable cause (Katz, 2011).

Charge Screening

Crown attorneys have a great deal of discretion in terms of whether or not they proceed with a charge based on the case presented to them by the police. It is at this stage of an investigation that Crown attorneys have ample opportunity to address any errors or inconsistencies in the case. The Crown can, at this moment, decide whether or not to proceed with the prosecution, since there must be reasonable and probable grounds to support a charge. In the province of Ontario's Crown Policy Manual (2005),[15] the section on charge screening dictates that every charge must be screened in accordance with the standards that there be a "reasonable prospect of conviction" and it is in the "public interest" to pursue the charge. The threshold for a "reasonable prospect of conviction" is an objective standard that applies to all cases and at any stage the charge can be discontinued.

The fairness and integrity of the criminal justice system demands that, because of the risk of wrongful conviction, inherently weak cases should not be prosecuted: "Under our criminal justice system, we place a high premium on the presumption of innocence, proof beyond reasonable doubt and the adversarial process. Thus, we should expect that citizens will not be put in jeopardy of conviction unless the prosecution has tendered a quantum of evidence sufficient to establish guilt beyond reasonable doubt" (Tanovich, 1994, 174). In both the Randy Druken and Gregory Parsons wrongful-conviction cases from Newfoundland and Labrador, the Crown's office simply accepted the police's belief in the guilt of these two individuals, in spite of glaring inconsistencies in each instance. The commission of inquiry that was convened to address these wrongful convictions (as well as that of Ronald Dalton) found that Wayne Gorman, the prosecuting attorney in all three cases, did not fulfil his role of acting "as a challenge function to the police" (Lamer, 2006, 270). It has been argued that charge screening is a critical part of the criminal justice system and that, to prevent miscarriages of justice, "its role needs to be enhanced, not diminished. Charge screening should be conducted at the earliest possible stage" (Dewart, 2009, para. 13). Furthermore, charge screening as a means of assessing the strength of a case should be continuous, should assess the credibility of witnesses and evidence, and should be independent of external pressures, including from the police.

Disclosure of Evidence Obligations

The Crown's office and the police department are closely tied in terms of their work in criminal cases. According to Ontario's Crown Policy Manual (2005), the police relationship with Crown counsel dictates that "police have the sole responsibility for charging decisions except where the consent of the Attorney General is required by statute. Crown counsel are solely responsible for determining whether a charge is to proceed once it has been laid." The police present evidence, investigate cases, and, when necessary, support the Crown's position in court. They may also consult Crown counsel on legal issues, and the Crown in turn may ask for police assistance in conducting further investigations. If an error has occurred during a criminal investigation with respect to the collection of evidence, interrogation of suspects, or eyewitness identification, the Crown may be unaware of the error and perpetuate a miscarriage of justice that began in the early processing of a case. Where the Crown's office has much power with respect to miscarriages of justice is in the area of disclosure of evidence. Any "relevant" evidence about a criminal case that comes to the attention of the prosecution is meant to be shared with the defence; in fact, that includes almost all the information at its disposal. In the past, when evidence was withheld that was exculpatory to the defence, it could result in a miscarriage of justice. Police are also considered to have disclosure obligations and in *R. v. McNeil*[16] the Supreme Court confirmed that, although the Crown and police are separate and distinct, the police have a corollary obligation to the Crown's duty and must disclose to the Crown all material relevant to the investigation.

It was only in 1991 that *R. v. Stinchcombe*[17] clarified the issue of disclosure of evidence by the Crown, and this landmark case has had a significant impact on criminal trials since that time. In the original trial, Stinchcombe was charged with several counts of criminal breach of trust, theft, and fraud. At the preliminary inquiry, the accused's secretary, a Crown witness, gave evidence favourable to the defence. Following this inquiry, the police interviewed a witness and took a statement; the defence was informed of the existence but not the content of this statement. It was only during the trial that defence counsel learned the witness would not be called and defence requests for disclosure of the contents of tape-recorded statements were refused. Stinchcombe was convicted of breach of trust and fraud. The Alberta Court of Appeal dismissed the case; however, the Supreme Court ruled that the Crown did have an obligation to disclosure the contents of the statement in *Stinchcombe*. Further, the Supreme Court established that the Crown has a legal (and ongoing) duty to disclose all relevant information to the defence, subject to a few exceptions.

Two years earlier, in 1989 the royal commission of inquiry examining the 1971 wrongful conviction of Donald Marshall, Jr, referred to by Justice John Sopinka in the *Stinchcombe* decision, had advocated for complete and automatic disclosure, limited only "where ... such disclosure will endanger the life or safety of such person or interfere with the administration of justice." In that instance, information about the true killer of Sandy Seale was known by the police and the Crown shortly following Marshall's conviction but was never disclosed to defence counsel. However, the court in *Stinchcombe* did not go so far as to establish limits on disclosure; in fact, the court neither advocated disclosure "without request" nor "put the onus on the Crown to bring to the Court's attention when they should have been unable or unwilling" to disclose information (Luther, 2002, 578). These were two recommendations that had emerged from the commission of inquiry in regard to the errors that had occurred in the Marshall case, more than twenty years earlier.

While *Stinchcombe* was welcomed with open arms by the defence bar, it has since been argued that courts have failed to apply even the limited-disclosure standard advocated by Justice Sopinka in that case (Luther, 2002; Phillips, 2002–3). Fred Kaufman (1998b, 1229) notes that, in spite of *Stinchcombe*, "there continue to be many cases in Ontario where disclosure issues delay the commencement of trials, result in adjournments, in stays of proceedings and in mistrials" – and most likely wrongful convictions. Given that this decision instructed Crown attorneys to disclose all relevant evidence to the defence, the contention appears to surround what constitutes "relevance." In effect, there is very little incentive for prosecutors to disclose all documents since penalties for failure to do so are few and far between (Phillips, 2002–3, 556). According to the test established in *R. v. Chaplin*,[18] evidence is considered relevant if there is "a reasonable possibility of the information being useful to the accused in making a full answer and defence"; it is then the duty of the Crown to meet this obligation. Unfortunately, the good-faith obligation expected of the prosecution in this regard is not always met. Moreover, there are others who argue that the Crown delegates its disclosure obligations to the police (Luther, 2002). Phillips believes that the spirit of the *Stinchcombe* decision will be met and full disclosure established only when the civil-procedure discovery model is adopted; he also advocates a broader understanding of what is relevant and how that is determined by the Crown, as well as stronger penalties for failing to disclose (2002, 554–6).

The Canadian legal landscape is replete with cases of wrongful conviction that have resulted in part from a lack of disclosure on behalf of Crown attorneys, cases that occurred both before and *after* the ruling in *Stinchcombe*. Prior to *Stinchcombe*, in 1959 Steven Truscott's wrongful conviction in Goderich, Ontario, could be blamed in part on a failure by the Crown to disclose crucial evidence to the defence regarding uncertainty surrounding the medical evidence in the case. Specifically, vital evidence from the autopsy report around the time of Lynne Harper's death was withheld from the defence at trial, evidence that would have likely cleared Truscott and affected a jury's verdict. Latterly, on a reference to the Supreme Court of Canada in 1966, the same doctor's reappraisal regarding the time of death was also withheld from the defence.[19] In 1971 in Nova Scotia, as noted above, the Crown prosecutor in the trial and subsequent wrongful conviction of Donald Marshall, Jr, not only failed to interview witnesses who had given contradictory statements, he also failed to disclose the contents of earlier inconsistent statements to the defence.[20] In 1972 Romeo Phillion was wrongly convicted for the murder of an Ottawa fireman, owing in part to a false confession he gave to the police; he served over thirty years for a murder he did not commit. While this wrongful conviction was based largely on Phillion's false confession, his inability to overturn his conviction resulted partly from a lack of Crown disclosure of key evidence. More than twenty years after his conviction, evidence surfaced from 1968 indicating that the police and the Crown knew that Phillion had an alibi for the time of the murder; this information was never disclosed to his lawyer at trial.[21]

In 1975 Erin Walsh was wrongfully convicted for the murder of Melvin Peters in Saint John, New Brunswick, in part based on a lack of disclosure of evidence by the Crown. The Crown withheld evidence of a ballistics report, evidence from civilian eyewitnesses who heard Walsh crying out for help as he had been taken to the car, and recordings of conversation between two Crown witnesses in jail stating that they had concocted a story to place the blame on Walsh.[22] Ivan Henry was convicted in 1983 in Vancouver for ten counts of rape, attempted rape, and indecent assault for which he spent twenty-seven years in jail. During and after his trial, the police and Crown withheld evidence from Henry's defence counsel, including statements made by complainants to police, reports from police officers at the scene of the crime, evidence that another perpetrator had been arrested for similar acts in the same neighbourhood, and medical and lab reports on semen from the crime scene. This evidence demonstrated material inconsistencies that would have undermined the Crown's identification evidence, which had secured Henry's conviction.[23]

Thomas Sophonow's conviction for the murder of Barbara Stoppel in Winnipeg in 1981 was partly attributable to a failure on the part of the Crown's office to disclose an incident of mistaken eyewitness identification, police reports on eyewitness identification, and a great deal of other significant evidence (Cory, 2001). In 1991 James Driskell was wrongly convicted of first-degree murder in Winnipeg, Manitoba; the foundation for this conviction was almost exclusively based on the testimony of two unsavoury witnesses (Ray Zanidean and John Gumieny), whose lack of credibility was known to the Crown at that time but never disclosed to the defence. In particular, the report of the Commission of Inquiry into Certain Aspects of the Trial and Conviction of James Driskell revealed that the Crown had failed to disclose, inter alia, "favourable" arrangements made with the witnesses regarding their own criminal charges (i.e., dropping charges and payments), as well as a witness's recantation, and had also failed to correct misleading or inaccurate evidence of one of the informer witnesses at trial.[24] Three wrongful convictions for murder that occurred in Newfoundland in the 1990s, those of Randy Druken, Gregory Parsons, and Ron Dalton, were all instances of overzealous prosecution; in Druken's case, the fact that the Crown failed to disclose evidence to the defence also had an impact. In addition, there have been other cases following *Stinchombe* where an erroneous conviction resulted in part from Crown attorney mistakes, including those of Robert Baltovich – Ontario (1992); Herman Kaglik – Northwest Territories (1992–3); and Kyle Unger – Manitoba (1992).

"Pleas of Convenience": Plea Bargaining

Plea bargaining is a routine part of the criminal justice system; it would be impossible to hold trials for all of the criminal cases that regularly come before the courts – the sheer numbers would create a backlog that would add months and years to already overburdened courts. Thus, Crown prosecutors will frequently offer a lesser penalty for a guilty plea in cases where the evidence appears overwhelming against the accused. The result is often beneficial to all concerned: the Crown can tidily close its case, the defence is spared a possibly long trial, and the accused is rewarded for saving court time and expense as well as for sparing victims and victims' families from having to relive painful events. In theory, plea bargaining works well, but in practice, for those individuals who are in fact not guilty but technically plead guilty to an offence they did not commit, it can result in a wrongful conviction. This custom raises issues about Crown expediency as well as the role of defence counsel in arranging such pleas for clients they know are innocent. Research into the incidence of false guilty pleas in Canada suggests that each year thousands of individuals may be entering guilty pleas for offences they did not commit (Sherrin, 2011, 5).

One case where an innocent person accepted a guilty plea for a crime he did not commit was that of Richard Brant, who pleaded guilty in exchange for a six-month sentence for shaking his son Dustin to death; the evidence for his culpability came from now discredited pathologist, Dr Charles Smith.[25] In May 2011 the Ontario Court of Appeal quashed Brant's conviction for aggravated assault in the death of his son, given that the scientific evidence that convicted him was later found to be false.[26] Anthony Hanemaayer was also a victim of a "plea of convenience." In his case, almost twenty years after the crime, he was acquitted by the Ontario Court of Appeal in 2008 for a sexual assault that occurred in 1987; twice-convicted murderer Paul Bernardo admitted to the assault in 2006. Hanemaayer was a construction worker in the area where the assault occurred when he was identified by the victim's mother as being the assailant; however, her glimpse of the attacker lasted only seconds. While that was the sole evidence against Hanemaayer, her confidence that he was the attacker and the forcefulness of her testimony convinced him that he would be found guilty and ultimately receive a lengthy sentence; he pleaded guilty to breaking and entering and assault with a weapon and received a sentence of two years less a day.[27]

A final example of these pleas of convenience are the cases of Shawn Hennessey and Dennis Cheeseman, who pleaded guilty to manslaughter for assisting James Roszko in the murder of four RCMP officers in 2005. Essentially, there was little to no evidence for these convictions and it appears that Hennessey and Cheeseman entered guilty pleas out of fear of receiving life sentences for first-degree murder convictions; Hennessey received ten years, while Cheeseman received seven. While they both lost appeals of their sentences, they have since been granted parole. University of Alberta law professor Steve Penney has stated in reference to this case: "It would be unfair to accept a plea agreement where the accused were basically presented with a situation where the Crown was bluffing, it wasn't prepared to proceed, didn't think there was a reasonable prospect of a conviction, and yet it threatened the accused with the prospect of the punishment for first-degree murder if they didn't agree to this particular plea deal."[28]

David Tanovich, law professor and veteran defence lawyer, describes two types of individuals who engage in these pleas of convenience: those who face testimony from unassailable Crown witnesses and those who are denied bail pending trial.[29] The "dirty little secret," says Tanovich, is that the second category of accused will often plead guilty to escape remand conditions and end the proceedings against them with time served as their sentence. The problem has also been linked to a desire to avoid the high costs of a trial that some accused persons feel will likely result in a conviction anyway. Regardless of the reasons for pleading guilty in these cases, given that the ultimate result is a wrongful conviction, such practices require greater scrutiny.

While it may well be routine for Crown attorney's to over-charge in order to later offer an incentive of a reduced charge in exchange for a guilty plea to individuals who accept these pleas of convenience, this practice may be construed as unethical, particularly in instances where the case against an accused is weak and where defence counsel is inexperienced or ignorant as to the ramifications of a guilty plea. To begin to address this problem, it has been suggested that, before accepting a guilty plea, judges should be required to engage in a factual inquiry and in direct communication with the accused to ensure that there is no reason to believe that the plea may be false, and that legal-aid funding be restructured in order to reduce the incentive for counsel to resolve cases quickly by guilty pleas without adequate inquiry into the potential defences (Sherrin, 2011).

Systemic Resistance

As noted earlier, there is a remarkable reluctance of the part of many actors in the criminal justice system to acknowledge errors and then rectify them; this intransigence has been referred to as "systemic resistance."[30] It is clearly evident in those cases where prosecutors refuse to admit that the wrong person was convicted, even following a defendant's exoneration (Medwed, 2012). In fact, when discussing the case of Charles Fain, who was exonerated by DNA identification technology in 2004, the prosecutor in the case was still convinced Fain was guilty (cf. Gross et al., 2005, 526). Prosecutors may also have great faith that the police "get it right," or that the police will arrest only those who are guilty. From this premise, their obduracy is not surprising, since they both are working for the same "side" and thus it makes sense that prosecutors will endeavour to prove the police are correct. Similar to the police, prosecutors suffer from tunnel vision and confirmation bias (Hill et al., 2008), as well as selective-information processing (defending beliefs in face of contradictory evidence) and belief perseverance (Burke, 2006). This resistance has elsewhere been referred to as cognitive dissonance, whereby "prosecutors modify their conceptions of work in order to reduce the cognitive dissonance between what they would like to do and what they can" (Johnson, 2002, 169, referred to in Bandes, 2005–6, 491). It is well known in cognitive psychology that people "are more likely to attend to, seek out and evaluate evidence that is consistent with their beliefs, and ignore or downplay evidence that is inconsistent with their beliefs" (Fugelsang and Dunbar, 2004, as referenced in Bandes, 2005–6, 492). This applies to both police and prosecutors and likely explains their apparent inflexibility when faced with evidence that contradicts their theory of what occurred in a particular case.

Structural and Systemic Reforms

As seen with policing, attempts at systemic reform are also evident in the prosecution services. On the federal level, the Public Prosecution Service of Canada[31] provides ongoing education and training to federal prosecutors on the prevention of miscarriages of justice. On the provincial level, prosecutorial services are answerable to the provincial attorneys general, who more or less operate as separate entities. While some provinces have similar models, only one province, Nova Scotia, has a separate director of public prosecutions (DPP),[32] which may be viewed as being not only separate but also independent of the government. The office of the DPP in Nova Scotia was established in 1990 by the Public Prosecutions Act,[33] which came about as a direct response to the wrongful prosecution of Donald Marshall, Jr in 1971 and was a recommendation of the royal commission of inquiry into his case. The inquiry had found that there was a need for a separate office in order to "improve the fairness – and the public's faith in the fairness – of the administration of justice in Nova Scotia."[34]

As seen with police forces, various provinces have also developed a number of initiatives that are aimed at addressing the role of Crown attorneys with respect to miscarriages of justice; many of these involve training sessions that have emerged in response to high-profile wrongful-conviction cases, as well as recommendations of commissions of inquiry.[35] The majority of the reform efforts address issues that are systemic in nature and may take the form of enhanced education and training, both internally and externally, with respect to preventing the known causes of wrongful convictions. For example, the training in Saskatchewan has focused on avoiding tunnel vision, whereas in British Columbia advocacy-training workshops address the exercise of Crown discretion.[36] In addition, many efforts take the form of adding sections to ongoing training sessions that specifically address how to avoid wrongful convictions by recognizing the factors that contribute to them (British Columbia, Alberta, Saskatchewan, Manitoba, Ontario, Quebec, Nova Scotia, Newfoundland and Labrador). For some provinces, such training and educational seminars include not only Crown counsel but also defence counsel, police, and the judiciary (e.g., Manitoba, Ontario).

Some provinces have developed their own stand-alone committees that are aimed at providing direction to Crown attorneys and reviewing individual cases of miscarriages of justice. The province of Ontario established the Ontario Criminal Conviction Review Committee in May 2006. The role of this committee, comprised of six senior Crown counsel and advised by the Honourable Patrick LeSage, is meant to act as a resource to Crown attorneys throughout Ontario in preventing wrongful convictions. In addition, it reviews cases where a miscarriage of justice is thought to have occurred, devises preventive educational and policy programs, and develops protocols and best practices for dealing with these cases.[37] The province of New Brunswick also created a standing committee, first called the Prevention of Miscarriages of Justice Committee and now referred to as the Conviction Review Committee.[38] Ultimately, these bodies could serve to increase professional accountability as well as enhance confidence in the criminal justice system overall.

U.S. Reform: Conviction Integrity Units

Recent years have seen the opening of a number of Conviction Integrity Units (CIUs), located in U.S. district attorneys' offices, that function as post-conviction review programs to secure exonerations for the wrongly convicted. While CIUs investigate claims of wrongful convictions occurring within their own jurisdictions, the prosecutorial offices are not making factual determinations of innocence. According to the National Registry of Exonerations in the United States, there are 151 exonerees who were freed in part owing to the work of CIUs; this accounts for 9 per cent of all of the exonerations in the United States since 1989. As of 2014, there were sixteen CIUs in existence: Lake County, Illinois (one); Dallas County and Harris County, Texas (two); Wayne County, Michigan (one); New York County, Brooklyn, and Oneida County, New York (three); Denver, Colorado (one); Santa Clara County, California (one); New Orleans, Louisiana (one)[39]; Pima County, Arizona (one); Cuyahoga County, Ohio (one); Philadelphia, Pennsylvania (one); Baltimore, Maryland (one); Multnomah County, Oregon (one); and the District of Columbia (one) (Center for Prosecutorial Integrity, 2014). However, given the short period of time in which these CIUs have operated, and their varying mandates,[40] the number of exonerations attributable to CIU work is small – 151 – and these have occurred in only six states: Illinois (15 exonerations), Texas (102 exonerations), New York (24 exonerations), California (6 exonerations), Maryland (3 exonerations), and Louisiana (1 exoneration).[41] The earliest exoneration through a CIU occurred in 2003 in California, with the highest numbers of overall exonerations occurring in the most recent years of 2014 (51 exonerations) and 2015 (58 exonerations).

In theory, these units could serve as another level of accountability for the prosecutor's office. Yet there are some practical problems with them in that they function solely within the prosecutors' offices with no real oversight, and further, it is the prosecutor's office that decides which cases to re-examine. Given that CIUs are internal mechanisms and their success depends on the prosecutors' ability to regulate themselves, they are inherently problematic (Malavé and Barkai, 2014). In their study of three CIUs, Malavé and Barkai further argue that CUIs in fact represent an "expedient, political reaction to the negative publicity surrounding wrongful convictions" and may fall victim to the possibility of being only "window dressing" and not a serious response to the problem (2014, 202). They point out that, since wrongful convictions are difficult to study and identify, it is equally difficult to measure the success of CIUs since there is no baseline from which to compare rates of exoneration, and both the public and law enforcement may view them with mistrust. At the same time, the strengths of these units lie in their greater access to information and resources than that possessed by the defence bar, as well as the enormous discretionary political power tied to the state attorney's office when it comes to affecting reforms.

The Role of Defence Counsel: Ineffective Assistance of Counsel

"A poor person may be without counsel when bail is set or denied, and during critical times for pretrial investigation. He or she may receive only perfunctory representation – sometimes nothing more than hurried conversations with a court-appointed lawyer outside the courtroom or even in open court – before entering a guilty plea or going to trial. The poor person who is wrongfully convicted may face years in prison, or even execution, without any legal assistance to pursue avenues of post-conviction review. While in prison, he or she may endure practices and conditions which violate the Constitution, but have no access to a lawyer to seek remedies for those violations." (Bright, 1999, 783)

Ineffective assistance of counsel has been established as a contributing factor to wrongful convictions in Canada and elsewhere. In reviewing the over 350 exonerations of wrongful convictions it has facilitated to date, the Innocence Project website of the Benjamin Cardozo Law School in New York discusses "inadequate defense" as a substantial causative factor.[42] Examples provided of this behaviour include: being asleep in the courtroom during trial, having been disbarred shortly after finishing a death-penalty case, failing to investigate alibis, failing to call or consult experts on forensic issues, and failing to show up for hearings. The issue of competent legal representation is especially problematic in the United States, given that capital punishment is still legal in thirty-one states. When the stakes are such that the outcome of a trial is literally a matter of life or death, having effective counsel is critical. Ironically, it is often in exactly these capital cases where some of the most egregious examples of lawyer misconduct have been cited.[43]

Poverty looms large as a contributing factor to inadequate legal representation since many wrongful-conviction cases involve representation by public defenders' offices, which are notoriously underfunded. Bernhard (2001) notes that "jurists, bar associations, journalists, and academics readily agree that poor people are too often badly represented in the criminal court" (225). It is not unheard of in the United States to find stories of lawyers "assigned to represent poor people charged with capital offences, who slept through the presentation of evidence, arrived at the courthouse intoxicated with alcohol or narcotics, were unable to recall a single relevant case, failed to conduct any investigation or failed to present any [mitigating] evidence" (Bernhard, 2001, 226). At the same time, there appears to be a judicial tolerance of malpractice that not only insulates ineffective lawyers but also stymies any efforts to increase accountability for bad lawyering (Bernhard, 2003).

Legal-aid and public defenders' offices have limited resources to allocate for criminal defence cases, and while American law dictates that those charged with serious crimes have the constitutional right to be represented by an attorney at no cost,[44] this does not, in and of itself, guarantee that said counsel will be effective. Some states will not fund post-conviction proceedings at all, and in many cases where funds are available states allow for only the bare minimum. For example, in Texas, which has the highest number of inmates on death row, the Texas Association of Criminal Defense warns lawyers who are appointed to these capital cases that they will likely need to perform about 250–750 hours of uncompensated work to represent their clients competently (Bright, 1997, 807).

Within the Canadian criminal law context, there appears to be a dearth of research and case law on the role of ineffective counsel in contributing to miscarriages of justice. However, it has been argued that most courts have adopted a "lawyer-control" mode of criminal defence (Ives, 2003–4, 251). This model accepts that only a few decisions are solely in the hands of the accused (mainly whether or not to testify, and what plea to enter) and that counsel has almost complete control over the conduct of the defence.[45] Accordingly, courts are generally reluctant to question any decisions made by counsel with respect to strategic and tactical determinations made during a trial (Ives, 2003–4, 252). Appellate courts are hesitant to second-guess counsel, who have all of the important information before them, underlining the difficulty in making a case for incompetency. Moreover, this also results in a presumption in favour of competency, putting an accused at a distinct disadvantage in bringing such a case before the courts.

In MacFarlane's seminal article regarding wrongful conviction in Canada, one of the eight immediate causes of wrongful conviction is inadequate defence work (2006). The wrongful conviction of Donald Marshall, Jr was attributable in part to ineffective counsel, as the royal commission inquiring into his case noted: "Defence counsel failed to provide adequate professional investigation, interview Crown witnesses or seek disclosure of the Crown case ... the defence counsel were aware of prior statements of [three witnesses], but did not request them ... Had defence counsel taken even the most rudimentary steps an accused should be entitled to expect from his or her counsel, it is difficult to believe Marshall would have been convicted ... the fact that the defence team may have believed Marshall to be guilty probably impacted its lackluster investigation" (Royal Commission on the Donald Marshall, Jr Prosecution 1989a, 277).

In an inquiry into another case, that of Guy Paul Morin, Justice Kaufman acknowledged that inadequate counsel can cause wrongful convictions (1998b, 1049), but he did not address the issue directly because it was outside his terms of reference.

Wilbert Coffin's case of an alleged wrongful conviction is a notorious, albeit historical, example of incompetent defence counsel. Convicted for first-degree murder in the shooting deaths of three American tourists in 1953 in the Gaspé peninsula in Quebec on nothing but circumstantial evidence, Coffin was hanged in 1956. While Coffin proclaimed his innocence to the end, his attorney presented virtually no defence: he called no witnesses (after claiming in his opening statement that he would call over fifty), and he refused to let Coffin testify in his own defence (Anderson and Anderson, 1998, 70). Coffin was also found guilty in part owing to political pressure to find the suspects and close the case: given the wide publicity the case incurred at that time and the fact that tourism in the province of Quebec depended heavily on Americans, an unsolved triple homicide could have had profoundly negative economic consequences.[46]

As members of the Canadian Bar Association (and other professional associations), criminal defence counsel must adhere to a Code of Ethics that can be understood as promoting effective representation of their clients. Each province has its own code of conduct and the Rules of Professional Conduct in Ontario define a "competent lawyer" as one who "has and applies relevant skills, attributes, and values in a manner appropriate to each matter undertaken on behalf of a client," including:

(a) knowing general legal principles and procedures and the substantive law and procedure for the areas of law in which the lawyer practices,
(b) investigating facts, identifying issues, ascertaining client objectives, considering possible options, and developing and advising the client on appropriate courses of action,
(c) implementing, as each matter requires, the chosen course of action through the application of appropriate skills, including,

    (i)   legal research,
    (ii)   analysis,
    (iii) application of the law to the relevant facts,
    (iv) writing and drafting,
    (v)   negotiation,
    (vi) alternative dispute resolution,
    (vii) advocacy, and
    (viii)problem-solving ability,

(d) communicating at all stages of a matter in a timely and effective manner that is appropriate to the age and abilities of the client,
(e) performing all functions conscientiously, diligently, and in a timely and cost-effective manner,
(f) applying intellectual capacity, judgment, and deliberation to all functions,
(g) complying in letter and in spirit with the Rules of Professional Conduct,
(h) recognizing limitations in one's ability to handle a matter or some aspect of it, and taking steps accordingly to ensure the client is appropriately served,

(i) managing one's practice effectively,
(j) pursuing appropriate professional development to maintain and enhance
     legal knowledge and skills, and
(k) adapting to changing professional requirements, standards, techniques,
     and practices.[47]

Moreover, this duty to behave competently has ethical obligations attached to it as well: "A lawyer should not undertake a matter without honestly feeling competent to handle it or being able to become competent without undue delay, risk, or expense to the client. This is an ethical consideration and is to be distinguished from the standard of care that a tribunal would invoke for purposes of determining negligence."[48] Lawyers who fail to adhere to the standards set out in this code are subject to disciplinary procedures.

As will be noted below, the notion of "competence" is a fluid one, and tactical decisions that defence counsel take on behalf of their clients can have inadvertently devastating consequences for them. The issue is complex, since lawyers should have free rein to conduct a defence as they see fit and not be overly burdened by procedural rules. At the same time, defendants want to be assured that decisions taken on their behalf are in their best interests and are going to advance their defence. Similarly, appellate courts are reticent to intervene and hesitate to second-guess counsel who have a better grasp of the information and facts of a particular case.

Essentially, Canadian courts have embraced the American approach to ineffective-counsel claims; the *Strickland*[49] test for ineffective counsel was adopted in *R. v. G.D.B.*[50] In this latter case, the accused had been charged with a number of sexual offences against an underaged child. During the trial, G.D.B.'s counsel made a tactical decision not to introduce in evidence a tape-recorded conversation between the complainant and her mother where she denied the alleged assaults took place; the accused was ultimately convicted of sexual assault and indecent assault. On appeal, it was argued that a miscarriage of justice had occurred in part because of the fact that counsel acted incompetently in failing to use this evidence. The Court of Appeal appointed a commissioner to inquire about fresh evidence and competency of counsel; it dismissed the accused's appeal. The Supreme Court, in examining the fresh evidence, did not find that counsel had been acting incompetently. It concluded that not introducing the tape appeared to have been a tactical decision based on the belief that it would undermine the credibility of the complainant's mother (the main witness) and would have forced the defendant to testify; in his counsel's opinion, he would have been a poor witness. The Court ultimately determined that counsel's actions were more a matter for professional ethics and that the accused had not met the due-diligence criterion for introducing the tape as fresh evidence; it also did not believe that introducing the tapes as evidence would have affected the outcome in the case.[51]

In the Canadian context the standard for competence is rather low, and a heavy burden is placed on the accused to demonstrate incompetence.[52] Using a reasonableness standard, the accused must prove that defence counsel did not act reasonably given the information available at that time; in other words, "but for" counsel's errors the results would have been different.[53] In *G.D.B.*, the court stated:

> The reasons contain a performance component and a prejudice component. For an appeal to succeed, it must be established, first, that counsel's acts or omissions constituted incompetence and second, that a miscarriage of justice resulted ... Incompetence is determined by a reasonableness standard. The analysis proceeds upon a strong presumption that counsel's conduct fell within the wide range of reasonable professional assistance. The onus is on the appellant to establish the acts or omissions of counsel that are alleged not to have been the result of reasonable professional judgment. The wisdom of hindsight has no place in this assessment ... Miscarriages of justice may take many forms in this context. In some instances, counsel's performance may have resulted in procedural unfairness. In others, the reliability of the trial's result may have been compromised.[54]

While the court did indeed establish the standard for ineffective counsel, as borrowed from *Strickland*, it did not find for it on the facts of *G.D.B.* In fact, Ives (2003–4) points out the difficulty in establishing this claim in Canada more generally: the vast majority of cases in the three years following *G.D.B.* failed.[55] More recent cases affirm that, consistent with *G.D.B.*, in order for a claim of ineffective counsel to succeed, it is necessary to show, first, that counsel's acts or omissions constituted incompetence (known as the performance component), and, second, that a miscarriage of justice resulted (known as the prejudice component).[56] There would seem also to be great appellate deference to defence counsel more generally. Courts are reticent to interfere with the conduct of counsel for a number of reasons, inter alia, not wanting to encourage a proliferation of similar challenges or to create backlogs in the courts, fear of impairing the independence of counsel, and undermining attorney-client trust (Ives, 2003–4).

In her analysis, Ives found that, while there are no guidelines per se, appeals courts have outlined a number of important considerations in ascertaining reasonable conduct on the part of counsel (footnotes omitted):

1. The explanation offered by trial counsel for why he or she made the decision and, in particular, whether the decision was based on an [*sic*] proper understanding of the facts and the applicable law;
2. The implications of adopting a different tactic or strategy and the advantages versus the disadvantages associated with each choice;
3. The degree of consistency between counsel's choice and the overall defence strategy;
4. The reasonableness of the overall defence strategy;
5. The instructions, if any, that the accused provided to trial counsel on the matter;
6. The response of the accused, if any, at the time the alleged deficiency occurred and after he or she has been convicted of the offence; and
7. The position, if any, taken by the trial judge in relation to the matter. (Ives, 2003–4, 257–8)

While case law has demonstrated that a successful claim of ineffective assistance of counsel is difficult to prove, it remains an option for those who feel inadequately represented. Furthermore, effective assistance of counsel[57] has been recognized by the courts as an aspect of fundamental justice and at the same time is a "primary guarantee of the reliability and fairness of the adversarial adjudicative process and, as such, an important safeguard against the risk of a miscarriage of justice" (Ives, 2003–4, 242).

   Given the difficulty in establishing claims of ineffective counsel, and the fact that such claims are a reactive rather than proactive measure, a case has been made for other remedies to address this problem. Dew (2006) argues that the most effective method for mitigating ineffective assistance of counsel is not through the appellate courts but through better education of lawyers. Specifically, he argues that educating lawyers on the causes and effects of wrongful convictions[58] would help, as would reformulating the ethical guidelines that govern defence lawyers; however, the crisis in legal-aid funding in Canada is likely to exacerbate this problem.[59]

The Role of the Judiciary

"Wrongful convictions do not occur in a vacuum of judicial indifference." (Sherrer, 2003, 539)

One of the hallmarks of being a judge is the ability to render decisions in a fair and impartial manner. In fact, the right to be tried by an independent and impartial tribunal is a principle of fundamental justice that is protected by section 7 of the Charter (*Ruffo v. Conseil de la magistrature*). Impartiality has been defined as "a state of mind in which the adjudicator is disinterested in the outcome, and is open to persuasion by the evidence and submissions," while bias "denotes a state of mind that is in some way predisposed to a particular result, or that is closed with regard to particular issues" (*R.D.S. v. The Queen*, headnote). Judges are expected to weigh evidence and make objective decisions free of preconceived perceptions and ideas about particular individuals and groups. When a judge advances a decision that reflects "the contexts that constitute his/her identity ... [he or she] runs the risk of being accused of one of the most serious allegations of judicial impropriety: bias" (Devlin, 1995).

   Judges are the ultimate arbiters in criminal cases and wield a great deal of power with respect to the admissibility of evidence, the conduct of preliminary hearings, and ultimately the verdict. At the same time, they are not immune to the challenges that other legal professionals face but are perhaps held to a higher standard of scrutiny. In the commission of inquiry pertaining to the cases of Ronald Dalton, Gregory Parsons, and Randy Druken, Justice Lamer refers to the fact that judges themselves are susceptible to tunnel vision: "Generated by a police and prosecutorial culture that allows the subconscious mind to rationalize a biased approach to evidence ... [tunnel vision] is mutually reinforcing amongst police officers, amongst prosecutors and in the interaction between these groups of professionals. It may even affect judges" (2006, 71). Moreover, judges are human, and while they are meant to render directions and decisions that are unbiased and impartial, it would difficult for any judge to present information to juries that is completely detached and neutral in the face of particularly heartfelt witness testimony.

The judiciary, then, shares a critical role with other legal professionals in both contributing to and preventing wrongful convictions. Judges at different stages of the adjudication process have varying responsibilities with respect to this issue: appellate judges play a remedial role and are retrospective in their ability to overturn convictions and correct past errors made by lower courts, while judges at first instance have the ability to be forward-looking and to prevent errors from occurring farther down the line (Delisle, 1987, 391). Trial judges and justices may influence the outcome of a trial and the safety of a conviction in a number of ways, including: decisions regarding the admissibility of evidence,[60] directions given to the jury (jury charge), and screening mechanisms such as the preliminary inquiry and directed verdicts. Given that judges may be "the most crucial actor in the real-life drama of an innocent person's prosecution and conviction" (Sherrer, 2003, 539–40), the judiciary can assume a more active, or rather proactive, role at every possible stage of the criminal process in order to prevent wrongful convictions.

Judicial error was a prominent feature in the wrongful conviction of Donald Marshall, Jr in 1971 in Nova Scotia. The royal commission examining this case found that not only were defence and crown counsel responsible for a number of errors, but the trial judge, Justice Louis Dubinsky, also made several errors of law that contributed to his wrongful conviction. Most fundamental was the judge's misinterpretation of the Canada Evidence Act,[61] which resulted in an error in limiting the cross-examination of an eyewitness's comments made outside the courtroom. John Pratico was an unreliable teenaged witness who had succumbed to pressure by the police and perjured himself by changing his statement to one that was consistent with the police version of events; he had actually witnessed nothing and had encountered Marshall following the event. At trial, Justice Dubinsky made a number of incorrect rulings regarding key evidence that further denied Marshall a fair trial. The royal commission found that "errors by the trial judge were so fundamental that a new trial should have been the inevitable result of any appeal."[62] Latterly, when Marshall's conviction was finally overturned after he served eleven years in prison, the presiding judge placed the blame on Marshall himself for his wrongful conviction, referring to him as the "author of his own misfortune," claiming that he lied and was attempting to commit a robbery that evening, and concluding that any miscarriage of justice was more apparent than real.[63] This was in direct contradiction to the later findings of the royal commission, which noted that the "criminal justice system failed Donald Marshall, Jr. at virtually every turn."[64] In another case, that of Steven Truscott, there is some debate as to whether the jury charge of Justice R.I. Ferguson was biased. Yet it can certainly be argued that he had overstepped the bounds of judicial propriety (Burtch, 1981). Justice Edward P. MacCullum, who chaired the commission of inquiry investigating the wrongful conviction of David Milgaard, held almost forty years after the fact, found that Milgaard's defence was prejudiced by a judicial error in applying the rules of evidence as they pertained to the circumstances regarding a witness's statement (although this contradicted an earlier Court of Appeal finding). He also found that the judge further prejudiced the case by "excessive intervention when witnesses were testifying."[65]

Preliminary Inquiry

Prior to the commencement of a trial for an accused charged with an indictable offence, a preliminary inquiry must be held if requested by the accused or Crown counsel.[66] It is during that time that a judge may exercise his or her discretion in determining whether the Crown has discharged the evidential burden and may prevent the prosecution of inherently weak cases. While a preliminary inquiry "is not a trial and must not be turned into a trial" (Fish, 1979, 633), it does allow for the disclosure and discovery of the Crown's case against the accused (Roach, 1999b, 162). In particular, a preliminary inquiry is used to determine whether or not there is sufficient evidence to put the accused on trial for the offence charged, and determinations are made regarding the sufficiency of the evidence through hearing evidence from both Crown witnesses[67] and defence witnesses, the latter of which the accused is allowed to cross-examine; ultimately, the end result is that the accused will be either discharged or ordered to stand trial.[68] Under section 548(1) of the Criminal Code, after hearing all of the evidence, a justice (usually a provincial court judge) must commit the accused to trial, "if in his opinion there is sufficient evidence to put the accused on trial for the offence charged or any other indictable offence in respect of the same transaction," or discharge the accused, "if in his opinion on the whole of the evidence no sufficient case is made out." The courts have determined that the test for committal is whether there is any evidence that, if believed by a reasonable jury, properly instructed, could result in a conviction.[69]

A preliminary inquiry may serve to prevent an accused from being tried on weak or insufficient evidence, possibly preventing a miscarriage of justice. One notable example is the case of Susan Nelles, a Toronto nurse who was accused of murdering sick infants and discharged after a preliminary inquiry in which the evidence against her was found to be solely circumstantial (Delisle, 1987, 229). The judge held that the Crown had not made out a sufficient case against Nelles; the evidence on the whole amounted to no evidence at all or was "of too dubious a nature" to merit a committal to trial.[70] One critique of the preliminary inquiry, however, has been that the standard for committal is so low as to allow an accused to proceed to trial despite the potential for an appellate court to find later that that same evidence was unreasonable (Bloos and Plaxton, 2000, 517). This low standard may thus render the preliminary inquiry ineffective in preventing wrongful convictions through its screening function. Moreover, Roach argues that the preliminary inquiry "may protect those such as Susan Nelles, accused of complex crimes with radically insufficient evidence, but will not protect the Donald Marshalls of the world who face weak and unreliable evidence on all the elements of the crime" (1999b, 161).

Directed Verdict[71]

A directed verdict may also serve as a means for the judiciary to prevent miscarriages of justice and may be entered by a trial judge if the Crown has not made out a prima facie case against the accused. Functioning as more than simply gate keeping, a directed verdict can prevent an entire case from moving into the hands of the jury for deliberation. It is this screening function that gives merit to the directed verdict as a guard against wrongful convictions based on manifestly unreliable evidence. However, the ultimate effectiveness of the directed verdict resides in the discretion of the trial judge to "test the chain of evidence for the weak links before he sends it out to the jury" (Devlin, 1966, 64).

Essentially, the directed verdict is a rule in common law and has no statutory basis.[72] At the close of the Crown's case, after the Crown has presented all of its evidence and before the defence is called upon to elect whether to call evidence, defence counsel may make a motion for a directed verdict.[73] In response, a judge may allow a directed verdict by withdrawing the case from the jury and entering a verdict of acquittal.[74] According to the Supreme Court of Canada, the test for a directed verdict, found in *United States v. Shephard*, as upheld in *R. v. Mezzo* and *R. v. Monteleone*, is whether there is any admissible direct or circumstantial evidence upon which a reasonable jury, properly instructed, could convict.[75] It is not the role of the judge to weigh the evidence or assess its quality or reliability; these issues are for the jury to decide.[76] The courts are very clear on this issue: if there is some evidence on every essential element of the offence which, if believed by a reasonable jury, properly instructed, would justify a conviction, the Crown has discharged the evidential burden of sufficiency and has raised a prima facie case against the accused: the case must go to the jury (*R. v. Charemski*).[77] On the other hand, if the Crown cannot adduce any evidence to prove any of the elements of the offence, then a directed verdict is warranted.[78]

The legal test for directed verdicts as it currently stands has been criticized for doing what it was not meant to – allowing weak evidence to be placed in the hands of the jury – and the circumstances that allow a trial judge to withdraw a case from the jury are often very narrow.[79] In fact, the Supreme Court of Canada in *R. v. Mezzo* held that the evidence would have to reach a "level of extreme dubiousness … in the sense of merely raising a suspicion or conjecture of guilt and no more" in order to be considered insufficient so as to warrant withdrawal from the jury.[80] Therefore, in the commission of inquiry examining three wrongful convictions in Newfoundland and Labrador, Justice Lamer believed that the current test for directed verdicts should be modified and codified in the Criminal Code so as to require a trial judge to enter a directed verdict *ex propio motu* (on the initiative of the judge). Lamer advocated for this even in those cases where defence counsel does not make an application but where there is "no evidence or the evidence is so manifestly unreliable on any essential element of the offence, that it would be dangerous to convict," thus raising the threshold of evidentiary sufficiency in order for cases to go to the jury and giving more discretion to the trial judge to "throw out cases where the evidence can colloquially be characterized as 'garbage'" (Lamer, 2006, 168). According to Lamer, "garbage" cases are those in which mere suspicion and circumstantial evidence of motive and opportunity are used to establish the identity of an accused, as was the case for Milgaard, Morin, Sophonow, and Parsons. Regardless, as noted with the preliminary inquiry, the judges' role in ferreting out miscarriages of justice through a directed verdict is somewhat restricted.

The Role of the Jury: Reliability and Instructions

In jury trials the jury has a specific role to play: to weigh the evidence and draw the correct inferences of guilt or innocence. However, given the number of wrongful convictions that have occurred in recent years in Canada and elsewhere, it is clear that a jury's verdict is not always reliable. By exercising their power through withdrawing cases from juries and directing acquittals, judges are challenging the "blind faith in the perceived, innate good sense of juries," or rather, the belief in the inherent competency of the jury not to return an unjust verdict of guilty in cases based on weak evidence (Lamer, 2006, 167–8). However, if judges were to exercise their discretion in this manner more frequently, there is the very real fear that they will begin to encroach upon the jury's role as the ultimate arbiter of fact. The court in R. v. Mezzo held that the dangers associated with sending jurors away to consider whether to convict on weak evidence could be remedied by proper direction from the trial judge. For example, in the case of eyewitness identification, it has been held that proper jury instruction is sufficient to turn the jury's mind to the inherent frailties of identification evidence.[81]

Sherrer takes a particularly controversial standpoint regarding the role of judges in influencing the outcome of trials (2003). He suggests that, by "subtle manipulation of the proceedings," judges are able to influence the outcome of a trial so that the jury's decision will reflect how the judge thinks the case ought to be decided (2003, 576–7). For Sherrer, this influence occurs through jury instructions or a voir dire[82] and significantly contributes to wrongful convictions – a fact he believes is revealed through comments by jurors following trials that they convicted someone they did not believe was guilty but that they felt they had no choice based on instructions, or impressions, from the trial judge (577). This viewpoint seems rather extreme and Canada Criminal Code prohibitions[83] against contacting and revealing the identity of jurors would bar any type of research into those factors that would influence jury decisions. However, it is also true that lay people serving on juries can be swayed by "experts" and that the increasing complexity of forensic evidence, which is sometimes presented with subtle, or inadvertent, manipulation, may force jurors to rely more and more on instructions from judges to understand it.

In spite of clear jury instructions from a judge, there is still a risk that evidentiary frailties may not be adequately cured by appropriate jury direction. According to Lamer, complex jury instructions[84] that would attempt to attune jurors to the frailties of unreliable evidence are inadequate in remedying the dangers in convicting on the evidence and are ineffective in ensuring that the jury draws the correct inferences of guilt or innocence (Lamer, 2006, 168). Delisle suggests that, while the jury is the ultimate trier of fact, the criminal justice system still seeks to control and promote rational decision making because, despite evidentiary rules and cautious jury instructions and warnings, a jury of "human beings, with all their frailties and wants, may act unreasonably through weakness of emotion and judgment" (1987, 390–1). Therefore, raising the bar for sending cases to the jury recognizes that, when faced from the start with inherently unreliable evidence, the jury may not always be trusted in the end to get it right.[85]

Conclusions

The role of each of the professionals involved in wrongful-conviction cases discussed thus far illustrates how individual actions or actors can serve, in varying ways, either to prevent or to contribute to a miscarriage of justice. Clearly, those performing these essential roles in the criminal justice system need to be vigilant and to have the courage to challenge and correct errors that occur, as well as to remain open to the possibility that they have failed to arrest, try, defend, convict, or sentence the "right" defendant. As Justice Lamer stated in his commission of inquiry: "I wish to indulge in this opportunity to extend my apology to all those who have suffered injustice in our legal system while I held this role. Since the ultimate problem is invariably systemic, those of us who form that system cannot simply say that any particular injustice has nothing to do with me" (2006, 101).

This is a laudable sentiment, but the difficulty is that few legal actors have the humility to make such an admission and ultimately act to rectify errors.

Chapter Five

False Confessions

"Police must be aware that as the level of inducement increases, the risk of receiving a confession to an offence which one did not commit increases, and the reliability of the confession diminishes correspondingly." (Justice Alan D. MacInnes, *R. v. Mentuck*[1] at para. 100)

Introduction

The idea that a person could confess to something they did not do is inconceivable to most individuals. However, high-profile cases of wrongful conviction where false confessions have played a role are indications that people routinely confess to things they have not done. In fact, studies in the United States have found that false confessions were the leading or primary cause of wrongful conviction in anywhere from 14 to 25 per cent of cases studied (Drizin and Leo, 2004, 902). The Innocence Project estimates that, in 27 per cent of its over 350 exonerations to date, the accused person made a false confession or a false admission; this is consistent with, but slightly higher than, the numbers from the National Registry of Exonerations (13 per cent) and the Canada data gathered for this book (10 per cent). As noted, while these numbers are not directly comparable, they reflect the reality that false confessions are a problem in many wrongful-conviction cases.

The purpose of this chapter to present a synopsis of the various factors that influence why individuals falsely confess to crimes, in particular the police interrogation techniques and individual psychological vulnerabilities. The chapter also explores confessions induced through the controversial "Mr Big" police sting, examines the different types of false confessions, and provides an overview of the protections against false confessions built into the legal landscape: the common law "confessions rule" and specific rights recognized under the Charter to protect against self-incrimination. Finally, the chapter discusses the manner in which the courts have treated confession evidence and the safeguards against false confessions.

Inducement of False Confessions through Criminal Investigations

Police Interrogation: The Reid Technique

A number of high-profile wrongful convictions where false confessions have played a role in recent years are indications that people do sometimes confess to things they have not done. While a variety of factors may explain why individuals falsely confess to crimes, the most influential are police interrogation practices. Kassin (2005) proffers that a presumption of guilt also influences the way police conduct interrogations – perhaps leading them to adopt a questioning style that is highly aggressive (219). However, police practices do not occur in a vacuum and particular psychological vulnerabilities, susceptibilities, or weaknesses can also influence receptiveness to authority figures. As Gudjonsson and MacKeith (1997) note, "often a combination of custodial, interrogative, and psychological vulnerabilities must be interpreted within the broader circumstances of the case." This section will focus on how both routine and undercover police interrogation practices, in conjunction with psychological vulnerabilities, may influence confessions.

The police represent the first point of entry into the criminal justice system. They make initial, often integral, decisions about arrest, charge, and evidence gathering. In the investigation of a crime, a central part of police practice focuses on obtaining a confession. Confessions are a particularly strong piece of evidence against an accused, even in cases where they are later retracted. In the past, police had the freedom to conduct interrogation practices with impunity; confessions were "extracted" from suspects using a number of physical techniques bordering on abuse and torture. In the United States, this "third degree" involved the direct and explicit use of physical violence, elaborate strategies of torture, physical and psychological coercive techniques that did not leave marks, threats of harm, and promises of leniency (Drizin and Leo, 2004, 909–10). Around the mid-twentieth century, police forces began to reform their interrogation strategies and developed more psychologically oriented techniques of interrogation thought to be more sophisticated and more humane (Leo, 1992, 40).

Modern-day police interrogation practices have become increasingly advanced and occur both in the interrogation room and during undercover operations. The Reid Technique, used routinely by police forces across the United States and increasingly by Canadian police forces, involves a detailed analysis of the facts of the case, as well as the interviewing and interrogation of suspects. The psychological methods that form an essential part of the Reid Technique are confrontational, manipulative, and suggestive (Inbau et al., 2001). In Inbau et al.'s instruction manual for police regarding the Reid Technique, there is a clear distinction between an interview and an interrogation. An interview is thought to be non-accusatory in nature, done early on in an investigation and with the purpose of gathering information, whereas an interrogation is inherently accusatory, conducted only when the interrogator is reasonably certain of the suspect's guilt, and involves active persuasion; its purpose is to learn the "truth" (Inbau et al., 2001, 5–8). This distinction reflects a belief on the part of police interrogators that, when they are undertaking interrogations and using the Reid Technique, they are relatively certain of the suspect's guilt and the end goal is to extract a confession. However, this technique has been referred to as "guilt-presumptive" (Moore and Fitzsimmons, 2011), where tunnel vision is a prescribed part of its methods (Findley and Scott, 2006). Moreover, a number of researchers have demonstrated that the Reid Technique may engender false confessions (Gudjonsson, 2002; Kassin, 1997; Ofshe and Leo, 1997a).

The Reid Technique itself involves several steps all aimed at eliciting a confession from the suspect. While the steps detail the means of eliciting a confession in a controlled and structured manner, they also require the interrogator to engage in frequent behavioural analysis (Behavior Analysis Interview) in order to "read" any verbal and/or non-verbal cues exhibited by the suspect. The manual also dictates that the presence of particular behavioural cues at certain moments during the interrogation process may be construed as indicative of guilt or innocence.[2] This rather subjective analysis will likely result in misinterpretation, misrepresentation, and error since ascribing meaning to particular non-verbal cues is an inexact science at best.

The first of the nine steps,[3] positive confrontation, which requires that the interrogator begin the interview by stating, in a friendly manner, that the suspect's guilt is assured; this is done with sympathy and understanding in an attempt to befriend the suspect. Step two, theme development, involves presenting a number of scenarios to the suspect that would justify why he/she committed the crime, often placing the moral blame for the act on others. This development of themes is calculated, recasts the suspect's behaviour so that he/she is no longer morally and/or legally culpable (Drizin and Leo, 2004, 912), and is put to the suspect in a rapid-fire and highly intense manner. The third step, handling denials, requires the interrogator to minimize the number of denials by constantly interrupting the suspect and restating the assertion that the suspect is guilty. Disagreements are ignored or overridden and denial is countered by shifting to other themes. In step four, overcoming objections, the interrogator will use the objections to further develop the theme of the interrogation. During step five, procurement and retention of the suspect's attention, the belief is that only suspects that have lasted this long are the guilty ones, and as the intensity of the interrogation increases, the interrogator becomes physically closer to the suspect and repeatedly reiterates the theme of what is presumed to have occurred. In step six, handling the suspect's passive mood, the suspect is said to feel defeated at this point (and may be crying); the interrogator acknowledges this and further intensifies and repeats the central statements. Step seven, presenting an alternative question, involves providing the suspect with two incriminatory choices regarding an aspect of the crime, based on an assumption of guilt. Step eight, having the suspect orally relate various details of the offence, follows from step seven, where the suspect has chosen an alternative and the interrogator reinforces the admission of guilt. The interrogator is then required to obtain a brief oral review of what occurred during the commission of the crime. The final step of this technique involves converting an oral confession into a written confession.

While the Reid Technique is increasingly used by police forces in Canada to extract confessions from allegedly guilty suspects, there are a number of problems with its use. Primarily, this form of interrogation is manipulative and relies on a number of dubious beliefs about the behaviour of guilty and innocent people. In other words, it is based on the belief that guilty suspects will appear guilty and innocent suspects will appear innocent (Moore, 2008, 4; Moore and Fitzsimmons, 2011). This belief is clearly problematic and research in recent years has demonstrated that the detection of deception is imprecise and no more reliable than guesswork (Granhag and Stromwell, 2004). Given the inherently intimidating environment where police questioning takes place and the variable nature of human behaviour, to presuppose how any given individual will behave, and prescribe meaning to that behaviour, is illogical. Another erroneous assumption of this technique is that innocent suspects are immune to its pressure tactics (Moore, 2008, 6). The number of high-profile wrongful convictions involving false confessions clearly attests to the fact that innocent people can be coerced and manipulated into making false confessions.

Undercover Interrogation: The "Mr Big" Sting

The Reid Technique demonstrates the lengths to which police will go to procure a confession from a criminal suspect. What are also of interest with respect to false confessions are *undercover* operations undertaken by the police to gain confessions, in particular the example of the "Mr Big" or "Big Boss" sting. While the majority of false confessions result through "ordinary" police interrogations such as the Reid Technique, the "Mr Big" sting is a particularly egregious example of overzealous policing that can and does result in false confessions. This unique sting operation has been used increasingly in recent years by the RCMP to investigate crimes that have proven difficult to solve.[4] In fact, Keenan and Brockman (2010) have studied eighty-one judicial decisions involving Mr Big stings that appeared before Canadian courts in some capacity between 1992 and 2010, the majority of which (fifty-six) occurred in British Columbia. Usually undertaken in cases where there is little or no evidence against a suspect, the "Mr Big" sting involves a highly detailed scheme whereby an individual who is suspected of having committed a serious crime is slowly enticed into joining a criminal organization. Police pose as members of this organization and attempt to enlist[5] the suspect in criminal acts with the prospect of rewards, in the form of money, promises of power, and so on. This takes place over a number of weeks or months where the individual becomes slowly involved in low-level activities to draw him into the gang. Part of the ruse involves implied (sometimes direct) threats of violence or imprisonment and actual staged incidents of violence towards those who betray or oppose members of the criminal group.[6]

The final step for the unwitting suspect to joining the gang is to confess all previous criminal actions to "Mr Big" or the Big Boss. In other words, "a suspect is encouraged to believe that he is associating with criminals who are operating in a major way, outside the law; and that to be taken in as a member of the criminal 'family,' he eventually will have to satisfy Mr. Big, the head of the organization, not only that he will be a worthwhile member, but also that there are no loose ends in his past that could bring trouble onto 'the family.'"[7] It is at this moment that the police record any criminal confessions and subsequently arrest the individual. Some scholars note that it is not surprising that this form of undercover investigation developed in the early 1990s, a time when rulings from the Supreme Court of Canada[8] had severely circumscribed the use of undercover investigative techniques against persons in custody (Moore, Copeland, and Schuller, 2009). The practice is coming under increasing scrutiny by the legal community and the courts regarding its potential to produce miscarriages of justice through false confessions.[9] In spite of the controversy surrounding it,[10] the technique has been extensively used in Canada. However, recent critiques by the Supreme Court of Canada, to be discussed below, may serve to limit use of this practice by the RCMP in the future.

While the methods used by the RCMP during "Mr Big" sting operations lack the formality and structure of the Reid Technique routinely used by Canadian police forces, both have the same putative aim: extracting a confession from the accused. Whereas police officers practising the Reid Technique will likely end their interrogation after a number of hours, or days, a "Mr Big" sting can take place over weeks and months, at considerable cost. Nonetheless, both forms of interrogation have the potential to induce false confessions; the sophisticated manipulations of the Reid Technique are aimed at breaking a suspect's will and producing confessions (whether true or false), while the inducements offered through a "M. Big" sting may a lure a suspect to confess simply for the possible financial rewards. Such confessions present a number of legal challenges, and prior to examining these challenges it is useful to examine individual suggestibility and how false confessions can be classified.

Suggestibility and Types of False Confessions

Not everyone succumbs to police interrogation practices and falsely confesses to crimes they have not committed. A growing body of research has begun to demonstrate not only what factors influence individual suggestibility to interrogation practices but also how a confluence of particular factors may lead to the production of a false confession. Gudjonsson (2002) has researched the psychology of interrogation practice extensively and discusses the factors that influence confession through the "Decision-Making Model of Confession." This approach, borrowed from rational-choice approaches to decision making, posits that decision making is influenced by perceptions regarding the available courses of action, or regarding the probability of each course of action occurring, and the benefits and harms associated with each course of action (Drizin and Leo, 2004). Suspects are influenced by their beliefs and ideas about probabilities regarding the outcome of their situation, which in turn may influence a decision to confess to a crime (whether they did it or not). Thus, even innocent suspects can be induced to confess by "leading them to believe that their situation, though unjust, is hopeless and will only be improved by confessing; or by persuading them that they probably committed a crime about which they have no memory and that confessing is the proper and optimal choice of action" (Ofshe and Leo, 1997a, 979). This two-step process, as described by Ofshe and Leo, involves first convincing the suspect that his situation is hopeless[11] and then eliciting the admission through the use of inducements (Ofshe and Leo, 1997a, 915–16).

Gudjonsson's research on suggestibility has empirically established that particular characteristics of interrogated individuals may affect their tendency to confess falsely to something they did not do (2002). His concept of interrogative suggestibility, defined as "the tendency of an individual's account of events to be altered by misleading information and inter-personal pressure within interviews," is thought to influence susceptibility to false confessions (Singh and Gudjonsson, 1992, 155). The Gudjonsson Suggestibility Scale measures susceptibility in controlled experimental situations and has been demonstrated to differentiate between real and faked suggestibility (Gudjonsson and Sigurdsson, 2004, 447). Factors that have been shown to have an impact on suggestibility include youth, intelligence, memory, anxiety, impulsivity, sleep deprivation, coping strategies, self-esteem, mood, and withdrawal from intoxicants (Sherrin, 2005, 633). Clearly, some individual personalities are more susceptible to interrogator suggestibility and, given the right circumstances, may be more likely to confess falsely. For these vulnerable individuals, the extent to which common law rules and Charter protections safeguard them remains uncertain.

While there have been a number of typologies of those who falsely confess, the original classification of such confessions emerged from the work of Kassin and Wrightsman (1985, 7) and included voluntary confessions, coerced-compliant confessions, and coerced internalized confessions. Later, Ofshe and Leo (1997b) modified this initial classification and suggested that there are five types of false confessions: voluntary, stress-compliant, coerced-compliant, coerced-persuaded, and non-coerced persuaded. The first type, the voluntary confession, involves statements or admissions freely given to the police, with little interrogation or pressure. Reasons proffered for voluntarily confessing to something one did not do include: desire for notoriety, attention, or fame; need to expiate guilt for real or imagined acts; inability to distinguish between fantasy and reality; and a pathological need for acceptance or self-punishment (Gudjonsson, 2002: Kassin, 1997; Leo, 2001).

One example of a voluntary false confession is that of Simon Marshall of Sainte-Foy, Quebec. Marshall, who has been variously described as schizophrenic, intellectually handicapped, and having a borderline personality,[12] admitted to a string of sexual assaults in 1997 and served five years in prison before his release in 2003. Following his release, he confessed to three more sexual assaults, but at that time DNA evidence proved he could not have committed these new assaults; the same DNA evidence indicated that he was also not guilty of the earlier assaults.[13] Clearly, Marshall's psychological problems and intellectual handicap put him at greater risk to police suggestibility owing to his inability to understand the impact of a confession, the repercussions of a guilty plea, and the deprivations of a prison sentence. In spite of his enhanced vulnerabilities, Marshall had approached the police on his own volition. As a result in part of his limited capacity, Marshall suffered from much taunting, abuse, and aggression at the hands of other prisoners during his time in prison. The Quebec Court of Appeal found that he had been a victim of a miscarriage of justice and in December 2006 Marshall was awarded $2.3 million for his wrongful conviction, the highest compensation in provincial history at that time. It was further found that police misconduct contributed to Marshall's conviction.

Another example of a voluntary false confession is the case of Romeo Phillion. In 1972 Phillion admitted to the 1967 murder of an Ottawa firefighter while being questioned by police regarding his involvement in a robbery. He immediately recanted but was convicted nonetheless and received a life sentence for murder; he was released on bail thirty-one years later, in 2003, while the federal minister of justice reviewed his conviction under section 696.1 of the Criminal Code.[14] The minister referred his case back to the Court of Appeal as if it were an appeal by Phillion; a new trial was ordered, but the Crown withdrew the charges in 2010 since it reasoned too much time had passed to pursue a conviction. After much legal wrangling in 2014,[15] Phillion was legally permitted to pursue civil action and seek financial redress from the province and the police for his ordeal; he died in 2015 without settling his lawsuit. Phillion did not apply for parole during his years in jail, since he steadfastly refused to admit guilt and responsibility for the murder.[16] Not only was his confession false, but suppressed evidence recently came to light that supported Phillion's alibi that he was two hundred kilometres from Ottawa when the murder took place. Gudjonsson has examined the Phillion case for the defence and found that "it contained many of the hallmarks of a false confession, including a desire to gain attention and cause mischief to police."[17] In this case as in Marshall's, personal psychological vulnerabilities to suggestibility may have contributed to the false confession and resulted in wrongful conviction and imprisonment.

The second type of false confession, the stress-compliant one, results from the great pressure of relentless questioning that occurs while a person is in custody and the only perceived way to end the questioning is to confess (Ofshe and Leo, 1997b). The types of psychologically manipulative techniques as practised by police officers when undertaking the Reid Technique could likely result in this type of confession, making these false confessions the most routine. In such scenarios, the police will generally use aggressive types of confrontation, in an intimidating environment, and block attempts by the suspect to deny guilt or responsibility. The suspect views a confession as a means to end an untenable situation, where he/she is psychologically exhausted and embattled. One example of a stress-compliant false confession is the case of *R. v. Chapple*,[18] where a day-care operator in Alberta was charged with aggravated assault after a child in her care suffered a serious head injury. The accused was subjected to an eight-hour interview, filled with lengthy monologues, constant interruptions, and persistent questioning, after which she made incriminating statements. The judge found her confession to be inadmissible on the grounds that it was the result of oppressive circumstances, where the defendant simply told the police what they wanted to hear.

Similar to the stress-compliant false confession is the third type, the coerced-compliant. In both situations, the suspect falsely confesses to end an overbearing interrogation. However, in a coerced-compliant false confession, "a suspect confesses in order to escape or avoid an aversive interrogation or to gain a promised reward" (Kassin, 1997, 225). This type of false confession most likely results from extensive physical abuse and aggression, so intolerable that the suspect confesses to gain the "reward" of an end to the beating. While there are many historical examples, a glaring one of coerced-compliant false confession is that of the Birmingham Six. The Birmingham Six were six Irish men convicted of two pub bombings in 1974 in England, where 21 people were killed and 182 injured. This occurred during the height of Irish sectarian violence in Northern Ireland and England during the 1970s; the arrested men were repeatedly beaten by the police until they signed confessions to the murders. It was only after sixteen years of imprisonment, much civil and criminal litigation, and a well-publicized media campaign that they were finally freed in 1991. These types of abusive police interrogative procedures were more common in the past than they are now; today, police are more inclined to use the psychologically manipulative practices of the Reid Technique.

The fourth type of false confession, the coerced-persuaded, is one where the individual has no memory of committing the crime but confesses nonetheless. In these cases, the suspect temporarily doubts the reliability of his/her own memory and believes that he/she probably committed the crime in question and confesses to it (Ofshe and Leo, 1997b). This type of false confession results from relentless questioning occurring over a number of hours or even days, the presentation of fabricated evidence, and an inherent psychological vulnerability to suggestion. The interrogator attacks the suspect's confidence in his/her own memory, offers the suspect an acceptable amnesia-based explanation for this lack of memory around the commission of the crime, and facilitates the construction of a confession to explain how and why the crime occurred (Ofshe and Leo, 1997b). One example of this type of false confession is the American case of Martin Tankleff in New York state. When he was seventeen years old, Tankleff confessed to the murder of his parents following hours of police questioning. The police lied to Tankleff and informed him that, just prior to his death, his father identified his son as the killer; overcome by grief, shock, and exhaustion, and believing he may have blacked out, Tankleff responded that if his father had said that, then it must be true. While Tankleff immediately retracted the false admission, it was presented as oral evidence at his trial. Notwithstanding the fact that there was no other real evidence, this so-called confession was instrumental in his conviction. Tankleff was incarcerated for seventeen years, a state appellate court overturned his conviction in 2008, and that same year the state attorney general's office decided not retry him for the murder.[19] This type of confession illustrates the powerful and manipulative nature of police questioning to the extent that it may affect a suspect's confidence in his/her own memory.

Finally, the fifth type, the non-coerced-persuaded confession, is similar to the coerced-persuaded type; the difference is that it is elicited not in response to coercive interrogation but rather to modern-day psychologically manipulative interrogation tactics and techniques (Leo, 1992, 44). Through subtle manipulation, the police are able to convince or persuade the suspect that he/she, in fact, did commit the crime but simply cannot recall the event. According to Ofshe and Leo, "a non-coerced-persuaded confession … is given by a suspect who has temporarily come to believe that it is more likely than not that he committed the offense despite no memory of having done so" (1997b, 215). The confession is quickly recanted once the suspect is removed from the interrogation situation. One example of a non-coerced-persuaded false confession is the American case of Gary Gauger in the state of Illinois. Gauger's parents were murdered in 1993. He discovered their bodies, and during an all-night interrogation and at police urging, he made some hypothetical statements regarding his parents' murder, speculating that he could possibly have killed them during an alcoholic blackout. Moreover, the police lied to Gauger while questioning him regarding the results of a polygraph and blood-stained clothing found in his room. His inculpatory statements, immediately retracted, were admissible and Gauger was convicted on two counts of murder. Two years later, the "confession" statements were found to be inadmissible, the charges dropped against Gauger were dropped, and two outlaw motorcycle-gang members were convicted for the murders.[20]

While Ofshe and Leo's (1997b) typology appears to be the most consistently referred to in the literature, there is still much debate around the most appropriate way to classify the different types of false confessions (Gudjonsson, 2002). For example, Gudjonsson is not in agreement with Kassin and Wrightsman's classification since he believes that not all compliant and internalized confessions are coerced and could result from other stresses or pressures (1985, 201). Whereas internal stresses are thought to emerge from the individual, custodial stresses emerge through the interrogation process and non-custodial stresses emerge from other people. Furthermore, there are individuals who falsely confess for other reasons, for example, to protect someone else, and these cases do not fit neatly into discrete categories. While it is not essential that there be agreement among legal researchers regarding this issue, overall efforts at classification aid in understanding the manner in which false confessions do occur. Although police interrogation practices will likely have an impact on the different types of false confessions that emerge, they are clearly not causative on their own; individual psychological vulnerabilities may exacerbate suggestibility under the right conditions. Given these considerations, it is important to understand how the courts have attempted to limit the impact of confession evidence through various legal strictures.

Legal Parameters: Common Law Confessions Rule and Charter Protections[21]

Canadian courts have long recognized the importance of restricting the admissibility of certain types of evidence, in order both to protect the accused person and to assure the fair administration of justice. Confession evidence is one area that has attracted much attention by the courts and legislatures for a number of reasons. Given that accused persons are subject to the authority of the criminal justice system, and are thus in a more vulnerable position than those administering justice, they necessarily benefit from extra protections. Particularly, certain groups of individuals, thought to be more vulnerable to police pressures on account of their youth, intellectual capacity, or mental status, are afforded special protections under the law. The courts have also recognized that being a suspect of a crime, in and of itself, puts one at a disadvantage, given the enhanced powers of the state. The courts have acknowledged the possibility of confessions being induced and at trial questions primarily arise with respect to the voluntariness of confessions given by accused persons to those in authority. In essence, a common law confessions rule is really about the common law limits on police interrogation.[22] Moreover, the issue of voluntariness is further linked to the notion of choice, and the "detained person is entitled to choose whether to make a statement to the authorities or not."[23]

Right to Silence: R. v. Hebert

Closely linked to the issues of confessions is the right to silence, enshrined in section 7 of the Charter.[24] Legal rights under the Charter comprise sections 7–14, and while not specifically defined as such, include protecting "… the rights of persons within the system of criminal justice, limiting the powers of the state with respect to investigation, search, seizure, arrest, detention, trial and punishment" (Hogg, 2007, 1028). What section 7 further conveys is the right to silence, both at the police investigative stage and at trial (Paciocco and Stuesser, 2015, 341). The right to silence essentially provides protection to individuals from the overwhelming power of the state. It is an attempt to balance individual rights with state power:

"On the one hand s.7 seeks to provide to a person involved in the judicial process protection against the unfair use by the state of its superior resources. On the other, it maintains to the state the power to deprive a person of life, liberty or security of the person provided that it respects fundamental principles of justice. The balance is critical."[25] One of the first cases that examined this right to silence with respect to confession evidence was that of *R. v. Hebert*.[26]

This case involved an individual who, when charged with robbery, told police he did not want to make a statement to them. He later made a number of incriminating statements implicating himself in the robbery to an undercover police officer sharing his jail cell. This case is of particular importance since, not only did it find that Hebert's rights had been violated by the improper police questioning, but it established that the right to silence (an objective right) is the most important right to be advised of, which in effect allows the suspect the right to choose to speak to authorities, or not.[27] While the Supreme Court ultimately found that Hebert's rights had been violated through improper police questioning and underscored the importance of the right to silence, it also outlined a number of limits to the right to silence, specifically:

1. The police may question the accused in the absence of counsel after the accused has retained counsel;
2. The right to silence only applies after detention;
3. The right to silence does not affect voluntary statements to a cellmate provided that person is not acting as a police informant or an undercover police officer;
4. The right to silence is not violated where undercover agents observe the suspect and do not "actively elicit information in violation of the suspect's choice to remain silent."[28]

In spite of this decision, there appears to be little consensus within the legal community about the extent of the role of the right to silence in affording protection to criminal suspects,[29] and even the court in *Hebert* only loosely defined those parameters.

Other rights linked to the right to silence are the right to counsel under section 10(b) of the Charter and the common law privilege against self-incrimination. As Justice McLachlin states in *Hebert*: "The detained suspect, potentially at a disadvantage in relation to the informed and sophisticated powers at the disposal of the state, is entitled to rectify the disadvantage by speaking to legal counsel at the outset, so that he is aware of his right not to speak to the police and obtains appropriate advice with respect to the choice he faces."[30] Thus, once an individual is informed of his/her right to silence through counsel, the assumption is that that right protects them. Moreover, the privilege against self-incrimination is based on the idea that an accused does not have to answer to the Crown until a case has been established against him. As Paciocco and Stuesser demonstrate, the principle is protected by a number of common law rules, "including the privilege against self-incrimination (the right of any witness in any proceeding to refuse to answer questions that may incriminate them), the right of accused persons to decide whether to testify at their own trials, and the rule excluding involuntary confessions" (2015, 307).[31] While the Court in Hebert was unanimous in its finding that section 7 included the right to silence, there was less clarity around the contours of that right, in effect reflecting what has been called the "Canadian ambivalence towards confessions" (Cournoyer, 2001, 2). There is particular concern over the application of the right in "Mr Big" undercover operations and it currently appears that the limited rights protected by the rules laid out in *Hebert* do not apply in the context of such operations (Smith et al., 2009, 178). The law on "Mr Big" operations is currently developing against the recent decision in *R. v. Hart*, to be discussed in more detail below.

Confessions Rule: R. v. Oickle

The confessions rule as it applies today was first articulated in *R. v. Oickle*.[32] In this case Oickle was accused of setting eight fires and after much questioning admitted to setting one of them. Later, at the urging of the police, the accused agreed to re-enact some of the fires and was ultimately charged with and convicted of arson. The Nova Scotia Court of Appeal excluded the confessions and entered an acquittal, but on further appeal to the Supreme Court the convictions were restored. There, Justice Frank Iacobucci restated an earlier confessions rule with particular reference to the courts' increasing recognition that false confessions can and do occur. Of note was the Court's acknowledgment of the importance of social-science research around the nature and types of false confession, particularly the work of Ofshe and Leo (1997a; 1997b). In addition, the courts recognized that the advent of DNA forensic analysis has allowed a number of previous confessions, and resultant convictions, to be proved unequivocally false, and wrongly convicted individuals have been exonerated. It seems that both research and practical developments indicate the need for particular vigilance around the admissibility of confession evidence.

In *Oickle* it was established that, in order for confessions made to persons in authority to be admissible, the Crown must establish beyond a reasonable doubt that the defendant has not been overborne by inducements, oppressive circumstances, or lack of an "operating mind." Moreover, the admissibility of statements or confessions must not have been induced through police trickery. Thus, the "contemporary" confessions rule requires a contextual analysis of all of the conditions surrounding the confession. The first of these relates to the presence of threats or promises that may give rise to questions of voluntariness.[33] Clearly, a threat or promise in exchange for a confession will render the confession inadmissible. While direct threats of violence or harm are obvious, the rule also covers more veiled threats involving a promise of leniency.[34] Inducements that address leniency from the courts or "hope of advantage" will, in most instances, be excluded.[35] The second factor addresses the issue of oppression,[36] and confessions that result from a desire to escape inhumane conditions, or interrogation to such a degree as to overbear the suspect's will, all constitute oppressive circumstances. The *Oickle* Court listed a number of oppressive tactics that can produce an unreliable confession, including deprivation of food, clothing, water, sleep, or medical attention, denial of access to counsel, the use of fabricated evidence, or aggressive questioning lasting for a prolonged period of time.

Citing a number of instances of oppression in Canadian criminal investigations, the Court emphasized that the use of oppressive tactics by police may lead not only to confessions motivated by a desire to escape from the inhumane conditions, but also to a situation in which a suspect actually "comes to doubt his or her own memory, believes the relentless accusations made by police, and gives an induced confession."[37] The third aspect of the confessions rule, the operating mind doctrine,[38] "requires that the accused possess a limited degree of cognitive ability to understand what he or she is saying and to comprehend that the evidence may be used in proceedings against the accused."[39] This consideration relates to the suspect's cognitive capacity, such that confessions may be considered inadmissible where it has been shown that a suspect did not possess the requisite capacity to comprehend fully what occurred. This particular consideration is included to protect the intellectually disabled, those who have limited capacity owing to intoxication, and young persons.

Given the particular vulnerability of young persons, there are a number of provisions within the Youth Criminal Justice Act which afford special protections to youth with respect to the statements they make to the police when they are criminal suspects.[40] The operating mind doctrine is quite limited in scope, however, and applies only when it can be said that the individual either did not know what he was saying or did not know that he was speaking to police and that the words would be used against him (Dufraimont, 2008c, 253). The threshold that the doctrine sets out represents a very low level of cognitive capacity, with the result that, on its own, the doctrine is unlikely to result in the exclusion of a significant number of confessions. Moreover, while the Court in *Oickle* noted that judges must remain aware of issues specific to each individual when considering whether to admit evidence relating to a confession, the decision has been criticized for failing to engage in any meaningful discussion of the specific kinds of personal characteristics and situations that might lead to a higher risk of false confessions for certain vulnerable individuals (Ives, 2007, 483).

The fourth and final aspect of the confessions rule addresses what is considered other police trickery.[41] Essentially, this refers to actions on the part of the police used to induce a confession that may be so appalling as to "shock the community." The doctrine is considered to be a distinct inquiry and Justice Iacobucci acknowledged that this aspect of the confessions rule goes beyond voluntariness; "its more specific objective is maintaining the integrity of the criminal justice system."[42] Justice Lamer, in the concurring opinion in *Rothman v. The Queen*,[43] introduced the concept of what it meant to "shock the community":

That a police officer pretend[s] to be a lock-up chaplain and hear[s] a suspect's confession is conduct that shocks the community; so is pretending to be the duty legal-aid lawyer[,] eliciting in that way incriminating statements from suspects or accused; injecting Pentothal into a diabetic suspect pretending it is his daily shot of insulin and using his statement in evidence would also shock the community; but generally speaking, pretending to be a hard drug addict to break a drug ring would not shock the community; nor would, as in this case, pretending to be a truck driver to secure the conviction of a trafficker; in fact, what would shock the community would be preventing the police from resorting to such a trick.[44]

It would seem that the distinction Lamer draws conveys the belief that impersonating an officer of the court (police, lawyer) would shock the community, but impersonating a criminal or other marginalized person would not. Rather than rely on the "dirty tricks" doctrine, courts today "tend to focus on how abusive the conduct is, and to consider the risk of unreliability as but one factor for consideration" (Paciocco and Stuesser, 2015, 360). While it is recognized that in investigating crime the police may occasionally deal with sophisticated and highly developed criminal activities and must have the tools to do so, it is also necessary that safeguards be in place so that police activity and police powers are not used excessively without regard for individual and collective rights.

Right to Silence Revisited: R. v. Singh

Case law continues to refine the parameters of Charter protections and it would seem that the right to silence is being gradually eroded. In *R. v. Singh*,[45] the Supreme Court attempted to clarify further the right to silence under section 7 and also examined the intersection between the right to silence (from *Hebert*) and the common law confessions rule (from *Oickle*). In this case Singh was accused of second-degree murder and made a number of incriminating admissions to the police, despite repeatedly attempting to end the police interview and asking to be returned to his cell. The issue before the Supreme Court was the admissibility of the statements made to the police on the grounds that they were involuntary and infringed his Charter right to silence. In dismissing Singh's appeal, the Court was significantly divided with respect to the intersection of the confessions rule regarding voluntariness and the right to silence. The majority found that "voluntariness, as it is understood today, requires that the court scrutinize whether the accused was denied his or her right to silence. The right to silence is defined with constitutional principles. A finding of voluntariness will therefore be determinative of the s. 7 issue. In other words, if the Crown proves voluntariness beyond a reasonable doubt, there can be no finding of a Charter violation of the right to silence in respect of the same statement."[46] In referring to the link between the confessions rule and the right to silence, Justice Louise Charron, writing for the majority, also found that "the confessions rule effectively subsumes the right to silence in circumstances where an obvious person in authority is interrogating a person who is in detention because, in such circumstance, the two tests are functionally equivalent. However, this does not mean that the residual power afforded to the right to silence under s. 7 of the Charter cannot supplement the common law."[47] It is thus argued that the confessions rule enhances or supplements the section 7 right to silence – rather than merely subsuming it.[48] Questions of voluntariness are closely linked to whether or not an accused person was denied his or her right to silence and both affect the admissibility of confession evidence. The characterization of the confessions rule and the right to silence as functional equivalents in this context has been criticized in that the case was a missed opportunity to clarify the distinction between the two, and that a clear distinction would have been in keeping with the fact that the Charter and the common law hold differing purposes and concerns (Walker, 2010).

Overall, the finding in *Singh* could allow for excessive police interrogation practices insofar as they permit the suspect to choose to remain silent and are not so extreme as to violate the operating mind principle. In other words, persistent police practices are permissible in order to elicit admissions or confessions from the accused, as long as he/she is made aware of his/her right to silence. In *Singh*, however, the dissent found that his statements to the police did in fact violate his right to silence and that the rationale of the confessions rule is distinct from the purposes of the Charter and that the two doctrines should be kept separate (Ross, 2007). Writing for the minority, Justice Morris Fish stated that "a confession that meets these common law standards does not invariably represent a 'free and meaningful choice' for the purposes of the *Charter*."[49] Thus, even if a confession could be considered voluntary under the confessions rule, at the same time it could have been obtained through state action that infringed section 7 of the Charter. The dissenting opinion appears to reflect a greater concern with the abuse of police powers over individual rights, while at the same time recognizing that the police have a particular responsibility to investigate crime and interrogate suspects. This does not, in and of itself, permit police badgering and relentless interrogation that disregards the notion of choice. While the majority decision in *Singh* affirms that the voluntariness of statements is closely tied to Charter rights, it has also been argued that it represents a blow to the right to silence (Litkowski, 2008, 1; cf. Ives and Sherrin, 2008).

Right to Counsel: R. v. Sinclair

A more recent decision appears to infringe further upon the right to silence. In *R. v. Sinclair*,[50] the accused was arrested for murder and spoke to counsel on two occasions. During police interviews that occurred over several hours, Sinclair stated he had nothing to say, and the police, while confirming his right to silence, did not allow him to re-consult his lawyer. He later made incriminating statements to the police and to an undercover officer in his cell; he also participated in a re-enactment at the murder site. At trial, the judge ruled that the interview, statements to the police, and the re-enactment were all admissible and that Sinclair's rights under section 10(b) of the Charter had not been infringed. ("Everyone has the right on arrest or detention ... (b) to retain and instruct counsel without delay and to be informed of that right.")

While the Court of Appeal affirmed this decision, the Supreme Court examined whether the right to counsel under the Charter required that a lawyer be present at all times throughout an interrogation; the Court was ultimately split three ways in its understanding of the issue. While the purpose of this section of the Charter was to support a detained person's right to choose whether or not to cooperate with the police, based on advice from counsel, in the Court the issue boiled down to differences of opinion as to when the right to consult counsel, following the initial consultation, ends. The majority position, rendered by Justice Louise Charron and Chief Justice Beverley McLachlin, represented a belief in the need for a narrow degree of protection for the accused, where the right to re-consult counsel was permitted only if there had been a change in circumstances.[51] The dissent, by Justices Louis LeBel and Morris Fish, conveyed a more expansive view, according to which the right to counsel should be considered as a continuing right, to be asserted at any point and consistent with the notion of jeopardy. For them, the right protects the accused from self-incrimination and also ensures the presumption of innocence. Absent these protections, the chances of a guilty plea increase, as well as the admission of incriminating statements. Ultimately, for the dissent, the right to counsel goes beyond a one-time consultation; the suspect has an inherent right not to be part of building a case against him or herself.

While also dissenting, Justice Ian Binnie's position was more intermediate; he argued for allowing the detainee *"reasonable* access to legal advice from time to time in the course of a police interrogation."[52] Sinclair's consultation with counsel over the phone constituted a total of 360 seconds of legal advice, which, to Binnie was not "enough to exhaust his s.10(b) guarantee."[53] Binnie's position reflects the belief that this and other cases (*Singh, Oickle*) have now lowered the bar so that "an individual (presumed innocent) may be detained and isolated for questioning by the police for at least five or six hours without reasonable recourse to a lawyer, during which time the officers can brush aside assertions of the right to silence or demands to be returned to his or her cell, in an endurance contest in which the police interrogators, taking turns with one another, hold all the important legal cards."[54]

Considered in combination with the above cases, *Sinclair* is representative of a slow encroachment on individual Charter rights in favour of the needs of law enforcement (cf. Boyle and Cunliffe, 2012). In particular, the cases represent a shift in the courts' view on section 10(b) rights, again in favour of the needs and interests of law enforcement (MacDonnell, 2012). The overall decision of the Supreme Court underlines the tension between balancing societal interests in solving crime and protecting the public, on the one hand, with the rights of accused persons under the Charter, on the other. Despite several lengthy, protracted considerations by the highest court in Canada, the law with respect to the right to silence and to ascertaining the voluntariness of confessions remains conflicted.

Case Law regarding Police Interrogation: The Reid Technique and the "Mr Big" Sting

Given that there is overlap between the confessions rule and the right to silence afforded through the Charter, recent lower court decisions regarding the admissibility of confession evidence, garnered either through overt police interrogation techniques or through covert undercover police practices, are not altogether clear or consistent. First of all, while the courts have generally accepted the use of the Reid Technique by the police, there have been a number of cases where the consistency of this technique with the confessions rule has been examined. In fact, in *R. v. M.J.S.*, it was noted that "the courts reserve the right and have the duty to determine when the accused's will to resist has been so broken by an interrogation that he is unable to say no to skilfully implanted suggestions that he make an admission against interest; and also when an accused's confidence in his memory is so shaken by the interrogation technique that he will agree with any suggestion made to him by an interrogator. The interrogation of suspects is fundamental to police work but overkill in interrogations can be harmful to the fundamental principles of a free and democratic society."[55] Specifically, in the *voir dire* examining this evidence in *R. v. M.J.S.*, questions were raised surrounding a confession to child abuse, which resulted from an intensive and at times oppressive police interrogation. The theme pursued in the interrogation surrounded the statement that, unless the "truth" was told, the accused's children would remain in the care of Social Services. As Provincial Court Judge Philip G.C. Ketchum noted: "After observing the demeanor of this accused, as well as his responses to the development of 'themes,' most of which were based on false information; and having regard to the time that this accused was under interrogation, as well as the intensity of those interrogations, and the repeated ignoring and overriding of any objections or denials from the accused, I am satisfied that these interrogations had the effect of creating an oppressive atmosphere."[56]

Furthermore, a "hypothetical admission that if the injuries were caused by the manner in which he held his infant, the accused was sorry that it happened," was presented as a confession of fact.[57] These admissions were made following seven and a half hours of questioning by three different interrogators and thirty-four denials by the accused. In this instance, the confession was not admissible since it was considered ambiguous and resulted only through threats and promises. The matter was put succinctly by Judge Ketchum: "When stripped to its essentials the Reid Technique is solely designed to convince the suspect that he is caught, that the police have overwhelming evidence that he is the culprit, and that there is no way that the suspect will be able to convince the interrogator or anyone else involved in the criminal justice system that he didn't do the crime."[58]

More recently, further case law has underlined the limitations of the Reid Technique and the extent to which it may produce false confessions. In *R. v. Chapple*,[59] the accused asserted her right to silence twenty-four times; she was ignored and a confession secured. In this case, Judge Michael Christopher Dinkel, of the Provincial Court of Alberta, reiterated Ketchum's earlier denunciation of the Reid Technique from twelve years previous and found that "its use can lead to overwhelmingly oppressive situations that can render false confessions and cause innocent people to be wrongfully imprisoned."[60] Furthermore, he went on to say that in this case "the interview had all the appearances of a desperate investigative team that was bent on extracting a confession at any cost ... Although there is no law prohibiting the use of the Reid Technique, I find that it has the ability to extinguish the individual's sacred legal rights to be presumed innocent until proven guilty and to remain silent in the face of police questioning. Innocence is not an option with the Reid Technique" (paras. 120–1). In this case the subsequent confession was said to have been the product of oppression, where the suspect's will had been overborne, and it was therefore excluded as evidence.

Though not always identified as an application of the Reid Technique, this approach to suspect questioning is not uncommon and there are several cases that highlight the need for oversight in police interrogation practices. In *R. v. Fitzgerald*,[61] an accused person stated 137 times that she wanted to remain silent when being questioned by the police. The court later found that the "right to silence was rendered meaningless"[62] and her statement subsequently rejected. In *R. v. Koivisto*,[63] the accused asserted his right to silence twenty-eight times, but the interrogating officer nonetheless ignored these requests. In *R. v. Mentuck*,[64] police continued to question the accused in spite of the fact that he asserted his right to silence sev-enty-five times.[65]

Courts are now ruling that the Reid Technique may be thus construed as essen-tially an attempt to override a suspect's right to silence. As Moore notes: "The social chemistry of the interrogation room is psychologically disconcerting from the outset. The suspect is informed that he need not say anything. If he opts to remain silent, the same agent who moments earlier informed him that he could remain silent proceeds to ask a litany of questions, and the questions persist, no matter how often the right to silence is invoked. On balance it does not appear to be providing much of a safeguard" (2008, 17). Furthermore, Justice Stromberg-Stein asks in *R. v. Rhodes*, "When does no mean no? How many times must a suspect say no? Can a suspect simply be ignored until his or her will is broken down or over-ridden?"[66] Clearly, repeated questioning may serve to break down a suspect's will, disorient and denigrate him/her, and at times ultimately prompt him/her to make a confession simply to end the interrogation. It has been argued that "persistent questioning, especially when coupled with the use of the Reid technique, should lead to a finding that the statement was not made voluntarily" (Litkowski, 2008, 18). While the manner in which such evidence is obtained should lead to a finding of involuntariness and inadmissibility, the extent of "persistent questioning" is difficult to establish and, more often than not, confessions obtained through this questionable technique are admitted.

Case law surrounding the admissibility of confession evidence obtained through the "Mr Big" sting demonstrates an increasing concern regarding the risks involved in admitting evidence obtained in this manner. In 2002 the Supreme Court had accepted in *R. v. Fliss*[67] that the tactics used during a "Mr Big" sting were legitimate police investigative techniques. Regardless, one issue the courts have grappled with more recently is the question as to whether the suspect was actually *detained* when incriminating statements were made. The *Hebert* doctrine set out the principle that a statement made to an undercover police officer in a place of detention is generally not admissible. In "Mr Big" sting operations, how-ever, it is difficult to argue that the suspect is detained when being questioned by undercover officers, whose true identity and purpose is unknown to them. In *R. v. McIntyre*,[68] the circumstances of the case illustrate the nuances inherent in *where* the confession takes place. McIntyre had been informed of his right to silence dur-ing arrest and detention and had chosen to remain silent. While incarcerated, an undercover agent placed with him was unable to procure any information, so a further sting operation was instituted. During a "Mr Big" sting-type operation that took place five months following his release, McIntyre made a number of self-incriminating statements implicating himself in a murder. The defence argued that the statements made to the undercover police by McIntyre while he was still a suspect in a murder investigation were inadmissible under sections 7 and 24(2) of the Charter. However, Justice Lewis C. Ayles of the New Brunswick Court of Appeal found that "there was no reason to protect the appellant from the power of the state. He was free in his comings and goings and he was in no way restricted by the police. There was no coercion in this case … the statement should therefore be received in evidence."[69] The statements were found to be admissible, the appeal was ultimately dismissed, and the conviction was upheld. What is interesting is that, if McIntyre had confessed to his cellmate (undercover police), it would have been inadmissible, but, because the confession was given to an undercover officer while he was not detained, it was admissible.

A further issue regarding the admissibility of such confession evidence has to do with to whom the admissions are made, in particular whether the statements are made to "persons in authority." The designation of who constitutes a person in authority has particular significance to the confessions rule, as designated in *R. v. Hodgson.*[70] Primarily, statements made to a person in authority are admissible only if it is established that they were made voluntarily and free from coercion (Weinstein, 2005). This requirement reflects a belief that state agents are in a position to hold coercive power over detainees so that special protections are necessary. The designation of a "person in authority" includes "the objective status of the person to whom the statement was made, and only where they are identified as someone formally engaged in the arrest, detention, interrogation or prosecution of the accused, is it then necessary to examine whether the accused believed that the person could influence or control the proceedings against him or her."[71] Put differently, suspects must reasonably believe that these persons are acting on behalf of the police or prosecution and could influence the proceedings against them. Ultimately, undercover agents are technically "persons in authority" in spite of the fact that this may not be known to the suspect at the time.

In the case of *R. v. Grandinetti,*[72] the Supreme Court established that, in order to be characterized as a person in authority, the recipient of the confession must have been acting in collaboration with the state and not against its interests. In this instance, Grandinetti was the subject of a "Mr Big" sting operation, and while attempting to secure a confession to the murder of his aunt, the undercover police officers posing as criminals convinced him that they had contacts with the police department which would influence the murder investigation. Grandinetti ultimately confessed to the undercover police officers and on appeal argued that the statements were made to persons in authority since he believed they could ultimately have an impact on the investigation through their connection to corrupt police. While his conviction was upheld at the Alberta Court of Appeal, and subsequently at the Supreme Court of Canada, Justice Rosalie Abella of the latter court agreed with the trial judge's prior designation that the definition of a person in authority was limited to people that the accused believed were acting in collaboration with authorities and not against its interests. Thus, the Court held that an accused must believe that their statement was made to a person in authority and also that this person was capable of influencing the outcome of the case against them, so as to engage the voluntariness analysis of the confessions rule.[73] It has been argued that this decision in fact reinforces the offering of inducements in exchange for a confession, which essentially violates the confessions rule and closes the door on undercover police officers ever being classified as persons in authority (Weinstein, 2005, 12, 14). Moreover, Moore, Copeland, and Schuller (2009) note that, "while the target of a Mr. Big investigation may not perceive himself to be subject to the coercive power of the state, the fact remains that the state is engaging in highly invasive behaviour and exercising a significant degree of control over the suspect through the creation and manipulation of scenarios" (359). Not only did the outcome in both *Hodgson* and *Grandinetti* eliminate the confessions rule as a means to exclude admissions arising from "Mr Big" operations (Poloz, 2015, 242), but it could also allow for the admissibility of confessions extracted through other types of police inducements and may result in police abuse of power.

In a 2000 Manitoba decision there was some recognition by the courts that the overpowering nature of inducements may force false confessions, and the confession obtained through the "Mr Big" sting in *R. v. Mentuck* was ultimately considered inadmissible. Mentuck was a suspect in the 1996 murder of a fourteen-year-old girl. With little evidence against him, the RCMP instituted a sting operation whereby they declared to have knowledge of his involvement in the murder and offered Mentuck significant inducements to confess (including $85,000). Mentuck denied the allegation to the undercover police on several occasions, but he finally confessed through a "Mr Big" sting operation. The trial judge in this case, Justice MacInnes of the Manitoba Court of the Queen's Bench, found that much of Mentuck's alleged confession contained information he had been told by the police or had viewed through earlier court proceedings. He found that there were overwhelming inducements to confess: undercover police had promised there was a terminally ill person ready to take the rap for Mentuck but they just needed the details; he was going to make substantial sums of money once he joined the organization; the contact threatened that he would lose his job if Mentuck failed to confess; and so on. As Justice MacInnes remarked, "it provided nothing but upside [*sic*] for the accused to confess and a downside of frustration and despair in maintaining his denial. I conclude that the confession, if not false, is certainly too unreliable for acceptance as an admission of guilt."[74] The confession was ultimately found to be unreliable and, in conjunction with the totality of evidence, was insufficient to convict Mentuck; he was found not guilty.

In 2007 questions regarding the constitutionality of aspects of the "Mr Big" sting operation were considered by the Ontario Court of Appeal in *R. v. Osmar*.[75] The court found that the use of the "Mr Big" sting was constitutional and not in violation of section 7 Charter protections against self-incrimination.[76] Osmar was convicted of first-degree murder in March 2002 for two deaths occurring one month apart in Thunder Bay, Ontario. Police were only able to charge Osmar with these murders following a confession he made during a "Mr Big" sting operation. Osmar appealed his conviction based partly on the grounds that statements he made to undercover police about the murders came about through trickery and elicitation, and constituted a violation of his Charter right against self-incrimination. In dismissing the appeal, Justice Marc Rosenberg referred to two earlier Supreme Court decisions which held that this right to silence is not infringed by undercover police operations where the suspect is not detained (*Hebert*) and also applies to "Mr Big" undercover operations (*McIntyre*).[77] In rejecting the arguments put forth by the appellant, Rosenberg stated that the case "does not violate the principles of fundamental justice" since there was no evidence of coercion, the appellant was not under any "pronounced psychological and emotional pressure," and there was no evidence of an "abuse of power" which would have rendered the confession unreliable. Further, Rosenberg recognized that, while the manner in which "Mr Big" operations are instituted may likely shock the community in some instances, it did not do so in this case.[78]

Most recently, *R. v. Hart*, decided by the Supreme Court of Canada, clarified the law around the admissibility of confessions evidence obtained through the

"Mr Big" sting. Hart was initially convicted in 2007 on two counts of murder for the drowning deaths of his three-year-old twin daughters; the main evidence against him was an admission during a "Mr Big" sting that he had pushed his daughters into a lake. In 2011 the Newfoundland and Labrador Court of Appeal found in *R. v. Hart*[79] that the state's control over the accused, owing to his vulnerability, limited education, and susceptibility to influence, in effect made his status that of a person in detention. Moreover, the statements the accused made were inconsistent and not corroborated by other evidence. Thus, the Court of Appeal ruled that, based in part on Hart's individual circumstance of poverty, social isolation, economic need, and the emotional attachments he formed with the police officers during the four months of the sting operation, he was effectively under state control and his statements were thus inadmissible because he was not advised of his right to silence prior to making them. The statements were thus excluded and a new trial was ordered.

The appeal of the acquittal to the Supreme Court of Canada in 2014 was dismissed and the Court found that the current law provides insufficient protection for the rights of suspects who become implicated in "Mr Big" operations. In coming to its decision to exclude Hart's confession, the Supreme Court of Canada was highly critical of this approach to obtaining evidence. It noted that "Mr Big" operations present a clear risk of unreliable confessions, since they often involve the use of powerful inducements as well as threats to the suspect, and that the nature of the operations, which involve illegal activities, paint a negative picture of the accused's character and can have a prejudicial effect at trial.[80] The Court further acknowledged that Mr Big operations have the potential for becoming abusive and present a clear risk of wrongful convictions.[81]

In excluding the evidence of Hart's confession, the Court created a two-pronged test for the admissibility of evidence procured through the "Mr Big" sting. The first involves a presumption of inadmissibility of such confessions that the state can rebut by showing that the probative value of the confession outweighs its prejudicial effect. Thus, the Court has introduced what has been described as a new common law rule of evidence as a pre-condition of admissibility (Poloz, 2015, 249). It involves a collective examination of "contextual factors," including the age and mental health of the accused as well as his/her disposition and vulnerability, the extent of inducements offered and threats made, and any indicia of reliability in the statement (para. 7). On the facts of *R. v. Hart*, the Court found that Hart's confession was inadmissible and had been influenced by a number of factors, including financial inducements offered to the suspect, Hart's individual vulnerability in terms of his mental capacity and previous social isolation, and the lack of confirmatory evidence of the facts of the confession.[82] The second prong of the test involves assessing police misconduct through the application of the doctrine of the abuse of process. The Court noted: "As this Court has said on many occasions, misconduct that offends the community's sense of fair play and decency will amount to an abuse of process and warrant the exclusion of the statement" (para. 117).

While the decision in *Hart* demonstrates the Court's recognition that "Mr Big" operations have the potential to provide prejudicial and unreliable evidence (Poloz, 2015, 249), it would also appear that, by allowing this controversial operation to continue, the Court is willing to accept a great deal of questionable police behaviour (Khoday, 2013). At the same time, the Court has raised the threshold for the admission of such evidence. Furthermore, it calls into question the validity of the sentences currently being served for convictions obtained through reliance on evidence obtained in this way.[83] The *Hart* decision was immediately followed by calls from the Association in Defence of the Wrongfully Convicted (AIDWYC)[84] for review of all "Mr Big" convictions, with particular concern being expressed for convictions that are not supported by adequate confirmatory evidence.[85]

Shortly after *Hart*, the Supreme Court in *R. v. Mack*[86] demonstrated that not all confessions obtained through "Mr Big" would be rendered inadmissible; the confession in that case was retained. However, in 2015, two Quebec Court of Appeal cases overturned convictions following the decision in *Mack*. In *Laflamme c. R.*,[87] a confession obtained through a "Mr Big" sting was not considered voluntary owing to the fact that the sting operation featured threats and staged violence that had amounted to coercion (Millan, 2015a). In *Perrault c. R.*,[88] the confession itself was considered reliable, since it was coherent and detailed and corroborated other facts about the crime. Regardless, in this case a new trial was ordered on the grounds that the trial judge had failed to instruct the jury adequately regarding the probative value of the confession (Millan, 2015b).

Confessions as Evidence

Confessions as evidence are particularly compelling because they are statements against one's own interest and are regarded as highly reliable (Moore and Fitzsimmons, 2011). Given the influence of confessions as evidence, the police are afforded considerable power in obtaining them. Yet there is a fine balance between protecting the rights of criminal suspects and allowing police the essential leeway to investigate crimes. While individual rights and freedoms necessarily restrict police powers, individuals must function in such a way that their rights do not infringe on those of others. As noted by Justice Lamer in *Rothman v. The Queen*, "it must also be borne in mind that the investigation of crime and the detection of criminals is not a game to be governed by the Marquess of Queensbury rules. The authorities, in dealing with shrewd and often sophisticated criminals, must sometimes of necessity resort to tricks or other forms of deceit and should not through the rule be hampered in their work."[89] However, the police should not be given the power to investigate crimes and interrogate suspects with impunity. As discussed earlier, the Reid Technique, so effective at eliciting confessions from suspects, should be used with great care since it also has the power to elicit confessions from the innocent.

In light of a number of recent high-profile wrongful convictions, arguments have been made for a national policy of mandatory video-taping of all police interrogations in order to eliminate any suspicions or "contamination" around confessions that occur during these practices (cf. Garrett, 2010a). The promise of this type of reform is great in terms of the prevention of miscarriages of justice, as argued in the 2005 report of the federal/provincial/territorial heads of the Prosecution Committee Working Group (Department of Justice, 2005b), which strongly advocated for this policy nationwide as well as for mandatory training of police and

Crown attorneys around the possibility of false confessions. The Group's second report, in 2011, reiterated these recommendations and advocated video-taping of the entirety of custodial interviews at a police facility in investigations involving offences of significant personal injury, along with a review of investigation standards and continual training (Department of Justice, 2011). A number of court decisions[90] have also recommended video- and audio-taping of all interrogations in serious crime cases, noting how the failure to record may render the admissibility of a confession questionable. Moreover, the recording of interrogations appears to be a standard practice for the RCMP and is being instituted in numerous provincial and municipal police forces throughout the country, as well as in the United States and abroad (Sullivan, 2004). At the same time, the subtleties involved in police interrogation practices that serve to induce both true and false confessions, through either the Reid Technique or the "Mr Big" sting, could hardly be moderated through video-taping police interviews. While video-taping may curb the more blatant forms of coercion and intimidation of suspects by the police, more sophisticated strategies will likely be missed by this policy. In fact, Cutler and Leo (2016) argue that, while recording interviews is an important first step, defence attorneys and others will need to familiarize themselves with the techniques and social psychology of interrogation practices in order to understand when persuasive and/or coercive tactics are at play.

Given the decision in *R. v. Hart*, and the presumption of inadmissibility of confessions obtained through the "Mr Big" sting, it is possible that the courts will find fewer questionable confessions to be admissible. The probative value/prejudicial effect balancing that is now required will likely force courts to apply greater scrutiny to confessions obtained in this manner. At the same time, the second-prong of the *Hart* test requires an analysis of any police misconduct in obtaining the confession, through the doctrine of abuse of process. In the few cases that have been decided since *Hart*, it would appear that the courts are being very cautious in considering such confession evidence. It remains to be seen whether or not this decision and test will curb the use of the technique and possibly force police to be more accountable.

As has been discussed, the courts have established a confessions rule that is meant to address the admissibility of confessions at trial, and even in cases where questionable confession evidence is admitted, defendants can raise other arguments about its inherent reliability. Unfortunately, these objective questions and issues fail to address what Sherrin has termed the "subjective vulnerabilities of suspects that may render their statements to authorities as unreliable" (2005, 639, 656); the confessions rule has not been generally interpreted or applied in a way that takes these vulnerabilities into account. Furthermore, mandatory videotaping of all interrogations cannot mitigate the effects of individual psychological vulnerabilities. Both Roach (2007) and Sherrin (2005) argue that, by relying on the voluntariness rule, the courts are missing the influence of other risk factors that may be external to the accused and that in turn may have an impact on false confessions, such as sleep deprivation, intoxication and withdrawal, youth, and intellectual incapacity. In spite of the long-standing legal protection offered by the confessions rule, and in light of more recent Charter considerations protecting the right to silence and the right against self-incrimination, individual susceptibility to police interrogation as well as other psychologically based vulnerabilities will invariably allow some inherently false confessions to go unnoticed and contribute to wrongful convictions.

Conclusions

While some would contend that these "enhanced" interrogation techniques are simply a more effective means of getting the "right" suspects to confess to the crimes they have committed, the increasing number of wrongful convictions that have resulted from false confessions would negate that argument. Furthermore, if the courts are attempting to maintain a balancing act between allowing the police the necessary leeway to do their jobs, and at the same time protecting individual liberties, it is difficult to justify enhanced interrogation as a means of achieving those ends. It is impossible for courts to regulate for every eventuality; therefore, what is required is greater transparency in the conditions surrounding the interrogation process. Some have even argued for the need to introduce expert testimony on interrogation and false confessions at trial (Cutler, Findley, and Loney, 2014). This would likely allow for more clarity around the nature and extent of the voluntariness of confessions obtained in this way and greater attention to individual rights. Police responsibility to investigate crime and interrogate suspects should not permit badgering and relentless interrogation of suspects, practices that disregard the principle of choice and the individual right to silence.

Chapter Six

Jailhouse Informants

"The danger is, that when a man is fixed, and knows that his own guilt is detected, he purchases impunity by falsely accusing others." (Lord Adinger in *R. v. Farler*[1])

Introduction

The use of jailhouse or in-custody informants in criminal investigations and trials has a long history in most common law jurisdictions. In many cases these individuals, who are often incarcerated themselves, bring information to authorities regarding confessions or other information pertinent to an ongoing investigation or trial. In exchange, the informants receive some sort of benefit for their cooperation, which could take the form of leniency in their own case with respect to sentence, monetary reward, dismissal of charges, or some other favour. Clearly, incarcerated individuals in the position to provide evidence to authorities stand to gain a great deal and the incentives to provide information, regardless of its factual nature, are compelling. In fact, jailhouse informants have been found to have contributed to wrongful convictions in 15 per cent of the over 350 exonerations uncovered by the Innocence Project[2]; the National Registry has determined them to be a factor in 7 per cent of the 2,143 cases to date; and the Canada data for this study concluded that the testimony of jailhouse informants contributed to wrongful convictions in 21 per cent of the cases in appendix A.

The purpose of this chapter is to present an overview of the difficulties inherent in using jailhouse informants in criminal investigations and trials. The challenges of using "criminals as witnesses" are outlined, specifically by addressing questions related to voluntariness, reliability, and credibility. Furthermore, the chapter discusses Canadian case law with respect to how courts have used this type of evidence, and, through illustrations from a number of high-profile wrongful convictions, such as that of Guy Paul Morin and Thomas Sophonow, it demonstrates how the use of jailhouse informants' testimony can contribute to error. Finally, the chapter surveys new Crown attorney policies on this subject in a number of provinces, policies that rest on the recognition that jailhouse informants' testimony, if it is to be used at all, must be greatly circumscribed.

Definitions

In very general terms, an informant is simply someone who provides information to a law-enforcement agency (Sherrin, 1997, 106). Black's law dictionary defines an informer as follows: "A person who informs or prefers an accusation against another, whom he suspects of the violation of some penal statute."[3] Zimmerman describes an informant as "a person who provides information, assistance or some other benefit to a law enforcement agency in exchange for some benefit, whether immediate or in the future, tangible or intangible, personal or third party" (1994, 83). This can include both citizen informants and criminal informants, of whom prison informants and jailhouse informants are a part.[4] Prison informants are those individuals who participate as witnesses in internal penitentiary tribunals and testify against fellow inmates who may be subjected to administrative segregation, involuntary transfer, or other sanctions (Genua, 2006). Jailhouse informants are comprised of individuals who are awaiting trial or sentence and in most cases testify regarding an alleged confession or admission of guilt, overheard from another inmate. This is usually, but not always, done in exchange for some benefit or leniency (Sherrin, 1997, 107). The focus of this chapter is on these latter individuals.

"Criminals as Witnesses"[5]

The central issue with respect to the use of jailhouse informants relates to the fact that such individuals have in essence, and in most cases, committed crimes or are facing some sort of charge and are considered to be inherently untrustworthy. In the Ontario Court of Appeal case of *R. v.* Trudel,[6] the court quotes the trial judge as saying, "The mere fact that any witness in this case has a criminal conviction does not, of itself, destroy or impair his or her credibility, but it may indicate a lack of moral responsibility to tell the truth." Given that jailhouse informants are often awaiting trial or sentencing for a crime allegedly committed by them, they may not present in the most credible manner. Consequently, their testimony may be tainted since it is often offered in exchange for some benefit to them. The inherent unreliability is in part due to the fact that such individuals will often fabricate evidence in response to various incentives (Sherrin, 1997; Trott, 1996; Zimmerman, 1994). Prison or jail conditions contribute to a general deprivation of the basic comforts of life; moreover, threats to a person's safety and well-being, as well as actual assaults, are not uncommon. Thus, it is understandable that, when facing an extended period of time in such conditions, a person would attempt to alleviate his or her own suffering, even it if involves stretching the truth or fabricating evidence. Further, the credibility and reliability of an in-custody informant's evidence is also affected by their appearance, mannerisms, criminal record, reputation in the community for truthfulness, interest in the matter, and motive (Genua, 2006).

   Sherrin (1997) points out that an existing deterrent to becoming a jailhouse informant is the fact that an individual may thereby be placing his or her own safety in jeopardy from other prison inmates. By becoming an informant,[7] these individuals can become pariahs in the prison environment and may be threatened or assaulted. In many cases, however, the potential threats are outweighed by the possible benefits. In the historic American case of *United States v. Cervantes-Pacheo,* the court found that "it is difficult to imagine a greater motivation to lie than the inducement of a reduced sentence."[8] Another U.S. case expresses the same sentiment: "Common sense would suggest that he [accomplice] often has a greater interest in lying in favour of the prosecution than against it, especially if he is still awaiting his own trial or sentencing. To think that criminals will lie to save their fellows but not to obtain favors from the prosecution for themselves is indeed to clothe the criminal class with more nobility than one might expect to find in the public at large."[9] While it seems likely that most jailhouse informants are motivated by an incentive or reward, other motivating factors include anger at another prisoner, desire to frame someone else for a crime he or she committed, the thrill of playing detective, fear, and survival (Sherrin, 1997, 111).

In cases where informants lie or fabricate evidence, some go to great lengths to bolster their stories, often with limited access to resources. A notable American case involved Leslie White,[10] a jailhouse informant who was ultimately the subject of a grand jury investigation regarding the use of informants in Los Angeles, California, jails in the late 1980s. White was skilled enough to fabricate several confessions; through impersonating prosecutors, police, sheriffs, and bail bondsmen on jail telephones, he was able to obtain enough information to corroborate the many confessions he allegedly heard. Similarly, in the Canadian case of *R. v. McInnis*,[11] an informant sought out information from the police that was considered crucial to the case, in the hopes of obtaining freedom (Skurka, 2002). Moreover in *Trudel*, the court noted that "informers are resourceful and well capable of obtaining information that they later plant into the mouth of the accused."[12]

In spite of the many flaws inherent in the use of informant testimony, this evidence is often given great weight in criminal trials. According to Sherrin, its credibility, or rather believability, is affected by a number of factors (1997, 117–18):

1. The trier of fact (in most cases the jury) is likely to associate informer testimony with the prosecution. The Crown Attorney is meant to represent the "people," is not attempting to *win*, and is thought to only be interested in seeking the truth (cf. Zimmerman, 1994). Thus, evidence the Crown's office presents, and by extension witnesses called to bolster this evidence, are often lent more credibility by juries.
2. Some informants might present well as witnesses; in some cases, they have been known to testify or offer testimony on several cases, and thus have experience in this regard. Furthermore, given the inducements available to informants, the incentives are great and the possibility of prosecution for perjury fails to serve as a deterrent.
3. Informants benefit from the fact that juries might not be conversant with the machinations and deprivations of prison life, and the great appeal of incentives to escape that situation, whether legal or not. Juries may not be in the best position to assess the credibility of the evidence of informants; they likely come across in a convincing manner, keeping control over their demeanour and body language (Genua, 2006, 4).
4. In assessing the credibility of informant testimony, it is difficult or almost impossible for the defendant to refute the testimony. It often becomes a question of "he said, she said," where juries are left having to assess the word of one alleged criminal over another.

Given the limitations inherent in their testimony, there continue to be difficulties around the use of jailhouse informants as witnesses; however, their significance in facilitating the job of law enforcement tends to overshadow these problems and police still rely on them extensively. It has also been argued that they are not only a useful tool in some criminal investigations but in fact are essential in obtaining information in high-profile cases, particularly in the area of organized crime. Zimmerman notes that informants are important in policing so-called invisible crimes, where there is no victim or a reluctant victim (1994, 83). Further, informants are thought to be essential for obtaining information on drug and conspiracy investigations. Informants have been used extensively in police operations in Canada in recent years, particularly in investigations and trials of members of outlaw motorcycle gangs.[13]

Canadian Case Law

Judicial pronouncements regarding the reliance on jailhouse informants have evolved in Canadian jurisprudence in recent years. While initially informants were barred from giving evidence owing to a belief in their incapacity to tell the truth and a jury's inability to detect their lies (MacFarlane, 2006, 469), the courts have allowed their testimony when accompanied by a warning to treat such testimony very cautiously. To date, no steadfast rule exists, but Supreme Court of Canada rulings serve to guide judges when dealing with witness testimony lacking corroboration. In *R. v. Vetrovec*, the appellants were convicted of conspiracy to traffic heroin and appealed based on the trial judge's charge to the jury with respect to corroboration, since one of the witnesses was an accomplice. Specifically, this case addressed the issue of the law of corroboration of accomplices, a very complicated and technical area of law. In this case, Justice Brian Dickson stated: "Identification evidence, for example, is notoriously weak, and yet the trial judge is not automatically required, as a matter of law, to instruct the jury on this point. Similarly, the trial judge is not required in all cases to warn the jury with respect to the testimony of other witnesses with disreputable and untrustworthy backgrounds. Why, then should we automatically require a warning when an accomplice takes the stand?"[14] Ultimately, the Court found that there was no special category for accomplices and that they should be treated like any other witness testifying at a criminal trial. But what was required was "a clear and sharp warning to attract the attention of the juror to the risks of adopting, without more, the evidence of the witness."[15] Therefore, the result of the decision in *Vetrovec* was a discretionary rule that asks trial judges to give warnings in appropriate cases. The ruling in *Vetrovec* has been followed in dozens of other cases where a witness's testimony is questionable and the judge is obliged to warn the jury; two more recent higher court decisions have further affected the consideration of jailhouse informant testimony.

In the case of *R. v. Brooks*,[16] a young child was murdered and the cause of death was acute brain injury, but there was no direct evidence establishing the accused as the killer. At trial, the Crown introduced testimony of two jailhouse informants to the effect that the accused had admitted to killing the child to stop her crying. In this case, both informants had previously offered to testify at other trials and had lengthy criminal histories; one had testified at a prior trial in return for a lighter sentence and the other had a history of psychiatric illness and substance abuse. There was no *Vetrovec* warning given at this trial and the accused was found guilty of first-degree murder; the Ontario Court of Appeal set aside the conviction and ordered a new trial. At the Supreme Court, there was not complete agreement on whether a *Vetrovec* warning should have been given in this particular case, but the Court was unanimous in refusing to establish a mandatory jury caution in the case of jailhouse informants as witnesses (Genua, 2006, 6). The majority ruled that the *Vetrovec* caution is normally required when the testimony of jailhouse informants or other "unsavoury" witnesses is offered by the Crown, and in *Brooks* the judge should have given the warning. Brooks's conviction was restored since the majority believed a jury would have convicted on the strength of the evidence, regardless of whether a warning was given or not. While this case underlines the importance of rigour when considering certain witness testimony, it also illustrates a lack of a clear majority ruling on this issue; the Court was in fact split 3–1–3. What is somewhat puzzling is that the Court did not require warnings to juries in all cases, nor did it indicate that such a warning should be repeated several times, or that juries should always be told "that jailhouse informants are usually motivated by self-interest and that such evidence has often proved to be untruthful and produced wrongful convictions" (Schmitz, 2000, 2).

With respect to what constitutes a proper warning, Justice John Major affirmed that "at a minimum, a proper Vetrovec warning must focus the jury's attention specifically on the inherently unreliable evidence. It should refer to the characteristics of the witness that bring the credibility of his or her evidence into serious question. It should plainly emphasize the dangers inherent in convicting an accused on the basis of such evidence unless confirmed by independent evidence."[17] Trial judges are directed to consider not only witness credibility but also the importance of the witness to the Crown's case. It is up to the trial judge's discretion as to when such a warning is warranted, as Justice Michel Bastarache noted:

> These factors affect whether the Vetrovec warning is required. In other words, the greater the concern over the credibility of the witness and the more important the evidence, the more likely the Vetrovec caution will be mandatory. Where the evidence of so called "unsavoury witnesses" represents the whole of the evidence against the accused, a "clear and sharp" Vetrovec warning may be warranted. Where, however, there is strong evidence to support the conviction in the absence of the potentially "unsavoury" evidence, and less reason to doubt the witness's credibility, the Vetrovec warning would not be required, and a lesser instruction would be justified.[18]

The decision in *R. v. Trudel*[19] established that specific instructions around warnings to juries are advisable. In this case both individuals were appealing a conviction for first-degree murder and the original trial had relied on extensive evidence from three other convicted persons. The Ontario Court of Appeal allowed the appeal[20] and one reason given was that the trial judge had not given the jury an adequate warning on accepting this evidence and further erred by admitting evidence of confessions by inmates since "their prejudicial effect outweighed their probative value."[21] Moreover, in this instance the court further delineated aspects of the *Vetrovec* warning. Specifically, it referred to the purpose of the warning as "to alert the jury that there is a special need for caution in approaching the evidence of certain witnesses whose evidence plays an important role in the proof of guilt. The caution is of particular importance where there are defects in the evidence of a witness that may not be apparent to a lay trier of fact. Perhaps the most important of these is the jailhouse informer."[22] Furthermore, the court established the four characteristics of a proper *Vetrovec* warning based on the fact that jury members may be incapable of adequately assessing witness credibility. In its ruling:

1. The evidence of certain witnesses is identified as requiring special scrutiny;
2. The characteristics of the witness that bring his or her evidence into serious question are identified;
3. The jury is cautioned that, although it is entitled to act on the unconfirmed evidence of such a witness, it is dangerous to do so; and
4. The jury is cautioned to look for other independent evidence which tends to confirm material parts of the evidence of the witness with respect to whom the warning has been given.[23]

Where evidence is presented by accomplices, children, and jailhouse informants, this type of warning may help juries in assessing credibility. But, regardless of who is giving the testimony, that testimony must meet the standards of admissibility before it is allowed into evidence. What is interesting about these decisions is the reluctance of Canadian high courts to *require* judges to provide a warning in cases where testimony from "unsavoury" witnesses is presented; the warning is ultimately discretionary. Given that informant testimony is the backbone of many criminal cases, and the fact that numerous prosecutions would likely not be brought forward without it, it is possible that higher courts do not wish to hamstring the system by forcing judges to give a *Vetrovec* or similar warning in all cases of informant testimony. At the same time, without a clear understanding of the inherent difficulties with this testimony, there is a risk of convictions based on fabricated testimony or, worse still, manipulations of the system in cases where informant testimony is proffered for nefarious ends.[24]

More recent decisions have added further nuances to the parameters of the *Vetrovec* warning. In *R. v. Hurley*,[25] an important aspect of the case was testimony from an informant who claimed that the accused had told him he had he had cleaned the room where the murder took place in order to remove DNA evidence of his presence. In this case, the trial judge "did not tell the jury that caution was required because Mr. Niemi was a jailhouse informant, that he was facing charges himself, or that he was aware a reward was offered for information about the killing. Although these facts were included in the trial judge's summary of Mr. Niemi's evidence, at no point in the jury charge were they linked to the need for extreme caution in relying on his evidence."[26] In this case, the Supreme Court stressed the importance of a trial judge identifying for a jury those characteristics of the witness that brings his or her credibility into serious question, including the fact that a witness may have a motive to lie in order to gain some advantage.

In *R. v. Khela*,[27] the case against the accused relied heavily on the testimony of two unsavoury witnesses; both had lengthy criminal records and were members of a prison-based gang. The trial judge's directions to the jury included admonitions to treat their testimony cautiously and to decide whether any other evidence confirmed or supported it. On appeal, the issue surrounded whether, in his *Vetrovec* warning, the trial judge had failed to instruct the jury that for evidence to be confirmatory of the jailhouse informants' testimony, it had to be both independent and material. The British Columbia Court of Appeal upheld the conviction on the grounds that the warning was thought to be sufficient, while the Supreme Court dismissed the appeals and found that a *Vetrovec* caution cannot be applied routinely in every situation. In a judgment delivered by Justice Morris Fish, the Court emphasized that a *Vetrovec* warning must contain the four cautions cited above, but "that failure to include any of the components in the terms outlined above may not prove fatal where, as in this case, the judge's charge read as a whole otherwise serves the purposes of a Vetrovec warning."[28] Fish went on further to emphasize that "a truly functional approach must take into account the dual purpose of the Vetrovec warning: first, to alert the jury to the danger of relying on the unsupported evidence of unsavoury witnesses and to explain the reasons for special scrutiny of their testimony; and second, in appropriate cases, to give the jury the tools necessary to identify evidence capable of enhancing the trustworthiness of those witnesses."[29]

Other judgments have found that, in the absence of evidence of collusion or collaboration, the testimony of one unsavoury witness can confirm the testimony of another,[30] and that for evidence to be confirmatory of an unsavoury witness, it must come from another source and tend to show that the unsavoury witness is telling the truth about the guilt of the accused.[31]

The Model Jury Instructions from the National Judicial Institute with respect to "Crown Witnesses or Unsavoury Characters" reflect these case-law developments.[32] While these warnings are discretionary, judges must take into account the credibility of the witness and the importance of the witness to the Crown's case. They state:

[1] *(Name of Witness)* testified for the Crown. I am now going to give you special instructions that apply to this witness. You have heard that (*identify for the jury the characteristics of the witness that bring his or her credibility as a witness into serious question, e.g., accomplice, jailhouse informant, unsavoury witness*). Testimony from this kind of Crown witness must be approached with the greatest care and caution because experience tells us (*identify for the jury the reasons why evidence from witnesses with these characteristics is suspect, e.g., having an interest in the outcome of the case, a strong motivation to lie, the ability to conceal true motives, a desire to minimize his or her own involvement, etc.*).

[2] It is dangerous to base a conviction on unconfirmed evidence of this sort. You should consider whether *(Name of witness)*'s testimony is confirmed by other evidence in deciding whether the Crown has proved *(Name of accused)*'s guilt beyond a reasonable doubt.

[3] You should look for independent evidence tending to show that *(Name of Witness)*'s testimony implicating *(Name of Accused)* is true. By "independent," I mean from a source unconnected to *(Name of Witness)*.

[4] However, if you find *(Name of Witness)*'s testimony trustworthy, you may rely on it even if it is not confirmed by other evidence.

(*Where there is confirmatory evidence, the following may be added:*)

[5] I now want to illustrate the kind of evidence from this case that you might find confirmatory by giving you some examples. I emphasize that these are only examples. You may not find the evidence I am about to mention helpful in confirming *(Name of witness)*'s testimony, or you may find confirmation in other evidence that I do not mention. It is up to you to decide.[33]

Furthermore, juries should be warned in instances of allegations of collusion between witnesses, and evidence that juries are entitled to consider as being confirmatory should be identified.

American Case Law

In the United States, the acceptance of jailhouse-informant testimony without disclosing information about any agreement with the informant is considered to be in violation of the *Brady* rule. This rule emerged from the case of *Brady v. Maryland*,[34] which established that prosecutors have a constitutional obligation to disclose exculpatory evidence to the defence. Moreover, with respect to informant testimony, case law has established that the prosecution must disclose information that an agreement has been made not to prosecute a witness in exchange for testimony (*Giglio v. U.S.*[35]) or to provide more lenient treatment in exchange for testimony (*US v. Sudikoff*;[36] *State v. Lindsey*[37]). Similar to the difficulties found in the Canadian case of *R. v. Stinchcombe*,[38] "under *Brady* and most state criminal discovery rules, the prosecutor has the discretion to determine *what* constitutes exculpatory evidence and *when* to disclose it" (Joy, 2008, 13).[39] In the American context, the confluence of jailhouse-informant testimony and a lack of disclosure regarding any agreements made between the prosecution and the witness or informant surrounding the production and use of this testimony has resulted in numerous wrongful convictions and a great deal of scholarship[40] (cf. Bloom, 2005; Gross, 2008; Joy, 2008; Medwed, 2006; Raeder, 2007; Thompson, 2011).

As discussed, informant testimony is a causative factor in wrongful convictions and the leading cause in capital cases (Warden, 2006). While wrongful convictions resulting from false informant testimony are inherently problematic, the most egregious cases are likely capital ones since the prisoner languishes for many years on death row, awaiting an execution for a crime he/she did not commit.[41] The story often follows a typical pattern: a horrific crime occurs (most often sexual assault and murder, with the victim frequently a woman or a child), there are few suspects, an already marginalized individual (one likely facing other charges/or a co-accused) admits to hearing a confession or can corroborate some existing evidence, this person offers to testify on behalf of the prosecution in exchange for leniency (dropped charges, payment, and so on), and a wrongful conviction results. There have been far too many examples of this pattern occurring; however, in those cases when such errors are exposed, the exposure frequently happens only at exoneration. Innocence projects throughout North America and elsewhere have only revealed the tip of the iceberg[42] in terms of actual convictions in error, and what these cases indicate is that countless other individuals have been or remain incarcerated because of the reprehensible actions of informants. At the same time, policy to address the use of criminal-informant testimony appears to be severely lacking (Roth, 2016).

Jury Directions to Ignore Inadmissible Evidence

While warnings or jury directions given by judges in certain situations[43] may prove to satisfy legal or case-law requirements, a further question remains as to whether such warnings do indeed have an effect or are helpful to juries when weighing such evidence. On their face, judges' instructions to juries either to ignore particularly prejudicial evidence or to look for independent corroboration or for other evidence appear to be an effective means of obtaining a fair trial and, in turn, avoiding wrongful convictions. Yet earlier research has demonstrated that such warnings do not, in fact, always have such an effect and may serve to draw unwanted attention to the problematic evidence (Broeder, 1959; Wolf and Montgomery, 1977). As discussed, in the case of unreliable or unsavoury witnesses, the *Vetrovec* warning is an attempt by judges to caution the jury regarding the acceptance of the unconfirmed testimony of unreliable witnesses. While there appears to be little empirical research[44] that examines the effect of jury instructions on informant evidence, studies that examine the impact of jury instructions on other forms of suspect evidence provide some comparisons.

What may be problematic from the start is that almost all of the research examining the impact of jury instructions or directions on jury decision making takes place in experimental settings with mock-jury simulations, and often with university students as participants, thus limiting generalizability to real-life settings. Leverick (2014) notes (as have others) that such research is fraught with many methodological challenges. Despite the fact that the social psychologists who undertake these studies staunchly defend their results, much of the research is hampered by inadequate sampling, inadequate trial simulation, an absence of jury deliberations in the research design, use of inappropriate dependent variables, and participants' awareness that they are role playing and that their decision has no real-life consequences (Leverick, 2014, 102).

Moreover, the results of much of this research have been equivocal. For example, Steblay et al. (2001) demonstrate that, taken as a whole, judicial instructions do not effectively eliminate jurors' use of inadmissible evidence (487). They also found greater juror non-compliance with instructions to ignore when the reason for rejection was not provided or rejection of the evidence was justified with an unexplained technicality or if the evidence was illegally obtained. There was a smaller effect when judicial reasoning was provided regarding the nature of the inadmissibility. Kassin and Sommers have concluded that juries will ignore inadmissible evidence if the reasons for disregarding it are substantive rather than procedural (1997, 1053). As Leverick notes, most of the research around the effects of jury directions relates to eyewitness identification evidence and the most common finding is that jury directions appear to lead to an increase in general scepticism about the evidence rather than greater sensitivity to it (2014, 107). While Findley (2013) argues that jury instructions regarding the unreliable or questionable nature of certain forms of evidence raises the risk that courts may latch onto the them as an excuse not to employ more effective exclusionary orders, in his view there is still a role for jury instructions (and expert testimony on evidentiary issues) if applied properly.

In her extensive review of jury directions, Leverick proffers the following factors as significant in increasing their efficacy: simplifying the language to make the directions accessible to laypersons, ensuring that the directives address the relevant considerations (see also Findley, 2013), and providing a written copy of the directives to the jury (2014). While Kassin and Sommers (1997) support the idea that judges should explain the basis of a ruling once a containment is introduced, they also discuss how juries may be "inoculated" at the start of a trial with a general warning that they may be hearing inadmissible evidence (1053). Roach goes a step further and recommends that courts exclude unreliable evidence outright, given the recent and historical examples of how specific forms of evidence have contributed to wrongful convictions (2007). Ideally, unreliable evidence should not be permitted at trial, but considering the inadequacies of jury directions to disregard when such evidence is presented, other means require consideration. As a further means of excluding unreliable evidence, Roach suggests that courts could make greater use of the common law rule that allows for the exclusion of evidence when its prejudice exceeds its probative value (2007, 228), given that the courts have failed to recognize the exclusion of unreliable evidence as a right under section 7 of the Charter. In his cogent arguments regarding the case for excluding problematic identification evidence as well as the testimony of jailhouse informants and coerced confessions, Roach underscores the inherent unreliability of much of that evidence and the challenges courts face in balancing the right of innocent persons not to be convicted and the role of the state in pursuing convictions.

Wrongful-Conviction Case Examples

Canadian case law has also included wrongful convictions that have resulted, in part, from the testimony of jailhouse informants; the two most extreme examples to date are Guy Paul Morin and Thomas Sophonow.

Guy Paul Morin

In October 1984 Christine Jessop, an eight-year-old girl from Durham County, Ontario, went missing; her body was found in December of the same year – she had been murdered and sexually assaulted. Guy Paul Morin was arrested for her murder in 1985. He was acquitted following a first trial in 1986 and was found guilty of first-degree murder at a second trial in July 1992. In 1995 the Ontario Court of Appeal allowed Morin's appeal and he was acquitted, based on DNA forensic analysis indicating that he could not have murdered Christine Jessop. A commission of inquiry chaired by Justice Kaufman in 1998 examined the many errors that occurred in this case and made 119 recommendations for change.[45] Factors that contributed to Morin's wrongful conviction included questionable forensic evidence, inadequate investigative procedures by the police, and the use of jailhouse-informant testimony.

In Morin's case, two jailhouse informants, Mr X and Robert Dean May, testified that Morin made statements to May, which were overheard by Mr X, regarding the murder of Christine Jessop. Both these individuals testified for the prosecution at both of Morin's trials, as well as at the commission of inquiry. Their testimony surrounded a so-called confession made by Morin on 30 June and 1 July, when, it was alleged, Morin became upset and cried out, "Oh fuck, why did I do it, oh fuck, man, fuck, I killed her, I killed that little girl" (Kaufman, 1998c, 405). An investigation regarding the circumstances of the alleged confession and the backgrounds of May and Mr X took place during the Kaufman Inquiry and revealed a variety of factors that called into question the reliability and credibility of their testimony. Both had lengthy criminal records and histories of psychiatric problems and had received benefits in relation to outstanding charges in exchange for their testimony. Furthermore, May recanted his initial testimony and then later recanted his recantation. Overall, Justice Kaufman found that both of these witnesses were inherently unreliable: "Two sociopaths, motivated to obtain benefits, who allege a 'bare-bones' confession containing no detail known only to the perpetrator, absent any real confirmation of what they said, should ring far more bells than were rung here" (488). Kaufman concluded that the prosecutors failed to evaluate effectively the informants' reliability, perhaps because both had consented to and passed polygraph examinations, but he did not find misconduct on the part of the prosecution. One of his recommendations was the institution of a blanket rule requiring an automatic *Vetrovec* warning whenever a jailhouse informant testifies. Since that time, as will be discussed below, the attorney general for Ontario has instigated a policy that would have likely disallowed the testimony of May and Mr X and ultimately prevented Guy Paul Morin's wrongful conviction.

Thomas Sophonow

The Sophonow case is one of the most egregious examples of the difficulties surrounding the use of jailhouse-informant testimony in Canada. Thomas Sophonow was arrested for the murder of sixteen-year-old Barbara Stoppel in 1982; his long ordeal involved three trials, two convictions, and forty-five months in jail for a murder he did not commit, prior to his acquittal by the Manitoba Court of Appeal in 1985. Sophonow's case was fraught with difficulties around eyewitness identification, disclosure of evidence, alibi evidence, and the use of jailhouse informants. A commission of inquiry, chaired by former Justice Peter Cory, examined the many factors that contributed to Sophonow's wrongful conviction.[46] One section of its report, devoted entirely to jailhouse informants, is entitled "Jailhouse Informants, Their Unreliability and the Importance of Complete Crown Disclosure Pertaining to Them."[47] There, Justice Cory gives a scathing account of such witnesses:

> Jailhouse informants comprise the most deceitful and deceptive group of witnesses known to frequent the courts. The more notorious the case, the greater the number of prospective informants. They rush to testify like vultures to rotting flesh or sharks to blood. They are smooth and convincing liars. Whether they seek favours from the authorities, attention or notoriety they are in every instance completely unreliable. It will be seen how frequently they have been a major factor in the conviction of innocent people and how much they tend to corrupt the administration of justice. Usually, their presence as witnesses signals the end of any hope of providing a fair trial.[48]

In Sophonow's case, eleven individuals volunteered to provide testimony to support Sophonow's guilt; the police and Crown attorneys ultimately narrowed the testimony down to three individuals: Thomas Cheung, Adrian McQuade, and

Douglas Martin. Cheung had twenty-six fraud charges dropped in exchange for his testimony, whereas McQuade and Martin had long histories of providing testimony to the police in exchange for some benefit. While the use of jailhouse informants was standard practice in criminal cases in Manitoba in the early 1980s, what is most disconcerting in this instance was that Sophonow's defence counsel was not made aware of the questionable histories of these witnesses at that time and was therefore unable to refute their testimony. Furthermore, in Cory's review of existing research on jailhouse informants, as well as a result of his thorough study of what occurred in Sophonow's case, he found that:

- jailhouse informants are polished and convincing liars;
- all confessions of an accused will be given great weight by jurors;
- jurors will give the same weight to "confessions" made to jailhouse informants as they will to a confession made to a police officer;
- "confessions" made to jailhouse informants have a cumulative effect and, thus, the evidence of three jailhouse informants will have a greater impact on a jury than the evidence of one;
- jailhouse informants rush to testify in particularly high-profile cases;
- they always appear to have evidence that could come only from one who committed the offence; and
- their mendacity and ability to convince those who hear them of their veracity make them a threat to the principle of a fair trial and, thus, to the administration of justice.[49]

Consequently, Cory developed a number of cogent recommendations regarding the very limited use that should be made of jailhouse informants. These recommendations, consistent with the Manitoba Guidelines of 1999, included the following: there should be a general prohibition on the use of such informants, except in very rare circumstances; only one informant should be permitted for each case; and clear instructions should be given to the jury on the dangers and unreliability of this type of testimony when it does occur. Many of these recommendations have become policy in a number of provinces, as discussed in the section that follows.

Provincial Policy Reform

Throughout the previous two decades, as outlined in the tables below, a number of provinces have established both policies on, and committees for, vetting the use of jailhouse-informant testimony in order to circumscribe the use of these witnesses.[50] The data in Tables 5, 6, and 7 have been separated by region: Table 5 encompasses the Atlantic provinces (Nova Scotia, New Brunswick, Newfoundland and Labrador, and Prince Edward Island); Table 6, the west coast and the prairies (British Columbia, Alberta, Manitoba, and Saskatchewan); and Table 7, central Canada (Quebec and Ontario).[51] As will become evident, there is a great deal of overlap between the policies and many have followed the recommendations of both the Kaufman and Sophonow inquiries; thus, features common to the provincial policies will be discussed together.[52]

Table 5. Jailhouse-informant policies – Atlantic provinces

Policy Components	Nova Scotia (NS)	New Brunswick (NB)	Newfoundland and Labrador (NL)	Prince Edward Island (PEI)
Date of Issue	14 May 2004 (based on Ontario's policy)	10 May 2003 1 September 2015	1 October 2007	November 2009 (based on Nfld's policy)
Presumption of use of informants	No presumption	Inherently suspect and reliance on this type of evidence should be the exception and not the rule.	Presumed unreliable unless other evidence confirms it; it is also presumed inadmissible unless charges are serious.	Informants should be prohibited from testifying, and only allowed in rare cases such as kidnapping, where they may know the whereabouts of a victim.
Test of admissibility	Only where there are sufficient indicia of reliability and a compelling public interest in doing so.	Evidence is sufficiently reliable and the public interest consideration is compelling.	Can be used if approved by the DPP[53] and if it is in the public interest because charges are serious.	The Crown should conduct a subjective assessment of the proposed testimony and consider:[54] background, past testimony as an informant, reliability of past information, convictions for dishonesty, circumstances of incarceration and of accused's confession.
Policy applies to:	Someone who receives one or more statements from an accused while both are in custody. The statements must relate to an offence committed outside of custody.	Someone who receives one or more statements from an accused while both are in custody. Statements must be related to an offence committed outside of custody.	Not specified	Not specified
Policy does not apply to:	Informers who allegedly have direct knowledge of the offence independent of accused's statements. Police undercover operations outside of custody. Police should not limit the use of informants to advance police investigations.	Informers who have evidence independent of alleged statements of the accused.	Not specified	Not specified

(Continued)

Table 5. Jailhouse-informant policies – Atlantic provinces (Continued)

Policy Components	Nova Scotia (NS)	New Brunswick (NB)	Newfoundland and Labrador (NL)	Prince Edward Island (PEI)
Inmate seeking benefit:	A benefit will be considered by the Committee.	When a benefit or immunity is used in exchange for testimony, a written public interest agreement must be entered into.	Negotiations for benefits should not be conducted by a Crown who is prosecuting the accused or be contingent on a conviction.	Negotiations for benefits should not be conducted by a Crown who is prosecuting the accused or be contingent on a conviction.
Pre-condition to assessment by Committee	Crown must consider 7 enumerated principles when determining whether there is compelling public interest in relying on in-custody informant evidence. Chief Crown attorney determines whether evidence should be referred to the Committee for review.	Crown must prepare an assessment of witness credibility. In difficult cases, this is carried out with police assistance.	Police must interview the witness to ensure credibility of evidence. Crown must perform, at a minimum, a subjective assessment of the informant's testimony.	Not specified
Assessed ineligible when:	Determined by the Committee	Not specified	More than one informant is prohibited	Only one informant should be used
In-Custody Informant Committee	Yes, composed of the chairperson and four other members (chief Crown attorney of the region, of the Appeals Branch, of another region) requires 4 of 5 to adduce evidence.	No	No	No
Mandate/Role of Committee	Committee to review whether there is compelling evidence in presenting the informant's evidence.[55]	N/A	N/A	N/A
Sole Decision Maker	Yes, the Committee cannot adduce evidence of an informant without the approval of the Committee.	The DPP must agree to the use of the testimony.	The DPP must agree to the use of the testimony.	Not specified

Additional Criteria

Assistance of Police	The Crown must be satisfied that the police have investigated the background of the informer so as to assist in assessment of reliability.	In establishing the reliability of the informant's evidence, the Crown will ask the police to assess: motives, how the information was obtained, disclosure, opportunity to collude, independent confirmation, informant's character, previous disclosures, and informant's safety.	The police must conduct a thorough interview to determine that evidence was obtained directly from the accused.	Not specified
KGB Statement	N/A	N/A	N/A	N/A
Role of the Attorney General	N/A	Only the attorney general can grant immunity from prosecution.	N/A	N/A
If the Informant Testifies				
Disclosure	There is a heavy onus on complete disclosure, subject to informer privilege and safety considerations. The prosecutor must ensure full and fair disclosure.[56]	The Crown should discose the informant's criminal record, prior testimonies, considerations (requested, offered, or received), and circumstances surrounding the statement.	Not specified; however, the judge must give the jury a strong direction as to the unreliability of informant testimony. Failure to give this warning to a jury should result in a mistrial.	N/A
Agreement between Informant and Crown (other than immunity)	N/A	Public Interest Agreement, as per Policy 11, Charge Screening	N/A	N/A
If the Informant Lies	When the prosecutor becomes aware of such evidence, the matter should be referred to an outside police agency for investigation. Prosecution is to be carried out by an independent prosecutor; purpose is to deter like-minded members of the prison population.	Not Specified	Not specified	Not specified

Table 6. Jailhouse-informant policies – West Coast and Prairies

Policy Components	British Columbia (BC)	Alberta (AB)	Manitoba (MB)	Saskatchewan (SK)
Date of Issue	2 October 2009	20 May 2008	5 November 2001	27 October 2011
Presumption of use of informants	1. Presumed to be unreliable unless other evidence confirms it. 2. Presumed inadmissible unless charges are serious and evidence compelling.	No presumption	Presumed inadmissible; "inherently suspect"	No presumption of ineligibility but, given the inherent difficulties of reliance on them, they are used only on rare occasions when they are the sole evidence for the prosecution.
Test of admissibility	Only if approved by a special committee or ADAG (Assistant Deputy Attorney General) and in the public interest owing to serious charges.	Only where there are sufficient indicia of reliability and compelling public interest to do so.	Only in unusual circumstances where the policy permits.	Only justifiable where it is in the public interest.
Policy applies to:	Not specified	Someone who receives one or more statements from an accused while both are in custody, related to an offence committed outside of custody.	Any inmate imprisoned anywhere in Canada.	Someone who allegedly receives one or more statements from an accused person relating to crimes, while both are in custody.
Policy does not apply to:	Not specified	Not specified	Informers who allege direct knowledge of the offence, independent of accused's statements; police undercover operations outside of custody. Police should not limit the use of informants to advance police investigations.	Not extended to those who have personal knowledge of the offence independent of the statements made to them by the accused.
Inmate seeking benefit:	If sought, Crown must adhere to policy memo on immunity agreements.	If sought, Crown must adhere to policy memo on immunity agreements.	A benefit will be considered by the Committee.	An informant may request favours for himself or his family including transfers, bail, lesser punishments, money, or protection – but no consideration is given for undiscovered criminality.
Pre-condition to assessment by Committee	Crown must report the details of the file and witness statement to the Informer Witness Registry, request police interview, and investigate the witness and the evidence.	Crown must consider 7 enumerated principles when determining whether there is compelling public interest in relying on in-custody informant evidence.	The statement must be reviewed to see if it could have been obtained from another source (e.g., media) and informer's background assessed.	In cases where the prosecution is based solely on unconfirmed or uncorroborated evidence, it must proceed with caution and inform the Committee.

Assessed ineligible when:	Not specified	Not specified	Informant has a previous conviction for perjury or other dishonest crimes; where testimony is sole evidence linking accused to the crime; more than one informant is prohibited (even if others meet the test).	When the informant commits another criminal offence prior to testifying as a witness.
In-custody Informant Committee	Yes, composed of three Crown attorneys, including the regional Crown counsel and one designated by the ADAG.	No, but review of decision to use informant is conducted by outside criminal justice director.	Yes, composed of five members: assistant deputy attorney (as chair), the appropriate director, senior Crown attorney in charge, general counsel, and prosecutor conducting the case.	Yes, comprised of three senior Crown trial prosecutors, the executive director of public prosecutions, and regional crown prosecutor.
Mandate/role of Committee	To consider the following: motives of the informant; how information was obtained; how it was disclosed to authorities; opportunity to collect/collude; other evidence that confirms story; corroboration of further evidence; character of informant; previous disclosures, whether informant was a state agent; safety issues.	To review whether there is compelling public interest in presenting the evidence of the informant.	Consider the proposed witness's evidence, the background of the witness, and the application of specific criteria to the facts of the case.	Assesses public interest and reliability criteria (confirmation of statement; corroboration context, details and circumstances of statement; access to external sources; general character; previous reliability as an informant; safety issues) to determine whether informant can testify on behalf of the Crown.
Sole decision maker	Yes, the Committee can review its decision if new circumstances arise; even if approved by the Committee, the Crown can decline to call an informant to testify.	No, if the outside director disagrees with the use of an in-custody informant, the assistant deputy minister, Criminal Justice Division, will make the final decision.	Yes, the Committee decides if the informant will testify.	Yes, in consultation with the assigned prosecutor.
Additional Criteria				
Assistance of Police	Yes, the police must investigate and attend the interview conducted by the Crown.	Yes, police provide the Crown with background information and must satisfy the Crown that the informant has been properly investigated.	Yes, police must conduct an investigation to assist in making a decision about the use of the informant.	Yes, police are consulted in assessing the reliability of informants. Police must also carry out direct contact with the informant relating to consideration.

(Continued)

Table 6. Jailhouse-informant policies – West Coast and Prairies (Continued)

Policy Components	British Columbia (BC)	Alberta (AB)	Manitoba (MB)	Saskatchewan (SK)
KGB Statement[57]	N/A	N/A	Yes, the informant must provide a videotaped statement prior to testifying.	Role is the same as in any other prosecution.
Role of Attorney General	Regardless of whether the informant testifies, the name and case information must be entered into the Informer Witness Registry.	N/A	The attorney general must be informed of the decision regarding any informant and keeps a registry of all decisions taken by the Committee.	Not specified
If the Informant Testifies				
Disclosure	Yes. Crown should disclose all information relevant to the credibility of the informant.	Yes. Crown must disclose once the personal safety of the informant has been ascertained. Even if the Crown does not intend to call the informant as a witness, a disclosure obligation exists subject to informer's privilege.	Yes. Crown must disclose: informant's criminal record; Manitoba Registry record of informer (if it exists); benefits, promises, undertakings, etc. given to the informant (but none conditional on conviction); any other evidence attesting to or diminishing credibility, including medical/psychological reports.	Complete disclosure is required, (subject to safety considerations), including: criminal record, any previous informant testimony given, any information in the Crown's possession respecting consideration (sought or given) and offers, written records, and circumstances under which the informant's information was known.
Agreement between Informant and Crown (other than immunity)	N/A	N/A	Yes. When the informer is approved, the department and informant sign a written agreement regarding testimony and it must be disclosed pre-trial.	Yes, but it must be in writing.
If the Informant Lies	Not specified	Crown is to prosecute vigorously to deter like-minded members of the prison population.	Crown is to prosecute vigorously to deter like-minded members of the prison population. Prosecution is to be carried out by an independent prosecutor.	Any consideration given to an informant is based on the testimony given in court being true. Thus lying would constitute an end to the agreement.

Table 7. Jailhouse-informant policies – Ontario and Quebec

Policy Components	Ontario (ON)	Quebec (QC)
Date of Issue	21 March 2005	10 September 1991 (revised 1998, 2000)
Presumption of use of informants	No presumption	No presumption
Test of admissibility	If there is a compelling public interest in adducing the informant's evidence at trial.	Not specified
Policy applies to:	Someone who receives one or more statements from an accused while both are in custody. The statements must relate to an offence committed outside of custody.	A person who has committed or participated in the commission of an offence or was part of a criminal organization and attempts to testify for the prosecution relative to an offence committed or testify against a criminal organization which he or she is or was connected to.
Policy does not apply to:	Informers who allegedly have direct knowledge of the offence independent of the statements of the accused; police undercover operatives outside the custodial setting. Policy should not limit the use of informers to advance police investigations.	Not specified
Inmate seeking benefit:	A benefit will be considered by the Committee.	A benefit will be considered by the Comité de contrôle
Pre-condition to assessment by Committee	A stringent screening and vetting process by the Crown; an analysis is conducted based on weighing the public interest for and against the informer testifying.	Not specified
Assessed ineligible when:	Not specified	Not specified
In-custody Informant Committee	Yes, composed of chairperson and four other members (local Crown, Crown from another region, director of Crown operation where case is tried).	Yes, Comité de contrôle is comprised of four member-representatives including the director general of public prosecutions; director general of correctional services; director general of policing, prevention, and public policy; and of the director of the specific police force.
Mandate/Role of Committee	To consider indicia or reliability, promises for safety given, informer privilege, and strength of case without informer.	Comité negotiates and concludes a written agreement with the witness outlining his/her obligations; ascertains that, at each step, each party respects the agreement; negotiates an agreement for the protection and reinstallation of the informant; and shares costs with police forces/RCMP for out-of-province cases.
Sole Decision Maker	Yes, but the Committee can review its decisions; regardless the Crown may decide not to call the informant as a witness.	Not specified

(Continued)

Table 7. Jailhouse-informant policies – Ontario and Quebec (Continued)

Policy Components	Ontario (ON)	Quebec (QC)
Additional Criteria		
Assistance of Police	A police officer must attend the meeting of the Committee with the Crown (police and Crown conduct extensive investigations).	A police officer is part of the Comité de contrôle.
KGB Statement	N/A	N/A
Role of Attorney General	Registry of In-Custody Informers established.	Not specified
If the Informant Testifies		
Disclosure	Heavy onus to make complete disclosure, subject to informer privilege and safety considerations. List of items for prosecutor to review to ensure full and fair disclosure.	Not specified
Agreement between Informant and Crown (other than immunity)	N/A	Not specified
If the Informant lies	When the prosecutor becomes aware of such evidence, the matter should be referred to an outside police agency for investigation. Prosecution is to be carried out by an independent prosecutor, the purpose of which is to deter like-minded members of the prison population.	Not specified

In/admissibility

In some provinces there is a presumption of inadmissibility of informant testimony (British Columbia, Manitoba, New Brunswick, Newfoundland and Labrador, and Prince Edward Island), and it would appear that reliance on this type of testimony, in most cases, occurs only in exceptional circumstances since the testimony is inherently suspect and deserves to be heard by the court only when there is a compelling public interest to be served. PEI policy is the most restrictive in this regard; in that province, jailhouse-informant testimony is prohibited outright and is allowable only in rare cases such as kidnapping when the whereabouts of the victim are unknown. In fact, most provinces require that there must be sufficient indicia of reliability before such testimony can be used. Some provinces (Newfoundland and Labrador, Prince Edward Island) require approval from the director of public prosecutions as well as other subjective assessments prior to its admission at court. The application of the policy is mainly restricted to those who receive one or more statements from an accused while both were in custody, related to offences committed outside custody (Ontario, Nova Scotia, New Brunswick, Alberta, Saskatchewan). Whereas it is not specified in BC, NL, or PEI policy, in Manitoba this policy can apply to any inmate imprisoned anywhere in Canada, and in Quebec it includes those who have committed or participated in the commission of an offence or those who are part of a criminal organization and are willing to testify against it.

Preconditions to Assessment

Some provinces have also established certain pre-conditions to assessment by a committee or, where there is no committee, to the use of this testimony more generally. In British Columbia, the Crown must report details of the file and witness statements to the Informer Witness Registry, request a police interview, and investigate the witness and the evidence. Ontario has a similarly rigorous formula whereby the Crown must weigh the public interest in having the informant testify; whereas in Alberta and Nova Scotia, the Crown must consider seven enumerated principles in determining whether the public interest is compelling enough to warrant reliance on this testimony. In Manitoba, the statement must be reviewed to see if it could have emanated from another source, as well as requiring an assessment of the informer's background, while in Saskatchewan the committee must be informed when the case is based solely on unconfirmed evidence (from the jailhouse informant). In New Brunswick, the Crown must assess witness credibility, as is the case in Newfoundland and Labrador, but in the latter province the police also have to interview the witness. Prince Edward Island and Quebec have no specified policy in this regard. Ineligibility requirements differ, and while some provinces are silent on the matter (New Brunswick, Ontario, Quebec, British Columbia, Alberta), others require that no more than one informant should be used in each case (Newfoundland and Labrador, Prince Edward Island, Nova Scotia) and still others require committee approval (Nova Scotia). Interestingly, in Manitoba, if the informant has a previous conviction for perjury or other dishonest crimes, or where the informant testimony is the sole evidence linking the accused to the crime, it is ineligible. Finally, in Saskatchewan, if the informant commits another offence prior to testifying, the testimony becomes ineligible.

In-Custody Informant Committees

Given the difficulties associated with this type of evidence, most provinces have developed committees, comprised of police officers and prosecutors, to vet any testimony proffered from jailhouse informants. In-Custody Informant Committees exist in British Columbia, Manitoba, Saskatchewan, Nova Scotia, Ontario, and Quebec but not in New Brunswick, Newfoundland and Labrador, Prince Edward Island, and Alberta. In Alberta, an outside criminal justice director reviews the decision to use an informant. These committees have various compositions, from three to six members, including Crown attorneys, directors of public prosecutions, regional Crown counsel, and other representatives from the attorney general's office. Unlike the other provinces with committees, in Quebec the Comité de contrôle also includes representatives from corrections and policing, prevention, and public policy. While worded somewhat differently, each committee has basically the same mandate: to consider indicia of reliability, promises for safety given, informer privilege, informer background, the strength of the evidence, and the strength of the case without the informer. Some committees are involved in concluding written agreements with informers, as well as ascertaining that they are followed up (Quebec). While in many provinces the committee has the final word, and can review its own decisions (Ontario, British Columbia, Manitoba, Saskatchewan, Nova Scotia), ultimately it is up to the Crown whether or not to call the informant as a witness. In New Brunswick and Newfoundland and Labrador, the director of public prosecutions must agree to the use of the testimony, whereas in Alberta the assistant deputy minister, Criminal Justice Division, makes the final decision.

Eligibility and Benefits

Some provincial policies do not apply to informers who have direct knowledge of the offence, independent of the statements of the accused, or police undercover operatives outside prisons (Ontario, Nova Scotia, Manitoba, Saskatchewan). Newfoundland and Labrador, Prince Edward Island, British Columbia, Alberta, and Quebec do not specify to whom the policy does not apply, whereas in New Brunswick informers who fall under federal witness protection or within the rule of informer privilege are not covered. In almost all cases, a benefit for the informant will be considered by the In-Custody Informant Committee. It has been established that negotiations for benefits should not be conducted by a Crown attorney who is prosecuting the accused, nor should they be contingent on a conviction (New Brunswick, Newfoundland and Labrador, Prince Edward Island). In British Columbia and Alberta, the Crown must adhere to the policy memo on immunity agreements, and in Saskatchewan an informant is permitted to request favours not only for himself but also for his family. Ultimately, no consideration is given when undiscovered criminality comes to light.

Role of Police, Attorney General

In most provinces, the police serve to assist Crown attorneys in vetting the use of informant testimony. In some cases, police officers attend meetings with the committee (Ontario) or are part of the committee (Quebec), as well as being involved in investigating the background and reliability of the informants (British Columbia, Alberta, Manitoba, Saskatchewan, Newfoundland and Labrador, Nova Scotia). In New Brunswick, the police are involved in vetting the informant's testimony and credibility. Only one province (Manitoba) requires that statements made by informants be video-taped prior to testifying, in the event that the trial testimony differs. Furthermore, in some provinces the attorney general must be informed of the decision regarding any informant and a registry is kept of all decisions made by the committee (British Columbia, Manitoba, Ontario). In New Brunswick, it is the attorney general who has the power to grant informants immunity from future prosecutions.

Disclosure and Perjury

In those cases where an informant is permitted to give testimony, some provinces (Nova Scotia, British Columbia, Alberta, Manitoba, New Brunswick, Saskatchewan, Ontario) place a heavy onus on the Crown to disclose to the defence all information relevant to the credibility of the informant, including previous record, previous informant testimony, benefits, promises and undertakings, informer privilege, and safety considerations. Neither Newfoundland and Labrador nor Prince Edward Island mentions disclosure considerations directly; however, they require the traditional approach whereby the judge instructs the jury on the reliability of informant testimony (similar to a *Vetrovec* warning). In some cases, a written agreement between the informant and the Crown attorney must be signed (Manitoba, Saskatchewan, Quebec) and disclosed. Given the problems with such testimony, in those cases where an informant who testifies has been found to be lying, some provinces have policies that allow them to end the agreement regarding consideration (Saskatchewan) or to prosecute the informant by an independent prosecutor for perjury, in order to deter like-minded members of the prison population (Alberta, Manitoba, Ontario, Nova Scotia, New Brunswick).

The fact that all ten provinces have adopted strict guidelines regarding the admission of informant testimony speaks volumes about how seriously the problems associated with this testimony are being taken, as well as representing an acknowledgment of the fact that such testimony is considered unreliable and that safeguards are essential in protecting defendants. Furthermore, these guidelines flowed from the lessons learned through the experience of wrongful convictions. While there is much variability and overlap in the provincial policies discussed, long gone are the days where Crown attorneys would allow informants to testify with impunity. At the same time, the extent to which such policies have now restricted the use of informant testimony remains to be seen. In 2001 former Justice Cory, as chair of the Sophonow Inquiry, stated with respect to jailhouse informants: "Usually, their presence as witnesses signals the end of any hope of providing a fair trial." Given the proliferation of provincial In-Custody Informant Committees and the related policies now in place, in those rare cases where their testimony continues to be used, it is hoped that fair trials can prevail.

Conclusions

It would seem that testimony offered by jailhouse informants (likely questionable at best, outright fabricated at worst) no longer plays such a significant part in evidence at criminal trials as it once did. This is in a large part due to recent case law, commissions of inquiry, and the cases of exonerated wrongly convicted persons that have established its inherent unreliability. Today, judges are now encouraged to warn juries about the dangers of convicting based on such testimony and across the country provincial policies severely limit the use of jailhouse-informant testimony. At this juncture, it would be premature to believe that the common law and policy reform in Canada have eradicated the problems inherent in this testimony. While most provinces have a presumption of inadmissibility, there are still many ways for informants to testify and the most skilled among them will likely continue to proffer false testimony in exchange for benefits, which are on offer under all the provincial policies. At the same time, the incentives to lie to escape prison persist: prisons are violent, frightening environments and most individuals will go to great lengths to avoid incarceration. Moreover, while some provincial policies dictate that informants who lie will be prosecuted to "deter like-minded members of the prison population," the extent to which this actually occurs is unknown. Perhaps police and Crown attorneys should be more circumspect in allowing the testimony of informants at all, especially in those instances where such testimony alone is the sole evidence against an accused. In these cases, questions regarding the utility of pursuing charges altogether, and the spectre of a wrongful conviction based on false testimony from a jailhouse informant who has much to gain and little to lose, need to be taken seriously.

PART TWO

Evidentiary Detection Methods:
Missteps and Innovations

Chapter Seven

DNA Evidence: Raising the Bar

"DNA evidence is not simply a matter of the pure application of science; people's perceptions and misunderstandings of the actual meanings of the science come into play and must be accounted for." (Gerlach, 2004, 46)

Introduction

The advent of scientific DNA (deoxyribonucleic acid) forensic analysis heralded a new era in criminal justice investigation and identification. DNA profiling gave law-enforcement officials a tool that could provide seemingly irrefutable evidence of innocence or guilt in those cases where biological evidence was present at the crime scene. To its credit, DNA evidence has allowed many innocent individuals to be eliminated as suspects in criminal cases, and has also permitted many "cold" cases to be solved by uncovering perpetrators many years after the fact. However, there are still problems associated with DNA use in an increasingly risk-based society.

The objective of this chapter is to provide an overview of the use of DNA evidence in police investigations, criminal trials, and exonerations. It examines the legal framework in Canada for the issuance of DNA warrants allowing genetic testing within specific investigations, as well as the DNA Identification Act[1] of 2000, which administers the National DNA Data Bank (NDDB) that facilitates broader use of DNA to investigate open and forthcoming criminal investigations. It also outlines the difficulties surrounding the use of DNA and explores how Canadian jurisprudence has clarified the limits of its application under the Charter of Rights and Freedoms. Case examples of wrongly convicted individuals who were later exonerated through DNA forensic analysis are presented, along with some cautionary concluding remarks.

DNA Technology

DNA technology has evolved considerably over the past thirty years; what was once unheard of has now become a commonplace practice in many criminal investigations. In essence, DNA technology allows criminal investigators to establish, with relative degrees of certainty, whether or not physical matter found at a crime scene is a match for that of the accused or another person. The technique of DNA testing of forensic evidence was first used in a case in Leicester, England, in the 1980s where two women had been sexual assaulted and murdered over a three-year period (Gerlach, 2004, 34). Through testing the samples of all men of a particular age in the surrounding communities, detectives were able to apprehend and convict Colin Pitchfork for this crime. The first American to be exonerated through the use of DNA identification technology was Gary Dotson, whose 1979 rape conviction was overturned in 1989 and charges dismissed (Gross et al., 2005). Furthermore, Kirk Bloodsworth was the first defendant in the United States sentenced to death in 1984 and later exonerated by DNA in 1993; to date, over three hundred Americans have been exonerated through DNA technology.[2]

In Canada, the RCMP first used DNA technology in 1989 in a sexual-assault case; the suspect[3] was exculpated, in part owing to forensic DNA analysis (Lussier, 1992). Since that time and through the establishment of the NDDB, Bank, DNA has played a large role in matching offenders to crime scenes, as well as matching crime scenes to other crime scenes. Of particular significance for the purposes of this chapter is the role that DNA can play in exoneration of the wrongly convicted. The well-known exonerations of Guy Paul Morin and David Milgaard through DNA analysis (which will be discussed in greater detail below) both occurred only after many years of political and legal wrangling and a great deal of media attention. Yet, while DNA is a powerful tool, it is only one part of identification evidence; it can, at most, prove the presence of an individual at a given crime scene. In some instances, DNA may also establish sexual or other incriminating contact, but it is not determinative of guilt in relation to the crime itself. At the same time, popular conceptions of DNA, gleaned through the media (particularly criminal investigative television), lend it much credibility. In fact, however, physical matter such as blood, saliva, or semen that can be tested for the presence of DNA is available in approximately only 10 per cent of cases of violent crime (Scheck, Neufeld, and Dwyer, 2000) and needs to be bolstered by other inculpatory evidence to support a conviction. Furthermore, when DNA typing was first used in the 1990s, it was criticized within the scientific community for confusing population genetic estimates for potential mismatches. Latterly, debates around population genetics have been resolved and consequently the certainty about DNA has increased significantly in a relatively short period of time (Garrett, 2008a; Gerlach, 2004; Gross et al., 2005).

Other Identification Evidence: Fingerprints

The taking of fingerprints[4] (dactyloscopy) – whether from suspects or from other evidence at crime scenes – remains a routine practice in most criminal investigations. This process has a long history dating back to the late nineteenth century and generally allows for the identification of individuals by linking them to their own criminal record and by comparing their fingerprints with those found at the crime scene (McCartney, 2006a). In fingerprint analysis, what is of significance is where the fingerprints were found and whether or not they were accompanied by other evidence, for example, suspect fingerprints left in blood (Hageman, Prevett, and Murray, 2002, 13). When examining fingerprints for identification purposes, experts make comparisons between known and unknown fingerprints. It is thought to be a more definite science than DNA; fingerprint analysis customarily involves subjective comparisons and consequently there are no population statistics for fingerprints, whereas DNA experts generally speak of the statistical probability of the evidence matching a suspect.

Fingerprint identification continues to be the most common identification technique used by law enforcement in Canada, though the scientific weaknesses of the process have come to light over the last few decades and have tempered the view that fingerprinting offers an infallible method of identifying criminal suspects (Cole, 2008). In fact, there is evidence and case law that point to wrongful convictions that have resulted through the misattribution of fingerprint evidence (Cole, 2006). Fingerprint analysis has been used in law enforcement mainly for identification purposes, and only infrequently to detect unknown perpetrators (McCartney, 2006a, 181). The Identification of Criminals Act allows for the taking of photographs of and fingerprints from an accused. When an accused fails to attend at a specific place and time for photographs and fingerprints, charges may be laid according to the Criminal Code (s. 145 and 512(2)(b)).

Given the lack of consensus in the field of fingerprint matching, standards vary considerably. Some experts in this field rely on what has been identified as a "points of identification method," whereby a specified number of matching points must be reached between two fingerprints in order to have a positive identification, whereas others rely on subjective judgments (Mnookin, 2001). The number of points regarded as essential for a match varies greatly across jurisdictions, and when fingerprints from a crime scene are only partial ones, there are further difficulties in certainty of proof. There is little legal dispute in Canada regarding the standard required for a fingerprint "match"; most police forces use Automated Forensic Identification Services (AFIS), which maintain and operate a computerized search and storage system.[5] For the most part, the assessment of the latent fingerprints from crime scenes is based mainly on human interpretations (National Academy of Sciences, 2009, 139). Even with AFIS, there are no standard test protocols and subjective assessments are the norm. Research has indicated that this subjectivity is evident even among the same experienced examiners who do not always agree with their own past conclusions (Dror and Charlton, 2006). As seen with other types of impression evidence, fingerprint analysis is ultimately a subjective science and not beyond challenge. The National Academy of Sciences, in a 2009 report on the state of forensic sciences in the United States, compared fingerprint analysis with other forms of experienced-based pattern recognition (such as tire impressions, tool marks and handwriting analysis).

The analysis of fingerprints is known as "friction ridge analysis" and consists of "experience-based comparisons of the impressions left by the ridge structures of volar (hand and feet) surfaces" (National Academy of Sciences, 2009, 136). Latent prints are examined through a procedure known as ACE-V – which stands for "Analysis, Comparison, Evaluation and Verification" – used as a means of comparative analysis since 1959 (National Academy of Sciences, 2009, 137). Factors to be considered in analysis include: condition of the skin, type of residue (oil or sweat or both), mechanics of touch, the nature of the surface touched, development and capture techniques, and the size of the latent print (137–8). Latent prints are then compared to known prints if there are sufficient details in both for comparison purposes. Visual comparison is followed by an evaluation of the agreement of the friction-ridge formations in the two prints and an identification or exclusion is the next step; the process is verified when another qualified examiner repeats the observation and comes to the same conclusion. This method of analysis has not been validated, does not guard against bias, is considered to be too broad to ensure repeatability and transparency, and does not guarantee that two individuals following it will obtain the same result (National Academy of Sciences, 2009, 142).

Perhaps because of the long history of fingerprint use in criminal investigation and identification, many fingerprint examiners – despite the subjective nature of their analyses – testify in the language of absolute certainty, which the courts in turn have accepted as being unassailable. But as Mnookin notes (2008): "Given the general lack of validity testing for fingerprinting, the relative dearth of difficult proficiency tests, the lack of a statistically valid model of fingerprinting, and the lack of validated standards for declaring a match, such claims of absolute, certain confidence in identification are unjustified. They are the product of hubris more than established knowledge" (139). There appears to be no definitive answer as to the validity and reliability of fingerprint evidence. On account of the uncertainties attached to the use of fingerprint evidence for identification purposes, DNA profiling was welcomed as a replacement for fingerprinting in the investigative realm and has now largely overtaken fingerprinting for that purpose.

The Genetics of DNA

Comparison of bodily fluids for identification purposes in criminal cases, prior to the advent of DNA profiling, was done through A-B-O serial typing of blood, semen, and saliva (Hageman et al., 2002). Rarely used today, this type of biotechnology is much less discriminating and serves simply to rule out individuals belonging to a particular group. Alternatively, a "match" could be inclusive of many individuals *in* a particular group.

On the other hand, DNA represents the biological material that is responsible for transmitting traits from one generation to the next.[6] Nuclear DNA (nDNA) is found in the set of forty-six chromosomes contained in the nucleus of human cells and is most commonly referred to in forensic DNA analysis, whereas mitochondrial DNA (mtDNA) is found in the cytoplasm of human cells in greater numbers and is useful in forensic analysis since it contains its own DNA (Hageman et al., 2002, 8). In cases where nuclear DNA is not available or has been degraded, mitochondrial DNA may be investigated. DNA identification technology has evolved considerably since it was first used in the late 1980s. For the purposes of forensic analysis, a match is sought between the DNA found at a crime scene and that of a suspect and is useful only if it is backed up by a statement as to the rarity of the profile.

The first type of DNA analysis used, in the late 1980s, was restriction fragment length polymorphism (RFLP), which involved examining the length differences of specific markers along the DNA molecule. Initially, this type of analysis was thought to be quite discriminatory, but it required more genetic material that was less degraded and the process itself could take up to two months (Hageman et al., 2002, 28). Another early technique was the DQ alpha polymarker system. This relied on a method of "molecular zeroxing," called polymerase chain reaction or PCR, which could produce millions of copies of a DNA molecule quickly and with small samples (Scheck and Neufeld, 2002a, 242). While this method was very sensitive, and allowed for the analysis of small, old, and degraded samples, it was not very discriminating and could yield only large frequencies. The most commonly used method today involves short tandem repeats (STR) of DNA fragment lengths from known and unknown samples. The STR method is thought to have both the "discriminatory power of the RFLP technique and the sensitivity of the DQ alpha" (Scheck and Neufeld, 2002a, 242). It is currently the standard in DNA testing and is in use today for forensic DNA analysis in the United States, the United Kingdom, and Canada.[7]

The process involved in DNA typing is fairly straightforward. Bodily fluids or tissue deposits are sought from a suspect to develop a forensic profile. DNA is then extracted from the biological sample and analysed through STR methods; profiles are then produced for interpretation and comparison (Hageman, Prevett, and Murray, 2002, 40). In order to establish if a match occurs, there must be no differences between the evidentiary DNA and the comparison profile, that is, they must share the same number and placement of bands in the genetic bar code, or they must share the same sequence at all forensic genetic addresses tested (Hageman et al., 2002, 41). From the match, inferences must be made as to the significance of that match. This involves the application of population genetics statistics in which the probability is considered that someone other than the suspect could match the profile found at the crime scene. Traditionally, this involved estimating the frequency of occurrence of that profile in a given population (Hageman et al., 2002, 42). The current approach is more flexible, suggesting that it is best to "use data for a single racial group taken as a whole rather than an average or a mix of values from subpopulations" (Gerlach, 2004, 43). Given the variability that ultimately enters into any considerations of probabilities, DNA evidence should be considered within the context of other evidence; questions of guilt or innocence should not rest on DNA evidence alone.

A DNA "match" in this sense is not conclusive of positive identification; rather, a match will have varying degrees of scientific strength, based in part on the number of matching genetic traits and the rarity of the profile (Hageman et al., 2002, 14). Profiling in this manner can also exclude an individual from consideration. An inconclusive result is more problematic for courts since it signifies that an individual profile cannot be included or excluded as a possible match. In the early days of DNA profiling and analysis, there was a great deal of debate around possible contamination occurring during DNA collection and around the reliability of laboratory techniques used in producing samples. The standardization of collection techniques and laboratory regulations, as well as comparison tools, has allowed for much less scepticism today regarding the reliability of DNA for identification purposes. The National Academy of Sciences (2009) found that, of all the forensic disciplines, DNA is the most stringent in that it has strict protocols in place for both laboratory and processing procedures.

Legal Framework: DNA Warrants and the DNA Identification Act

As DNA science became increasingly common and reliable in the forensic context, the need for legal authorization of police use of the science to solve crimes led to two changes in the law: the introduction of DNA warrants to authorize collection and testing of DNA in a specific investigation and the establishment of a national DNA databank to facilitate use of the science in open investigations and crimes yet to be committed. Given the many legal questions that needed to be addressed in order for a databank to be established, the Canadian government began with the more limited and less controversial amendments to the Criminal Code[8] and the Young Offenders Act[9] to allow for the collection and use of DNA samples in specific investigations.

The first part of this process involved Bill C-104, an Act to Amend the Criminal Code and the Young Offenders Act (Forensic DNA Analysis), which was passed in June 1995 and allowed for the issuance of warrants to seize DNA samples from suspects. These warrant procedures continue to exist under the Criminal Code and permit a judge to issue a warrant for seizing bodily substances for DNA testing if particular criteria are met (ss. 487.04–487.09) and if the judge is of the opinion that it is in the best interest of the administration of justice. Specifically, the criteria include: that a designated offence has been committed, that bodily substances were found at the place of the offence or on or around the victim, that the person was a party to the offence, and that forensic analysis of bodily substance from that person will provide evidence about whether the substance found at the crime scene was from that person. Section 487.04 states that forensic DNA analysis, "in relation to a bodily substance that is taken from a person in execution of a warrant under section 467.05," means "analysis of the bodily substance and the comparison of the results of that analysis with the results of the analysis of the DNA in the bodily substance referred to in paragraph 487.05(1)(b), and includes any incidental tests associated with that analysis."

The DNA Identification Act, which authorized the establishment of Canada's National DNA Data Bank, came into force as of 10 December 1998, but the NDDB itself was launched only in July 2000. In essence, the NDDB aims to help law-enforcement agencies identify individuals who have allegedly committed specific types of offences. DNA profiles are also stored for use in future investigations, and the NDDB therefore facilitates broad and long-term use of the DNA belonging to those who are included in the databank after having committed a designated crime. The NDDB is comprised of two parts, a Crime Scene Index (CSI) (s. 3) and a Convicted Offenders Index (COI) (s. 4).

The CSI contains anonymous DNA profiles that are derived from bodily substances found where an offence was committed, on the victim, on the victim's clothing or belongings, or on anyone or anything else associated with the crime scene (s. 3(a-d)). The COI contains identifiable DNA profiles from the bodily substances of individuals who have committed a primary designated offence (s. 4). The Criminal Code (s. 487.04) contains a long list of primary designated offences, which generally relate to serious personal injury such as assaults, sexual offences, and other crimes against the person, many of which involve the loss or exchange of bodily substances that could be used to identify a perpetrator through DNA analysis. Secondary designated offences are typically of a lesser degree of severity, do not often involve the loss or exchange of bodily fluids, and include those for which a person is liable to a maximum sentence of five or more years imprisonment if found guilty; some of these offences are listed in the Controlled Drugs and Substances Act.[10] A judge can also order that DNA from an individual convicted of a secondary designated offence be collected and retained. The DNA Data Bank Advisory Committee, which includes representatives from the Office of the Privacy Commissioner of Canada, the police, and the legal, scientific, and academic communities, meets regularly to monitor the databank and discuss policy and operational issues.

The same year as the launch of the DNA Identification Act, the federal government passed Bill S-10,[11] an Act to Amend the National Defence Act, the DNA Identification Act, and the Criminal Code, in order to ensure consistency with the new DNA legislation. The courts have the power (though s. 487.051) to take bodily samples from adults and youth found guilty of certain offences.[12] Samples may be taken from persons in either of the following ways: by plucking hair (including the root sheath); by taking of buccal swabs by swabbing the lips, tongue, or inside cheeks of the mouth to collect epithelial (skin) cells; or by taking blood by pricking the skin (s. 487.06(1)(a)(b)(c)). Furthermore, this act allows the police to compare DNA profiles in either the CSI or COI crime scence or convicted offenders index with profiles that are already contained in the databank for the purposes of investigating unsolved crimes (s. 4(1)). While individuals who are subsequently acquitted of the crimes with which they are charged can have their DNA removed from the databank (s. 9(2)(a)), the DNA profile of those found guilty of a primary designated offence can be kept indefinitely (s. 9(1)).[13] What is interesting to note is that the taking of a DNA sample is one of the few instances under criminal law where the state has the right to intrude on the physical integrity of the person without that person's consent (Oscapella, 2012).

DNA profiling, through testing and banking, takes place in Canada via the NDDB, in conjunction with six regional forensic RCMP labs in Halifax, Regina, Ottawa, Winnipeg, Edmonton, and Vancouver, and two provincial forensic labs in Ontario (Centre for Forensic Sciences, CFS) and Quebec (Laboratoire de Sciences Judiciaires et de Médecine Légale du Québec, LSJML). The process itself is fairly straightforward: the NDDB processes the samples from convicted offenders and then uploads the profile information to the COI. Forensic laboratories process the biological samples left at crime scenes and upload the profile information to the CSI. The NDDB will run a search between the CSI and the COI, and if a match occurs the identifying (but coded) information is brought to the Canadian Police Services and Information Centre (CPSIC). This information is forwarded back to the forensic laboratory, where the convicted offender's identity information is passed on to an investigator (National DNA Databank of Canada, 2006, 13). Since its inception, the NDDB has entered 343,212 samples into the COI and 128,395 into the CSI; as of 15 February 2017, it has matched 43,845 crime scenes to offenders and 4,996 crime scenes to other crime scenes.[14] Given that the content of the NDDB is growing at a phenomenal rate, the likelihood of these numbers increasing is great; as new types of crimes become designated offences, more and more profile and index samples will be entered into the databank.[15]

Because the NDDB became functional only in June 2000, the DNA Identification Act contained provisions to address those cases of individuals who were incarcerated at that time but whose offences may have warranted inclusion in the databank by reason of the nature of the offence committed. This retroactive application involves applying the DNA Identification Act to a limited number of offenders who have committed certain designated offences and had been sentenced prior to 30 June 2000 and were still serving sentences.[16] This included dangerous offenders, dangerous sexual offenders, and those convicted of murder, sexual offences, or manslaughter (for which they received a sentence of more than two years) (National DNA Databank of Canada, 2006, 20). For retroactive DNA warrants, it is the responsibility of the Crown attorney's office to make the NDDB order.

Privacy considerations enter into discussion regarding the use and storage of DNA samples. In recognition of this, the Criminal Code (s. 487.08(1)) circumscribes the use of samples taken from suspects, specifying that they can only be used "in the course of an investigation of the designated offence for the purposes of forensic DNA analysis."[17] Given that the taking of DNA samples may also reveal other biological information such as genetic traits and inherited diseases (Gerlach, 2004, 69), one fear is that this information could be used to discriminate against persons for insurance or other purposes. The DNA profiles used for the databank samples are considered to be anonymous; they hold information from thirteen core tests or "loci," specify only gender, and contain no medical or physical information from the donor (National DNA Databank of Canada, 2006). Profiles are identified by a bar-code number and donor identity of the convicted offender is held separately from the genetic information derived from the sample (National DNA Databank of Canada, 2006, 7). Each sample collection kit is given a unique serial number or bar code so that each offender is linked solely to one number. On submission, fingerprints on the identification form are matched to those on the collection card. The biological sample is then split from the personal information to comply with the privacy provisions. Databank scientists receive only a biological sample identified by the serial number – personal information is sent to the criminal records services of the RCMP (Hageman et al., 2002, 127). Consideration is also given to how samples were initially collected and labs will reject samples for a number of reasons: if they come from a non-designated offence, if there is an inadequate amount of biological sample, if an improper collection kit was used, if no order is included in the submission, or if biological samples were not taken correctly (Hageman et al., 2002). This information is protected by law and is to be used only for law-enforcement purposes.

The list of offences that are subject to DNA sampling has expanded considerably since the law was enacted. When the federal government enacted the Anti-Terrorism Act[18] in 2001, it contained a range of terrorism offences that, as primary designated offences, were subjected to the taking of DNA samples. Subsequently, amendments to the DNA Identification Act itself enlarged the legislation's reach. The first set of amendments occurred in 2005, through Bill C-13,[19] but only a limited number of its provisions have come into effect. The amendments expanded the list of primary designated offences to include, inter alia, child pornography, breaking and entering, extortion, sexual exploitation of a disabled person, and intimidation of a justice system participant or journalist. It also created a list of offences whereby the courts *cannot* refuse to make a DNA order (the nineteen most serious offences in the Criminal Code) and included provisions whereby if a person is found "not criminally responsible on account of mental disorder for a designated offence, he or she may be ordered to provide a sample of bodily substance for DNA analysis" (MacKay, 2007, 11). Further, the mental-disorder provisions are also retroactive and the amendments allowed a NDDB order to be made after sentencing. In 2007 the law was amended again and, primarily through Bill C-18,[20] the number of offences for which a NDDB can be made was expanded to include attempted murder and conspiracy to commit murder. In addition, the amendments contained provisions to make it an offence for failing to appear for a DNA sample, ensured that information in the databank can be used to investigate all criminal offences, and simplified the procedures to destroy samples taken from individuals convicted of non-designated offences (MacKay, 2007). These amendments also affected the National Defence Act,[21] ensuring that the relationships between the civilian and military justice systems with the NDDB are the same and that the provisions affecting the collection, storage, and usage of samples are applied in the same manner.

Prior to the most recent amendments to the DNA Identification Act, the law itself was reviewed on two occasions. Statutory reviews were undertaken by the House of Commons Standing Committee on Safety and National Security (2009) and the Senate Standing Committee on Legal and Constitutional Affairs (2010).[22] While both found a number of flaws with the current system, including a lack of resources, both also recommended that the government be permitted to take DNA samples automatically upon conviction for *all* designated offences, further widening the net. The most recent amendments to the DNA Identification Act occurred through the controversial Bill C-10, the Safe Streets and Communities Act,[23] introduced by the Conservative federal government in 2012. This omnibus crime bill contained amendments to a number of statutes that had been introduced previously but not passed. In effect, it created a number of new criminal offences, while also increasing mandatory minimum sentences and eliminating conditional sentences for some offences. As well, it expanded pre-trial detention restrictions and introduced harsher sentencing principles for young offenders. With respect to the DNA Identification Act, it had previously allowed the destruction of DNA collected from young offenders (s. 10.1(1)) according to the provisions of the Youth Criminal Justice Act.[24] Bill C-10 replaced this provision with one that allows the indefinite retention of DNA from those youth convicted of a serious violent offence, or a presumptive offence (murder, attempted murder, aggravated sexual assault, manslaughter), or a second conviction for serious violence (ss. 202–3). Furthermore, it affected the storage of DNA samples taken from adult offenders who had received a pardon (now referred to as record suspension). Parliament later amended the DNA Identification Act in December 2014 to support missing-person cases and further assist criminal investigations.[25] This new National Missing Persons DNA Program, operational by 1 April 2017, will facilitate the investigation of cases involving missing persons and unidentified human remains.[26]

Each time the federal government amends the DNA Identification Act, the changes appear to be consistent with a more conservative approach to law enforcement. When designated offences were first introduced into the Criminal Code in

1995, they numbered only thirty-seven very serious violent or sexual offences; fifteen years later, more than 265 offences are qualified as designated offences (Canada, House of Commons, Standing Committee on Public Safety and National Security, 2009, 37–8). Gerlach argues that this shift towards more conservatism in criminal justice policy had actually occurred earlier; the policy process behind the enactment of the DNA warrant and databank legislation in the mid-1990s through to 2000 itself reflected a shift towards greater emphasis on public safety and a movement away from the protection of individual rights (2004, 68). In fact, the Office of the Privacy Commissioner of Canada has stated that the expansion of the scope of the DNA scheme, by progressively adding new offences, has not achieved the stated aim of a safer and more just society (Campbell, 2009).[27] If the initial rationale for collecting samples was for linking the DNA of offenders who have committed serious violent and/or sexual offences with DNA from crime scenes where similar offences occurred, that has definitely changed. Clearly, the government must balance the individual right to privacy against that of public security; this is especially difficult when genetic material is involved in the practice of law enforcement. While specific processes are contained within the legislation to address these concerns (i.e., restrictions on the number of genetic markers to be retained, anonymity guarantees, restrictions on the types of offences that can be considered as designated for DNA profiling, etc.), in essence the continuing expansion of the NDDB and the simple fact that it contains genetic materials that have proven useful in solving crimes tend to override these privacy protections.

The Promise of DNA

As an investigative tool, DNA forensic analysis holds great promise. At this juncture, it has been well established that DNA has allowed for the identification of suspects and elimination of others in many criminal cases where physical evidence was present at a crime scene. DNA evidence provides law enforcement with a fairly quick and reliable means of establishing whom to pursue in criminal investigations. Further, the establishment of DNA databanks has allowed for many unsolved cases to be solved through matching crime scene with convicted-offender DNA. At trial, DNA results provide an important piece of evidence, often for the prosecution, that the individual in question was present at the crime scene, although other evidence is equally necessary to support a charge against a person. In recent years, popular media conceptions have influenced how juries treat DNA and other forensic evidence. The so-called CSI effect, a term coined by American prosecutors, reflects the idea that jurors have been so influenced by criminal investigative television shows (such as *CSI*) that they are reticent to convict individuals where no physical or scientific evidence is present. This, in turn, creates unrealistic expectations for real-life investigators to provide irrefutable scientific evidence (Ballard, 2006). At the same time, empirical research has tended to show that, if it does exist at all, the CSI effect on jury decision making is marginal at best and may be a media-created phenomenon (Cole and Dioso-Villa, 2007; Shelton et al., 2006). In fact, Godsey and Alou (2011) believe that there may be a "Reverse CSI-Effect": when jurors are faced with cases where there is forensic evidence produced by the prosecution, too much weight may be given to this evidence, to a defendant's detriment.

Scheck and Neufeld (2002a) support the extraordinary significance of DNA as an investigative tool; they point to the numbers of exonerations that DNA has facilitated, as well as the certainty with which its conclusions can be taken. Perhaps that is the greatest potential of DNA forensic analysis: its ability to eliminate individuals as possible suspects in cases where physical evidence is present. In that sense, it can and does serve a largely preventive function – by eliminating potential suspects whose DNA profile does not match that taken from victims or that found at the crime scene. In fact, the Federal Bureau of Investigation (FBI) reported an early exclusion rate of 25 per cent of suspects in sexual-assault cases where DNA was obtained (Connors et al., 1996). Prior to the introduction of DNA as an investigative tool, problems with other types of evidence went unchallenged: difficulties around eyewitness error, false confessions, and the lies of jailhouse informants could not be successfully contested by other, "scientific" evidence indicating that the police had the wrong individual. The introduction of DNA into the investigative process has no doubt prevented a large number of convictions in error.

Outside of the criminal justice system, DNA has also played a role in determining issues in civil court. For example, DNA sampling can help in determining paternity in child-custody and support cases. Through the use of private laboratories, citizens can submit DNA samples for testing for a number of medical conditions. Further, immigration departments are requesting proof of kinship through DNA analysis to allow landed immigrants to bring relatives into the country. Yet, in an increasingly risk-based society, growing ever more reliant on new and more invasive methods of surveillance, the promise of DNA is overshadowed somewhat by the potential for misuse and misinterpretation.

Problems with DNA: The "Illusion of Certainty"[28]

The possibility for problems or errors is present at every stage of the DNA profile: sample collection and preservation, laboratory processing and analysis, overstatement of evidence, and interpretation of results – in other words, overall procedural laxity (Gerlach, 2004; McCartney, 2006a; Scheck and Neufeld, 2002a). Nonetheless, the processes used and standards applied in both sample collection and laboratory processing have evolved and have been refined to a great degree since such profile matching was first used in the 1980s, so that current margins of error are very small. While the underlying methods used for forensic testing have increasingly proven to be scientifically valid and reliable, human error or misrepresentation can occur in the process of application. Errors are most likely to happen when the laboratory results are interpreted and presented in court. The first opportunity for error occurs around the visual comparison of two DNA fragments – which involves a subjective standard – and the second opportunity occurs around estimating the "statistical likelihood of a false match within a given population" (Gerlach, 2004, 152). In recent years, accreditation of laboratories and the establishment of strict shared criteria for interpretation (cf. CODIS) have helped to alleviate much of this controversy.

Issues or questions regarding DNA can be raised at various stages in criminal justice processing. Initially, when police begin their investigation, steps must be taken to establish that proper procedures were followed in seeking out the DNA warrant and in the collection of the DNA samples. One concern with respect to the search for suspects in criminal cases has to do with the issue of "mass screening" or DNA dragnets. Mass screening or "targeted intelligence screening" involves seeking DNA samples from large numbers of individuals who fit a certain gender, race, and age profile and live in a specific geographic area, similar to the alleged suspect in a criminal case. While individuals are not required to provide DNA in response to requests made as part of a dragnet sweep, and police have no authority to upload volunteer samples onto the NDDB, failure to volunteer to provide a DNA sample in a mass screening can raise suspicions regarding an individual's involvement in a given investigation. The United Kingdom has a long history of mass screenings, first for fingerprints; subsequently, from 1999 to 2005, 120 mass screens for DNA had taken place in that country, resulting in the collection of over four thousand samples.[29] While rarely undertaken in Canada, the first screening of this nature took place during a police investigation into a series of rapes that had occurred in Vermillion, Alberta, in 1994, when ninety men were asked to submit DNA samples (men who were asked were known to have been "out on the town" when the latest attack occurred) (Gerlach, 2004, 185). Eighteen months later, after testing over 240 samples, the police were neither able to find a suspect nor solve the case.

A second mass screening took place in Port Alberni, British Columbia, in 1996, following the brutal rape and murder of an eleven-year-old girl. Given that DNA warrant legislation had been passed at that point, the police could have legally seized samples from individual suspects, but ultimately they were able to accomplish the DNA testing by requesting voluntary samples, which were obtained from 411 individuals (Gerlach, 2004, 186). A third dragnet took place in Sudbury, Ontario, in 1998 after the brutal stabbing of a store clerk. In spite of testing over eighteen hundred samples, no one was arrested for this crime.[30] More recently, while investigating the disappearance of over eighteen women and girls in northern British Columbia, along Highway 16, the RCMP in Prince George collected approximately six hundred "volunteer" DNA samples from cab drivers. This was based on the theory that a cab driver may have been one of the last people to have contact with one of the missing women; however, drivers who refused to volunteer found their names on the list of suspects. As with other dragnets, this sweep through Prince George has produced no reported investigative leads but has conversely generated much anger towards the police.[31]

Given that there are no regulations that govern the practice of mass screening and despite the fact that this costly process rarely results in identifying the perpetrator, it will nonetheless likely continue as a form of police interrogation (Gerlach, 2004, 187). This kind of investigation raises concerns regarding the retention of samples, consequences for refusal to submit a sample, and violation of civil liberties around the right against self-incrimination. At the same time the Criminal Code dictates that the results from such dragnets must be destroyed once it has been established that the crime-scene DNA was not from those individuals (s. 487.09(3)).

From the point of collection of DNA samples, it is necessary that the prosecutorial team establish the chain of custody or "exhibits continuity" to ensure that the DNA sample has integrity through each part of the analytic process, so as not to risk cross-contamination; this continuity applies to evidence collection, delivery, analysis, and, finally, testimony (Hageman et al., 2002, 90–4). While standards have improved considerably since DNA first entered the criminal justice system, the spectre of cross-contamination of samples can create questions of reasonable doubt with juries.[32] It would appear that difficulties around the use of DNA evidence continue to occur during the court process and there are three areas where this is of specific consideration: the effect on juries, the apparent pro-prosecution bias, and the consequent disadvantage to defence counsel.

Juries are most often comprised of laypersons whose knowledge of population genetics is, at best, limited. Thus, when experts (often population geneticists) report the odds of chance DNA matches, the wording used can have a large impact on the jury's sense of guilt or innocence (Gerlach, 2004, 45). These probability ratios tend to be very persuasive to jurors, who may believe that DNA evidence is proof of identification, linking the accused to the crime scene and ultimately to the crime (Findley and Grix, 2003 271). Furthermore, the language used to convey the significance of a particular "match" may be unfamiliar to most jurors (and many lawyers). The significance of a match is often conveyed as a probability that "a randomly selected, unknown, unrelated person would have the same DNA profile as the suspect" (Findley and Grix, 2003, 278). While there are many ways to convey this type of probability, it is often done with odds ratios regarding the calculation of the likelihood of a chance match. In cases where DNA samples include mixtures of more than one person, this in turn distorts the probability ratio (ibid.). Judges may help in clarifying this information to jurors, but juries are required to have at least a rudimentary understanding of what these ratios mean and the extent to which they are reflective of guilt or innocence.

Moreover, as discussed, a steady diet of criminal investigative television and media news reporting on crime has saturated much of the public domain about the significance of DNA. The influence of popular culture plays a role in jurors' understanding of the implications of DNA evidence and ultimately on their expectations about the power of such evidence, which in turn can influence decision making. As McCartney (2006a, xii) notes, the notion of the infallibility of DNA has pervaded popular culture and also permeated the criminal justice system. While it is clear that "a 'match' alone without more is not itself conclusive of an individual's guilt" (Findley and Grix, 2003, 277), it may be compelling enough for a jury to ignore other exculpatory evidence and focus solely on DNA. The fact that the accused was present at a crime scene at some point is not evidence that he or she committed a crime and this detail seems to get lost in the language of probability ratios, "autorads," and "genetic loci."

It has been argued that the presentation of DNA profiling in courts, in and of itself, is reflective of a pro-prosecution bias, with respect to who is presenting the evidence and manner in which it is presented (Gerlach, 2004; Hageman et al., 2002). The alleged "prosecutor's fallacy" refers to the faulty legal reasoning occurring around the conclusions of DNA matching that is thought to favour the prosecution or rather "equating the probability of a random match with the probability of the appellant's innocence" (*R. v. Terceira*, para. 58). Given that these numbers are often expressed in highly unlikely terms, the tendency is to believe that the probability of random match is very unlikely, ergo, the probability of the defendant's innocence equally so. From this form of logic, the only choice is to convict. What is necessary to balance this type of reasoning are equally compelling arguments from defence counsel that raise doubts about the strength of that probability.

Given that in Canada the role of the main forensic laboratories (RCMP, CFS, and LSJML) is to provide services for law-enforcement agencies, this may also enforce a pro-prosecution bias. Gerlach goes so far as to state that their scientific objectivity may be compromised as a result (2004, 91). More often than not, the RCMP forensic experts testify on behalf of the prosecution and the "absence of a counter-expertise in forensic science of DNA analysts readily available to the defense further reinforces the sense that the science and technology are beyond challenge" (Gerlach, 2004, 157). As a result, defence lawyers appear to be at a disadvantage with respect to knowledge of and access to DNA technologies; unlike prosecuting attorneys, they do not have the resources of the police, police experts, or government forensic experts at their behest. Consequently, many clients of defence counsel lack the resources to seek out such expert advice independently. In his research with defence counsel, Gerlach (2004) demonstrated that, while they were aware of their ignorance of these issues, access to more information was hindered by lack of time, resources, and inability to engage experts of their own owing to lack of funds.[33]

The Role of DNA in Post-Conviction Exonerations

It is at the level of post-conviction review that DNA profiling can play an increasingly significant role. For those who believe they were wrongly convicted, access to DNA testing and profiling may allow for the revisiting of their conviction. This is of particular significance for those who were wrongly convicted prior to the 1990s, when DNA testing was in its infancy; however, many other challenges can also impede this process. Primarily, not only does there need to be physical evidence present from the initial crime scene, but that evidence has to have been preserved, which is often not the case.[34] The issue is less of a problem since 2000, since crime-scene profiles have been collected and uploaded onto the NDDB and are therefore more accessible. At the same time, the availability of evidence remains an issue for possible wrongful convictions that took place prior to 2000 or where evidence, after many years, is either lost or destroyed.[35]

The final roadblock to presenting post-conviction DNA evidence would be to have this evidence examined by a court. While the general rule for appealing a criminal conviction in Canada is that the appeal be filed within a thirty-day window following conviction, there is some flexibility regarding this rule for "out of time" appeals, depending upon who is requesting it (Crown or defence counsel) and if due diligence has been demonstrated. As will be discussed in chapter 9, following the exhaustion of all avenues of appeal, individuals can apply to have their conviction reviewed by the minister of justice through section 696.1 of the Criminal Code, whereby DNA results may be presented as "fresh evidence" demonstrating proof of innocence. In the United States access to post-conviction DNA testing is often obstructed, since many states have statutes of limitation regarding the presentation of new evidence that can prove innocence (Scheck and Neufeld, 2002a, 244). While all fifty states have post-conviction DNA-testing statutes, many are limited in application in regard to who can access DNA. DNA may be inaccessible in cases where there was an original guilty plea, when a person is still incarcerated, or when a person had already had a request for DNA denied; moreover, many states fail to safeguard DNA evidence and excessive delays in proceedings are the norm.[36] Further, Garrett notes that, regardless of the statutes, the system continues to lack procedures to ensure full access to evidence of innocence at the time of trial, and then fails to properly assess claims of innocence brought during appeals (2008a, 2010a). Nevertheless, there may be other legal avenues available to some prisoners, depending upon the state in which they are incarcerated, that will allow prosecutors to consent to DNA testing in extraordinary circumstances.

In criminal cases, progression through the criminal justice system is lengthy and protracted; from arrest to trial, months and sometimes years can go by as a result of overloaded dockets in courts, delays requested by attorneys to facilitate evidence gathering, and general scheduling conflicts. The advent of DNA technology adds a further delay to the process. Although the RCMP aims to test forensic samples within thirty days, and despite increased spending on and improvements to staffing levels, backlog in the testing of DNA evidence has been a general problem in the Canadian system. In 2005–6 the average testing time was 114 days; by 2011, reviews of lab turnaround times showed little improvement, with some tests taking up to a year.[37] The latest annual report (2015–16) of the NDDB revealed that, as of 31 March 2016, it had received 444,152 DNA profiles, of which 326,989 DNA profiles were contained in the Convicted Offenders Index and 117,163 in the Crime Scene Index.[38] For that year there were 5,044 convicted-offender-to-crime-scene hits and 578 crime-scene-to-crime-scene hits; these numbers were the highest reached since the inception of the databank. In both 2005 and 2007, as discussed, the federal government introduced amendments that expanded the reach of the DNA Identification Act by increasing the number of Criminal Code offences that would permit DNA sampling. Clearly, the government is attempting to spread the DNA "net" to capture and retain biological samples of increasing numbers of individuals, effectively spreading its surveillance to more and more citizens.

Scheck, Neufeld, and Dwyer (2000) have great faith in the potential offered by DNA – as the success of the Innocence Project attests. Associated with the Benjamin Cardozo Law School, New York University, the Innocence Project has facilitated the exoneration of over three hundred and fifty incarcerated individuals through the use of DNA forensic analysis. At the same time, Rapp (2000) warns of the danger of overemphasizing the importance of this arguably significant and fundamental tool. Primarily, he believes that too strong a focus on the potential of DNA will result in the assumption that other, more basic reforms to the criminal justice system are unnecessary to help prevent wrongful convictions. The reality is that DNA, as derived from physical evidence left at a crime scene, is available only in a small percentage of cases. The great majority of wrongful convictions result from mistaken eyewitness identification, false confessions, reliance on jailhouse informants, and professional misconduct – problems occurring within the administration of justice which are impossible to rectify through DNA profiling. Reforms that focus solely on DNA and ignore the importance of addressing the causes of wrongful conviction will help just a small percentage of individuals.

At the Exclusion of All Else

It has been argued that the presentation of DNA evidence has effectively raised the bar in establishing that a wrongful conviction occurred.[39] In effect, defendants are now in a position where they must "prove" their innocence through DNA. While fifty American states have statutes that legislate the authorization of post-conviction DNA testing, many of these laws are limited in scope and substance.[40] In the vast majority of cases where there is no DNA, establishing innocence post-conviction is much more problematic. Furthermore, when DNA is not present, it may be used as a justification for why an individual cannot be cleared. As Roach (2006) indicates, it is now more difficult for wrongful-conviction cases to be recognized in the absence of DNA. In essence, this is creating a new threshold of truth for wrongful convictions. The fact that post-conviction DNA exonerations occur at all should indicate that other factors might also be involved in wrongful convictions.

In their comprehensive examination of exonerees in the United States from 1989 to 2003, Gross et al. (2005) found that, of the 340 exonerations, 144 of them were cleared through DNA evidence. Sixty per cent of the exonerations were for homicide, whereas 36 per cent were for rape or sexual assault; over 88 per cent of the rape exonerations had been convicted through mistaken eyewitness identification. They argue that, given that DNA played such a significant role in rape exonerations, the false conviction rate would be measurably higher if a similar tool were developed that was capable of discerning other types of errors: "There are other undetected miscarriages of justice in rape cases without testable DNA, and a much larger group of undetected false convictions in robberies and other serious crimes of violence for which DNA identification is useless" (531). Since the stakes have now changed with the introduction of DNA technology regarding the threshold for establishing that a wrongful conviction has occurred, and since there will continue to be errors in criminal investigations that play a role in wrongful convictions, it would be wise to expend greater efforts at researching the contributing factors.

Canadian Case Law

Canadian courts have addressed issues related to the admissibility of DNA evidence for a number of years, even prior to DNA warrant legislation. One of the first was the 1989 case *R. v. Borden*,[41] where the defendant provided a DNA sample following his identification and arrest as the possible perpetrator of a sexual assault. This DNA was compared with another sample that was collected from an earlier similar but unsolved crime, and it proved to be a match. Borden was then charged with and convicted of both assaults. The Court of Appeal of Ontario overturned the conviction for the earlier assault on the grounds that Borden had not consented to the use of his DNA sample for the earlier, unsolved crime. On the Crown's appeal to the Supreme Court, the earlier Court of Appeal decision was upheld on the grounds that Borden had not been asked, nor did he give his consent, to use his sample to investigate the earlier crime (Gerlach, 2004, 67). In essence, the Court agreed that the respondent's section 8 Charter right to be secure from unreasonable search and seizure had been violated. This case occurred prior to the enactment of statutory authorization to seize bodily samples; thus, consent was considered necessary to make the seizure lawful at that time.

Another case, R. v. Stillman,[42] also occurred prior to the emergence of DNA legislation, but it highlighted the need for the DNA warrant scheme that exists today (Gerlach, 2004, 74). In this case the accused had been found guilty of first-degree murder of a fourteen-year-old girl. While he had repeatedly refused, on the advice of counsel, the police's request to provide hair samples and teeth impressions, such samples were taken by force. Furthermore, the police retrieved a discarded tissue from the accused for DNA samples. In this instance, the Supreme Court believed that sections 7 and 8 of the Charter had been violated and upheld the accused's right to freedom from the excessive use of force to seize bodily samples with reference to the hair and teeth samples; however, a different conclusion was reached regarding the seizure of the tissue. While the seizure of the used tissue was found to have violated the accused's right under section 8, that was only because the accused was in custody and had no means of controlling this type of collection of his bodily samples. In any case, the tissue was admitted under section 24(2) of the Charter, the Court being influenced in this analysis by the fact that it had not been forcefully seized. Justice Cory commented at that time, through obiter dictum, that "it would seem that the recent provisions of the Code permitting DNA testing might well meet all constitutional requirements."[43] It was thus found, in both Borden and Stillman, that the "taking of bodily substances could not be justified as a search incidental to an arrest and violated the accused's rights under sections 7 and 8 of the Charter" (MacKay, 2007, 2). Subsequent to the incidents that occurred in Borden and Stillman, a DNA warrant scheme was enacted to allow, without specific consent from the accused, for the collection of DNA samples and for the comparison of these with those found at crime scenes, when the police have reasonable and probable grounds as well as authorization from a judicial officer (Weinper and Sandler, 2003, 442). The existing provisions override the potential challenges to forced DNA collection based on common law notions of bodily integrity, which were central to the legitimate Charter complaints established in Stillman; armed with a DNA warrant, police can now collect DNA samples without having to obtain consent from the suspect for the physical intrusion (Gerlach, 2004, 198).

More recent cases have challenged the constitutionality of the DNA warrant provisions on different grounds. In R. v. Brighteyes,[44] the court found that the DNA provisions did not violate section 8 of the Charter (the right to be secure against unreasonable search or seizure). In this case, the court found that the warrant provisions did violate section 7 ("Everyone has the right to life, liberty and security of the person and the right not to be deprived thereof except in accordance with the principles of fundamental justice"), since they involved the coercive taking of conscriptive[45] evidence, but they were justifiable under section 1 (which "guarantees the rights and freedoms set out in it (Charter) subject only to such reasonable limits prescribed by law as can be demonstrably justified in a free and democratic society"). In R. v. S.A.B.,[46] the defendant was convicted of sexual assault of a minor, the victim became pregnant, and the fetus was aborted; fetal tissue was taken for DNA sampling. Evidence was presented at trial that, of the seven DNA samples taken from the fetus, five established that the probability that the defendant was *not* the father was one in ten million; the sixth was damaged and inconclusive; and the seventh did not produce a match and was described (by a Crown expert) to be a mutation. On appeal to the Supreme Court of Canada, the appellant challenged whether a warrant for DNA evidence from an individual respects the right to be free from unreasonable search and seizure under section 8 of the Charter and argued that the expert's opinion lacked factual foundation. In rejecting the first argument, Justice Arbour found: "On balance, the law provides for a search and seizure of DNA materials that is reasonable. In light of the high probative value of forensic DNA analysis, the interests of the state override those of the individual" (para. 61). She further decided that the trial judge weighed "carefully and appropriately the evidence tendered by the DNA expert. His verdict was not based solely on the DNA results" (para. 63). The Court ultimately dismissed the appeal and found those sections of the Criminal Code relating to DNA to be constitutional.

In *R. v. Terceira*,[47] the defendant was found guilty of first-degree murder; the victim had been sexually assaulted and died from asphyxiation. The appellant based his appeal on several factors, including the admissibility of DNA evidence and jury instructions on the same subject. While the Court of Appeal heard evidence regarding the significance of the statistical probability of a match, on dismissing the appeal, the court held that the admissibility of probability statistics should be left to the discretion of the trial judge, to be decided on a case-by-case basis (Chesen, 2007). The DNA warrant and databank legislation also apply to young offenders, in more or less the same manner that Criminal Code violations apply to youth, although it would seem that the courts tend to exercise caution when applying databank orders to young persons. In the case of *R. v. R.C.*,[48] a thirteen-year-old had been convicted of assault with a weapon. Overall, the offence was minor in nature: the youth had stabbed his mother in the foot with a pen and struck her in the face with his fist. He pleaded guilty to assault with a weapon (a primary designated offence) and breach of an undertaking. While section 487.051(2) of the Criminal Code allows the taking of a DNA sample in such cases, the judge decided against it in this instance on the grounds that the impact of the order on the youth's privacy and security interests would be "grossly disproportionate to the public interest in the protection of society and the proper administration of justice." The Nova Scotia Court of Appeal allowed the Crown's appeal and directed that a DNA sample be taken. The Supreme Court allowed the appeal and affirmed the earlier judgment; in support of the trial judge's ruling, Justice Fish found that the judge in the first instance "weighed the public interest in ordering that a DNA sample be taken from him and retained in the DNA Data Bank against the impact of such an order on his privacy and security interests. She concluded this exercise in light of the principles and objects of youth criminal justice legislation, and found that the impact of the order would be grossly disproportionate" (para. 69).

In general, Canadian courts continue to assess and reassess how DNA warrants and databank legislation are acceptable under the protections of the Charter. The above cases and others have demonstrated that arguments for "limiting the use of DNA evidence based on the Charter have failed" (Gerlach, 2004, 202). Courts have the power to seize and later bank a convicted offender's DNA and retain it indefinitely; it is likely that they will continue to exercise that power with increasing frequency given the ever-expanding list of designated offences. In balancing individual rights against the assumed societal protection to be granted through the seizure of DNA, the courts tend to concur: societal protection now trumps individual privacy interests in the use of genetic information for the purposes of investigating crimes. Furthermore, not all defendants have the resources to challenge alleged rights' violations with respect to how, when, and where samples are obtained.

Wrongful-Conviction Case Examples

A number of wrongful-conviction exonerations have occurred in recent years in Canada through the use of DNA forensic analysis, often transpiring many years after the fact. When DNA evidence is present at a crime scene and can exclude a suspect as the perpetrator of the crime, DNA is often championed as the panacea to all that ails the criminal justice system. As discussed earlier, however, faith in DNA's ability to "solve" crimes may prove to be misplaced, and the case of George Pitt illustrates this point well. Pitt is currently serving a life sentence in a maximum-security prison in New Brunswick for the 1993 murder of six-year-old Samantha Toole. Pitt was the boyfriend of Gloria Toole (Samantha's mother) and both he and Gloria had been drinking heavily the night Samantha went missing. Samantha was discovered missing at 10:00 a.m. the next morning and was found near death later that same evening in a river not far from her home. Ultimately, the cause of death was drowning, but Samantha had been sexually and physically assaulted.

A circumstantial case was established against Pitt, who had a lengthy criminal record. The most damning evidence was that Pitt was seen washing a comforter from the master bedroom at 4:00 a.m. – he claimed to have spilled beer on it. DNA evidence indicated that there was a centimetre-square spot of Samantha's blood on the comforter (there was also a large unidentified blood stain), as well as plant material similar to that growing near the river; at the time of trial, a witness claimed to have seen Pitt walking near where the body was found (Shulgan, 2006). Moreover, a number of individuals had come and gone from Toole's apartment during the evening, most of whom had consumed vast quantities of alcohol. Pitt's two appeals to the New Brunswick Court of Appeal in 1996 were dismissed. Nonetheless, persistent journalists were able to uncover new evidence, such as four hairs found on Samantha Toole that had never undergone DNA forensic analysis. Given that advances had occurred in DNA technology since Pitt was first convicted, his defence team requested that vaginal and anal swabs from the victim, as well as other evidence, be retested. DNA analysis revealed that the hair strands belonged to Samantha or her mother – and no foreign DNA was found on either swabs or night clothing belonging to the victim. While these findings did not exonerate Pitt, they also did not provide other evidence as to who committed these crimes (Shulgan, 2006). The impact of the circumstantial evidence, coupled with the inconclusive DNA results, did not raise sufficient enough doubt or evidence for Pitt's case to be re-examined. Rather than provide answers, in this case the DNA analysis has simply raised further questions about Pitt's involvement in Samantha's murder.

Canada's most famous DNA exoneree is undoubtedly David Milgaard. Milgaard served over twenty-two years for the murder of Gail Miller, in Saskatoon,

Saskatchewan, in 1969. It was only through an unremitting media campaign occurring over many years, and the tireless efforts of his mother, Joyce, that Milgaard's conviction was set aside by the Supreme Court in 1992. Yet Milgaard's true "innocence" was not established until 1997, when DNA evidence conclusively proved that he could not have murdered Gail Miller; it also proved that Larry Fisher was the murderer. Another renowned DNA Canadian exoneree is Guy Paul Morin. Morin was convicted of murdering nine-year-old Christine Jessop in Durham County, Ontario, in 1992. After an acquittal, followed by a conviction for first-degree murder, Morin was finally exonerated in 1995 through DNA forensic analysis. A further example of an overturned wrongful conviction through DNA analysis is the Newfoundland case of Gregory Parsons. Parsons was convicted for the assault and murder of his mother in 1994; he was later exonerated through DNA analysis in 1998. In these three cases, each of the individual men has received government compensation and the errors that contributed to their convictions have been thoroughly examined through extensive and costly commissions of inquiry.[49]

What these cases reveal is that actors in the criminal justice system, particularly the police and prosecution service, at times have focused on one individual and tailored the available evidence to fit the suspect profile. Milgaard, Morin, Parsons, and, to a lesser extent, Simon Marshall were the fortunate ones; physical evidence was present at their crime scenes. In each case, it was only much later that DNA forensic analysis of physical evidence from the crime scene facilitated their exonerations for the crimes that they clearly did not commit. Without the presence of DNA evidence, these individuals might still be serving sentences in prison. Moreover, once discovered, this evidence allowed for a fairly rapid exoneration. Those less fortunate wrongly convicted, whose cases turn on less tangible, more subjective evidence (such as false confessions, mistaken eyewitness identification or police misconduct), must work far harder to establish their innocence. Clearly, the presence of DNA at a crime scene and the resultant weight it is afforded in most criminal investigations has raised the bar considerably regarding establishing innocence, to the extent that it exceeds the grasp of many wrongly convicted persons.

The Preservation of Evidence

Clearly, while the utility of DNA science has been amply demonstrated by the number of cold cases that have been solved through its application to old case materials, many exonerations could not have happened if such materials had not been preserved. While over thirty-five American states have legislation that compels the preservation of evidence upon conviction, at the same time, the existing laws differ in terms of time frames for retention and categories of crime that require evidence preservation.[50] Likewise, space concerns limit the amount of evidence that can be stored and thus many states have policies to destroy evidence of older, unsolved cases. Moreover, most statutes allow for premature disposal; thus, even in cases where legislation exists to facilitate post-conviction testing of biological evidence, a great deal of evidence disappears or goes missing.

Given the many jurisdictional issues that govern the administration of criminal law in Canada, it is not surprising that there is a lack of coherence in provincial and territorial evidence preservation policies; indeed, there are no legislated standards at all in this regard.[51] Every police force, coroner's office, and forensic investigation agency in the country has its own procedure for the preservation and retention of evidence; some of these are written protocols while others are more informal.[52] Retention periods often vary according to a number of issues related to the crime, including the seriousness of the crime, access to evidence, costs of preservation, and the overall probability that the evidence will be needed for future reference.

A few examples of preservation policies illustrate the lack of uniformity and coherence across the country.[53] The current policies in the city of Toronto, for example, require the permanent retention of autopsy photographs; other practices in Canada regarding the retention of evidence in criminal cases are "arbitrary and inconsistent."[54] Furthermore, with respect to criminal cases, the Toronto Police Services, under Bylaw 689–2000, has a detailed "schedule of retention periods for their records; for example: crime scene fingerprints are retained permanently in all homicide cases; for 5 years (after appeals) in robbery and sexual assault cases; and for 5 years (after occurrence) in the more minor indictable offences. Photographs are retained for 5 years (after appeals)."[55]

At the same time, in the province of Ontario, the Policing Standards Manual for Sexual Assault Investigation mandates that police services develop their own local protocols around, inter alia, "the collection, preservation and transfer of medical/ forensic evidence (including provisions to allow for a Sexual Assault Evidence Kit to be stored for up to six months when a victim chooses to attend the hospital to have the examination completed but chooses not to report the assault to the police at that time)." The six-month time frame is quite limiting, and given that this is not a directive per se, but rather a standards manual that provides guidelines to police forces, there is likely a great deal of variability in how police forces in Ontario, or any province for that matter, preserve evidence in sexual-assault cases. Moreover, in Quebec, the Service de Police de la Ville de Montréal has a policy regarding the preservation of evidence in criminal cases that ranges from three months up to indefinite retention, based on a court order and in cases "pour l'évènement, criminel ou non, avec décès ou avec enquête du coroner, politique ministérielle ou disparition non localisée."[56]

A recent case brought before the Ontario Court of Appeal by the Innocence Project at Osgoode Hall Law School involved a petition for the court to find that all evidence in cases carrying a life sentence be preserved until the offender dies, unless he/she gives permission to have it destroyed or seeks a court order to that effect. The case concerned Amina Chaudhary, found guilty of killing a child in 1984, and centred around the right to preserve forensic evidence in her case; the autopsy files had been lost and lawyers were arguing that the rest of the file was at risk.[57] Chaudhary's defence counsel contended that the loss of the remaining files would likely compromise any attempts at post-conviction review. This Charter challenge was argued in part on the idea that the life-long preservation of evidence is a constitutional right, which had been dismissed by the judge at first instance. Justice Michael R. Dambrot found that a Charter violation would occur only in cases where the evidence was destroyed or lost on account of negligence. In the Notice of Application, the claim was thus rejected based on the fact that the declaration was "much too encompassing and much too undefined" – Chaudhary had sought "all evidence and exhibits"[58] – and that the test for public interest standing in this case was not met.[59]

On appeal, however, Chaudhary's counsel sought declaratory relief for speculative harm; in other words, the claim was not based on past harms, but rather counsel believed that there is "reasonable apprehension of harm" in the future.[60] Ultimately, the Court of Appeal dismissed the appeal, given that the appellant "does not challenge the findings made by Dambrot J. but now seeks the declaratory remedy on a basis that is not set out in the record and was not the subject of adjudication by Dambrot J."[61] Moreover, the judges endorsed what they describe as "thoughtful, obiter observations regarding the preservation of evidence" made in first instance:

> Unlike preservation of *Stinchcombe* material before trial, preservation after appellate rights are exhausted does not give rise to a legal principle that can be identified with sufficient precision to yield a simple a [sic] standard. It would be preferable for there to be a carefully developed legislated scheme, which could then be reviewed by the Courts for *Charter* compliance.
>
> But if there is an obligation on the Crown arising from the *Charter* to preserve *Stinchcombe* material after appellate rights have been exhausted, and if the task of developing the response to this issue must fall to the Courts, the response should be developed in a nuanced and incremental manner. Unlike preservation of relevant material before trial, it requires consideration of the differing types of material covered by *Stinchcombe*, what subsequent use there may be for such material, questions of dangerousness and perishability, and questions of feasibility and cost.[62]

While these obiter observations have no standing in precedent they do raise what are significant concerns that the courts will likely be facing in the future.

Conclusions

It is an incontrovertible fact that the use of DNA forensic analysis has substantially changed law-enforcement practice; however, given the enormous potential for the use (and abuse) of genetic material, it must be treated cautiously. As Justice Charron notes in *R. v. Rodgers*:

> There is no question that DNA evidence has revolutionized the way many crimes are investigated and prosecuted. The use of this new technology has not only led to the successful identification and prosecution of many dangerous criminals, it has served to exonerate many persons who were wrongfully suspected or convicted. The importance of this forensic development to the administration of justice can hardly be overstated. At the same time, the profound implications of government seizure and use of DNA samples on privacy and security of the person cannot be ignored. A proper balance between these competing interests must be achieved within our constitutional framework.[63]

What has become evident is an ever-broadening trend of designating more and more offences as subject to DNA forensic analysis and retention in the databank, not only in Canada but also in the United States and the United Kingdom.[64]

In her book on forensic identification and the "risk society," McCartney (2006a) makes a compelling argument that "reform of the criminal process in the risk

society" will result in "eroding the presumption of innocence, negating protections against wrongful conviction, and downgrading the status of 'fairness'" (103).
She further argues that, in the United Kingdom, risk-society considerations have
trumped the need for vigilance around avoiding wrongful convictions. These
arguments are equally true in the Canadian context, as evinced by the uncritical acceptance of DNA technology (as well as the development of the National
DNA Data Bank), an ever-increasing list of designated offences, and an increasing
reliance on DNA profile matching. Gerlach describes this as an example of how
crime management is turning more and more towards an actuarial language of
probability and statistical distribution of criminal traits (2004). Perhaps that is the
downside of our growing dependence on DNA and other emerging forensic technologies. But it also begs the question as to whether or not it is inevitable.

During the House of Commons Standing Committee Hearings prior to the passage of the first amendments to the DNA Identification Act in 2005, the privacy
commissioner of Canada at that time, Jennifer Stoddart, echoed those reservations:

> Our concern is that we are moving away from the DNA scheme that was set out in the
> 1998 Act and approved by Parliament. We are moving away from a limited Data Bank
> that only contains DNA samples from those convicted of the most serious violent and
> sexual offences where the nature of the crime is such that it is likely to leave DNA at
> the crime scene. I fear that we are moving towards a registry of all convicted offend-
> ers. And we are doing this without regard to the original rationale for the legislation
> and without any compelling evidence that would justify the inclusion of these new
> offences. (Stoddart, 2005)

Stoddart recommended that caution be exercised around adding an ever-
increasing number of offences to the primary and secondary designation lists.
This appears advisable given that, as has been argued, "bodily integrity, the right
against self-incrimination, the rules against police 'fishing expeditions' and the
presumption of innocence are being eroded in order to accommodate biotechnology" (Gerlach, 2004, 204). Recently, in a report for the British Columbia Civil Liberties Association, it was recommended that, before adding more offences to the
growing list that now warrant DNA sampling, Parliament undertake a review to
ascertain whether there is empirical evidence to support the increase, given the
nature of the privacy intrusions involved; and that DNA samples not be used to
conduct DNA familial analyses (identifying a suspect through biological relatives)
absent justification on the part of the Crown (Oscapella, 2012). While these cautions
are prescient, considering the increasingly conservative slant to most changes in
criminal law policy in the previous decade, it is doubtful they will be heeded. Even
if Gerlach is exaggerating the extent to which privacy protections are being violated through the use of DNA technology, what is needed is further research and
study into how this very powerful investigative tool could better serve the needs
of law enforcement while at the same time safeguarding individual civil liberties,
a difficult balance at best.

Chapter Eight

Forensic Evidence and Expert Testimony

"Expert witnesses have an essential role to play in the criminal courts. However, the dramatic growth in the frequency with which they have been called upon in recent years has led to ongoing debate about suitable controls on their participation, precautions to exclude 'junk science,' and the need to preserve and protect the role of the trier of fact – the judge or the jury." (Justice Ian Binnie, in *R. v. J.(L.J.)*[1])

Introduction

In recent years, criminal prosecutions have relied upon increasingly more sophisticated forms of evidence and the use of expert witnesses to assist the triers of fact in deciding upon the merits of a particular case. Yet it is now recognized that expert testimony and forensic evidence, while meant to represent objective and scientifically sound reasoning, have led to wrongful convictions through a lack of impartiality, unsubstantiated claims, and distortion of the fact-finding process (Department of Justice, 2005b).

The first part of this chapter provides an overview of the use of forensic evidence at trial, with particular attention paid to the possibility of error and its repercussions. These issues are illustrated by some wrongful-conviction case examples that demonstrate how forensic-science evidence, and experts' defence of it, has contributed to miscarriages of justice. While a brief overview of some of the types of forensic evidence is presented, this is not meant to be exhaustive, given the frequent and persistent changes occurring in the field of forensic sciences. In addition, the emergence of social-science evidence in courts is discussed.

The second part of the chapter focuses on the uses of expert testimony, and it will be argued that at times the manner in which expert testimony is offered, around forensic and other matters, can be misleading, resulting in misinterpretation and misrepresentation. This is followed by discussions of forensic pathology and discredited expert testimony. American and Canadian jurisprudence offers some examples of how the courts' attempts to structure the use of expert testimony have evolved over time.

I. Forensic Evidence: "Junk" or Genuine Science?

Courts are turning more and more to the testimony of experts and "scientific" evidence for help in deciding the guilt or innocence of defendants in criminal trials.

The past twemty years has evinced a virtual plethora of case law around the use of emerging forensic science, along with growing public, media, and research interest in this field. Aside from DNA evidence (as discussed in the previous chapter), many developments in other areas of scientific discovery have allowed for past convictions based on faulty science to be re-examined, as well as new charges to be brought or dropped. As Walker and Stockdale (1999) note, forensic evidence offers great promise with respect to avoiding miscarriages of justice; however, this scientific "revolution" has not been without its complications. The role of the expert witness has increasingly come under scrutiny – with one issue of concern being that expert evidence should not "usurp the function of the trier of fact by approaching the ultimate issue to be decided" (Trotter, 2005, 195). Unfortunately, when experts are called to Canadian courts to testify about the relative weight to be given to particular evidence, there is a tendency for the triers of fact to treat such evidence as infallible. While Canadian case law dictates that judges must provide warnings to juries about the weight to be given to expert testimony, questionable science, presented by an alleged "expert," dressed up as reliable and based on fact, can be very compelling to a layperson who is unfamiliar with the topic and requires assistance in making a decision. As stated, the field of forensic science is in perpetual growth; it is not the objective of this chapter to provide an exhaustive or complete account of continuing developments in the field. Rather, the chapter focuses on how mistakes made in interpreting forensic sciences have contributed to wrongful convictions and on the need for vigilance to prevent similar errors in the future.

Wrongful-Conviction Case Examples

A number of cases have come to light in recent years that illustrate how forensic evidence can be misused, misinterpreted, and misunderstood and can ultimately influence a conviction in error. What is of particular importance is that these cases are a small example of what can happen when science, admittedly pure, is applied and interpreted in a biased and suggestible fashion. Further, these are cases where the errors in forensic science have become known and the convicted individuals have been exonerated – in essence, such people are the "lucky" ones. There are likely countless other cases where forensic errors have either not yet been exposed or, if they have been, have not yet facilitated exoneration.

The cases of Steven Truscott, James Driskell, and Guy Paul Morin will be briefly discussed with a view to demonstrating how forensic science played and continues to play a key role in the circumstances of their cases.

STEVEN TRUSCOTT
The Steven Truscott case, one of the oldest wrongful convictions in Canadian history, represents a conviction based largely on circumstantial evidence, some of which relates to time of death based on stomach contents. In June 1959 twelve-year-old Lynne Harper was found raped and strangled in the woods near Clinton, Ontario; she had gone missing on the 9 June and was found two days later. Steven Truscott, fourteen years old at the time, was the last individual to be seen with Harper, giving her a ride on his bicycle early in the evening of 9 June. Therefore,

for the coroner's office, establishing the time of death was essential to either eliminating Truscott or including him as a suspect for consideration in Harper's murder. Dr John Penistan, the district pathologist, examined the contents of Lynne
Harper's stomach shortly after her death and estimated the time of death to have
been one and one half to two hours after her last meal – an exactitude that is lu-
dicrous, even following the standards of the time. Moreover, this ascertained the
time of death to have been between 7:15 and 7:45 – pointing the finger directly
at Steven Truscott. If the science based on Penistan's investigation was correct,
Truscott was the only individual capable of murdering her within that time frame.
Not surprisingly, Truscott was found guilty of murdering Lynne Harper and was
sentenced to death in 1959.

Given his young age, the public outcry over the sentence, and a growing
sentiment in Canada against the death penalty, in 1960 Truscott's sentence was
commuted to life imprisonment. Seven years later, the Supreme Court heard a reference on the Truscott case, but his appeal was rejected because the Court was not
convinced by the evidence. It has recently come to light that, during the time of the
Supreme Court hearing, Dr Penistan reviewed his case notes and wrote that the
time of death could have been up to twelve hours after Harper's last meal; however, this evidence was never disclosed to the defence, or to the Court. Truscott
was ultimately released from jail after serving ten years and lived anonymously
until he resurfaced in 2001 attempting to clear his name. Media attention and a
book (Sher, 2001) shed new light on the questionable scientific and circumstantial
evidence presented at the original trial. An application was prepared for ministerial review (see chapter 9) and in 2005 the minister of justice sent the case back to
the Court of Appeal. The court heard very strong arguments about the dubious
nature of much of the "scientific" (including stomach contents and forensic entomology) and the circumstantial evidence that had been used to convict Truscott
in the first instance. With respect to stomach contents, fresh and undisclosed evidence now pointed to the fact that the "scientific" certainty around the time of
death at the original trial has been called into question by a number of factors and
Harper's death likely occurred many hours after it was originally thought (Court
of Appeal for Ontario, 2006).

The Ontario Court of Appeal also heard forensic entomological evidence at
Truscott's 2006 appeal. Forensic entomology involves the study of insects within
a legal context, while medicolegal entomology, more particularly, involves the use
of insect evidence in abuse and death cases (VanLaerhoven and Anderson, 2013).
In order to ascertain, among other things, the time elapsed since death or the post-
mortem interval (PMI), entomologists study the eggs and larvae of arthropods,
specifically blowflies, found on corpses (Chaubert and Wyss, 2003). This type of
science is an aid to investigators since it may allow them to narrow the time of
death and thus limit the number of possible suspects who may have had contact
with the deceased. Insects found on decomposing bodies at crime scenes are generally studied to ascertain their life cycle (Campobasso and Introna, 2001; Goff,
2000; Kanaki, Stiakakis, and Michalodimitrakis, 2003), because that will provide
some information about the time of death by determining the age of the larvae and
the length of time taken to complete their development. Decomposition of tissue is
also affected by environmental temperature, light, and humidity; further, blowflies

are sensitive to extreme heat and do not lay eggs after dark. Entomological information is often only used in cases where examination of other indicators of time of death are not possible; as with other types of forensic science, it is inexact.

New testimony at the Court of Appeal around the presence of insects, preserved through detailed descriptions from the original crime scene and autopsy, provided a different (some say more accurate) account of the time of Lynne Harper's death. Testimony from a number of forensic entomologists was heard, and while some of it was contradictory, the defence attorney's position was that compelling entomological evidence suggested that the time of Lynne Harper's death would have been sometime immediately before or after sunset (around 9:00 p.m.) on the evening of 9 June 1959 (Court of Appeal for Ontario, 2006). The Court of Appeal decision in August 2007 acquitted Truscott and found that, based on fresh evidence, a miscarriage of justice likely occurred.[2] Ultimately, the expert medical and entomological evidence about the original time of Harper's death was found to be scientifically untenable and the fresh evidence cast considerable doubt on the Crown's claim that she died before 8 p.m.[3]

JAMES DRISKELL

James Driskell[4] was convicted of killing Perry Harder in 1991, based partly on hair-microscopy evidence. Harder and Driskell were small-time criminals and had a history of criminal involvement together. Harder disappeared in June 1990 and was found in a shallow grave in September 1990, having been shot in the chest. Forensic scientists examined hairs from the gravesite and compared those to hairs taken from a van owned by Driskell. The case was based on the hair and confession evidence from informants, and the microscopy evidence established that the hair could have come from the victim. At the original trial, forensic scientists found that "one hair from the vacuumed debris and two from the van carpet *were consistent* with those believed to be Mr. Harder's" (emphasis added, Lucas, 2006, 2). This terminology was explained: "If the hair is consistent, that means it either came from the same person as that known sample or from somebody else who has hair exactly like that" (transcript of testimony of Tod Christianson in *R. v. Driskell*, 148–9, from Lucas, 2006, 2). In 2002 another forensic scientist established, through more sophisticated means of detection (mtDNA), that the hairs from the van were not from the victim.

It was later revealed that the informants in this case were compromised. One was paid a large amount of money ($20,000 and other expenses) in exchange for his testimony and granted immunity from charges of arson. Furthermore, much exculpatory evidence was not revealed to the defence at the time of the trial. Driskell spent twelve years in jail until his release on bail in 2003, awaiting conviction review by the minister of justice. His conviction was overturned in 2005, and while the federal government ordered a new trial, the proceedings against Driskell were eventually stayed by the Manitoba Department of Justice.

GUY PAUL MORIN

The case of Guy Paul Morin[5] underlined the weak nature of hair-microscopy evidence and is of particular significance with respect to the use and misuse of forensic evidence generally and the testimony of experts. In 1985 Morin was arrested for the murder of Christine Jessop, an eight-year-old girl from Durham County, Ontario. At the time of the murder, he had no criminal record and lived with his parents, who were neighbours of the Jessop family. Christine Jessop disappeared in October 1984 on her way home from school; her body was found over two months later, some fifty kilometres away. Morin became a suspect in this case, partly because Christine Jessop's mother described him as a "weird-type guy" and also because of somewhat odd comments he made to police during interviews; he was arrested four months later (Kaufman, 1998b, 65). Following an acquittal from the first trial, Morin was found guilty at his second trial in 1992. It was only in 1995 that DNA evidence cleared Morin and he was finally acquitted.

Hair and fibre[6] evidence presented at both of Morin's trials was relied upon quite heavily by the prosecution but turned out to have little probative value. At Morin's trial, the hair and fibre evidence produced by forensic examiners from the Centre for Forensic Sciences in Toronto was proffered as proof of physical contact between the victim and Morin. Specifically, hairs found on Christine Jessop's necklace and fibres from her clothing and from a recorder case at the site where her body was found were thought to have come from Guy Paul Morin, or were said to be similar to fibres found in his car and home. Morin and his parents stated that Christine Jessop had never been in their car or home, but the Crown argued that the fibre "matches" were actually an indication that Guy Paul Morin had abducted and killed Christine Jessop (Kaufman, 1998c, 65).

Conversely, the defence team argued that these alleged "matches" had little probative value, there was no common source for the fibres found, and contamination could likely have happened with this evidence through the manner in which it was collected. Also of significance is how the forensic experts presented their findings at the Morin trial. Kaufman (1998c) indicated that the variety of ways in which forensic scientists discussed the relative value of hair and fibre comparisons ("*consistent with*," "*could have*" come from a particular source, "*cannot be excluded*," etc.) likely had an impact on Morin's wrongful conviction. The hair- and fibre-sample similarities were presented as factual links, when they were, at best, suggestive. Moreover, during the commission of inquiry into this case, it was revealed that the fibre evidence had been contaminated while in the possession of the Centre for Forensic Sciences, and that this fact had been suppressed (Kaufman, 1998c, 83). In brief, the commission found that the hair and fibre comparisons had little or no probative value, scientific findings were overstated, and limitations to these findings were not "accurately or adequately communicated to the police, prosecutors, the defense and to the courts" (Kaufman, 1998c, 249).

Types of Forensic Evidence

Forensic science has been described as "the systematic and painstaking identification, analysis and comparison of the physical residues of crime in order to establish what happened, when, where and how it happened, and who might have been involved" (Walker and Stockdale, 1999, 121). Thus, forensic science plays a role in both police investigation and criminal prosecution, for both prosecuting and defence attorneys. Forensic scientists become involved at the beginning of an investigation and assist the police in determining if a crime has occurred; they participate in the collection and preservation of any evidence that may be relevant to the investigation. Forensic scientists also assist the prosecution and the defence when called on to provide evidence to the courts. Given that forensic scientists are considered to be "expert witnesses," they can provide information to the courts on both fact and opinion; the difficulty occurs when the courts (and even the scientists themselves) are unclear as to which is which (Walker and Stockdale, 1999, 120).

Various types of scientific evidence[7] have been presented in the past during criminal trials and conveyed as "expert" or reliable which have later proven to have been "bad" science or "good" science used in a fraudulent manner. At times, courts will accept forensic evidence without questioning the methodology or the basis of reliability since they are attending to precedence. Courts tend to deal with questions about the weight of evidence and thus can admit evidence that lacks sound empirical backing; also problematic is taking judicial notice of forensic evidence in a particular case without questioning how it was used (Beecher-Monas, 2007, 121). As the detection capacities of forensic science increase, so do the means of answering questions raised at crime scenes about when and how individuals were killed, and even who was responsible for the crime. Problems occur when such evidence is accepted without scrutiny and ultimately forms the basis of a conviction in error. Both American and Canadian courts have increasingly accepted more and more precise forms of "science" as evidence that have come under scrutiny in recent years; a few will be considered here.

IMPRESSION EVIDENCE: FOOTWEAR OR FEET

Impression evidence can take the form of shoe prints or footprints, teeth marks or tire marks, and such evidence can be used to establish contact between a perpetrator and victim. Footwear-impression evidence has been routinely accepted by the courts in Canada; in those cases, footwear impressions made in blood, mud, or other materials are compared to the prints of shoes worn by the accused. In fact, in *R. v. Hall*, the court stated that "expert evidence comparing footprint impressions has been received in criminal cases in this province (Ontario) for at least 25 years."[8] In addition, *barefoot*-impression evidence has also been scrutinized by the courts. The case of *R. v. Dimitrov*[9] addressed the hypothesis that footprint impressions left in boots can be linked to wear patterns from the feet of a specific suspect. In this instance, a connection could not be validated using scientific principles and the evidence was excluded; the case established that such evidence was "novel science" that had yet to become generally accepted in the relevant field.

IMPRESSION EVIDENCE: FORENSIC ODONTOLOGY

The terms forensic odontology and forensic dentistry, used synonymously, involve the interpretation of dental evidence from crime scenes (Sweet and Wood, 2013). A forensic odontologist's work consists of both identifying remains through the use of dental records and identifying the cause of bite marks on skin or other surfaces. Consequently, forensic odontologists are involved in either (or both, depending on the provincial authority) death investigation or criminal or quasi-criminal investigation. Identifying deceased persons appears to be the most common task of forensic dentists (Pretty and Sweet, 2001) and in most cases is fairly straightforward; ante-mortem and post-mortem dental records are compared in order to make a positive identification following death. In those cases where ante-mortem dental records are unavailable, forensic dentists may complete a profile from the dental remains and suggest characteristics that may facility in the search for ante-mortem materials (Sweet and DiZinno, 1996). It is the area of bite-mark analysis that is much more tentative as a science and clouded with controversy.

Bite-mark analysis as an area of impression expertise (Kiely, 2006, 317) is a sub-discipline of forensic dentistry. While there are existing guidelines regarding the collection of bite-mark evidence established by both the American Board of Forensic Odontology[10] and the British Association of Forensic Odontology,[11] the practice itself is inherently subjective and there is a dearth of rigorous scientific research supporting its conclusions. In order for it to gain credibility as a forensic science, studies are needed to establish the uniqueness of human dentition and how it is represented on human skin and other substrates (Pretty, 2006), as well as how this type of evidence can be used in a way that will facilitate the investigation of crimes.[12] At present, the idea that forensic odontologists are able to identify a person by comparing the accused's teeth with teeth marks left on the victim's body has little theoretical or empirical support (Beecher-Monas, 2007, 97). Yet bite marks, often associated with violent rape/homicide, appear to be increasingly accepted in U.S. courts, despite the controversy surrounding this type of evidence.[13] The case of Kennedy Brewer, convicted and sentenced to death in the United States for the murder of a three-year-old child, was based almost entirely on faulty bite-mark evidence. Dr Michael West, a now discredited forensic odontologist, testified at his trial that nineteen indentations on the victim's body were made by Brewer's top two teeth. Brewer was exonerated after fifteen years when it was established that the bite marks were likely from insects since the body had been left in the water for days.[14]

While bite-mark evidence has been used in Canadian courts, it has been mainly taken as an indication of the force of a sexual assault (cf. *R. v. Ho*,[15] *R. v. J.A.A.*[16]). In *R. v. Kines*,[17] a Manitoba Court of Appeal case from a directed acquittal, bite-mark identification was used to ascertain the identity of the perpetrator of the murder of a three-year-old child. In that case a forensic odontologist testified that the accused had a "very highly unusual" dentition that lined up with most of the bite marks on the body.[18] The expert believed that the accused was "most likely" the biter and that he was "very confident" in his identification of the accused. The case was ultimately submitted back for retrial on the grounds that the judge had not differentiated "the question of whether the Crown met its burden on a directed verdict test (the evidentiary burden)" from the question "whether the Crown met its burden of proof beyond a reasonable doubt (the burden of proof)."[19]

IMPRESSIONS EVIDENCE: TIRE MARKS
Tire-impression evidence taken from a crime scene may be used to establish that an accused person's car was in the vicinity of a crime; as in shoe-print analysis, examiners look at style, brand, class, and individual wear patterns of tires (Kiely, 2006, 316). In most cases, police are the forensic experts with respect to identifying and matching tire-mark evidence, and recently a number of reported decisions in the United States have used this type of evidence. In Canada, tire-mark evidence has been used in insurance cases to establish evidence of driving patterns;[20] however,

it has also been used in a number of criminal cases to bolster the case against an accused or to complement other evidence. In *R. v. Dhillon*,[21] tire-mark evidence taken in 1977 regarding the tread pattern and size of tire marks contributed to the accused's murder conviction in 2001, in conjunction with DNA evidence that had not been analysed at the earlier time. In *R. v. Butorac*,[22] a tire-track impression on one of the victim's wrists was found to have come from a tire on the perpetrator's car. Finally, tire-mark analyses have been used in a number of cases of dangerous driving causing death to establish recklessness.[23] What these cases demonstrate is that, by itself, tire-track evidence is insufficient to find beyond a reasonable doubt that an accused is guilty of a crime. Clearly, impression evidence is still an inexact science and at face value it can establish the presence of an individual at a crime scene but is insufficient on its own to designate a given individual as the perpetrator of a crime.

IMPRESSION EVIDENCE: FIREARMS AND TOOL MARKS

Firearms identification has long been an investigative tool used by police. In terms of forensic analysis, the objective of firearm identification is to determine whether particular ammunition was discharged from a particular firearm through the identification of fired bullets, cartridge cases, or other ammunition components (Dahlstrom et al., 2013). Further, it is a branch of tool-mark identification, or friction-ridge identification, which examines the markings made by a harder surface (tool itself) against a softer surface (Chaklos and Kuehner, 2007, 333). Tool marks also occur in the commission of a crime when an instrument such as a crowbar, wire cutter, or screwdriver is used and the manufacturing processes dictate the types of marks left behind (National Academy of Sciences, 2009). Identification procedures involve microscopic comparisons based on pattern matching. With respect to firearms, and similar to other impression evidence, identifying that a particular firearm was responsible for a shooting does not, by itself, provide information about who perpetrated the crime; correlating evidence must be compelling enough to establish proof beyond a reasonable doubt. Databases have been developed in the United States regarding the striation patterns of particular firearms and ammunition; these are then used by police forces to identify characteristics and types. Linking ammunition from a particular firearm used in a crime to ammunition found elsewhere is often used as a means of evidence collection in criminal cases (cf. *R. v. Abdow*,[24] *R. v. Belic*,[25] *R. v. Willis*[26]). Ballistic experts are frequently called in criminal cases to comment on the possible trajectories of bullets in order to narrow down or implicate possible suspects (cf. *R. v. Melaragni*).[27] In the case of *R. v. Daunt*,[28] the accused was convicted of second-degree murder, but he claimed that he shot the victim in self-defence. Later, an expert in tool-mark and firearm identification demonstrated that the shooting could not have occurred as Daunt claimed; in fact, the court found that "the paths of the two bullets into and through the body of the deceased man as he sat in his vehicle did not jibe with the claim of the appellant that he fired only to warn Truswell off. The Crown contended, by inference at least, that the appellant fired the fatal shot from point-blank range and that he must have had one or the other of the two possible intents in murder."[29]

In spite of its long history as a police investigative tool, there is still no clearly defined process of firearm and tool-mark determination and the scientific knowledge base remains fairly limited (National Academy of Sciences, 2009). Moreover, a statistical foundation of certainty simply does not exist (Spiegelman, and Tobin, 2013).

ARSON INVESTIGATIONS

Arson investigation is another area of forensic analysis that has recently benefited from increases in scientific knowledge. Following a fire where death has occurred, burn patterns and points of origin are often examined to establish whether or not a fire should be considered accidental or intentional and whether there were accelerants[30] present. What may have been true about arson investigative practices many years ago may no longer be. For example, fires were always thought to burn upwards but now have been understood to burn down from the ceiling; fires caused by accelerants were once believed to reach very high temperatures, but it is now known that temperature is also affected by ventilation; crackled glass was long thought to be a sign of accelerant use, but it is now believed to result when water hits hot glass; and flashover effects (which occur when an interior fire reaches a very high temperature and everything in the room ignites) have been found to resemble arson (Lounsberry, 2007). Faulty arson findings have been used to convict several U.S. prisoners who were later found to have been innocent (cf. Arson Review Committee, 2006).[31]

Canadian courts rely on expert testimony in arson cases, as illustrated in the homicide conviction in *R. v. Fry*,[32] where five people died in a fire and it was found that

> the explosion may have been delayed because liquid gasoline does not burn; rather, the vapours created by the gradual evaporation of gasoline burn when they come in contact with an open flame. According to the expert opinion evidence, once the vapour pool ignited, it would have created an "air hammer" that traveled from the ground floor up through the townhouse. The pressure front precedes the flame front and causes damage before the flame actually arrives. In this case, the "air hammer" blew out windows in the front and rear of the residence, carrying shards of glass up to 109 feet. It also caused significant structural damage. The expert opinion evidence was that the second explosion occurred when the canister attached to the propane torch ruptured and that this explosion propelled the torch back out the family room window and onto the rear patio where investigators found it.[33]

As with other cases when trace evidence is used to determine the cause of a crime, there are many compounding factors that affect its inherent reliability. For one, in most arson cases, firefighters cause considerable damage to the evidence in efforts to control the extent of the fire. At the same time, when accelerants (such as gasoline, diesel fuel, kerosene, lighter fluid, turpentine, or butane) are used to start a fire, they undergo changes as a result of the intense heat, thus making detection, identification, and analysis problematic (Ottley, 2010, 270).

FORENSIC ANTHROPOLOGY

The burgeoning field of forensic anthropology has also played a growing role in facilitating some criminal investigations; the past two decades have witnessed a significant increase in forensic anthropologists providing evidence for investigations around suspicious deaths.[34] According to Reichs (2007, 455), forensic anthropology is a branch of "applied physical anthropology concerned with the identification of human remains in a legal context." Forensic anthropologists are able to assess age, race, stature, and gender from skeletal remains and formulate opinions around the cause of death in some instances. Put differently, their discipline is known as the study of "non-visually identifiable remains" (Pollanen et al., 2013, 22). A forensic anthropologist may be useful in death investigations in managing crime scenes, building preliminary biological profiles, and accurately identifying the post-mortem interval; however, not all provinces have a fully integrated approach to the use of forensic anthropology in death investigations (Pollanen et al., 2013, 21).

In general, there are significant problems in the field of forensic science, including the failure of forensic scientists to explain the strengths and weaknesses of their data, scientists and other "experts" expressing opinions that exceed their expertise, and a lack of objectivity in testifying (Beecher-Monas, 2007, 102). Forensic-identification sciences, including fingerprint comparisons, as well as the analysis of handwriting, bite marks, voiceprints, tool marks, firearms, tire prints, and shoe prints, have been described as types of "non-science forensic science" which "have little or no basis in actual science" and "neither borrow from established science nor systematically test their hypotheses" (Saks and Faigman, 2008, 150). Furthermore, Saks and Faigman include evidence in arson and explosives cases and aspects of forensic pathology as unreliable, owing to an "irrational reliance on unspecified, unsystematic 'experience' coupled with plausible sounding arguments" (150). They argue that these so-called non-science forensic sciences lack scientific origins, maintain unsupported assumptions, make exaggerated claims, fail to employ the scientific method of hypothesis testing, and are technological failures (168). For them, hair-microscopy analysis and forensic anthropology have also been found to be unreliable.

While the field of forensic science and pseudo-science is burgeoning, this appears to be occurring at the same time that the courts are reticent to hold it up to greater scrutiny. Forensic sciences tend to focus on the ability to individualize, which involves being able to say that some trace evidence was made by a particular source to the exclusion of all other possible sources (Saks and Faigman, 2008, 154). These claims are rarely held up to empirical analysis and lack any hypothesis testing but tend to be accepted without any substantive questioning in the courts. Moreover, a recent and highly significant report by the National Academy of Sciences (National Academy of Sciences, 2009) in the United States further undermined the unreliability of much of these so called forensic sciences and cautioned the courts against their further use. The report identified significant problems in the forensic sciences in the United States to the extent that these disciplines are in need of "serious overhaul," while also noting that forensic DNA analysis was an exception; the protocols for DNA analysis, it stated, "represent a precisely specified, and scientifically justified, series of steps that lead to results with well-characterized confidence limits, and that is the goal for all methods of forensic science" (NAS, 177). While the increase in the types of scientific "proofs" that can be offered to courts is laudable, these developments must be approached with care, since, as with other types of evidence, they are not unassailable (as is commonly believed) and future research may later discredit what is currently accepted as scientifically plausible.

Other Questionable Evidence

HAIR MICROSCOPY

In the past, hair evidence was considered trace evidence[35] and how it was used in courts provoked controversy. Hair-microscopy examination had become an important form of forensic science by the mid-1950s, decades prior to the advent of DNA profiling in the late 1980s. This type of evidence was the generally accepted means of comparing known (K) hairs (from the defendant or the victim) with those found at the crime scene (Q or questioned hairs) (Lucas, 2006). Hair microscopy was used in many cases to establish whether or not specific hair evidence found at a crime scene in fact belonged (or not) to the accused. In its simplest form, the investigation involved examining hairs under a microscope; the examiner could usually identify what racial group (Caucasian, Mongoloid, or Negroid) and where on the body (scalp, pubic, or limbs) they came from (Scheck, Neufeld, and Dwyer, 2000, 162). Unfortunately, this type of science is beset with a number of weaknesses: hairs from the same head may mismatch, there is disagreement among experts about criteria for comparisons, and some hairs are hard to distinguish (Scheck, Neufeld, and Dwyer, 2000). In fact, of the over three hundred and fifty exonerations facilitated thus far through the Innocence Project of the Benjamin Cardozo Law School, 51 per cent relied on improper or invalidated forensic evidence and of that number 24 per cent involved hair evidence.[36]

Today, human hairs can be analysed for mtDNA (mitochondrial DNA), although it is much less discriminating than nDNA (nuclear DNA). Given that the hairs that are most frequently encountered often have no or little nucleated material, they are less amenable to nDNA analysis (Lucas, 2006, 6) and therefore the conclusions drawn from their analysis are less definitive. In fact, many forensic labs in Canada no longer use hair-microscopy comparisons. In those cases when hair is examined at all, it is determined whether or not it is of human or animal origins and if it possesses a root sheath suitable for DNA analysis; the body area of origin is also identified (Lucas, 2006, 24). Microscopic-hair analysis is particularly problematic, since there is scare scientific support for its methodology. The idea is that each hair is unique, but there is little empirical support for this theory (Beecher-Monas, 2007, 114). In the United States, hair analysis by the FBI requires that it be done alongside mitochondria DNA testing.

In recent years, hair-microscopy evidence has come under scrutiny by various provincial governments in Canada. In 2003 the attorney general of Manitoba established a committee to examine errors that resulted from an overreliance on hair-microscopy evidence in homicide cases over a fifteen-year period (Manitoba, 2004, 2005). The Manitoba Forensic Evidence Review Committee was created in part as a response to the wrongful conviction of James Driskell[37] and also, more generally, as a result of growing disquiet with this form of evidence. Because of its somewhat narrow mandate, the committee ultimately reviewed only two cases.[38] DNA samples were obtained from the two convicted men and analysed in an American laboratory; in both instances, the original hair-microscopy comparisons were shown to be wrong. The two cases were referred back to Manitoba Department of Justice for review.

Two other formal reviews have taken place, in the provinces of British Columbia and Ontario, following the same parameters as the Manitoba review (in effect examining cases of homicide and other serious violence where hair microscopy was used in evidence) (Department of Justice, 2011). In British Columbia, the review committee, comprised of retired judges, defence lawyers, police, and crown counsel, was established to examine select cases of homicide, sexual assault, robbery, and other indictable offences from the previous twenty-five years. To be included the case needed to involve hair-microscopy evidence where the accused pleaded not guilty, asserted factual innocence, and had unsuccessful appeals. This committee ultimately reviewed two homicide and two sexual-assault cases but found no evidence that a miscarriage of justice had occurred in any of them (MacFarlane, 2012). In Ontario, the Ontario Criminal Conviction Review Committee, mandated by the Ministry of the Attorney General, undertook a similar review of forensic lab databases and police and prosecution files where hair samples were gathered in murder and manslaughter conviction cases from 1985 to 2000. This review of approximately 146 cases is ongoing.[39] Less formal reviews of this evidence are said to be occurring on an ad hoc basis in other provinces (Department of Justice, 2011). As MacFarlane argues, hair microscopy provides nothing more than an educated guess; its probative value is slight, its prejudicial effect is great, and its use should be restricted to aiding police in investigations and never at trial (2012, 6).

POST-HYPNOTIC EVIDENCE
In the past, it has been the practice of some Canadian courts to accept evidence from witnesses to crimes that was obtained through hypnosis. In David Milgaard's trial for the murder of Gail Miller in 1969, the Crown used post-hypnotic evidence from two adolescent witnesses to help convict him. That testimony was later established to be perjured and procured through misleading means (see chapter 9). More recently, the Supreme Court of Canada ruled by a 6–3 margin, in *R. v. Trochym*,[40] that the long-held practice of admitting evidence obtained from witnesses who have been hypnotized is unreliable. In this case, a key witness, following hypnosis, changed her testimony to fit more closely with the police's timing of the murder; Trochym was then found guilty of killing his girlfriend. While the Court's judgment in *Trochym* rules out using such evidence at trial in the future since it is considered "unscientific," it does allow the police to use hypnosis for investigative purposes.[41]

Robert Baltovich's original conviction for the murder of Elizabeth Bain, which was later set aside, also rested partly on post-hypnotic evidence. Bain disappeared in June 1990; her car was later found containing a quantity of blood indicating she was dead, but her body has never been found. During the search for Bain, the police used the controversial method of "hypnotically enhanced memory" on many of the witnesses they questioned. A largely circumstantial[42] case was made against Baltovich and he was found guilty of second-degree murder in 1992. His appeal that same year challenged the judge's address to the jury and the use of the alleged "hypnotically enhanced memory" testimony of witnesses. On account of inordinate delays and the search for new evidence,[43] Baltovich's appeal was not heard until 2004. At that time, the Court of Appeal set aside his original conviction and ordered a new trial; the judges were not persuaded that an acquittal was appropriate given the existence of other evidence upon which a properly instructed jury could reasonably convict.[44] A new trial was to begin in 2008, but in April of that year the prosecution called no evidence and Baltovich was ultimately acquitted by the jury after a deliberation of fifteen minutes.[45]

FORENSIC PATHOLOGY

Pathology is a branch of science that is concerned with the causes and nature of disease processes (Wecht and Weedn, 2007, 387). At the same time, not all pathologists are capable of discerning cause of death from human remains. Anatomical or clinical pathologists are trained to examine cells, tissues, or organs for evidence of disease, while forensic pathologists are trained in the application of pathology to medical-legal matters (investigating violent, sudden, suspicious, unexplained, unexpected, and medically unattended deaths in order to determine the cause and manner of death – generally through autopsy) (Wecht and Weedn, 2007, 388). Forensic pathologists produce expert reports, provide consultative advice to police, prosecutors, and defence attorneys, and offer testimony in criminal and civil cases (Pollanen et al., 2013, 12). In particular, autopsy evidence[46] presented at criminal trials, with respect to cause and manner of death, has been used to convict individuals for murder – at times mistakenly.

In recent years, controversy about forensic pathology has revolved principally around cases of sudden, unexplained death of apparently healthy babies aged two years or less. The investigation of such cases requires that the pathologist reviews, not only the circumstances occurring immediately prior to the child's death, but also the child's previous medical, family, and social history, including past contact with the social service or justice system regarding issues of abuse and/or neglect. In these instances, pathologists must document emergency and resuscitation efforts (since they may also cause injury), examine the crime scene, conduct post-mortem exams, and analyse laboratory findings. The biggest problems appear to occur when these pathologists are expert witnesses in court; there, difficulties stem from the fact that pathologists' frame of reference is based on their medical opinion, with its attendant criteria for scientific acceptability, whereas lawyers adhere to a standard of legal proof with its differing requirements (Campbell and Walker, 2012). Paediatric forensic pathologists have been referred to as "gatekeepers" because their claims regarding the cause of death will have an effect on how the medical and legal systems deal with child death (Ballenden, Laster, and Lawrence, 1993, 124). Regardless, forensic investigation is an inexact science and there can be dispute among experts regarding cause of death and "cases of sudden infant death ... are often indistinguishable from deaths involving intentional suffocation" (Brookman and Nolan, 2006, 878). As discussed below, the testimony of two then renowned paediatric forensic pathologists as experts at a number of criminal trials in Canada and the United Kingdom illustrate the difficulties with this type of evidence.

SOCIAL-SCIENCE EVIDENCE[47]

While the "hard" sciences, such as biology, chemistry, and physics, have begun to play an increasing role in providing expertise to triers of fact in criminal cases, the more "soft" or social sciences, such as psychology, sociology, and criminology, have also been influential. Social sciences are concerned with issues surrounding human motivation and behaviour. Paciocco (1999) notes that the admission of this type of evidence in Canada began in the 1980s but was formally heralded in 1990 by the decision in *R. v. Lavellée*,[48] where the court rejected the tradition of excluding expert behaviour evidence and admitted evidence that established "battered women syndrome" as a legitimate defence. What is of significance about the use of social-science evidence in courts of law is that most laypersons likely have their own pre-conceived ideas and understandings about human behaviour that in turn can influence decision making (Bala, 2005). In particular, *R. v. D.(D.)*[49] underlines the problems surrounding the admission of this kind of evidence. That case involved the admissibility of expert testimony on delayed disclosure of child sexual abuse, and it was established that ultimately the trial judge[50] has the responsibility to provide the jury with the same information about delayed disclosure that an expert witness would have (Bala, 2005, 285).

In the majority judgment in *R. v. D.(D.)*, Justice Major of the Supreme Court of Canada called for caution in the interpretation and admission of social-science evidence in courts of law, indicating the potential for unfairness towards the accused as well as the possibility that this type of evidence may be confusing or overwhelming to juries (Bala, 2005, 283). Chief Justice McLachlin, in a dissenting opinion, stated: "I see no reason to judge social sciences by a different standard than other sciences."[51] In this instance, the Court accepted that triers of fact, while knowledgeable about human behaviour, might need assistance at times in making decisions in specific cases. For example, in the case of *R. v. Spence*,[52] the Court addressed the issue of social-science evidence relating to race, since the victim was East Indian, the perpetrator African Canadian. The defence wanted to challenge potential jurors for cause in the belief that East Indian jurors would be sympathetic to the victim, which could aggravate or compound racial prejudice against the accused. The trial judge refused, but on appeal the majority of the court set aside the conviction and stated that, if the accused wanted to, he was entitled to include the interracial nature of the crime in questions to the jury. The conviction was restored, however, at the Supreme Court on the grounds that the defence was unable to demonstrate an "air of reality" that racial prejudice would be aggravated in this case.

Many of the cases where social-science evidence may be of some relevance involve accused persons who have ongoing relationships with the complainants through familial and other ties (Bala, 2005). Social-science research has demonstrated that individuals in these circumstances do not always behave according to pre-conceived ideas about what constitutes "normal" behaviour. Thus, when attempting to understand the behaviours and reactions of individuals involved in criminal cases of this nature, it is especially important for expert testimony to enlighten the triers of fact about these matters.

CHARACTER EVIDENCE

The courts are generally reluctant to admit evidence about a defendant's bad character and propensity to commit a particular offence. This is understandable given that character evidence can be extremely subjective and open to differing and contradictory interpretations. Further, in the case of *R. v. Mohan*,[53] discussed in greater detail below, Justice Sopinka provides considerations as to what Canadian courts will allow with respect to evidence of an individual's character. In this case, the

Court decided that the accused is permitted to "adduce evidence as to disposition both in his or her own evidence or by calling witnesses."[54] This evidence regarding character is limited to evidence of the accused's "reputation in the community with respect to the relevant trait or traits." However, with few exceptions, an accused is not permitted to present the evidence of an expert witness that the accused is incapable of committing a particular crime.[55] Where the accused advances evidence of his or her good character, the prosecutor may answer that evidence by presenting details on the accused's previous conviction(s) for other offences.[56]

In the case of *R. v. J. (J.-L.)*,[57] Justice Binnie acknowledged the role of the trial judge as gatekeeper with respect to expert evidence. In this instance, the Court recognized the importance of psychiatric evidence of disposition – when the disposition at issue is "characteristic of a distinctive group." At the same time, the Court established factors to assist in evaluating novel scientific evidence:

1. whether the theory or technique can be tested;
2. whether it has been subjected to peer review and publication;
3. whether there is data on the known or potential rate of error or whether agreed-on standards exist; and
4. whether the theory or technique used has been generally accepted.

Thus, the courts will accept evidence regarding the behaviour, nature, and characteristics of a distinctive group of individuals – with an alleged propensity to commit a specific offence – only when it falls within the narrow confines of a standard profile. In essence, this limits the nature and types of evidence that would be admissible. This case established that novel science with respect to disposition needs to be evaluated individually, for each relevant case.

Generally speaking, the prosecution may not advance evidence of the accused's prior disreputable behaviour where the evidence does not relate directly to the charge under prosecution. There is an exception that allows for similar-fact evidence of bad character to be raised if it is sufficiently similar to the charge for which the defendant is being prosecuted. In limited instances, the prosecution can then advance evidence of the defendant's bad character provided the judge is satisfied that, on a balance of probabilities, the probative value of such evidence outweighs its prejudicial effect.[58] Even where such evidence is introduced, however, the judge must warn the jury about how to assess its value properly.

II. Expert Evidence at Trial

"Expert evidence must be necessary in the sense of assisting the trier of fact by providing special knowledge that the ordinary person would not know. Its purpose is not to substitute the expert for the trier of fact."[59]

Use of Experts in the Courts: Canadian Case Law[60]

In Canadian courts, establishing whether or not an individual can testify as an expert occurs during a *voir dire*, where it is determined (outside of earshot of the jury) if evidence tendered by one side or the other is admissible. It is during the *voir dire* that it must be established if the witness possesses the requisite expertise to offer an opinion in the relevant area (Paciocco and Stuesser, 2015, 216). When giving their opinions at trial, expert witnesses must keep their testimony to within their area of expertise and they must adhere to the rules of evidence. According to Paciocco and Stuesser (2015), there are at least five forms in which that expert evidence can be presented:

- a submission to "train" the trier of fact by providing information to help him or her assess and draw conclusions from the evidence;
- an opinion that is based solely on the expert's own observations;
- an opinion that is based in whole or in part on hearsay or inadmissible information, which may be accompanied by a warning by the judge about the weight to be attributed to the opinion if the facts upon which it is based cannot be supported by evidence;
- an opinion on an inference arising from the facts of the case or relating to evidence that has been presented to the courts; and,
- in cases where the evidence is highly technical, a submission in layman's terms to assist the jury (228–33).

There is a very limited rule allowing laymen to present opinion evidence at trial when it has been determined that there is no other adequate way for them to communicate knowledge that they possess and that is relevant to the case. Expert witnesses, on the other hand, are allowed to provide conclusions about facts within their area of expertise in court. Exceptions are made for expert witnesses in this regard since it is believed that they will provide the triers of fact with more information and expertise on a particular subject to help in decision making (Paciocco and Stuesser, 2015, 196).

The case of *R. v. Mohan*[61] is an important one in Canadian jurisprudence because it established the criteria for the reception of expert-opinion evidence as to character (Delisle et al., 2015). In this case the defendant was a paediatrician who was accused of sexually assaulting four teenaged, female patients. Defence counsel wanted to draw on the expertise of a psychiatrist who would testify to the fact that the type of individual who would have committed such an offence did not fit the profile of the defendant. In this case, the Court established the following four-part test to govern the admissibility of expert testimony:

1. Expert opinion is "necessary": it provides information likely to be outside the experience and general knowledge of a judge, lawyers, or jury.
2. Expert opinion is "relevant": this requires both a finding of logical relevance and a determination that the benefits of the evidence (in terms of materiality, weight, and reliability) outweigh its costs (in terms of the risk that it may be accepted uncritically by the trier, its potential prejudicial effect, and the practical costs associated with its presentation) (Paciocco and Stuesser, 2015, 214).
3. Absence of an exclusionary rule: expert evidence will be inadmissible if it "runs afoul of an exclusionary rule of evidence separate and apart from the opinion rule itself" (*R. v. Mohan*, para. 26).

4. The expert must be properly qualified: An expert must "possess special knowledge and experience going beyond that of the trier of fact" (*R. v. Béland*,[62] para.16).

Thus, in order for expert evidence to be admissible at trial, it must be relevant to the issue being discussed, it must be helpful to the trier of fact, and the judge must establish if the expert is truly an "expert" and determine the reliability and validity of the proposed evidence (Delisle et al., 2015). Furthermore, judges can still exclude expert witnesses following a decision to admit such evidence if the manner in which it is presented causes "the prejudicial effect of the evidence to outweigh its probative value." The expert-opinion evidence rules apply anytime a witness (expert or not) offers observations that require specialized training or experience (Paciocco and Stuesser, 2015, 205).

There are risks involved in placing too much emphasis on expert-witness testimony, as Justice Sopinka warned in *Mohan*: "There is a danger that expert evidence will be misused and will distort the fact-finding process. Dressed up in scientific language which the jury does not easily understand and submitted through a witness of impressive antecedents, this evidence is apt to be accepted by the jury as being virtually infallible and as having more weight than it deserves" (para. 19). The criteria outlined in *Mohan* provide guidelines for admitting such evidence and have established a template for a "case-by-case assessment" (Paciocco, 1999, 321). Furthermore, in Canadian jurisdictions, juries receive a great deal of assistance from the judge when making judgments, far more than in American courts. In *R. v. McIntosh*, the Crown's case relied heavily on eyewitness testimony and the issue at appeal was whether the trial judge erred in refusing to admit expert evidence on the issue of eyewitness identification. The appeal was dismissed and expert-evidence testimony in this case was considered to be within the normal experience of the jury.[63]

A recent opinion by the Ontario Court of Appeal further refined the criteria for assessing the admissibility of expert evidence at trial. In *R. v. Abbey*,[64] a young man who was an alleged associate of a notorious street gang was accused of the murder of a rival gang member. In the weeks following the murder, Abbey had a teardrop tattooed on his cheek, and the prosecution wished to call an expert in sociological research on gangs to testify about gang membership and the significance of the teardrop tattoo. This expert testimony, and that of other gang members, was being presented to bolster the prosecution's case regarding the meaning of a teardrop tattoo within urban street-gang culture more generally (Campbell, 2011, 20). The expert was to testify that the tattoo possibly signified the commission of a murder, among other things. However, the expert evidence was ultimately rejected by the trial judge at a *voir dire* on the grounds that it was not considered reliable and was thought to represent a novel scientific theory; Abbey was ultimately acquitted.

On appeal, speaking for the majority, Justice David H. Doherty underlined the importance of both defining and limiting the scope of an expert's testimony and introduced a more distinct framework for the *Mohan* criteria. This process involves two separate phases. The first requires a decision as to the admissibility of the evidence (as per *Mohan*), and involves asking whether the opinion relates to a subject matter that is the subject of expert opinion, whether the witness is qualified, whether there are any exclusionary rules, and whether the proposed opinion is logically relevant to a material issue.[65] The second step of the *Abbey* test has been referred to as the "gate-keeping" function, whereby a judge must exercise his/her discretion to determine whether the benefits of using the expert witness testimony outweigh its costs. The benefit side of the analysis involves considering its probative value, significance, and reliability; reliability considerations involve not only the subject matter but also the method used by the expert to arrive at the opinion as well as "the expert's expertise and the extent to which the expert is shown to be impartial and objective."[66] The cost side of the analysis involves a consideration of the risks inherent in the admissibility of such evidence, risks related to uncritical acceptance of an alleged "expert" opinion when cloaked with "the expert's impressive credentials, the impenetrable jargon in which the opinion is wrapped and the cross-examiner's inability to expose the opinion's shortcomings [which] may prevent an effective evaluation of the evidence by the jury."[67]

In *Abbey*, the Ontario Court of Appeal found that the trial judge had committed a number of errors with respect to the expert evidence:

> First, he did not properly delineate the nature and scope of Dr. Totten's evidence before addressing its admissibility. Second, in testing the reliability of Dr. Totten's proposed opinion evidence, the trial judge relied almost exclusively on concepts and criteria that were inappropriate to the assessment of the reliability of Dr. Totten's opinion while failing to consider the criteria that were relevant. Third, in examining the methods used by Dr. Totten to enhance the reliability of his opinion, the trial judge imposed too high a standard of reliability, misapprehended parts of Dr. Totten's evidence and considered evidence that was irrelevant to the reliability of the opinion. Fourth, in assessing the reliability of Dr. Totten's opinion, the trial judge went beyond questions of threshold reliability and considered features of Dr. Totten's evidence that should have been left to the jury in their ultimate assessment of that evidence. Fifth, the trial judge erred in holding that because Dr. Totten's opinion had not been peer reviewed, it followed that his opinion was not based on proven facts and could not be admitted into evidence.[68]

The court found that the outright exclusion of this evidence, along with other improperly excluded testimony from other gang members, rendered the verdict unsafe and a new trial was ordered. If such expert testimony had been admitted in a more limited fashion at the trial stage, it could "have provided a context for understanding why an urban street gang member may have a teardrop tattoo transcribed on his cheek, but not necessarily answer the question as to the meaning of the teardrop tattoo on Abbey's cheek at that particular time. The latter question was for the jury to decide, given the totality of the other evidence" (Campbell, 2011, 22).

Given that there are no hard-and-fast rules for deciding admissibility, judges must ascertain whether the *Mohan* criteria are met in each case and it is up to the party who is calling the witness to convince the judge of the merit of the witness's testimony. This allows for a great deal of interpretation to occur, since the question of what a jury would find "necessary" has not been defined by the courts (Bala, 2005). The decision in *Abbey* has now further delineated the process for deciding admissibility and has established that there may be cases where a judge finds for admissibility but, through his/her gatekeeping function, assesses the costs of admissibility as too high and ultimately rejects such evidence. Because the state of scientific evidence, particularly forensic evidence, is continually advancing, expert testimony itself is in a constant state of flux. Moreover, expert testimony ruled relevant for a particular case may not be relevant for another similar case.

Use of Experts in the Courts: American Case Law

A long-held rule around the use of expert testimony in the United States involves the *Frye*[69] (1923) case. Frye was convicted of murder and filed an appeal based on the fact that the courts would not allow the presentation of evidence (specifically the presentation of the results of a polygraph test, which he had passed) that might have had an impact on the outcome of the case. The federal appeals court affirmed the lower court decision not to admit the evidence, since this type of evidence had not gained general acceptance in the field at that time[70] (Kiely, 2006, 40). Thus, this case established that expert testimony as evidence could be admitted only if it had been generally accepted in the scientific community. This rule was superseded in 1993 by *Daubert v. Merrel Dow Pharmaceuticals, Inc*[71] – which has been described as the case where the U.S. Supreme Court took "steps to block junk science" (Scheck, Neufeld, and Dwyer, 2000, 164). It was a complicated case about birth defects that were alleged to have resulted from a drug meant to alleviate morning sickness in pregnant women; the issues at trial revolved around what type of research is deemed acceptable in the relevant scientific community, and to what standard of reliability such research should be held.

Ultimately, the courts decided that experts could be used in criminal trials and their reliability safeguarded through screening by the trial judge, cross-examination, and the presentation of contrary evidence (Delisle et al., 2015). In other words, *Daubert* established a "reliable foundation" test. Furthermore, another American case, the *Khumo Tire Company Ltd v. Patrick Carmichael*,[72] later established that the scientific method is not important for all forms of expertise since not all expert opinions are based on science. Where the expert opinion is not based in scientific explanation, the question that should be asked is "whether experience and research permit the expert to develop a specialized knowledge that is sufficiently reliable to justify placing before the trier of fact" (as found in Paciocco and Stuesser, 2015, 220–1).

In the United States, an interdisciplinary approach to legal scholarship (Headley, 2002) appears to be an acceptable norm in the courts. Expert witness testimony is allowed if such testimony addresses issues that have been rigorously established in the relevant scientific community or has been supported by the specific discipline from which it emerged – scientific or not. While these cases have established a standard of acceptability in terms of these types of evidence, the ability to cross-examine and to present other, likely contradictory evidence allows the prosecution and the defence the opportunity to challenge alleged "scientific" evidence that is inconsistent with their own arguments. While opening the door for heated debate in some cases about the relative merits of specific expert testimony, this also creates the possibility for a conviction to be based (in part) on convincing, and not necessarily valid, expert testimony. Whereas a standard of acceptability is essential, at the same time it allows the party with more access to resources to present expert-witness testimony favourable to their case and, at times, at the expense of the truth.

Discredited Expert Testimony (Canada) – Dr Charles Smith

The many errors made by the former Dr Charles Smith in his analysis of forensic pathological evidence are some of the most egregious in Canadian history. Smith was the chief paediatric pathologist at the Hospital for Sick Children in Toronto, Ontario, for many years and considered a leading expert on paediatric forensic pathology. During that time, he was involved in over forty autopsies of children whose deaths occurred under questionable circumstances. Following questions raised surrounding evidence Smith had presented in some of the more recent cases, in 2005 Ontario's chief coroner ordered a review of forty-five cases in which he had been the chief or consulting pathologist from 1991 to 2002 (one dated back to 1988). The purpose of the review was to establish whether or not Smith's findings on all of the cases he had been involved with could be supported by the facts. The conclusions reached were staggering: the pathologists who reviewed the cases found that the results were questionable in at least twenty of them, of which twelve had resulted in convictions (Goudge, 2008, 4). A common theme that emerged from this initial inquiry was that the consulting team disagreed with Smith's findings around the timing of injuries, many of which included fractures (Office of the Chief Coroner, 2007). More specifically, the panel of forensic pathologists found that in twenty cases Smith had provided an opinion regarding the cause of death that was not "reasonably supported by the materials available for review" (Office of the Chief Coroner, 2007, 4).

The release of the findings from the chief coroner's review resulted in a public outcry and in 2007 the Ontario government established an inquiry[73] into the oversight of Ontario's paediatric forensic pathology system, headed by Justice Stephen Goudge of the Ontario Court of Appeal, who was assisted by an expert medical and scientific panel. The twenty questionable cases became the focus of the inquiry and the Goudge Report was to make recommendations regarding the practice and oversight of paediatric forensic pathology in Ontario, and to restore and enhance public confidence in the system.

The Goudge Report outlined a number of specific errors (2008, 16–19) that appeared consistently across the cases examined. Dr Smith's testimony at trial clearly demonstrated that he did not understand his role as an expert witness, which was to provide evidence as an impartial observer rather than support the Crown's case (Goudge, 2008, 16). Moreover, Smith had no training in paediatric forensic pathology, he was unprepared for complex matters, he overstated his knowledge, he testified outside his own limited area of expertise, and from time to time he would even rely on his personal experience as a parent to bolster his testimony (Campbell and Walker, 2012). The inquiry established that Smith's opinions were at times "speculative, unsubstantiated, and not based on pathology findings" (Goudge, 2008, 18). When testifying, Smith used language that was unscientific and lacked the candour expected and required of an expert witness; at the same time, he made false and misleading statements to the court (Campbell and Walker, 2012). Smith's licence to practice medicine was revoked by the College of Physicians and Surgeons of Ontario in January 2011.[74]

Shortly following the release of the Goudge Report in October 2008, the government of Ontario acted quickly to implement many of its 169 recommendations, the majority of which were aimed at modifying the institutions and practices related to forensic pathology in Ontario (Goudge, 2008, 18). According to the Ministry of Community Safety and Correctional Services, the Coroners Amendment Act, 2009,[75] effectively implemented all the legislative reforms recommended by the Goudge Commission of Inquiry.[76] Such reforms included not only new regulatory structures around death investigations but also a "new register for all forensic pathologists participating in death investigations, a new oversight structure known as the Death Investigation Oversight Council, and a new accountability relationship between the chief forensic pathologist and the chief coroner of Ontario" (Sossin, 2014, 249). A further result has been a new focus on professionalizing the entire field of forensic science, including formal certification of pathologists in forensic pathology and new post-graduate training programs at several Canadian universities (Pollanen et al., 2013). Sossin (2014) describes the impact of the inquiry on policy change in the province of Ontario as "transformative and direct" (244), but a number of other factors may have also played a role, including: the government that called the inquiry was the same one that implemented the changes; the presence of great political will to address the damage done by Charles Smith; and an overall need for and desire to "modernize" the system of death investigation in the province.

The reach of Smith's errors was far and wide; information on sixteen of the controversial cases that were reviewed by Smith are contained in Table 8. The pattern for a number of the cases was the same: an accidental child death occurs, Smith is called into to perform an autopsy or review autopsy results, Smith finds for non-accidental injuries, charges are laid, a plea agreement is struck, the family member accepts a plea as the lesser of two evils, and lives are ruined. The cases of Brant, Kumar, Marquardt, Waudby, and Sherrett-Robinson illustrate this pattern. Richard Brant was convicted of aggravated assault following the 1992 death of his infant son, Dustin, in Belleville, Ontario. While the autopsy indicated he had died from complications associated with pneumonia, Smith concluded that Dustin's death was the result of Shaken Baby Syndrome. Brant was charged with manslaughter, but following a guilty plea to the reduced charge of aggravated assault, he was sentenced to six months in prison. While professing his innocence, Brant felt pressured to accept the plea agreement given that Smith was the leading expert in paediatric forensic pathology at that time. Further, Smith's opinions were considered unassailable and Brant would have faced up to fifteen years in jail if found guilty of manslaughter.[77] Dinesh Kumar's experience was strikingly similar to Brant's. Following the death of his infant son in 1992 in Toronto, Ontario Kumar was charged with second-degree murder. He was pressured to accept a plea agreement of criminal negligence causing the death of his infant son, a case that was largely based on Smith's testimony that the infant had died of Shaken Baby Syndrome. Kumar's conviction was set aside in 2011 by the Ontario Court of Appeal, following the Goudge Commission of Inquiry.[78] Tammy Marquardt was

Table 8. Problematic cases involving former Dr Charles Smith[79]

Name	Victim	Cause and Year of Death	Smith Testimony	Charge	Conviction – Plea Agreement	Outcome	Guilty Plea
Richard Brant	Dustin (infant)	Complications associated with pneumonia (1992)	Shaken Baby Syndrome (SBS)	Manslaughter	Aggravated Assault – 6 months prison	Conviction quashed 2013	Yes
Dinesh Kumar	Gaurov (infant)	Undetermined (1992)	SBS	Second-degree murder	Criminal negligence causing death – 90 days (weekends) jail	Conviction set aside 2011	Yes
Tammy Marquardt	Kenneth – 2 years	Epileptic seizure or natural causes (1993)	Asphyxiation – strangulation or suffocation	Murder	Murder – life sentence (served 14 years)	Conviction set aside 2010	No
Sherry Sherrett-Robinson	Joshua – 4 months	Undetermined (1996)	Asphyxiation	Murder	Infanticide (one year in prison)	Acquittal 2009	No
Brenda Waudby	Jenna – 21 months	Assault (1997)	Chronic child abuse	Second-degree murder	Child abuse	Conviction overturned 2012	Yes
William Mullins-Johnson	Valin – 4 years	Undetermined (1994)	Strangulation and sexual assault	First-degree murder	Murder – (trial) life sentence (served 13 years)	Conviction overturned 2007	No
Louise Reynolds	Sharon – 7 years	Dog bites (1997)	Multiple stab wounds to the head	Second-degree murder	Charges dropped owing to second autopsy	Civil case against Kingston Police settled	No
ONeil Blackett[80]	Tamara – 1 year	(2009)	Asphyxiation due to multiple traumatic injuries	Second-degree murder	Manslaughter – (sentenced to 3.5 years)		Yes
Maria Shepherd	Kasandra 3 years	Natural causes (1991)	Blow to the head	Manslaughter	Manslaughter (sentenced to 2 years)	Conviction overturned 2016	No
William and Mary Colville	Tiffani 3 mths	Undetermined causes (1993)	Asphixia	Manslaughter – aggravated assault and failing to provide the necessities of life	Failing to provide the necessities of life (William – 5 mths custody, Mary – suspended sentence + probation)		Yes

(Continued)

Table 8. Problematic cases involving former Dr Charles Smith (Continued)

Name	Victim	Cause and Year of Death	Smith Testimony	Charge	Conviction – Plea Agreement	Outcome	Guilty Plea
Maureen Laidley	Tyrell 4 years	Accidental head injury (1998)	Non-accidental head injury	Second-degree murder	Charges withdrawn		N/A
Marco Trotta[81]	Paolo 8 mths	SIDS (1993)	Multiple fractures – chronic abuse	Murder	Second-degree murder, aggravated assault, and assault causing bodily harm (life sentence – served 8 years)	Retrial – found guilty of assault causing bodily harm, and manslaughter – (suspended sentence and time served)	No
Anisa Trotta	Paolo 8 mths	SIDS (1993)	Multiple fractures – chronic abuse	Murder	Criminal negligence causing death, failure to provide the necessities of life (5 years – served 3 years)	Retrial – charges stayed	No
Lianne Gagnon-Thibeaut	Nicholas 11 mths	Undetermined or accidental head injury (1995)	Non-accidental blunt force trauma	No charges laid		Another child removed by the Children's Aid Society	N/A
S.M.	Amber 16 mths	Accidental fall (1988)	Severe shaking	Manslaughter	Acquittal		No
Camille Mohamed[82]	Baby M	Unascertained (1992)	Asphixia	Second-degree murder	Manslaughter – 2 mths house arrest, suspended sentence, 3 years probation	Pardon 2006	Yes
Roy Simmons	Tyler 3 mths	(1990)			Manslaughter and incest – jailed for seven years		No

convicted of the murder of her two-year-old son in Scarborough, Ontario, in 1993. The bulk of evidence used to convict Marquardt was Smith's testimony, where he had concluded that the infant had died either of strangulation or of suffocation. Marquardt was released after serving fourteen years of a life sentence; her two other children were seized by the Children's Aid Society and adopted. Expert testimony on appeal could not determine the cause of her son's death but speculated that it may have been due to a seizure brought on by asthma and pneumonia. Marquardt's conviction was set aside in 2010 and a new trial ordered; the Crown ultimately withdrew the charges against her.

Brenda Waudby was convicted of child abuse in 1999, following the 1997 death of her infant daughter in Peterborough, Ontario. Like Kumar and Brant, Waudby was initially charged with a more serious crime – murder – but agreed to a plea deal on child abuse. Waudby accepted the plea in part because she feared losing custody of her other two children.[83] The case against her was based on Smith's testimony that her daughter had suffered from chronic abuse. A youth who had been babysitting her daughter the night of the incident later confessed to having beaten and assaulted the child.[84] Waudby's conviction was overturned in an Ontario Superior Court in 2012.[85] In 1999 Sherry Sherrett-Robinson was convicted of infanticide for the murder of her four-month-old son in Trenton, Ontario. As with Waudby, Kumar, Brant, and Marquardt, the case against Sherrett-Robinson was based largely on Smith's testimony that her son's death was suspicious; she had agreed to the plea deal to avoid a conviction for first-degree murder and served a year in jail. A review of her case resulted in Sherrett-Robinson's acquittal by the Court of Appeal in 2009; while the cause of death of her son remained unascertained, it was likely accidental. Another victim of Charles Smith's discredited testimony, Maria Shepherd, was finally acquitted by the Ontario Court of Appeal in 2016, twenty-five years following the death of her stepdaughter Kasandra. Shepherd spent two years in jail on a manslaughter conviction for the death; while she claimed that she had hit the child with little force, Smith's testimony that she had died from cranio-cerebral trauma convinced the court of her guilt.[86]

In a number of other cases, it appears that, while Smith's initial evidence may have been problematic, there was nonetheless sufficient cause for the charges to be continued. In Oneil Blackett's case, he pled guilty to the death of his stepdaughter, Tamara, as a sign of remorse (according to his lawyer), despite the fact there were a number of concerns with Smith's evidence.[87] Given the sufficiency of evidence in that case, it has not been revisited by the courts. Moreover, in Marco and Anisa Trotta's case, while Smith's problematic testimony may have contributed to their original convictions in 1998 for the 1993 murder of their eight-month-old son, Paolo, there was other copious evidence of a history of horrific and chronic child abuse. Their convictions were quashed by the Supreme Court in 2007, owing to the fact Smith's testimony was discredited though the Goudge Commission of Inquiry. Regardless, there was enough evidence to warrant a retrial, where charges were stayed against Anisa Trotto, while Marco Trotto pled guilty to assault causing bodily harm and was found guilty of manslaughter.[88] He was sentenced to time served and one-year probation. For William and Mary Colville, a second autopsy on their three-month-old daughter, Tiffani, who had died in 1993, showed evidence of overlooked rib fractures. For Smith, these multiple rib fractures were indicative of death by asphyxiation and ultimately charges of manslaughter, aggravated assault, and failing to provide for the necessities of life were laid against both parents. While the court dismissed the first two charges in 1995, guilty pleas were entered for failing to provide the necessities of life: Mary Colville received a suspended sentence and two years' probation and William Colville was sentenced to five months in custody.[89] In Camille Mohamed's case, she gave birth in 1992 and later claimed not to have known she was pregnant. The baby was found dead shortly after birth and Mohamed was charged with second-degree murder; she pled guilty to manslaughter and was given a suspended sentence, probation, and community service. Mohamed was pardoned in 2006.[90]

In three other cases, the legal results of Smith's testimony were less problematic. S.M. was charged with manslaughter for her daughter's death in 1988; what looked like an accidental fall was interpreted as Smith as death through severe shaking. Nonetheless, S.M. was acquitted in 1991.[91] Maureen Laidley's son died through an accidental head injury in 1998. Regardless, Smith's autopsy findings resulted in a charge of second-degree murder; however, three other pathologists refuted Smith's findings and ultimately charges were dropped.[92] For Lianne Gagnon-Thibeault, when her son died from an accidental fall, Smith's testimony of cerebral edema was later refuted by two other expert witnesses. While no criminal charges were actually laid in her case, the Children's Aid Society removed another child from her care.[93] While these three cases did not result in findings of criminal responsibility, the ramifications for the families were likely huge; their grief over the loss of their children was overshadowed by the spectre of being held criminally responsible for their deaths. The enormous emotional, psychological, and financial costs of such experiences are difficult to imagine. The Office of the Attorney General of the province of Ontario has since offered compensation to the victims of Charles Smith's egregious errors. The eligibility amounts range up to $250,000 for those directly involved; children removed from their homes may claim up to $25,000; relatives of the accused may claim $12,500.[94] The actual amounts claimed have not been disclosed. Some argue that these "recognition" payments are not only ungenerous but exploit Smith's victims, who are "weak, and exhausted, and poor" and thus less likely to engage in civil litigation to seek higher settlement amounts.[95]

Two cases in particular illustrate the nature and affect of Smith's ineptitude. For Louise Reynolds, from Kingston, Ontario, evidence Smith presented at a preliminary hearing had been instrumental in bringing charges against her in 1997, when he determined that her seven-year-old daughter, Sharon, had died of multiple stab wounds to the head. Reynolds spent two years in jail awaiting trial on the charge of murder and it was later established through another autopsy undertaken while Reynolds was jailed that, in fact, the "stab wounds" had actually come from dog bites. Smith reviewed the case and changed his original view, concurring that the wounds could have been from a dog. The Crown withdrew its charge against Reynolds in 2001 and she attempted to sue the police and Smith for negligence, bad faith, and misfeasance of public office in the conduct of an autopsy and preparation of a post-mortem report (*Re. Louise Reynolds*).[96] While initially denied, Reynolds appeal was later allowed because the court found that her statement of claim had disclosed a reasonable cause of action for negligence and misfeasance in public office and that her case should be allowed to proceed to trial to enable the court to rule on Dr Smith's immunity claim.[97] Ultimately, Reynolds discontinued the case against the Kingston Police Service, and the balance of the case was settled on terms that are confidential.[98]

Findings from another autopsy performed by Smith resulted in the conviction of William Mullins-Johnson for the first-degree murder of his four-year-old niece, Valin; he was incarcerated for twelve years as a result. Dr Smith's autopsy findings had revealed that Valin had been sexually assaulted and died of strangulation. Mullins-Johnson had long claimed his innocence, but he was released from jail only when it was discovered that Smith had lost particular tissue samples that would have been instrumental in demonstrating that Valin had died from natural causes.[99] On appeal in July 2007, the court found that there was no reliable pathological evidence to support the conclusion that Valin was sexually assaulted or that she died as the result of a crime; Mullins-Johnson's conviction was quashed and an acquittal entered in October 2007.[100] In October 2010 Mullins-Johnson received $4.25 million in compensation as well as an apology from then Attorney General Chris Bentley for his ordeal.[101]

Discredited Expert Testimony (United Kingdom) – Sir Roy Meadow[102]

In the United Kingdom similar controversies occurred around the expert testimony of a once-renowned paediatric forensic pathologist during the 1990s. Professor Sir Roy Meadow was a prominent paediatrician and expert witness at many trials in England and Wales where parents had been accused of murdering their children. In the case of Angela Cannings, Meadow surmised that the death of her three children could only be the result of murder. Prior to her arrest in 1999 for the sudden death of her son and third child Matthew, Cannings had lost a daughter in 1989 and a son in 1991 to what was initially determined to be Sudden Infant Death Syndrome (SIDS), or cot death as it is known in Great Britain. Cannings was found guilty in 2002 and had her conviction quashed by the Court of Appeal in 2003.[103] Her case led the attorney general to review almost three hundred other cases where parents had been convicted of harming or killing their children. Recent research has now been able to find common neurological links amongst children which in fact may have caused SIDS in many cases.[104] Other cases reviewed by Meadows that later were established to have been mistaken include those of Sally Clark (she served three years for killing two of her sons; shortly following her release, she committed suicide); Donna Anthony (she served six years for murder convictions in the case of a son and daughter); and Trupti Patel (she was ultimately cleared in the killing of three of her children). In Clark's case, Sir Meadow provided statistics to indicate that the risk of two infants dying of SIDS in a family by chance were "approximately a chance of 1 in 73 million."[105] His testimony, dressed in scientific language, and his credibility, resulting from over thirty years in the field and countless examples of expert testimony given at trial, ultimately swayed judges and juries as to the veracity of his claims.

The Court of Appeal decision in *Cannings* established that in relation to unexplained infant deaths in the United Kingdom, where the outcome of the trial depends exclusively on a serious disagreement between experts, it will often be unsafe to proceed. A conviction could be unsafe where there was a sudden and unexplained infant death, where there was a dispute between medical experts as to whether the infant had been unlawfully killed, and where there was no extraneous evidence of physical harm (Goldsmith, 2006). The *Cannings* decision influenced a review of infant death cases, led by then attorney general, Lord Goldsmith, into all convictions from the previous ten years of parents convicted of the unlawful killing of an infant or child under age two. Of this examination of almost three hundred cases, twenty-eight appeared to be unsafe and were identified for possible referral to the Court of Appeal or the Criminal Cases Review Commission. What also emerged from this review were a number of other, non-SIDS-related questionable convictions, designated as instances of Shaken Baby Syndrome (SBS) – a triad of injuries thought to constitute evidence of child abuse, now referred to as non-accidental head injury (NAHI). Given the growing medical controversy surrounding the identification of cases of SBS or NAHI – these cases were considered separately by Goldsmith. In the *R. v. Harris*[106] case examining issues of SBS, the court found that such cases needed to be determined on their individual facts. What also emerged from this review were guidelines on the way the prosecution team instructs expert witnesses. These guidelines address issues around the disclosure of material, certification of credibility, competence, and the necessity of limiting expert-opinion evidence to the expert's own specific area of knowledge.[107] Both the Smith and Meadow cases underline the importance of appropriate checks and balances around this type of testimony, the responsibility of defence and Crown counsel to challenge questionable scientific evidence, and the need for certification protocols for scientists.

Discredited Expert Testimony (United States) – Fred S. Zain et al.

Fred Zain was a notorious American forensic investigator whose fraudulent actions led to a number of wrongful convictions (Giannelli, 2010). Zain stands out for his incompetence as a forensic laboratory technician in the states of both West Virginia (1977–89) and Texas (1989–93); he worked as a serologist[108] for years despite having falsified not only his credentials but also numerous test results.[109] A special judge was appointed by the Supreme Court of Appeals of West Virginia in 1993 to investigate allegations that Zain had given false testimony in criminal prosecutions and to decide whether "habeas corpus relief should be granted to prisoners whose convictions were obtained through [the] willful false testimony of Fred S. Zain."[110] Zain's problematic testimony and discrepant results had begun to appear in the 1980s in a number of cases, including *State v. Thomas Sayre*,[111] *State v. Dale S. O'Neil*,[112] *State v. Ronald Bennett*,[113] *State v. Micah D. Truitt*,[114] and *State v. James E. Richardson*.[115] In Justice Thomas Miller's report, he found that Zain intentionally and systematically gave inaccurate, invalid, or false testimony or reports, and that in some cases the misconduct was so egregious that it should be considered newly discovered evidence in any criminal prosecutions in which Zain offered evidence; 134 cases were identified as in need of re-examination.[116] As noted in the inquiry, Zain's misconduct was evident on a massive scale and included:

(1) Overstating the strength of the results; (2) overstating the frequency of genetic matches on individual pieces of evidence; (3) misreporting the frequency of genetic

matches on multiple pieces of evidence; (4) reporting that multiple items had been tested when only a single item had been tested; (5) reporting inconclusive results as conclusive; (6) repeatedly altering laboratory records; (7) grouping results to create the erroneous impression that genetic markers had been obtained from all samples tested; (8) failing to report conflicting results; (9) failing to conduct or to report conducting additional testing to resolve conflicting results; (10) implying a match with a suspect when testing supported only a match with the victim; and (11) reporting scientifically impossible or improbable results [503].

Such errors were not only "the result of systematic practice rather than an occasional inadvertent error" but also reflected a "pro-prosecution" attitude. Additionally, the investigation exposed systemic problems with the operating procedures of the state crime lab, a whitewash by the serology department regarding evidence of Zain's widespread abuse, and prosecutors who turned a blind eye to his misdeeds (Giannelli, 2010, 1314). After he left West Virginia, Zain worked in a laboratory in Texas where he was involved in DNA profiling and testified in at least one death-penalty case. An independent investigation into his work in Texas also demonstrated his incompetence.[117] Zain was later indicted on three counts of perjury in West Virginia and perjury, record tampering, and evidence fabricating in Texas; he died in 2002 prior to a final ruling on many of these charges (Giannelli, 2010).

Another notorious and problematic forensic expert in the United States was Joyce Gilchrist of the Oklahoma City Police Department. Gilchrist worked as a police forensic analyst for over twenty years, testified in hundreds of cases, and helped to send twenty-three people to death row; eleven have since been executed.[118] It later came to light that in a number of cases she had relied on faulty and misleading evidence, fabricated laboratory reports, withheld evidence, and provided improper testimony regarding facts she could not possibly have known.[119] In 2001, following a number of exonerations of cases where Gilchrist had testified from 1980 to 1993, the Oklahoma State Bureau of Investigation conducted a review of over 1,700 cases; of these, 196 were deemed in further need of review.[120] In spite of the fact that the contents of the report remain confidential, the National Registry of Exonerations lists the following exonerees who were all wrongly convicted in part on the basis of to Gilchrist's testimony: Jeffrey Pierce, David Johns Bryson, James Dean, Kathy Gonzalez, Curtis McCarty, Robert Miller, Ada JoAnn Taylor, Debra Sheldon, Joseph White, and Thomas Winslow.[121] While the errors of a number of other police forensic analysts who were involved in wrongful convictions in the United States through flawed forensic analysis and problematic testimony, such as Arnold Melnikoff of the state of Montana crime lab (problematic hair analysis) and Pamela Fish of the Chicago Police Department (false testimony), have surfaced, there are likely hundreds of others whose errors remain undetected or who have never been held accountable.[122]

The above anecdotal evidence demonstrates how problematic such flawed science and subsequent testimony can be, and how it can contribute to wrongful convictions in some cases, but systematic study of known wrongful-conviction cases reveals its greater extent. Garrett and Neufeld found in their study exploring forensic-science testimony of prosecution experts in the trials of 137 known innocent exonerees (who had been exonerated through DNA evidence) that in 82 cases (60 per cent) the forensic analysts provided invalid testimony,[123] whereas in a total of 85 cases, or 63 per cent, either invalid testimony was offered or exculpatory evidence withheld (2009, 14). The errors appeared to occur at two levels: first, the misuse of empirical population data, and second, conclusions regarding the probative value of evidence that were unsupported by empirical data (Garrett and Neufeld, 2009, 9). Most problematic were errors in serology in 100 cases and hair-microscopy analysis in 65 cases, but faulty evidence was also presented for bite-mark, shoe-print, and fingerprint comparisons. Of most concern was that this evidence was not from a handful of analysts but rather from seventy-two forensic analysts employed by fifty-two laboratories or medical practices in twenty-five states. Moreover, Garrett and Neufeld found that such experts were mostly employed exclusively by the prosecution; defence counsel rarely cross-examined prosecution experts or retained their own on account of financial constraints (2009, 11). These numbers are consistent with Garrett's later work (2011), where, in examining the factors that influenced the first 250 Innocence Project DNA exonerations, he found the use of invalid forensic evidence in 61 per cent of the 153 cases where the prosecution called forensic analysts to testify at trial (9). Later data from the Innocence Project indicates a slightly lower percentage: 47 per cent of cases showed invalidated or improper forensic evidence. The National Registry of Exoneration data are also slightly less, with 23 per cent of the cases showing false or misleading forensic evidence; the Canadian data for this project indicate that in 27 per cent of the cases there were instances of mistaken or problematic forensic or expert evidence. While not directly comparable, all of these different data indicate significant problems with this type of evidence and testimony.

Systemic Reform Efforts

In light of a growing number of wrongful-conviction cases, various governmental bodies in the United Kingdom, the United States, and Canada have attempted to regulate some aspects of the forensic sciences and their use by the courts. In the United Kingdom in 2008, the development of the office of the Forensic Science Regulator was appointed to provide independent advice on quality standards to both government and the criminal justice system. While sponsored by the Home Office, the regulator is a public appointee and is involved in identifying and leading in the development of new and improved quality standards, monitoring the standards in place, and providing advice and guidance to service providers.[124] Moreover, in its very detailed Codes of Practice and Conduct[125] for forensic providers and practitioners in the criminal justice system, it established guidelines regarding the use of experts at trial, as well as standards for accreditation and validation of science and expertise. Such a regulatory body may go a long way to addressing some of the glaring difficulties attached to such evidence in the past.

In the United States, one example of reform is seen in the state of Texas, where the Texas Forensic Science Commission was established in 2005 in order to address the matter of criminal courts keeping up to date with changes in forensic sciences. Crime laboratories in that state have been plagued by lost and tainted evidence, poorly conducted tests, and misleading testimony for a number of years. The commission, comprised of prosecutors, defence attorneys, forensic scientists, and legal experts, was set up to oversee and investigate problems in forensic-crime laboratories. Its role is to investigate complaints that allege professional negligence or misconduct by a laboratory, facility, or entity in the state of Texas that would substantially affect the integrity of the results of forensic analysis. Thus, its mandate is to develop a process for reporting professional negligence or misconduct; investigate allegations of professional negligence or misconduct; promote the development of professional standards and training; and recommend legislative improvements.[126] Towards this end, the commission has developed a number of specific committees and panels, as well as publishing a series of reports related to the delivery of forensic-science services.

In Canada, as we have seen, the federal-provincial-territorial Heads of Prosecution Committee Working Group has published two reports that address the problems attached to miscarriages of justice, specifically as they relate to forensic sciences and expert evidence. The first report, in 2005, recommended increased training and education for prosecutors around the proper use, examination, and cross-examination of expert witnesses, as well as training regarding reliance on novel scientific techniques or theories (backed by indicia of reliability and necessity). It also recommended that, on the same subject, governments consider establishing a central repository to catalogue and track case law, newsletters, and articles; the reliability of current techniques; the latest developments and advancements in specific fields of expertise; literature and study guides; directories of organizations of experts; prosecution policie; and teaching aids. Finally, it recommended reminding prosecutors of their disclosure obligations under the Criminal Code (s. 657.3) when tendering expert evidence at trial (2005, vi).

The Working Group's second report, in 2011, once again addressed the problems with forensic evidence and expert testimony. With respect to the recommendations in the 2005 document, the drafters of this report acknowledged that a central repository, while helpful, had not been created. At the same time, however, they expressed the belief that the subcommittee created to draft the report functions as a "conduit for the exchange of this sort of information among the prosecution services and police agencies represented on it" (158). It further recommended the continuation of efforts on several fronts: multidisciplinary legal education[127] among the bar, the judiciary, the scientific community, and the police regarding scientific concepts, developing areas, methods, and techniques; education for prosecutors on how to examine and cross-examine expert witnesses properly; federal government updates to the provinces and territories on these subjects; networking of expert witnesses; case conferences between Crown and defence experts in order to narrow or potentially resolve the scientific issues in a given case; and reciprocal disclosure of expert evidence in advance of the trial (158–9). While not included as a recommendation, the 2011 report also raised the possibility of using a procedure referred to as "hot-tubbing" or the presentation of concurrent evidence (2011, 138). Essentially, this practice from Australian courts and arbitration proceedings involves soliciting the viewpoints of multiple experts at the same time, through a panel. The court or tribunal thus chairs a discussion where the experts can ask questions and seek clarification on the issues. The benefit of this approach is said to be that all participants are thus able to identify key issues and establish common ground to expedite the trial process. It is quite likely, however, that procedural difficulties around presenting concurrent evidence, in terms of admissibility and reliability, would impede such a process in criminal proceedings in Canada.

Given that the majority of forensic-science laboratories in Canada are part of provincial governments, it is worth considering whether the privatization of crime laboratories would help to remedy problems with this evidence. During the commission of inquiry that examined the wrongful conviction of Guy Paul Morin, it was clearly established that scientists from the Centre for Forensic Sciences in Ontario made many grave errors in interpreting and contaminating the evidence used against Morin and the importance of this questionable evidence was overstated. While the CFS made many attempts to address the difficulties outlined in the Morin Inquiry, both before its creation and while it was under way, the idea that the CFS should become an independent agency or Crown corporation attracted much interest. This suggestion was supported by the Criminal Lawyers Association, AIDWYC, and the Canadian Bar Association of Ontario but rejected by the CFS itself and Justice Kaufman. Kaufman (1998c) believed that the relationship between the CFS and the police and prosecution[128] was not responsible for the mistakes made by the Centre in examining and testifying about forensic evidence. He argued that the appearance of impartiality would likely be addressed by the changes the CFS had undertaken in its practices. Yet, though he acknowledged that "independence does not guarantee impartiality" (Dr Tilstone in Kaufman, 1998c, 425), Kaufman ignored the fact that a persistent connection between the CFS and the state, and ultimately the agents of the state (police and prosecution), irrespective of whatever steps the CFS takes to distance itself from its past errors, could override the issue of impartiality. The inherent connections between state agents cannot be erased by cursory changes to process; the larger issue of independence of forensic scientists requires revisiting.[129]

At the same time, the establishment of independent forensic-science laboratories will hardly address all of the difficulties associated with the use of expert testimony. As discussed above, the continual developments in forensic sciences, the courtroom battles between experts for both the prosecution and the defence, and instructions given to juries by judges about the relative weight to be afforded such evidence all influence the nature and extent of the use of forensic evidence at criminal trials. With respect to the influence of forensic evidence on convictions made in error, it is likely that greater recognition and acknowledgment of the tenuous nature of much of this evidence by the courts, by the experts themselves, and by the public at large will likely have an effect in circumscribing the impact of this type of evidence on convictions.

Conclusions

Expert witnesses have always been treated differently than other witnesses before the courts; they are permitted to give their opinion and are not restricted to discussing the "facts" alone (Levine, Wallach, and Levine, 2007). Opinion evidence is in a category of its own and both jurisprudence and developments in the sciences have caused the courts to treat it cautiously. Clearly, the use of expert witnesses and expert testimony in criminal courts has evolved, and continues to evolve;

what is also clear is that there is a growing disbelief in its unassailability and that courts are now recognizing both its limitations and the potential that such testimony has to contribute to miscarriages of justice. Edmond (2002) raises the important concern as to whether the objective use of scientific evidence is ever possible. Whereas in the past such evidence was regarded as providing substantiation of the "truth," as offering incontrovertible scientific fact to a jury, it has now become a battleground for experts, leaving the triers of fact with the unenviable job of deciding whether experts for the defence or for the prosecution are the more credible ones. Such a task is evidence of "the brittle nature of legal extrapolation from scientific fact" (Walker and Stockdale, 1999, 133). This also raises further questions as to whether it is in fact possible to regulate the use of this type of evidence at all.

An important conclusion from the findings of National Academy of Sciences report bears repeating here: a great deal more research regarding the premises and techniques being used in most areas of forensic science is needed in order that such evidence can be properly considered by the courts. What is required is greater scrutiny of the scientific research presented to the courts, scrutiny that allows the courts to understand research methods, materials, procedures, results, and conclusions, in addition to levels of uncertainty; without that, scientific evidence can be at best misleading, and at worse patently false (National Academy of Sciences, 2009, 185–6). More specifically, research is also needed around the most appropriate language to use in expressing the probabilities of results so that they will be not only meaningful but also comprehensible to the legal process (Sangha et al., 2010, 376). Sangha et al. (2010, 378–93) offer a number of recommendations to strengthen the scientific certainty of much of the forensic evidence presented to the courts, including national accreditation, the development of standards and guidelines, proficiency testing, individual certification, and overall increased research funding linked to improvements.

Similarly, the Goudge Inquiry, described earlier, advanced a number of important considerations regarding what experts should *not* do when presenting evidence in courts. Importantly, it acknowledged that experts should avoid advocating for one party, being unprepared, overstating their opinions, providing unscientific or unbiased views, attacking colleagues who possess differing opinions, providing evidence beyond their expertise, and, finally, offering casual, misleading, or speculative opinions (Goudge, 2008, 185–8). What that inquiry ultimately endorsed for the courts was an "evidence-based" approach to the reception of expert testimony at trial, which involves addressing questions of reliability, not only of the theory or technique itself, but also of the use made of it by the expert. In addition, the inquiry advocated unbiased and objective experts who were transparent and able to avoid the temptation of offering extraneous information. Finally, this approach requires experts at trial to articulate clearly their opinions, as well as their reasoning and level of certainty.[130] The extent to which courts have responded to this call remains to be seen.

PART THREE

Responses to Miscarriages of Justice

Chapter Nine

Conventional Remedies through the Courts and Conviction Review

"You don't run a justice system, especially if you are trying to find wrongful convictions, through a politician, and that is what we have at the moment." (James Lockyer[1])

Introduction

A number of remedies exist for those who believe they have been the victim of an erroneous prosecution, a wrongful conviction, and even a wrongful imprisonment. Nevertheless, as will be demonstrated, such matters take an inordinate amount of time, are inaccessible to many, and are often inadequate.

This chapter examines remedies through the courts and conviction review through the federal Department of Justice. Some conventional remedies through the courts include an appeal of a criminal conviction, tort or civil action, and challenging an alleged Charter violation, all of which represent a possible means to address legal errors that may have contributed to a wrongful conviction. At the same time, conviction or ministerial review occurs only after all attempts at appeal have been unsuccessful. Moreover, these reviews must be based on new and significant matters that were not available at trial, and conviction review is often considered a last resort. What becomes apparent is that such remedies are seldom effective in providing a means to having a conviction revisited or overturned.

Conventional Remedies through the Courts[2]

In Canada, once an individual has been convicted of a criminal offence, there is a thirty-day period within which they can appeal their conviction. An appeal can be based on an interpretation of law, fact, or mixed law and fact.[3] Many erroneous convictions can be and are rectified in the second instance through appellate courts. In such cases, errors made in the first instance at trial are addressed by provincial or territorial Court of Appeal judges and remedied through setting aside the original verdict (quashing the conviction) and entering an acquittal or ordering a new trial.[4] However, the process of appeal is neither simple nor straightforward.

The power to appeal a conviction is conferred through section 686(1)(a) of the Criminal Code, which allows a Court of Appeal to set aside a verdict if (i) it is unreasonable or cannot be supported by the evidence; (ii) if it is based on a legal error; or (iii) if there was a miscarriage of justice. Criminal appeals, from the point of view of public policy, represent a contradiction in terms, since they "have the advantage of restoring public confidence in criminal justice by correcting errors while, paradoxically, undermining public confidence by exposing malpractice and errors in the first place" (Malleson, 1994, 156–7). At the same time, there are self-imposed limits to the power to safeguard against wrongful convictions (Furgiuele, 2007, 237–8). Essentially, courts have adopted a restrictive approach in applying this provision and thus some convictions in error will not be overturned through this means. Some would argue that the restrictive approach reflects a crime-control model of justice (Malleson, 1994, 156), whereby courts prefer to err on the side of caution to ensure that the guilty do not go free.

The reticence of appellate courts to overturn trial verdicts has been characterized as creating an "appellate disadvantage," by means of which deference is shown to decisions made by judges and juries in the first instance (Furgiuele, 2007, 242, 244). It is based on the belief that triers of fact (trial judges and juries) are at an advantage because they see and hear witnesses first-hand and arguably are in a better position to assess the evidence (Furgiuele, 2007, 242). Moreover, "while s. 686(1)(a)(i) is meant to guard against wrongful convictions ... the dominance of the concept of appellate disadvantage can work to rob the courts of use of their judgment in pronouncing on the reasonableness of a verdict, thus sending judges scurrying to find other avenues by which they may be able to allow an appeal" (Furgiuele, 2007, 243).

Furgiuele (2007) argues that, in order for the appeal process under section 686 to safeguard against wrongful convictions, appellate courts would need to lessen their adherence to the concept of appellate disadvantage and deference to trial judges and juries, and be more open to question the findings of fact at trial. In the report of his inquiry into the wrongful conviction of Guy Paul Morin, Justice Kaufman cautioned against the tendency to overestimate the advantage of the jury and trial judge and recommended that appellate powers under section 686(1)(a)(i)[5] be expanded in order to be able to set aside a conviction that is unreasonable or unable to be supported by the evidence when there is a "lurking doubt" or "sense of disquiet" about the accused's guilt, although "lurking doubt," in and of itself, is not grounds for an appeal in Canadian courts (Furgiuele, 2007, 273; Kaufman, 1998b, 1178, 1189). This standard is modelled after the British approach to criminal appeals, under which the Court of Appeal may allow an appeal if it has a "lurking doubt"[6] about the guilt of the accused such that the verdict is "unsafe or unsatisfactory"[7] (Furgiuele, 2007, 252). Justice Kaufman stated: "[A] slightly broadened scope for appellate intervention permits the Court to do directly what some judges now do indirectly. It recognizes the most important, though not the exclusive, function of a criminal appellate court: to ensure that no person is convicted of a crime he or she did not commit" (Kaufman, 1998b, 1189–90).

In order to improve the appeal process further, Furgiuele (2007) suggests that appellate disadvantage could be alleviated through video-taping trial proceedings and requiring juries to provide reasons for their verdicts. Video-taping of trial proceedings would provide appellate courts the opportunity to view and assess the physical evidence, to see witness testimony first-hand, and to hear the reasons offered by trial judges for their verdicts. Requiring juries to provide reasons for their verdicts would also allow appellate courts to review their factual findings and decisions made regarding evidence (Furgiuele, 2007, 271–3). Finally, Furgiuele recommends a legislative amendment to section 686(1)(a)(i) to allow appeal courts to set aside a verdict on the basis that it is "unsafe or unsatisfactory," as per the British standard, instead of "unreasonable," which may lower the reluctance of appellate courts to intervene in trial verdicts using the powers granted to them under section 686 (2007, 274). Combined with the establishment of an independent conviction-review body, this type of amendment would better reflect the "intent and purpose of remedying and preventing factual injustices wherever possible" (Howden, 2002, 598).[8]

The cases listed in appendix A illustrate the role of courts of appeal with respect to redressing miscarriages of justice. As Table 9 below indicates, many of these cases were remedied through the various courts of appeal, in a variety of fashions. While the majority seems to involve outright acquittals (twenty-nine, or 41 per cent of all cases), in many cases following an acquittal the court ordered a new trial. In those latter cases a number of other options are available: the accused may be acquitted/convicted on retrial (eight cases, one case respectively), the prosecutor can enter a stay of proceedings (eleven cases), or charges can be dismissed or withdrawn (ten cases). In some more unusual, high-profile cases, the Supreme Court ordered a new trial upon review of the evidence (five cases); in three of those cases the charges were withdrawn, in one case the charges were stayed, and in the last case the Court of Appeal entered an acquittal.

These cases reveal a great deal about the error-correction function of courts of appeal. While a number of the appeals resulted in an acquittal (41 per cent), a larger number also resulted in a referral back to the lower courts for retrial (48 per cent, thirty-three cases), thus indicating that while the appeals judges were satisfied that a particular conviction was unsafe, there was still merit to the charge itself, sufficient for a retrial. In terms of these cases, the most desired outcome – acquittal on retrial –occurred in only eight cases. This outcome is preferred from the perspective of the wrongly convicted since it indicates true innocence – the individual has been found not guilty of the charge by a judge and jury. While a withdrawal of charges (ten at appeals courts, five from the Supreme Court) and stay of proceedings (eleven cases) are also indicative of some measure of blamelessness, they do not go as far as an acquittal. When a Crown's office withdraws charges, it sends a message that there was not enough evidence to proceed, not necessarily that the accused is considered innocent per se. Worse still is a stay of proceedings because it leaves the accused in legal limbo for a year and the Crown can reinstitute charges at any time during that year (cf. Roach, 2006). While most stay-of-proceeding cases resulted in the charges being withdrawn or dropped, this imposes a rather cruel waiting game on an accused who has already spent years attempting to clear his or her name. Moreover, a stay of proceedings has an impact on the future pursuit of civil damages, since the result is not a factual finding of innocence and an accused must continue to prove innocence.

It could thus be argued that, with respect to miscarriages of justice, courts of appeal play a significant role in terms of correcting the errors of the lower courts in some instances. Those cases that are successful on appeal demonstrate that upon review the verdict was found to be unreasonable, or was based on a legal error or was a miscarriage of justice. At the same time, it is impossible to know to what extent the courts fail to address miscarriages of justice in those cases where there is insufficient evidence to appeal and convictions remain safe. While appealing a

Table 9. Wrongful-conviction cases on appeal

Appeal Court – conviction set aside, orders new trial, prosecutor enters a stay of proceedings	Appeal Court – conviction set aside, orders new trial, acquitted on retrial	Appeal Court – conviction set aside, orders new trial, charges dismissed, dropped or withdrawn	Appeal Court – enters an acquittal	Appeal Court – conviction set aside, orders new trial, convicted on retrial on a lesser charge	Supreme Court of Canada – orders new trial, Crown withdraws charges
Beaulieu (AB, 1992–7)	Dalton (NL, 1989–2000)	Kaminski (AB, 1992–2003)	McArthur (AB, 1986–99)	Cain (ON, 1986–2004)	Hay (ON, 2004–14)
Druken (NL, 1995–2000)	Hart (NL, 2007–14)	Nepoose (AB, 1987–92)	Truscott (AB, 1984–6)		Duguay (QC, 1990–2003)[9]
Parsons (NL,1994–98)	Baltovich (ON, 1992–2008)	Bjorge (AB, 1994–2005)	Henry (BC, 1983–2010)		Taillefer (QC, 1990–2006)
Kelly (NT, 2000–1)	Dimitrov (ON, 1999–2005)	Wood (AB, 1990–2005)	Huffman (BC, 1993–5)		Proulx (QC, 1991–2)[10]
Driskell (MB, 1991–2005)	Furmusa (ON, 1990–8)	Robinson (BC, 1994–2003)	Murrin (BC, 1994–2000)		Milgaard (SK, 1970–97)
Unger (MB, 1990–2005)	Leadbeater (ON, 1993–7)	Follard (ON, 1994–9)	Walsh (NB, 1975–2008)		
Mallory (ON, 2000–7)	Plamandon (QC, 1986–2014)[11]	Karthiresu (ON, 1995–2000)	Johnson (NS, 1993–2002)		
Stewart (ON, 2000–7)	Tremblay (QC, 1984–2010)	Marquardt (ON, 1995–2011)	Marshall (NS, 1971–83)		
Trudel (ON, 1996–2007)		McTaggart (ON, 1988–90)	Klyne (MB, 2006–7)		
Sauvé (ON, 1996–2007)		Phillion (ON, 1972–2010)	Sophonow[12] (MB, 1983–99)		
Hinse (QC, 1964–97)[13]			Brant (ON, 1995–2011)		
			Hanemaayer (ON, 1989–2008)		
			Hill (ON, 1996–9)[14]		
			Kumar (ON, 1995–2011)		
			McCullough (ON, 1991–2000)		
			Morin (ON, 1992–5)		
			Mullins-Johnson (ON, 1993–2010)		
			Nelson (ON, 1996–2001)		
			Norris (ON, 1980–91)		
			Sherrett-Robinson (ON, 1996–2009)		
			Staples (ON, 1970–2001)		
			Truscott (ON, 1959–2007)[15]		
			Webber (ON, 2008–11)		
			White (ON, 1995–2010)[16]		
			Anderson (PEI, 2008–9)		
			Cooper (PEI, 2003–5)		
			Dumont (QC, 1992–2001)		
			Pepin (QC, 1987–2002)		
			Shepherd (ON, 1992–2016)		

conviction may not represent a particularly effective remedy to wrongful convictions, some legal scholars believe that the success of the appeals process in certain cases is indicative that the system functions as it should by correcting its own errors (Hickman, 2004; Marshall, 2002). This seems a rather simplistic rendering of the function of the criminal justice system with respect to wrongful convictions. Mechanistically, an appeals court may indeed correct an error made by the lower court; however, from the perspective of the wrongly accused and convicted, the costs (both human and fiscal) of this process are onerous and lengthy with little guarantee of a successful outcome.

Other private-law remedies exist as a means to address wrongful convictions through the civil law, as discussed in chapter 3. Torts that would have some relevance to the wrongly convicted include false imprisonment, malicious prosecution, negligence, and negligent investigations.[17] In spite of the fact that civil litigation remains a possibility to address a wrongful conviction or imprisonment, it is often complicated, protracted, uncertain, and expensive (Kaiser, 1989, 112; Sheehy, 1999). Certainly, it is possible to pursue governments for torts committed by their servants and agents. Yet, while there are statutory prohibitions[18] against Crown immunity from torts in all common law provinces in Canada, Cohen and Smith (1986) note that private law in general and torts in particular are singularly ill-suited to deal with issues that fundamentally concern the nature of the state and the relationship of the individual to the state and the law.

Another remedy potentially available to the wrongly convicted would be to demonstrate that a right or freedom protected by the Canadian Charter of Rights and Freedoms had been violated. Particular rights protected through the Charter that, when ignored or abrogated, could potentially effectuate a wrongful conviction include full disclosure of all relevant evidence, prosecutorial burden of proof beyond a reasonable doubt, the right to make full answer and defence, the right to silence, the right against self-incrimination, the right against unlawful search and seizure, the right against arbitrary detention, the right to be informed of the reasons for detention, the right to trial within a reasonable time, and the overall right to exclude incriminating evidence (Sherrin, 2008). As discussed in chapter 1, Sherrin believes that the actual impact of these rights in terms of protection from a wrongful conviction is negligible. Moreover, as with any civil litigation, proving that such a violation has occurred and seeking appropriate damages would represent quite a challenge. In ordering a remedy for a Charter breach through section 24(1),[19] the court has the power to dismiss a charge, stay the proceedings, quash a search warrant, or exclude evidence. Only recently, in the case of *Ward v. Vancouver (City)*, has the Supreme Court provided direction about the granting of monetary damages as remedy.[20] Courts are cautious in this regard, since it is considered a "new endeavour" (para. 21); they must make pronouncements as to whether damages are an "appropriate and just" remedy and in an amount that is "appropriate and just" (para. 19).

Conviction-Review Process[21]

The power to revisit a conviction at the post-appeal stage has long been part of the Canadian criminal law. The Royal Prerogative of Mercy, part of the Criminal

Code,[22] was the first of such remedies and allows for the granting of pardons. Yet, while the authority to grant pardons has been used in the past to correct judicial errors, that role is now undertaken mainly by criminal appellate courts (Trotter, 2001). The right to conviction review was introduced in Canadian law in 1923 and is procedurally similar to what occurs today. Former section 1022 of the Criminal Code dealt with ministerial review and allowed the minister of justice to order new trials and refer cases or points to the Court of Appeal for its opinion (Department of Justice, 1998a). Since 1968, the Criminal Code has contained an explicit provision (s. 690) that provides for conviction review, undertaken by lawyers appointed by the Department of Justice. Following a long period of ad hoc review, the Criminal Conviction Review Group (CCRG) was formed in 1993, consisting of a group of lawyers working for the Department of Justice whose duty it was to report to the assistant deputy minister of justice. For many years the CCRG reviewed convictions thought to be in error and made recommendations to the minister regarding remedies. But, for a variety of reasons, discussed below, the conviction-review process was considered inadequate and section 690 of the Criminal Code was amended and replaced by sections 696.1–696.6 in 2002.

The opportunity for conviction review is now available to most individuals who have been convicted of an offence under criminal law, including both summary and indictable offences and convictions under the Criminal Code and the Controlled Drugs and Substances Act.[23] Furthermore, conviction review is also available to individuals who have been designated as dangerous or long-term offenders. In all cases a review does not occur until all avenues of appeal have been exhausted (provincial Court of Appeal and, in some cases, the Supreme Court of Canada), and must be based on new and significant information. Recently, the Ontario Court of Appeal in *McArthur v. Ontario* established that "it is the duty of the Minister of Justice to determine whether or not the applicant has exhausted his or her rights of judicial review or appeal with respect to the conviction as a pre-condition to conducting a ministerial review."[24] This decision also ascertained that "s. 696.1 does not require an offender to seek leave to appeal to the Supreme Court of Canada in order for his rights of appeal to have been 'exhausted.'"[25] This case has opened the door for applicants to file directly for review following a provincial Court of Appeal decision, which may in turn expedite the process somewhat.

The conviction review process takes place in four stages[26]:

1. *Preliminary Assessment*. CCRG legal counsel assess the merit of the case and ascertain that all necessary information is present, including trial transcripts, appeal factums, and so on. In order to be accepted for review, new and significant information must be presented that was previously unavailable at trial or appeal and could ostensibly have affected the outcome of the case. The applicant is not required to convince the minister of innocence per se, only that there is a reasonable basis to conclude that a miscarriage of justice likely occurred.
2. *Investigation*. Lawyers examine the extent to which the new information presented in support of an application is reliable or reasonably capable of belief, and relevant or related to guilt or innocence (Department of Justice, 2003, 3).

Each case is unique and thus demands the examination of specific issues during the investigation, which could include:

a. interviewing witnesses;
b. scientific or forensic analysis (DNA testing, polygraph examinations);
c. consultation with police, prosecutors, and defence lawyers involved in the original prosecution or appeal; and
d. obtaining all relevant and/or personal information and documents.

3. *Investigation Report.* The report is made available to the applicant who has the opportunity to view it and make any comments. At this time any further investigation is completed and the report and legal advice from the CCRG lawyers are forwarded to the minister. While the applicant can view the investigation report, he or she is not privy to the advice that the CCRG makes to the minister since solicitor-client privilege is said to apply in this instance.
4. *Decision by the Minister.* Lawyers[27] investigating the case for the CCRG then forward all submissions, the investigation report, and legal advice to the minister of justice. The minister reviews the information and makes a decision whether to dismiss or allow the application. At that time, the minister may refer a specific question to the Court of Appeal for its opinion. If the minister is "satisfied that there is a reasonable basis to conclude that a miscarriage of justice likely occurred" (Criminal Code, s. 696.3), he or she may:

a. order a new trial;
b. order a new hearing in the case of a dangerous or long-term offender; or
c. refer the matter to the Court of Appeal of a province or territory as if it were an appeal by the convicted person or dangerous or long-term offender.

Once a new trial has been ordered, a number of alternative remedies are open to Crown counsel of the province from whence the case emerged. They include the holding of a new trial or the withdrawal of charges and the offering of no evidence by the prosecution, resulting in a not-guilty verdict (Roach, 2006). Further, a stay of proceedings can also be brought forward by the office of the prosecution. As discussed in the inquiry examining the wrongful conviction of James Driskell,[28] the effect of ordering a new trial vacates the conviction, restores the presumption of innocence, and creates a reasonable expectation that there will be public accounting, such as a judicial hearing, in order to resolve the case (LeSage, 2007, 128–9). More problematic is a stay of proceedings under section 579 of the Criminal Code, which "does not result in an adjudication of guilt and … leaves the accused vulnerable to future subsequent prosecution" (Roach, 2006, 1). A stay of proceedings effectively puts the charges on hold and allows the Crown to recommence the proceedings on the same indictment within the year; ultimately, the accused has not cleared his/her name and may still be viewed as guilty by the public.

Therefore, each of these remedies has differing repercussions for the wrongly convicted. It is important to distinguish the relatively inquisitorial function of the conviction-review process from the post-review process in which the courts are engaged; each level of review is bound by differing actors, differing levels of court involvement, and differing procedures.

Statistics

While the number of applications for conviction review received in a given year by the CCRG remains relatively stable, the actual number of applications completed in the same year is small.[29] This is in part due to the complexity of the process, the amount of information needed to assess the merits of an application, and the protracted nature of the investigation.[30] As the table below indicates, many more applications are received in a year than there are decisions and outcomes. Nonetheless, the number of applications received for conviction review in a year is clearly not indicative of the virtual numbers of convictions in error occurring in a jurisdiction.

In terms of applications, it has been noted that, over a thirteen-year period (2002–15), the CCRG received 273 applications, a yearly average of 21 (Leverick et al., 2017). In only 16 cases did the minister find for the likelihood that a miscarriage of justice occurred, which translates into a referral rate of 5.8 per cent. At the same time, of the 16 cases referred back to courts of appeal, most were successful, in that 4 were acquitted and in the other 12 cases a new trial was ordered but in only one of those was a conviction obtained (on a lesser charge). Of the referrals, in five cases the proceedings were stayed by the Crown, one had the charges withdrawn, three cases resulted in an acquittal, and two are still before the courts. While the minister refers only a small number of applicants to the courts of appeal (5.8 per cent), the cases that are referred have a better outcome (93 per cent) (Leverick et al., 2017). It could be argued that, while the bar is very high for cases to be accepted for review by the CCRG, the ones that are ultimately referred result in a positive outcome.

When an application is declined, this indicates that in assessing the merits of a case, legal counsel for the Department of Justice are of the opinion that there is insufficient information available on a case to warrant a review or that the information provided is not convincing enough to demonstrate the existence of a miscarriage of justice.

Criticisms of the Process

The conviction-review process has been criticized[31] over the years for a variety of reasons. These criticisms are of two specific types, those concerning the process itself and those aimed at the role of the minister of justice as the arbiter of conviction review. The first group of criticisms target length of time, costs, secrecy, and inaccessibility. The criticisms that relate to the role of the minister of justice are directed at conflict of interest, difficulties with the adversarial system, and the principle of finality. Final criticisms address the language of the guidelines and the gaps in the 2002 amendments.

Process/Procedural Criticisms

One main criticism of conviction review is that the process is protracted (Braiden and Brockman, 1999; Campbell, 2005). The application process itself is onerous, since individuals must supply all the necessary documentation on their case,

Table 10. Applications to the minister of justice for conviction review[32]

Date	Applications Received	Progress of Applications: Preliminary Assessments	Progress of Applications: Investigations	Ministerial Decisions
1 April 2015–31 March 2016	7 applications (5 completed,[33] 1 partially completed,[34] 1 screened out[35])	6 preliminary assessments, 6 completed	0 completed, 1 under way[36]	0 applications dismissed, 0 granted
1 April 2014–31 March 2015	11 applications (5 completed, 5 partially completed, 1 screened out)	5 preliminary assessments, 5 under way	1 completed, 1 under way	0 applications dismissed, 2 granted
1 April 2013–31 March 2014	13 applications (8 completed, 5 partially completed, 0 screened out)	5 preliminary assessments, 6 under way	1 completed, 0 under way	0 applications dismissed, 0 granted
1 April 2012–31 March 2013	12 applications (3 completed, 5 partially completed, 4 screened out)	9 preliminary assessments, 4 under way	1 completed, 1 under way	1 application dismissed, 0 granted
1 April 2011–31 March 2012	16 applications (11 completed, 1 partially completed, 4 screened out)	11 preliminary assessments, 2 awaiting preliminary assessments	1 proceeding, 1 completed, 1 under way, 11 abandoned	1 application dismissed
1 April 2010–31 March 2011	9 applications (3 completed, 2 partially completed, 4 screened out)	9 preliminary assessments, 4 awaiting preliminary assessments, 2 under way	2 completed, 1 under way, 0 abandoned	1 application dismissed, 0 granted
1 April 2009–31 March 2010[37]	22 applications (7 completed, 6 partially completed, 9 screened out)	10 preliminary assessments, 9 awaiting preliminary assessments, 3 under way	0 completed, 0 abandoned, 8 not proceeding, 2 proceeding, 2 under way	1 application dismissed, 1 granted
1 April 2008–31 March 2009	25 applications (4 completed, 17 partially completed, 4 screened out)	6 preliminary assessments, 10 under way	0 completed 2 under way	0 applications dismissed, 1 granted
1 April 2007–31 March 2008	32 applications (7 completed, 23 partially completed, 2 screened out)	17 preliminary assessments, 3 under way	4 completed, 4 under way	1 application dismissed, 3 granted
1 April 2006–31 March 2007	18 applications (4 completed,14 partially completed, 0 screened out)	8 preliminary assessments,18 under way	3 completed, 7 underway	1 application dismissed, 1 granted
1 April 2005–31 March 2006	39 applications (2 completed, 36 partially completed, 1 screened out)	13 preliminary assessments, 20 under way	2 completed, 11 underway	0 applications dismissed, 1 granted
1 April 2004–31 March 2005	35 applications (7 completed, 26 partially completed, 2 screened out)	13 preliminary assessments, 20 under way	6 completed, 12 underway	1 application dismissed, 5 granted
1 April 2003–31 March 2004	29 applications (2 completed, 23 partially completed, 4 screened out)	10 preliminary assessments, 10 under way	3 completed, 5 under way	6 applications dismissed, 0 granted
1 April 2002–31 March 2003	11 applications (3 completed, 6 partially completed, 2 screened out)	7 preliminary assessments, 8 under way	2 completed 16 under way	0 applications dismissed, 1 granted

including appeal factums and trial transcripts, prior to the start of the investigation. Furthermore, any new evidence must be investigated thoroughly and new witnesses must be questioned. This slow-moving process is exacerbated by the fact that, by the time a conviction review is filed, an individual has exhausted all of his or her appeals, which have already taken a considerable amount of time. According to Boyd and Rossmo, the standard of due process is not addressed in these cases (1994). Two examples, to be discussed in more detail later, clearly illustrate this difficulty: David Milgaard's first request for conviction review received a response after three years, whereas Clayton Johnson's request received a response after three and one half years. The Department of Justice (1998a) justifies the inordinate delays that occur in a conviction review on the grounds that they are simply part of the thorough nature of the process. They also attribute some of the delay to applicants who adjust or supplement their filed documentation with further submissions.

The conviction-review process is costly to the applicant and there is a lack of financial assistance available (Rosen, 1992). Applicants must supply all completed transcripts, appeal factums, and copies of supporting materials, a considerable amount of documentation that in most cases likely involves extensive legal and photocopy costs.[38] Many lawyers represent their clients pro bono when making review applications and it is not uncommon for lawyers working for lobby groups such as AIDWYC/Innocence Canada to submit applications on their client's behalf. Further, some individuals are incarcerated when applying for conviction review, which increases the costs as well as the delays, although imprisoned applicants are given priority.

A great concern with the conviction-review process surrounds how evidence is assembled, reviewed, and evaluated. Specifically, questions concern the types of evidence and documents collected by the minister and the evidentiary burden of proof (Rosen, 1992); there appear to be few established rules of procedure or guidelines regarding this process (Braiden and Brockman, 1999, 24). Furthermore, the language used to describe the process is very broad, as is the discretion of the minister, thus resulting in much discrepancy in interpretation. In recent years, the minister of justice has outlined specific principles[39] meant to guide discretionary powers in cases of conviction review (Department of Justice, 1998a). They include[40]:

1. The remedy applicable under section 690 (now 696.1–696.6) is extraordinary. It is intended to ensure that no miscarriage of justice occurs when all conventional avenues of appeal have been exhausted.
2. The section does not exist to permit the minister to substitute his/her opinion for a jury's verdict or result on appeal.
3. The procedure is not intended to create a fourth level of appeal.
4. Applications should ordinarily be based on new matters of significance that either were not considered by the courts or that occurred or arose after the conventional avenues of appeal had been exhausted.
5. Where the applicant is able to identify such "new matters," the minister will assess them to determine their reliability. The minister will also determine whether matters are reasonably capable of belief, relevant to the issue of guilt, and could reasonably have affected the original verdict.

6. The applicant need not convince the minister of innocence or prove conclusively that a miscarriage of justice has actually occurred, only that there is a basis to conclude that a miscarriage of justice likely occurred.

These guidelines provide little direction for counsel in submitting a review application but rather function more as a codification of the process as it already functions. Additionally, there is no statutory test that dictates what specific remedy should be ordered once the minister is satisfied that a remedy is required (Department of Justice, 1998b).

Once an investigation has begun, there is also a perception that the process itself is inaccessible to interested parties and that it is conducted behind closed doors (Braiden and Brockman, 1999, 23). Defence counsel, applicants, members of Parliament, and advocacy groups are often denied access to information during the investigation, since the recommendations made to the minister by CCRG lawyers are considered protected by solicitor-client privilege. Moreover, as part of the investigation, the investigators need not reveal the nature of the information sought from interviews with legal professionals and witnesses or make the responses public (Boyd and Rossmo, 1994). Since 1994 counsel have been permitted to comment upon the investigation brief that discloses all of the information gathered which will be considered by the minister in reaching a decision. The Department of Justice has addressed the issue of transparency around conviction review in its annual report and argues that privacy protections safeguard the information contained in the brief and appendices from the public (2005a, 15).[41] The applicant can make written submissions with respect to these findings, but such submissions have no legal weight with respect to the minister's final decision.

Criticisms Relating to the Role of the Minister of Justice

The notion of conflict of interest is an inherent part of the conviction-review process. It is the minister of justice as attorney general who is being asked to review his or her own practices, or the practices of his/her provincial counterparts (Braiden and Brockman, 1999, 25). In other words, having the power to grant a remedy in a case where a miscarriage of justice occurred is essentially incompatible with the role of prosecutor. In those rare instances where the minister orders a remedy, a member of the executive branch of government is essentially overruling the judiciary. Rosen (1992) believes that this practice reflects a prosecutorial bias on the part of the Department of Justice, resulting in "deference to judicial determinations of guilt and an insufficiently rigorous questioning of the foundations of criminal convictions" (15–16). The exceedingly low number of remedies granted per year may be reflective of this reticence; for example, in 2005–6, thirty-nine applications were received but only one remedy was granted.

A further criticism, centred on the role of the minister of justice, focuses on the fact that the review process is essentially using the adversarial system to address errors made in the same system (Braiden and Brockman, 1999, 27). In other words, the system is being used to police itself. The Department of Justice clearly delineates what a conviction review is *not* meant to be: it is not another level of appeal or a substitution for a judicial review[42] of a case. Political relationships, individual roles, and the climate of bureaucracy have contributed to the delicate balancing of these issues. At the same time, using the adversarial system to address its own errors limits the possibility of remedies and also the possible remedies. In essence, as the final voice in the conviction review process, the minister of justice is not meant to second-guess decisions rendered by the courts or determine guilt or innocence.

In Canada the principle of finality,[43] embedded in the procedural rules of the court, is founded on the notion that an appellate system should not enable the endless relitigation of the same issues (Criminal Lawyers Association, 2000). Conviction review may therefore undermine the principle of finality, for it "reminds us that the contested events are capable of review and reinterpretation" (Malleson, 1994, 159). It is quite likely that this principle influences, whether directly or indirectly, the conviction-review process. When revisiting a conviction, the minister of justice must question the principle of finality, and in some cases ignore it when considering possible remedies. The principle may prompt appellate courts to take a restrictive approach to interfering with a criminal conviction (Braiden and Brockman, 1999, 21), as well as leading the minister of justice to be reticent when undertaking a conviction review (Kaiser, 1989, 133). On the other hand, it is arguable that appellate review of errors in law and procedure made by trial judges can serve to promote the principle of finality by encouraging the consistent and uniform application of the law, thereby reducing uncertainty and the likelihood of future appeals (Malleson, 1994, 160). In jurisdictions without a final review body, such as Australia, the principle of finality affects the task of correcting wrongful convictions, since the system of appeals alone is limited and current post-appeal mechanisms ineffective (Hamer, 2014). As noted in *Re. Acosta Andres, Azola Blanco and Veliz Garcia*,[44] if errors that occur in the administration of justice are not revisited because of an unwarranted reliance on the principle of finality, then that principle could become "an instrument of injustice."

Other Criticisms

As noted above, the guidelines that established the parameters for the minister of justice in making decisions around conviction review underlined that, above all, such review is considered to be an *extraordinary measure*. Such language establishes precedent not only for how this process is used but also how it is interpreted. Referring to conviction review, and by extension the spectre of miscarriage of justice, as extraordinary, exceptional, and infrequent likely serves to perpetuate myths about the infallibility of the judicial process and creates an unrealistic portrait of the reality. As discussed in chapter 1, the accepted estimate of convictions in error in the United States is .5 to 1 per cent, with a similar projected figure for Canada. To continue to provide an "*extraordinary*" response to a problem that is increasingly considered to be *ordinary* obfuscates reality and allows miscarriages of justice to remain unaddressed.

The guidelines also establish that, in order for a case to be eligible for conviction review, it must be "based on new matters of significance that either was not considered by the courts or that occurred or arose after the conventional avenues of appeal had been exhausted." Information considered by the CCRG is "new" if the courts had not examined it during the original trial or appeal, or if the applicant became aware of it following court proceedings. According to the Department of Justice (2003, 2), information is deemed to be significant if it is reasonably capable of belief, relevant to the issue of guilt, and could have affected the verdict if it had been presented at trial. Furthermore, information that would qualify as both new and significant would do one or more of the following:

1. establish or confirm an alibi;
2. include another person's confession;
3. identify another person at the scene of the crime;
4. provide scientific evidence that points to innocence or another's guilt;
5. prove that important evidence was not disclosed;
6. show that a witness gave false testimony; and
7. substantially contradict testimony at trial.

The assessment of whether information is "new and significant" is similar to the test applied by the courts in determining the admissibility of new or "fresh" evidence on appeal. As established in *R. v. Palmer*,[45] fresh evidence must be relevant and reasonably capable of belief, such that, if taken with the other evidence presented at trial, it could reasonably be expected to have affected the verdict. Conviction review additionally requires the applicant to satisfy the minister that there is a reasonable basis to conclude that a miscarriage of justice likely occurred, based on this new and significant information. The test created by the minister of justice to *get* a court hearing through conviction review is thus considered higher than the test that will be applied *at* a court hearing (Wolch and McLean, 2004, 65).

This raises the question as to whether the bar has been set too high. In some cases, it may not be new information per se that will exonerate an individual, but rather a reinterpretation of old information that is not eligible for consideration under this process. Many erroneous convictions likely cannot reach this threshold and thus go unchallenged. The standard of new and significant information will be of little value to the wrongly convicted individual who was represented by incompetent counsel, unless it can be established that he/she failed to introduce important evidence. Furthermore, erroneous eyewitness identification, which, as discussed in chapter 2, is the most frequent cause of wrongful convictions (Huff, Rattner, and Sagarin, 1986; Kassin et al., 2001; Wells and Olson, 2003), would require much concrete evidentiary and contradictory proof in order to be refuted through this process. Witnesses who unequivocally identify suspects at trial are viewed as inherently believable, in spite of the established unreliability of human memory. Finally, those who falsely confess to committing crimes as a result of aggressive police interrogation tactics (Drizin and Leo, 2004; Leo and Ofshe, 1998) must in turn reinvestigate and eventually solve the crimes for which they have been convicted. A confession, even a false one, goes a very long way to convincing a judge and jury of culpability. Thus, these individuals must fight hard to establish their innocence and the "new and significant information" standard for conviction review creates an enormous burden of proof for them.

Furthermore, as stated in the guidelines above, in order to succeed, an applicant need not convince the minister of innocence nor prove conclusively that a miscarriage of justice has actually occurred, but rather must demonstrate that such a miscarriage *likely* occurred. Upon being satisfied of a likely miscarriage of justice, the minister of justice may order a new trial or refer the matter to the Court of Appeal. Importantly, this notion of the likelihood of occurrence of a miscarriage of justice is not a legislative standard per se but rather a matter of policy governing the exercise of the powers of the minister under section 696.1 of the Criminal Code. Consequently, this "satisfaction" is inherently a subjective matter to which precedent cannot apply. Each case is to be decided on its own merit, with little guidance as to what exactly constitutes "satisfying" proof for the minister.

2002 Amendments

The conviction-review process has gone through some transformations in recent years, the amendements of 2002 being in part an effort to address dissatisfaction with procedural elements. In particular, this dissatisfaction centred on the role of the minister of justice, procedural delays, secrecy, lack of accountability, and prosecutorial bias (Department of Justice, 1998a). At that time, extensive consultations with the provinces occurred and some changes were implemented. According to the Department of Justice, the review process was transformed into the "Reform Model," which in essence represented "a compromise between a separate review body similar to the English model and the status quo of section 690 of the *Criminal Code*" (Department of Justice, 2003). The changes to this section included:

1. guidelines regarding when one is eligible for review;
2. criteria for when a remedy may be granted;
3. expansion of the category of offences for which a review is available to include summary convictions (i.e., more minor offences);
4. authority for investigators to compel the production of documents and the appearance of witnesses;
5. regulations that set out how to apply and govern the review process generally;
6. requirement that the minister of justice submit an annual report to Parliament;
7. a physically separate CCRG, which moved to another building; and
8. a proposal to appoint a special adviser[46] to oversee the review process and provide advice directly to the minister.[47]

The amendments have served to make both the procedures and the criteria for review somewhat more explicit for applicants. The investigative lawyers now have the power to compel witnesses and investigate summary convictions (Canada Gazette, 2002). Given the expense and protracted nature of this process, however, it is unlikely that individuals convicted of summary conviction offences, the least serious of criminal offences, will begin this onerous process in anything other than exceptional circumstances. Most of the other amendments address procedural issues, such as annual reports, eligibility criteria, and so on. One wonders whether the amendments were a genuine attempt by the government to address the gaps and difficulties with the review process or an effort to appease the various groups that lobbied for change by appearing to "do something."

Case Example: David Milgaard

Gail Miller, a twenty-year-old nurse's aide, was sexually assaulted and murdered in Saskatoon, Saskatchewan, in 1969. David Milgaard, sixteen years old, who was considered a drifter and drug user, happened to be in Saskatoon on the day of the murder. Through the coercion of juvenile witnesses by the police, Milgaard become the prime suspect and was ultimately convicted of Miller's murder, receiving a sentence of life imprisonment in 1970. In 1971 Milgaard's appeal was rejected by the Saskatchewan Court of Appeal and his leave to appeal to the Supreme Court of Canada that same year was dismissed. In December 1988 Milgaard's legal team applied for a conviction review based on new evidence. The new evidence indicated that there was a serial rapist in the vicinity during that time and one of the key witnesses implicating Milgaard had later recanted his testimony. In February 1991 the minister of justice denied this application. A second application was made in August 1991 that was almost identical to the first. By then, the Milgaard case had gained prominence in the media and, in reversing her original opinion, the minister of justice directed the Supreme Court[48] to review Milgaard's conviction and consider whether:

(a) the continued conviction of David Milgaard in Saskatoon, Saskatchewan, for the murder of Gail Miller, in the opinion of the Court constitute[s] a miscarriage of justice? and

(b) depending on the answer to the first question, what remedial action under the Criminal Code, if any, is advisable? [*Reference re Milgaard*]

In 1992 the Supreme Court of Canada set aside Milgaard's conviction and ordered a new trial based on the fresh evidence regarding a serial rapist who had not been pursued by the police at that time and the recanted testimony of several of the original witnesses. According to the Court, this evidence was "credible evidence that could reasonably be expected to have affected the verdict of the jury" (*Reference re Milgaard*). The attorney general for the province of Saskatchewan decided not to pursue another trial and stayed the charges against Milgaard. While Milgaard was freed in 1992, after almost twenty-three years in prison, he was not formally acquitted or exonerated until five years later when DNA identification evidence unequivocally proved his innocence and the Saskatchewan government formally apologized to him for his ordeal. In 1999 Milgaard and his family received $10 million, the largest compensation settlement for a case of wrongful conviction at that time in Canada. Milgaard's case is of particular interest when discussing the issue of conviction review since it illustrates how the process initially failed to prove that a miscarriage of justice occurred, in spite of his innocence. It was only after a second review was requested, following much lobbying from Milgaard's family and political advocacy groups, that his case was reconsidered. Larry Fisher was convicted of the rape and murder of Gail Miller in 1999.[49]

Case Example: Clayton Johnson

Clayton Johnson was found guilty of murdering his wife in 1993 and sentenced to life imprisonment. His wife's death in 1989 was initially ruled as an accident, occurring after a fall down the basement stairs, alleged to have occurred shortly after Johnson left for work. Suspicion quickly fell on Johnson because of his involvement with a younger woman following his wife's death and when it was revealed that he had taken out a life-insurance policy on his wife's life six months prior to her death. Pathologists who initially reinvestigated Mrs Johnson's accidental fall declared that her head injuries could have been the result of blows from either a baseball bat or a two-by-four piece of wood. Johnson was convicted at trial based in a large part on questionable evidence from pathologists who had not seen the original police reports and a witness who had changed her initial testimony.[50] Johnson's appeal to the Nova Scotia Court of Appeal was dismissed in 1994, and one year later the Supreme Court of Canada also dismissed his application for leave to appeal.

In March 1998, with the assistance of AIDWYC, Johnson applied for conviction review. The new and significant information to support the review included opinions solicited from twenty-two experts in forensic pathology, engineering, biomechanics, physics, and human postural dynamics, and further evidence that supported the improbability of the alleged crime (Public Prosecution Service, 2002). Moreover, it was established that crucial blood-splatter evidence was not given to experts who testified at the original trial. In September 1998 the minister of justice referred the case back to the Nova Scotia Court of Appeal in order to allow the new forensic evidence to be heard. The minister specifically asked the court:

> In the circumstances of this case, would the information provided by or on behalf of Clayton Norman Johnson or obtained during the review of his section 690 Criminal Code application for the mercy of the Crown be admissible as fresh evidence on appeal to the Court of Appeal? [and]
>
> If the Court of Appeal concludes that the information would be admissible on appeal, the Minister has asked the Court, pursuant to paragraph 690(b) of the Criminal Code, to proceed to hear the case as if it were an appeal by Mr. Johnson.[51]

Johnson was released from prison while awaiting arguments from both the Crown and the defence following the testimony of several pathologists who concluded that Mrs Johnson's death was due to a freak accident that resulted in her fatal head injuries. In 2002, after three and a half years, the Nova Scotia Court of Appeal overturned Johnson's first-degree murder conviction and ordered a new trial. Given that expert witnesses had been found to refute the murder claims and present evidence of accidental death, the Crown decided not to proceed. Johnson's case illustrates how the conviction-review process can work but also demonstrates its flaws: it took three and a half years before a remedy was given – and this only after a lengthy, extensive, and expensive investigation. Johnson later received $2.5 million in compensation for the five years he spent in prison.

Other Considerations regarding Conviction Review

For those individuals who believe they have suffered a miscarriage of justice, the conviction-review process truly represents the last resort for some form of exoneration. With sufficient time, resources, and the introduction of new and significant information pertaining to their case, such individuals can apply for review. Yet, as the numbers indicate, the chances of being granted a remedy are slim. The creation of an independent review commission in Canada, similar to the Criminal Cases Review Commission in the United Kingdom,[52] is therefore worthy of consideration.

The most recent consultation that occurred around the amendments to the conviction-review process in Canada in 2002 involved examining the possibility of establishing an independent review commission, similar to the CCRC. This suggestion was rejected; the provinces were satisfied that the review process should remain in the hands of the federal minister of justice, and the feeling was that the Canadian prosecutorial system was too dissimilar to that of the United Kingdom for such a commission to work in Canada (Canada Gazette, 2002). It has been suggested that calls for change to the current system are premature since there has not been sufficient study of the potential of the ministerial-review process, which would serve the important function of highlighting the substantive similarities and differences between the Canadian process and the independent process in existence that in the United Kingdom. The need for further investigation into the reasons for the low number of applications for review in Canada has also been highlighted, and it has been argued that this may result from a variety of factors, such as the role of the Charter in weeding out cases of abuse of conduct and procedural irregularities, rather than simply being due to a lack of confidence in the ministerial-review scheme (Somji, 2012). Furthermore, the Department of Justice has argued elsewhere that a review mechanism similar to the CCRC would detract from the notion of judicial finality by creating another level of appeal, would be too costly, and would result in many more pro forma requests. Finally, the Department of Justice contends that, as it stands, the review process is considered to be independent from the prosecutions conducted by the provincial attorneys general and thus satisfies the requirement for an independent review mechanism (1998a).

The arguments put forth by the Department of Justice against the establishment of an independent commission are unfounded and rejecting the idea outright appears to be somewhat shortsighted for a number of reasons. Primarily, the CCRG is not, nor will it ever be, independent of the Department of Justice. A truly independent commission would have enhanced credibility within the legal community. Establishing a commission that is at arm's length, both literally and figuratively, from the federal government would create a process outside of the purview of threats of prosecutorial bias and also allow for a more expeditious processing of cases. Moreover, the principle of finality is not meant to be an instrument of injustice; errors made at an earlier point in the process must and should be later acknowledged and rectified. It is indeed true that such a commission would likely result in an increased number of requests, but it is impossible to estimate exactly how many more cases would come forward or be dealt with if an independent commission were established.

The many high-profile cases heard in Canada, the United States, and abroad attest to the fact that a wrongful conviction is no longer an "extraordinary" occurrence. Therefore, it makes sense that measures to address this problem should no longer be out of the ordinary but rather accessible, affordable, and readily available to those who believe they have been wrongly convicted. Furthermore, the onerous nature of the process would likely dissuade those whose cases were questionable to undertake a review. In addition, including input from other experts, such as forensic specialists, psychiatrists, and police, as is evidenced in the record of the United Kingdom's Criminal Cases Review Commission, would strengthen the investigation report and likely result in more convictions being sent back to courts of appeal for reconsideration. Given that the causes of wrongful convictions are multifaceted, the importance of including a number of voices that function outside of the legal realm cannot be overstated. An independent commission that would have greater access to such professionals would likely process cases faster and, in turn, foster greater confidence in its ability to address miscarriages of justice expediently, transparently, and equitably. Investing more resources in an independent commission is far less costly than the millions of dollars regularly spent on commissions of inquiry that investigate the circumstances of individual cases of wrongful convictions (cf. Campbell, 2005).

Conclusions

The ultimate goal for individuals seeking conviction review is exoneration. The hardship and misfortune that accompany a wrongful conviction are difficult to manage at best and untenable at worst. When a conviction review results in an acquittal or the setting aside of a conviction, it does not necessarily constitute exoneration per se. Clearly, the advent of DNA forensic analysis has raised the bar on exonerating those wrongly accused and convicted. It is one of the few tests that can provide true (more or less) exculpatory evidence in some cases. At the same time, it is limited to those cases where physical evidence exists and the unfortunate reality is that wrongful convictions often occur in cases where there is no physical evidence linked to the accused, or even in cases where no crime has actually occurred at all. In the language of conviction review, a preponderance of factors that indicate a miscarriage of justice likely occurred does not constitute exoneration. In order to avoid future miscarriages of justice, perhaps what is needed is a greater awareness of the causes of wrongful conviction for those who contribute to these errors at the earlier stages, namely, police and prosecution. Preventing wrongful convictions from occurring in the first instance, such as at the investigative stage, is far less costly, in both fiscal and human terms, than are the many years involved in attempting to overturn a conviction at a later date.

An overview of the conviction review process in Canada has made clear that the justice system is not in a credible position to review itself. Much can be learned from the United Kindom's experience with the Criminal Cases Review Commission. While not without its own flaws, the system is at arm's length from the home secretary, is responsible for reviewing several hundred cases per year, has been successful in many of the cases sent back to the Court of Appeal, and employs many experts in compiling its investigative briefs.

Individuals who have been wrongly convicted suffer a great deal, psychologically, morally, physically, and financially. So, as Howden notes, "an effective process of conviction review must go beyond mere formal review of applications or fear about lack of finality and concern for preventing misuse of the process to a proactive investigative stance. It should ensure, to the best of human capability, that real possibility of injustice will be uncovered and will occur in as expeditious a manner as possible" (Howden, 2002, 582). As long as the power to determine whether the system fails remains solely in the hands of the lawmakers, the Canadian government will ultimately continue to fail these individuals.

Chapter Ten

Commissions of Inquiry: Lessons Learned

"The inquiry must shine light into dark corners where the public interest in uncovering the truth is more important than preserving private secrets." (Van Harten, 2003, 242)

Introduction

Commissions of inquiry are a distinctive means of addressing wrongful convictions. In general, their focus is to outline the circumstances that have contributed to miscarriages of justice by ascribing blame and providing policy recommendations for change, among other things. Commissions are often chaired by retired judges, are incredibly costly, and generally last months, even years. Their thoroughness is particularly significant with respect to establishing why errors occur and making pointed recommendations for change. At the same time, the implementation of their sometimes sweeping recommendations is somewhat deficient.

This chapter examines the various commissions of inquiry specifically aimed at addressing the causes of several high-profile wrongful convictions in Canada. Early commissions of inquiry that examined the circumstances of wrongful convictions include those involving Donald Marshall, Jr of Nova Scotia, Guy Paul Morin of Ontario, and Thomas Sophonow of Manitoba. More recently, commissions have taken place examining the wrongful convictions of Gregory Parsons, Ronald Dalton, and Randy Druken of Newfoundland, David Milgaard of Saskatchewan, and James Driskell of Manitoba. This chapter discusses all of these cases. It also discusses the Goudge Commission of Inquiry into Pediatric Forensic Pathology, which examined a number of miscarriages of justice in Ontario stemming from the actions of Dr Charles Smith.

Commissions of Inquiry[1]

Commissions of inquiry are generally mandated by provincial governments or the federal government on an ad hoc basis to investigate the circumstances surrounding problems of public concern (Macdonald, 2011). Royal commissions or public inquiries were first established over 150 years ago as a means for the state to conduct independent, non-government-affiliated investigations regarding the conduct of public businesses or the fair administration of justice (Sellar, 1947), and also include consultative committees and risk assessments (Salter, 1990). Each province, as well as the federal government, has passed legislation that enables the establishment of independent inquiries. A public inquiry can be "chartered" to have designated persons (frequently judges) investigate almost any issue of public concern (Scheck and Neufeld, 2002b). Some commissions inquire into and provide recommendations on general issues of public policy, others investigate in the wake of disturbing events or major disasters; while an inquiry may be classified as either advisory or investigative in function, many inquiries do both (Macdonald, 2011). Unlike conviction review, in which any individual can apply to the minister of justice to review his or her conviction, the wrongly convicted cannot demand that a public inquiry be held to investigate the circumstance of his or her case. Rather, a public inquiry is mandated by the provincial or federal government at the behest of the Executive Council, through an order-in-council. In most cases, commissions of inquiry have specific mandates to investigate the circumstances surrounding the administration of justice. The process of a commission of inquiry is far more public than a conviction review, and in most instances extensive lobbying by advocacy groups and unremitting media attention has likely had an impact on whether or not an inquiry is called.[2] While the executive of a government authorizes the commission, decides the terms of reference, chooses the commissioner, and can impose a time limitation, inquiries are inherently independent. Moreover, a public inquiry enjoys the advantage of independence from government, which lends them some credibility, when compared to the public service that is considered an arm of government (Law Reform Commission of Canada, 1977, as found in Stutz, 2008; Witelson, 2003).

The commissioners, who are often retired judges, frequently hold sweeping powers that allow them to engage in a fact-finding mission in order to "uncover the truth."[3] Judges, as heads of inquiries, help to instil confidence in their impartiality and may enhance the prospects that the public will accept the inquiry's findings and recommendations (Stutz, 2008, 504). Their role, through formal hearings, is to outline the errors that led to an injustice, with the aim of preventing similar problems in the future. The Supreme Court of Canada has noted, in the inquiry into the tainted-blood scandal, that the function of a commission of inquiry is threefold: to investigate, educate, and inform society.[4] For example, commissions of inquiry have investigated issues such as the non-medical use of drugs, train accidents, the sinking of an offshore drilling rig, and mysterious infant deaths in a children's hospital.[5] In a sense, the commissions tend to recreate the circumstances surrounding a particular injustice, ascertain the causes of a specific issue or event, ascribe blame, and make recommendations. They generally offer policy recommendations to address the specific problems they have identified.

Media coverage of commissions of inquiry serves to focus public attention on the issues raised. Given that governments are not bound by the policy recommendations stemming from commissions, their function may be solely symbolic. Nonetheless, they are able to reveal larger social, political, and organizational problems (Roach, 1994). Furthermore, according to Justice Cory in the *Blood System* case, there are remedial and restorative merits to the recommendations that emerge from commissions: "A public inquiry before an impartial and independent commissioner which investigates the cause of tragedy and makes recommendations for change can help to prevent a reoccurrence of such tragedies in the future,

Table 11. Public inquiries vs criminal prosecutions

	Public Inquiries	Criminal Prosecutions
Focus:	Inquisitorial	Adversarial
Powers:	Investigative: tailored to address specific issues; prevention/advisory	Apply pre-existing standards to a discrete event in the past; sentencing
Public Participation:	Facilitates public participation; defines public issues in public view	Affected interests may be denied standing
Evidence:	Can collect evidence from many different sources; rules are more permissive	State must prove guilt beyond a reasonable doubt; must follow strict rules of criminal procedure
Outcome:	Policy recommendations: formulate and apply new standards of conduct	Acquittal/finding of guilt (acquittal does not mean that an event could not have been prevented or that the state is not culpable)

and to restore public confidence in the industry or process being reviewed."[6] According to Justice John Gomery, inquiries, if conducted fairly, may serve as a useful form of independent, impartial investigation and policy making (Gomery, 2006, 729).

Given that public inquiries are not criminal prosecutions, individuals who testify at them are not subject to the same rules of evidence and procedure as in a criminal prosecution. Nonetheless, there is some debate over witnesses's constitutional rights with respect to self-incrimination when called to provide testimony at an inquiry (Scott, 1990).[7] Accused persons testifying at public inquiries run the risk of publication of detailed allegations against them, and consequently their right to remain silent may be infringed (Roach, 1994, 415). As Table 11 indicates, criminal prosecutions and public inquiries have similar and at times parallel functions with respect to seeking out the circumstances and ascribing blame regarding an event. But there are also differences, as Roach observes (1994, 420–41). The following summarizes the similarities and differences.

Clearly, the aims, objectives, and results of public inquiries differ from those of criminal prosecutions. While both can establish culpability for wrongdoing, the determinations from inquiries do not entail civil or criminal legal consequences.[8] The ultimate outcome of a commission of inquiry is greater awareness of how an injustice occurred, followed by comprehensive policy recommendations capable of changing criminal justice practice. As stated earlier, the risk is that policy recommendations stemming from an inquiry may have a more symbolic than real value. Conversely, the outcome of a criminal prosecution has a narrower aim – ascertaining guilt or innocence for one particular instance, with little if any effect on larger circumstances that may have influenced the occurrence of the crime. At the same time, the sentence following a conviction also conveys a form of public denunciation of the act in question and reveals the state position regarding particular acts.

While the outcome of an inquiry may not be as immediately discernible as that of a criminal trial, it can establish the accountability of those responsible for the injustice that occurred. Roach identifies the symbolic value of public inquiries with respect to three processes of accountability (1995). Primarily, public inquiries provide a means of exposure and are able to hold individuals accountable through their power to compel witnesses to explain their actions.[9] Furthermore, public inquiries have organizational accountability by "articulating new standards of proper conduct and applying them to past events" (Roach, 1995, 272). In essence, organizations may be held accountable through public condemnation of their behaviour as improper, rather than illegal. Finally, public inquiries can serve to hold society accountable, since they must answer to interest groups and the public in general. This latter form of accountability serves a social purpose by forcing individuals and organizations to respond to public criticisms regarding conduct.

In Canada in recent years, seven[10] commissions of inquiry have addressed the issue of wrongful convictions, examining the roles of the agents in the criminal justice system and how they contributed to these miscarriages of justice. A considerable amount of time, energy, and resources has been devoted to establishing why such wrongful convictions occurred, and how similar errors could be prevented in future criminal investigations and prosecutions. It is beyond the scope of this chapter to examine the many recommendations made and the extent to which they have been implemented by the provinces.[11] At the same time, however, it is useful to examine the larger issues that led to these commissions, the political climate within which they occurred, and the force of their recommendations.

I. Royal Commission on the Donald Marshall, Jr Prosecution

In 1971 Donald Marshall, Jr was convicted of murdering Sandy Seale and sentenced to life imprisonment in the province of Nova Scotia. While Marshall was present during the commission of the murder and was himself wounded in the attack, the police thought his version of events lacked credibility. The police investigative practices in this case were poorly conducted; the crime scene was not cordoned off, nor did the police search the area or question witnesses – all of which resulted in Marshall becoming a target early on in the investigation. Two juvenile witnesses, one on probation and the other considered "unstable," were coerced by the police into providing testimony that corroborated the police version of the events. Lack of disclosure of exculpatory evidence on the part of the Crown, combined with an inadequate standard of professional representation on the part of the defence, as well as judicial errors in law, resulted in Marshall's wrongful conviction and subsequent imprisonment for eleven years. It was later revealed that Marshall, a Mi'kmaq, was also the victim of racism (Wildsmith, 1991). In fact, ten days following Marshall's conviction, another witness came forward, claiming Roy Ebsary to be the real killer. The RCMP followed this lead but, after an incompetent and incomplete investigation, concluded that Marshall was the killer. The new lead in the case was not disclosed to Marshall's defence lawyer or to the Crown counsel in charge of Marshall's appeal. Ebsary was later convicted of manslaughter in the death of Sandy Seale in 1985; he served one year in jail.

The case was reinvestigated in 1982 as a result in part of information about the real killer that Marshall had obtained while he was incarcerated. The police coerced Marshall in the reinvestigation to admit, falsely, that the murder had occurred during the commission of a robbery. The next year, the Court of Appeal, while entering an acquittal, blamed Marshall for his wrongful conviction owing to his admission of the attempted robbery, and found that any miscarriage of justice was "more apparent than real." Unfortunately, these comments had a negative impact on Marshall's negotiations with the Department of the Attorney General for compensation, resulting in an unfairly low monetary award.

In 1986 the Executive Council of Nova Scotia established a royal commission to investigate the circumstances surrounding this case. Justice Alexander T. Hickman, former chief justice of Newfoundland, served as chairperson. The Council charged the Marshall Commission with issuing recommendations to help prevent such tragedies in the future and to review and assess the system of administration of criminal justice in Nova Scotia in the context of this case. The wide-ranging recommendations included:

- establishment of an independent review mechanism to investigate wrongful convictions and constitute judicial inquiries to consider compensation claims;
- improvement of race relations between the criminal justice system and blacks, Mi'kmaq, and other visible minorities in Nova Scotia through policy, affirmative action in law-school admissions and hiring of federal correctional staff, and culture-specific justice initiatives;
- improvement of the administration of criminal justice in Nova Scotia through the creation of a statutory office of director of public prosecutions, guidelines for prosecutorial discretion, and full and timely disclosure of evidence; and
- improvement of police practices by establishing an executive director to oversee aspects of police-community relations, fostering better relations between police and visible minorities, developing policies on racial stereotyping, better training, and video-taping police encounters with vulnerable populations.

Once released, the Marshall Commission report engendered controversy for its critical indictment of the criminal justice system. Moreover, the report went beyond the facts of the Marshall case and the role of individual actors[12] so as to identify the structural causes of convictions in error. In this regard, the report identified racism as contributing to Marshall's wrongful conviction: "The evidence is ... persuasive and the conclusion inescapable that Donald Marshall Jr. was convicted and sent to prison, in part at least, because he was a Native person" (Royal Commission on the Donald Marshall, Jr Prosecution, 1989a, 17). Moreover, the commission established that Marshall received unfair and unjust treatment from the police, Crown, defence, and the judiciary partly because he was impoverished, young, and lacking social influence.[13] Finally, the police were accused of using tunnel vision to target Marshall unfairly by ignoring other evidence that pointed to the contrary, and the prosecution failed to disclose considerable evidence that would have been favourable to the defence.

While many of the recommendations stemming from the commission's report were ultimately implemented and substantial change in the administration of justice occurred as a result (Solicitor General of Nova Scotia, 1992), they did not (and could not) eradicate wrongful convictions in that province. Kaiser advises a healthy scepticism concerning the commission's impact given that the flaws responsible for the injustices visited on Marshall will not disappear overnight (1990, 364). Still, this commission of inquiry held the criminal justice system accountable in a way that the courts never could. Moreover, the Marshall

Commission is considered particularly important historically: "It was only with the Report of the Marshall Royal Commission in 1989 that the potential ineptitude of our criminal justice system was laid bare. *This was the first time in Canadian legal history that a wrongful conviction was ever formally acknowledged by a public institution.* The weaknesses of our system were amply demonstrated in subsequent public inquiries such as this one" (Lamer, 2006; emphasis added).

As discussed, the Marshall Inquiry was significant in exposing how wrongful convictions could result from a lack of disclosure on the part of the Crown attorney and the police. While policy change in the province of Nova Scotia attempted to address this issue, in 1990 it was the landmark ruling of *R. v. Stinchcombe* that established the common law obligation of disclosure on the part of the Crown. Speaking for the majority in *Stinchcombe*, Justice Sopinka made specific reference to the Marshall case: "The right to make full answer and defence is one of the pillars of criminal justice on which we heavily depend to ensure that the innocent are not convicted. Recent events have demonstrated that the erosion of this right due to non-disclosure was an important factor in the conviction and incarceration of an innocent person" (13). Furthermore, the Nova Scotia government reported publicly on implementation of the Marshall Inquiry's recommendations annually for four years following release of its report (with a federal/provincial/Aboriginal forum established to further the recommendations for fifteen years) and prior to that the province had appointed a director of public prosecutions to lead an independent prosecution service (Stutz, 2008, 505). Another implemented recommendation involved changes to the Nova Scotia Human Rights Act[14] to provide for protection from discrimination based on, among other things, Aboriginal origin.

II. The Commission on Proceedings Involving Guy Paul Morin

Christine Jessop, aged nine, went missing on her way home from school in October 1984. Her body was found two months later, over 50 kilometres from where she went missing. Police first charged Guy Paul Morin with her murder in 1985. They initially targeted Morin because he was a neighbour of the Jessops and considered to be an unusual character.[15] He secured an acquittal of this charge in 1986. A new trial was later ordered in 1992, and the court found Morin guilty of first-degree murder and sentenced him to life imprisonment with no possibility for parole for twenty-five years. After serving six months of this sentence, he was released on bail pending his appeal. In 1995 the Ontario Court of Appeal acquitted Morin when DNA evidence demonstrated unequivocally that he could not have murdered Christine Jessop.[16] Senior Crown counsel and the attorney general of Ontario conceded Morin's innocence, apologized, and compensated Morin for his ordeal.

Morin's initial wrongful conviction 1992 was due in part to a number of factors, including faulty forensic science, unprofessional police practices, over-reliance on unreliable jailhouse informants, and a lack of disclosure on the part of the prosecution. In particular, the strength of the forensic evidence was greatly exaggerated by the scientists and its limitations downplayed or ignored. During his second trial, the prosecution relied heavily on hair and fibre findings allegedly indicating physical contact between Jessop and Morin. It was later found that the hair evidence had no probative value in proving Morin's guilt, and that the limitations of the hair comparisons made by the forensic scientists at that time were not communicated to the police or the prosecution at trial. Morin would neither have been arrested nor charged with this crime if such limitations had been known by the police at that time (Kaufman, 1998a, 5). Further, scientists with the Centre of Forensic Sciences had known of the contaminated state of fibre evidence presented at trial and failed to communicate this to the police, prosecution, defence, or the courts. Like the hair evidence, the fibre similarities were not probative in demonstrating direct contact between the victim and the accused. The scientists used misleading language at trial and thereby contributed to further misunderstanding.

Over-reliance on jailhouse informants also contributed to this miscarriage of justice. Two fellow inmates allegedly overhead a confession by Morin to the murder of Jessop, which was later presented as evidence of Morin's guilt. One of the informants was diagnosed as a pathological liar, who recanted his testimony after the second trial and later recanted his recantation (Kaufman, 1998a, 9). The other informant admitted to lying in the past and hearing voices. He made a deal with the police, telling them he would "give them anything they wanted if they got him into a halfway house" (Kaufman, 1998a, 10). Both informants rejected an offer to withdraw from testifying during the second trial. The prosecution later revealed this information to the jury in an effort to enhance the credibility of the informants; had the informants accepted the offer, it would have deprived the Crown of the only direct evidence against Morin and might have resulted in his acquittal (Kaufman, 1998a, 13). Police practices in this case also contributed to Morin's wrongful conviction, since the police failed to preserve evidence at the scene of the crime and to canvas the area during the investigation. Furthermore, the police organization of the investigation was inadequate and there was an over-reliance on the results of the polygraph, as well as on criminal profiling.

As a result of widespread media coverage of Morin's ordeal and his subsequent exoneration, a commission of inquiry into his case was ordered by the lieutenant governor in Council of the province of Ontario in 1996. The commission was mandated to inquire into the conduct of the investigation of the death of Christine Jessop, the conduct of the Centre of Forensic Sciences regarding the maintenance, security, and preservation of forensic evidence, and the criminal proceedings involving the murder charge (Kaufman, 1998c, 5). At the same time, the commission was not mandated to make any conclusions or recommendations with respect to the criminal responsibility of any person. Chaired by Justice Fred Kaufman, a former judge of the Quebec Court of Appeal, the commission had a threefold mandate: 1) to investigate the proceedings that led to Guy Paul Morin's arrest and conviction, 2) to advise regarding recommendations for change to prevent future miscarriages of justice, and 3) to educate members of the community as to the administration of justice (Kaufman, 1998c, 2). The lengthy final report detailed the many errors that affected the outcome of this case as well as offering 119 recommendations for change. The recommendations centred on three general areas: reform of forensic-science practices; restrictions on the use of jailhouse informants; and improvements to investigative practices. Additional recommendations addressed issues such as education for criminal justice professionals around the causes of wrongful convictions; improved police procedures around the collection, use, and limitations of evidence; increased police accountability; and directives regarding the role of the judge with respect to instructions given to the jury and the exercise of judicial discretion.

The commission's report was released in 1998. Evidence offered during the hearings suggests that some reforms were already in place at that time to address the flawed practices that contributed to Morin's wrongful conviction. For example, Dr James Young, assistant deputy solicitor general of Ontario, responsible for the Centre of Forensic Sciences, apologized for its role in the Morin conviction. During the inquiry, he outlined corrective measures undertaken by the CFS in response to the problems identified by the inquiry, including policy guidelines addressing the relationship between the Centre's scientists and prosecutors and the responsibilities of each (Kaufman, 1998c, 8). Also, during the inquiry, the Crown Policy Manual was changed to reflect a new policy on in-custody informers[17] (Kaufman, 1998c, 14). While these are laudable reforms, other recommendations have not yet been implemented. The extent to which they will be depends upon the political will of those who administer criminal justice in Ontario and on the availability of resources. Justice Kaufman stated: "Adequate resourcing can only benefit the public of Ontario in the long term" (1998c, 2). As was the case with the Marshall Inquiry, several of the recommendations presented in the report require a financial commitment on the part of the provincial government in order to be realized. Furthermore, given the evolving state of forensic sciences, and the problems later found with paediatric forensic pathology evidence in the province of Ontario (discussed below), it is clear that the presentation of science in the courtroom remains controversial (cf. Campbell, 2011).

III. The Inquiry regarding Thomas Sophonow

Thomas Sophonow's ordeal began in March 1982 when he was arrested for the murder of Barbara Stoppel in Winnipeg, Manitoba. Stoppel was sixteen years old in December 1981 when she was strangled while working a shift at a donut shop; she died two days later. Sophonow was originally a resident of Vancouver but was visiting Winnipeg at the time of the murder. During the initial investigation of the case, police appeared to have targeted Sophonow as the prime suspect early on. Their tentative identification of Sophonow, which caused him to be pursued as a suspect, arose from an improperly administered photo-pack of suspects. The subsequent police interrogation of Sophonow was not recorded, nor was a written transcript presented to him for his review and comment. In fact, his knowledge of how the shop door (where the murder took place) was locked, which further implicated him in the murder, was transmitted to him via the police during an initial interview. Moreover, the police admitted to playing "mind games" with Sophonow, telling him untruths and half-truths to obtain a confession. The interview itself was traumatizing and devastating to Sophonow, and Justice Cory later advised, during the commission of inquiry, that the "the greatest responsibility for this tragic miscarriage of justice must fall upon the investigating officers" (Cory, 2001). The Crown was also at fault in that it withheld evidence regarding the unreliability of eyewitnesses, which in turn had an impact on Sophonow's conviction.

Sophonow's first trial ended in a mistrial in 1982, and his second trial began in 1983, resulting in a conviction. The Manitoba Court of Appeal ordered a new trial in 1984, based on the grounds that trial judge had not fairly and adequately put the theory of his defence before the jury; this decision was appealed to the Supreme Court of Canada and the Court refused to hear it. Sophonow's third trial in 1985 resulted in another conviction. Subsequently, the Court of Appeal agreed to a new trial because the trial judge, once again, had not fairly and adequately put the theory of Sophonow's defence before the jury. The court then observed that Sophonow had already spent forty-five months in custody and another trial would constitute his fourth. The guilty verdict was set aside and the Crown's appeal of the acquittal was later dismissed by the Supreme Court of Canada.

Concurrent with a reinvestigation of Barbara Stoppel's murder in 2000, whereby another suspect was identified,[18] the provincial government of Manitoba publicly apologized to Sophonow and announced the creation of a commission of inquiry. This inquiry was chaired by retired Chief Justice Cory and mandated to:

- Inquire into the conduct of the investigation of the death of Barbara Stoppel and circumstances surrounding the criminal proceedings commenced against Thomas Sophonow;
- Advise on whether, in the circumstances of the cases, including entry of the final verdict of acquittal by the courts, Thomas Sophonow is entitled to financial compensation because of imprisonment while pending trial, appeals and re-trials for an offence he had not committed, and the basis for entitlement on the facts of the case;
- Make recommendations relating to the current administration of justice (Cory, 2001).

Justice Cory's recommendations, published in 2001, were wide-ranging and comprehensive. They centred on:

- improvements to police procedure during an investigation with respect to interviewing practices, investigation of suspects, and the use of eyewitness identification;
- curtailment of the use of jailhouse informants and directives regarding the disclosure of alibi evidence;
- specific directives regarding enhanced Crown disclosure of evidence and improved Crown relationship with the defence;
- creation of a completely independent entity to review cases where a wrongful conviction is alleged; and
- compensation for Thomas Sophonow.[19]

Even before the commission terminated, Justice Cory noted that the Winnipeg Police Service had taken steps to improve its procedures in many areas. Clearly, the publicity surrounding an inquiry of this nature affects parties implicated in the conviction to the degree that changes are implemented even before its termination. Further, in 2001 the province of Manitoba developed strict guidelines regarding the use of jailhouse informants based on a presumption of inadmissibility, and created an In-Custody Informant Committee that severely circumscribes their use.

*IV. The Lamer Commission of Inquiry Pertaining to the Cases of Ronald Dalton,
Gregory Parsons, Randy Druken*[20]

Newfoundland and Labrador is a relatively small province geographically, with an even smaller population. Incidents of crime, especially violent crime, are rare. For instance, in Newfoundland and Labrador in 2014, there were 6,725 incidents of violent Criminal Code violations, compared to the Canadian rate of over 369,359 incidents.[21] Furthermore, in 2014 there were two homicides in all of Newfoundland and Labrador, while there were 516 homicides in the rest of the country, the majority occurring in Alberta (104) and Ontario (155).[22] Hence, it should not be surprising that a commission of inquiry was called to examine three questionable homicide convictions that occurred in the early 1990s. Chaired by Antonio Lamer, retired chief justice of the Supreme Court of Canada, the inquiry began in 2003. The final report was submitted three years later, in June 2006, and contained a comprehensive set of recommendations, specific to each case. The Lamer Inquiry addressed the wrongful conviction and imprisonment of three individuals. According to its terms of reference, the inquiry was meant to investigate the administration of criminal justice regarding the arrest and prosecution of both Gregory Parsons and Randy Druken, as well as the lengthy delay experienced by Ronald Dalton with respect to the appeal of his conviction.

RONALD DALTON

The terms of reference allowed Justice Lamer to inquire into Dalton's appeal of his murder conviction for the death of his wife, as well as any findings with respect to practices or systemic issues that may have influenced the inordinately slow pace of the appeal.[23] On 15 August 1988 Ronald Dalton's wife, Brenda, choked to death; two days later, he was charged with her murder. In December 1989 Dalton was convicted of second-degree murder with no possibility of parole for ten years; the appeal of his conviction took more than eight years, which Dalton spent in a maximum-security prison. The difficulties in this case are mainly centred on the appeal of Dalton's conviction because he was faced with an inordinate number of delays related to accessing the transcripts of his trial (necessary for the development of appeal factums) and his application for legal aid. While the majority of Dalton's difficulties necessarily stemmed from the errors made on the part of counsel involved in his case and their subsequent actions, it could not have helped his cause that he was incarcerated in New Brunswick for a conviction that occurred in a Newfoundland court.

Dalton began his appeal in 1989 with a lawyer who later declined to continue with the case in 1992. A second lawyer was finally engaged by Dalton in 1995 and he also experienced many delays in preparing his appeal. The result was in part due to a lack of access to documents as well as various conflicts with the Legal Aid Commission regarding the number of hours allotted to this case. Furthermore, counsel made many broken promises to Dalton, as well as exaggerated and misleading representations. It was only in April 1997, eight years following his conviction, that Dalton found another lawyer who was finally able to move his case forward. Dalton's appeal was heard in January 1998 and a new trial was ordered. In June 2000 Dalton was finally acquitted of the murder of his wife.

Following an examination of these issues, Lamer came up with a series of recommendations, many related to legal-aid allocation, as well as resource allocation from the government of Newfoundland and Labrador (Lamer, 2006, 326–7). In particular, recommendations with respect to the Legal Aid Commission addressed the need to:

1. Establish an outreach program to help prisoners complete legal-aid applications, including developing a pamphlet for laypersons;
2. Monitor the progress of files, so services can be delivered more expeditiously;
3. Make counsel aware of all communications between defendants and the commission; and
4. Use the "claw-back"[24] mechanism only in extreme cases.

Lamer also discussed the role that the government of Newfoundland and Labrador could play in preventing future miscarriages of justice by:

1. Committing more resources to address court-transcription delay problems, since transcription should commence immediately upon filing notice of appeal;
2. Addressing Court of Appeal rules to allow the courts to intervene more quickly when a case does not require that much time; and
3. Providing appellate counsel with electronic recording of trial proceedings and limiting transcription.

In response to some of the problems occurring in this case and prior to completion of the Lamer Inquiry report, a new Crown policy was adopted in that province with respect to appeals to the Court of Appeal. In general, these policy changes allowed more time for the supplying of appeal factums, authorized the Crown's office to act on behalf of unrepresented persons with regard to requesting transcripts, and established a dating system to bring matters forward (Lamer, 2006, 52–3). Given the limitations of the terms of reference of this inquiry, Justice Lamer did not rule on whether Ronald Dalton was wrongly convicted for his wife's murder in the first instance. The court later established that Brenda Dalton choked on cereal and in the emergency room an inexperienced doctor pumped oxygen in her stomach in an attempt to resuscitate her. An autopsy performed the next day, conducted by a local pathologist, found a mark on her throat he identified as a sign of strangulation, which in turn led to Dalton's arrest. At his second trial, a number of forensic pathologists testified that the cause of death was choking, not strangulation, and Dalton was subsequently acquitted.

GREGORY PARSONS

The terms of reference of the inquiry instructed Justice Lamer to inquire into the death of Catherine Carroll (Parsons's mother) and the circumstances surrounding the criminal proceedings against Gregory Parsons for her murder. Lamer was further instructed to make any findings with respect to practices or systemic issues that may have contributed to or influenced the investigation and prosecution of Parsons. Catherine Carroll was found murdered in her home on 2 January 1991; eight days later, Gregory Parsons was charged with murder. Carroll had a long history of substance abuse and suffered from extensive psychiatric problems. The police began to focus their investigation on Parsons following incriminating statements made to police, days after her death, by Carroll's lawyer and psychiatrist that she feared Gregory. Given that they had a suspect, the police then made no effort to investigate any other person or discover an alternative explanation for Carroll's death (Lamer, 2006, 79). All the signs of tunnel vision were evident: evidence consistent with guilt was exaggerated, evidence inconsistent with guilt was ignored, irrelevant evidence was treated as supportive of guilt, and investigative practices were skewed in favour of establishing guilt (Lamer, 2006, 79).

A number of other factors influenced the case against Gregory Parsons. For one, after an altercation with Gregory prior to her death, Carroll had applied for a peace bond but had not followed up on it. Subsequent to her death, over two dozen persons came forward claiming that Carroll had informed them that Parsons had threatened and assaulted her. At the same time, there was no direct evidence of these alleged threats or assaults; all the evidence was simply hearsay. In essence, most of the evidence against Parsons was circumstantial, but this did not prevent the police from arresting him on 10 January 1991; he was committed to trial for first-degree murder in July 1992. Parsons was found guilty of second-degree murder of his mother in February 1994, with parole eligibility set at fifteen years.

When Parsons appealed his conviction, it was immediately quashed by the Court of Appeal in 1996, and a new trial ordered. Three basic errors were successfully argued on appeal:

1. The hearsay statements about Carroll's fear of her son's violence were inadmissible and should not have been allowed at trial;
2. An audiotape ("kill tape") containing a song composed by Parsons and some friends that mentions violence and killing should not have been admitted into evidence; and
3. A prejudicial statement made by the prosecution during closing arguments should have warranted a charge from the judge to diminish its adverse effects.

While awaiting the second trial, advances in DNA technology allowed for previously collected evidence from the Carroll crime scene to be tested. By 1998, it was discovered that bodily substances on the trial exhibits contained DNA belonging to another, unknown male[25] and not Gregory Parsons. Subsequently, a stay of proceedings was entered to the charge of murder against Parsons in February 1998 and by November 1998 Parsons was acquitted and received a public apology.

In his extensive review of the evidence around the Parsons case, Lamer cited a number of factors that could be improved with respect to police and Crown practices that contributed to the wrongful conviction in this case (2006, 327–9). Recommendations that relate to the conduct of the Royal Newfoundland Constabulary (RNC) include:

1. Improving note-taking, interviewing, and statement-taking practices by following the recommendations made by Justice Kaufman in the Morin Inquiry;
2. Video-taping all interviews taking place at the police station and audio-taping all field interviews;

3. Establishing policy and protocol to assist officers in obtaining independent expertise; and
4. Developing policy standards with respect to qualifications, training, and criminal investigation for police.

Other recommendations address the role of the director of public prosecutions and include:

1. Establishing a system to ensure evidence in every major case is critically assessed by the Crown attorney;
2. Establishing and maintaining a Crown culture that is sensitive to injustice; and
3. Establishing a policy to allow adequate time to prepare cases and assign junior counsel to facilitate this process; encouraging mentoring.

Furthermore, the inquiry established that the Crown Policy Manual should address when it is appropriate to exercise discretion not to call evidence that is inherently unreliable, and to establish guidelines for appropriate limits of Crown advocacy and for interviewing child witnesses. In addition to directives for chief justices, the recommendations noted the need for the minister of justice to amend the Criminal Code to allow jurors to be interviewed subject to stringent conditions by commissioners conducting inquiries into wrongful convictions, as well as the need for reviewing the threshold for directing a verdict of acquittal.

RANDY DRUKEN

The terms of reference of the inquiry directed Justice Lamer to examine the conduct of the investigation into the death of Brenda Young and the circumstances around the criminal proceedings for murder against Randy Druken. Furthermore, Lamer was meant to report any findings respecting practices or systemic issues that may have contributed to or influenced the investigation and prosecution of Randy Druken.

Brenda Young, an on-and-off girlfriend of Randy Druken, was found murdered in her home in June 1993. Druken was charged in August 1993 and convicted of second-degree murder in March 1995. He received a life sentence of imprisonment with parole eligibility at fourteen years. Druken was an obvious suspect in this crime, for in addition to being on mandatory supervision for a stabbing at the time of the murder, he was a known drug user, had a lengthy criminal record, and had been involved in a tumultuous and previously violent relationship with Brenda Young. In spite of Druken having an alibi for the time of the crime and there being no direct evidence against him, circumstantial evidence was shaped by the police in order to make a case against Druken. In his analysis, Lamer once again pointed to tunnel vision on the part of the RNC in focusing on Randy Druken and not following any other leads, as well as ignoring exculpatory evidence.

Further mistakes made in the investigation of Druken for the murder of Brenda Young included liberties taken in interviewing key witnesses and inter-witness contamination (Lamer, 2006, 180).[26] Equally damaging for Druken was the use of a jailhouse informant, an individual with a history of fraud who had attempted to inform on another case and whose version of the "facts" of this case (allegedly obtained from Druken) was inconsistent. This witness also failed a polygraph test, a factor that was not shared with defence counsel until the trial had begun. Furthermore, in August 1998 this informant sent a statement to the minister of justice indicating that he had been coerced in this case into giving false testimony to the RNC and the Crown prosecutor's office.[27] At the same time, the RNC undertook forensic testing of evidence retained from the crime scene years earlier and it was revealed that another person had been there – Paul Druken[28] – Randy's brother. In June 1999 the Court of Appeal allowed Druken's application for appeal based on the existence of fresh evidence and ordered a new trial. The second investigation into Brenda Young's murder discovered that Paul Druken had been present at the crime scene and that key testimony had been tainted and was unreliable. Given that there was no new evidence implicating Randy Druken, a stay of proceedings on the murder charge was entered in August 2000; a third investigation came up with the same result.

Justice Lamer made a series of recommendations in this case that were similar to those in the Parsons case and related to both police and Crown practices. With respect to the police, several of the recommendations were directed at the practice and use of the polygraph and polygraph evidence; and the modernization of police investigative practices around the use of technologies such as surveillance systems, digital-camera equipment, and computer workstations. Crown policy recommendations addressed the use of jailhouse informants consistent with the recommendations made by Justice Cory in the Sophonow Inquiry, as well as the use of prosecutorial discretion around:

1. Withdrawal of charges when there are no reasonable and/or probable grounds to lay a charge, no probability of a conviction, or when it is not in the public interest to proceed;
2. Use of a stay of proceedings only when there is a reasonable likelihood that proceedings will be recommenced;
3. Commencing a trial and electing to call no evidence and requesting an acquittal when there is no probability of a conviction or reasonable likelihood of recommencement of the proceedings;
4. Calling no further evidence and requesting an acquittal at trial when the Crown determines that the evidence is so unreliable that it would be dangerous to convict;
5. Consulting with the senior Crown attorney where there are doubts as to the proper course of action;
6. When terminating a prosecution, requiring a written report to be filed with the director of public prosecutions and made available to all Crown attorneys; and
7. Expressing in open court the basic reasons for exercising the discretion to withdraw a charge, enter a stay of proceedings, or enter no evidence.

Clearly, the issues of police tunnel vision and Crown culture dominated the Parsons and Druken criminal investigations, and likely had an impact on Dalton's initial trial (which was not part of the Lamer mandate). In these cases, the police focused on the targeted individuals, actively sought witness testimony consistent with their version of the case, and ignored any evidence that provided alternative explanations. Also, the Crown culture that existed in the early 1990s in St John's affected the Crown's over-zealous pursuit of these suspects and its unquestionable acceptance of the police theory of what occurred.

Following the release of the inquiry report, the minister of justice for Newfoundland and Labrador stated that all forty-five of Justice Lamer's recommendations would be implemented. Furthermore, in light of the problems in the police force, the RNC has taken many remedial steps. They include raising standards for training and qualifications, improving evidence-collection methods, and implementing major-case management strategies so that no officer works alone on a case. As for the Crown, after the release of the inquiry's report, the minister of justice appointed retired Newfoundland Supreme Court Judge Williams to carry out an independent review of the office of the director of public prosecutions. To date that has not yet begun.

V. Commission of Inquiry into the Wrongful Conviction of David Milgaard

The commission of inquiry into the wrongful conviction of David Milgaard was a long time coming; Milgaard has been regarded as one of the longest-serving wrongly convicted individuals in Canada.[29] He was initially convicted of murdering Gail Miller on 31 January 1969, when he was sixteen years of age; he ultimately served over twenty-two years in jail for a murder he did not commit. Prior to Milgaard becoming a suspect in this case, the police had been investigating what looked to be the actions of a serial rapist in the area. They focused on Milgaard as a suspect in the Miller case only after an acquaintance, Albert Cadrain, gave inculpatory statements (later refuted by a number of other witnesses) to the police regarding blood seen on Milgaard's clothing on the morning of the murder. Once the police narrowed in on Milgaard as a suspect, the serial-rapist storyline was abandoned. After extensive questioning, interviewing, and reinterviewing, two other adolescent witnesses (Nichol John and Ronald Wilson) changed their stories to mirror the police version of events; one even admitted to witnessing the stabbing. This occurred over a three-day period, whereby several exculpatory statements became inculpatory ones.

Milgaard was arrested in May 1969 and convicted of the murder of Gail Miller in January 1970; his fight to clear his name began immediately. The Saskatchewan Court of Appeal dismissed his appeal in January 1971 and leave to appeal to the Supreme Court of Canada was dismissed in November 1971; Milgaard was denied parole in June 1979. His only option at this point was to apply for a review of his conviction from the minister of justice – a process that was fraught with difficulties for him. Milgaard made his first application for conviction review in 1988 and three years later received a response from the minister of justice that his request was rejected, without explanation. Given that one of the requirements for conviction review is to provide new evidence that had not been previously considered by the courts, Milgaard reapplied for review in August of 1991 once his counsel became aware that Larry Fisher may have murdered Gail Miller and that one of the original witnesses had recanted his testimony. At that time, there was much popular support for Milgaard's innocence and the minister of justice referred Milgaard's case back to the Supreme Court for a hearing in November 1991. In turn, the Supreme Court directed the minister to quash the conviction and ordered a new trial. Rather than go ahead with the trial, by April 1992 the Crown attorney had entered a stay of proceedings. The Government of Saskatchewan did not order a new trial and Milgaard was finally released from jail.

His fight for justice was not over – he remained free but was left in legal limbo regarding his innocence. It was not until July 1997 that DNA technology had become sophisticated and reliable enough to demonstrate that Milgaard had not murdered Gail Miller, and in fact Larry Fisher had. Negotiations for compensation on the part of the Saskatchewan government began immediately and two years later David Milgaard was presented with $10 million, at that time the largest amount ever awarded to an individual wrongly convicted by Canadian courts. Larry Fisher was convicted for Gail Miller's murder in November 1999; his appeal was considered on the merits and the conviction affirmed by the Saskatchewan Court of Appeal in September 2003 and then the Supreme Court of Canada in August 2004. The commission of inquiry promised at the time of the DNA exoneration of Milgaard was delayed until all the legal issues surrounding Fisher's conviction were resolved.

The inquiry was chaired by Justice Edward P. MacCallum of the Alberta Court of Queen's Bench. Its terms of reference were to study the investigation into the death of Gail Miller and the criminal proceedings that resulted in Milgaard's wrongful conviction for her murder for the purpose of making findings and recommendations with respect to the administration of justice in the province of Saskatchewan. Further, the commissioner was meant to determine whether the investigation should have been reopened at an earlier point based on information subsequently received by the police and the Department of Justice. Beginning in April 2004, the commissioner heard from 114 witnesses, over more than 190 hearing days; the previous testimony of 19 others was read into the record. Milgaard himself testified via video. The hearings themselves were not without controversy. Early on, Milgaard expressed the opinion that he did not want to testify at the inquiry since he and his counsel felt the psychological damage inflicted by rehashing his traumatic experiences would prove too difficult. Justice MacCallum came very close to ordering him to attend, under threat of loss of standing and withholding legal aid for his case. Ultimately, a compromise was reached, whereby Milgaard testified via video recording from his home in Vancouver. His mother, Joyce, angrily left the proceedings on one occasion following several procedural rulings that went against her son. She later apologized to MacCallum through her lawyer.

MacCallum's final report concluded that there was no evidence of police misconduct and that the police did not suffer from tunnel vision (2006, 403). While neither Nichol John nor Ron Wilson initially implicated Milgaard, both did after continued questioning. MacCallum stated that there was no evidence of outright coercion; however, given their young ages and the seriousness of the circumstances, both witnesses likely felt pressured to implicate Milgaard. MacCallum indicated that "there is a clear distinction to be made between coercing evidence from a witness in the sense of compelling assent or belief and using persuasive techniques such as repetitive questioning and suggestion" (2006, 401), a fine and difficult line to draw. Moreover, the individual conducting the polygraphs of John and Wilson failed to record the circumstances of the interview or the questions asked, making it impossible to verify the nature of the proceedings. At the same time, MacCallum did not find any evidence of misconduct on the part of the prosecutor, noting that disclosure to the defence "met the standards of the day" (2006, 404). It appears that both the Crown and defence counsel were not aware either of the 1968 sexual assaults that had occurred in the same area or of any possible connection(s) to the Gail Miller murder at the time of the Milgaard's trial. The inquiry found that the Saskatoon police did not share this information, or their suspicion of a possible connection between these sexual assaults and Miller's murder, with the prosecution. Also, the prosecutor exercised his discretion by not disclosing evidence from witnesses who could have supported Milgaard's version of events, but MacCallum described this non-disclosure as "a product of an honest, if mistaken, belief that the evidence was not useful to the defense" (2006, 404).

Justice MacCallum noted a legal error in this case that likely contributed to Milgaard's wrongful conviction. While the Saskatchewan Court of Appeal found that the trial judge had made a procedural error in failing to hold a *voir dire* regarding Nichol John's statements, it ruled that Milgaard suffered no prejudice as a result – a conclusion MacCallum believed was in error (2006, 406). Holding a *voir dire* around this evidence would have likely revealed a number of inconsistencies in the conduct of the interview(s) and the statements made. In any event, MacCallum found that the investigation and prosecution of Larry Fisher (the real killer) for three rapes and one indecent assault committed in Saskatoon in 1968 and 1970 evinced no cover-up, nor was there any evidence that the authorities conspired to deal with Fisher's charges in a manner that would have prevented Milgaard from knowing about them. The Saskatoon police files relating to the Fisher sexual assaults were "apparently lost or destroyed in the course of movement to new premises, or culled" (MacCallum, 2006, 407). MacCallum also noted that Linda Fisher's report to the Saskatoon police in August 1980 expressing her belief that her ex-husband, Larry Fisher, was responsible for Gail Miller's murder should have gone further than it did. This lead could have been followed up and possibly been the basis for an application for conviction review. MacCallum also reviewed a number of other issues related to Milgaard's wrongful conviction, the majority of which he deemed non-probative. At the same time, he concluded that "the criminal justice system failed David Milgaard because his wrongful conviction was not detected and remedied as early as it should have been" (MacCallum, 2006, 410).

MacCallum's recommendations focused on the police, on criminal procedure in homicide cases, and on the issue of wrongful convictions more generally (2006, 413–14). With respect to the police, MacCallum supported mandatory sharing of investigation reports between all police forces assisting in major cases, clearly written agreements between municipal police forces and the RCMP to avoid confusion, mandatory audio-and-video-recording of statements from youth in major cases whether as witnesses or suspects, and referral of every complaint made to the police regarding the safety of a conviction to the director of public prosecutions. On the matter of procedure, MacCallum recommended that in indictable-offence cases exhibits should be scanned and stored electronically and in homicide cases all trial exhibits capable of yielding forensic samples should be preserved for a minimum of ten years; additionally, all prosecution and police files relating to indictable offences should be retained in their original form for a year, then scanned and preserved electronically. MacCallum supported the establishment of dedicated medical services in one or more major centres where autopsies in sudden-death cases are performed by qualified forensic pathologists, as well as the establishment of an independent review agency along the lines of the United Kingdom's Criminal Cases Review Commission to replace ministerial review under the section 696 of the Criminal Code. He also questioned the rather limiting criterion of factual innocence for paying compensation to the wrongly convicted, stated that prosecutors should refrain from unsolicited contact with the National Parole Board, and, finally, recommended informing victims of crime regarding the resolution of their cases.

VI. Commission of Inquiry into Certain Aspects of the Trial and Conviction of James Driskell

James Driskell was co-accused in a criminal investigation into a stolen-car-parts ring and jointly charged with Perry Harder for possession of stolen property. Prior to the preliminary hearing, Harder disappeared; his body was found nine months later in a shallow grave, having been shot three times. Driskell was charged with murdering Harder, his alleged motive being to stop Harder from testifying against him at the trial for theft. James Driskell was convicted in 1991 for murder, largely based on the testimony of two jailhouse informants and forensic-hair evidence found in Driskell's car that was said to have come from the victim. It was later revealed that the informants in this case were compromised. One was paid a large amount of money ($20,000 and other expenses) in exchange for his testimony and granted immunity from arson charges. Latterly, DNA testing that was done on the hair evidence revealed that it could not have belonged to Harder. Furthermore, much exculpatory evidence was not revealed to the defence at the time of the trial. Driskell spent thirteen years in jail until his release on bail in 2003, awaiting conviction review by the minister of justice. His conviction was overturned in 2005, and while the federal government ordered a new trial, the proceedings against Driskell were eventually stayed by the Manitoba Justice Department. The stay was allowed to lapse following the one-year expiry term and the case was never returned to court for a determination of the final status of the prosecution (LeSage, 2007, 145).

The Driskell Inquiry began in July 2006 and was headed by Justice Patrick LeSage, a former chief justice of the Ontario Superior Court; the report was released in February 2007. The mandate of this inquiry was rather unusual and included an examination of:

1. The conduct of Crown Counsel, considering whether it fell below professional and ethical standards expected of prosecutors at that time;
2. Whether the Winnipeg police failed to disclose material information to the Crown at any time and if it contributed to a likely miscarriage of justice;
3. Whether the conduct of the Crown or the police should be referred to an appropriate body for further review or investigation;
4. The role of the RCMP laboratory;
5. Whether any aspect of this case should be further studied, reviewed, or investigated and if so, by whom;

6. Whether and in what way a determination or declaration of wrongful conviction can be made in cases like this;
7. Systemic recommendations arising out of the facts of the case that the Commissioner considers appropriate.

The powers granted to Justice LeSage were far-reaching. His extensive review of the case revealed a variety of problems with respect to the investigation and trial of James Driskell. The main one was a failure to disclose information to Driskell's defence regarding the backgrounds of and deals made with two questionable informants, who became central to the case against him. Both the police and Crown's office failed in their professional duty to disclose information about the motives behind the informants' testimony. Given that the case rested heavily on informant evidence, if defence counsel, judge, and jury had been aware of the inconsistencies in that testimony[30] at trial, it is highly unlikely that a guilty verdict would have been returned. The Inquiry also revealed that the chief of police for Winnipeg, Jack Ewatski, conducted an internal investigation into the Driskell case in 1993, partly in response to media reports that a witness had recanted his testimony. While Ewatski's report confirmed allegations of witness impropriety, he nevertheless concluded there was no evidence to indicate Driskell was not guilty and withheld the report until ordered by a judge in 2003 to release it.[31] Equally damning was the analysis of hair evidence found in a van belonging to Driskell which scientists from the RCMP laboratory in Winnipeg testified at trial to be microscopically "consistent" with the known hairs from the body of the deceased. In the early 1990s hair-microscopy analysis was a routine forensic procedure, but it is now known for its imprecision and microscopy errors have been responsible for a number of wrongful convictions. Human hair can currently be analysed for mitochondrial DNA, which has a much greater accuracy of identification. LeSage also found that the RCMP lab had no verification protocol in place at the time to "check" their own conclusions regarding the hair microscopy; and that these conclusions were not scientifically justifiable and may have negatively influenced the jury.

The subsequent twenty-one recommendations that emerged from the inquiry addressed the role of the province (ten), the provincial government and the Winnipeg Police Service (three in each case), the RCMP (one), the federal government and other jurisdictions (three), and the judiciary (one). The recommendations focused on improving police practices regarding disclosure, note taking, statement taking, and report writing. In addition, LeSage questioned the practice of proceeding by way of "direct indictment"[32] and emphasized the importance of preliminary hearings in establishing the facts of the case. He further recommended regular, informal meetings between representatives of the bench, bar, and police services as well as homicide-file reviews. Another recommendation was that disclosure policy be extended to the post-conviction phase, and LeSage underlined the importance of disclosure of any benefits given to so-called "unsavoury" witnesses. Finally, given the difficulties inherent to a stay of proceedings (which happened in this case) – a process that simply "suspends" the proceedings, leaves residual stigma, and does not close the matter – LeSage recommended that such decisions following a conviction review should be made only by the attorney general or the director of public prosecutions.

While LeSage stated that the conduct of some Crown attorneys involved in the case "fell below then existing professional standards expected of lawyers and agents of the Attorney General" (LeSage, 2007, 111), he did not recommend that this conduct be referred to the Law Society of Manitoba (Recommendation #20). The rationale for this was that three of the four Crown attorneys no longer practised in Manitoba and it would be unfair to single out the remaining prosecutor; however, LeSage did recommend that all cases resembling Driskell's that were prosecuted by prosecutor George Dangerfield be further reviewed (Recommendation #6). LeSage did not believe that criminal charges should be pursued against the Crown attorneys or the individual police officers involved in the case (Recommendation #21), since it was deemed that "a further police investigation is not likely to uncover any additional information" (LeSage, 2007, 112). Similarly, while failure to disclose material to the defence by some members of the Winnipeg Police Service contributed to Driskell's wrongful conviction, Justice LeSage did not require that these police officers' actions be referred to the Law Enforcement Review Agency (Recommendation #22), for three of the four police officers involved had since resigned and the fourth was about to and thus the agency would have no jurisdiction. LeSage explained that the passage of time (sixteen years) would make it difficult to pursue anyone for the serious breaches of basic disclosure obligations in this case.

Immediately following the release of the report, the attorney general for Manitoba, Dave Chomiak, announced that the province accepted the recommendations in their entirety and an adviser, retired Court of Queen's Bench Justice Ruth Kindle, was appointed to assist in implementing them. Chomiak issued an apology to Driskell on behalf of the province as well as a good-faith payment of $250,000, prior to resolving compensation issues.[33] As a response to the inquiry, the province implemented a number of changes.[34] With respect to disclosure, the attorney general appointed a disclosure manager to lead the Manitoba Justice Disclosure Unit, as well as expanding post-conviction disclosure policies for information sharing between police, the Crown, and defence counsel. The policies on direct indictments and on Crown stays of proceeding are to be reviewed and revised and quarterly meetings to be held among representatives of the judiciary, the Crown, the defence bar, and police and correctional authorities. Finally, the province will consider the possibility of other external reviews in cases of suspected wrongful convictions as well as committing more resources – in the form of more prosecutors, additional support staff, and more resourses and technology – to ensure that demands for disclosure are met.

VII. Goudge Commission of Inquiry into Pediatric Forensic Pathology[35]

More recently, in 2007, a Commission of Inquiry into Pediatric Forensic Pathology began proceedings in the province of Ontario, chaired by Justice Stephen T. Goudge of the Ontario Court of Appeal. The commission specifically examined the work of Dr Charles Smith, employed by the Hospital for Sick Children in Toronto from 1981 to 2005. While Smith performed the job of a paediatric forensic pathologist, he in fact had no formal training or certification in forensic pathology, nor did he have much experience in death investigations prior to being hired (Goudge, 2008). An initial review of Smith's work had been conducted in 2005, at the behest of the chief coroner for Ontario, Dr Barry McLellan, following a number of incidents where questions had been raised about Smith's testimony at trial. A panel of pathologists external to the coroner's office studied forty-four cases and concluded that twenty of them were problematic; of those, twelve had resulted in findings of guilt by the courts. These twenty cases became the focus of the commission of inquiry; the objectives of the inquiry were to examine the errors made by Smith in his analyses, to make recommendations regarding the practice and oversight of paediatric forensic pathology in Ontario, and to restore and enhance public confidence in the system.

As discussed in chapter 8, the Goudge Report, released in 2008, outlined a number of specific errors that appeared consistently across the cases examined (Goudge, 2008, 16–19). These included Smith's lack of understanding of his role as an impartial observer, a lack of preparation on complex matters in testifying, and an overall lack of professionalism in testifying, including relying on personal experiences as a parent to bolster his testimony, bias towards the Crown's case, and criticisms of other professionals. In fact, the inquiry established that Smith's opinions were at times "speculative, unsubstantiated, and not based on pathology findings" (Goudge, 2008, 16). The result of Smith's testimony was that a number of cases that the courts had ruled were infant homicides were in fact cases of sudden infant death where no crime had occurred at all. The inquiry addressed how such errors could have possibly occurred in the first instance, attempted to rectify injustices in some cases, and offered a number of recommendations to prevent future miscarriages of justice of this kind.The report contained 169 recommendations, the great majority aimed at modifying institutions and practices related to forensic pathology in the province of Ontario (Goudge, 2008, vol. 3). In response, the government acted quickly; according to the Ministry of Community Safety and Correctional Services, the Coroners Amendment Act 2009[36] effectively implemented all the legislative reforms recommended by the Goudge Commission. Efforts were aimed at centralizing and expanding forensic pathology services in Ontario.[37] Most importantly, the position of chief forensic pathologist was established, as well as an Ontario Forensic Pathology Service, which "would bring all of the province's forensic pathology services under one umbrella to ensure consistency, accountability and oversight."[38] Moreover, a further recommendation from the Goudge Commission (which was accepted by the government) advised the creation of a governing Council "to oversee the duties and responsibilities of the Office of the Chief Coroner for Ontario" (Goudge, 2008, 590). In addition, a complaints committee was also established to address concerns related to "the non-medical roles of coroners and pathologists (e.g., providing evidence in criminal proceedings)."[39] At the same time, changes have occurred with respect to the practice of forensic pathology; the Coroners Amendment Act codifies a set of standards and best practices for the investigation of suspicious deaths. On an institutional level, the Office of the Chief Coroner is required to produce an annual report by the Paediatric Death Review Committee and the Deaths under Five Committee. Finally, the provincial government opened a new state-of-the-art Forensic Services and Coroner's Complex in Toronto in September 2013.[40]

The effect of the Goudge Commission's report on the practice of forensic pathology in the province of Ontario was expansive. As noted, the extensive changes to forensic pathology, in particular increased oversight, accountability, and transparency, will most likely enhance professionalism and lead to greater proficiency in pathologists' conclusions and testimony in courts. Moreover, in February 2011, the Ontario College of Physicians and Surgeons instituted disciplinary proceedings against Smith and stripped him of his licence to practise medicine, the maximum penalty allowable, as well as imposing a small fine.[41] These facts, in addition to the overturning of convictions that resulted from Smith's problematic testimony, may help to enhance public confidence in this system. Clearly, in this instance the commission of inquiry not only exposed a system that was highly unprofessional, unregulated, and lacking in accountability, but also forced a number of significant changes that were long overdue.

Inquiry Recommendations Overview

By way of an overview of the many recommendations emanating from the seven commissions of inquiry to date, Table 12 links these recommendations to the specific chapters in this volume that address those same issues.

Reach of Inquiries: Challenges, Strengths, and Limitations

Each commission of inquiry held extensive powers that included the ability to issues subpoenas and hold hearings, recruit where necessary government and independent sources, issue reports that dealt with the causes of wrongful conviction, and make policy recommendations about remedies to prevent wrongful convictions in the future (Scheck and Neufeld, 2002b). Given that they have no binding power, it is unclear if the recommendations stemming from the commissions of inquiry can realistically affect policy in this regard. As each inquiry demonstrated, wrongful convictions are not the result of one simple error made by one individual. Rather, they are a culmination of oversights and mistakes, intentional or otherwise, that are compounded one upon the other. It is difficult to ascribe individual blame in such situations. The complex nature of the issues involved in these cases suggests that one simple policy change will have little overall effect, and that what is needed are more concerted efforts.

Consequently, it is difficult, even impossible, to state to what extent all of the many recommendations from the inquiries have been implemented. Stutz points out the difficulties inherent to understanding what constitutes the actual implementation of recommendations from an inquiry, since they may range from "an announcement that the government accepts a recommendation, to declaring a policy change, to passing legislation, to allocating funds, to establishing a new program or institution, or to some form of verification that the change has been made" (2008, 512). He then delineates those factors that are under a commissioner's control, such as the preparation of feasible recommendations and planning for their implementation through ongoing consultation, from those that are not, such as follow-up arrangements, political climate, and professional interest in taking action (2008). Roach notes the need for a systemic audit of the extent to which provinces have actually implemented many of the policy changes recommended by inquiries (2010, 106). He also notes that there is further uncertainty regarding the extent to which the recommendations and changes occurring in one province have affected developments in other provinces and that the federal government

Table 12. Commissions of inquiry recommendations overview

Commission of Inquiry – cases	Province	Recommendations[42]	Chapter
Donald Marshall, Jr	Nova Scotia, 1986–9	1. Create an independent review mechanism 2. Improve race relations 3. Establish a director of public prosecutions, guidelines for discretion and full Crown disclosure 4. Improve police practices	1. Chapter 13 2. Chapter 1 3. Chapter 4 4. Chapter 3
Guy Paul Morin	Ontario, 1996–8	1. Reform of forensic sciences 2. Restrictions on jailhouse informants 3. Improve police investigative practices	1. Chapter 8 2. Chapter 6 3. Chapter 3
Thomas Sophonow	Manitoba, 2000–1	1. Improve police procedure 2. Curtail use of jailhouse informants 3. Enhanced Crown disclosure 4. Independent entity to review cases 5. Compensation	1. Chapter 3 2. Chapter 6 3. Chapter 4 4. Chapter 13 5. Chapter 11
Lamer Commission: Dalton	Newfoundland and Labrador, 2003–6	1. Legal-aid allocation 2. More resources to address transcription delay 3. Address Court of Appeal rules re. time delays 4. Consider electronic recordings	1–4. Chapter 4 2. Chapter 9
Lamer Commission: Parsons	Newfoundland and Labrador, 2003–6	1. Change to police training and investigative procedures 2. Changes to Crown practice and culture	1. Chapter 3 2. Chapter 4
Lamer Commission: Druken	Newfoundland and Labrador, 2003–6	1. Changes to police practice 2. Use of jailhouse informants 3. Address prosecutorial discretion	1. Chapter 3 2. Chapter 6 3. Chapter 4
David Milgaard	Saskatchewan, 2004–6	1. Changes to police procedure 2. Preservation of trial exhibits 3. Dedicated forensic pathologists 4. Establish an independent review agency	1. Chapter 3 2. Chapter 7 3. Chapter 8 4. Chapter 13
James Driskell	Manitoba, 2006–7	1. Improve police practices around disclosure, note taking, statements, and reports 2. Disclosure of benefits to jailhouse informants 3. Re-examine the use of direct indictments and stay of proceedings	1. Chapter 3 2. Chapter 6 3. Chapters 4, 9
Goudge Commission of Inquiry	Ontario, 2007–8	1. Modification of institutions and practices related to paediatric forensic pathology	1. Chapter 8

has never amended the Criminal Code based on any inquiry recommendations. At the same time, the findings of several of the inquiries have been referred to in reported decisions throughout Canada, including those of the Supreme Court of Canada.[43] Furthermore, several of the commissions of inquiry have addressed the inherent unreliability of jailhouse informants; in turn, most provinces have responded with Crown policies that strictly curtail the use of such testimony, as well as establishing In-Custody Informant Committees.[44] In addition, issues of disclosure of evidence have been addressed through the advent of the Canadian Charter of Rights and Freedoms, and also through direction provided by the *Stinchcombe*[45] decision and the recommendations stemming from the royal commission on the Donald Marshall, Jr case.

While some of recommendations of the inquiries address obvious discernible aspects of the administration of justice, others, as discussed, are more intangible and can be measured only by a reduction in the numbers of wrongful convictions. Given that it is impossible to measure wrongful convictions in the first instance, reductions to this unknown number are also unidentifiable. A corollary to this concern is the question as to whether the impact of many of the recommendations can ever actually be measured. The commissions of inquiry have demonstrated that it takes many years for the extent of errors that contribute to wrongful convictions to come to light. Thus, measuring the impact of recommendations stemming from the study of wrongful convictions will likely also take many years. Nonetheless, a public acknowledgment of the roles that different agents in the criminal justice system have played in contributing to wrongful convictions can serve to hold governments accountable. As Salter states, "inquiries play a pivotal role in the delineation of public issues and public debate, even when their recommendations are not implemented" (Salter, 1990, 174). Furthermore, an inquiry may also have an effect in informing and educating the public, through developing a considerable amount of valuable research and allowing for the cathartic airing of opinions and concerns around important social issues (Macdonald, 2011).

Roach has posited that public inquiries differentiate Canada from the United States (1994). In the United States, prosecutions and civil lawsuits are often the response to scandals and disasters (Roach, 1994, 426). The litigious nature of many of the relationships between the state and individuals in that country illustrates an approach to solving contention and dissent that is unfamiliar to most Canadians. In fact, provincial legislation often caps damages that can be awarded in cases of civil litigation. In Canada, too, public inquiries allow for public statements regarding proper conduct surrounding the behaviour of agents of the government – something unknown in the United States. Indeed, they have been described as providing "the key structural response for the investigation and analysis of errors and for the dissemination of remedies" (Wolson and London, 2004, 678).

Governments are faced with the challenge of deciding when commissions of inquiry are the appropriate instrument to be used to investigate problems in the administration of justice, and under what circumstances. Clearly, the arduous and costly nature of such inquiries prohibits their use in all known cases of wrongful conviction. They generally take years to complete, and commissioners are faced with the burdensome task of assimilating masses of information. Some have also argued that inquiries are simply a tool for governments to delay action (Stutz, 2008) or a means of infringing on the rights of private citizens and giving too much power to judges (Macdonald, 2011). As Justice Gomery notes, commissions may be criticized for their long duration and costliness, "if one takes the position that a price can be put upon the search for truth and justice."[46] The impact of such commissions, while difficult to measure, would likely be lost if they were ordered too routinely. At best, commissions of inquiry represent government-supported efforts at addressing, through public information and policy recommendations, problems in the functioning and administration of the criminal justice system. At worst, they are an expensive exercise that essentially underlines or reiterates known systemic flaws.

Chapter Eleven

Compensation: The "Obstacle Course"

"'We pay the money, we have the public inquiry,' said Mr. Ruby, Donald Marshall Jr.'s former lawyer, 'but we can't make them whole again.'"[1]

Introduction

The objective of this chapter is to explore the issues surrounding what has been described by Kaiser (1989) as the "compensatory obstacle course" to monetary indemnification for a wrongful conviction and imprisonment in Canada. The chapter begins with discussion of the deprivations of wrongful conviction and the symbolic meaning of compensation for those so victimized. The next sections discuss, with some examples, Canada's international and national obligations towards this type of compensation. This is followed by a section on the semantics surrounding the issue of exonerations, and an introduction to some of the legal and psychological differences between the various statutory designations that may follow from the recognition of a miscarriage of justice, as represented by a wrongful conviction. Both the American and British systems of compensation are explored, and some reflections are offered on the role that restorative solutions may have in compensating the wrongly convicted.

When miscarriages of justice occur, it is reasonable to expect that governments will be held financially accountable in order to rectify wrongdoings to which they may have inadvertently contributed (Campbell, 2005). Persons who are wrongly convicted and imprisoned suffer myriad destructive and long-term consequences as a result of their ordeal. Grounds has found evidence for enduring personality change in the many wrongly convicted individuals he has interviewed, thought to be brought about by years of suffering, countless losses, pain, and humiliation, often occurring several years following exoneration and release (Grounds, 2004, 165). Therefore, a natural expectation is that those responsible for wrongful convictions will be made to provide monetary compensation in an attempt to redress the wrongs committed. Not only does this rationale for compensation exist on the societal level, whereby society is expected to assume responsibility for the miscarriage of justice, but compensation must also address the devastating effects on the individual (Kaiser, 1989, 100).

During the Sophonow Inquiry, as discussed in the previous chapter, Justice Cory sought to ascertain appropriate compensation for Thomas Sophonow for the

fifteen years he was considered a murderer. In doing so, Cory examined a wide
variety of factors said to result from the experience of wrongful conviction and
imprisonment,[2] as well as Sophonow's own role in contributing to his wrongful
conviction. The effects of this wrongful conviction included:

- a host of deprivations, such as liberty, civil rights, reputation, enjoyment of life,
  and potential normal experiences, and intercourse with friends, neighbours and
  family;
- other forgone developmental experiences, such as education and social learning in the workplace;
- humiliation and disgrace, as well as pain and suffering;
- physical assaults while in prison by fellow inmates and staff;
- accepting and adjusting to prison life, knowing that it was unjustly imposed;
  prison discipline, including extraordinary punishments imposed legally;
  prison visitation and diet;
- effects on the claimant's future, specifically the prospects of marriage, social
  status, physical and mental health, and social relations generally; and
- effects of post-acquittal statements made by public figures, police officers, and
  the media.[3]

As the above list indicates, all aspects of an individual's life are affected through
his/her victimization by a wrongful conviction. Clearly, monetary compensation
cannot restore lost years, lost livelihoods, lost opportunities, and lost relationships. Nevertheless, the wrongly convicted themselves describe the symbolic
importance of compensation in terms of societal acknowledgment of responsibility for their suffering (Campbell and Denov, 2004). Kaiser further outlines
the benefits said to accrue from compensation, which include: minimizing social
stigma, contributing to a feeling of vindication, helping to integrate the accused
in mainstream society, assisting in future planning, and contributing to the support of dependents (1989, 102). He observes that the payment of compensation
represents a partial fulfilment of the obligations of the state in the face of its
injustice, as well as restoring public respect by the assumption of responsibility
(1989, 102).

As discussed in earlier chapters, the investigation of a wrongful conviction and
the assignment of blame and responsibility for errors is a difficult and intermi-
nable process. So, too, are the means of obtaining compensation. The compensation process, as it currently stands in Canada, requires the wrongly convicted to
fulfil a number of responsibilities prior to being considered for compensation; it
is far from automatic. In the case where a wrongly convicted person has not been
the subject of a commission of inquiry, in which compensation considerations
were part of the terms of reference, that individual must jump through numerous
hoops. Primarily, as will be discussed below, the person must have been acquitted of the charge through a Court of Appeal or have received a pardon in order to
be considered for compensation. Further, an inquiry must be appointed to establish the amount of compensation and ascertain the division of responsibility federally, provincially, and municipally. Finally, the person must wait for the cheque,
so to speak.[4]

Canadian Obligations: Internationally

The Canadian government has a legal obligation, both nationally and internationally, to provide compensation to the wrongly convicted. Canada ratified the International Covenant on Civil and Political Rights (ICCPR) in 1976, which constitutes a binding obligation in international law, on both the federal and provincial levels (Kaiser, 1989). Two articles in this covenant address the issue of compensation for the wrongly convicted:

- Article 9(5): Anyone who has been a victim of unlawful arrest or detention shall have an enforceable right to compensation.
- Article 14(6): When a person has by a final decision been convicted of a criminal offense and when subsequently his conviction has been reversed or he has been pardoned on the grounds that a new or newly discovered fact shows conclusively that there has been a miscarriage of justice, the person who has suffered punishment as a result of such conviction shall be compensated according to law, unless it is proved that the non-disclosure of the unknown fact in time was wholly or partly attributable to him.

In essence, Canada, as a signatory to the ICCPR, has an obligation to create a statutory or regulatory provision to meet this obligation. In place of legislation, the Canadian government has established guidelines.

Canadian Obligations: Nationally

There is no current existing statute in Canadian law that dictates federal, provincial, or territorial obligations for compensation to the wrongly convicted. In recognition that the state bears (some) responsibility for the actions of its agents, in 1988 the Canadian government adopted a set of guidelines which assign the necessary conditions for compensation to be awarded to persons wrongfully convicted and imprisoned in Canada. These Federal-Provincial-Territorial Guidelines address the rationale for compensation, the conditions of eligibility for compensation, and the criteria for quantum of compensation (see appendix E). The conditions of eligibility for compensation are the following:

1. The wrongful conviction must have resulted in imprisonment, all or part of which has been served.
2. Compensation should only be available to the actual person who has been wrongfully convicted and imprisoned.
3. Compensation should only be available to an individual who has been wrongfully convicted and imprisoned as a result of a *Criminal Code* or other federal penal offence.
4. As a condition precedent to compensation, there must be a free pardon granted under Section 683(2) [now 749(2)] of the *Criminal Code* or a verdict of acquittal entered by an Appellate Court pursuant to a referral made by the Minister of Justice under Section 617(b) [now 696.1(b)].

5. Eligibility for compensation would only arise when Sections 617 and 683 [now 696.1 and 749] were exercised in circumstances where all available appeal remedies have been exhausted and where a new or newly discovered fact has emerged, tending to show that there has been a miscarriage of justice.

As compensation should be granted only to those persons who did not commit the crime for which they were convicted (as opposed to persons who are found not guilty), further criteria require:

a. if a pardon is granted under Section 683 [now 749], a statement on the face of the pardon based on an investigation, that the individual did not commit the offence; or
b. if a reference is made by the Minister of Justice under Section 617(b) [now 696.1(b)], a statement by the Appellate Court, in response to a question asked by the Minister of Justice pursuant to Section 617(c) [now 696.1(c)], to the effect that the person did not commit the offence.

While the entitlement criteria under the guidelines are broader than under the ICCPR, there are other stringent criteria that must be met before compensation is awarded. Section B of the guidelines dictates that the wrongly convicted must also have been wrongly imprisoned, and that compensation is available only for that person, not for family members. This exclusion unfairly eliminates those who have suffered a wrongful conviction and the entire attendant devastating consequences that follow, but who have narrowly missed being imprisoned. In addition, the family members of wrongly convicted persons also suffer a great deal, often losing an important source of emotional and financial support. They are further stigmatized through having a family member in jail, however unjustified that imprisonment is, and often spend countless time, effort, and finances working towards exoneration. Currently, their losses are not recognized or compensated through these guidelines.[5]

Furthermore, section B(4) indicates that a condition precedent to compensation is that a free pardon has been granted under section 749 of the Criminal Code or a verdict of acquittal[6] entered by an Appellate Court pursuant to a reference made by the minister under section 696.1 of the Criminal Code.[7] Such criteria narrow the numbers of eligible applicants considerably. More importantly, the guidelines require that the Court of Appeal make a finding on the *innocence* of the individual in order to be considered eligible for compensation. This goes beyond the normal mandate of the Court of Appeal since it requires that the court make a statement or finding to the effect that the person did not commit the offence, which is far more than a verdict of not guilty. Given the narrow nature of the criteria required for this designation, the courts rarely if ever make such a finding.[8]

Guidelines as Policy Statement

While not a substitute for a statutory obligation, the guidelines represent a national policy statement regarding ex gratia payments (Kaiser, 1989, 111). They attempt to address Canada's obligations under the ICCPR in a manner that is somewhat less limiting than the conditions set out in that document. For example, under the ICCPR, entitlement to recovery may be affected by non-disclosure on the part of the accused. The Federal-Provincial Guidelines provide that such blameworthy conduct or lack of due diligence on the part of the claimant may affect only the amount of the compensation, not the entitlement (Cory, 2001). In all cases, compensation for non-pecuniary[9] losses under the guidelines is not to exceed $100,000 (indexed to $350,000 by today's standards), whereas there is no cap for pecuniary[10] losses. Regardless, the pecuniary/non-pecuniary distinction has not always been made when compensation has been awarded in the past. The guidelines are also an important policy statement in that they establish the state's obligation to those who have suffered through errors of the criminal justice system.[11] Nonetheless, the process itself is not particularly straightforward. Two further criticisms of the guidelines are that they do not specifically oblige the relevant government to act and the fact that they do not represent a significant departure from previous practice or policy (Kaiser, 1989, 121–2). While the guidelines represent an important precedent in theory, in practice they do not go far enough in recognizing Canada's obligation under the ICCPR to the wrongly convicted.[12]

The "Semantics" of Exoneration: The Threshold of Innocence

One issue of significance when considering compensation for the wrongly convicted is the legal status of an individual's case following release from prison. Once an individual has been convicted of a crime he or she did not commit, a large part of that person's attention is understandably directed towards clearing his or her name. In their interviews with the wrongly convicted, Campbell and Denov (2004) noticed that, for all of them, focusing on the appeal of their conviction was an effective coping strategy to deal with their incarceration. Then, once released, the wrongly convicted are faced with a dilemma with respect to their request for compensation: how the criminal justice system has designated their status will have a bearing on whether or not they are successful. Given that in Canadian law at the present time there are no specific legal procedures that determine and declare that a wrongful conviction has in fact occurred (Roach, 2006), how the courts ultimately designate an individual following a wrongful conviction is of importance. Further, the difficulty in proving that a wrongful conviction has actually occurred is compounded by how the courts have defined the situation.

Exoneration in the strict sense of the word means a removal of a charge, responsibility, or duty. With respect to a wrongful conviction, exoneration involves an official act declaring a defendant not guilty of a crime for which he or she had previously been convicted (Gross et al., 2005, 524). This can occur through a number of ways. When a convicted individual presents his or her case to a provincial Court of Appeal in Canada, that court has a number of options on how to proceed. It can enter an acquittal, or it can dismiss the appeal and then the individual can ask for leave to appeal to the Supreme Court of Canada. The Court of Appeal can also quash the conviction, which means in essence to vacate or void the conviction; nevertheless, this does not designate exoneration. The court can then order a new trial, whereby the Crown attorney's office can then proceed to a verdict (guilty or not guilty) or: "1. Withdraw the charge; 2. Proceed with the trial but elect to not call any evidence, or stop calling further evidence and ask the judge or jury to acquit; or 3. Enter a stay of proceedings" (Lamer, 2006).

Clearly, in the case of a withdrawn charge and an acquittal, it would be difficult to argue that an individual was completely exonerated of a charge. While the accused is immune from any future prosecution for the same conduct through an acquittal, it also indicates that the Crown was unable to prove its case against the accused. Unmistakably, the worst outcome for the wrongly convicted would be a stay of proceedings. A stay of proceedings is under the sole jurisdiction of the Crown[13] and essentially puts the charge against the individual on "hold"; proceedings can then be recommenced at any time within the following year. If charges are not reintroduced within that year period, then they are "deemed never to have been commenced." Nonetheless, as previously discussed, the accused is still open to future prosecution for that same offence, and this process has been described as creating a sort of "legal limbo" (Roach, 2006, 13).

While Crown policy across the country varies as to the use of a stay of proceedings, common sense would dictate that a stay should be invoked only in cases where there is a possibility that additional evidence may come to light in the future which would likely incriminate the accused. Roach has argued that a stay of proceedings should be used only when there is an indication that an active investigation will continue and there is a reasonable likelihood that the proceedings will be recommenced (2006). Clearly, in the eyes of the public (or the wrongly convicted), a stay does not represent exoneration. When entering a stay of proceedings, the Crown attorney is sending the message that the charge has been put aside for the moment and could re-emerge. For the wrongly convicted, they are neither acquitted nor exonerated;[14] the spectre of a future prosecution is an undeniable reality.

As discussed, the guidelines for compensation limit eligibility to those who have been acquitted through a Court of Appeal (by way of conviction review) or who have received a free pardon and who have been designated as having not committed the offence in question.[15] Consequently, those whose cases result in a stay of proceedings are essentially ineligible for compensation. The case of James Driskell is illustrative of this problem. James Driskell served twelve years in prison for the murder of Perry Dean Harder and was released in 2003 awaiting conviction review. His conviction was overturned in 2005 and a new trial ordered at which time the attorney general of Manitoba entered a stay of proceedings in his case. A commission of inquiry, as discussed in the previous chapter, was ordered to examine the circumstances of Driskell's arrest and conviction (but was not mandated to consider compensation) and the final report was released in early 2007. One strong recommendation to emerge from this report[16] was the elimination of Crown stays in Manitoba, particularly for ministerial-review (s. 696) cases. This recommendation is based on the fact that a stay of proceedings can be ordered with any public hearing while the final report is pending, thus essentially denying the wrongly convicted public recognition that a miscarriage of justice has occurred (Lamer, 2006, 137). While Driskell was initially ineligible for compensation because of his legal status, he did receive an immediate "good faith" payment of $250,000 and was later awarded $2.4 million in 2011. Partly because of a civil suit that he launched, the inquiry did not consider the issue of compensation. Clearly, there is a need to revise how compensation is awarded in such cases, where innocent individuals are denied the opportunity for compensation based on somewhat arbitrary legal designations.

Compensated Cases

In spite of the difficulties inherent in the compensation process, thirty-three[17] Canadians have received compensation for being wrongly convicted and imprisoned (see Table 13, which ranks the individuals by amount compensated, beginning with the highest award).[18] A number of ex-gratia compensation awards have been assigned through commissions of inquiry (Sophonow, Morin) and some individuals have had original compensation amounts increased as a result of findings of these commissions (Donald Marshall, Jr, Randy Druken, Gregory Parsons). The majority of the other individuals have received compensation directly from provincial ministries once the mistakes occurring in their cases became known. As Table 13 indicates, many individuals had to wait an inordinately long time for compensation; while Linda Huffman waited only 3 years, Steven Truscott waited 49, and the average wait was 16.2 years from date of the original conviction. Given the many adjustment problems experienced by the wrongly convicted upon their release to the community (cf. Grounds, 2004), waiting years to be compensated likely exacerbates their situation. Further, the amount of compensation, ranging from $36,000 to $13.1 million, appears to be largely based on the number of years an individual has spent in prison and the amount of time he or she has waited for compensation. The majority of individuals were wrongly incarcerated for murder (seventeen), while others were incarcerated for sexual assault (seven), armed robbery or theft (five), child abuse/infanticide (two), break and enter (one), and assault (one). These individuals came from across the country: compensation was awarded thirteen times in Ontario, four times in Quebec, three times in Newfoundland, British Columbia, and Alberta, twice in Nova Scotia and Manitoba, and once in Saskatchewan, Northwest Territories, and New Brunswick. What is interesting are the low numbers of compensation awards in certain provinces, particularly in the prairies and the Maritimes. While this may be indicative of low numbers of wrongly convicted individuals in these provinces, it is more likely reflective of governmental reticence to acknowledge these types of errors.

The Canadian Department of Justice has been in process of revamping its guidelines for compensation of the wrongly convicted for a number of years. Given that the current guidelines are almost thirty years old and appear inconsistently applied across the country, this process is long overdue. However, there is no target date for completion of the work.

Compensation in the United States

In the United States, geographic location largely determines whether or not one can receive compensation for a wrongful conviction. Statutes providing compensation exist for the federal government, in the District of Columbia, and in thirty-two states and all require varying degrees of proof, while many have restrictions such as requiring a pardon.[19] The thirty-two states that compensate the wrongly convicted are: Alabama, California, Colorado, Connecticut, Florida, Hawaii,

Table 13. Compensated cases

Name	Year of conviction	Crime	Time spent in jail	Amount of compensation	Years from conviction to comp.	Years from exon. to comp.
Rejean Hinse**	1964, QC	Armed robbery	5 years	$13.1 million	47 years (2011)	14 years (1997)
David Milgaard*	1969, SK	Murder	23 years	$10 million (including $750,000 to mother)	30 years (1999)	7 years (1992)
Ivan Henry**	1983, BC	Sexual assault	27 years	$8 million (BC), excluding an undisclosed amount from Vancouver and federal government	33 years (2016)	11 years (2005)
Steven Truscott†	1959, ON	Murder	10 years (38 years on parole; sentenced to hang in 1959; commuted to life in 1960)	$6.5 million (plus $100,000 to wife)	49 years (2008)	1 year (2007) (parole granted in 1969)
William Mullins-Johnson*	1994, ON	Murder	12 years	$4.25 million	16 years (2010)	3 years (2007)
Thomas Sophonow*	1983, MB	Murder	3 years, 9 months	$2.6 million	18 years (2001)	1 year (2000)
Clayton Johnson**	1993, NS	Murder	5 years	$2.5 million	11 years (2004)	2 years (2002)
Simon Marshall*	1997, QC	Sexual assault	7 years, 4 months	$2.3 million	9 years (2006)	2 years (2004)
Steven Kaminski**	1992, AB	Sexual assault	7 years	$2.2 million	14 years (2006)	3 years (2003)
Randy Druken*	1995, NFLD	Murder	7 years	$2.1 million	11 years (2006)	6 years (2000)
Gregory Parsons*	1994, NFLD	Murder	54 days	$1.3 million (awarded in two parts)	8 years (2002, 2005)	4, 7 years (1998)
Guy Paul Morin*	1992, ON	Murder	18 months	$1.25 million (including $550,000 to mother)	4 years (1996)	1 year (1995)
Benoit Proulx**	1991, QC	Murder	2 months	$1.1 million	10 years (2001)	9 years (1992)
Herman Kaglik*	1992 and 1993, NWT	Sexual assault	52 months	$1.1 million	8 years (2000)	2 years (1998)
Donald Marshall, Jr*	1971, NS	Murder	11 years	$945,679 (including $174,265 to mother)	13 years (1984, 1991)	1, 8 years (1983)
Jason Dix**	1996, AB (in custody and acquitted at trial)	Murder	22 months	$765,000	6 years (2002)	4 years (1998)
Ronald Dalton*	1989, NFLD	Murder	8.5 years	$750,000	19 years (2008)	8 years (2000)
Richard Norris*	1980, ON	Break and enter; indecent assault	8 months	$507,450	13 years (1993)	2 years (1991)

(Continued)

Table 13. Compensated cases (Continued)

Name	Year of conviction	Crime	Time spent in jail	Amount of compensation	Years from conviction to comp.	Years from exon. to comp.
Kenneth Norman Warwick (alias Norman Fox)*	1976, BC	Sexual assault	8.5 years	$412,500	9 years (1985)	1 year (1984)
Joseph Dean Webber**	2007, ON	Armed robbery, forcible confinement, extortion	1.6 years	$392,500	4 years (2011)	1 year (2011)
Michael McTaggert**	1987, ON	Robbery	20 months	$380,000	14 years (2001)	11 years (1990)
James Driskell*	1991, MB	Murder	12 years	$250,000 (2008 – interim good-faith payment) $2.4 million (2011)	17 years (2008)	3 years (2005)
Tammy Marquardt*	1995, ON	Murder	14 years	$240,132	15 years (2010)	< 1 year (2010)
Rejean Pepin*	1986, QC	Armed robbery	7 months	$188,000	15 years (2001)	14 years (1987)
Linda Huffman*	1993, BC	Theft	60 days (served through electronic monitoring)	$105,512[19]	3 years (1996)	2 years (1994)
Wilfred Truscott**	1984, AB	Assault	1 year	$36,000	2 years (1986)	< 1 year (1986)
Gary Staples**	1970, ON	Murder	2 years	Not disclosed	32 years (2002)	30 years (1972)
Erin Walsh**	1975, NB	Murder	10 years	Not disclosed	33 years (2008)	< 1 year (2008)
Peter Frumusa**	1989, ON	Murder	8 years	Not disclosed	15 years (2004)	6 years (1998)
Gordon Folland*	1995, ON	Sexual assault	3 years	Not disclosed	11 years (2006)	7 years (1999)
Sherry Sherrett-Robinson**	1999, ON	Infanticide	1 year	Not disclosed	12 years (2011)	1 year (2011)
Brenda Waudby**	1999, ON	Child abuse	Unknown	Not disclosed	12 years (2011)	N/A[20]
JackWhite*	1995, ON	Sexual assault	Suspended sentence	Not disclosed	15 years (2010)	1 year

* Indicates ex-gratia payments, including those determined under 1988 guidelines (20 cases)[21]
** Indicates payments granted in civil suit, by court order, or agreed upon in settlement (13 cases)[22]

Illinois, Iowa, Louisiana, Maine, Maryland, Massachusetts, Michigan, Minnesota, Mississippi, Missouri, Montana, Nebraska, New Hampshire, New Jersey, New York, North Carolina, Ohio, Oklahoma, Tennessee, Texas, Utah, Vermont, Virginia, Washington, West Virginia, and Wisconsin.[23] Given the differing cultural, social, and political environments across the country, the manner in which compensation is provided varies considerably. Some restrictions include ineligibility in cases where individuals were convicted as a result of a confession or guilty plea (irrespective of whether or not it was falsely obtained), or where there is evidence that the individual in some way contributed to his/her conviction. Furthermore, few states provide substantial awards and some are undeniably paltry (in Montana compensation is limited to tuition support with no monetary assistance [Bernhard, 2004, 706]). In some states compensation is capped and most states tax compensation amounts (e.g., the New Hampshire total is $20,000, whereas the cap in Florida is $2 million, with caps of $500,000 in Maine, Mississippi, and Massachusetts[24]); some states also supply support services, including employment training, counselling, and tuition fees (e.g., Connecticut, Florida, Illinois, Louisiana, and Massachusetts.)[25] The likelihood of recovery is quite limited, with only 37 per cent of known wrongly convicted individuals having received compensation (Mandery, 2005, 497).

The Justice for All Act of 2004 was an attempt to rectify some of these inequities by addressing issues surrounding the use of DNA and victims' rights.[26] This omnibus legislation was meant to enhance the protections of the wrongly convicted through two sections, the DNA Sexual Assault Justice Act[27] and the Innocence Protection Act.[28] These acts provide funding for victim services and are aimed at ensuring access to post-conviction DNA testing for those wrongly convicted in prison or on death row. Specifically, the Innocence Protection Act provides funding to states to defray the costs of post-conviction DNA testing, as well as for training counsel to improve the quality of representation at death-penalty trials. The issue of compensation is also addressed in this legislation, which provides awards for unjust imprisonment ranging from $50,000 per year for non-capital cases to $100,000 per year for capital cases. The compensation provisions contained in this act (ss. 431 and 432), however, apply just to federal cases; only five states have adopted the same standards for compensation.[29] While section 432 reiterates the United States' position that states should provide compensation for wrongful convictions, there are no enforcement mechanisms. Moreover, there is no requirement that state governments follow the sums outlined in this act, and each state is entitled to use its own compensatory mechanisms – if they exist at all. Thus, the current inconsistencies across the United States with respect to compensation for wrongful conviction and imprisonment do not appear to be adequately addressed by this legislation.[30]

The different approaches regarding compensation for the wrongfully convicted in the United States as well as the wide discrepancies in approach across the various states make it difficult to compare the trends on compensation in the United States to those in Canada. However, it is worth noting that, as in Canada, there have been reports of large compensation packages for individuals wrongfully convicted in the United States. For instance, Anthony Graves received $1.45 million from the state of Texas for the twelve years he spent on death row as a result of a wrongful conviction for which he was exonerated in 2010; Marty Tankleff was awarded $3.4 million in 2014 by the state of New York after spending seventeen years in prison for a double homicide he did not commit.[31] The largest American payment is believed to be the $25 million awarded to Thaddeus Jimenez by the city of Chicago for the sixteen years he spent in prison for a wrongful conviction for murder.[32] Nevertheless, these large figures are not the norm in the United States, and because of the above-noted policies, many American wrongful convictions end with minor compensation or none at all.

Compensation in the United Kingdom

For many years, compensation for miscarriages of justice in the United Kingdom was provided at the discretion of the home secretary through either an ex-gratia payment or a statutory scheme in cases involving negligence by the police or other public authority (Taylor, 2004). In April 2006 the home secretary introduced changes limiting payments to those eligible under the statutory scheme. This statutory obligation is to provide compensation in the form of a monetary award for a miscarriage of justice, as contained in the Criminal Justice Act 1988. According to this legislation, "when a person has been convicted of a criminal offence and when subsequently his conviction has been reversed or he has been pardoned on the ground that a new or newly discovered fact shows beyond a reasonable doubt that there has been a miscarriage of justice, the Secretary of State shall pay compensation for the miscarriage of justice to the person who has suffered punishment as a result of such conviction or, if he is dead, to his personal representatives, unless the non-disclosure of the unknown fact was wholly or partly attributable to the person convicted (sec.133(1) subject to subsection (2))." While this section of the law is thought to meet the British obligation for compensation under the ICCPR (s. 14(6)), on closer examination the scheme limits access to compensation for the wrongly convicted in a number of ways (Spencer, 2010). First of all, only those actually convicted are eligible; those on remand (awaiting trial) and then later acquitted are not. Second, only those whose convictions are quashed "outside the normal process of appeal" are eligible for compensation; thus, those whose appeal occurs during the normal time frame of nine to ten months in prison are also ineligible. Finally, only those cases where a new or newly discovered fact emerges to exonerate a convicted person are eligible, so no compensation is available for those who have been wrongly convicted as a result of misconduct on the part of legal professionals. British case law has illustrated the difficulties that the courts have grappled with in attempting to ascertain what constitutes a miscarriage of justice for the purposes of section 133.[33] What is inherently problematic about this scheme is that a number of demonstrably innocent people will receive absolutely no compensation as a result.

Some complaints about the current system are that it is difficult to establish eligibility; the process is long and protracted; compensation is limited to the individual, excluding family members; and it does not take sufficient account of non-financial losses accrued through emotional distress, character assassination, and the stigma of being labelled as a criminal (Taylor, 2004). Moreover, to add insult to injury, the government deducts what are called "saved living expenses" for prison board and lodging from compensation awards. For example, Michael Hickey and Vincent Hickey were wrongly convicted of murdering thirteen-year-old Carl Bridgewater in 1978 in the West Midlands of England. While their convictions were quashed by the Court of Appeal nineteen years later and they were awarded compensation, the amount was ultimately subject to a 25 per cent deduction to pay for their saved "board and lodgings" expenses.[34] Similarly, an attempt to bring compensation payments to the wrongly convicted in line with compensation to other victims of crime, capping individual awards at £500,000, was greeted with public uproar.[35] Regardless, the government has capped the maximum amount of compensation payable at £1 million, which applies only in cases when an applicant has been imprisoned for at least ten years; in all other cases it is £500,000.[36]

Furthermore, the home secretary, as minister of justice, is the only individual with the power to decide eligibility for compensation. An independent assessor is then assigned in each case to decide the amount of compensation, which is determined in a manner similar to the procedures in dealing with claims made under civil action, subject to the following guidelines under the Criminal Justice Act:

133(4a) In assessing so much of any compensation payable under this section or in respect of a person as is attributable to suffering, harm to reputation or similar damage, the assessor shall have regard in particular to –

(a) the seriousness of the offence of which the person was convicted and the severity of the punishment resulting from the conviction;
(b) the conduct of the investigation and prosecution of the offence;
(c) any other convictions of the person and any punishment resulting from them.

More recently, in 2011, the Supreme Court ruled on the precise meaning of "miscarriages of justice" with respect to interpreting section 133 and broadened its scope somewhat to cases where a new or newly discovered fact "so undermines the evidence against the defendant that no conviction could possibly be based upon it."[37] Legislation in 2014 reversed this decision, adding to section 133 the stipulation that a miscarriage of justice has occurred "if and only if the new or newly discovered fact shows beyond reasonable doubt that the person did not commit the offence."[38] This effect of this amendment is that it is more difficult now for those seeking compensation, which is considered the exception rather than the rule (Lipscombe and Beard, 2015).

One final means of gaining compensation for a wrongful conviction in the United Kingdom and the United States would be through civil action filed through the courts for malicious prosecution or wrongful arrest. In such instances the applicant must be able to establish that the authority was negligent and, as in Canada, these cases are very challenging to argue successfully in the courts since it is almost impossible to establish that a single person was intentionally at fault. Furthermore, the doctrine of immunity often protects police and prosecutors against these types of actions. While it is again difficult to compare the compensation paid in British cases to the situation in Canada because of great differences in the approach taken by each government, the strict limits on compensation combined with the fact that the British government continues to try to restrict the cases that would qualify for compensation suggest that large payments for wrongful convictions will remain a rare occurrence in Britain.[39] The British Home Office has indicated that the highest payment given for a wrongful conviction was £2.1 million (approximately CDN$3.8 million in 2014), with an average payout of £250,000.[40]

Questions of State Accountability

Compensating the wrongly convicted with monetary indemnity for their suffering represents a moral and legal obligation on the part of the state towards its members who have fallen victim to errors of the criminal justice system. As it stands in Canada, the current compensation scheme is difficult to access, arbitrarily applied, and in need of overhaul. The thirty-three cases listed in Table 13 make it clear that few individuals are ever compensated for their ordeal, that they must wait many years for compensation, and that the amounts awarded vary considerably. The number of people who receive compensation is far below the actual number of wrongly convicted if one accepts Zalman's error rate of 0.5 to 1.0 per cent of all convictions annually in the United States being in error and McLellan's extrapolation of that number to Canadian cases (872 cases in 2010).[41] Being compensated for a wrongful conviction is a legal "crap-shoot," dependent on media influence, individual perseverance, and political will. Admittedly, while it is essential that the state establish particular criteria for eligibility for compensation, at present it is unclear who exactly is eligible, under what circumstances, and for how much. The restrictive manner in which successive governments have interpreted the compensation guidelines in Canada reveals a great deal about the Canadian government's interpretation of its obligation to citizens whom it has treated unfairly.

When considering the role of the state with respect to wrongful convictions, questions of moral responsibility[42] are fundamental and concern the nature of the state and the relationship of the individual to the state and, by extension, to the law (Cohen, 1986, 22). Kaiser invokes Dworkin's concept of moral harm in attempting to situate the issue of wrongful convictions within a larger framework (Kaiser, 1989). In this instance, bare harm that is said to result from the loss of liberty per se is differentiated from the iniquity of moral harm occurring from wrongful imprisonment. When the state has had a role in causing such harm through the flawed administration of justice, it has a responsibility to rectify the situation through policy, statute, and compensation. As Justice Cory noted in the Sophonow Inquiry: "In the case of wrongful conviction, it is the State which has brought all its weight to bear against the individual. It is the State which has conducted the investigation and prosecution on the individual that resulted in the wrongful conviction. It is the State which wrongfully subjected the individual to imprisonment" (Cory, 2001).

What is clear is that, in cases of wrongful conviction, the state has improperly exercised its powers. Those targeted in incidents of wrongful conviction are often individuals who are already somewhat marginalized and powerless to protect themselves from the system (Martin, 2001a). For such vulnerable individuals, the actions of the state have devastating effects – and from a societal point of view, these acts serve to demonstrate that the state is capable of error. It is how the state rectifies that error that serves to restore, enhance, or destroy its credibility.

Providing compensation to the wrongly convicted is a means of holding the state accountable for its errors. Regrettably, compensation often occurs many years after the fact and is not an automatic requirement following an exoneration from a wrongful conviction. Also, through compensation, the focus is generally aimed at errors that have emanated from within the criminal justice system itself. But justice is administered within a larger societal context, influenced by a variety of other factors that are beyond the purview of such remedies. The narrow nature of such a focus was underlined in the royal commission that examined the wrongful conviction of Donald Marshall, Jr, an Indigenous person: the discrimination that occurred in that case, based on both race and status, had its roots in "social, political, and economic structures, institutions and values that are not part of the criminal justice system" (Royal Commission on the Donald Marshall, Jr Prosecution, 1989a, 150). At the same time, providing remedies to the wrongfully convicted that go beyond the criminal justice system are unlikely.

Restorative Solutions

As discussed above, there is little question that the wrongly convicted suffer many deprivations as a result of their conviction and imprisonment. Financial compensation goes a long way to addressing the difficulties that many face as a consequence of many years of imprisonment. Grounds presents a compelling case for the long-term psychological adjustment issues that many wrongly convicted individuals and their families must cope with upon release (2004). In essence, more is needed to address these larger, more pressing adjustment problems. Burnett (2005) presents an interesting case for a restorative-justice approach to the wrongly convicted. By equating victims of miscarriages of justice with other victims of crime, she argues for the application of a restorative-justice framework as a possible means of not only addressing the great needs that the wrongly convicted have following release but also of providing an appropriate alternative to the formal response of the criminal justice system. Restorative justice, as a movement both within and outside the criminal justice system, attempts to respond to crime and criminals from a healing, reparative perspective. Restorative-justice initiatives move away from questions of blame and punishment and towards addressing harms and healing.

Following Zehr's (2002) method of responding to the needs of those harmed by a crime, as well as examining the most appropriate means of "putting things right," Burnett argues for a victim-compensation fund for the wrongly convicted, similar to that for victims of the 11 September 2001 terrorist attacks in the United States (2005). Among other measures, she calls for the assignment of a caseworker to undertake a complete needs assessment and develop a long-term plan for the wrongly convicted and their families. While admirable as an alternative means to address compensation, a restorative-justice scheme would also, by extension, rely on the willingness of governments to accept responsibility for errors that have occurred in the administration of justice. As discussed, with compensation generally, there appears to be little political appetite to do so at this juncture. Nonetheless, a compensation scheme that incorporates restorative-justice ideals would provide a more humane approach to better addressing the long-term consequences that the wrongly convicted suffer, and would go beyond mere monetary indemnification. At the same time, it would represent a strong political message of accountability and responsibility on the part of governments for these miscarriages of justice.

Conclusions

The issues outlined above illustrate the difficulties inherent in the compensation process as it currently exists in Canada. Not only are the guidelines applied in what seems to be an arbitrary manner, but they also fail to meet Canada's international obligation under the International Covenant on Civil and Political Rights. The guidelines are limited to compensation of only the wrongly imprisoned themselves and are restricted to those who have been granted a pardon or found by appeal courts to have not committed the offence. This differs significantly from an acquittal, leaving a number of innocent individuals (who cannot "factually" prove they are innocent) without access to compensation. Moreover, compensation can be awarded only following an inquiry that assesses governmental responsibility – an arduous and protracted process. Essentially, while the guidelines do not *oblige* a government to act, legislation does. Guidelines provide only a framework for considering compensation, whereas compensation statutes bring uniformity to the process, are fairly easy to use, resolve claims rapidly, and are politically popular (Bernhard, 2004, 708–10). While the British Criminal Justice Act, which contains a statutory scheme for compensation, appears to be a more equitable means of addressing this problem in that it allows the British government to provide compensation for the wrongly convicted in certain circumstances, it is far from perfect. It sets rather strict limits on who is eligible for compensation and the courts and legislature are also attempting to restrict access further. That said, legislating such schemes not only facilitates the process to a limited extent for the wrongly convicted, it also sends a clear message that state governments are acknowledging some degree of responsibility for errors occurring through the administration of justice.

The Impact of Public Lobbying on Wrongful Convictions: The Role of the Media, Lobby Groups, and Innocence Projects

"There is probably no other area of reporting on the system of justice that provokes such a violent reaction against journalists than revelations of the ultimate weakness or our judicial system – that it can send innocent people to jail." (Stephens and Hill, 1999, 281)

Introduction

There are a number of mechanisms that play a critical role in exposing miscarriages of justice; within the Canadian context, these include the media, lobby groups, and innocence projects. In recent years, the media have played an increasingly important role in drawing attention to miscarriages of justice. Unrelenting coverage of specific cases has often had the effect of forcing governments to revisit them and at times has resulted in exonerations. Simultaneously, a number of lobby groups have emerged to take up the cause of the wrongly convicted, in part owing to inadequacies in the criminal justice system in addressing its own errors. Finally, innocence projects, which are comprised of law-school and journalism student groups that take on suspected cases of wrongful conviction, have also been successful in finding grounds for appeal, conviction review, and exoneration, as well as, in some cases, influencing criminal justice policy. This chapter discusses the impact of these and other forms of public lobbying in drawing attention to and attempting to redress wrongful convictions.

The Construction of Crime by the Media

The theory of social constructionism provides one viewpoint for understanding the impact that the media has on public perceptions about crime and victimization. A simplistic rendering of this theory posits that individual reality is a product of our own creation, influenced by personal knowledge and input from others. Further, individual knowledge about the world comes from a variety of sources: personal experiences, significant others, other social groups, and institutions and the mass media (Surette, 1998). All of these sources work together to influence and create constructions about reality, which in turn also allow certain social conditions to be labelled as social problems. With respect to crime, public perceptions are influenced by the claims-making process of officials, interest groups, and the media (Spector and Kitsuse, 1977). Most information about crime and law breaking is conveyed through the media, and hence perceptions about crime, criminal justice, and victimization are influenced by how this news is conveyed. At the same time, large multinational corporations own media sources, thus shaping views on news issues. Politics also play a role in determining what news is reported, who is quoted, and what particular slant a story takes. The same issues are often conveyed by news sources completely differently, given the political perspective of which news medium is doing the reporting.

Nobles and Schiff[1] provide a sophisticated and nuanced perspective on what they describe as the "miscommunication between law and the media" through the application of autopoietic systems theory (2000). Put differently:

> The legal system, which claims to operate on the basis of just/unjust ... finds itself confronting a paradoxical situation in which law poses the problem of its own justice or, at least, applies that distinction to its own observations of external reality. Law's functional identity based on its ability to "do justice" is itself subject to the legal system's coding of legal/illegal, lawful/unlawful. Justice may, therefore, be either lawful or unlawful with the resultant paradoxes of "lawfully unjust" or "unlawfully just." Within the environment constructed by law, the paradox of justice/injustice is resolvable only by transforming it into the distinction lawful/unlawful – [a] distinction that may be made by law, and law alone. (King and Schutz, 1994, 280, references omitted)

Similarly, Nobles and Schiff (2000, 5) regard miscarriages of justice as communicative events, constructed by the law but interpreted by the media. While the media claim to be presenting information to the public in an "objective" manner, autopoietic systems theory would deny the possibility of objective reporting when translating communications from one subsystem to another. As they note, "when journalists seek to translate their understanding of legal processes into news, and lawyers attempt to turn journalists' stories into evidence or arguments for reform, we have a situation which is both consensus, and a multiplicity of understandings and misunderstandings" (Nobles and Schiff, 2000, 5). Thus, the nexus between law and the media is necessarily fraught with layered meanings, differences of interpretation, and ultimately varying versions of the truth. This communicative situation between law and media is known as a "structural coupling" (Nobles and Schiff, 2000, 95).

Overturning a conviction[2] – reversing the coding of a previous communicative event – is interpreted by the media as a "crisis" in the legal system; however, the legal system rejects this labelling. According to Nobles and Schiff (2000, 100), the codification of crisis is internal to the media alone, and the legal system resists this interpretation since otherwise its authority to "do justice" will be undermined. The solutions advanced by the media to respond to the alleged crisis posed by a miscarriage of justice are addressed to and on behalf of "the public," which is in turn a construction by the media. This serves to reinforce the (mis)communication between the media and the law, because news articles addressed to the public rarely attempt to communicate the meanings of legal codes in their own complex and technical terms (Nobles and Schiff, 2000, 105). The guilty/acquittal binary is understood by the media to represent actual guilt/innocence; in other words, media often conceptualize or interpret the overturning of a conviction as the acknowledgment of factual innocence, when in fact only the guilty/not-guilty binary is operative in the legal system.

Walker (2002b) rejects the application of the "heuristic device of autopoiesis" to the study of miscarriages of justice and believes that this perspective on law "as a system of self-referential communications is hardly likely to explain the complexities of law, politics and culture and how they have impacted upon the criminal justice process during the past decade. Indeed, the arid setting of boundaries between 'systems' seems peculiarly inappropriate in this context. Thus, one might ask where the boundaries lie of the 'systems' of the law and the media (and politics)?" (4). Moreover, Walker points out that this perspective simplifies the notion of individual rights, which are impossible to understand within the distinct system of law alone, since their meaning is also embedded in other systems. Thus, while the media provide the public with truncated frameworks for understanding how and why miscarriages of justice may have occurred, these perspectives are not shared in legal discourses and are naturally limited, failing to address or explain both the structural and functional forces also operating simultaneously, forces that go beyond the criminal justice system itself.

Impact of the Media on Wrongful Convictions: Provocateur or Watchdog?

As noted, the media are the main source for information about crime for most members of the general public. Continually updated information about crime, victimization, and violence are provided to the general public through print news, television, and the Internet; the latter's round-the-clock availability has facilitated even greater access and some believe has created an insatiable public appetite for news. Yet, while crime reporting may take up a great deal of space in news reporting, it is clearly disproportionate to the actual incidence of crime, which in turn may create unrealistic fears regarding victimization. Highly sensationalized accounts of particularly heinous crimes play a role not only in informing the public but also in shaping perspectives about the nature and extent of criminal victimization. The result is that many individuals have a skewed perspective about the extent of violent crime occurring in society; this imbalance in turn contributes to a heightened fear of crime, a fear that is often disproportionate to the reality of being victimized (Kidd-Hewitt, 1995). One study indicated that, while United Kingdom newsprint media in the early 1990s devoted 64.5 per cent of crime reporting to stories of personal violence, in fact only 6 per cent of crime then involved personal violence (Williams and Dickinson, 1993). Regardless, the media functions for profit; and for many news sources, the more sensational the coverage, the more likely that it will bring in advertising and sales dollars.

Provocateur

Media representations of crime can also inadvertently contribute to miscarriages of justice as a consequence of their role in crime news reporting.[3] With respect to contributing to (or provoking) miscarriages of justice, particularly when heinous crimes occur (most often brutal murders of so-called "innocent"[4] victims), media outlets will often provide extensive and graphic coverage. To the extent that police permit, journalists will report highly stylized details of these crimes, possible suspects, potential leads, and other information about the crime in question. This in turn exerts enormous pressure on the police to solve these crimes, and to do so expeditiously. While public pressure to solve a crime immediately does not always result in the wrong person being accused or convicted, police may, in their desire to solve these cases, cut corners in investigative practices. Public opinion, particularly when hostile, can also play a role in judicial errors; before a suspect is even identified, it is not uncommon that the media foment collective hysteria about a "killer on the loose." In repeatedly writing about a particular case, the media may be inadvertently contributing to an atmosphere of fear. Martin (2001a) points out how this can occur in the larger institutional context within which a crime occurs; the high-profile nature of a case, in conjunction with the marginalized status of the accused as an "outsider" and suspect or unreliable evidence, may all precipitate a wrongful conviction. Thus, while the media provide information about crime and victimization to the public in general, they also play an inadvertant role in the criminal justice process, one that can have unforeseen consequences for an accused person.

One effect of extensive media reporting on cases before the courts is the possibility of influencing the impartiality of the jury. Jurors may be affected by salacious reporting and render verdicts based on inaccuracies gleaned from media reports, rather than on the evidence and arguments presented in the courtroom. While it is likely impossible to shield jurors completely from media accounts of some crimes, particularly those involving extensive reporting, there are, as discussed below, a number of legal remedies, in Canada and elsewhere, for mitigating the effect of prejudicial pre-trial publicity (Naylor, 1994, 497–500). One United Kingdom case that illustrates how prejudicial pre-trial publicity[5] can influence the outcome of a trial was that of Michelle and Lisa Taylor. Both were convicted of murdering Michelle's lover's wife; Michelle's motive for the actual killing of her lover's wife was alleged to be jealousy, while her sister's motive was a concern for the lover's treatment of her sister. In 1993 the Court of Appeal cleared both sisters, partly on the grounds of prejudicial reporting of their trial; the other grounds for appeal were that the prosecution had failed to make contradictory witness statements available to the defence. During their trial in 1992, headlines such as "love crazy mistress butchers wife" and "'killer' mistress at her lover's wedding"[6] were not uncommon. In that case, the court found that the media generally and tabloids more specifically "went beyond intimating a set of facts but actually constructed a set of facts using manipulated photographs from a video-recording in order to present a story other than, and in the eyes of the media better than, the truth" (Stephens and Hill, 1999, 265).

On appeal, both convictions were quashed by Lord Justice McCowan, who, in referring to the prejudicial reporting, stated that he found "it quite impossible to say that the jury were not influenced in their decision by what they read in the press" and that the press coverage had been "unremitting, extensive, sensational, inaccurate and misleading."[7] The Court of Appeal requested that the solicitor general address this issue; however, the solicitor general rejected the application and refused to have the offending newspapers (the *Sun*, the *Daily Mirror*, the *Daily Express*, and the *Daily Mail*) charged under the Contempt of Court Act, 1981. When the Taylor sisters later attempted to challenge this decision, they were unsuccessful, as two divisional court judges decided it was not open to judicial review (Shaw, 1995). In another case, three police officers who had been charged with conspiring to pervert the course of justice over the case of the Birmingham Six[8] were released and had their prosecution stayed as the court accepted their claim that adverse publicity had made a fair trial impossible (cf. *R. v. Reade* [1993]); Naylor, 1994, 492). In addition, negative newspaper reporting regarding individuals who have committed particularly heinous crimes can ultimately affect parole and release decisions occurring many years after the original offence (cf. Myra Hindley[9]). What appears clear is that, in criminal courts, the fact that the prosecution must discharge the burden of proof matters little "to those covering the story because, quite simply the media works on 'probabilities' rather than 'beyond reasonable doubts'" (Stephens and Hill, 1999, 265).

Watchdog

In its role as watchdog, the media can increase public awareness about miscarriages of justice. In fact, the media have been referred to as the "last court of appeal" (Savage et al., 2007) or the "court of last resort" for the wrongly convicted (Warden, 2002, 843). In recent years, with increased media access and exposure of many cases of the wrongly convicted, the media has now cast doubt on the fundamental reliability of the criminal justice system (Warden, 2002, 804). The horror of a wrongful imprisonment can be conveyed through interviews and media reports around specific cases. By forcing what are, at times, obscure cases into the public eye, the media serve to remind the public at large about the continued victimization and imprisonment of the wrongly convicted. This watchdog role can have an effect, in turn, on politicians and policy makers who have the power to intervene and rectify these injustices. Savage et al. (2007) point out that the media can contribute to campaigns of miscarriages of justice through publicity, influence, and the power to investigate. And, of course, the publicity the media bring to a case can attract legal support as well as political interest.

Yet this form of advocacy does not come without a price as media reporting can convey its own "tunnel vision"; the orientation and slant of a particular report may influence public opinion, or be viewed as "pressurizing" the judiciary (Savage et al., 2007, 95). Clearly, the media take sides in these debates; it is rare to find fair and balanced arguments about specific cases. Often particular journalists will advocate for individuals who have been wrongly convicted, using quotes and reporting that supports their partisan approach. While admirable, such reporting hardly represents an impartial or evenhanded means of representing a case and may in turn alienate public opinion about particular cases. Journalists, having lost faith in the criminal justice system and believing that courts are not in the business of seeking the "truth" or rather the "real truth" (but are more concerned with "the case" or "guilt" or "innocence"), are bound to seek and publish the "truth" and to look for the story beyond the "legal truths," regardless of how such reporting helps or hinders a particular case (Stephens and Hill, 1999, 273, 276).

Given that the media may play a watchdog role in keeping members of the criminal justice system accountable, journalists walk a fine line with respect to what they can and cannot report to the public about criminal cases, and when. In Canada, both statute and case law have had an impact on media coverage of criminal trials, at times outlawing media coverage completely or finding the press in contempt for reporting on specific cases. There are two competing objectives at play – "the protection of privacy and the constitutional right of all criminal defendants to undergo a fair trial" (Canadian Judicial Council, CJC, 2007, 14) – and this involves balancing the rights of the accused to a fair trial and the freedom of the press to report on criminal trials. In fact, journalists can be held in contempt of court for reporting on cases before the courts (once a case is under consideration of the courts or sub judice); however, the law with respect to contempt is currently in a state of flux (CJC, 2007, 3).[10]

With respect to reporting on criminal trials, the press in Canada, as in other democracies, is free to report what it chooses, but the courts have the authority to issue publication bans in order to ensure a fair trial for the accused; such bans would be considered unconstitutional in the United States, where much greater freedom of the press is allowed (Evans, 1995). Moreover, sanctions can be and are applied in those cases where such bans are not respected, but they are not enforceable outside of Canadian borders.[11] The courts have long established that such restrictions do not violate freedoms of the press, of speech, or of expression, all protected under the Charter. At the same time, more recent case law has addressed the issue of the protection of the identity of confidential sources. While there is no law per se that grants immunity to journalists' sources, in 2008 the Ontario Court of Appeal specifically recognized that, while protecting journalist-informant relationships was important, immunity did not apply. Thus, freedom of the press is not absolute. Justice John Laskin noted that "the court must ensure that the privacy interests of the press are limited as little as possible. But the court must also balance against the privacy interest of the press, the state or other societal interests in getting at the truth."[12] This decision was later affirmed by the Supreme Court.[13]

While statutory protections regarding the publication of information include section 11(d) (presumption of innocence) and 2(d) (freedom of expression) of the Charter, the leading case on publication bans is *Dagenais v. Canadian Broadcasting Corporation* (1995).[14] In this case the trial judge had issued a publication ban that prevented the Canadian Broadcasting Corporation from airing a fictionalized mini-series entitled "The Boys of St. Vincent." This 1992 docudrama was based in part on events involving the sexual abuse of young boys by Christian Brothers at the Mount Cashel Orphanage in St John's, Newfoundland. The airing of the series would have coincided with the hearings of four Christian Brothers who were being tried for sexual abuse of young boys at another Catholic school, in Ontario, at that same time. An injunction was granted by the Superior Court judge which prohibited the broadcast of the mini-series anywhere in Canada until the end of the four trials, as well as publicizing the Crown application for an injunction and related materials. The Ontario Court of Appeal affirmed the decision to grant the injunction but limited its scope; later, the Supreme Court of Canada held that the ban was too broad and established the following factors to be considered in the issuing of a publication ban, namely, that: "(a) such a ban is necessary in order to prevent a real and substantial risk to the fairness of the trial, because reasonably available alternative measures will not prevent the risk; and (b) the salutary effects of the publication ban outweigh the deleterious effects to the free expression of those affected by the ban."[15] The decision in *Dagenais* thus established that judges have common law discretionary authority to tailor a ban[16] to specific circumstances and that they must ensure that the ban covers no more information than is necessary (CJC, 2007, 15). With respect to miscarriages of justice, it is clear that this balancing of the right to a fair trial and freedom of the press is a precarious one and the implications for the wrongly convicted are great.

Finally, the role of family members as "watchdogs" in exposing miscarriages of justice to the press cannot be overstated. In many cases, if not for the persistence of outside family members, who themselves are victims of miscarriages of justice,[17] several wrongly convicted individuals would not have been released. One lawyer has noted that "families ... are the best people to take any case forward because nobody can impeach their motives ... they are essentially the best protagonists of change ... I am a firm believer in families being the hero of any campaign because without them there is nothing. All those other organizations exist only because of them ... ultimately it's the families which drive you and which lead the change" (Savage et al., 2007, 99).

The overturning of the David Milgaard's wrongful conviction and imprisonment in 1992 would not have been possible without the assistance of his mother, Joyce. She raised money and recruited lawyers, journalists, and private investigators to reinvestigate a crime that she believed her son could not have possibly committed. In 1990 the press covered Joyce Milgaard attempting to physically hand a forensic pathologist's report to then federal Justice Minister Kim Campbell, which outlined details and evidence that would exonerate her son. Headlines that followed this incident amidst a growing popular sentiment that Milgaard was in fact innocent, such as "Joyce Milgaard Snubbed by Kim Campbell,"[18] were indicative that the popular press saw the minister's behaviour as appalling – and reported it accordingly. One year later, Joyce Milgaard held a vigil outside a Winnipeg hotel to confront then Prime Minister Brian Mulroney, who did in fact speak to her. Regardless of this press coverage, Campbell refused to overturn Milgaard's conviction on the basis of new evidence in February 1991. A new application in August of the same year resulted in a direction to the Supreme Court in November 1991 to review Milgaard's case; Milgaard was released in 1992 but exonerated only in 1997 when DNA forensic analysis proved that Larry Fisher committed the murder.[19] Many years later, at the commission of inquiry into the errors that occurred in this case, it was found that "[Milgaard's] mother's unflagging commitment to her son's cause is widely credited with his conviction being overturned by the Supreme Court in 1992."[20] Savage et al. (2007, 100) describe the function of families as one of resilience – sticking with a campaign for exoneration long after others have given up.[21]

The media serve a number of functions that are at times in opposition: "At its best, the media's role as a watchdog of society can ferret out wrongdoing that goes undetected by other institutions. It can expose corrupt politicians, uncover accounting frauds at big corporations and spring the wrongly convicted from jail. But the competitive pressures also drive various media outlets to chase every detail of a story – sometimes even the trivial and the deeply personal. That can erode the media's credibility and the public's faith in the media's ability to serve as a watchdog" (Dorschner and Hoag, 2005).[22] On balance, however, media attention to wrongful convictions in Canada has likely contributed to a much wider public recognition that such miscarriages of justice can and do occur.

Independent Lobby Groups

The movement to facilitate the exoneration of innocent people has a long history in the United States, Canada, and the United Kingdom; such early movements began through grass-roots organizations, with little funding and little initial support.[23] In the United States, what could be described as the first type of innocence project, the *Court of Last Resort*, was a drama series that ran on the NBC network from 1957 to 1958. It was hosted by the detective novelist Earl Stanley Gardner and focused initially on improving the administration of justice but later evolved to investigate actual individual claims of false imprisonment and wrongful conviction (Buck, 2005, 1–2). Gardner worked with private investigators and experts in forensics and the law to review and possibly reverse miscarriages of justice.

In 1983 Centurion Ministries began operating under the direction of the Reverend James McCloskey in Princeton, New Jersey, and continues its work today as a secular non-profit organization that helps the wrongly convicted seeking exoneration (Buck, 2005, 2; McCartney, 2006a). It follows a "no representation model," whereby it investigates cases of possible innocence and then refers them to pro-bono legal counsel, thus providing no direct representation (Suni, 2002, 927). Centurion Ministries restricts itself to taking on individuals who are "completely innocent" of the crime and also assists exonerees in reintegrating into society.[24]

The Death Penalty Information Center (DPIC) is an independent lobby group in the United States aimed at providing general information about the death penalty, including a database on all executions in the country since 1977. While it is not an innocence lobby group per se, it provides information on a number of death-row inmates who have been exonerated since 1973, as well as a number of reports and articles regarding the issue of wrongful conviction in capital cases. The DPIC has reported that, since 1973, 157 people from 26 states have been released from death row either because their conviction was overturned through an acquittal at retrial, or because all charges against them were dropped, or because they were given an absolute pardon by their state governor based on new evidence of innocence.[25] Moreover, the DPIC provides information on a number of cases of individuals put to death by the state who may in fact have been innocent.[26] A report published by the DPIC in 2004, entitled "Innocence and the Crisis in the American Death Penalty,"[27] outlines how questions of innocence have emerged as a significant issue in death-penalty debates, to the extent that public opinion about capital punishment has changed as a result. The report notes that the advent of DNA forensic analysis and the release of many exonerees from death row have also led to a reduction in the overall number of death sentences handed down by the courts, perhaps reflecting a reluctance on the part of the judiciary to contribute to the spectre of the execution of an innocent person.

In Canada, the Association in Defence of the Wrongly Convicted (now Innocence Canada) began its work in 1993, having grown out of the Justice for Guy Paul Morin Committee.[28] AIDWYC/Innocence Canada functions as a non-profit organization that advocates on behalf of the wrongly convicted. It primarily reviews and supports claims of innocence in homicide cases where all levels of appeal have been exhausted. A number of lawyers work on a pro-bono basis for the organization and develop briefs to be submitted to the minister of justice for conviction review under section 696 of the Criminal Code. To date, AIDWYC/Innocence Canada has assisted in the successful exoneration of twenty-one individuals.[29]

In the United Kingdom, the organization JUSTICE has a long history and first began operation in 1957, serving to investigate cases of alleged innocence; it did so for over forty years until the establishment of the Criminal Cases Review Commission[30] in 1997, at which time it disbanded, a decision that has been described as premature (Naughton, 2006). Also evident in various forms in the United Kingdom are "justice campaigns"; they occur when groups of individuals band together and effectively bring attention to particular cases of miscarriages of justice. These groups act as "'extra-judicial' 'extra-legal,' 'non-governmental' or 'unofficial' sources of influence over the machineries of law enforcement and criminal justice" (Savage et al., 2007, 85). They have also been described as instrumental in bringing about policy reform for a number of key criminal justice and policing practices.[31] These campaigns have had varying outcomes and varying levels of success; some focus on obtaining justice in individual cases through quashing of convictions, but their outcomes may have a wider, more general effect on policy and legislative reform (Savage et al., 2007, 89).

The Scottish-based Miscarriages of Justice Organization (MOJO) offers assistance to those in prison and afterwards in coping with a wrongful conviction.[32] While its main objective is one of support in reintegration upon release, it also offers advocacy services for innocent persons in prison, including referrals for legal representation, forensic services, and media contacts. One of its founding members, Paddy Hill, was himself wrongfully imprisoned for sixteen years as one of the infamous Birmingham Six. In recognition of the adjustment problems many of the wrongly convicted experience on release (Grounds, 2004), MOJO is attempting to raise money to establish a retreat to facilitate their return to the community.

Innocence Projects

Emergence

Innocence projects are generally comprised of groups of students (from either law, journalism, or criminology) working in conjunction with faculty members and lawyers from the community to provide pro-bono support to establish the innocence of those who claim a wrongful conviction. There are a number of projects that exist throughout North America, Europe, and Australia, all of which offer more or less the same service, through varying mandates and outcomes. Tables 14 through 17 contain a non-exhaustive list of innocence projects in Canada, the United States, the United Kingdom and Ireland, and Australia and New Zealand currently functioning that are affiliated with a university. The first Innocence Project to be affiliated with a university law school, which served as a model for many others to follow, was founded by Barry Scheck and Peter Neufeld in 1992 at the Benjamin Cardozo Law School of Yeshiva University, New York, and it adopted a "full representation model" which essentially functions as a legal clinic

Table 14. Innocence projects – Canada

Project	School	Faculty	Link
Innocence McGill	McGill University	Faculty of Law	http://www.mcgill.ca/innocence/
Conviction Review Project I	Université d'Ottawa	Faculty of Law, Common Law Division	anne@weinsteinlaw.net
Innocence Ottawa	Université d'Ottawa	Department of Criminology, Faculty of Social Sciences	https://innocenceottawa. wordpress.com/news/
Osgoode Hall Innocence Project	York University	Osgoode Hall Law School	Innocent@yorku.ca
UBC Law Innocence Project	University of British Columbia	Faculty of Law	http://www.innocenceproject.law. ubc.ca
Regroupement Projet Innocence Montréal (autrefois comité sur les erreurs judiciaires)	Université de Montréal	Faculté de droit	helene.dumont@umontreal.ca
Projet Innocence Québec	Université de Québec à Montréal	Faculté de droit	https://www.innocencequebec.com

(Buck, 2005, 1; Cromett and Thurston-Myster, 2005; Huff, 2004; McCartney, 2006b). Since that time, dozens of other projects have developed in the United States.

The first legal clinic/innocence project in the United Kingdom[33] was established at the University of Bristol in 2005 and seeks to ascertain "factual innocence" rather than determine technical miscarriages of justice; one year later, innocence projects emerged at Cardiff Law School, the University of Leeds, and the University of Westminster, all of which were part of the larger Innocence Network until it folded. The first Innocence Project in Canada was established at Osgoode Law School of York University in 1999 (McCartney, 2006b). Subsequently, innocence projects emerged at McGill University, Faculty of Law; University of Ottawa, Faculty of Law (Common Law Division); University of British Columbia, Faculty of Law; and University of Ottawa, Criminology Department (Innocence Ottawa). Two francophone projects were founded in the province of Quebec, both from within faculties of law; Regroupement Projet Innocence Montréal is attached to the Université de Montréal, and Projet Innocence Québec is part of the Université de Québec à Montréal. In Australia, innocence projects were established at Griffith University, Queensland, and the University of Technology, Sydney, in 2001. The advent of DNA forensic analysis and widespread media reporting about miscarriages of justice likely facilitated the development of the large network of innocence projects now operating in common law jurisdictions throughout the northern hemisphere. While all may have more or less similar mandates, they differ with respect to how cases are accepted, processed, and followed.

The Role of Innocence Projects: Forms and Function

The first Innocence Project at Cardozo Law School emerged in response to the growing use of DNA forensic analysis in the late 1990s, which raised concerns

Table 15. Innocence projects – United States[34]

Project	School/Affiliation	Faculty	Coverage	Link
Loyola Law School Project for the Innocent	Loyola Law School		California	http://www.lls.edu/academics/ experientiallearning/clinics/ socialcriminaljusticeclinics/ projectfortheinnocent/
Innocence and Justice Clinic	Wake Forest University	School of Law	North Carolina	http://innocence-clinic.law.wfu.edu
Oklahoma Innocence Project	Oklahoma City University	School of Law	Oklahoma	innocence@okcu.edu
Northern Arizona Justice Project	Northern Arizona University	Department of Criminal Justice	Arizona	http://nau.edu/arizona-innocence-project/
Arizona Justice Project	Arizona State University	Sandra Day O'Connor College of Law	Arizona	info@azjusticeproject.org
Innocence Project Northwest	University of Washington	School of Law	Washington	https://www.law.washington.edu/clinics/ipnw/
Innocence Project	Texas Southern University	Thurgood Marshall School of Law, Earl Carl Institute for Legal and Social Policy	Texas	http://www.tsulaw.edu/centers/ECI/centers/ criminal_justice
Innocence Project	Yeshiva University	Benjamin N. Cardozo School of Law	New York	info@innocenceproject.org
Post-Conviction Innocence Clinic	New York Law School		New York	http://www.nyls.edu/academics/office_ of_clinical_and_experiential_learning/ clinics/post_conviction_innocence_ project/
Boston College Innocence Program Clinic	Boston College	Law School	Massachusetts	http://lawguides.bc.edu/c. php?g=350980&p=2367585
Mid-Atlantic Innocence Project	American University	Washington College of Law	District of Columbia, Maryland, and Virginia	innocenceproject@wcl.american.edu
Northern California Innocence Project	Santa Clara University	Law School	California	http://law.scu.edu/ncip/
Hawai'i Innocence Project	University of Hawai'i	William S. Richardson School of Law	Hawai'i	www.innocenceprojecthawaii.org
Corey Wise Innocence Project	University of Colorado, Boulder	Law School	Colorado	kristy.martinez@colorado.edu
New England Innocence Project	Pace University	Law School	Connecticut, New Hampshire, Massachusetts, Rhode Island, Vermont, Maine	intake@newenglandinnocence.org

(Continued)

Table 15. Innocence projects – United States (Continued)

Project	School/Affiliation	Faculty	Coverage	Link
Pace Post-Conviction Project	Pace University	Law School, Barbara C. Salken Criminal Justice Clinic	Westchester County and New York City	www.innocenceprojecthawaii.org
Florida Innocence Project	Nova Southeastern University	Shepard Broad Law Center	Florida	http://www.floridainnocence.org/
Innocence Clinic	University of Miami	School of Law	Florida	http://www.law.miami.edu/academics/clinics/innocence-clinic
Ohio Innocence Project	University of Cincinnati	College of Law, Rosenthal Institute of Justice	Ohio	https://www.law.uc.edu/oip
Pennsylvania Innocence Project	Duquesne University	School of Law	Pennsylvania	delosae@duq.edu
Illinois Center on Wrongful Convictions	Northwestern University	School of Law, Roderick MacArthur Justice Center	Illinois	http://www.law.northwestern.edu/legalclinic/wrongfulconvictions/
Illinois Innocence Project	University of Illinois at Springfield	Center for Legal Studies	Illinois	illinoisinnocenceproject@uis.edu
Medill Justice Project	Northwestern University	Medill School of Journalism, Media, Integrated Marketing Communications	Illinois	medilljusticeproject@northwestern.edu
Wrongful Conviction Clinic	Indiana University	Robert H. McKinney School of Law	Indiana	https://mckinneylaw.iu.edu/practice/clinics/clinics-wrongful-conviction.html
Innocence/Wrongful Conviction Clinic	University of Tennessee	College of Law	Tennessee	http://law.utk.edu/clinics/innocence/
Texas Innocence Network	University of Houston	Law Center	Texas	http://texasinnocencenetwork.com/
Innocence Project Texas	Texas Tech University School of Law in Lubbock	Texas A&M University School of Law, Fort Worth	Texas	info@ipoftexas.org
Actual Innocence Clinic	University of Texas at Houston	School of Law	Texas	Tiffany Dowling tdowling@law.utexas.edu
Actual Innocence Clinic	South Texas College of Law Houston		Texas	Catherine Burnett cburnett@stcl.edu
Rocky Mountain Innocence Center	University of Utah	S.J. Quinney College of Law	Utah, Nevada, and Wyoming	http://rminnocence.org/what-we-do/
University of Kentucky Innocence Project	University of Kentucky	College of Law	Kentucky	http://law.uky.edu/course-catalog/law-971-innocence-project-externship
West Virginia Innocence Project	West Virginia University	College of Law	West Virginia	http://wvinnocenceproject.law.wvu.edu
Institute for Actual Innocence	University of Richmond	School of Law	Virginia	http://law.richmond.edu/academics/clinics-skills/in-house/innocence/index

Project	University	School	Location	Website/Contact
Innocence Project Clinic	University of Virginia	School of Law	Virginia	http://www.law.virginia.edu/html/academics/practical/innocenceclinic.htm
Wisconsin Innocence Project	University of Wisconsin	School of Law	Wisconsin	http://law.wisc.edu/fjr/clinicals/ip/
Hamline Innocence Clinic	Hamline University	School of Law	Minnesota, North Dakota	innocencemn@ipmn.org
Montana Innocence Project	University of Montana	School of Law	Montana	http://www.mtinnocenceproject.org
North Carolina Center on Actual Innocence	Duke University/University of North Carolina/North Carolina Central Univeristy/Elon University/Campbell University	School of Law	North Carolina	http://www.nccai.org
Michigan Innocence Clinic	University of Michigan	Michigan Law	Michigan	http://www.law.umich.edu/clinical/innocenceclinic/Pages/default.aspx
Cooley Innocence Project	Western Michigan University	Cooley Law School	Michigan	http://www.cooley.edu/clinics/innocence_project.html
Innocence and Justice Project New Mexico	University of New Mexico	School of Law	New Mexico	http://lawschool.unm.edu/ijp/index.php
Innocence Project of South Dakota	University of South Dakota	School of Law	South Dakota	ipsd@usd.ed
Arkansas Innocence Project	University of Arkansas	School of Law Legal Clinic, Robert A. Leflar Law Center	Arkansas	Robert A. Leflar Law Center, 1 University of Arkansas, Fayetteville, AR 72701
Innocence Project Clinic	University of Baltimore	School of Law	Maryland	http://law.ubalt.edu/clinics/innocenceproject. cfmmnethercott@ubalt.edu
The Exoneration Project	The University of Chicago	The Law School	Illinois	https://www.exonerationproject.org
George C. Cochran Innocence Project	The University of Mississippi	School of Law	Mississippi	http://innocenceproject.olemiss.edu
California Innocence Project	California Western	School of Law	California	https://californiainnocenceproject.org
Northern California Innocence Project	Santa Clara University	School of Law	San Diego, CA	http://law.scu.edu/ncip/
Idaho Innocence Project	Boise State University		Idaho	https://innocenceproject.boisestate.edu
Pennsylvania Innocence Project	Temple University	Beasley School of Law	Philadelphia, PA	http://innocenceprojectpa.org
Justice Brandeis Innocence Project	Brandeis University	The Schuster Institute for Investigative Journalism	Massachusetts	www.brandeis.edu/investigate/innocence-project
Midwest Innocence Project	University of Missouri, Kansas City	School of Law	Missouri	Office@TheMIP.org

Table 16. Innocence projects – United Kingdom[35] and Ireland

Project	School	Faculty	Link
University of Leeds Innocence Project	University of Leeds	Faculty of Law	innocenceproject@leeds.ac.uk
University of Southampton Innocence Project	University of Southampton	School of Law	J.MacLean@soton.ac.uk
Glasgow Caledonian Innocence Project	Glasgow Caledonian University	School of Law	m.bromby@gcal.ac.uk
Cardiff Law School Innocence Project	Cardiff University	Cardiff Law School	https://www.cardiff.ac.uk/law-politics/courses/law/pro-bono
Irish Innocence Project	Griffith College Dublin	Law School	innocenceproject@gcd.ie
The Innocence Project	Durham University	Durham Law School	https://www.dur.ac.uk/law/societies/dups/
Innocence Project Bournemouth	Bournemouth University	Law Department	https://www.causes.com/causes/43287-bournemouth-innocence-project
Innocence Project	Bangor University	School of Law	https://www.bangor.ac.uk/law/innocence.php.en
Innocence Project	Lancaster University	School of Law	http://www.lancaster.ac.uk/law/undergraduate/extra-curricular-opportunities/the-innocence-project/
Innocence Project	Nottingham Trent University	School of Law	https://www4.ntu.ac.uk/legal_advice_centre/about_us/index.html
Innocence Project	Sheffield Hallam Univeristy	School of Law	http://www4.shu.ac.uk/mediacentre/
Cambridge University Innocence Project	Cambridge University	Faculty of Law	https://www.cusu.cam.ac.uk/societies/directory/innocenceproject/
Innocence Project London	University of Greenwich	School of Law	30 Park Row, London SE10 9LS United Kingdom
Miscarriages of Justice Project	University of Leicester	School of Law	http://luls.org.uk/pro-bono/the-miscarriages-of-justice-project/
Innocence Project	Plymouth University	School of Law, Criminology and Government	https://www.plymouth.ac.uk/courses/undergraduate/llb-law/innocence-project
Innocence Project	University of Portsmouth	School of Law	http://www.port.ac.uk/institute-of-criminal-justice-studies/research/strategic-projects/criminal-justice-clinic
Miscarriages of Justice Review Centre	University of Sheffield	School of Law	http://www.sheffield.ac.uk/law/about/mjrc
Innocence Project	University of Strathclyde	Law Clinic, Journalism Department	https://www.lawclinic.org.uk/updates/strathclyde-innocence-project
Innocence Project	Bangor University	Bangor Law School	https://www.bangor.ac.uk/law/innocence.php.en
Winchester Innocence Project	Winchester University	Media, Communications and Journalism	https://winchesterinnocence.wordpress.com

Table 17. Innocence projects – Australia and New Zealand

Project	School	Faculty	Contact Info
Griffith University Innocence Project	Griffith University	Griffith Law School	https://www.griffith.edu.au/ criminology-law/innocence-project
The Sydney Exoneration Project	University of Sydney	Sydney Law School, Psychology Department	http://www.psych.usyd.edu.au/lab/ notguilty/?page_id=22
Bridge of Hope Innocence Initiative	RMIT University	Justice and Legal Studies	http://www1.rmit.edu.au/ browse;ID=l6hmgxtdqgafz
Criminal Justice Review Project	Edith Cowan University	Sellenger Centre for Research in Law, Justice and Social Change	pamela.henry@ecu.edu.au
Innocence Project New Zealand	University of Otago	Department of Psychology, School of Law	http://innocencenetwork.org/ location/innocence-project-new-zealand/

about the ability of the criminal justice system to function effectively (Cromett and Thurston-Myster, 2005; Weathered, 2003, 78). To date, the Innocence Project has accepted only cases that have DNA evidence and it is often working on two hundred cases at any given time (Medwed, 2003, 1106). The project receives upwards of fifteen hundred requests annually from inmate applicants alleging innocence, and co-founder Barry Scheck has noted that approximately 40 per cent of the cases it takes to conclusion result in exonerations (Weathered, 2003, 78). The Innocence Project has exonerated over three hundred and fifty people in the United States to date, twenty of whom were serving time on death row.[36] The efficacy of the original Innocence Project is likely attributable to its stringent selection criteria: the fact that it confines itself to cases where there is DNA evidence enhances its chances of successful exoneration considerably. While most other Innocence Projects investigate cases that do not involve DNA evidence (Medwed, 2003, 1107), the overall effectiveness of Innocence Projects is in large part attributable to DNA forensic analysis (Buck, 2005, 2).

The Osgoode Hall Innocence Project at York University in Toronto, Ontario, allows students to work on cases supervised by faculty, and after a thorough screening process, it attempts to reinvestigate cases and seek proof of innocence. Eligibility criteria are restricted to the following[37]:

- A conviction for a serious offence – the applicant must have been convicted of a serious criminal offence. No indictable offence is prima facie excluded. Summary conviction offences are excluded unless the Innocence Project feels that there are compelling reasons why the application should proceed further.
- All rights of appeal have been exhausted – prospective clients must normally have appealed their conviction(s) to the applicable court of appeal of the province.
- A claim of factual innocence is seriously advanced – cases are accepted only if, on his/her own facts, the applicant is not guilty of the offence at issue or any included criminal offence(s). Other policy considerations may also be considered.

- Alternative resources are unavailable – the project must limit itself to assisting individuals who do not have the resources necessary to pursue a remedy privately.

In those cases that warrant it, this Innocence Project may seek a formal remedy of conviction review through a written application to the federal minister of justice under section 696.1 of the Criminal Code. Osgoode Hall also assists in requests for compensation and clemency, as well as in legal research and advocacy. It has been instrumental in having the charges withdrawn in the case of Romeo Phillion, wrongly convicted and imprisoned for over thirty years for the murder of Leopold Roy.

Innocence projects assume differing approaches based on the level of legal representation offered to a client. These models are either "no representation," "limited representation," or "full representation" (Suni, 2002, 926). "No representation" innocence projects establish no formal legal relationship with the inmate applicant and are not bound by any professional obligations or duties. "Limited" and "full" representation models can be differentiated by whether or not they continue to represent inmates "even if they determine that there is not a credible claim of actual innocence" (Suni, 2002, 928). Innocence projects that adhere to the full-representation model will proceed with a case until its conclusion, regardless of whether or not they continue to view their client as actually innocent, whereas limited-representation innocence projects litigate only on behalf of cases "with the most merit" (Medwed, 2003, 1102), in other words, those cases that "continue to present viable claims of absolute, factual innocence" (Suni, 2002, 929).

It appears that, in practice, the majority of innocence projects follow the limited-representation model (Medwed, 2003, 1105).[38] As a consequence, there are professional and ethical issues that emerge since limited representation makes it more difficult to ascertain when the attorney-client relationship has been established or whether the innocence project is fulfilling an objective role (Medwed, 2003, 1123; Suni, 2002, 929). Determining if an attorney-client relationship exists during the investigation is important, because "the existence of such a relationship brings with it substantial duties relating to, among other things, confidentiality, exercise of independent professional judgment, competence and diligence" (Suni, 2002, 931).

Innocence projects as part of law schools may be either comprised of student volunteers with minimal supervision or function as in-house law clinics, where students are supervised by faculty members and can earn credits towards their degree. A third but less common form places students in externships with public-defender organizations alongside a classroom component (Medwed, 2003, 1100).[39]

Despite the variety of forms assumed by innocence projects, there remain similarities in their basic functioning,[40] perhaps the most fundamental of which is case screening and selection. Among the criteria for case selection, innocence projects have to decide whether they are going to restrict themselves to cases with DNA evidence. The advantages to accepting only cases with DNA evidence is that not only are screening and selection much easier, but, since many exonerations have resulted from DNA forensic analysis of evidence, these cases are thought to be more likely to yield a successful outcome (Medwed, 2003, 1107). One early drawback to laboratory DNA testing in the United States was related to cost ($2,500 to $5,000; cf. Medwed, 2003, 1098n.4); however, technology has advanced to the degree that private-laboratory costs are now much lower (e.g., depending on the laboratory, from $180 to $395 to process and test one forensic sample[41]). Non-DNA cases are more time-consuming at all stages of the process: from initial case selection through to investigation, litigation, and exoneration – given that other evidence must be sought out and examined and a determination made as to its relevance (Medwed, 2003, 1107).

Regardless of their specific mandate, innocence projects have also achieved other successes beyond exonerations. Among the more notable examples, in 2003 Illinois Governor George Ryan cited the investigative work of journalism students at the Medill Innocence Project as a contributing factor in his decision to declare a moratorium on the death penalty as well as grant clemency to the state's death-row inmates (Buck, 2005, 2; Roberts and Weathered, 2009, 46; Warden, 2002, 846). Moreover, judges are now beginning to recognize the work of innocence projects. At the Conference of Chief Justices in 2005, a resolution was submitted calling for judges to support the efforts of innocence projects across the country; though this resolution passed, it proved controversial since such support would have constituted an acknowledgment that "there are critical weaknesses in their justice systems" (Post, 2005).

At the same time, innocence projects raise awareness about the many factors responsible for wrongful convictions in the first place. For instance, it is common for innocence projects to stress the importance of establishing policies and procedures for the preservation of evidence (Naughton, 2006; Weathered, 2003, 81). With regard to false confessions, innocence projects have campaigned for all police interrogations to be recorded (Cromett and Thurston-Myster, 2005; Roberts and Weathered, 2009, 47; Findley, 2006, 255n.88). In addition, campaigns have addressed the need for changes to eyewitness identification, supporting the police use of "a double blind, sequential display process and to control the information given to the witness" (Cromett and Thurston-Myster, 2005; Findley, 2006, 255n.89). Another matter of particular concern to innocence projects is the compensation of exonerated individuals (Findley, 2006, 256; Huff, 2004, 115). Finally, in recent years several states have introduced reforms making DNA testing more accessible to inmates at the post-conviction stages – reforms that are, at least in part, attributable to the work of innocence projects (Huff, 2004, 115; Roberts and Weathered, 2009, 47).[42]

Pedagogy: Do Innocence Projects Teach Students about Law?

The objective of most innocence projects is to provide law students with the opportunity to investigate "real, live" alleged miscarriages of justice and hone their research and writing skills at the same time; this mainly takes the form of post-conviction representation of innocent people. Innocence projects are a relatively new form of clinical legal education, as opposed to legal-aid clinics and clinics offering legal representation to indigent persons that have long been a part of formal legal education in law schools (Stiglitz et al., 2002). In innocence projects, when performing "autopsies … on criminal cases in which the system failed" (Findley, 2006, 262), students acquire and develop a number of skills and aptitudes essential to litigation practice, such as critical thinking, legal analysis, interviewing, counselling, fact finding,[43] and case management (Medwed, 2003, 1135; McCartney, 2006b). Similarly, when dealing with scientific evidence, students gain experience in "how to consult independent experts, demand access to raw data and lab analyst case bench notes, and retest the evidence, when appropriate" (Findley, 2006, 248). A further educational benefit of innocence projects is that they "radicalize" law students, instilling a progressive reform-oriented mindset (McCartney, 2006b; Findley, 2006, 263).

For faculty members attempting to balance the pedagogical and social-justice roles of innocence projects, there are two possible contrasting supervisory styles: directive and non-directive (Medwed, 2003, 1132). Ideally, students are given "ownership" of their cases, such that they receive non-directive supervision, although complex cases may warrant greater attention from faculty. Directive supervision, wherein faculty assumes primary responsibility for the handling of a case, has the advantage of ensuring that "students do not flounder excessively or lose faith in their abilities" (Medwed, 2003, 1131). But, at the same time, too much direction on the part of faculty is less popular since it reproduces the traditional hierarchical relationship students have with law-school faculty (Medwed, 2003, 1132).

Since innocence projects typically take on large and complex cases, there is "no uniform experience" for students (Findley, 2006, 240). In general, the educational value for students working on these cases varies a great deal, for it can take months, even years, to achieve a resolution. This leads Findley (2006, 240) to suggest the need for law clinics and innocence projects to offer students a more intensive and consistent experience, particularly in terms of legal writing and litigation skills.

Innocence Projects in Journalism Schools

While innocence projects have traditionally emerged from law schools, guided by criminal law professors and practitioners, a relatively recent phenomenon has been the creation of innocence projects in journalism departments or schools in universities. Journalism-based[44] innocence projects operate according to the no-representation model; that is, once they have concluded the investigative work, they then refer the case to pro-bono attorneys. In October 2009 students involved in Northwestern University's Medill Justice Project worked to uncover evidence proving the innocence of Anthony McKinney, who had spent thirty-one years in jail for the murder of a security guard, a murder many believe he did not commit. In an unprecedented action, the state's attorney for Cook County issued a subpoena asking for "all unpublished interviews; all notes, memoranda, reports, and summaries made by the students; all electronic communications involving the case; and the grade each student who worked on the case received each quarter, the grading criteria, and course syllabi,"[45] as well as e-mails exchanged between the students and Professor David Protess.[46]

The prosecutor's office stated that it required these documents to make "an accurate of assessment of witnesses' credibility and other essential issues." Further, the prosecutor's office believed that the journalism students in this case were acting not as journalists per se but rather as investigators cooperating with the legal team and so were not protected under the Illinois Reporter's Privilege Act[47] from being compelled to reveal sources and turn over notes. While the school initially complied and turned over some documentation that had already been on-the-record, it later fought to keep grades, grading criteria, evaluations of student performances, expenses, syllabi, e-mails, unpublished student memos, and off-the-record interviews private. This type of harassment has been described as an "unwarranted fishing expedition" and an attempt to discredit the work done by the Innocence Project. Since the original subpoena, a number of other lawsuits have been filed regarding what information is protected and what is not, while Professor Protess has been removed from his position at Northwestern University. Anthony McKinney was never exonerated and died in 2013 after spending thirty-five years in prison.[48] The roadblocks that the students involved in the Innocence Project have faced in this case may be unusual; however, they reveal once again the intransigence that the state often displays in the face of calls to re-examine an earlier conviction.

Conclusions

General awareness regarding the fact that miscarriages of justice can and do occur has clearly increased in the last few decades, so much so that media reports of these cases are not as extraordinary as they once were. Paradoxically, however, this reporting has also served to inure the public to the idea of wrongful convictions, which have come to be seen as commonplace, little more than unavoidable failures of the criminal justice system. To counter this complacency, what is now required is greater reporting about the failures of the system that result in these errors and about the known factors that contribute to miscarriages of justice, in order to educate the public about how mistakes happen and, ultimately, how they can avoided.

At the same time, the proliferation of innocence projects and lobby groups in most common law jurisdictions is also indicative of a deep dissatisfaction with the ability of standard criminal justice procedures to produce a fair outcome or to function effectively in providing adequate recourse when an initial conviction is in error. While innocence projects can help to fill those gaps created by an over-taxed legal system with all of its inherent deficiencies, as well as providing unique learning experiences for students so they may ultimately assist in overturning erroneous convictions, more is needed. In order for innocence projects to be more effective, greater direction and guidance is required by senior counsel with years of experience working within the criminal justice system. The pro-bono involvement of larger numbers of practising lawyers with established innocence projects would benefit students and possibly the wrongly convicted.

The rise in the innocence movement is an indication that more and more students graduating from law schools will be aware of the spectre of miscarriages of justice. These students, some of whom may have already worked on wrongful-conviction cases, will likely be more sensitive to where mistakes can happen, how they occur, and how to better raise issues on appeal. One result of this greater awareness and understanding of wrongful convictions could possibly be fewer errors in the future.

Chapter Thirteen

Lessons from Other Jurisdictions

"Most significantly, we still need statutory change to our system of criminal justice and a specific body that can address the continuing problem of the wrongful conviction of the innocence and deliver ... the machinery that can guarantee to investigate fully alleged wrongful convictions." (Naughton, 2010)

Introduction

Given that most common law jurisdictions struggle with the problem of wrongful convictions, it is not surprising that many have developed means of redressing these errors of justice, from both within and outside the formal criminal justice system. Specifically, the United Kingdom and Norway have developed commissions to redress miscarriages of justice, independent of the realm and purview of government. The Criminal Cases Review Commission (CCRC) of England, Wales, and Northern Ireland, as well as the commissions of the same name in Scotland and Norway, serve as examples of review bodies for suspected miscarriages of justice. In the United States, given that the death penalty still exists in thirty-one states, the spectre of a miscarriage of justice has very grave implications. Recently, various state legislatures have developed innocence commissions and commissions of inquiry to revisit arguably questionable convictions. This chapter will critically examine and compare post-conviction exoneration policies and practices for the wrongly convicted in selected jurisdictions.

United Kingdom: Criminal Cases Review Commission

On 21 November 1974 bombs went off in two pubs in Birmingham, England, killing twenty-one people and injuring scores of others. This occurred during the height of the Irish "Troubles"[1] and was evidence that the terrorist campaigns that had been occurring in Northern Ireland between Loyalist paramilitary groups and the outlawed Irish Republican Army for several years had extended their reach to England (Keegan, 1999, 1777). Under emergency legislative measures – specifically, the Prevention of Terrorism Act (1974) – six men[2] were quickly targeted, arrested, and ultimately convicted of setting these bombs; however, they were innocent. All of the usual factors that contribute to wrongful convictions were present: coerced false confessions, faulty forensic science, and the use of other highly circumstantial evidence (Walker, 1999a, 47). It was only after sixteen years of imprisonment, much civil and criminal litigation, and a well-publicized media campaign that the "Birmingham Six" were finally freed on 14 March 1991.

It was on the very same day the "Birmingham Six" convictions were quashed that the British government established a Royal Commission on Criminal Justice (known as the Runciman Commission) to examine the workings of the criminal justice system from arrest through trial to conviction and appeal (Kyle, 2004, 660). When the commission reported two years later, it recommended a number of sweeping changes to arrest, trial, and criminal procedure in the United Kingdom. Interestingly, the most extensive of its recommendations were directed at miscarriages of justice.[3] At that time, individuals who claimed to be wrongly convicted could apply to the home secretary, through the C3 Division of the Home Office,[4] for a review of their conviction. The home secretary possessed the statutory power to refer the case back to the Court of Appeal, and generally required that new evidence be presented which would test the safety of the conviction. The commission recognized that the role of the home secretary as an executive power was in conflict with the role of reviewing individual cases thought to be in error (this also was manifest in reticence on the part of the home secretary to refer cases back to the Court of Appeal). Consequently, it recommended that a new independent body be established, with wide powers of investigation and review, to replace the home secretary in referring cases of alleged miscarriages of justice to the Court of Appeal. Thus, via the enactment of the Criminal Appeal Act of 1995, the Criminal Cases Review Commission was established.[5]

The CCRC is an independent public body, appointed by the queen, that has the power to review convictions and sentences in cases emanating from England, Wales, and Northern Ireland. Its membership is made up of eleven commissioners; one-third of these must be lawyers with ten years experience and two-thirds must have knowledge of the justice system.[6] It is important to note that the CCRC is *not* an innocence commission, in the American sense (Zellick, 2006, 561), and it does not profess to be one.[7] The role of the CCRC is not to establish the innocence of a defendant (and, as discussed earlier, there are many ways to understand the construct of innocence). In essence, the commission has the task of investigating and reviewing individual cases in order to ascertain the safety of a given conviction; it also possesses the unique power to commission experts to examine evidence and offer their opinions on its value (Roach, 2010, 92). While the commissioners have varying degrees of knowledge about the criminal justice system – they include accountants, scientists, coroners, psychiatrists, and former police officers (Leigh, 2000) – they are also assisted by case-review managers. The commission itself possesses a large number of powers; it may:

1. Review convictions on summary conviction and on indictment;
2. Review sentences on indictment (where the matter was dealt with in criminal proceedings in England, Wales, and Northern Ireland); and
3. Review findings of not guilty by reason of insanity and cases where the person was under a disability when he/she did the act or made the omission charged against him or her. (Criminal Appeal Act, 1995, ss. 9–12)

The Court of Appeal can also direct the commission to investigate any matter in an appeal and to report on it to the court (Leigh, 2000, 366). The CCRC can consider out-of-time appeals and appeals of deceased individuals (Zellick, 2006).[8] Also, the terms of reference under which it can refer cases to the appellate courts are wider than those applied to previous case referrals under the home secretary (Kyle, 2004, 662).

The criteria for eligibility under which the CCRC can refer cases to the Court of Appeal are contained in section 13 of the Criminal Appeal Act, 1995:

(1) A reference of a conviction, verdict, finding or sentence shall not be made under any of sections 9 to 12 unless –
   (a) the Commission consider that there is a real possibility that the conviction, verdict, finding or sentence would not be upheld were the reference to be made,
   (b) the Commission so consider –
      (i) in the case of a conviction, verdict or finding, because of an argument, or evidence, not raised in the proceedings which led to it or on any appeal or application for leave to appeal against it, or
      (ii) in the case of a sentence, because of an argument on a point of law, or information, not so raised, and
   (c) an appeal against the conviction, verdict, finding or sentence has been determined or leave to appeal against it has been refused.

Essentially, these criteria outline the "real possibility" test for consideration of a reference (to be discussed below) and require that new or fresh evidence must be presented in support of a review.

Cases are assessed to establish grounds for appeal, and, following a preliminary assessment, a more intensive review is then undertaken by a case-review manager and a commissioner. The commission may investigate matters by itself or rely on other resources, such as forensic specialists, police forces, and law-enforcement bodies. Review of a case may be continued at this stage if there is the belief that there are grounds under which an appeal would be likely to succeed (if the circumstances of the case as presented are true). The commission staff will examine documents and interview witnesses and applicants. In cases where there is a belief in the possibility of reversal, the case is then presented to a committee of three commissioners, who make a final decision whether to refer the case, not to refer the case, or direct that further investigation be done. In the situation where a case is initially refused, the applicant, after viewing the reasons, can make further representations before a final decision is taken (Zellick, 2006, 563). The CCRC's involvement in the case ends at this point, and the final decision lies with the Court of Appeal.

As indicated in Table 18, in almost twenty years, the commission has reviewed more than 20,000 cases and referred more than 600 to the appeal courts; it receives two or three new applications every working day. The time frame for investigating cases is usually one or two months, but more complex cases take from one to three years, depending on whether an individual is incarcerated.[9] Overall, 60–70 per cent of the forty to fifty cases referred each year to the Court of Appeal result in the conviction or sentence being overturned (Zellick, 2006).

Table 18. Figures[10] from the CCRC, April 1997–June 2017

Total Applications	22,431 (including ineligible cases)
Cases Waiting	332
Cases under Review	641
Completed	21,469 (including ineligible)
Referrals	632
Heard by Court of Appeal	624 (418 allowed, 193 dismissed)

Shortly following its inauguration, the CCRC was hailed as a great improvement over the previous C3 division of the Home Office. It had the advantage of being independent from the government, as well as having increased access to resources and expertise (James et al., 2000), and it was able to address a large backlog of cases rather quickly that it had inherited from the Home Office. It is believed that, because it is separate from government and not dependent on public support to continue its work, the CCRC is not as susceptible to public pressure as the Home Office once was. Nonetheless, the initial support for the commission waned in later years and there is now a burgeoning groundswell of voices, particularly among the innocence network in the United Kingdom, that point to its relative ineffectiveness in fulfilling its original mandate: to investigate and, in fact, *review* alleged miscarriages of justice. Nobles and Schiff (2010) point out that, in reality, it is difficult to measure the efficacy of the CCRC, since there is no benchmark figure for the total number of miscarriages of justice that occur. At the same time, they calculate that the CCRC accounts for .58 per cent of all of the successful appeals to the Court of Appeal, Criminal Division, and thus makes only a minuscule difference. Moreover, the CCRC has rejected just over 96 per cent of the applications it receives (Roach, 2010, 92). There are a number of complaints[11] about its current functioning, as discussed by Walker and Campbell (2010). They include:

1. *Insufficient resources to address all cases properly*: When the CCRC began addressing the backlog from the C3 department of the Home Office, it also had to manage a large number of new cases – for example, within its first year of operations, it had over one thousand new cases to deal with, as well as an accumulation of 851 old cases (James et al., 2000, 145). The commission made a bid for more resources at that point, and was given substantially less than it requested. Clearly, insufficient resources contribute to the delay in processing cases. Furthermore, once a case is referred to the Court of Appeal by the CCRC, the court may also take a long period of time to hear the appeal.
2. *"Real possibility" test*[12]: The statutory test[13] for referring a case to the Court of Appeal by the CCRC under the Criminal Appeal Act of 1995 is that there must be a "real possibility that the original conviction, verdict, finding or sentence would not be upheld were the reference to be made" (s. 13(1)(a)). With respect to a conviction, the "real possibility" would result from arguments or evidence that were not raised at the original hearing. This would also include "exceptional circumstances," as in the case of inadequate counsel, although the CCRC seems loathe to refer such cases to the Court of Appeal (INUK, 2007). Given that there is no objective standard to identify a complete and thorough

investigation, it would follow that the idea of a "real possibility" is also undefined; some argue that this is done at the expense of getting to the truth of whether the applicant is innocent (Keirle, 2010; Kerrigan, 2010). When the CCRC believes the conviction is unsafe, the role of the investigators is to find "something new" in order to justify a referral to the Court of Appeal (Nobles and Schiff, 2001, 287).

3. *Over-Reliance or deference to the Court of Appeal*: An early criticism of the CCRC was that it had to rely on the Court of Appeal and could not decide cases on their own merit (Malleson, 1995, 929). This continues to be true; the powers of the CCRC allow it only to review cases and then either reject them or refer them to the Court of Appeal. Consequently, the CCRC tends to second-guess how the Court of Appeal will interpret particular case evidence and refer only those cases that it believes will be received favourably by the court. Naughton has repeatedly argued that this second-guessing effectively impedes its independence and makes it a more restrictive system than the one it replaced (2006; 2010).

4. *Limitations of investigative powers*: From time to time, an investigating officer has been appointed to help in fact-finding in some cases, and that person is not routinely an officer from a different police force than the original investigating one (James et al., 2000, 142). Since police misconduct has long been associated with miscarriages of justice (cf. Martin, 2001a), it would seem prudent to use other police forces to reinvestigate questions or evidence from the initial inquiry. Police are unlikely to find other officers complicit in a miscarriage of justice given the strength of police solidarity and fraternity (Slapper and Kelly, 1996).

5. *Subjective language*: Sections of the Criminal Appeal Act of 1995 have been written in somewhat subjective language and have proven difficult for the CCRC to interpret (Leigh, 2000, 368). Similarly, this applies to standards of application as well – given the constant state of flux of criminal evidence, as well as criminal law and procedure, it is not always clear which standards the CCRC should apply when examining old evidence, or in fact what is considered "fresh" evidence (Malone, 2010). Furthermore, there is little guidance for the CCRC with respect to the criteria for deciding when a conviction is unsafe (Keegan, 1999). Thus, it is difficult to determine in advance whether a given case will be successfully referred to the Court of Appeal by the CCRC given this lack of uniform standards.

6. *Investigative role*: The CCRC is said to have an investigative role that is, in essence, inquisitorial in approach (Leigh, 2000, 371). However, the stated mandate of the CCRC is to investigate cases where there is new evidence (Keegan, 1999). Elsewhere, it has been argued that the CCRC does little investigative work and solely "reviews" whatever briefs are sent to it by applicants (INUK, 2007). Further, its investigative task is not directed at uncovering miscarriages of justice per se, but rather is linked to the standards of referral for cases at the Court of Appeal (Nobles and Schiff, 2001, 287). This requirement effectively eliminates all cases where old evidence was rejected or misinterpreted but may have been indicative of innocence. Moreover, whether the CCRC has the time, staff, and resources to investigate and find new evidence is questionable.

7. *Legal representation*: The issue of poor legal representation at trial has been found to have an impact on erroneous convictions in a number of cases (Dwyer et al., 2000; Griffin, 2001). Regardless, poor representation at trial or bad "lawyering" is not considered adequate to meet the real-possibility test, and the Commission therefore has neither the power nor the mandate to consider such arguments (Green, 2010). In practice, the Court of Appeal does not address this issue when examining the safety of a conviction. It would make sense that either the CCRC or the Court of Appeal should take into account the considerable effect that inadequate counsel can have on the outcome of a case and find a means of addressing the problem during review. Furthermore, given the amount of time and effort needed to prepare an investigative brief, the allotment of ten hours of legal-aid assistance in preparing an application appears insufficient (Bird, 2010; Griffin, 2001, 1278).

8. *Appointment of commissioners*: Commissioners are appointed to the CCRC by the queen based on a recommendation from the prime minister. However, because the CCRC is an independent *public* body, it has been argued that such appointments are too political in nature (Slapper and Kelly, 1996).[14] Questions have also been raised about the legal expertise within the commission and the adequacy of the training of staff involved in investigations (Kyle, 2004, 674; Maddocks and Tan, 2010).

Most fundamentally, then, the CCRC has been accused of being overly meticulous in seeking a "real possibility" that a conviction would be reversed by the Court of Appeal (James et al., 2000, 147). As Naughton points out, the CCRC limits its considerations to whether convictions are lawful or not; it does not question the role of the criminal justice system itself in creating miscarriages of justice and further acting against their rectification (2010, 3). As discussed above, the CCRC has been blamed with second-guessing the Court of Appeal in referring only those cases that it is fairly certain the court will quash, which appears to be outside of its mandate.[15] Similarly, the low referral rate can be explained as indicative of considerations as to how the Court of Appeal will realistically view the new evidence, thus eliminating those cases that fail to meet the court's standards (Leigh, 2000, 367). Decreasing the turnaround time for assessing cases for referral could possibly reduce wait times, but it could also result in certain cases being rejected due to a mere cursory review of the evidence.

It has been suggested that the CCRC could increase its productivity through publicizing the availability of legal advice so that more applications have a better chance at being eligible for review (James et al., 2000, 149). Given the complexity involved in many wrongful-conviction cases, it appears that an increase in access to and availability of legal assistance is essential (Bird, 2010). Many wrongful convictions come to light only as a result of the diligence of dedicated lawyers working pro bono, often years after the fact. Aside from human-rights arguments against wrongful convictions, even cost-benefit calculations favour better legal representation earlier on, to avoid the costs of lengthy trials, appeals, and terms of imprisonment. At the same time, Roach notes that the CCRC focuses on a wider range of issues than do U.S.-style innocence projects, which are more concerned with cases of "factual innocence," such as legal issues relating to whether appellate courts would quash a conviction and accept new evidence on appeal (Roach, 2010, 93).

A further problem with the CCRC is that its sheer existence creates a false sense of security; the illusion is that, if the system does fail, such errors will necessarily be caught by this body that functions outside of the system (Naughton, 2010; Nobles and Schiff, 2001; Roach, 2010; Schehr, 2005). If this is indeed the case, then the crisis in confidence created by wrongful convictions has resulted in a response that affirms the system's legitimacy (Roach, 2010, 113, 121). If the CCRC eventually eliminates such miscarriages of justice, one consequence might be that innocence projects, functioning outside of the judicial system, would then become redundant. In fact, the opposite is true. As such projects proliferate, so does recognition of their increasingly important role in forcing the re-examination of suspected miscarriages of justice (Naughton, 2010). In any event, Roberts and Weathered (2009) point out that innocence projects perform a decidedly different function than that of the CCRC (and have differing philosophical foundations), in that their search is for "factual innocence" rather than seeking new evidence that may cast doubt on the safety of the conviction (51), which is the role of the CCRC. They argue further that these roles are in fact compatible given that innocence projects may seek new evidence for the courts to consider that may point to innocence – and that this may also serve to meet the standard of establishing that the conviction was "unsafe," as required by the Court of Appeal via the CCRC (Roberts and Weathered, 2009, 59).[16]

The many criticisms of the CCRC underline the difficulties encountered when attempting to address systemic errors through the system itself. Initial fears that the existence of the CCRC would have little impact on miscarriages of justice appear to have been realized to a degree. At the same time, the antagonistic relationship that existed between the Court of Appeal and the Home Office prior to the CCRC appears not to have been replicated. Nonetheless, while the CCRC was initially effective in clearing the backlog of cases awaiting review, there appears to be ongoing problems around its relationship with the Court of Appeal. Keegan argues that the CCRC is definitely an improvement over the C3 Division of the Home Office, but it is still a system "riddled with many challenges" (1999, 1781). Because of its "real possibility test," as opposed to the more common-sense approach of the Court of Appeal, the CCRC likely refers fewer cases than was originally anticipated (Newby, 2010).

Scottish Criminal Cases Review Commission

Scotland has a long historical disconnection with England that is also reflected in contrasting models for criminal investigation and adjudiciation (Walker, 1999b, 323). While it remains part of Great Britain, Scotland now has its own parliament and a separate and distinct criminal process. The latter includes an independent Criminal Cases Review Commission, created in 1999. Its mandate is to investigate and review convictions and sentences from Scottish courts where an alleged miscarriage of justice took place and refer those considered meritorious back to the Court of Appeal. The Scottish Criminal Cases Review Commission can refer both summary and indictable offences and it is not limited to only considering issues raised by the applicant but may also undertake independent investigations of its own.[17] In Scottish law, the statutory test for referral, by virtue of powers under the Criminal Procedure (Scotland) Act 1995, is when the commission believes: "that a miscarriage of justice may have occurred; and that it is in the interest of justice that a reference should be made" [s. 194C (1)(a)(b)].

The SCCRC[18] generally receives about 100 cases per year (with a record 165 in 2005–6) and normally accepts cases where the convicted person has already attempted to appeal through normal channels and been unsuccessful (SCCRC, 2006). From its inception in 1999 through to 2016, the SCCRC received 2,166 applications and made 127 conviction referrals (of which 116 were heard by the courts) to the High Court of Justiciary, sitting as a court of appeal; this translates to an initial referral rate of 3.5 per cent, and of that number 76 cases were overturned, which is a success rate of 59 per cent.[19] Under special circumstances, the commission will accept cases for review where no appeal has taken place.[20] While it is very similar to the English model in many respects, symbolic differences are evident in the language and terms of reference used by the SCCRC. For example, the SCCRC application forms asks: "Do you believe that you have suffered a miscarriage of justice in relation to the conviction and/or sentence imposed?" The term "miscarriages of justice" is absent from the English commission's application form; its mandate is limited to cases where leave to appeal has already occurred or been refused, where a new factor is present that the courts have not considered before, or where there are "exceptional circumstances" (CCRC application form). This narrower frame of reference may be reflective of a different approach to its work, or perhaps it may stem from the CCRC's experience with a larger number of cases and its clear idea of the kind of evidence the Court of Appeal in that jurisdiction is willing to accept when quashing convictions.

Nobles and Schiff (2010) point out that, even given the differently worded tests for referring cases, the SCCRC refers about half as many cases as the CCRC to the relevant court of appeal, with a similar rate of overturned convictions.[21] Moreover, these differing statutory powers, as well as different appeal courts, may in fact undermine comparisons (Nobles and Schiff, 2010, 155). In Scotland, the High Court of the Justiciary must consider whether there has been a miscarriage of justice, whereas in England and Wales the Court of Appeal, Criminal Division, must consider whether a conviction is "unsafe" – with the result that referrals are made only if there is a "real possibility" that the conviction will not be upheld.

In their analysis of the first ten years of the operation of the SCCRC, Leverick et al. (2009) found that the commission was far more than a "sifting" mechanism for the Court of Appeal in cases where fresh evidence emerged. This was borne out by the number of cases referred to the appeal court which were later quashed on the basis of additional evidence not raised by the appellant but identified by the SCCRC during its own investigations (Chalmers and Leverick, 2010, 616). Similarly, the cases referred to the SCCRC went beyond those involving evidence that came to light since the conviction, but rather also involved other issues such as an error of law at trial (26 per cent), irregularities at trial (19 per cent), and misdirection by the original trial judge (17 per cent). It would therefore seem that the relationship of the SCCRC and the appeal court is in fact a harmonious one and the cases most likely to succeed on appeal are those that involve errors of law and trial misdirection. Chalmers and Leverick (2010) opine that this is presumably due to the fact that the SCCRC has not attempt to construct miscarriages of justice in anything but legal terms (619).

Questions have been raised as to whether or not the United Kingdom in fact needed two separate review commissions. Walker (1999b) contends that, aside from powers to take precognitions[22] on oath from private sources under the Criminal Procedure Act 1995, the Scottish CCRC does not differ significantly from its English counterpart. One interpretation is that the existence of a separate Scottish CCRC reflects local authiorities' "pandering to historical symbolism," rather than "a determination to combat miscarriages of justice" (James et al., 2000, 150). The historical relationship between England and Scotland, fraught with caution, conflict, and suspicion, is likely part of the reason for the creation of the SCCRC. While it could be argued that a second CCRC is wasteful from a resource perspective, it is unlikely that the Scots would abandon their CCRC in order to be subsumed by its English counterpart, given their historical mistrust of England and their current political trajectory towards independence.

Norwegian Criminal Cases Review Commission

Norway developed its own Criminal Cases Review Commission in 2004, largely based on the English model. As was the case in England, this commission also grew out of a series of highly publicized cases of wrongful conviction in that country. The legislative framework for the Norwegian CCRC is found in the Norwegian Criminal Procedure Act (CPA) of 1981 (para. 391). The Norwegian CCRC is relatively smaller than its English counterpart (a chairperson, four members, and three alternate members). Its mandate is to decide whether individuals who seek review of their conviction or sentence should have their cases retried in court, and it has the final authority to reopen a case and refer it to the applicable court for an appeal.[23] The main criteria for referral also demand that new evidence or new circumstances must be present that may lead to an acquittal. Other referral criteria include: if the conviction is in contravention of international law, if anyone involved in the case has committed a criminal offence that may have affected the case, if a judge or jury member was disqualified, if the Supreme Court has departed from a legal interpretation that it had previously relied on that could affect the outcome of the case, or if there are special circumstances.[24]

The responsibility to produce all relevant information about a case falls on the commission, not the applicant. Furthermore, the commission has wide responsibilities: it may call the applicant or other witnesses to informal questioning, it may hold hearings or apply for evidence to be heard in court, and it can petition the court for a background report on the applicant (including an assessment of his/her mental health) or for coercive measures[25] to be applied. It may make orders for compulsory disclosure, appoint experts or hold inquiries, and, in special circumstances, request that prosecuting authorities conduct criminal investigations (NCCRC, 2004). In its first year of operation (2004), the NCCRC had 232 petitions for review (a much greater number than the anticipated 100); 61 were completed that year, of which 23 were heard on their own merit, 5 were referred to the court for review, and a number were dismissed as not falling within the commission's mandate. While this may seem a rather high number of rejections, the commission believes that since individuals may now apply directly to it for a review, rather than to the court via a solicitor, this may have contributed to the large number of rejections based on incomplete or weak cases (NCCRC, 2004). Since 2004, when it was first established, the Norwegian commission has received 1,973 petitions, concluded 1,861 of them, and reopened 251 cases, which reflects a reopening rate of approximately 16 per cent.[26]

The legal system in Norway operates on an inquisitorial basis, common in Western Europe and other parts of the world, characterized "by an active role for the fact-finder, by decisions based on full judicial inquiry and by truth-seeking rather than proof-making" (Frieberg, 2011). Consequently, the examining or investigating judge or magistrate takes on an active role in investigating the case, rather than sitting as an impartial observer as is common in the adversarial system. There are safeguards inherent in the inquisitorial system to guard against wrongful convictions: the court plays an active role in collecting evidence and determining guilt, and, in order to uncover the "truth," judges read the prosecutor's investigative file as well as determine the verdict and sentence. Still, errors can and do occur (Gilliéron, 2013). In particular, there is a risk of wrongful conviction through penal-order proceedings, a simplified procedure that allows for a conviction without a trial, similar to plea bargaining in the adversarial system. Such proceedings occur without a hearing of the defendant and the problems arise in part from careless investigation on the part of the police and the short deadlines available to oppose the penal order.[27]

CCRC Model for Canada

From time to time, calls have been made for establishing an independent review commission in Canada, similar to the CCRC. In fact, when parts of the Criminal Code that dealt with conviction review were amended in 2002, this idea was addressed and ultimately rejected as a possible option. One of the reasons given, inexplicably, was that "the Canadian experience with cases of wrongful conviction bears little resemblance to that of the United Kingdom" (Canada Gazette, 2002). Presumably, in this instance, counsel was referring to the system of prosecutions in the United Kingdom, which differs from the Canadian system. In the United Kingdom, a head prosecutor serves the entire country, whereas in Canada an attorney general and court of appeal can be found in each province.

Yet leaving the power to revisit convictions in the hands of the minister of justice continues to be problematic. On the practical side, very few applications are made each year to the Canadian Criminal Conviction Review Group, and there is clearly a conflict of interest when the minister of justice is involved in the administration of justice in individual cases (Zellick, 2006, 556). In addition, six commissions of inquiry (as discussed in chapter 10) that examined the factors that led to individual wrongful convictions each advocated for the establishment of an independent commission in Canada, along the lines of the CCRC.[28] Walker and Campbell (2010) address the possibility of an independent commission for Canada, but one with significant changes. Primarily, they support the creation of a body that would take a more holistic view of miscarriages of justice, that would demand cooperation between lobby groups, courts, prisons, and parliamentary committees, and that would address both the individual and systemic factors that contribute to miscarriages of justice.

United States of America

Death Penalty

"[The death penalty] ... is inconsistent with evolving standards of decency." (State of New Jersey, 2007)

There have long been arguments against the use of the death penalty in Western jurisdictions. They have centred on moral and religious questions regarding the right of the state to take a life, and other concerns have been raised about the disproportionate distribution of the death penalty among mainly indigent and African American defendants. For the wrongly convicted in the United States, the death penalty looms large, since there is little or no margin for error. Clearly, once an individual has been executed, there is no recourse to exoneration, except posthumously, which has been done only on very rare occasions. Moreover, once an individual receives a death sentence, there may be exorbitant (in many respects) legal loopholes to jump through in order to reverse or commute such a sentence to life imprisonment. In any case, the death penalty process is lengthy, costly, and onerous; appeals average ten years and can take up to two decades. After having reinstated capital punishment in 1976, the United States has executed 1,447 individuals, and there are currently 2,905 people on death row in thirty-four states (sixty-two are housed by the federal government).[29] While thirty-one states (as well as the federal government and the U.S. military) have death-penalty statutes, two of these states have had no executions since 1976 (Kansas, New Hampshire). There were twenty executions in 2016 in only five states[30] and in recent years fourteen states have suspended executions. Means of execution have also evolved over the years; since 1976, execution methods have included firing squad, hanging, gas chamber, electrocution, and lethal injection (all death-penalty states currently use lethal injection).[31] The death penalty is also considerably expensive for states to undertake: a recent California study indicated that executions have cost that state over $4 billion since 1978 (Alarcon and Mitchell, 2011). What is also particularly unsettling is that, from 1973 to 2016, there have been 157 exonerations of prisoners on death row, prisoners who otherwise would have been put to death.

Alone among Western nations in retaining the death penalty, the United States' peculiar perseverance in this regard has been the subject of much academic and legal commentary (cf. Whitman, 2003; Zimring, 2003). In his compelling essay on political, legal, and cultural developments that have had an impact on the death penalty in the United States, Garland (2005) argues that the American retention of the death penalty is not a result of American "exceptionalism." Rather, it is a complex confluence of government structures and a "particular kind of politics" – specifically, a system that politicizes criminal justice through its system of elected criminal justice officials (prosecutors, judges, and sheriffs). Garland also argues that, in spite of its retention of the death penalty, the United States is on the same abolitionist trajectory as other Western nations. In essence, the commitment to the death penalty is political and symbolic, "not social or structural, and so it is ... open to change" (2005, 361).

Indeed, there appears to be a burgeoning groundswell of support to abolish the death penalty in many traditionally conservative states. Moreover, in 2005, the U.S. Supreme Court found the death penalty unconstitutional for crimes committed by juveniles in the case of *Roper v. Simmons*.[32] Earlier, in *Atkins v. Virginia*[33] in 2002, the Court ruled that executing the intellectually handicapped was unconstitutional. A large influence on this movement towards abolition has likely been the growing number of death-row and other prisoners who have been wrongly convicted and later exonerated, many through DNA evidence. State responses have included the formation of task forces to examine specific issues (Massachusetts), the development of innocence commissions (North Carolina), and striking down the death penalty as unconstitutional (New York and Kansas).

Another current argument against the use of the death penalty is that it can be viewed as "cruel and unusual punishment." Primarily, this centres on a growing concern that the supposedly more "humane" process of lethal injection[34] is not in fact humane at all. Following a brief de facto moratorium on executions in the United States in recent years, owing to questions around lethal-injection protocols, the Supreme Court ruled on the issue, although it did not address the constitutional validity of the death penalty itself. In *Baze et al. v. Rees, Commissioner, Kentucky Department of Corrections*,[35] one of the questions before the Court was whether or not the pain and suffering caused by lethal injection violated the 8th Amendment right against cruel and unusual punishment. The Court adopted a "substantial risk of serious harm" test and decided that the risk of improper administration of the three-drug cocktail was not so substantial or imminent as to constitute an 8th Amendment violation. Given the current short supply of the drugs necessary (specifically sodium thiopental) for lethal injection in the United States, the Court considered questions around the ability of one drug, midazolam, to block the pain caused by the other drugs in the 2015 case of *Glossip v. Gross*.[36] This drug had been responsible for a number of "botched" executions in the past.[37] The Court ruled in favour of the continued use of midazolam, in conjunction with pancuronium bromide and potassium chloride, since the majority did not consider it be cruel and unusual punishment under the 8th Amendment. This controversial decision, as well as various opinions read from the bench, underlines the ongoing conflict around the death penalty in the United States.

Other concerns about the application of the death penalty focus on the time individuals must wait on death row (averaging a decade), the conditions of confinement, and the attendant psychological, social, and emotional deprivations. The conditions have been found to be so oppressive that some waive their appeals and welcome their execution – these individuals have been labelled as death-penalty "volunteers" (Blume, 2005).

Death-Penalty Considerations in Canada

The last execution in Canada took place fifty years ago, in 1962; nonetheless, the death penalty was in place until 1976 and fully abolished only in 1998.[38] From time to time, the issue of capital punishment resurfaces and it was raised in Parliament as recently as 1987, when it was defeated on a free vote of 148 to 127, despite public opinion at that time that indicated support for capital punishment. More recently, in 2001, the Supreme Court reaffirmed its rejection of the death sentence in the case of *USA v. Burns and Rafay*.[39] Sebastian Burns and Atif Rafay had been accused of a triple homicide in Washington State which has retained the death penalty; the case in Canada centred around an extradition request. What is of interest is that the decision in this case hinged on the spectre of a miscarriage of justice; the ruling established that the Canadian government should not extradite individuals to other countries where the death penalty was a possible sanction. The Supreme Court found that

> legal systems have to live with the possibility of error. The unique feature of capital punishment is that it puts beyond recall the possibility of correction. In recent years, aided by the advances in the forensic sciences, including DNA testing, the courts and governments in this country and elsewhere have come to acknowledge a number of instances of wrongful convictions for murder despite all of the careful safeguards put in place for the protection of the innocent. The instances in Canada are few, but if capital punishment had been carried out, the result could have been the killing by the government of innocent individuals. The names of Marshall, Milgaard, Morin, Sophonow and Parsons signal prudence and caution in a murder case. Other countries have experienced revelations of wrongful convictions, including states of the United States where the death penalty is still imposed and carried into execution [para. 1].

In essence, this decision demonstrated that extraditing an individual to another country where he or she may face the death penalty is a clear violation of section 7[40] of the Canadian Charter of Rights and Freedoms (Roach, 2006).

American Legislation

In 2004 the Department of Justice of the United States government passed the Justice for All Act.[41] This omnibus legislation was meant to enhance the protections of victims and the wrongly convicted. Victim protection came through the Scott Campbell, Stephanie Roper, Wendy Preston, Louarna Gillis, and Nila Lynn Crime Victims' Rights Act,[42] whereas protection for the wrongly convicted was contained in two other sections, the DNA Sexual Assault Justice Act[43] and the Innocence Protection Act.[44] The victim-protection aspect of the legislation established what are considered rights for victims of crime in federal criminal proceedings, as well as the means for enforcing them. Rights protected within the first of these measures include the "right of reasonable protection, the right of notification regarding release on parole, escape or other proceedings regarding the accused (as well as the right to be heard at such proceedings), the right of restitution, and the right to be treated with fairness ... with respect for the victim's dignity and privacy" (s. 3771(a)) (OVC, 2006). In essence, the act protects existing rights, expands the definition of a victim, establishes the rights of victims to participate in any public proceedings regarding the accused, and further enshrines enforcement of victims' rights. It has been noted, however, that the act falls short of allowing a victim the right to file a lawsuit against the federal government when these rights are not protected (OVC, 2006, 2).

The DNA Sexual Assault Justice Act is meant to, inter alia, establish funding and standards for forensic laboratories and forensic testing of DNA (ss. 303, 305), as well as attempt to address the backlog of DNA samples in criminal and missing persons' cases (s. 311). For the wrongly convicted, the Innocence Protection Act has a section titled "Exonerating the Innocent through DNA Testing," which addresses death-penalty reform by ensuring access to post-conviction DNA testing for those wrongly convicted in prison or on death row. Section 411 establishes the conditions that must be met for physical evidence to be tested or retested. Specifically, the Innocence Protection Act provides funds to states to defray the costs of post-conviction DNA testing. It also allows for a new trial or sentencing hearing to be scheduled in the event that the applicant's DNA does not match the evidence, and it sets time limitations for such testing in capital cases.

In his commentary on the U.S. Supreme Court decision in *District Attorney's Office v. Osborne*,[45] Garrett (2010b) notes that, while the Court may have denied Osborne relief in this instance to post-conviction DNA testing, it underscored the importance of the Innocence Protection Act as a model for an adequate set of post-conviction DNA-access procedures. Furthermore, it ruled that, while most states have post-conviction discovery rules, they must also adopt adequate and non-arbitrary procedures to provide access to DNA testing – a ruling that can be interpreted as putting pressure on states to facilitate innocence (Garrett, 2010b, 103). Though this decision did not in fact recognize an "open-ended constitutional right of access to postconviction DNA testing" (ibid., 105), what it did do was underscore the liberty interests attached to existing post-conviction procedures, to which most prisoners have access. In other words, the Osborne decision can be understood as a ratification of the Innocence Protection Act model (Garrett, 2010b, 127) and thus may lead to more exonerations in the future.

Another section of this act, titled "Improving the Quality of Representation in State Capital Cases" (s. 421), establishes grants for training counsel to improve the quality of representation at death-penalty trials and at appeals. This is in part a response to the extensive research that indicates that many individuals are on death row as a result of poor or even incompetent legal representation (Mello, 1995; Vick, 1995; Weisberg, 1995). Finally, section 431 of the act, titled "Compensation for the Wrongfully Convicted," increases compensation for federal cases of wrongful conviction and stipulates that states should provide "reasonable compensation to any person found to have been unjustly convicted of an offence against the State and sentenced to death" (s. 432). The term "reasonable," however, is left undefined.

In spite of its far-reaching mandate, the law as it stands is a much milder version than the originally proposed legislation (Zalman, 2006). That legislation was an attempt to rectify perceived inequities around access to the use of DNA and victims' rights.[46] Moreover, the Justice for All Act of 2004 is federal legislation and therefore applies only to federal cases; it is up to state governments to establish similar statutes on their own, which is highly dependent on their political willingness to do so.

Innocence Commissions

In light of growing public concern about wrongful convictions, the possibility of establishing a national "innocence commission" has been raised from time to time in the United States. Scheck and Neufeld (2002b) have argued for the feasibility of such a commission. In this regard, they believe that a Canadian public-inquiry model for a national innocence commission could work in the United States, if certain conditions were met, specifically:

1. If the commission were chartered to investigate wrongful convictions at its own discretion;
2. If it had sufficient power to order "reasonable and necessary" investigative services, as well as to subpoena documents, compel testimony, and bring civil actions; and
3. If its findings were transparent, publicly accountable, and required a formal public response from the relevant branch of government to its recommendations (103–4).

This vision of a national innocence commission is that it would function in a fashion similar to the National Transportation Safety Board, which is responsible for investigating transportation accidents and making recommendations for preventing similar tragedies in the future.

At the state level, a number of innocence commissions have already been established. More generally, Roach notes that innocence commissions "have ranged from self-appointed study commissions with an interest in systemic reform of the criminal justice system to temporary or permanent state-appointed inquiries into specific cases and/or systemic causes of wrongful convictions to permanent state-appointed commissions with a mandate to investigate claims of miscarriages of justices [sic] and to re-open judicial proceedings in individual cases" (2010, 89). Roach then further divides such commissions into bodies mandated either to correct erroneous convictions (error correction) or to identify and address the causes of wrongful convictions (systemic reform), or both. There is clearly an inherent tension between these two roles; the mandates are both similar and distinct, making them difficult to reconcile (ibid., 107). While the CCRC, and both the Scottish and Norwegian commissions, could be described as examples of the error-correction-model (state-financed public institutions), a number of existing state commissions (privatized/voluntary) either have mixed mandates or focus on systemic reform of one type or another.

In 2002 the state of North Carolina developed the Actual Innocence Commission, a self-appointed body comprised of law-enforcement, criminal justice, and legal-academic personnel serving voluntarily. In general, the objectives of the commission were to make recommendations that would reduce or eliminate the possibility of wrongly convicting the innocent. This wide-ranging mandate encompassed the promotion of awareness regarding the factors that cause wrongful convictions, a task that was to be accomplished through research and discussion.[47] For example, the commission studied the issue of eyewitness identification (Mumma, 2004, 652) and, in conjunction with researchers in this area, developed a document that contained improved procedures for conducting line-ups. While its recommendations in this area were not binding on law enforcement they were nonetheless shared with local and state police chiefs' and sheriffs' associations.

What developed out of this commission was an Innocence Inquiry Commission in the state of North Carolina in 2006, the first of its kind in the United States. Its mandate is to investigate and evaluate post-conviction claims of factual innocence and provide claimants with a level of review outside of the regular court system. While it may have broader investigative powers than the CCRC, some believe that this body, by restricting its mandate to cases of factual innocence, has limited its reach with respect to error correction (Roach, 2010, 95). The commission is comprised of attorneys, police officers, community members, and victim advocates, has broad subpoena powers, and can send cases of wrongful conviction to a panel of three judges to make a final ruling. It has received 1,837 claims since it began operating in 2007 and has rejected many of them for a variety of reasons, including no new evidence (27 per cent), no way to prove innocence (20 per cent), incomplete factual innocence (20 per cent), failure to return the questionnaire (13 per cent), no reliable evidence (9 per cent), claimant failed to cooperate (1 per cent), and the claim was procedural (3 per cent).[48] It has exonerated nine individuals to date, and of those nine cases,[49] one contained sufficient evidence to merit judicial review but did not prove innocence by clear and convincing evidence and the claimant was denied relief (*State v. Reeves*[50]). The eight other claimants were able to prove innocence and were released (*State v. Taylor*,[51] *State v. Kagonyera and Wilcoxson*,[52] *State v. Womble*,[53] *State v. McCollum/Brown*,[54] *State v. Grimes*,[55] *State v. Sledge*,[56] *State v. McInnis*[57]). A further case was found by the commission to have insufficient evidence to merit judicial review and the investigation was closed (*State v. McNeil*[58]). In the case of *State v. Isbell, Mills, Williams*,[59] the commissioners were not unanimous in their votes and the investigation was closed. In the *State v. Knolly Brown*[60] in June 2016, the Innocence Commission declared Brown as factually innocent, vacated his conviction, and dismissed the case,[61] while in the *State v. Robert Charles Bragg*, heard in late 2016, the commission found sufficient evidence of factual innocence to merit judicial review and referred the case forward for a hearing before a three-judge panel.[62] A decision is still pending.

A number of other American states have developed innocence commissions in recent years that include broader mandates. While some may have error-correction functions, others also have time-limited mandates to make recommendations regarding systemic reform. Most are not able to require that their recommendations be implemented, nor do they continue functioning after their reports are delivered (Roach, 2010, 96). The state of California set up the Commission on the Fair Administration of Justice in August 2004, comprised of prosecutors, defence attorneys, law professors, a judge, a rabbi, and law-enforcement officials. Before ceasing operations in 2008, the commission released official recommendations addressing the causes of wrongful convictions (eyewitness misidentification, false confessions, the use of jailhouse informants, problems with scientific evidence, professional responsibility, and accountability of prosecutors and defence lawyers) and proposing remedies.[63] Further attempts to pass bills on these subjects in the California legislature were unsuccessful. Only one bill, designed to improve the state compensation scheme, was ultimately successful, becoming law in October 2009.[64] The state of Connecticut established the Connecticut Advisory Commission on Wrongful Convictions in 2004 and its objective "is to make recommendations that will reduce or eliminate the possibility of the conviction of an innocent person in the State of Connecticut."[65] Further, it examines the causes of wrongful conviction, makes recommendations for change, and educates the public about this issue. It also has the mandate to conduct investigations in individual cases to determine the cause(s) of wrongful convictions. A report published by the commission in 2009 contained recommendations related to compensation, electronic recording of interrogations, and the use of double-blind administration of eyewitness line-ups (State of Connecticut, 2009). Similarly, the Florida Innocence Commission was created in 2010 by that state's Supreme Court both to study the causes of wrongful conviction and to implement measures to prevent such miscarriages of justice from occurring in the future; the commission was also mandated to review individual cases. It has completed its work and is no longer active. In its final report it made recommendations regarding the use of jailhouse informants, scientific evidence, preservation of evidence, professional responsibility, and increased funding of the criminal justice system (Florida Innocence Commission, 2012).

While not a commission per se, the Louisiana State Law Institute was authorized by the state legislature in 2010 to study and make recommendations on procedural matters that often lead to wrongful convictions, including the preservation of forensic evidence, confessions and admissions, a code of evidence, and other issues relating to the finality and accuracy of criminal convictions. Its recommendations were expected in 2013 but are still pending.[66] In 2010 the state of Oklahoma Bar Association established the Oklahoma Justice Commission, dedicated to "enhancing the reliability and accuracy of convictions." The responsibilities of this commission encompass: identifying the causes of wrongful conviction, including law-enforcement, forensic, and judicial procedures); proposing remedial strategies and procedures aimed at reducing the possibility of convictions in error; and outlining implementation plans.[67] The New York State Bar Association (NYSBA), in 2008, created a Task Force on Wrongful Convictions which examined both DNA and non-DNA exonerations across the state to identify causal factors. It also established a number of subcommittees to focus on specific issues, as well as developing a series of recommendations for change. The Task Force published its final report in 2009 but still continues to work towards eliminating wrongful convictions through policy and practice.[68] Furthermore, a Justice Task Force was created at the Court of Appeals for the state of New York in 2009, aimed at isolating causative factors of wrongful convictions as well as recommending reforms.[69]

The state of Wisconsin, following the release of Steven Avery in 2003 for a sexual assault he did not commit, introduced a suite of legislative measures known as the Criminal Justice Reform Package.[70] This package was compiled by a criminal justice task force and focused on minimizing the factors leading to wrongful convictions (improved eyewitness procedures, mandatory recording of interrogations, and the preservation of biological evidence); the bill became law in December 2005.[71] Following the work of the Avery Task Force, the Wisconsin Criminal Justice Commission was created, comprised of individuals from the state bar, Marquette University Law School, the Wisconsin Attorney General's Office, and the University of Wisconsin Law School. Aimed at raising issues not addressed by the Avery Task Force, this commission reviewed – and later made recommendations regarding – the use of expert testimony, jury instructions to address eyewitness error, jailhouse-informant testimony, junk science, false confessions, prosecutorial discretion, tunnel-vision confirmation bias in criminal investigations, crime-lab standards and funding, defence-attorney training and funding, and appellate standards of review.[72] The state of Virginia established the self-appointed Innocence Commission of Virginia, which had the task of examining known exonerated cases of wrongful conviction and making appropriate policy recommendations. The commission was comprised of the Innocence Project of the National Capital Region, the Administration of Justice Program at George Mason University, and the Constitution Project, and tendered a report in 2005. It outlined a number of factors that contributed to wrongful-conviction cases in the state, as well as containing a series of cogent recommendations to improve the reliability of Virginia's criminal justice system.[73]

The Connecticut Innocence Commission has been around since 2003 and its mandate involves the making of policy recommendations as well as working with legislative committees on the reform of practices that contribute to wrongful convictions. The state of Pennsylvania established a special advisory committee on wrongful convictions in 2006; the committee is mandated to examine cases of those wrongly convicted of violent crimes who were later exonerated. A report, issued in 2011, contains a series of recommendations that address: eyewitness misidentification, false confessions, indigent defence services, informant testimony, prosecutorial practice, post-conviction relief, redress, and the use of science.[74] In 2008, through its Court of Criminal Appeals, the state of Texas created the Texas Criminal Justice Integrity Unit to review the strengths and weaknesses of the Texas criminal justice system and to bring about meaningful reform through education, training, and legislative recommendations.[75] It also established the Timothy Cole Advisory Panel on Wrongful Convictions in 2009: Timothy Cole was wrongly convicted of sexual assault and served fourteen years in jail, where he died in 1999 as a result of an asthma attack. Texas granted its first posthumous exoneration in his case ten years later. The panel has since submitted a report to the Task Force on Indigent Defence, which contains recommendations regarding eyewitness-identification procedures, recording of custodial interrogations, open-discovery policies, post-conviction procedures, and the feasibility of creating an innocence commission to investigate wrongful convictions.[76]

Finally, some American states are specifically addressing suspected wrongful convictions through commissions of inquiry, similar to what takes place in Canada, as discussed in chapter 10. In the state of Illinois, in the wake of evidence that there were innocent men on death row, Governor George Ryan declared a moratorium on executions in 2000 and in 2003 all 167 death-row inmates had their sentences commuted to life imprisonment. In 2002 Ryan appointed a special commission to study capital punishment. It released a set of recommendations but skirted the issue regarding retention of capital punishment per se (State of Illinois, 2002). The commission's recommendations covered investigative practices, limitations on eligibility for capital punishment, and prosecutorial decision making in trial and review of capital cases. Many of the recommendations became part of a death-penalty reform bill in 2004, which did not ultimately become law. However, Illinois abolished the death penalty in March 2011, the sixteenth state to do so, a decade after the moratorium on executions, in part because of a growing recognition that the process of imposing the penalty is inherently flawed. At the same time, Governor Pat Quinn commuted the death sentences of the remaining fifteen inmates on death Illinois' death row to life imprisonment.[77]

Massachusetts (a non-death-penalty state) took an approach almost diametrically opposed to that of the Ryan Commission. Governor Mitt Romney ordered the creation of a commission in 2004 to determine the safeguards necessary to ensure that capital punishment would be administered fairly and accurately in the event that the state passed a law authorizing the practice (Hoffmann, 2005). While Massachusetts had abolished the death penalty in 1984, the commission's report established the conditions under which it could be brought back and severely limited how and when it could be imposed. This report was criticized for being overly reliant on scientific evidence and for the insertion of a "no doubt" standard of proof at capital sentencing (Hoffmann, 2005). In the end, Massachuetts did not reintroduce capital punishment. A similar attempt to re-establish the death penalty in the state of New York in 2005 was also unsuccessful.[78]

Conclusions

The previous two decades have witnessed great strides by several Western jurisdictions to rectify convictions in error. At first glance, the British and Norwegian models of Criminal Case Review Commissions appear to be sincere attempts to provide another level of review for questionable convictions. More than ten years on, the flaws of the much-heralded United Kingdom CCRC are becoming apparent. This commission appears overburdened, underfunded, excessively deferential to the Court of Appeal, and severely limited by its mandate in sending cases to the Court of Appeal for review; its referral rate of less than 4 per cent of all requests speaks for itself. It is difficult to compare the United Kingdom CCRC to the Scottish and Norwegian systems, owing to their differing mandates and referral criteria.

In Canada, if the provincial attorneys general or the federal minister of justice were ever to reconsider the feasibility of a CCRC model in the Canadian context, they would do well to learn from the United Kingdom's mistakes. A commission that was adequately funded by legally trained personnel, truly independent of the Department of Justice, and with far-ranging powers of referral and safeguards in place to support applicants throughout the process would likely be in a better position to address miscarriages of justice than the current system.

Support for the death penalty continues to be on the decline. In the United States, where the death penalty was reinstated in 1976, American states are imposing it in far fewer numbers than in previous years and executing fewer and fewer individuals. States that still hold death-penalty statutes are questioning its application and even establishing moratoria on its use until problems in implementation are addressed. While there will always be pockets of the Canadian population that support the death penalty, it is highly unlikely that it will ever be reinstated in this country. Nonetheless, one American development that is worthy of further consideration is the establishment of innocence commissions. Historically, Canada has been relatively open to examining the errors that occur in cases of wrongful conviction and in attempting to rectify them through policy recommendations. Since the 1980s, there have been six commissions of inquiry to address eight wrongful-conviction cases. Each of these commissions had a discrete man-date to examine one or more particular cases; their many recommendations were far-reaching, and while not legally binding, some of them have been implemented (see chapter 10). An independent, free-standing commission established to exam-ine current and ongoing cases of wrongful convictions, with the power to make policy recommendations and hold provincial governments accountable, along the lines recommended by Scheck and Neufeld (2002b), may be feasible in this con-text. Roach points out that the North Carolina experience of two separate com-missions, or one that clearly delineates its error-correction and systemic-reform functions, is a possible model to follow (2010, 101).

Governments, which are ultimately responsible for the performance of state actors, must remain vigilant to conviction errors that occur in their jurisdictions. The existence of such errors of justice calls into question the validity and reliability of the criminal justice system and weakens public confidence. While the examples discussed above illustrate well-meaning attempts to address wrongful convictions after they occur, their relative ineffectiveness has demonstrated the need to prevent wrongful convictions from occurring in the first place. A whole host of commis-sion of inquiry reports and rigorously conducted research outlines the determin-ing factors behind wrongful convictions. The implementation and enforcement of many of the policy recommendations that have already been made would be an appropriate place to begin.

Chapter Fourteen

Final Conclusions

"Regardless of whether the errors of the criminal justice system are episodic or epidemic, they still warrant review and reform, not because reform will lead to an error-free process, but because the participants in the system deserve our attention and efforts." (Gould, 2008, 241)

Introduction

The occurrence of wrongful convictions and wrongful imprisonment in Canada is no longer a matter of dispute. The many high-profile cases examined by commissions of inquiry, and the many others played out in the media, clearly illustrate that innocent people go to prison for crimes they did not commit; some of them spend years and decades in jail before they are exonerated, and some continue to remain behind bars. These errors occur because innocent people are mistakenly identified as being the perpetrators of crimes, they sometimes confess to things they have not done, and they are often unfairly targeted by the police and prosecution and unscrupulous jailhouse informants. The normative assumption at the start of this book that the criminal justice system in Canada is deeply flawed has been affirmed throughout; errors clearly occur and mechanisms in place to correct them are also defective. Conviction review, through section 696 of the Criminal Code, occurs very infrequently and is inaccessible as a source of relief for most wrongly convicted. At the same time, obtaining compensation from the state for a wrongful conviction is far from an automatic process, despite Canada's national and international commitments to do so.

Moreover, the "rhetoric" of innocence, as narrowly understood as occurring through DNA proof of non-involvement in a given crime, has come to dominate the discourse about wrongful convictions in the criminal justice system. Feige (2003) notes that this restrictive lens may serve to hijack criminal justice legislation and decision making by focusing policy on protecting only a small number of demonstrably innocent individuals, while simultaneously neglecting protections for the rights of *all* accused. Given that biological evidence is present only in a very small number of criminal cases, focusing solely on these cases serves to isolate other convictions that may also be in error but lack the necessary biological evidence to prove otherwise it. In fact, many innocence projects will take on only alleged wrongful-conviction cases that have DNA evidence, because they are easier to solve definitively and often are of long standing, pre-dating the advent of DNA forensic analysis in the early 1990s. Advances in the use of, and access to, DNA forensic analysis will most likely result in fewer and fewer wrongful convictions in the future; where biological evidence is present, police forces and prosecutions would be remiss not to preserve and analyse it. What this does mean is that, for those cases without biological evidence, the bar has been substantially raised; what it does *not* mean is that the problem of wrongful convictions has been solved.

This volume has attempted to provide a context for situating the issue of miscarriages of justice within theoretical, social, and legal frameworks of analysis. It has done so by examining the role of contributing factors to wrongful convictions, by exploring how emergent technologies have both facilitated the exoneration of the wrongly convicted and prevented miscarriages of justice, and by critically analysing the current policy and practical responses to this issue. Research that goes beyond a specific focus on failures of the system can provide a better understanding of the way in which the criminal justice system systemically generates errors (Zalman, 2006, 484). As a result, a study of this nature also, it is hoped, engenders other possible means to prevent similar errors from occurring; future efforts at research and advocacy regarding miscarriages of justice in Canada may be informed by this compilation and analysis of theory, research, policy, and case law.

Wrongful-Conviction-Generated Reforms and Possible Remedies

At this juncture, some changes to criminal justice procedures have come about as a result in part of wrongful convictions. Aided to a certain extent by extensive media exposure, lobbying by interested groups, and the work of commissions of inquiry, a certain number of reforms have occurred within the criminal justice system to address many of the systemic difficulties that result in convictions in error. In the area of eyewitness identification, efforts to prevent erroneous identification in the future have fostered a number of policy changes, including: double-blind line-up administration, cautions around witness instruction, the taking of confidence statements, recording of procedures, more balanced line-up composition, and the use of cognitive interviews. The extent to which such reforms have been implemented across the country within all municipal, provincial, and federal police forces is impossible to ascertain. In order to address police misconduct, recourse may be had to the tort of negligent investigation, which now allows citizens to sue the police if it can be proven that they acted negligently in pursuing them in a criminal action. In addition, the tort of malicious prosecution allows citizens to pursue prosecutors, but it must be proven that the proceedings against them were unfounded. Yet, while police and prosecutors are not immune from liability for blatant errors, these remedies are slow, expensive, and rarely successful and thus hardly act as deterrents. Then there is the problem of tunnel vision, evident on the part of both police and prosecutors, involving a single-minded and overly narrow focus on a particular theory regarding who perpetrated a crime while ignoring evidence to the contrary. No amount of legislation or policy reform can effectively address the narrow-mindedness of tunnel vision.

Guilt-presumptive interrogation practices as seen through the use of the Reid Technique and the "Mr Big" sting have often led to false confessions. While reliance on protections under the Charter and case law have attempted to circumscribe the use of these practices, it would appear that the right to silence in the face of police interrogation has been substantially eroded (cf. *R. v. Sinclair*). A number of possible reforms to counter the false confessions that emerge through these practices have been suggested; however, the courts are reticent to restrain police powers. Many police forces may temper the use of the Reid Technique, but they also continue to rely on it to elicit confessions. At the same time, the RCMP's use of the "Mr Big" sting has now been restricted to a degree by the decision in *R. v. Hart*, although it remains to be seen whether the new two-pronged test of admissibility will ultimately have an impact on its use. Testimony from jailhouse or in-custody informants has also been considerably restrained in recent years. Responding in part to a number of wrongful convictions that resulted from fabricated evidence provided by fraudulent witnesses and the recommendations of a number of commissions of inquiry, most provinces and territories have established committees to vet this testimony as well as registries to track individuals who offer it. Along with strong warnings to juries from judges about the dangers of convictions based on such testimony, these measures may help in addressing the problem. Yet it is still possible for the more skilled informant to provide testimony in exchange for benefits, which continue to be offered under all provincial policies, and the attraction of other inducements – including the prospect of avoiding imprisonment – remains great.

One way of viewing these changes is that they are "responses" to specific aspects of the problem but fail to address the systemic nature of wrongful conviction in and of itself, and hence the continued need for a true "remedy." Given that such a remedy must be systemic in nature, it necessarily involves a number of steps. First of all, the mechanism for conviction review, to establish if a miscarriage of justice likely occurred, needs to be independent in nature. Six commissions of inquiry examining the circumstances surrounding wrongful convictions have made this very recommendation.[1] In these inquiries, examining the wrongful convictions of nine men, judges and former judges have advocated for the need for the review process to be truly independent from government, similar in nature to the conviction-review commissions in England and Wales, Scotland, Norway, and North Carolina. In fact, Justice Edward P. MacCallum, who chaired the commission of inquiry into the case of David Milgaard, notes that the system of conviction review in Canada is reactive and places too heavy an onus on the wrongfully convicted (2006, 411). Not only does this system require years of work and financial security, it is also based on the premise that wrongful convictions occur infrequently, and that any remedy from the minister would be extraordinary. As MacCallum and others have observed, it remains highly problematic that the Canadian criminal justice system retains responsibility to correct its own errors. He goes on to say:

> The federal Minister of Justice should not be the gatekeeper to determine whether an alleged wrongful conviction should be returned to the Court for further review. The involvement of a federal politician in the review of individual cases of alleged wrongful conviction invites public advocacy and accusations of political influence ... As long as responsibility for conviction review remains with the federal Minister of Justice, there will be the potential for political pressure and public advocacy to play a role in

the decision making process, or, at the very least, for the perception to exist that the decision can be so influenced. The conviction review process must not only be truly independent, it must be seen to be independent. (Ibid., 411)

A separate body similar to the CCRC model would have symbolic significance to the public and to victims of miscarriages of justice, even though, as it stands, any recommendations coming from such bodies are fettered by the procedures and decisions of courts of appeal. In their review of the CCRC as a model for Canada, Walker and Campbell (2010) note that any reform should offer a more holistic approach to miscarriages of justice, and while continuing innocence work, it should also focus on policy recommendations, working as a "criminal justice inspectorate" (203–4). Moreover, they argue that a Canadian CCRC should be actively involved in government reform, by having a voice at the table when important criminal justice policy and procedural debates are occurring, as well as through involvement in "routine" or "mundane" miscarriages of justice that are overturned through normal appeals processes. Perhaps a model combining a CCRC with the mandate of an innocence commission, as seen in some American states, would be appropriate. The development of an innocence commission charged with investigating cases, along with the responsibility for policy recommendations and reform, independent of and separate from government (similar to what Roach [2010] advocates), would not only be a vast improvement on the work done by the existing CCRG but would also go a long way to preventing future miscarriages of justice.

A wrongful conviction causes much chaos in the life and family of the wrongly convicted; this occurs on many levels and the wrongly convicted may incur numerous psychological, emotional, and financial difficulties. Not only does the wrongly convicted individual often become a wrongly imprisoned one, this loss of freedom is often accompanied by loss of employment, loss of family and friends, and loss of reputation, to name but a few consequences. In addition, family members, friends, and colleagues are also greatly affected, both emotionally and financially. Grounds (2004) has noted the severe and psychological adjustment problems of the wrongly convicted upon release, including enduring personality change, Post-Traumatic Stress Disorder, and, in some cases, depression, anxiety, paranoia, and alcohol and drug dependence. In Westervelt and Cook's (2012) examination of the adjustment of death-row exonerees upon release, they found further evidence of the aftermath of trauma among the men they interviewed: feelings of dislocation and disconnection, grief over losses, damage to relationships, and bouts with anger, guilt, and mistrust (9). Similarly, in Campbell and Denov's (2004) study on the effects of wrongful imprisonment, they found that the wrongly convicted, in addition to the hardships associated with prison conditions, suffer as a result of the indeterminacy of their release date given their inability to admit guilt and participate in their own supposed rehabilitation. Many researchers from different traditions have come to similar conclusions that trauma is at the core of the experience of the wrongly convicted (Westervelt and Cook, 2012).What these studies demonstrate is the need for a further remedy, one that recognizes the difficulties that the wrongly convicted have experienced and provides for some form of psychological support upon release.

Adjustment difficulties are the norm upon release from prison. After living many years in the hostile environment of a prison, many ex-prisoners have problems adapting to the demands of modern society, negotiating new technologies in attempting to find gainful employment, and re-establishing relationships with family members. However, for most ex-prisoners, release from prison is gradual and they are required to live in supported living conditions for a time to facilitate their adjustment and to monitor their progress. The wrongly convicted, in contrast, are sometimes released directly from prison[2] and are often left to their own devices, with little support and direction as to how to adapt to their newfound freedom. While redress from the criminal justice system through compensation is a significant first step for many exonerees, what is equally important is the provision of the necessary supports for successful reintegration; more specifically, post-release services are required that address the social, psychological, and financial difficulties inherent in adjustment. In its 2009 report, the New York Innocence Project (2009b) outlined a number of necessary and significant social-service-type supports which would facilitate adaptation, including payment of attorneys' fees associated with filing for compensation, transitional assistance with housing, transportation, education, workforce development, physical and mental-health care, an official acknowledgment of the wrongful conviction, automatic record expungement, and assistance with child support and child custody.

Further to this is the recommendation that exonerees develop a "release" plan for returning to their communities and families (Innocence Project, 2009b). Others who advocate for supported release of the wrongly convicted include Lonergan (2008), Weigand (2009), and Lawrence (2009). In fact, some advocacy groups, such as MOJO Scotland (Miscarriages of Justice Organization), a human-rights organization that assists innocent people and their families in prison and on release, also provides support to the wrongly convicted in reintegrating into their communities. Finally, using a framework of restorative justice, Westervelt and Cook (2012) call for the development of "reintegration networks" to support exonerees upon release. While including many of the above recommendations, these networks would be similar to "circles of support" for released sex offenders and also include assistance from ex-exonerees and/or death-row survivors as mentors to help new exonerees meet the demands of release. In addition, such networks would allow for exonerees to participate in a community-reintegration forum, where they could publicly share their experiences and thereby "shed negative stigma" and regain their "innocent identity by integrating the experiences of trauma ... participants in this forum would include those who are responsible for the injury so they could hear, firsthand, how the harm has affected the person injured and his or her companions" (234–5). Westervelt and Cook recognize that, given the intransigence of criminal justice officials to acknowledge their errors or any wrongdoing to which they may have contributed, even in the face of an exoneration, having them participate in such a forum may be unrealistic. At the same time, however, they advocate for the inclusion of others in such networks, including community members, surviving victims, and the families of victims and exonerees. These recommendations underscore the importance of continued support upon release as a significant remedy – support that goes well beyond simple financial compensation – for the wrongly convicted.

The "extraordinary" nature of the remedy of conviction review reflects a pervasive attitude among many members of the criminal justice system – that in fact the system gets it "right" in most instances and "wrongful" convictions are indeed exceptional events. Regardless of one's position on the frequency of occurrence of wrongful convictions, the real possibility exists that errors will continue to occur in any criminal justice system. Thus, it is the responsibility of the actors in that system to educate themselves about the many causes of wrongful conviction and at the same time be more vigilant with respect to pursuing the "right" suspect, that is, one towards whom the evidence realistically points. While human-rights arguments demand this level of vigilance, policy makers may be further convinced by fiscal arguments. In a study done by Conroy and Warden (2011) examining the financial burden attached to eighty-five wrongful convictions in the state of Illinois from 1989 to 2010, they established that the cost to taxpayers had been $214,000,000; broken down, this number calculated incarceration costs at $18,500,000, court costs at $31,500,000, and settlement and judgment costs at $156,000,000. There is no reason to believe that the costs in Canada are any less per person, outside of the extraordinary costs incurred in capital cases. Perhaps a true "remedy" to this issue requires a sea change – one that recognizes the reality of wrongful convictions, that makes mandatory the ongoing education of police, prosecutors, and the defence bar regarding the possible sources of conviction error, and that demands greater caution in proceeding with charges where the evidence is limited.

The Canadian system of conviction review is inaccessible to many, owing in part to its protracted nature, limited eligibility criteria, and high burden for establishing that a miscarriage of justice "likely" occurred. In addition, seeking and obtaining compensation for a wrongful conviction, through the Federal-Provincial-Territorial Guidelines, places further demands on the wrongly convicted. A significant problem for these individuals is that the guidelines do not oblige the government to act and much is dependent on the whim of a particular politician or attorney general or on the effects of media campaigning. While it could be argued that state governments regain authority or build legitimacy by enhancing procedural justice through the post-conviction practices of exoneration and compensation, that argument is belied by these practices' impossible thresholds, their infrequent occurrence, and, in the few cases that are successful, their inadequate compensatory limits (Campbell, forthcoming). Thus, one further remedy to address the problem of wrongful convictions in Canada would be to facilitate access to compensation and other supports upon exoneration. Perhaps the system in the United Kingdom is an example in this regard. In that country a statutory scheme exists that allows for wrongly convicted exonerees to apply for compensation under section 133 of the Criminal Justice Act, 1988, which gives the justice secretary the discretion to pay compensation to a wrongly convicted person "when his conviction has been reversed or he has been pardoned on the ground that a new or newly discovered fact shows beyond reasonable doubt that there has been a miscarriage of justice." While the ambit of this scheme was recently narrowed in R(Adam) v. Secretary of State for Justice to those cases where "fresh evidence shows clearly that the defendant is innocence of the crime of which he has been convicted,"[3] it nonetheless allows a rather straightforward (albeit limited) avenue for redress, a path that is significantly absent in the Canadian scheme.

Problem Solved? One Step Forward, Two Steps Back

While great strides have occurred with respect to changes in criminal justice policy and developments in forensic science (particularly the use of DNA) that will, one hopes, decrease the likelihood that miscarriages of justice will continue to occur, there is no reason for complacency. Given that the criminal justice system is administered by human beings, errors, though perhaps not of the same nature, will persist. One recent development that raises the spectre of miscarriage of justice is the mega-trial phenomenon. As Campbell (2011) notes, the phenomenon of the long and complex trial – generally aimed at organized crime, gangs, and terrorism, and involving large numbers of defendants and copious amounts of complex evidence – places undue burdens on defence counsel, prosecutors, judges, and accused persons in terms of time and resources, which may raise concerns about the effectiveness of the administration of justice.[4]

The LeSage-Code Report, released in 2008 by the Ontario Ministry of the Attorney General, contained a series of recommendations regarding the quick and efficient movement of large, complex cases through the criminal justice system. The Canadian Parliament later passed the Fair and Efficient Criminal Trials Act[5] in 2011, incorporating many of the recommendations in the LeSage-Code Report, in order to address the difficulties inherent in this phenomenon. The act itself contains a number of provisions to reform the mega-trial process, including: allowing greater scope for judges to proceed on direct indictment; allowing for the appointment of a case-management judge to rule on preliminary issues;[6] allowing for the delayed enforcement of a severance order;[7] allowing for rulings at mistrials to be binding on later decisions; and, finally, allowing for greater protection of the identity of jurors and the swearing of up to 14 jurors[8] (MacKay, 2011).

Mega-trials often involve charges brought in the name of efficiency; however, the monumental amounts of evidence available at these trials can stretch into the millions of pages of documents. Consequently, defence counsel are overburdened to such an extent that the right to full answer and defence becomes virtually impossible, and pressures to plea bargain overwhelming. In the province of Quebec, while Operation SharQC resulted in the initial arrest of 155 people for gang-related activities, it also resulted in Justice James Brunton releasing 31 of the accused on the grounds of inordinate delay.[9] Moreover, Brunton criticized the prosecutors for going ahead with such a large trial prior to ensuring that the system was capable of handling it (MacKay, 2011). While a further 104 accused accepted plea agreements on charges of conspiracy to commit murder, the first trial to hear evidence in this case came to an abrupt end in October 2015. At that time, Justice Brunton issued a stay of proceedings on charges against five so-called gang members for conspiracy to commit murder and first-degree murder, on the grounds that crown prosecutors' delays in disclosing important evidence amounted to a "serious abuse of process."[10] An administrative investigation regarding the delay in disclosure of evidence in this case, as well as the management of mega-trials more generally, is being conducted by the Directeur des poursuites criminelles et pénales (DPCP) (head of the provincial prosecutor's office).[11]

Final Thoughts

"Twenty years for nothing, well that's nothing new, besides, no one's interested in something you didn't do." (The Tragically Hip's "Wheat Kings," 1992)[12]

The title of this book – *Miscarriages of Justice in Canada: Causes, Responses, Remedies* – represents an ambitious gesture to address the entirety of the problem of wrongful conviction from a Canadian perspective. More specifically, my objective has been to transcend a simple reiteration of the existing literature and offer a broader overview of the many factors that may contribute to a miscarriage of justice, as well as a larger, systemic context for understanding how such miscarriages continue to occur. While I have also endeavoured to provide a comparison of the Canadian record in policy, case law, and practice around miscarriages of justice with that of other jurisdictions, this effort may have fallen short in certain respects. Where the comparisons seemed the most useful in underscoring differences and similarities, they were included. But research and writing deadlines precluded further, more in-depth comparisons. Given the relatively recent enactment of the Charter, the Supreme Court of Canada continues to refine the contours of the legal rights found within sections 7–14, and this in turn affects the practical application of those rights. Consequently, such developments filter down to police practices, criminal-trial procedural rules, and restrictions on the admissibility of evidence, which all have an impact upon the safety of convictions. Keeping abreast of these developments substantially delayed the termination of this volume and upcoming decisions will likely further affect how the courts interpret individual rights. The ever-evolving nature of criminal law precludes any real definitive conclusions about many of these issues.

A study of this nature has revealed a number of avenues for continued examination of the problem of miscarriage of justice. In particular, the wrongly convicted who have been released, whether exonerated or not, offer a wealth of possibilities for future study. Much could be garnered by examining the strategies they use in adjusting to the many challenges they face upon release and reintegration, as well as the nature of the errors that fostered their wrongful conviction in the first instance. Moreover, an examination of the impact of significant Supreme Court decisions that affect those factors that contribute to miscarriages of justice would prove a fruitful subject of inquiry. More specifically, an analysis of the aftermath of case law and criminal justice policy following significant decisions in the higher courts, such as *R. v. Sinclair*, *R. v. Stinchcombe*, and *Hill v. Hamilton-Wentworth Regional Police Services Board*, could reveal a great deal about the extent to which the lower courts and governments have been guided by the highest court in their rulings and policy decisions. Such study may provide insights into the limits of these judicial rulings on practice, into the role of the courts in policy change, and into how those factors influence the evolution of the law over time.

Wrongful convictions represent coherent examples of practical failures in criminal justice policy and the criminal justice system itself. What this book has revealed is that, time and again, mistakes were made that resulted in innocent people being sent to jail for crimes they did not commit. Errors occurred on the part of police, Crown attorneys, defence counsel, witnesses (whether sincere in their beliefs or not), and judges; errors sometimes occurred at one stage in the process that were then further compounded at later points, which resulted in wrongful convictions. The fact that the majority of these errors were avoidable is deeply disturbing; the same can be said of the inflexibility that many of these actors displayed when later faced with their own mistakes. On that basis, both reform and remedy should in fact be quite simple – just as the actors in the criminal justice system have generated and compounded errors that resulted in wrongful convictions, so too do they have the power to learn from past mistakes, to practise greater vigilance in the exercise of their job, and to be open to the possibility of their own error. The costs of a wrongful conviction, be they emotional, psychological, or economic, are frankly too great to proceed otherwise.

Appendices

Wrongful Convictions in Canada[1]

Evidentiary / Procedural Issue	Casual or Contributing Factor	Percentage of Wrongful Conviction Cases
Fabricated, erroneous, or unreliable eyewitness identification	31	44.28%
Problematic police investigation or police misconduct	27	38.57%
Police/Crown Failure to disclose evidence	21	30%
Mistaken or problematic forensic or expert evidence	19	27.14%
Fabricated or problematic witness or complainant testimony	19	27.14%
Unreliable co-accused testimony or jailhouse informant testimony	15	21.43%
Erroneous judicial instructions	13	18.57%
False confessions	7	10%
Racial prejudice	7	10%
Overzealous or malicious prosecution	6	8.57%
Poor legal representation	2	2.85%

Wrongful Convictions

Accused	Prov/ Ter	Charge(s)	Year Convicted / Exonerated	Sentence / Time spent in Prison	Case Outcome	Ministerial Review	Compensation	Casual & Contributing Factors
Wilfred Beaulieu[2]	AB	Sexual assault (two counts)	1992 / 1997	4 years / 4 years	Acquittal – one count New trial – one count (Crown entered a stay of proceedings)	Yes	Denied	– Fabricated complainant testimony – Problematic police investigation
Darcy Bjorge[3]	AB	Possession of a stolen vehicle Fraud	1994 / 2005	3 years – concurrent on each count	Possession – new trial ordered (Charges stayed at re-trial) Fraud – dismissed	Yes	–	– Erroneous eyewitness identification
Steven Kaminski[4]	AB	Sexual assault	1992 / 1999	7 years / 7 years	Conviction overturned – new Trial ordered, provincial authorities declined to proceed	Yes	$2.2 million – (estimated) Federal Government	– Problematic complainant testimony
Richard McArthur[6]	AB	Assault causing bodily harm	1987 / 1990	4 years	Acquitted – Crown did not seek retrial	Yes	–	– Erroneous eyewitness identification
Wilson Nepoose[6*]	AB	Murder (2nd degree)	1987 / 1992	Life / 4 years	Acquitted – Crown did not seek retrial	Yes	–	– Unreliable eyewitness identification – Witness perjury – Problematic police investigation – Failure to disclose evidence – Racial prejudice
Connie Oakes[7*+]	AB	Murder (2nd degree)	2013 / 2016	14 years / 2.5 years	Conviction overturned, Court of Appeal ordered new trial Crown entered a stay in proceedings	Yes	–	– Co-accused gave false testimony – Unreliable eyewitness identification
Wilfred Truscott[8]	AB	Assault, mischief causing damage to personal property	1984/ 1986	18 months / 12 months	Overturned	No	$36,000	– Problematic complainant testimony

Name	Province	Offence	Conviction / Exoneration	Sentence	Outcome	Factual innocence?	Compensation	Contributing factors
Danny Wood[9]	AB	Murder (1st degree)	1990 / 2005	Life 25 / 15 years	Conviction quashed and referred back to the Court of Appeal, heard as a new appeal. New Trial ordered. Charges stayed at retrial	Yes	–	– Crown failure to disclose evidence – Unreliable eyewitness identification
Ivan Henry[10]	BC	Sexual assault (Ten counts)	1983 / 2010	Dangerous offender – indeterminate / 27 years	Conviction quashed, acquitted on all charges	No	$8 million – British Columbia + Undisclosed amounts (Vancouver, federal government)	– Police misconduct – Crown failure to disclose evidence
Linda Huffman[11]+	BC	Theft	1993 / 1995	60 days (electronic monitoring) / 60 days	Acquitted	No	$105,512	– Problematic police investigation
Corey Robinson[12]	BC	Murder (2nd degree) Charged twice	1996 / 2003	Life 10 years / 9 years	Acquitted Dismissed at retrial	No	–	– Problematic police investigation – Problematic forensic evidence
Kenneth Norman Warwick (Norman Fox)[13]	BC	Sexual assault	1976 / 1984	10 years / 8 years	Pardon granted (recommended by solicitor general and minister of justice)	No	$275,000	– Erroneous eyewitness identification
James Driskell[14]	MB	Murder (First degree)	1991 / 2003	Life 25 / 13 years	Conviction quashed, new trial ordered by minister of justice, proceedings stayed	Yes	$4 million – provincial government, police, Crown	– Problematic forensic evidence (hair microscopy) – Unreliable eyewitness identification (recanted) – Failure to disclose evidence – Erroneous judicial instructions

(Continued)

Wrongful Convictions (Continued)

Accused	Prov/ Ter	Charge(s)	Year Convicted / Exonerated	Sentence / Time spent in Prison	Case Outcome	Ministerial Review	Compensation	Casual & Contributing Factors
Cody Klyne[15]	MB	Dangerous driving Fleeing police	2006 / 2007	– / –	Overturned	No	–	– Erroneous eyewitness identification
Thomas Sophonow[16]	MB	Murder (2nd degree)	1982 – Mistrial 1983 – Conviction 1985 – Acquittal 2000 – Exoneration	Life / 4 years	Acquittal	No	$2.6 million – provincial government	– Unreliable eyewitness evidence – Jailhouse–informant testimony – Erroneous judicial instructions – Crown failure to disclose evidence – Mistaken expert evidence
Kyle Unger[17]	MB	Murder (1st degree)	1992 / 2009	Life 25 / 14 years	Minister of justice ordered a new trial Charges withdrawn	Yes	Denied by provincial government	– "Mr Big" sting operation (false confession) – Jailhouse–informant testimony – Problematic forensic evidence (hair microscopy)
Felix Michaud[18]	NB	Murder (1st degree)	1993 / 1996 & 2001 (convicted twice, acquitted at third trial)	Life 25 / 9 years	Overturned – lack of evidence Charges stayed, then dropped	No	–	– Unreliable co–accused testimony – Crown failure to disclose evidence – Jailhouse–informant testimony
Erin Walsh[19]	NB	Murder (2nd degree)	1975 / 2008	Life 10 / 28 years	Conviction quashed, acquittal entered	Yes	Yes – provincial government (undisclosed amount)	– Crown failure to disclose evidence – Unreliable co–accused testimony
Ron Dalton[20]	NL	Murder (2nd degree)	1989 / 2000	Life 10 / 8 years	Acquitted at retrial	No	$750,000 – provincial government	– Mistaken foresic/expert evidence

Name	Province	Charge	Year convicted / exonerated	Sentence / time served	Outcome	Compensated	Compensation	Contributing factors
Randy Druken[21]	NL	Murder (2nd degree)	1993 / 2000	Life 14 / 6 years	Conviction quashed New trial ordered Charges stayed	No	$2 million – provincial government	– Jailhouse–informant testimony – Unreliable eyewitness identification – Police misconduct – Overzealous prosecution
Nelson Hart[22]	NL	Murder (1st degree) (two counts)	2007 / 2014	Life 25 / 8 years	Overturned by the Court of Appeal Charges withdrawn	No	–	– "Mr Big" sting operation – False confession
Gregory Parsons[23]	NL	Murder (2nd degree)	1994 / 1998	Life 15 / 40 days	Conviction quashed, new trial ordered Stay of proceedings Acquittal	No	$1.3 million – provincial government	– Problematic police investigation – Unreliable eyewitness identification – Overzealous prosecution – Trial judge's errors
Herman Kaglik*[24]	NT	Sexual assault	1992 / 1998	6 years / 52 months	Exonerated	No	$1.1 million – federal government (+legal fees)	– Problematic complainant testimony – Crown failure to disclose evidence – Police misconduct – Racial Prejudice
Steven Jones Kelly[25]	NT	Sexual assault	2000 / 2001	3 years / 8 months	Conviction quashed – charges stayed	No	–	– Erroneous judicial instructions – Fabricated complainant testimony
Gerald Barton[26]	NS	Statutory rape	1970 / 2011	Probation / –	Overturned	No	Denied	– Fabricated complainant testimony – Problematic police investigation
Clayton Johnson[27]	NS	Murder (1st degree)	1993 / 2002	Life 25 / 5 years	Quashed conviction, Court of Appeal ordered new trial Acquitted at new trial	Yes	$2.5 million – provincial government	– False confession – Problematic forensic/ expert evidence – Police misconduct – Overzealous prosecution

(Continued)

Wrongful Convictions (Continued)

Accused	Prov/ Ter	Charge(s)	Year Convicted / Exonerated	Sentence / Time spent in Prison	Case Outcome	Ministerial Review	Compensation	Casual & Contributing Factors
Donald Marshall, Jr [28*]	NS	Murder (Non–capital)	1971 / 1982	Life / 11 years	Acquitted	Yes	$1.5 million (lifetime pension)	– Lack of Crown disclosure – Unreliable eyewitness testimony – Police misconduct – Erroneous judicial instructions – Racial prejudice
Robert Baltovich [29]	ON	Murder (2nd degree)	1992 / 2008	Life 17 / 8 years	Court of Appeal set aside conviction Ordered a new trial Crown chose to call no evidence	No	–	– Erroneous judicial instruction – Unreliable eyewitness identification (through hypnosis)
Richard Brant [30*]	ON	Aggravated assault	1995 / 2011	6 months / 6 months	Guilty plea set aside, acquittal entered (following Goudge Inquiry)	No	–	– Problematic expert evidence (forensic pathology) – Problematic police investigation
Rodney Cain [31]	ON	Murder (2nd degree)	1985 / 2004	Life 12 years / 19 years (reduced to 10 in 1987)	Conviction quashed New trial ordered Convicted on a lesser charge (manslaughter)	Yes	–	– Unreliable eyewitness identification – Recantations or perjured admissions by witnesses
Dimitre Dimitrov [32]	ON	Murder (2nd degree)	1999 / 2005	Life 12/ 4.5 years	Conviction quashed New trial ordered Acquitted at second trial	No	–	– Problematic expert/ forensic evidence and testimony (police) – Erroneous judicial instruction
Gord Folland [33]	ON	Sexual assault	1994 / 1998	4 years / 2.5 years	Conviction overturned New trial ordered Charges withdrawn	No	Confidential settlement – defence lawyer	– Problematic complainant testimony – Jailhouse–informant testimony – Poor legal representation

Peter Frumusa[34]	ON	Murder (1st degree)	1990 / 1998	Life 25 / 8 years	Exonerated	No	Confidential settlement – provincial government, crown attorneys, Niagara Regional Police	– Jailhouse-informant testimony – Problematic police investigation
Anthony Hanemaayer[35]	ON	Assault Break-and-enter assault while threatening to use a weapon	1989 / 2008	2 years less a day / 16 months	Acquitted on appeal – Paul Bernardo confessed to the crime	No	Denied	– Erroneous eyewitness identification – Police/Crown withheld evidence
Leighton Hay[36]	ON	Murder (1st degree)	2004 / 2014	Life 25 / 1 0 years	Conviction quashed, new trial ordered Charges dropped	No	–	– Erroneous eyewitness identification – Mistaken expert evidence
Jason Hill[37*]	ON	Robbery	1996 / 1999	3 years / 20 months	Conviction quashed Overturned at second trial	No	Denied	– Erroneous eyewitness identification – Erroneous judicial instruction – Problematic police investigation – Racial prejudice
Kulaveeringsam "Kulam" Karthiresu[38]	ON	Murder (2nd degree)	1995 / 2000	Life / 6.5 years	Conviction quashed – new trial ordered Charges withdrawn	No	–	– Unreliable eyewitness identification – Problematic witness testimony
Dinesh Kumar[39]	ON	Criminal negligence causing death	1992 / 2011	90 days / 90 days 2 years probation	Court of Appeal set aside the guilty plea	No	–	– Problematic expert testimony (forensic pathology)
Stephen Leadbeater[40]	ON	Sexual assault	1993 / 1999	5 years / 7 months	Court of Appeal acquittal Retrial ordered Charges were dropped	No	–	– Police and crown misconduct – Fabricated complainant testimony – Failure to disclose evidence

(Continued)

Wrongful Convictions (Continued)

Accused	Prov/ Ter	Charge(s)	Year Convicted / Exonerated	Sentence / Time spent in Prison	Case Outcome	Ministerial Review	Compensation	Casual & Contributing Factors
Richard Mallory Robert Stewart[41]	ON	Murder (1st degree) (2 counts) Murder (2nd degree) (2 counts)	2000 / 2007	Life 25 / 15 years	Convictions overturned by the Court of Appeal New trial ordered Stay in proceedings	No	–	– Unreliable eyewitness identification – Jailhouse-informant testimony – Erroneous judicial instruction – Police misconduct
Tammy Marquardt[42] + *	ON	Murder (2nd degree)	1995 / 2011	Life 10 / 14 years	Conviction quashed by the Court of Appeal New trial ordered Charges withdrawn	No	$250,000 – provincial government	– Problematic expert evidence (forensic pathology)
Chris McCullough[43]	ON	Murder (2nd degree)	1991 / 2000	Life 18 / 9 years	Conviction overturned New trial ordered Charges dropped	No	–	– Unreliable co-accused testimony (jailhouse informant) – Unreliable eyewitness testimony – Problematic expert evidence
Michael McTaggart[44]	ON	Armed robbery (2 counts)	1988 / 1990	5 years / 2 years	Conviction overturned	No	$380,000	– Police failure to disclose evidence – Erroneous eyewitness identification
Allan Miaponoose[45]*	ON	Sexual assault	1994 / 1996	1 year / 1 year	Conviction quashed Acquittal entered	No	–	– Problematic complainant testimony – Problematic police investigation – Erroneous eyewitness identification – Racial prejudice

Name	Prov.	Offence	Years	Sentence / Time served	Court outcome		Compensation	Contributing factors
Guy Paul Morin[46]	ON	Murder (1st degree)	1992 / 1995	Life 25 / 18 months	Court of Appeal set the conviction aside, entered an acquittal	No	$1.25 million – provincial government	- Jailhouse-informant testimony - Unreliable expert/forensic evidence - Problematic police investigation - Unreliable witness testimony
William Mullins-Johnson[47] *	ON	Murder (1st degree)	1994 / 2007	Life 25 / 12 years	Court of Appeal quashed the conviction, entered an acquittal	Yes	$4.25 million – provincial government	- Problematic expert evidence (forensic pathology) - Racial prejudice
Jamie Nelson[48]	ON	Sexual assault	1996 / 2001	3 years / 3 years	Court of Appeal reversed the verdict, entered an acquittal	No	–	- Fabricated complainant testimony
Richard Norris[49]	ON	Break-and-enter Indecent assault	1980 / 1991	23 months / 8 months	Court of Appeal entered an acquittal	No	$507,000 – provincial government	- Unreliable eyewitness testimony
Romeo Phillion[50]	ON	Murder (2nd Degree)	1972 / 2010	Life 10 / 31 years	Court of Appeal overturned the conviction, ordered a new trial / Charges withdrawn	Yes	Denied	- False confession - Failure to disclose evidence - Police misconduct
John (Jack) Salmon[51]	ON	Manslaughter	1971 / 2015	10 years / 4 years	Court of Appeal quashed the conviction, entered an acquittal	No	–	- Flawed forensic evidence - Unreliable eyewitness identification
Maria Shepherd[52] +	ON	Manslaughter	1992 / 2016	2 years less a day / 9 months	Court of Appeal overturned the conviction, entered an acquittal	No	–	- Flawed forensic evidence and testimony (forensic pathology)
Sherry Sherrett-Robinson[53] +	ON	Infanticide	1999 / 2009	1 year / 1 year	Court of Appeal overturned the conviction, entered an acquittal	No	Undisclosed amount	- Flawed forensic evidence (forensic pathology)

(Continued)

Wrongful Convictions (Continued)

Accused	Prov/ Ter	Charge(s)	Year Convicted / Exonerated	Sentence / Time spent in Prison	Case Outcome	Ministerial Review	Compensation	Casual & Contributing Factors
Gary Staples[54]	ON	Murder (2nd degree)	1972 / 1974	Life 10 / 22 months	Court of Appeal quashed the conviction New trial ordered Acquitted at second trial	No	Undisclosed amount – Hamilton Police	– Failure to disclose evidence – Unreliable eyewitness identification – Unreliable complainant evidence
James Sauvé and Richard Trudel[55]	ON	Murder (1st degree) (2 counts)	1996 / 2004 (New trial ordered 2007	Life 25 / 17 years	Court of Appeal overturned the conviction New trial ordered Charges stayed	No	–	– Unreliable eyewitness testimony – Jailhouse–informant testimony – Erroneous judicial instruction – Police misconduct
Steven Truscott[56]	ON	Murder (1st degree)	1959 / 2007	Death (commuted to life) / 10 years	Overturned Court of Appeal entered an acquittal	Yes	$6.5 million – provincial government	– Failure to disclose evidence – Mistaken expert evidence – Overzealous prosecution – Problematic police investigation
Brenda Waudby[57] +	ON	Child abuse	1999 / 2013	– / –	Murder charge was stayed by the Crown (2001) Child–abuse conviction was overturned (2013)	No	Undisclosed amount	– Flawed forensic evidence (forensic pathology) – Crown withheld evidence
Joseph Dean Webber[58]	ON	Armed robbery Forcible confinement Extortion	2007 / 2010	7.5 years / 1.5 years	Court of Appeal set aside the conviction, entered an acquittal	No	$392,500 – provincial government	– Erroneous eyewitness identification

Name	Province	Offence	Years	Sentence / Time served	Outcome	Retrial	Compensation	Contributing factors
Jack White[59]	ON	Sexual assault	1995 / 2010	Suspended sentence / –	Court of Appeal quashed conviction, ordered a new trial the Crown withdrew the charges	No	Confidential settlement – employer	– Fabricated complainant testimony – Ineffective assistance of counsel
Jillian Anderson[60]+	PEI	Sexual exploitation	2008 / –2009	5 months / –	Conviction overturned by the Supreme Court of PEI	No	–	– Problematic complainant testimony – Police misconduct – Erroneous judicial instruction
John Charles Cooper[61]	PEI	Assault with weapon Uttering death threats	2003 / 2005	2 years / 29 months	Conviction overturned on appeal	No	Denied	– Problematic complainant testimony – Problematic police investigation
Hughes Duguay[62]	QC	Murder (1st degree)/ manslaughter	–1990 / 1995– 1995 / 2003	– Life – 12 years / 8 years	Court of Appeal withdrew guilty plea, quashed the conviction, entered a stay of proceedings	No	–	– False confessions – Failure to disclose evidence – Erroneous judicial instruction
Billy Taillefer[63]	QC	Murder (1st degree)	–1990 / 1995– 1995 / 2006	– Life / 12 years	Conviction quashed, new trial ordered, Acquittal after retrial	Yes		– False confessions – Failure to disclose evidence – Erroneous judicial instruction
Michel Dumont[64]	QC	Sexual assault Kidnapping Uttering threats	1992 / 2001	52 months / 34 months	Court of Appeal entered an acquittal	Yes	Denied	– Erroneous eyewitness identification – Overzealous prosecution – Failure to disclose evidence – Erroneous judicial instruction
Rejean Hinse[65]	QC	Aggravated robbery	1964 / 1997	15 years / 5 years	Acquitted	No	$8.6 million – federal government $4.5 million – provincial government	– Problematic police investigation – Erroneous eyewitness identification

(Continued)

Wrongful Convictions (Continued)

Accused	Prov/ Ter	Charge(s)	Year Convicted / Exonerated	Sentence / Time spent in Prison	Case Outcome	Ministerial Review	Compensation	Casual & Contributing Factors
Simon Marshall[66]	QC	Sexual assault	1997 / 2003	5 years / 5 years	Court of Appeal acquittal	No	$2.3 million – provincial government	– False confession[67] – Problematic police investigation
Rejean Pépin[68]	QC	Armed robbery	1987 / –	3 years / 7 months	Court of Appeal acquittal	No	$188,000 – province and federal government	– Erroneous eyewitness identification
Yves Plamondon[69]	QC	Murder (1st degree) (3 counts)	1985 / 2014	Life / 28 years	Acquitted (one charge) Charges stayed (two)	No	Pending	– Jailhouse-informant testimony – Failure to disclose evidence
Benoit Proulx[70]	QC	Murder (1st degree)	1991 / 1992	Life/ 2 months	Court of Appeal acquittal	No	$2.3 million – provincial government	– Unreliable eyewitness identification – Malicious prosecution
André Tremblay[71]	QC	Murder (1st degree)	1984 / 2010	Life/ 16 years	Reference to Court of Appeal New trial ordered Crown called no evidence, acquittal	Yes	–	– Failure to disclose evidence – Jailhouse-informant testimony (recantation)
David Milgaard[72]	SK	Murder (1st degree)	1970 / 1997	Life / 23 years	Exonerated	Yes	$10 million – provincial government	– Unreliable eyewitness identification – Problematic police investigation

* indicates cases in which the defendant was Indigenous
+ indicates cases in which the defendant was female

Suspected Wrongful Convictions[73]

Accused	Prov. / Ter.	Charge(s)	Year Convicted	Sentence / Time spent in Prison	Reasons for Suspicion
Yvonne Johnson*[74]	AB	Murder (1st degree)	1989	Life 25 / 17 years	– The Crown's medical witness testified at trial that Johnson's role in the fight would not have resulted in the victim's death; – Three other people were charged with Johnson; however, she was the only Indigenous individual and the only one to be charged with first-degree murder.
Joe (John) Warren[75]	AB	Murder (1st degree) (2 counts)	1983	Life 25 / 21 years	– There is no physical evidence linking Warren to the crime; – The conviction rests largely on fraudulent testimony provided by a jailhouse informant; – Another suspect has admitted to being the killer.
Darren Koehn[76]	BC	Murder (2nd degree)	1994	Life 10 / unknown	– The conviction was largely based on testimony provided by a forensic pathologist whose report has been found to be flawed; – The defence called almost 20 character witnesses who testified to Koehn's lack of violence; – The police believed that the death was a result of ritual torture because Koehn's mother was Wiccan.
Frank Ostrowski[77]	MB	Murder (1st degree)	1987	Life 25 / 23 years	– Police informant testified against Ostrowski in exchange for having the charges against him dropped; – Information regarding the police informant was not disclosed to the defence at trial. – The case is current before the Court of Appeal.
Walter Dillespie Robert Mailman[78]	NB	Murder (2nd degree)	1984	Life 10 / –	– The conviction is based on problematic testimonies; one witness was coerced and the other testimony was given by the woman who was originally charged for the murder but charges were dropped in exchange for her testimony; – One of the key witnesses immediately recanted his testimony after the trial; – There is no physical evidence linking either man to the crime; both men had alibis. – Evidence favourable to the defence was never disclosed by the police or prosecution.
George Pitt[79]	NB	Murder (1st degree)	1994	Life 25 / –	– The conviction was based on evidence that Pitt tried to cover up the crime as he washed the victim's comforter at 4 a.m. – Biological evidence tested after the trial clears Pitt.
Glenn Assoun[80]	NS	Murder (2nd degree)	1999	Life 18.5 / 16 years	– There was no physical evidence linking Assoun to the crime; – Currently released on bail pending investigation into possible miscarriage of justice by the Criminal Conviction Review Group.
Amina Chaudhary[81]	ON	Murder (1st degree)	1984	Life 25 / 26 years	– Her conviction was based on the testimony of Dr Charles Smith, whose testimony in other cases has been widely discredited; – Autopsy photos have been lost. – The Innocence Project at York University's Osgoode Hall is examining this case.

(Continued)

Suspected Wrongful Convictions (Continued)

Accused	Prov. / Ter.	Charge(s)	Year Convicted	Sentence / Time spent in Prison	Reasons for Suspicion
John Moore[82]	ON	Murder (2nd degree)	1978 / 1982	Life 10 / 10 years	– Moore was not present when the murders took place but was convicted under a now unconstitutional part of the Criminal Code, s. 21(2), which suggests he "ought to have known" that the robbery was going to take place and the possible consequences that could arise;
Chris Bates[83]	QB	Murder (2nd degree) Charges dropped in 2000 in exchange for guilty plea to armed robbery	1993	Life 10 / 5.5 years	– Innocence Ottawa at the University of Ottawa has taken on the case. – There is no physical evidence linking Bates to the crime; – The conviction is primarily based on conflicting testimony of Bates's ex-girlfriend, police coercion, and fabricated evidence; – Private investigators have provided new evidence suggesting more likely suspects; – Innocence Canada submitted a request and a formal conviction review of the case (overturn the guilty plea to robbery) is currently pending.
Wilbert Coffin[84]	QB	Murder (1st degree)	1953	Capital punishment / executed 1956	– The evidence against Coffin was circumstantial, the trial was conducted in French (despite Coffin being English), Coffin's counsel was ineffective and entered no defence, and the political atmosphere in 1950s Quebec contributed to a quick resolution of the case; – Former Senator Jacques Hébert wrote two books about the possibility of Coffin's wrongful conviction; – In 2007 the House of Commons unanimously adopted a motion calling for a swift investigation into the case;
Jacques Delisle[85]	QB	Murder (1st degree)	2012	Life 25 / In custody	– The Criminal Conviction Review Group is currently reviewing the case. – Delisle has admitted to assisting his disabled wife in her suicide; – Four forensic experts have concluded suicide as the likely cause of death; – The Criminal Conviction Review Group is currently reviewing the case.
Leon Walchuk[86]	SK	Murder (2nd degree)	2000	Life 16 / In custody	– Experts are now questioning the type of arson evidence that was used at Walchuk's trial (a pre-eminent arson expert from the US reviewed the case in 2006 and found no accelerant was used); – The minister of justice turned down CCRG's recommendation for review in 2009, and while no accelerant was found, cited still "compelling evidence" of murder. – Osgoode Hall Innocence Project is investigating the case and it is being sent for judicial review before the Federal Court of Appeal.

The Inquiry regarding Thomas Sophonow: Eyewitness Identification – Recommendations

Manitoba Justice
www.gov.mb.ca

Live line-up

- The third officer who is present with the prospective eyewitness should have no knowledge of the case or whether the suspect is contained in the line-up.
- The officer in the room should advise the witness that he does not know if the suspect is in the line-up or, if he is, who he is. The officer should emphasize to the witness that the suspect may not be in the line-up.
- All proceedings in the witness room while the line-up is being watched should be recorded, preferably by videotape but, if not, by audiotape.
- All statements of the witness on reviewing the line-up must be both noted and recorded verbatim and signed by the witness.
- When the line-up is completed, the witness should be escorted from the police premises. This will eliminate any possibility of contamination of that witness by other officers, particularly those involved in the investigation of the crime itself.
- The fillers in the line-up should match as closely as possible the descriptions given by the eyewitnesses at the time of the event. It is only if that is impossible, that the fillers should resemble the suspect as closely as possible.
- At the conclusion of the line-up, if there has been any identification, there should be a question posed to the witness as to the degree of certainty of identification. The question and answer must be both noted and recorded verbatim and signed by the witness. It is important to have this report on record before there is any possibility of contamination or reinforcement of the witness.
- The line-up should contain a minimum of 10 persons. The greater the number of persons in the line-up, the less likelihood there is of a wrong identification.

Photo pack line-up

1. The photo pack should contain at least 10 subjects.
2. The photos should resemble as closely as possible the eyewitnesses' description. If that is not possible, the photos should be as close as possible to the suspect.

3. Everything should be recorded on video or audiotape from the time that the officer meets the witness, before the photographs are shown through until the completion of the interview. Once again, it is essential that an officer who does not know who the suspect is and who is not involved in the investigation conducts the photo pack line-up.
4. Before the showing of the photo pack, the officer conducting the line-up should confirm that he does not know who the suspect is or whether his photo is contained in the line-up. In addition, before showing the photo pack to a witness, the officer should advise the witness that it is just as important to clear the innocent as it is to identify the suspect. The photo pack should be presented by the officer to each witness separately.
5. The photo pack must be presented sequentially and not as a package.
6. In addition to the videotape, if possible, or, as a minimum alternative, the audiotape, there should be a form provided for setting out in writing and for signature the comments of both the officer conducting the line-up and the witness. All comments of each witness must be noted and recorded verbatim and signed by the witness.
7. Police officers should not speak to eyewitnesses after the line-ups regarding their identification or their inability to identify anyone. This can only cast suspicion on any identification made and raise concerns that it was reinforced.
8. It was suggested that, because of the importance of eyewitness evidence and the high risk of contaminating it, a police force other than the one conducting the investigation of the crime should conduct the interviews and the line-ups with the eyewitnesses. Ideal as that procedure might be, I think that it would unduly complicate the investigation, add to its cost and increase the time required. At some point, there must be reasonable degree of trust placed in the police. The interviews of eyewitnesses and the line-up may be conducted by the same force as that investigating the crime, provided that the officers dealing with the eyewitnesses are not involved in the investigation of the crime and do not know the suspect or whether his photo forms part of the line-up. If this were done and the other recommendations complied with, that would provide adequate protection of the process.

Trial instructions

1. There must be strong and clear directions given by the Trial Judge to the jury emphasizing the frailties of eyewitness identification. The jury should as well be instructed that the apparent confidence of a witness as to his or her identification is not a criteria of the accuracy of the identification. In this case, the evidence of Mr. Janower provides a classic example of misplaced but absolute confidence that Thomas Sophonow was the man whom he saw at the donut shop.
2. The Trial Judge should stress that tragedies have occurred as a result of mistakes made by honest, right-thinking eyewitnesses. It should be explained that the vast majority of the wrongful convictions of innocent persons have arisen as a result of faulty eyewitness identification. These instructions should be given in addition to the standard direction regarding the difficulties inherent in eyewitness identification.

3. Further, I would recommend that judges consider favourably and readily admit properly qualified expert evidence pertaining to eyewitness identification. This is certainly not junk science. Careful studies have been made with regard to memory and its effect upon eyewitness identification. Jurors would benefit from the studies and learning of experts in this field. Meticulous studies of human memory and eyewitness identification have been conducted. The empirical evidence has been compiled. The tragic consequences of mistaken eyewitness identification in cases have been chronicled and jurors and Trial Judges should have the benefit of expert evidence on this important subject. The expert witness can explain the process of memory and its frailties and dispel myths, such as that which assesses the accuracy of identification by the certainty of a witness. The testimony of an expert in this field would be helpful to the triers of fact and assist in providing a fair trial.
4. The Trial Judge must instruct and caution the jury with regard to an identification which has apparently progressed from tentative to certain and to consider what may have brought about that change.
5. During the instructions, the Trial Judge should advise the jury that mistaken eyewitness identification has been a significant factor in wrongful convictions of accused in the United States and in Canada, with a possible reference to the Thomas Sophonow case.

Federal/Provincial/Territorial Heads of Prosecution Committee Working Group (2005), Recommendations regarding the Use of Eyewitness Identification Evidence

1. The following are reasonable standards and practices that should be implemented and integrated by all police forces:
   a. If possible, an officer who is independent of the investigation should be in charge of the lineup or photospread. This officer should not know who the suspect is to avoid the possibility of inadvertant hints or reactions that could lead the witness before the identification takes place, or increase the witness' degree of confidence afterward.
   b. The witness should be advised that the actual perpetrator may not be in the lineup or photospread, and therefore the witness should not feel that they must make an identification.
   c. The suspect should not stand out in the lineup or photospread as being different from the others, based on the eyewitness' previous description of the perpetrator, or based on other factors that would draw extra attention to the suspect.
   d. All of the witness' comments and statements made during the lineup or photospread viewing should be recorded verbatim, either in writing or if feasible and practical, by audio or videotaping.
   e. If the identification process occurs on police premises, reasonable steps should be taken to remove the witness on completion of the lineup to prevent any potential feedback by other officers involved in the investigation and cross contamination by contact with other witnesses.
   f. Show-ups should be used only in rare circumstances, such as when the suspect is apprehended near the crime scene shortly after the event.
   g. A photospread should be provided sequentially, and not as a package, thus preventing "relative judgments."

2. For prosecutors, the following practical suggestions should be considered:
   a. Assume the identity of the accused is always at issue unless the defence specifically admits it on the record. Timely preparation and a critical review of all of the available identification evidence, including the manner in which it was obtained, is requested as it will affect the conduct and quality of the trial.
   b. Allow the witness a reasonable opportunity to review all previously given statements and confirm that the statements were accurate and a true reflection

of their observations at the time. Carefully canvass the full range of indicia of the identification, including any distinguishing features that augment this evidence. Remember that it is the collective impact of all of the evidence that will be considered in support of a conviction. Defects in one witness' identification can be overcome by the consideration of other evidence.

c. Never interview witnesses collectively. Never prompt or coach a witness by offering clues or hints about the identity of the accused in court. Do not condone or participate in a "show-up" lineup. Never show a witness an isolated photograph or image of an accused during an interview.

d. When meeting with witnesses in serious cases, it is wise, if it is feasible and practical, to have a third party present to ensure there is no later disagreement about what took place at the meeting.

e. Never tell a witness that they are right or wrong in their identification.

f. Remember that disclosure is a continuing obligation. All inculpatory and exculpatory evidence must be disclosed to the defence in a timely fashion. In the event that a witness materially changes their original statement, by offering more or recanting previously given information during an interview, the defence must be told. In these circumstances it would be prudent to enlist the services of a police officer to record a further statement in writing setting out these material changes.

g. Always lead evidence of the history of the identification. It is vitally important that the trier of fact not only be told of the identification but all the circumstances involved in obtaining it, e.g., the composition of the photospread.

h. Be wary of prosecutions based on single-witness identification. While not required by law to secure a conviction, ascertain whether there is any corroboration of an eyewitness' identification in order to overcome any deficiencies in the quality of that evidence.

3. The use of expert evidence on the frailties of eyewitness identification is redundant and unnecessary in the fact-finding process. A proper charge and caution by the trial judge can best deal with the inherent dangers of identification evidence.

4. Workshops on proper interviewing should be incorporated in regular and ongoing training sessions for police and prosecutors.

5. Presentations on the perils of eyewitness misidentifications should be incorporated in regular and ongoing training sessions for police and prosecutors.

[The purpose of the recommendations was to reinforce the need to be diligent and vigilant in preserving the integrity of the identification process. Furthermore, they would also serve as a constant reminder of the potential abuse by otherwise faulty or tainted eyewitness testimony should the mandated safeguards be relaxed.]

Canadian Judicial Council, National Judicial Institute: Eyewitness Identification Evidence, Model Jury Instructions

[1] Identification is an important issue in this case. The case against (NOA) depends entirely (or to a large extent) on eyewitness testimony.

[2] You must be very careful about relying on eyewitness testimony to find (NOA) guilty of any criminal offence. Innocent people have been wrongly convicted because reliance was placed on mistaken eyewitness identification. Even a number of witnesses can be honestly mistaken about identification. Eyewitness identification may seem more reliable than it actually is because it comes from a credible and convincing witness who honestly but mistakenly believes that the accused person is the one he or she saw committing the offence.

[3] There is little connection between great confidence of the witness and the accuracy of the identification. Even a very confident witness may be honestly mistaken. A very confident witness may be entirely wrong with respect to his or her identification evidence.

[4] Eyewitness identification is a conclusion based on the witness's observations. The reliability of the identification depends on the basis for the witness's conclusion.

[5] Consider the various factors that relate specifically to the (each) eyewitness and his/her identification of (NOA) as the person who committed the offence charged:

(Select the applicable factors from each category below and review them with the jury. The list is not intended to be exhaustive.)

1. Reliability of the eyewitness

Did the witness have good eyesight?
Was the witness's ability to observe impaired by alcohol or drugs?
Does the witness have a reliable memory?
Is the witness capable of communicating the observations s/he made at the time?
How accurate was the eyewitness's judgment of distance?

(Review relevant evidence and relate to the issues.)

2. The circumstances in which the witness made his/her observations

Had the witness seen the person on a previous occasion?

Did the witness know the person before s/he saw him/her at the time?
How long did the witness watch the person s/he says is the person on trial?
How good or bad was the visibility?
Was there anything that prevented or hindered a clear view?
How far apart were the witness and the person whom s/he saw?
How good was the lighting?
Did anything distract the witness's attention at the time s/he made the
    observations? (e.g., stress from the production of a weapon, injuries, another
    event occurring simultaneously)
Was the perpetrator wearing a disguise?

(When cross-racial identification is in issue it may be appropriate to caution the
jury regarding the frailties of this type of identification.)
(Review relevant evidence and relate to the issues.)

3. The description given by the eyewitness after s/he made the observations

How long after the events did the eyewitness give the first description?
How specific was the description? (e.g., details of the physical description –
    weight, height, clothing, hair colour, facial hair, glasses)
Did the witness describe any features which are peculiar to the accused? (e.g.,
    tattoos, scars)
Did the witness miss any obvious physical feature of the accused?
How does the description compare to the way (NOA) actually looked at the time?
Did the witness ever give a different description of this person?
What are the differences between the descriptions? Are they significant or minor?
Has the eyewitness expressed uncertainty about his/her identification?

(Review evidence and relate to issue.)

4. The circumstances of the procedure followed for identification

(These factors are to be used when there was a photo or physical line-up.)

How long was it between the observation and identification procedure?
Did the eyewitness see a picture of (NOA) prior to the identification procedure,
    such as a television newscast? Or on the internet?
Did anybody show (NOA)'s picture to the witness to assist in the identification
    prior to the identification procedure?
Was anything done to draw the witness's attention to a specific photo or person?
Was anything done to confirm the witness's selection?
Was the line-up procedure fair? Did the other participants in the line-up share the
    physical characteristics of the accused? Were the photos similar? (e.g., size of
    the photo and colour)
Were photographs of other people shown at the same time?
Was anyone else present when the witness made the identification?

What did the witness say when s/he identified (NOA)?

Did the witness ever fail to identify (NOA) as the person whom s/he saw?

Has the witness ever changed his/her mind about the identification?

Was the witness exposed to other persons' accounts or descriptions?

Did the witness change his or her description after such exposure?

Was the identification the witness's own recollection of his/her observations or something put together from pictures shown or information received from a number of other sources?

(Review relevant evidence about the circumstances of identification.)

Read paragraph [6] when the in-court identification of (NOA) is the eyewitness' first identification of (NOA) as the offender. Otherwise go directly to paragraph [7].

6. (NOW) identified (NOA) for the first time in the courtroom while (NOA) was sitting in the prisoner's dock. This identification is entitled to little weight. This is because there is a danger that a witness will assume that the person sitting in the prisoner's dock is the offender.

Read the following sentence if (NOW) was shown a line-up or previous procedure to identify and failed to identify (NOA).

As well, (NOW) did not identify (NOA) in the line-up (or previous occasion) after the event and this seriously undermines any subsequent identification.

7. Remember, the Crown must prove beyond a reasonable doubt that it was (NOA) who committed the offence charged. Consider the evidence of the identification witness along with the other evidence you have seen and heard in deciding that question.

In the rare case where the jury could conclude that the in-dock identification is the only evidence of identification read the following instruction.

If you conclude that the in-dock identification is the only evidence of identification then it would be unsafe to convict (NOA).

Glossary:

NOA = Name of Accused
NOA2 = Name of Accused 2
NOC = Name of Complainant
NOC2 = Name of Complainant 2
NOD = Name of Declarant
NOW = Name of Witness
NOW2 = Name of Witness 2
NOAW = Name of Accused-Witness (Accused who testifies)
NO3P = Name of Third Party

Canada's 1988 Federal-Provincial Guidelines on Compensation for Wrongfully Convicted and Imprisoned Persons

The following guidelines include a rationale for compensation and criteria for both eligibility and quantum for compensation. Such guidelines form the basis of a national standard to be applied in instances in which the question of compensation arises.

A. Rationale

Despite the many safeguards in Canada's criminal justice system, innocent persons are occasionally convicted and imprisoned. Recently three cases (Marshall, Truscott, and Fox) have focused public attention on the issue of compensation for those persons that have been wrongfully convicted and imprisoned. In appropriate cases, compensation should be awarded in an effort to relieve the consequences of wrongful conviction and imprisonment.

B. Guidelines for Eligibility to Apply for Compensation

The following are prerequisites for eligibility for compensation:

1. The wrongful conviction must have resulted in imprisonment, all or part of which has been served.
2. Compensation should only be available to the actual person who has been wrongfully convicted and imprisoned.
3. Compensation should only be available to an individual who has been wrongfully convicted and imprisoned as a result of a *Criminal Code* or other federal penal offence.
4. As a condition precedent to compensation, there must be a free pardon granted under Section 683(2) [now 749(2)] of the *Criminal Code* or a verdict of acquittal entered by an Appellate Court pursuant to a referral made by the Minister of Justice under Section 617(b) [now 696.1(b)].
5. Eligibility for compensation would only arise when Sections 617 and 683 [now 696.1 and 749] were exercised in circumstances where all available appeal remedies have been exhausted and where a new or newly discovered fact has emerged, tending to show that there has been a miscarriage of justice.

As compensation should only be granted to those persons who did not commit the crime for which they were convicted (as opposed to persons who are found not guilty), further criteria would require:

a. if a pardon is granted under Section 683 [now 749], a statement on the face of the pardon based on an investigation, that the individual did not commit the offence; or
b. if a reference is made by the Minister of Justice under Section 617(b) [now 696.1(b)], a statement by the Appellate Court, in response to a question asked by the Minister of Justice pursuant to Section 617(c) [now 696.1(c)], to the effect that the person did not commit the offence.

It should be noted that Sections 617 [696] and 683 [749] may not be available in all cases in which an individual has been convicted of an offence which he did not commit, for example, where an individual had been granted an extension of time to appeal and a verdict of acquittal has been entered in Appellate Court. In such a case, a Provincial Attorney General would make a determination that the individual eligible for compensation, based on an investigation which has determined that the individual did not commit the offence.

C. Procedure

When an individual meets the eligibility criteria, the Provincial or Federal Minister Responsible for Criminal Justice will undertake to have appointed, either a judicial or administrative inquiry to examine the matter of compensation in accordance with the considerations set out below. The provincial or federal governments would undertake to act on the report submitted by the Commission of Inquiry.

D. Considerations for Determining Quantum

The quantum of compensation shall be determined having regard to the following considerations:

1. *Non-pecuniary losses*
   a) Loss of liberty and the physical and mental harshness and indignities of incarceration;
   b) Loss of reputation which would take into account a consideration of any previous criminal record;
   c) Loss or interruption of family or other personal relationships.

Compensation for non-pecuniary losses should not exceed $100,000.

2. *Pecuniary Losses*
   a) Loss of livelihood, including the loss of earnings, with adjustments for income tax and for benefits received while incarcerated;
   b) Loss of future earning abilities;

c) Loss of property or other consequential financial losses resulting from incarceration.

In assessing the above mentioned amounts, the inquiring body must take into
account the following factors:
a) Blameworthy conduct or other acts on the part of the applicant which contributed to the wrongful conviction;
b) Due diligence on the part of the claimant in pursuing these remedies.

3. *Costs to the Applicant*

Reasonable costs incurred by the applicant in obtaining a pardon or verdict of
acquittal should be included in the award for compensation.

Notes

Chapter 1

1 Lawrence Greenspon, "Wrongful Convictions: Experiences, Implications and Working towards Justice," University of Ottawa, 10 April 2002. The play "Blood on the Moon," performed by the Great Canadian Theatre Company, recounts the trial of Patrick Whelan from his point of view and raises questions about the legitimacy of his conviction (http://www.gctc.ca/plays/blood-moon).

2 As found in T.P. Slatterly, *"They Got to Find Me Guilty Yet"* (Toronto: Doubleday and Company 1972).

3 Fenians were a group of Irish nationalists in the nineteenth-century United States working to liberate Ireland from British rule. D'Arcy McGee was vocal in his opposition to them.

4 This theme is further discussed in chapter 11. Many jurisdictions require a finding of factual innocence prior to awarding compensation to the wrongly convicted.

5 It is beyond the scope of this chapter to examine this important issue in greater detail. See, for example, the Maher Arar Commission of Inquiry (O'Connor, 2006a, 2006b). See also Campbell (2013) for a study of how preventive-detention strategies in both Canada and the United States serve to create miscarriages of justice.

6 *R. v. Mullins-Johnson,* 2007 ONCA 720 (CanLII), para. 24.

7 Ibid., para. 25.

8 Discussed further in chapter 10.

9 Historically, individuals have been convicted for crimes that never actually occurred. Examples are cases where forensic evidence and expert testimony have been used to secure a finding of guilt but the verdicts are later overturned when it is demonstrated that no crime has occurred at all. See chapter 8.

10 Michael Petrunik, personal communication.

11 This more extreme position by Naughton includes all criminal convictions in the Crown Court and Magistrates' Courts in England and Wales that are overturned on appeal by the Court of Appeal (Criminal Division) (Naughton, 2005a, 166). Naughton (2005a, 2005b) offers a governmentality framework from which to understand miscarriages of justice and argues that the current study of the subject is too narrow, since it focuses mainly on exceptional cases of those who are also wrongly imprisoned, while ignoring more routine cases (2001, 2003). Clearly, inclusion of these tens of thousands of cases annually would substantially increase estimates of wrongful convictions and significantly alter perceptions of the nature and extent of

this issue. Regardless, it is not an opinion that is shared by many wrongful-conviction scholars.

12 From *Kansas v. Marsh*, 548 U.S. 163, 208 (2006) (Souter, J., dissenting), (Scalia, J., concurring), as found in Gross (2008).

13 *United States v. Garsson*, 291 F. 646, 649 (S.D.N.Y. 1923).

14 For similar arguments about the myth of innocence surrounding death-penalty cases, see Marquis (2005); for alternative arguments, see Steiker and Steiker (2005).

15 A number he extrapolates from the Gross et al. (2005) study of 340 exonerations through innocence projects from 1989 to 2003. He describes this figure as "conservatively" high.

16 At the same time, he is rather dismissive of criticisms regarding the fallibility of actors in the criminal justice system, which may reflect his position as a judge. This is particularly evident in the opening salvo of his article: "Almost all criminal defendants plead guilty, and almost all of them do because they are guilty" (Hoffman, 2007, 663).

17 Extrapolating from these numbers, and based on an average annual felony-conviction count of one million and a prison rate of 40 per cent, Zalman offers the following rather frightening annual estimates: assuming a 2 per cent error rate, the result would be 20,000 wrongful convictions and 8,000 wrongful imprisonments; a 1 per cent error rate, 10,000 wrongful convictions and 4,000 wrongful imprisonments; a .5 per cent error rate, 5,000 wrongful convictions and 2,000 wrongful imprisonments; and a .027 per cent error rate, 270 wrongful convictions and 108 wrongful imprisonments (Zalman, 2012, 225–6).

18 Elsewhere Gross (2008) cautions against extrapolating a wrongful-conviction rate from capital studies' estimates since he believes that the rate for false convictions is higher for murders in general and capital murders in particular than it is for other felony convictions. This may be in part due to the fact that greater resources are devoted to capital cases, through repeated review at various stages, thus increasing overall knowledge about what has occurred in these convictions, including the highlighting of errors (Gross and O'Brien, 2008).

19 www.law.umich.edu/special/exoneration/Pages/about.aspx.

20 The Home Office is the lead government department in the United Kingdom for, inter alia, policing and crime, similar to the Department of Justice in the United States and Public Safety Canada.

21 From *The Times*, 17 Aug. 1990, 14, found in Walker (2002a).

22 Further refining his number, based on estimates of those having served a custody sentence greater than three months (presumably, those whose convictions were in error but did not receive custodial sentences are not included), McLellan arrives at a total of 210 wrongly convicted individuals annually. He oddly conflates his estimate by including wrongly accused or remand populations with those who are actually wrongly convicted, which increases the number to 291.

23 In these cases, the convictions were either quashed or overturned on appeal, charges were dismissed, or the individual was acquitted at retrial owing to insufficient evidence or received a pardon.

24 See, for example, *Annual Report of the Office of the Correctional Investigator 2012–2013*, Part IV, Aboriginal Issues, 28 June 2013. See also Roach (2015).

25 The numbers do not add up to 70, nor do the percentages add up to 100, given that detailed information is not available for all of the cases and, as stated, more than one factor sometimes contributes to a wrongful conviction.

26 https://www.law.umich.edu/special/exoneration/Pages/about.aspx.

27 As of 22 February 2017. The numbers change frequently since the website is updated on a daily basis. The total is likely even larger because it does not include information on "group exonerations," which have been described as cases where police officers deliberately frame innocent defendants in mainly drug and gun crimes. Gross and Shaffer note that there are probably another "1100 convicted defendants who were cleared since 1995 in 12 'group exonerations'" and that the information on these cases is rather obscure (2012, 3).

28 Information on "perjury or false accusation" pertains to cases where "a person other than the exoneree falsely accused the exoneree of committing the crime for which the exoneree was later exonerated, either in sworn testimony or otherwise." This factor, present in over half of the exonerated cases, is not often singled out in the literature and is frequently included under police or prosecutorial misconduct.

29 The percentages are based on my own calculations of the number of cases showing evidence of that particular contributing factor.

30 http://www.innocenceproject.org/causes-wrongful-conviction#sthash.jb6GIr7U.dpuf.

31 http://www.law.umich.edu/special/exoneration/Pages/contactcorrection.aspx.

32 As noted, there are some wrongful-conviction cases where no crime has occurred at all.

33 Care must be taken not to confuse models with theories. Roach demonstrates that models of criminal justice describe the operations of the criminal justice system and the discourses that surround it, and provide normative statements as to what values ought to and in fact do influence the criminal law (1999a). Put simply, theory is more concerned with understanding ideas that allow for the systematization of knowledge of the social world (Ritzer, 2010). There is a long and rich history of sociological theories of crime, and while models provide more concrete descriptors of the material world, theories provide wider perspectives from which to understand social phenomena.

34 On reading Lofquist (2001), it is clear that he is referring to the "causes" of wrongful conviction, not examining the wider issue more generally.

35 This is by no means an exhaustive review of sociological theory as it pertains to miscarriages of justice; regardless, I am indebted to Chris Bruckert for her insight and guidance in this area.

36 Tunnel vision will be explained in greater detail in chapter 2; however, research has indicated that it is a significant contributing factor in a number of wrongful convictions.

37 Race and Wrongful Convictions in the United States, National Registry of Exoneration, March 2017, http://www.law.umich.edu/special/exoneration/Documents/Race_and_Wrongful_Convictions.pdf.

38 While some refer to the residential-school experience as an example of the cultural genocide of Indigenous peoples, this term is not without controversy.

39 In examining the restrictions in place for wrongly convicted individuals seeking exoneration, McLellan further argues that the reticence of state governments to compensate exonerees is an example of risk-based thinking which underlies an aversion to release anyone the state believes may be capable of causing further harm (2012b).

40 http://www.merriam-webster.com/dictionary/perfect%20storm.

41 Walker discusses the influence of the European Convention on Human Rights, which protects, inter alia, life (art. 2), humane treatment (art. 3), liberty and security of the

person (art. 5), fair trials and pre-trial process (art. 6), non-retrospective penalties (art. 7), and privacy and freedom from intrusion (art. 8) (1999, 38).

42 Canadian Charter of Rights and Freedoms, Part I of the Constitution Act, 1982, being Schedule B to the Canada Act 1982 (U.K.), 1982, c. 11 [Charter].

43 The impact of the seminal case of *R. v. Stinchcombe* is discussed in greater detail in chapter 2.

44 Section 11(d) of the Charter states: "Any person charged with an offence has the right ... (d) to be presumed innocent until proven guilty according to law in a fair and public hearing by an independent and impartial tribunal."

45 Criminal Code, R.S.C., 1985, c. C-46.

Chapter 2

1 J.M. Doyle, *True Witness: Cops, Courts, Science and the Battle against Misidentification* (New York: Palgrave Macmillan 2005), 21.

2 Jennifer Thompson, "I Was Certain, but I Was Wrong," *New York Times*, 18 June 2000, 4 at 15.

3 Jennifer Thompson-Cannino and Ronald Cotton tour publicly, recounting their story together. They have also published, with Erin Torneo, *Picking Cotton* (2009).

4 Luus and Wells (1994, 348) have found very little correlation between accuracy and witness confidence; however, the relationship between accuracy and confidence may not be so straightforward. The greater problem appears to surround the influence of feedback on confidence since feedback may artificially inflate confidence and thus reduce its correlation with accuracy (Bradfield, Wells, and Olson, 2002).

5 http://www.innocenceproject.org.

6 Gross and Shaffer (2012) provide an interesting breakdown of how such misidentifications are manifested. In particular, they reveal that honest mistakes are different than lies, the latter category including deliberate misidentification of the defendants as the perpetrator of the actual crime and accusations that the defendant committed fabricated crimes (41). For these categories, the incident rates differ from one type of crime to another.

7 Garrett's analysis is particularly revealing. Of the 190 cases, 63 per cent involved a discrepancy in description, while in 9 per cent the witnesses did not see the face; in 21 per cent, they were initially uncertain; in 40 per cent, they made an initial non-identification; in 3 per cent, they were hypnotized; in 28 per cent, they heard suggestive remarks; in 34 per cent, they viewed a suggestive line-up; and in 34 per cent, they identified the suspect in a show-up situation. See http://www.law.virginia.edu/html/librarysite/garrett_eyewitness.htm.

8 Given the plethora of recent research in this area, it would be impossible to cover all of the findings in a satisfactory manner; however, Wells and Olson (2003) provide an excellent overview of the main issues and findings.

9 See, for example, Loftus (1979), Loftus and Ketcham (1991), Loftus, Doyle and Dysert (2008).

10 See, for example, Wells (1984, 2006), Wells and Bradfield (1998), Wells and Hasel (2008), Wells and Loftus (2012), and Wells et al. (1998; 2000).

11 Innocence Project, http://www.innocenceproject.org/understand/Eyewitness-Misidentification.php (retrieved 11 June 2009).

12 The content of the line-up is under police control. It also comprises a "functional size" – which literally means the number of members in the line-up who fit the eyewitness's description of the suspect (Wells and Olson, 2003, 279). For example, if a witness described the suspect as having red hair and being six feet tall, and the suspect is the only line-up member who matches those characteristics, then the functional size of the line-up would be 1.0. Furthermore, a "blank" line-up does not contain the actual suspect or culprit and is used mainly in experimental situations.

13 Recent experimental research has demonstrated that the "optional deadline procedure" (involving briefly presenting the line-up, removing the line-up from view, and then giving the participants the option of either making an identification or viewing the line-up again), when compared to forced deadline or standard line-up procedures, resulted in a greater probability of correct identification (Brewer and Palmer, 2010).

14 388 US 218, 235 (1967).

15 Ibid., 388 U.S. 223–7.

16 [1989] 1 S.C.R. 3.

17 From M. Roth, "Why Police Composites Don't Always Hit the Mark: New System for Police Sketches Takes into Consideration That Witnesses Typically Recall the Entire Face, not Individual Features." See http://www.post-gazette.com/pg/07084/772371-84.stm (retrieved 25 Aug. 2009).

18 Cf. *R. v. Marcoux* [1976] 1 S.C.R. 763, where the Court found that Marcoux's refusal to take part in a line-up was admissible to the jury. Even more problematic was the case of *R. v. Henry* (2010) BCCA 462, where Henry had refused to participate in a line-up so the police physically forced him to do so and held him in a headlock for a photograph line-up. The court later found that the trial judge erred in allowing the jury to believe that Henry's refusal to participate was an admission of guilt and in failing to review other innocent explanations for Henry's resistance. He was acquitted on a number of charges of sexual assault after serving twenty-six years in prison as a dangerous offender.

19 It is beyond the scope of this chapter to present an overview of the voluminous research to date on estimator variables in eyewitness identification. See, for example, Cutler, Penrod, and Martens (1987), Kramer, Buckhout, and Eugenio (1990), Loftus, Loftus, and Messo (1987).

20 See chapter 3 for a discussion of the case of *Hill v. Hamilton-Wentworth Regional Police Services Board*, [2007] 3 S.C.R. 129, 2007 SCC 41, which deals with the problems encountered in the cross-race identification of an Indigenous suspect.

21 388 U.S. 293, 301–2 (1967).

22 Although an element of suggestion does not, in itself, exclude evidence.

23 388 U.S. 218, 235 (1967).

24 409 U.S. 188, 198–9 (1972) [*Biggers*].

25 432 U.S. 98, 114 (1977) [*Braithwaite*].

26 In *Biggers*, identification based a one-on-one confrontation between the witness and the defendant that occurred several months after the crime was held to be admissible since the witness had been with the perpetrator for well over fifteen minutes, had refused to identify the perpetrator during previous line-ups and show-ups, and was certain of her identification. In *Braithwaite*, an identification of the defendant from a single photo placed on the eyewitness's desk was upheld because the eyewitness viewed the perpetrator for two to three minutes, was a trained police officer, gave a detailed

description of the perpetrator, identified the defendant from the photo within two days, and was certain of his identification.

27 *Braithwaite*, at 432 U. S. 114.

28 Canadian case law setting out the rules on eyewitness identification is covered in detail in Department of Justice (2005b).

29 *R. v. Tebo*, [2003] O.J. No. 1853.

30 *R. v. Burke*, [1996] 1 S.C.R. 474, at para 52, citing *R. v. Sutton*, [1970] 2 O.R. 358 (C.A.).

31 *R. v. Hibbert* (2002), 163 C.C.C. (3d) 129 (S.C.C.) [*Hibbert*].

32 In-dock identifications, similar to show-ups, are highly problematic, and in *Hibbert* Justice Arbour, writing for the majority, noted: "It is important to remember that the danger associated with eyewitness in-court identification is that it is deceptively credible, largely because it is honest and sincere. The dramatic impact of the identification taking place in court, before the jury, can aggravate the distorted value that the jury may place on it. I am not persuaded that the instruction quoted above, to the effect that such identification should be accorded 'little weight,' goes far enough to displace the danger that the jury could still give it weight that it does not deserve" (para. 50).

33 *Hibbert*, at p. 10.

34 Ibid., 21.

35 Ibid., 28. The problems associated with "in-dock" identifications have also been noted in *R. v. A.(F.)*. and *R. v. Tebo*. Paciocco and Stuesser (2015) warn that juries should be warned that such identifications have virtually no weight (574).

36 Paciocco and Stuesser (2015), 573.

37 *R. v. McIntosh* [1997] O.J. No. 3172 [*McIntosh*].

38 Ibid., at 28.

39 *R. v. Bennett* (2003) Ont CA 179 C.C.C. (3d) 244.

40 Most of the information on Sophonow's case was taken from the commission of inquiry examining the errors in his case, chaired by Justice Cory. See https://websites. godaddy.com/blob/6aaa6fc2-99d9-4af2-a3b4-51e9d74ea37a/downloads/Thomas %20Sophonow%20Inquiry.pdf?2bd500cf (retrieved July 2017).

41 See chapter 10 for more detailed information on this and other commissions of inquiry.

42 See appendix B for an overview of the Sophonow Inquiry recommendations regarding best practices for police and Crown prosecutors in eyewitness identification.

43 https://websites.godaddy.com/blob/6aaa6fc2-99d9-4af2-a3b4-51e9d74ea37a/ downloads/Thomas%20Sophonow%20Inquiry.pdf?2bd500cf (retrieved July 2017).

44 *R. v. Hinse* [1997] S.C.J. No. 1. While Hinse was acquitted by the Supreme Court of Canada in 2007, he did not receive compensation for his criminal conviction at that time because the criteria for compensation for a wrongful conviction in Canada are currently so narrow he did not meet them. The Federal-Provincial Guidelines (discussed in greater detail in chapter 11) stipulate that an individual must be acquitted by an appeals court in order to be eligible. Moreover, Hinse's case was not the object of a conviction review (see chapter 9), another criterion of eligibility. Recently, in a Quebec Superior court hearing, pursuant to a civil matter, Hinse was awarded $8.6 million for his ordeal by the Canadian government, which was overtuned. The Quebec government reached a settlement prior to the judgment and has paid out $4.5 million in compensation for damages and interest to Hinse (*Hinse c. Québec (Procureur général)*). The town of Mont-Laurier also paid out $1 million.

45 Hill's case is significant because it established the tort of negligent investigation. It is discussed in greater detail in the next chapter examining police misconduct (*Hill v. Hamilton-Wentworth Regional Police Service Board*, 2007 SCC 41 [2007] 3 S.C.R. 129).

46 See appendix B for those recommendations.

47 RCMP, Operational Manual, 25.4, Sequential Photograph Packs. While this is only an RCMP policy, it is thought to serve as a guideline for provincial, territorial, and municipal police forces.

48 R.S., 1985, c. I-1.

49 As discussed, the double-blind or blind presentation dictates that the officer presenting the photograph pack should neither be involved in the investigation nor know which person is the actual suspect. This is done to protect the police officer from consciously or unconsciously influencing the witness's choice. Given that this is not always possible in small police forces, the Innocence Project Report suggests the use of the "folder system" whereby ten folders are used, five containing photographs of fillers, one containing the suspect's photograph, and four being empty. The folders are shuffled around and the witness views them one at time, away from the officer administering the line-up (Innocence Project, n.d.).

50 See appendix C for a list of the recommendations from the Working Group Report, published in 2004.

51 http://www.innocenceproject.org/causes-wrongful-conviction/eyewitness-misidentification.

52 Ibid.

53 National Academy of Sciences (2014). *Identifying the Culprit: Assessing Eyewitness Identification*. Washington, DC: National Academies Press.

54 This is discussed in greater detail in the next section of this chapter; however, the committee provides an example of the New Jersey Criminal Model Jury Instructions, available at https://www.njcourts.gov/attorneys/criminalcharges.html.

55 The research in this area is complex and confusing. See, for example, Lindsay and Wells (1985) and Steblay et al. (2001) for the earlier debates, and Clark et al. (2014), Gronlund et al. (2014), Mickes et al. (2012), and Steblay et al. (2011) for more recent research.

56 *Hibbert*, at para. 79.

57 https://www.nji-inm.ca/index.cfm/publications/model-jury-instructions/?langSwitch=en. Last revised in 2012.

58 See also *R. v. Jack* (1992), 70 C.C.C. (3d) 67 (Man. C.A.); *R. v. Jeffrey* (1989), 35 O.A.C. 321 (C.A.); *R. v. Wristen* (1999), 141 C.C.C. (3d) 1 (Ont. C.A.).

59 409 U.S. 188, 199–200 [1972].

60 Ibid.

61 See *Hibbert*.

62 *Hibbert* at para. 52.

63 *McIntosh*.

64 This decision was also followed in *R. v. Myrie* [2003] O.T.C. 219. *Mohan*, discussed in greater detail in chapter 8, is the leading Canadian case outlining the criteria necessary for allowing expert witnesses, of any stripe, to testify.

65 *R. v. Henderson* [2009] M.J. No. 145. Henderson was nonetheless convicted for murder.

66 Ibid., at paras. 44, 51.

67 (2009) 240 Man R. (2d) 24 (Man. C.A.).

68 Ibid., at para. 41.

69 Some of these ideas are also discussed in Campbell (2011).

70 (2008) QCCQ 6868.

71 (2006) SKCA 145.

72 Ibid., at para. 41.

73 http://www.justice.gc.ca/eng/dept-min/pub/pmj-pej/pmj-pej.pdf.

74 In its second report, released in October 2011, the Federal-Provincial-Territorial Heads of Prosecutions Subcommittee again endorsed this position.

75 *R. v. Corbett* [1988] 1 S.C.R. 670; *R. v. Seaboyer*, [1991] 2 S.C.R. 577; *R. v. Khelawon*, [2006] 2 S.C.R. 787, 2006 SCC.

76 [1986] 1 S.C.R. 802, and again *R. v. Hibbert*, [2002] 2 S.C.R. 445.

77 [1989] 1 S.C.R. 3 and discussion in Roach (2007).

Chapter 3

1 "Dirty Harry" refers to a 1971 Clint Eastwood movie of the same name; the moniker has come to represent police who violate ethical and professional boundaries in the pursuit of justice.

2 *Lamer Commission of Inquiry pertaining to the Cases of: Ronald Dalton, Gregory Parsons and Randy Druken*, 71–2.

3 See chapter 10 for a detailed discussion of commissions of inquiry.

4 *Commission on the Proceedings involving Guy Paul Morin*, 1013.

5 https://websites.godaddy.com/blob/6aaa6fc2-99d9-4af2-a3b4-51e9d74ea37a/downloads/Thomas%20Sophonow%20Inquiry.pdf?2bd500cf.

6 The commission's terms of reference dictated, inter alia, that Justice Lamer inquire into the conduct of the investigation and the circumstances surrounding the criminal proceedings in the deaths of Catherine Carroll (Parsons) and Brenda Young (Druken). For Ronald Dalton, the issues were more related to the delay involved in hearing his appeal, and so tunnel vision did not affect his case in the same manner. *Lamer Commission of Inquiry*, 5.

7 Ibid., 110–28.

8 Ibid., 207–20.

9 *Commission of Inquiry into the Wrongful Conviction of David Mllgaard*, 304.

10 Ibid., 403.

11 Betty Ann Adam, "Saskatoon Police 'in Shock' over Fisher DNA Match: Brown," *StarPhoenix*, 15 September 2006.

12 Toronto police constable James Forcillo was recently found guilty of attempted murder in the 2013 shooting death of Sammy Yatim. He is the eleventh police officer to be charged with murder or manslaughter since 1990 and the inception of the province's Special Investigations Unit, but the first to be convicted. Canadian Press, 25 January 2016, "List of Ontario Police Officers Charged with Murder or Manslaughter since 1990," http://thechronicleherald.ca/canada/1337083-list-of-ontario-police-officers-charged-with-murder-or-manslaughter-since-1990.

13 *R. v. Nasogaluak*, 2010 SCC 6, [2010] 1 S.C.R. 206.

14 From *Donoghue v. Stevenson*, [1932] A.C. 562 (H.L.).

15 *Cooper v. Hobart*, [2001] 3 S.C.R. 537, 2001 SCC 79.

16 *Childs v. Desormeaux*, [2006] 1 S.C.R. 643, 2006 SCC 18.

17 2007 SCC 41 [2007] 3 S.C.R. 129 [*Hill*].

18 Fillers or foils in a line-up are generally individuals who physically resemble the suspect but are not themselves suspects in the crime.

19 Interveners in *Hill*.

20 This included the fact that two other similar robberies had occurred while Hill was in custody; the suspect descriptions in these cases matched those in the earlier robberies, and Crime Stoppers tips emerged implicating Frank (a Hispanic man). Two charges were subsequently dropped against Hill, since it appeared that Frank had committed the crimes; of the remaining eight charges, six were withdrawn by the Crown and one remained based on two eyewitness identifications (Sutherland, 2007).

21 The civil actions brought were negligence, malicious prosecution, misfeasance in public office, defamation, and breach of Charter rights (ss. 7, 9, 11) (Sutherland, 2007). The Ontario Court of Appeal found that there was a tort of negligent investigation but that it did not apply in Hill's case. The appeal to the Supreme Court dealt with only the negligence claim.

22 *Hill*, para. 3.

23 Ibid., para. 36.

24 Ibid.

25 Ibid., para. 35.

26 *The Path to Justice: Preventing Wrongful Convictions*, chapter 10, http://www.ppsc-sppc.gc.ca/eng/pub/ptj-spj/ch10.html.

27 Ontario Ministry of Community Safety and Correctional Services, Policing, http://www.mcscs.jus.gov.on.ca/english/police_serv/MajorCaseManagement/mcm.html.

28 Ibid.

29 Justice Archie Campbell (2006), *Bernardo Investigation Review: Summary* (2006). Retrieved at: https://www.attorneygeneral.jus.gov.on.ca/inquiries/cornwall/en/hearings/exhibits/Wendy_Leaver/pdf/10_Campbell_Summary.pdf.

30 Ibid.

31 *The Path to Justice*, chapter 10.

32 While there has been an increase in the use of body-worn cameras by the police in recent years, there is little empirical support to date for their efficacy. See Witherspoon (2014).

33 https://www.aclu.org/know-your-rights-photographers.

Chapter 4

1 http://www.ppsc.gc.ca/eng/bas/index.html.

2 See discussion in *Krieger v. Law Society of Alberta*, [2002] 3 S.C.R. 372.

3 http://www.law.northwestern.edu/legalclinic/wrongfulconvictions/exonerations/il/alejandro-hernandez.html (retrieved 18 June 2010).

4 See, for example, the case of the Birmingham Six or the Guildford Four, discussed in greater detail in chapter 13.

5 Frank Ostrowski, a Winnipeg man, was convicted of murder in 1987 for ordering the killing of a fellow drug dealer who was believed to be an informant; the Crown's case against him was based on the idea that Ostrowski was fearful that the informant would "rat" on him to the police regarding his own involvement in cocaine trafficking.

In fact, another informant, Matthew Lovelace, who himself faced charges of possessing cocaine, testified against Ostrowski and in exchange the charges against him were dropped, a fact that was never revealed to Ostrowski or his defence counsel. Ostrowski was released on bail in December 2009; in 2014 the then minister of justice, Peter MacKay, ordered that Ostrowki's case go back to the Manitoba Court of Appeal for reconsideration. In February 2017 it was heard by the Court of Appeal of Manitoba. CBC News, "Frank Ostrowski Relieved but Still Angry Ottawa Reviewing Murder Conviction," http://www.cbc.ca/news/canada/manitoba/frank-ostrowski-relieved-but-still-angry-ottawa-reviewing-murder-conviction-1.2849171; http://www.cbc.ca/news/canada/manitoba/frank-ostrowski-court-of-appeal-1.3980710 (retrieved 26 Feb. 2016).

6 Ibid. In addition, the province of Manitoba opened an external review, chaired by Roger Salhany, former justice of the Ontario court, into all of Dangerfield's cases where the convicted person continues to claim innocence (MacDonald, 2009). Both the results of Salhany's review of Dangerfield's cases, as well as a further review of Ostrowski's case by lawyer John Briggs, the former head of the Nova Scotia Law Reform Commission, informed MacKay's decision to send it back to the Court of Appeal. B. Owen, "Manitoba Appeal Court to Review 27-Year-Old Murder Conviction," 24 Nov. 2014, http://www.winnipegfreepress.com/local/Murder-conviction-review-283772031.html.

7 *Royal Commission on the Donald Marshall, Jr Prosecution* (1989a).

8 Adopted by the Supreme Court of Canada in *Nelles v. Ontario* [1989] 2 S.C.R. 170 [*Nelles*].

9 Ibid.

10 Two of these cases were heard at the Supreme Court of Canada: cf. *Proulx v. Quebec* (2001) and *Miazga v. Kvello Estate* (2009).

11 *Dix v. Canada (Attorney General)* [2002] A.J. No. 784 [*Dix v. Canada*].

12 The controversial RCMP sting operation, "Mr Big," is discussed in greater detail in chapter 5.

13 *Dix v. Canada*, n.44.

14 This amount included $200,000 for general damages, $93,453 for legal fees, $106,201 for pre-trial loss of income, $15,209 for future loss of income, and $300,000 in punitive damages. The punitive damages included $100,000 on the grounds that the police had dealt with Dix aggressively, in a way that would offend most citizens, and $200,000 on the grounds that the prosecutor knowingly used false information to keep him in jail and for failure to disclose other information (*Dix v. Canada*).

15 Memoranda issued by the Attorney General's Office (Criminal Law Division).

16 [2009] 1 S.C.R. 66.

17 *R. v. Stinchcombe* [1991] 3 S.C.R. 326 [*Stinchcombe*].

18 [1995] 1 S.C.R. 727 at 557.

19 https://www.aidwyc.org/cases/historical/steven-truscott/.

20 *Royal Commission on the Donald Marshall, Jr Prosecution* (1989a), 4.

21 https://www.aidwyc.org/cases/historical/romeo-phillion/.

22 Faculty of Arts, Crime and Punishment, University of New Brunswick, "Cases: Wrongful Convictions," www.unb.ca.

23 "When Justice Fails: Charter Violations, Wrongful Convictions and Compensation," https://www.aidwyc.org/ivan-henry/.

24 LeSage, *Commission of Inquiry into Certain Aspects of the Trial and Conviction of James Driskell*, 98–112.

25 Dr Charles Smith's role in a number of wrongful accusations and convictions is discussed in greater detail in chapter 8. Dinesh Kumar also accepted a plea of convenience to a ninety-day jail term for the death of his infant son in 1992, frightened by the strength of the alleged scientific evidence against him presented by Smith.

26 T. Tyler, "Conviction Quashed in Case involving Disgraced Pathologist Charles Smith," *Toronto Star*, 11 May 2011.

27 T. Tyler, "Acquitted Man Demands Justice Reforms," *Toronto Star*, 26 June 2008. The attorney general of Ontario has refused to compensate him for his ordeal.

28 D. Staples, "Roszko Accomplices Launch Appeal," *Edmonton Journal*, 2 April 2009, http://netk.net.au/Canada/Roszko5.asp.

29 K. Makin, "Case Put Focus on Justice System's 'Dirty Little Secret,'" *Globe and Mail*, 14 January 2009.

30 James Lockyer, University of Ottawa, Faculty of Law, "Wrongful Convictions" (28 Nov. 2006).

31 The Public Prosecution Service of Canada was established in 2006 as a separate federal government organization, and replaced the Federal Prosecution Service, which had been part of the Department of Justice Canada.

32 Similar, but at the same time different, models for a prosecution service separate from provincial attorneys general are found in British Columbia and Quebec.

33 S.N. 1990, c. 21.

34 *Royal Commission on the Donald Marshall, Jr Prosecution: Digest of Findings and Recommendations* (1989a), 15.

35 For example, in the wake of the recommendations made by Justice Kaufman in the Inquiry into the Proceedings involving Guy Paul Morin, the province of Ontario immediately instituted Crown policies and training related to the use of jailhouse informants and scientific evidence and the conduct of witness interviews. See Department of Justice (2005b; 2011).

36 *The Path to Justice: Preventing Wrongful Convictions*, chapter 10, http://www.ppsc-sppc.gc.ca/eng/pub/ptj-spj/ch10.html, 166–75.

37 https://news.ontario.ca/archive/en/2006/05/24/Attorney-General-Taking-Steps-To-Help-Prevent-Wrongful-Convictions.html.

38 *The Path to Justice*, chapter 10, 166–75.

39 The New Orleans CIU (the Conviction Integrity and Accuracy Project) closed in early 2016 because of a lack of funding.

40 The CIUs vary in terms of how they are structured administratively, whether they are pro-active or reactive in regard to suspected cases of wrongful conviction, and the types of cases they will accept (i.e., whether DNA must be present, the absence of a guilty plea, whether procedural safeguards and privileges must be waived, the source of referrals, and relationships with the defence bar and innocence projects). See Center for Prosecutorial Integrity, 2014.

41 National Registry of Exonerations, http://www.law.umich.edu/special/exoneration/Pages/detaillist.aspx?View=faf6eddb-5a68-4f8f-8a52-2c61f5bf9ea7&FilterField1=Group&FilterValue1=CIU&&SortField=ST&SortDir=Asc.

42 https://www.innocenceproject.org/causes/inadequate-defense/.

43 Cf. Bright (1994), (1997), (1999); Dripps (1997); Levinson, (2001).

44 *Gideon v. Wainwright*, 372 U.S. 335 (1963).

45 Cf. Layton and Proulx (2001), as referred to in Ives (2003–4, 251).

46 Shortly following Coffin's execution, Jacques Hébert, then a reporter/publisher, latterly a senator, took up the case and wrote two books, *Coffin était innocent* (1958) and *J'Accuse les Assassins de Coffin* (1963), which strongly argued that a wrongful conviction had occurred in this case. A commission of inquiry took place in 1964, headed by Judge Roger Brossard, and examined the events surrounding the murder and trial; it found that Coffin was given a fair trial. Nonetheless, at the behest of Coffin's surviving family members, AIDWYC took up his case in 2006, fifty years following his execution, and presented a brief to the minister of justice for conviction review. The minister has yet to decide upon the merits of the case.

47 Code of Professional Conduct (2010), Law Society of Upper Canada, https://www.lsuc.on.ca/with.aspx?id=2147502071#ch3_sec1-1-definitions.

48 Ibid.

49 *Strickland v. Washington*, 466 U.S. 668 (1984) (U.S.S.C.) [*Strickland*].

50 [2000] S.C.R. 520 [*G.D.B.*].

51 Ibid.

52 More recently, in *R. v. Meer* [2016] SCC 5, the Court affirmed the strict criteria as found in *G.D.B.* for a finding on ineffective assistance of counsel. However, the earlier strong dissent at the Alberta Court of Appeal in *Meer* outlines the possibility that such a finding can also occur when there has been procedural unfairness, regardless of the outcome of the trial (*R. v. Meer*, [2015] ABCA 141).

53 *Strickland*, at para. 694.

54 *G.D.B.*, at paras. 26–8.

55 Of the sixty cases heard in the three years after *G.D.B.* (2000–2) that claimed ineffective assistance of counsel for a variety of reasons, ranging from incompetency based on failure to properly call and examine witness to failure to raise constitutional issues or call the accused to testify, only six have been successful (Ives, 2003–4, 247).

56 Cf. *R. v. Weagle*, *R. v. Schofield*, *R. v. Godron*, *R. v. MacKenzie*.

57 Claims of ineffective assistance of counsel are sometimes seen in cases involving women accused of murdering their male partners, where a battered women's syndrome defence would have been appropriate but was not put forward by counsel. In some instances, these women allege that they pled guilty without adequate legal advice, that the trials were poorly run, that counsel did not call them to the stand, or that no expert evidence or evidence of past histories of victimization were offered by counsel (Schneider, 2000).

58 Dew (2006) argues that this would specifically address those cases where counsel do not believe in their client's innocence, which can in turn have an impact on the overall conduct of the defence. The case of *R. v. Delisle* is an example where the defence did not call the accused to testify on his own behalf, since he did not believe his client was innocent (para. 247). In this case, the appeals court found that his right to a fair trial was prejudiced and ordered a new trial on the grounds that his lawyer had committed a "significant error" by not allowing the accused to testify.

59 See, for example, the Canadian Bar Association publication *Moving Forward on Legal Aid: Research on Needs and Innovative Approaches*, which discusses this "silent crisis" in detail and offers solutions: https://www.cfmlawyers.ca/wp-content/uploads/2012/06/CBA-Legal-Aid-Renewal-Paper.pdf.

60 During a *voir dire*, issues regarding admissibility of evidence are determined (Paciocco and Stuesser, 2015, 17–18). Here the rules of admissibility allow for unreliable or unnecessary evidence to be excluded, which could possibly benefit the accused person.

61 R.S.C., 1985, c. C-5.

62 *Royal Commission on the Donald Marshall, Jr Prosecution* (1989a), at 22.

63 Ibid., at p. 19.

64 Ibid.

65 *Commission of Inquiry into the Wrongful Conviction of David Milgaard*, http://www.publications.gov.sk.ca/freelaw/Publications_Centre/Justice/Milgaard/05-Chapter4.pdf.

66 Criminal Code, R.S.C. 1985, c. C-46, ss. 536(4), 536.1(3).

67 The accused is permitted to cross-examine Crown witnesses at this stage.

68 Criminal Code, R.S.C. 1985, c. C-46, ss. 540–1.

69 *R. v. Arcuri*, [2001] 2 S.C.R. 828; *United States v. Shephard*, [1977] 2 S.C.R. 1067.

70 *R. v. Nelles* (1982), 16 C.C.C. (3d) 97 (Ont. Prov. Ct.) as cited in Delisle (1987) at 229–30.

71 Thanks to Laura Case for her excellent work on developing the ideas in this section.

72 *R. v. Rowbotham*, [1993] 4 S.C.R. 834 [*Rowbotham*].

73 *R. v. Boissonneault* (1986), 29 C.C.C. (3d) 345 (Ont. C.A.).

74 *Rowbotham*, n.105.

75 *United States v. Shephard*, [1977] 2 S.C.R. 1067; *R. v. Mezzo*, [1986] 1 S.C.R. 802; *R. v. Monteleone*, [1987] 2 S.C.R. 154 [*Mezzo*].

76 *R. v. Monteleone*, [1987] 2 S.C.R. 154; *R. v. Mezzo*, [1986] 1 S.C.R. 802 [*Mezzo*].

77 [1998] 1 S.C.R. 679.

78 Ibid.

79 Laura Case, personal communication.

80 *Mezzo*, paras. 59, 62.

81 *R. v. McIntosh* (1997), 117 C.C.C. (3d) 385 (Ont. C.A.).

82 In American law, a *voir dire* is different than in Canadian law; it refers to the process through which potential jurors are questioned by the judge or a lawyer to determine their suitability for jury service; see *Peretz v. United States*, 501 U.S. 923 (1991).

83 Section 649: "Every member of a jury, and every person providing technical, personal, interpretative or other support services to a juror with a physical disability, who, except for the purposes of (a) an investigation of an alleged offence under subsection 139(2) in relation to a juror, or (b) giving evidence in criminal proceedings in relation to such an offence, discloses any information relating to the proceedings of the jury when it was absent from the courtroom that was not subsequently disclosed in open court is guilty of an offence punishable on summary conviction."

84 In the case of William Mullins-Johnson, wrongly convicted by flawed expert testimony in 1993, the jury instructions given by the judge in that case were ninety pages long.

85 Laura Case, personal communication.

Chapter 5

1 [2000] M.J. No. 447 [*Mentuck*].

2 During the first step of the technique, a suspect who is deceptive is said to drop his eyes, change posture, and offer vague denials, whereas a truthful suspect will allegedly lean forward, maintain eye contact, and appear legitimately shocked or angry. See http://www.reid.com/educational_info/critictechnique.html.

3 www.reid.com/educational_info/critictechnique.html.

4 The "Mr Big" sting is not permitted by the courts in the United States and the United Kingdom, although evidence collected by the RCMP in Canada through this technique

may be used in those jurisdictions (see *U.S. v. Burns*). It has been used by the RCMP since the 1980s and, as of 2008, it had been employed on 350 occasions in undercover operations. In 75 per cent of these operations, the person of interest was either cleared or charged; of the cases prosecuted, in excess of 95 per cent resulted in convictions. The other 25 per cent of the cases remain unsolved. See: http://bc.rcmp-grc.gc.ca/ViewPage.action?siteNodeId=23&languageId=1&contentId=6943.

5 Unwitting "targets" meet the undercover operatives in a number of ways: while in police custody (with the operatives posing as prisoners), by being informed they are a grand-prize winner, through a third party, through a place of employment or school, through a staged breakdown of a vehicle, or through the enticement of money (Keenan and Brockman, 2010, 53–8).

6 See *R. v. Hathaway, R. v. E.(O.N.)*.

7 *R. v. C.K.R.S.* [2005] B.C.J. No. 2917 at 31.

8 See in particular the cases of *R. v. Hebert* and *R. v. Broyles*.

9 One notable case where a "Mr Big" sting produced a true confession is that of Michael Bridges in Brandon, Manitoba. While he was a suspect in the murder and disappearance of Erin Chorney in 2002, the police had no evidence against Bridges, nor a body. Following an elaborate sting operation, Bridges confessed to the murder and burying the body; the police later found Chorney's remains and Bridges was convicted of first-degree murder. See also *R. v. Copeland*.

10 See, for example, the case of Kyle Unger (discussed in greater detail in chapter 10). In 1991 Unger confessed to murdering a teenager to an undercover operative through a "Mr Big" sting. His conviction was based on faulty forensic evidence and his alleged confession. He served fourteen years in jail and was released after DNA testing on hair samples proved he could not have been the killer. In 2009 the federal minister of justice ordered a new trial; however, the prosecution called no evidence and a judge acquitted Unger of murder.

11 The techniques involve accusation, cutting off of denials, attacking alibis, and confronting the suspect with real or non-existent evidence.

12 Tu Thanh Ha, "Quebec Man Cleared of Sex Crimes after Serving Five Years in Prison," Montreal *Gazette*, 11 Aug. 2005.

13 CBC News, "Wrongfully Convicted: High-Profile Cases where the Courts Got It Wrong," http://www.cbc.ca/news/canada/canada-s-wrongful-convictions-1.783998.

14 This section of the Criminal Code, R.S.C. 1985, c. C-46, allows for individuals who have exhausted all of their avenues of appeal to apply to the minister of justice to review their conviction in order to ascertain if a miscarriage of justice likely occurred. It is discussed in greater detail in chapter 9.

15 In 2012 Phillion launched a lawsuit seeking compensation of $14 million for his ordeal from the Ontario attorney general, the Ottawa Police Services Board, and two former police officers. While this lawsuit was dismissed by the Ontario Superior Court in 2013, in 2015 the Supreme Court of Canada upheld Philion's right to pursue damages.

16 For the wrongly convicted and imprisoned, continuing to maintain their innocence while incarcerated can have detrimental effects. For one, it increases the perception that they would impose a greater risk if released, since their continual denials of guilt are interpreted as a lack of effort towards their own "rehabilitation." Related to this is the indeterminacy of their release date, owing to their lack of involvement in their correctional plan; given the irresolution of their cases, the time boundaries for most

other prisoners marked for possible parole are out of reach to them (Campbell and Denov, 2004).

17 K. Makin. "Convicted Murderer Romeo Phillion Fears He May Not See the Outcome of His Exoneration Bid," *Globe and Mail*, 21 Jan. 2008, http://www.theglobeandmail.com/news/national/35-year-old-murder-case-to-be-relived/article17978841/.

18 2012 ABPC 229.

19 B. Lambert, "No Retrial in '88 Double Killing on Long Island," *New York Times*, 1 July 2008, http://www.nytimes.com/2008/07/01/nyregion/01tankleff.html?ref=martintankleff&_r=0.

20 National Registry of Exonerations, http://www.law.umich.edu/special/exoneration/Pages/casedetail.aspx?caseid=3234.

21 Some of these ideas have also been discussed in Weitzman and Campbell (2012).

22 *R. v. Oickle* [2000] 2 S.C.R. 3 [*Oickle*].

23 *R. v. Hebert* [1990] S.C.J. No. 64, at 23 [*Hebert*].

24 "Everyone has the right to life, liberty and security of the person and the right not to be deprived thereof except in accordance with the principles of fundamental justice."

25 *Hebert*, at 64.

26 Ibid. While this case considered the right of a detained person to silence under section 7 within the context of the confessions rule, it also considered the privilege against self-incrimination, the philosophy of the Charter, and the purpose of the right in question (para. 20).

27 Ibid., paras. 80, 52.

28 Delisle et al. (2004, 382).

29 Cf. Litkowski (2008), Moore (2008), and Stuesser (2002).

30 *Hebert*, at 52.

31 Note that the witness's right to refuse to answer under the right against self-incrimination has been modified by the Canada Evidence Act, R.S.C. 1985, c. C-5, s. 5, and replaced with protection by immunity. Though the right remains protected under Canadian law, this is not necessarily the case in all contexts. For instance, there is arguably insufficient protection for the right in the context of undercover operations. For further discussion, see Dufraimont (2012) and Paciocco and Stuesser (2015) at 311.

32 *Oickle.*

33 Ibid., at paras. 48–57.

34 Along the lines of "it would be better for you if you confessed" type statements.

35 Inducements may include a number of things: a direct or implied notion that the polygraph is infallible (*Oickle*, at 551); indicating to the accused that confessing would be helpful in obtaining treatment for his problems (ibid., at 545); cooperating would spare him being repeatedly visited by the police (ibid.); minimizing the allegations by placing the blame elsewhere and implying a promise or prospect of leniency based on lack of or diminished intention (ibid.); and presentation of several themes, mostly based on false information, which, when viewed cumulatively, suggest benefits to the accused or those close to him if he adopts them as his truthful explanation for the events (ibid.).

36 *Oickle*, at 58–62.

37 Ibid., at 58.

38 Ibid., at 63–4.

39 *R. v. Whittle*, [1994] S.C.J. No. 69.

40 Youth Criminal Justice Act, 2002, c. 1, ss. 146, 147, 151 all limit the manner in which police may question young persons who are suspected of criminal activity. Sherrin (2005, 654) does not believe that the criminal law provides adequate protections to young persons making false admissions or confessions to the police. He maintains that the protections that do exist under statute have not been supported through case law.

41 *Oickle*, at 65–7.

42 Ibid., at 65.

43 *Rothman v. The Queen* [1981] 1 S.C.R. 640 [*Rothman*].

44 Ibid.

45 *R. v. Singh* [2007] S.C.J. No. 48 [*Singh*].

46 Ibid., at 37.

47 Ibid., at 39.

48 Ibid.

49 Ibid., at 79.

50 *R. v. Sinclair*, 2010 SCC 35 [*Sinclair*]. Thanks to Justice Patrick Healy for clarifying the limits of this decision.

51 Such as a line-up identification, or if new information was introduced that would change the position of jeopardy of the accused, or if there was a material change in circumstances.

52 *Sinclair*, para. 105. Emphasis in original.

53 Ibid., para. 83.

54 Ibid., para 98.

55 *R. v. M.J.S.* [2000] A.J. No. 391, at 30.

56 Ibid., at 21.

57 Ibid., at 30.

58 Ibid., at 45.

59 2012 ABPC 229.

60 Ibid., at para. 122.

61 [2009] B.C.J. No. 2333.

62 Ibid., at para. 28.

63 [2011] O.J. No. 2794.

64 *Mentuck*.

65 K. Makin, "Gag Order Obscures Man's Innocence," *The Province*, 23 Oct. 2000, A3, d2.

66 *R. v. Rhodes* [2002] B.C.J. No. 1113 at 110.

67 2002 SCC 16, [2002] 1 S.C.R. 535.

68 *R. v. McIntyre* [1993] N.B.J. No. 293.

69 Ibid., at 55.

70 [1998] 127 C.C.C. (3d) 449 (S.C.C.) [*Hodgson*].

71 Ibid., at 83.

72 [2005] 191 C.C.C. (3d) 449 [*Grandinetti*].

73 Ibid., at paras. 34 and 36, as qtd. in Poloz (2015).

74 *Mentuck*, para. 100.

75 [2007] O.J. No. 244 [*Osmar*].

76 In this case, defence counsel was not able to introduce expert testimony by Dr Richard Ofshe, a renowned expert on false confessions, regarding the reliability of the appellant's statements to the undercover officers in the context of the "Mr Big" strategy. Justice Rosenberg found that the Dr Ofshe's testimony did not meet the

Mohan test, given that the areas that he wished to testify about were not matters whereby an ordinary person would form an incorrect judgment.

77 *Osmar*, at 25.

78 Ibid., at para. 48.

79 *R. v. Hart*, 2012 NLCA 61.

80 *R. v. Hart*, 2014 SCC 52 [*Hart*].

81 Ibid.

82 Ibid., at paras. 126–49.

83 Terry Pedwell, "Stricter Rules Needed in 'Mr Big' Police Stings: Supreme Court," *Global News*, 31 July 2014, http://globalnews.ca/news/1484222/supreme-court-to-rule-on-mr-big-stings/; Kevin Martin, "Supreme Court Ruling on Mr. Big Stings Show Judges Want Caution, but Technique Still Viable," *Calgary Sun*, 15 Aug. 2014, http://www.calgarysun.com/2014/08/15/supreme-court-ruling-on-mr-big-stings-show-judges-want-caution-but-technique-still-viable.

84 The Association in Defence of the Wrongly Convicted (AIDWYC; later renamed Innocence Canada) is a non-profit organization located in Toronto, Ontario, that champions the cause of the wrongly convicted and is staffed by lawyers working pro-bono. Its former director, Rubin "Hurricane" Carter, served twenty-three years in a New Jersey prison on a wrongful conviction for a multiple murder. The organization's role in addressing wrongful convictions is addressed further in chapter 12.

85 David Dias, "AIDWYC Wants Audit for all Mr. Big Convictions," *Legal Feeds*, 14 Aug. 2014, http://www.canadianlawyermag.com/legalfeeds/aidwyc-wants-audit-for-all-mr-big-convictions-5879/.

86 *R. v. Mack*, 2014 SCC 58, [2014] 3 S.C.R. 3.

87 *Laflamme c. R.*, 2015 QCCA 1517 (CanLII).

88 *Perreault c. R.*, 2015 QCCA 694 (CanLII).

89 *Rothman*.

90 See *Oickle*, at 46; also *R. v. Moore-McFarlane* [2001] O.J. No. 4646 and *R. v. Ahmed* [2002] O.J. No. 4597.

Chapter 6

1 *R. v. Farler* (1837), 8 Car. & P. 106, at 108, as found in *R. v. Vetrovec* (1982) 1 S.C.R. 811 [*Vetrovec*].

2 https://www.innocenceproject.org/causes/incentivized-informants/.

3 http://blackslawdictionary.org/informer/.

4 Others classify informants as incidental and recruited or confidential informants; the former supply information to the authorities about a specific incident, while the latter provide information on an ongoing basis and are typically paid by the police for their work (Blintiff, 1993 as found in Bloom, 2005).

5 Cf. Trott, 1996.

6 *R. v. Trudel* [2004] O.J. No. 248, at p. 71 [*Trudel*].

7 Other terms found in the literature on informants include "rat" and "snitch." Some legal scholars refuse to use such morally laden terms since "the issue here is not the morality of informing, but whether their testimony is untruthful, and whether the falsity is or should be obvious to prosecutors" (Raeder, 2007). I have adopted this reasoning.

8 *United States v. Cervantes-Pacheo*, 826 F.2d 310, 315 (5th Cir 1897).

9 *Washington v. Texas*, 388 U.S. 14, 87 S.Ct. 1920, 1925, 18 L.Ed.2d 1019 (1967).

10 http://articles.latimes.com/1988-12-02/local/me-1115_1_jailhouse-informant.

11 [1999] 44 O.R. (3d) 772.

12 *Trudel*, para. 78.

13 A notable example is that of Yves Trudeau, a long-time member of the Hells Angels biker club in Sherbrooke, Quebec, who turned informant in 1985. In exchange for his testimony against other gang members and a guilty plea to forty-three counts of manslaughter, Trudeau was given a life sentence and was eligible for parole in 1994, when he was released under a new identity. See https://www.pressreader.com/canada/montreal-gazette/20071128/281668250630793.

14 *Vetrovec*, at para. 7.

15 Ibid., at para. 17.

16 *R. v. Brooks* [2000] 1 S.C.R. 237 [*Brooks*].

17 Ibid., at para. 94.

18 Ibid., at para. 4.

19 This complex case, and one of the most expensive in Canadian legal history, surrounded the shooting deaths of Michel Giroux and Manon Bourdeau in 1990. Trudel, Sauvé, and two others were charged with first-degree murder in the settling of accounts with Giroux over unpaid drug debts, and the case was largely based on now discredited testimony from an informant. While originally decided in 1996, in 2007 the court issued a stay of proceedings based on unreasonable delay (*R. v. Trudel*, [2007] O.J. No. 113).

20 Leave to appeal to the Supreme Court was dismissed on 6 Jan. 2005 (*R. v. Trudel* (appeal by Sauvé) [2004] S.C.C.A. No. 246).

21 *Trudel*, at paras. 1–2.

22 Ibid., at para. 76.

23 Ibid., at para. 82.

24 Clifford Olson was convicted of murdering eleven children and youth in the 1980s and made a controversial plea agreement whereby he confessed to eleven murders and provided information to the RCMP regarding the whereabouts of some of his missing victims in exchange for monies paid ($10,000–$100,000 for each child victim) to his wife and son (http://www.cbc.ca/news/canada/story/2011/09/30/clifford-olson-death.html). While he was not a typical "jailhouse informant" per se, the agreement illustrates the extent that the authorities will go to in order to obtain convictions, particularly when there is little other evidence.

25 [2010] 1 S.C.R. 637.

26 Ibid., at para. 8.

27 [2009] 1 S.C.R. 104 [*Khela*].

28 Ibid., at para. 44.

29 Ibid., at para. 47.

30 *R. v. Roks*, [2011] ONCA 526.

31 *Khela*, at para. 37; *R. v. Kehler*, [2004] 1 S.C.R 328, at para. 15, as cited in *R. v. Pelletier*, [2012] ONCA 566, at para. 67.

32 Revised in April 2016.

33 https://www.nji-inm.ca/index.cfm/publications/model-jury-instructions/final-instructions/rules-of-evidence/crown-witnesses-of-unsavoury-character-vetrovec-warning/.

34 *Brady v. Maryland*, 373 U.S. 83 (1963) [*Brady*].

35 *Giglio v. U.S.*, 405 U.S. 150 (1972).

36 *United States v. Sudikoff*, 36 F.Supp. 2d 1196 (C.D. Cal. 1999).

37 *State v. Lindsey*, 621 So. 2d 618 (La. Ct. App. 1993).

38 *R. v. Stinchcombe*, [1991] 3 S.C.R. 326.

39 The issue of disclosure does not arise in the same way in Canadian law since Crown prosecutors are obliged to disclose all relevant evidence, whether it is inculpatory or exculpatory.

40 Additionally, there is much current debate surrounding the granting of immunity to prosecutors when *Brady* violations come to light (cf. *Connick v. Thompson*; also Bandes, 2011).

41 As of 2005, the following individuals who were convicted based in part on jailhouse-informant testimony spent many years on death row and were later exonerated: Randall Dale Adams, Joseph Amrine, Gary Beeman, Dan L. Bright, Anthony Siliah Brown, Shabaka Brown, Willie A. Brown, Larry Troy, Albert Ronnie Burrell, Michael Ray Graham, Jr, Joseph Burrows, Earl Patrick Charles, Perry Cobb, Darby Tillis, James Creamer, Verneal Jimerson, Dennis Williams, Willie Rainge, Kenneth Adams, James Creamer, Robert Charles Cruz, Rolando Cruz, Alejandro Hernandez, Joseph Burrows, Gordon (Randy) Steidl, Muneer Deeb, Charles Irvin Fain, Neil Ferber, Gary Gauger, Alan Gell, Charles Ray Giddens, Perry Cobb, Larry Hicks, Steven Smith, Madison Hobley, Richard Neal Jones, Curtis Kyles, Fredrico M. Macias, Steve Manning, Walter McMillian, Juan Roberto Melendez, Gary Gauger, Adolph H. Munson, Larry Osborne, Aaron Patterson, Alfred Rivera, James Robison, Jeremy Sheets, Charles Smith, Steven Manning, Rolando Cruz, Madison Hobley, Steven Smith, Christopher Spicer, Gordon (Randy) Steidl, John Thompson, Dennis Williams, Ronald Williamson, and Nicholas Yarris (Warden, 2006).

42 Cf. Naughton (2007).

43 Such directives occur at the time the evidence is presented or at the end of the trial in the form of a jury charge; they may take the form of directives to ignore or admit the evidence or limiting instructions regarding under what circumstances such evidence should be considered.

44 See, for example, Neuschatz et al. (2007).

45 This inquiry will be discussed in greater detail in chapter 10.

46 This case and the subsequent inquiry are discussed in greater detail in chapter 10.

47 The inquiry's report was published in 2001: https://websites.godaddy.com/blob/6aaa6fc2-99d9-4af2-a3b4-51e9d74ea37a/downloads/Thomas%20Sophonow%20Inquiry.pdf?2bd500cf.

48 Ibid.

49 Ibid.

50 Comprehensive provincial/territorial policies on the use of confession evidence, eyewitness identification, and forensic analyses were unavailable for comparison purposes for this volume.

51 The policies for Nunavut, Yukon, and the Northwest Territories were unavailable for this analysis.

52 Each of the provinces has individual policy documents setting out the policies summarized in this section. Most of these are publicly available online: British Columbia: http://www2.gov.bc.ca/assets/gov/law-crime-and-justice/criminal-

justice/prosecution-service/crown-counsel-policy-manual/inc-1-in-custody-informer-witnesses.pdf; Alberta: https://justice.alberta.ca/programs_services/criminal_pros/crown_prosecutor/Pages/incustody_informant_evidence.aspx; Saskatchewan: http://publications.gov.sk.ca/documents/9/93151-In%20Custody%20Informants.pdf; Ontario: https://www.attorneygeneral.jus.gov.on.ca/english/crim/cpm/; New Brunswick: http://www2.gnb.ca/content/dam/gnb/Departments/ag-pg/PDF/en/PublicProsecutionOperationalManual/Policies/In-custodyInformantEvidence.pdf; Newfoundland and Labrador: http://www.justice.gov.nl.ca/just/prosecutions/index.html; Prince Edward Island: https://www.princeedwardisland.ca/sites/default/files/publications/guide_book_of_policies_and_procedures_for_the_conduct_of_criminal_prosecutions.pdf; Nova Scotia: https://novascotia.ca/pps/publications/ca_manual/ProsecutionPolicies/In-custodyInformersMay04.pdf. Manitoba's policy can be accessed in hardcopy: Manitoba Department of Justice, Prosecutions, Policy Directive, Guideline No. 2: DIS:1, March 2008. Some of the main policies have been summarized by the Public Prosecution Service of Canada: http://www.ppsc-sppc.gc.ca/eng/pub/ptj-spj/ch7.html#fnb271.

53 Director of Public Prosecutions.

54 The Crown should also consider the circumstances surrounding the disclosure, any benefits sought or received by the informant, use of tests to ensure reliability (polygraphs), extent to which the statement is corroborated by other evidence, the specificity of the statement, and whether the details/leads are known only by the culprit.

55 The committee must also consider the extent to which the statement is confirmed, the details of the statement, circumstances under which it was made, the informant's general character, any medical or psychiatric reports concerning the informer, whether the informant has given reliable information in the past, and whether any consideration has been given by the authorities in the past.

56 Factors to be considered include: the informant's criminal record, information regarding any new charges against the informant, medical or psychiatric reports, information regarding previous testimony as an informant, any information on negotiations with the informant for consideration, safety measures taken on behalf of the informant, any record of an agreement, and the circumstances under which the informant and the information came to the attention of the authorities.

57 KGB Statements emerged from a young offender case, *R. v. B. (K.G.)*, [1993] 1 S.C.R. 740, where the court ruled that prior video-taped (KGB) statements could be used as original evidence when a witness gave contradictory evidence in court.

Chapter 7

1 DNA Identification Act 1998, c. 37.

2 http://www.innocenceproject.org/.

3 *R. v. Parent* (1988) 65 Alta L.R. (2d) 18 (Alta. Q.B.).

4 The inclusion of a section on fingerprinting in a chapter on DNA evidence may seem curious but it is significant that both are forms of identification evidence. While both have differing identification capacities and accuracies, fingerprint evidence was the original form of identification evidence used by police in solving crimes and has now been usurped by DNA.

5 These include LIVESCAN, OmniTrak, and others. Generally, both crime-scene and arrestee fingerprints and palm prints are stored and compared with each other.

6 For a more thorough and scientific explanation of DNA, see Hageman et al. (2002).

7 Projected future DNA technologies may involve the analysis of single nucleotide polymorphisms (SNPs), using large automated detection arrays, to provide information about such things as geographic ancestry, eye colour, hair colour, facial features, and stature; this has been referred to as the "genetic eyewitness" (Fourney et al., 2013).

8 Criminal Code, R.S.C. 1985, c. C-46.

9 Young Offenders Act, R.S.C. 1985, C.Y-1.

10 S.C. 1996, c. 19.

11 S.C. 2000, c. 10.

12 In the case of a conviction for a primary designated offence, the court is obliged to make the order for a DNA sample, unless the impact of this order would be "grossly disproportionate" to public interest or societal protection; in the case of a conviction for a secondary designated offence, courts can order samples if it is thought to be in the best interests of the administration of justice (MacKay, 2007).

13 DNA profiles remain accessible to the police and others in the criminal justice system, unless a pardon is obtained (MacKay, 2007).

14 http://www.rcmp-grc.gc.ca/nddb-bndg/stats-eng.htm.

15 The Criminal Code also contains provisions for the destruction of bodily substances taken and the removal of the results of forensic DNA analysis. This may occur, for example, when there is a finding that the suspect's DNA did not match the crime-scene sample; the suspect is acquitted; a year has elapsed following the discharge of the preliminary inquiry; information against the suspect has been dismissed or withdrawn; or a stay of proceedings has been issued (s. 487.09(1)). A provincial court judge can order that this information not be destroyed if he/she is "satisfied that the bodily substance or results might reasonably be required in an investigation or prosecution of the person for another designated offence or another person for the designated offence or any other offence in respect of the same transaction" (s. 487.09(2)).

16 The case of R. v. Rodgers challenged the constitutionality of these provisions and the courts found that, while taking DNA without consent may in fact "constitute a seizure within the meaning of section 8 of the Charter, the collection of DNA samples for data bank purposes from designated classes of convicted offenders is reasonable" (MacKay, 2007). In such cases, seizure of samples is allowable only when a designated offence has occurred and only through a judge's order.

17 An identifying system called CODIS (Combined DNA Index System) is now used in both American and Canadian DNA databank computer networks for cataloguing and comparing STR (short tandem repeat) DNA profiles. Furthermore, there is general acceptance of 13 core CODIS STR loci among all Canadian laboratories.

18 Anti-Terrorism Act, S.C. 2001, c. 41.

19 Act to Amend the Criminal Code, the DNA Identification Act and the National Defence Act, S.C. 2005.

20 An Act to amend the Criminal Code, the DNA Identification Act and the National Defence Act, S.C. 2007, c. 22.

21 R.S.C., 1985, c. N-5.

22 Canada, House of Commons, Standing Committee on Public Safety and National Security, *Statutory Review of the DNA Identification Act: Report on the Standing Committee*

on Public Safety and National Security (2009), http://publications.gc.ca/collections/collection_2009/parl/XC76-402-1-1-01E.pdf; Canada, Senate, Standing Senate Committee on Legal and Constitutional Affairs, "Public Protection, Privacy and the Search for Balance: A Statutory Review of the *DNA Identification Act*," Final Report, 2010, www.parl.gc.ca/Content/SEN/Committee/403/lega/rep/rep09jun10-e.pdf.

23 Safe Streets and Communities Act, S.C. 2012, c. 1 (Bill C-10).

24 Youth Criminal Justice Act, S.C. 2002, c. 1.

25 http://www.rcmp-grc.gc.ca/en/the-national-dna-data-bank-canada-annual-report-2014-2015?wbdisable=true; National DNA Data Bank of Canada, 2014–15.

26 http://www.rcmp-grc.gc.ca/en/the-national-dna-data-bank-canada-annual-report-2015-2016#a2; National DNA Data Bank of Canada, 2015–16.

27 At that time the Office of the Privacy Commissioner also expressed concerns about overly broad applications for information, violations of the fundamental right to respect for private life, familial searching that may produce false positives and false negatives, and the sharing of information with foreign jurisdictions.

28 The notion that DNA evidence can provide the "illusion" of certainty is borrowed from a report written by Christopher Shulgan in *Toro*, April 2006, referring to the George Pitt case.

29 "Rights Fears over DNA Plan," BBC news, 30 July 1999, news.bbc.co.uk/2/hi/uk_news/408097.stm, as found in McCartney, 2006a, 38.

30 http://www.rcmp-grc.gc.ca/wanted/sweeney_suspect_e.htm. Recently, the Sudbury police have used DNA phenotyping, a new form of profile extraction that allows scientists to identify ethnic make-up, face shape, and eye colour to develop a composite sketch of the alleged perpetrator. This method is costly (upwards of $6,000); however, the police are hopeful that it will help solve the case (https://thestar.com/news/canada/2017/01/25/sudbury-police-using-new-technology-in-effort-to-solve-1998-homicide.html).

31 M. Vonn, "Can a DNA Dragnet Undermine an Investigation? A Case Study in Canada," *GeneWatch*, 24, no. 5 (2011), http://www.councilforresponsiblegenetics.org/GeneWatch/GeneWatchPage.aspx?pageId=377.

32 In the notorious O.J. Simpson case, his acquittal for the murders of Nicole Simpson and Ron Goldman in 1995 was based in part on doubt created by defence counsel regarding deliberate contamination of the blood evidence collected from the crime scene while it was in the custody of the police.

33 Independent laboratories charge upwards of $350 per Legal DNA Profile (Autosomal STR), with varying other costs for comparison profiles and trial testimonies (see, for example, www.genetrackcanada.com/fee#tab-9).

34 The case of Steven Truscott illustrates this point. In 1959, when he was fourteen years old, Truscott was convicted of sexually assaulting and murdering Lynne Harper. In 2007 Truscott was exonerated by the Ontario Court of Appeal for this crime. The court refused to find him "innocent" per se, stating that was beyond their role, and acquitted him. It is likely that efforts to exonerate Truscott would have been facilitated if physical evidence from the victim and the crime scene were still available; by all accounts, this evidence was either destroyed or lost (Sher, 2001).

35 Putting the issue into context, an Innocence Project review of cases between 2004 and 2010 showed that 22 per cent of these cases were closed because evidence had either been lost or destroyed: http://www.innocenceproject.org/Content/DNA_Exonerations_Nationwide.php.

36 https://innocenceproject.org/access-post-conviction-dna-testing/.

37 "Backlog, Quality Concerns Plague RCMP DNA Testing," CBC News, 1 May 2007, http://www.cbc.ca/news/canada/backlog-quality-concerns-plague-rcmp-dna-testing-ag-1.633414; "DNA Lab's Slow Results Impeding B.C. Court Cases," CBC News, 1 June 2013, http://www.cbc.ca/news/canada/british-columbia/dna-lab-s-slow-results-impeding-b-c-court-cases-1.1305381.

38 http://www.rcmp-grc.gc.ca/en/the-national-dna-data-bank-canada-annual-report-2015-2016#a2.

39 James Lockyer, University of Ottawa, Faculty of Law, 28 Nov. 2006.

40 https://www.innocenceproject.org/access-post-conviction-dna-testing/.

41 *R. v. Borden* (1994) 3 S.C.R. 145.

42 *R. v. Stillman* (1997) 1 S.C.R. 607 (S.C.C.).

43 Ibid., at para. 92.

44 *R. v. Brighteyes* (1997) A.J. No. 363.

45 Conscriptive (vs. non-conscriptive) evidence is a legal designation with respect to how such evidence was obtained: "If the evidence is non-conscriptive, its admission will not render the trial unfair and the court will proceed to consider the seriousness of the breach and the effect of exclusion on the repute of the administration of justice. If the evidence is conscriptive and the Crown fails to demonstrate on a balance of probabilities that the evidence would have been discovered by alternative non-conscriptive means, then its admission will render the trial unfair" (*R. v. Stillman*, at paras. 364–5).

46 *R. v. S.A.B.* (2003) 2 S.C.R. 678.

47 *R. v. Terceira* (1999) S.C.J. No. 74.

48 *R. v. R.C.* (2005) S.C.J. No. 62.

49 This list is not meant to be exhaustive. Another individual also exonerated through DNA and compensated by the government for his ordeal is Simon Marshall of Quebec. Marshall is intellectually handicapped and confessed to a series of sexual assaults in 1997; he was incarcerated until 2003. Following his release, Marshall confessed again to three more sexual assaults, but at that time DNA evidence indicated he was not guilty. Early DNA evidence had never been tested.

50 Innocence Project, "Preservation of Evidence, Fact Sheet," https://www.innocenceproject.org/preservation-of-evidence.

51 The wrongful conviction of Leighton Hays illustrates that, even though fact that Canada does not have legislation that mandates access to forensic materials for testing, courts will often exercise their powers to ensure that such testing occurs. In Hays's case, he was convicted of a nightclub murder in 2002 based in part on eyewitness misidentification. One of the gunmen had been described as having a specific kind of hair, "two inch picky dreads"; however, when Hays was arrested, he had short hair. A large part of the Crown's case rested on the belief that Hays cut his hair shortly after the shooting in order to disguise his identity. Proving that the haircut took place would confirm the eyewitness testimony and the theory that Hays had attempted to disguise himself. Hairs were found in Hays's apartment that were used as evidence against him and he was convicted of first-degree murder. On appeal, his defence team sought access to the hairs found in his apartment for testing, the objective being to ascertain if these hairs indeed had been from his head or were facial hairs from shaving. While the Crown initially opposed this request, it was granted by the Supreme Court in 2010. By

2013, the testing had demonstrated the hairs were facial ones and not indicative of a haircut, thus disproving the Crown's theory. The court admitted the scientific evidence at this juncture and Hays's conviction was quashed and a new trial ordered; the charges were dropped one year later (https://www.aidwyc.org/hay-exonerated/).

52 *Chaudhary v. Attorney General of Canada et al.*, 2010 ONSC 6092, para. 6 [*Chaudhary*].

53 The author submitted an Access to Information request to the RCMP to view its policies on preservation of evidence, and while the Laboratory Services Manual was provided, much of the information on this matter was exempted by virtue of section 16(2) of the Access to Information Act.

54 "Child Killer's Case Prompts Push to Save Wvidence" (https://www.reddeeradvocate.com/.../child-killers-case-prompts-pusch-to-save-evidence/).

55 *Chaudhary*, para. 7.

56 Author's translation: For cases involving a death (criminal or non-criminal), a coroner's inquest, departmental policy, or disappearance. *La Gestion des Objets Trouvé et des Pièces à Conviction par l'Enquèteur et la Responsible de la salle des effets: Matrice sur la Durée de Detention des Biens et les Modalities de leur Disposition. Marco Levasseur.*

57 *Chaudhary.*

58 Ibid., para. 17.

59 Ibid., para. 22.

60 Y. Taddese, "How Long Should Crown Have to Keep Evidence? Innocence Project Seeks Declaration to Preserve until Accused Dies," *Law Times*, 23 Sept. 2013.

61 *Chaudhary v. Ontario (Attorney General)*, 2013 ONCA 615, para. 10.

62 Ibid., para. 11.

63 *R. v. Rodgers* [2006] 1 S.C.R. 554, at para. 4.

64 In fact, the United Kingdom's databank contains over a million profiles of innocent individuals, which is specifically designed to match DNA found at crime scenes with suspects. As noted in the BCCLA report, "intrusive collections of DNA have become the norm in UK police investigations" (Oscapella, 2012).

Chapter 8

1 *R. v. J.(L-J.)* (2000) 2 S.C.R. (600) at para. 25.

2 *R. v. Truscott* [2007] ONCA No. 575.

3 Ibid., at paras. 777–8.

4 Driskell's case was the subject of a commission of inquiry and is discussed in greater detail in chapter 10.

5 Because of the complex and problematic circumstances surrounding Morin's case, it was also the subject of a commission of inquiry, in 1998, and is discussed more extensively in chapter 10.

6 Fibre evidence involves comparing fibres of synthetic or animal origin, which may have come from clothing, carpets, furniture, etc. (Kaufman, 1998b, 85).

7 Under the heading of physical sciences are fingerprints, trace evidence (hair), firearm and tool-mark identification, and arson investigations. Forensic biological evidence includes forensic pathology, toxicology, serology, DNA analysis, forensic entomology, forensic odontology, and forensic anthropology (Wecht and Rago, 2007). Recently, Pollanen et al. (2013) have identified the following as nine "core" forensic disciplines: forensic pathology, forensic anthropology, forensic odontology, forensic nursing,

forensic entomology, forensic physical evidence, forensic toxicology, forensic biology, and forensic psychiatry. In this brief review, particular topics on the above lists are not covered owing to lack of space and their distance from wrongful-conviction and innocence scholarship.

8 *R. v. Hall* [2004] O.J. No. 5007.

9 [2003] O.J. No. 5243.

10 http://abfo.org/resources/id-bitemark-guidelines/.

11 www.bafo.org.uk.

12 Bite-mark identification, as well as fingerprints and handwriting, are based on the idea that people have unique attributes. Beecher-Monas (2007) questions this assumption and believes that it has not been tested; her preference is to rely on the theory that some people may *share* attributes (100).

13 As of 2007, bite-mark evidence had been admitted in at least fifty cases in the United States following the *Daubert* decision, which is discussed later in the chapter. In many cases, the courts have taken judicial notice of its reliability and draw on precedent in accepting it, without questioning its validity (Beecher-Monas, 2007, 96n.7).

14 https://www.innocenceproject.org/cases/kennedy-brewer/.

15 [1999] O.J. No. 4720 127 OAC 132.

16 [2011] 1 S.C.R. 628.

17 2012 MBCA 97.

18 Ibid., at para. 3.

19 Ibid., at para. 7.

20 Cf. *R. v. Samuels* [2005] O.J. No. 1873; *R. v. Laurin* [2012] O.J. No. 4357.

21 [2001] B.C.J. No. 1946.

22 [2010] B.C.J. No. 1518.

23 See *R. v. Penner* [2009] A.J. No. 447; *R. v. Dougan* [2008] O.J. No. 5292.

24 [2011] A.J. No. 218.

25 2011 ONCA 671.

26 [2008] O.J. No. 1875.

27 [1992] O.J. No. 4176.

28 [2007] Y.J. No. 63.

29 Ibid., at para. 37

30 Canines are often used to detect for accelerants; however, even when laboratory tests indicate that accelerants are not present, in a majority of those cases courts have relied on the unconfirmed testimony of dog handlers on the basis that the canine's highly developed sense of smell is more accurate than laboratory tests (Ottley, 2010, 266). Mechanical devices, such as hydrocarbon-gas detectors, are used as well, but canines are considered superior.

31 See, for example, the case of Cameron Todd Willingham. Willingham was executed by the state of Texas in 2004 for the arson murder of his three daughters. He was convicted in 1992 based in part on the testimony of a forensic expert who claimed, after studying the burn patterns in the home, that the fire was intentionally set. Since that time, other forensic experts, relying on more advanced science, have debunked this conclusion and there is a growing grass-roots movement to grant Willingham a posthumous pardon (http://camerontoddwillingham.com/). See also Giannelli (2013).

32 2011 BCCA 381.

33 Ibid., at para. 11.

34 See, for example, Skinner et al. (2010).

35 Trace evidence includes fibre, glass, paint, hair, soil, plastics, and adhesives (Woods, 2007). Collecting and examining this type of evidence is an intricate process, a thorough examination of which is beyond the scope of this chapter. Here, as with identification evidence, the use and misuse of such evidence can have an impact on the safety of a conviction.

36 https://innocenceproject.org/causes/misapplication-forensic-science/.

37 Driskell was wrongfully convicted for murder and served twelve years before his release; his conviction was due to a large degree to invalidated hair-microscopy evidence. His case is discussed in greater detail in chapter 10.

38 In 2004 the committee expanded its work to review cases of sexual assault and robbery where hair-comparison evidence had been used; however, no further cases that fit the criteria were studied.

39 http://www.ppsc-sppc.gc.ca/eng/pub/ptj-spj/ch10.html.

40 *R. v. Trochym* [2007] SCC 6.

41 Ibid., at 63.

42 James Lockyer, a lawyer and director of AIDWYC/Innocence Canada, also refers to the impact of "junk circumstantial evidence" on wrongful convictions – whereby an individual may be deemed guilty based on their conduct after a crime has been committed. In essence, this involves ascertaining from a person's conduct after a crime that he or she likely committed that crime. For example, in the Guy Paul Morin case, he was not involved in the search for Christine Jessop's body after she went missing; this was construed as evidence that he did not search for her because he already knew where she was, having killed her (Lockyer, University of Ottawa, Faculty of Law, 28 Nov. 2006). See also *R. v. White* ([2011] 1 S.C.R. 433), where the court underlines the importance of judges cautioning juries about misinterpreting post-event conduct ("demeanour evidence," para. 185) as indicative of guilt, since the misuse of such evidence may result in a wrongful conviction.

43 Baltovich's defence team presented evidence that demonstrated, inter alia, that Bain had previously met Paul Bernardo and had been seen with a "blond" man on the day of her disappearance (Finkle, 1998). Bernardo was convicted of nine charges related to the sexual assault and murders of Leslie Mahaffy, Kristen French, and Tammy Homolka in 1995, and is serving a life sentence as a dangerous offender.

44 http://www.cbc.ca/news/canada/i-get-to-live-the-rest-my-life-free-baltovich-acquitted-1.698182.

45 Ibid.

46 Forensic pathologists work in different types of death-investigation systems in Canada, and depending on the statutory milieu of the province, they may have the authority to perform autopsies or that responsibility may lay with others, such as coroners (Pollanen et al., 2013).

47 Some of theses ideas have been discussed in Campbell (2011).

48 [1990] 1 S.C.R. 852.

49 [2000] 148 C.C.C. (3d) [*R. v. D.(D.)*].

50 One difficulty with allowing the judge to play the role of so-called "expert" in such instances is that the accused does not have a chance to refute or qualify any instructions that a judge makes to the jury. At the same time, a jury is likely to find

any admissions from a judge about a particular issue at trial far more compelling than similar evidence from an expert witness (Bala, 2005, 286).

51 *R. v. D.(D.)*, at 27.

52 [2005] S.C.J. no. 74.

53 [1994] 2 SCR 9 [*Mohan*].

54 Ibid., at para. 31.

55 In the case of *R. v. Handy* ([2002] 2 S.C.R. 908), the Court held that reasoning based on "bad personhood" or "general disposition" is normally inadmissible; however, specific evidence of propensity to behave in a specific way may be admitted depending on the probative value and risk of prejudice. Moreover, similar-fact evidence (of character) may be introduced to show a prior violent relationship between the accused and the victim [*Handy*]. In *R. v. MacDonald* ([2002] O.J. No. 3315), the court allowed the victim to testify about past abuse suffered in order to support specific inferences that the accused was disposed to act violently *towards the victim* and that he had this disposition when he attacked the victim; the evidence was not used to demonstrate "bad personhood" per se.

56 Criminal Code, R.S.C. 1985, c. C-46, s. 666 (Previous Convictions).

57 *R. v. J(L.J.)*.

58 *Handy; R. v. Johnson*, 2010 ONCA 646.

59 *R. v. J(L.J.)* (headnote).

60 Some of these ideas have been discussed in detail in Campbell (2011).

61 *Mohan*. While *Mohan* established the scientific requirement for admitting expert evidence, this was later affirmed in *R. v. McIntosh* ([1997] 117 C.C.C. (3d) 385 (Ont. C.A.)) [*McIntosh*], which is referred to in Ontario as the *McIntosh* test (Paciocco, 1999, 313).

62 [1987] 2 S.C.R. 398.

63 *McIntosh*, at 28.

64 2009 ONCA 624.

65 Ibid., at para. 75.

66 Ibid., at para. 87.

67 Ibid., at para. 97.

68 Ibid., at para. 97.

69 *Frye v. United States*, 293 F. 1013 (D.C. Cir., 1923).

70 While polygraphs or lie-detector tests may be used as part of police investigative procedures, courts in both Canada and the United States continue to disallow the use of polygraph evidence at trial. In the American case of *U.S. v. Scheffer* (523 US 303 [1998]), a more sophisticated version of the polygraph was presented and dismissed as unreliable.

71 113 S Ct. 2786 [1993].

72 143 L. Ed (2d) 238 [1999] [U.S.S.C.].

73 *The Goudge Inquiry into Pediatric Forensic Pathology* (http://www.attorneygeneral.jus. gov.on.ca/inquiries/goudge/index.html) is discussed in greater detail in chapter 10.

74 Christie Blatchford, "Charles Smith's Punishment Deemed 'a Slap on the Wrist,'" *Globe and Mail*, 1 Feb. 2011.

75 C. 15, Amending the Coroners Act 1990, c. 37.

76 Previously, Ontario's forensic-pathology services had been decentralized, operating in regional forensic-pathology units and hospitals where autopsies were carried

out. See http://news.ontario.ca/mcscs/en/2008/10/strengthening-ontarios-death-investigation-system.html.

77 "Conviction Quashed in Case involving Disgraced Pathologist Charles Smith," *Toronto Star*, 12 July 2013, http://www.thestar.com/news/ontario/2011/05/04/conviction_quashed_in_case_involving_disgraced_pathologist_charles_smith.html.

78 "Man Acquitted in Baby Son's Death," *Globe and Mail*, 20 Jan. 2011, http://www.theglobeandmail.com/news/national/man-acquitted-in-baby-sons-death/article576987/; "Dinesh Kumar, AIDWYC Exonerations: Individual Cases," http://www.aidwyc.org/cases/historical/dinesh-kumar/.

79 Following the Ontario chief coroner's review of forty-five of Smith's cases where he had been chief or consulting pathologist, twenty cases were found to have questionable results, and among these were nineteen cases of children who died in unusual circumstances. Table 8 lists sixteen of the nineteen cases; information was unavailable for the other three. Much of the information contained here was obtained from Jill Mahoney and Tenille Bonoguore, "14 Causes Tainted by Charles Smith's Evidence," *Globe and Mail*, 10 Aug. 2010, http://www.theglobeandmail.com/news/national/14-cases-tainted-by-charles-smiths-evidence/article562711/?page=all ("Smith Blunders").

80 Ibid. While Smith's testimony was questionable in this case, Blackett plead guilty to manslaughter.

81 In the cases of Marco and Anisa Trotta, while Smith erred on this autopsy findings – for example mistaking an old, partly healed skull fracture for a recent injury – in Paolo's case, Marco Trotta was convicted at retrial as there was sufficient evidence of a long history of abuse.

82 In this case, Camille Mohamed did not know she was pregnant and the child died at birth, unassisted. (http://www.theglobeandmail.com/news/national/14-cases-tainted-by-charles-smiths-evidence/article562711/?page=all).

83 Liam Casey, "Brenda Waudby Moves on Sixteen Years after Charles Smith Debacle," *Toronto Star*, 23 Sept. 2013, http://www.thestar.com/news/gta/2013/09/23/brenda_waudby_moves_on_16_years_after_charles_smith_debacle.html.

84 The youth pled guilty to manslaughter in December 2006 and was sentenced to twenty-two months in prison.

85 Alyshah Hasham, "Brenda Waudby Officially Innocent of Child Abuse," *Toronto Star*, 27 July 2012, http://www.thestar.com/news/gta/2012/06/27/brenda_waudby_officially_innocent_of_child_abuse.html; Sarah Deeth, "Judge Overturns Waudby's 1999 Child Abuse Conviction," *Peterborough Examiner*, 27 June 2012, http://www.thepeterboroughexaminer.com/2012/06/27/crown-apologies-to-brenda-waudby.

86 https://www.thestar.com/news/crime/2016/02/29/woman-seeks-acquittal-in-stepdaughters-1991-death.html.

87 https://www.theglobeandmail.com/news/national/14-cases-tainted-by-charles-smiths-evidence/article562711/?page=all.

88 Michelle Mandel, "Trotta Hears the Train Coming: Oshawa Man Seeks to Quash Conviction of Killing Son," *Toronto Sun*, 8 Feb. 2011, http://www.torontosun.com/news/columnists/michele_mandel/2011/02/08/17200896.html.

89 https://www.theglobeandmail.com/news/national/14-cases-tainted-by-charles-smiths-evidence/article562711/?page=all.

90 Ibid.

91 Ibid.

92 Ibid.

93 http://www.cbc.ca/radio/thecurrent/the-current-for-january-12-2017-1.3932086/
charles-smith-scandal-how-a-mother-wrongly-accused-of-killing-her-son-fought-
back-1.3932116.

94 https://www.thestar.com/news/ontario/2010/08/12/compensation_to_smiths_
victims_paltry_and_insulting_lawyer_says.html.

95 "Given Injustice, $250,000 Is a Pittance," *Globe and Mail*, 20 Aug. 2010, http://www.
theglobeandmail.com/globe-debate/editorials/given-injustice-250000-is-a-pittance/
article1212936/.

96 A number of questions have been raised about Smith's role in this case, since he was
both an investigator through the initial autopsy and a witness at the preliminary
hearing. T. Cohen, "Ontario Woman Jailed over Daughter's Murder Fights to Sue
Pathologist," Canadian Press, 12 Feb. 2007.

97 *Reynolds v. Kingston (City)Police Services Board* [2007] O.J. 900.

98 Personal communication, Peter Wardle, 15 April 2015.

99 See also Campbell (2012).

100 *R. v. Mullins-Johnson* [2007] ONCA 720. In addressing the question of innocence, the
court stated that the acquittal re-established Mullins-Johnson's legal innocence (para.
22). It went on to say that (a) it did not have the jurisdiction to address the question of
factual innocence, and (b) for policy reasons (relating to the fact that declarations of
innocence would degrade the meaning of the not-guilty verdict) it could not support a
finding of innocence (paras. 24–5).

101 Theresa Boyle, "Man Wrongfully Convicted in Smith Case Gets $4.25 Million,"
Toronto Star, 22 Oct. 2010, http://www.thestar.com/news/ontario/2010/10/22/
man_wrongfully_convicted_in_smith_case_gets_425_million.html.

102 Sir Roy Meadow's case is discussed in greater detail in Campbell and Walker (2007;
2012).

103 *R. v. Cannings* [2004] EWCA Crim 1 [*Cannings*].

104 Scientists now believe that babies who die of SIDS are likely born with a condition (or
conditions) that cause unexpected responses to stressors, likely linked to the function
of the developing brain and nervous system: https://www.nichd.nih.gov/sts/
campaign/science/Pages/causes.aspx.

105 *R. v. Clark* [2003] EWCA Crim 1020.

106 *R. v. Harris* [2005] EWCA Crim 1980.

107 United Kingdom Attorney General's Office, "Attorney General Announces Results of
Shaken Baby Syndrome Cases Review, and New Guidance for Expert Witnesses," 4
Feb. 2006.

108 Serology is the scientific study of bodily fluids (blood and serum) and involves the
diagnostic identification of antibodies in the serum (Ryan and Ray, 2004, 247).

109 Zain's work came under scrutiny following the prosecution of Glen Woodall,
sentenced in 1987 to two life terms for a double rape. Zain's testimony regarding
the blood and hair analysis at trial was later found to be false, and Woodall was
exonerated through evolving (at that time) DNA forensic analysis (Scheck et al., 2000,
111).

110 *In the Matter of an Investigation of the W.Va. State Police Crime Lab., Serology Div.*, 438
S.E.2d 501, 510–11 (W. Va. 1993) [Investigation-Report].

111 "This was a sexual assault case in which the typing results were identical to the victim. The reported conclusion was ambiguous but implied a match with the defendant. The report should have stated no information on the semen donor." Investigation-Report, appendix.

112 "Some samples critical to the final conclusion reflected a difference between the worksheet and the data sheet, with the data sheet reflecting the victim's type and the worksheet reflecting a mixture which included the defendant. The worksheet showed evidence of alteration." Ibid.

113 "ABO grouping test results ... indicated A, B, and O activity on a napkin ... yet the result was reported as 'A.' Data sheets also showed one enzyme type ... to be not callable on the napkin, yet it was reported ... Another enzyme ... was shown in parentheses on the data sheets which usually meant inconclusive, yet it, too, was called ... The data in this case does not support the attribution of donor stated in the case report." Ibid.

114 "[The] data sheet showed 'O' activity on a knife ... yet the report stated that ABO 'A' was found on the knife. It also showed '635 Jkt R Sleeve' with 'O' activity, but this was not reported at all. There appears to be an incorrect attribution of donor." Ibid.

115 "There was no evidence that Lewis testing was performed on the swab, but the report implies that it was. The conclusion did not include any frequency, but a transcript was reviewed to see how these results were explained in court by Mr. Zain. He incorrectly multiplied the non-secretor frequency ... by 50% since the stain included semen (from males only) and finally by the PGM 1+ frequency, even though there may have been masking by the victim's PGM type. That the semen could not have originated from a secretor based on the absence of any blood group factors is not a certainty as stated in his testimony ... The value of the serological testing was overstated in both the report and the testimony." Ibid.

116 S. Weinberg, "Keystone Cops at the Police Lab, *Pacific Standard*, 18 June 2009, http://www.psmag.com/politics-and-law/keystone-cops-at-the-police-lab-3631. Ultimately, five prisoners in West Virginia were released, as was one in Texas.

117 Dr I.C. Stone report – unable to locate.

118 "Under the Microscope: Did Gilchrist Help Put Innocent People in Prison?" CBS News, 24 July 2002, http://www.webcitation.org/query?url=http%3A%2F%2Fwww.cbsnews.com%2Fstories%2F2001%2F05%2F08%2F60II%2Fmain290046.shtml&date=2009-05-08.

119 *McCarty v. State*, 765 P.2d 1215, 1218 (Okla. Crim. App. 1988).

120 D. Baldwin, "Gilchrist Case Report Sent to Governor," 17 July 2002, http://newsok.com/article/1056685.

121 National Registry of Exonerations, University of Michigan Law School, http://www.law.umich.edu/special/exoneration/Pages/detaillist.aspx.

122 Weinberg (2009).

123 In their study they found six types of invalid testimony: non-probative evidence was presented as probative, even though empirical population data was used incorrectly (16); exculpatory evidence was discounted (18); an inaccurate frequency or statistic was presented (18); statistics were provided without empirical support (18); non-numerical statements were provided without empirical support (19); and conclusions were presented that evidence originated from the defendant when it did not (20).

124 http://www.homeoffice.gov.uk/agencies-public-bodies/fsr/regulator/.

125 http://www.homeoffice.gov.uk/publications/agencies-public-bodies/fsr/codes-practice-conduct?view=Binary. While the Codes lay out core requirements for most laboratory-based forensic-science disciplines, there are separate codes for disciplines such as forensic pathology which have their own oversight bodies. The provision of forensic-pathology services is under the control of the Pathology Delivery Board, Home Office. This board functions through the home secretary and formally recognizes and regulates the work of pathologists who have sufficient training and experience to act on behalf of coroners and police in suspicious death and homicide cases; these pathologists are also entered in the Home Office Register of Forensic Pathologists (http://www.homeoffice.gov.uk/science-research/forensic-pathology/).
126 http://www.fsc.state.tx.us/.
127 The recently established Centre for Forensic Science and Medicine, attached to the University of Toronto, will likely fill that role. It describes itself as " a new interdisciplinary initiative dedicated to advancing teaching and research in the forensic disciplines, at the interface with the law and social science" and offers regular seminars to those in the legal, medical, and academic professions on a variety of topics related to the forensic sciences (http://www.forensics.utoronto.ca/Page969.aspx).
128 Although perhaps representative of institutional bias.
129 This recommendation is also supported by the Federal/Provincial/Territorial Heads of Prosecutions Subcommittee on the Prevention of Wrongful Convictions (2011).
130 Goudge Inquiry into Pediatric Forensic Pathology, Report, 73 at 376, 387–90, 427, as found in D. Paciocco, "Taking a 'Goudge' out of Bluster and Blarney: An 'Evidence-Based Approach' to Expert Testimony," *Canadian Criminal Law*, 13, no. 2 (2009): 146–7.

Chapter 9

1 In reference to the conviction review process. See https://www.pressreader.com/canada/calgary-herald/20061226/281685430361126.
2 An earlier version of parts of this chapter can be found in K. Campbell (2005).
3 Criminal Code, R.S.C. 1985, c. C-46, s. 675 (Right of Appeal of Person Convicted).
4 Criminal Code, R.S.C. 1985, c. C-46, s. 686(1)(2) (Powers of the Court of Appeal).
5 In fact, it has been argued that this section of the Criminal Code is the most relevant to wrongful convictions (Sangha et al., 2010, 99).
6 *R. v. Cooper* (1969), 53 Cr. App. R. 82.
7 Criminal Appeal Act 1968 (U.K.), 1968, c. 35, s. 2.
8 The possibility of an independent review commission for Canada is discussed in greater detail in chapter 13.
9 The charges against Hughes Duguay were stayed.
10 While Benoit Proulx's conviction was overturned at the Quebec Court of Appeal, the Crown's appeal to the Supreme Court resulted in a finding that Proulx had been a victim of malicious prosecution and had been convicted on insufficient evidence.
11 Yves Plamondon had originally been convicted on three counts of first-degree murder and on appeal he was acquitted on one of the charges and a stay entered on the other two.
12 Thomas Sophonow's case is a rather complex one and is discussed at greater length in chapter 10. His first trial ended in a mistrial, he was convicted at a second trial, and a third trial was ordered, where he was acquitted.

13 Following the stay of proceedings, Rejean Hinse took his case to the Supreme Court, where he was acquitted.

14 Jason Hill's case was unusual. As discussed in chapter 2, Hill's first appeal ended in a retrial. At his second trial he was acquitted. Hill then sued the police for malicious prosecution, negligent procedure, and a breach of Charter rights. Owing to the circumstances of his case, the tort of negligent investigation was established by the Supreme Court.

15 In Stephen Truscott's case, while under conviction review, the minister of justice at that time, Irwin Cotler, grappled with how to rectify what he recognized had been a miscarriage of justice. Ultimately, the case was sent back to the Court of Appeal as an appeal, at which point Truscott was acquitted.

16 The Ontario Court of Appeal heard Jack White's case in 2010, after being ordered to review the conviction by the Supreme Court of Canada in 2009. The Court of Appeal formally withdrew the charges against White in 2010.

17 Cf. McLellan (2012a).

18 See, for example, Proceedings against the Crown Act, R.S.O. 1990, c. P.27. In fact, Charney and Hunter (2011) note that it is "common practice for plaintiffs suing governments for the alleged tortious conduct of their servants and agents to plead that the conduct complained of was both a common-law tort and a violation of the *Charter* and to claim damages on both grounds" (394).

19 "24. (1) Anyone whose rights or freedoms, as guaranteed by this Charter, have been infringed or denied may apply to a court of competent jurisdiction to obtain such remedy as the court considers appropriate and just in the circumstances."

20 [2010] 2 S.C.R. 28.

21 Some of the ideas discussed in the following sections regarding the conviction-review process as well as the case examples can be found in K. Campbell (2008).

22 The Criminal Code (ss. 748 and 748.1) authorizes the governor in council to grant the following types of clemency: 1. Free Pardon: based on innocence, it is a recognition that the conviction was in error and erases the consequences and records of the conviction. 2. Conditional Pardon: criminal record is kept separate and apart from other criminal records prior to pardon eligibility under the Criminal Records Act (five years for a summary offence, ten years for an indictable offence); or parole in advance of eligibility date under the Corrections and Conditional Release Act for offenders serving life and indeterminate sentences for those who are ineligible for parole by exception. 3. Remission of fine, forfeiture, and pecuniary penalty: erases all, or part of, the monetary penalty that was imposed. See http://www.canada.ca/en/parole-board/services/clemency/what-is-the-exercise-of-clemency-royal-prerogative-of-mercy.html.

23 S.C. 1996, c. 19.

24 *McArthur v. Ontario* (Attorney General) 2013 ONCA 668 at para 4.

25 *Her Majesty the Queen v. Lindley Charles McArthur, et al.* (Ontario) (Criminal) (By Leave), 2012–12–03, 35695.

26 The following information is a summary of that found in Department of Justice (2003).

27 In most cases, the lawyers working at the CCRG conduct the review process. In high-profile cases or where the prosecution of the applicant was undertaken by the Department of Justice itself (such as for drug offences, or those occurring in northern regions), outside counsel will be appointed to conduct the review.

28 See chapter 10.

29 The numbers in the appendix A are not directly comparable to the statistics kept by the CCRG, given the longer time spans and the inaccuracies of the methodology. Only 28 per cent of the cases listed in appendix A were assessed by the CCRG.

30 In a given year a number of new and old applications are actively under review. For example, in 2005–6, twelve preliminary assessments were completed and twenty were under way; six investigations were completed and eighteen were under way; and six reports were completed and twelve were under way (Department of Justice, 2005a).

31 Some of these criticisms are also discussed in Campbell (2008) and Walker and Campbell (2010).

32 This table is adapted from Denov and Campbell (2003, 2005), with additional help from Nathalie Vautour, CCRG.

33 An application is considered to be "completed" when a person has submitted the forms, information, and supporting documents required by the regulations.

34 An application is considered to be "partially completed" when a person has submitted some but not all of the forms, information, and supporting documents required by the regulations.

35 An application is considered to be "screened out" if the person is not eligible to make an application for ministerial review, which would include convictions in civil court, or if new matters of significance were not raised.

36 An application is considered to be "under way" if it commenced during the reporting period or if it commenced beforehand but continued during the reporting period.

37 During this period, the CCRG introduced a new category, inquiries, which includes those who contact the CCRG for general information about the conviction-review process or other information but do not formally request the booklet *Application for a Conviction Review*. For the 2010 annual report, the CCRG received eleven such inquiries; for 2011, twenty-three; and in 2012, twenty.

38 It has been previously noted that most of these materials are necessary for each level of appeal and are likely already available (Campbell, 2005).

39 These are known as the Thatcher principles and are contained in the Thatcher 690 application decision. W. Colin Thatcher was convicted of murdering his wife in 1984. He applied for a conviction review in 1989 and received the minister's response in 1994. At that time, the minister of justice denied the application and further set out the nature of the conviction-review process and the role of the minister therein.

40 Parts of these guidelines have been codified in law (Criminal Code, ss. 696.1–696.6) through amendments to the conviction-review process in 2002. Furthermore, regulations accompanying these amendments contain information on the application process.

41 Following much lobbying, the minister of justice waived solicitor-client privilege in *Re Truscott*, and publicly released an edited copy of the brief of that case in 2005, likely due to its high-profile nature.

42 In Canadian jurisdictions a judicial review is a mechanism of administrative law. It constitutes an appeal from the decision of an administrative body, whereby a court rules on the appropriateness of the decision made by a tribunal or administrative agency.

43 This principle does not apply in the same manner in the United States, since American appellate courts have greater and more liberal powers and the possible grounds for appeal are more numerous (Department of Justice, 1998b). American states vary in terms of remedies and more collateral remedies such as civil action are available.

44 (No. 2), Judgment No. 570, 20 December 1983. The Administrative Tribunal, para. 1.

45 [1980] 1 S.C.R. 759.

46 Bernard Grenier, a retired Quebec provincial court judge, was appointed as special adviser in November 2003.

47 These last two amendments were non-legislative changes and reflect an attempt to distance the process from the Department of Justice Canada.

48 This request was considered to be unprecedented at that time, since in essence the minister of justice was asking the Supreme Court, which normally interprets law, to interpret fact (Boyd and Rossmo, 1994). The reference was made because one of Milgaard's original lawyers, Calvin Tallis, had been appointed to the Saskatchewan Court of Appeal and could thus not hear the review.

49 In 2004 the Supreme Court of Canada refused to hear Fisher's appeal, thus allowing for an inquiry to proceed on Milgaard's case in 2005. The mandate of the commission of inquiry, as examined further in chapter 10, was to examine the investigation into the death of Gail Miller and the criminal proceedings against David Milgaard.

50 https://www.aidwyc.org/cases/historical/clayton-johnson/.

51 R. v. Johnson, [1998] NSJ No 381, 131 CCC (3d) 343.

52 To be discussed in greater detail in chapter 13.

Chapter 10

1 Some of the ideas discussed in the following sections have been previously discussed in Campbell (2005).

2 The case of David Milgaard illustrates this point. He was convicted of raping and murdering Gail Miller in 1970 and served twenty-two years in prison before being exonerated through DNA in 1997. He was later awarded $10 million by the Saskatchewan and federal governments, the largest criminal compensation at that time in Canada. Following many years of lobbying by Milgaard's family, legal counsel, and AIDWYC, the Saskatchewan government finally held an inquiry into how and why this injustice occurred.

3 *Canada (Attorney General) v. Canada (Commission of the Inquiry on the Blood System)*, [1997] 3 S.C.R. 440 at 30 [*Blood System*]. Prior to this case, there was also a Royal Commission of Inquiry on the Blood System in Canada in October 1993, headed by Justice Horace Krever. Given that contaminated blood had been found circulating in the health-care system, its objective was a sweeping investigation of the conduct of both government and non-government organizations and agencies involved with the supply of blood and blood products.

4 *Blood System*, at para. 30

5 *Final Report of the Commission of Inquiry into the Non-Medical Use of Drugs* (1973); *Report of the Commission of Inquiry into the Hinton Train Collision* (1986); the Royal Commission on the Ocean Ranger Marine Disaster, *Report* (1984–5); *Report of the Royal Commission of Inquiry into Certain Deaths at the Hospital for Sick Children and Related Matters* (1984).

6 *Blood System*, at para. 30.

7 In the past, courts have supported the power to compel witness testimony in inquiries so long as it does not infringe on the rights of the witness in future proceedings (Ratushny, 2009), thus protecting the section 13 Charter right against self-incrimination. More recently, a decision by the Supreme Court of Canada (*R. v. Nedelcu*) has weakened this right considerably.

8 *Blood System*, at 34; also Gomery (2006, 792).

9 To this effect, Justice Gomery notes that during the Sponsorship Inquiry, "powerful people were obliged to answer questions about their actions and involvement ... whether they wanted to or not. They were expected to explain their actions, and to account for the manner in which they had discharged their public responsibilities, to an independent body carrying out its investigation in public" (Gomery, 2006, 787). The sponsorship scandal and subsequent inquiry examined high-level government corruption regarding the misuse and misdirection of public funds intended to promote the federal government through advertising in the province of Quebec in the late 1990s.

10 Technically, there have been six inquiries that examined the wrongful conviction of specifically named individuals. The seventh is the Goudge Commission of Inquiry into Pediatric Forensic Pathology in the province of Ontario. This inquiry was not aimed specifically at a wrongful conviction per se but rather examined the conduct of one pathologist, Dr Charles Smith, whose testimony as an expert witness resulted in a number of miscarriages of justice.

11 For a more thorough examination of the results of commissions of inquiry addressing wrongful convictions, see Botting (2010).

12 In publicly criticizing the police, Crown counsel, and the judiciary, the Marshall Commission was castigating these individuals for failing to follow proper procedure in the course of their jobs.

13 This was demonstrated in the commission's report, where the criminal investigations of two members of the Nova Scotia government were used to illustrate how a two-tiered justice system favours those with power and influence.

14 R.S.N.S. 1989, c. 214.

15 Prior to his becoming a suspect in the murder of Christine Jessop, Guy Paul Morin was described by the Jessops as a "weird-type guy," a bee-keeper, and a clarinet player, ostensibly because these hobbies were considered odd. It was noted that this characterization directed some suspicion towards Morin (Kaufman, 1998a).

16 DNA evidence indicated that sperm found on the underclothing of Christine Jessop could not have possibly belonged to Guy Paul Morin.

17 The inquiry discovered that there was some dispute over the exact nature and extent of the benefits given to two informants, Mr May and Mr X (Kaufman, 1998c, 422–36).

18 No other suspect has ever been tried for Barbara Stoppel's murder; the case remains unsolved.

19 In this instance, Commissioner Cory apportioned blame and responsibility and ordered that the total of $2.6 million in compensation was to be divided as follows: 50 per cent from the city of Winnipeg, 40 per cent from the province of Manitoba, and 10 per cent from the government of Canada. Sophonow experienced substantial delays in collecting this compensation. See chapter 11, n.4.

20 Henceforth referred to as the Lamer Inquiry.

21 http://www.statcan.gc.ca/tables-tableaux/sum-som/l01/cst01/legal50a-eng.htm.

22 http://www.statcan.gc.ca/tables-tableaux/sum-som/l01/cst01/legal50b-eng.htm; http://www.statcan.gc.ca/tables-tableaux/sum-som/l01/cst01/legal50c-eng.htm.

23 Under the inquiry's terms of reference, Justice Lamer was not mandated to examine why Dalton was initially charged with his wife's murder.

24 The "claw-back" mechanism involves a recalculation of payment to a lawyer who has previously represented a defendant but who is now seeking legal-aid funding on the same matter (Lamer, 2006, 17).

25 The DNA found at the crime scene belonged to Brian Doyle, a childhood friend of Parsons. Doyle later confessed to the crime and entered a guilty plea.

26 Several key witnesses in this case lived in the same building as Brenda Young and openly discussed the case among themselves following police inquiries. Through repeated questioning, several witnesses changed their story to fit the police version of events.

27 The informant in this case was charged with attempting to obstruct justice and received a five-year prison sentence.

28 Paul Druken died of a drug overdose on the day the RNC received the report containing the result of the forensic testing implicating him (Lamer, 2006, 175).

29 The longest-serving (known) wrongly imprisoned person was likely Romeo Phillion, who was convicted of murder in 1972 and released on bail in 2003, thirty-one years later, pending a conviction review of his case by the minister of justice. Both he and Milgaard would likely have been released earlier if they had admitted guilt and followed the normal conditional-release processes. But both were steadfast in their desire for exoneration and never wavered in their innocence claims. As Phillion said: "Parole is for the guilty. Not the innocent. If you're innocent, don't take parole." See *R. v. Johnson*, [1998] NSJ No. 381, 131 CCC (3d) 343.

30 Specifically, that the informants had been paid for their testimony ($20,000), that one informant had perjured himself, and that an immunity deal had been arranged for one informant with regard to arson charges in exchange for the testimony of the other.

31 Editorial, "Ewatski Must Go," *Winnipeg Free Press*, 22 Sept. 2006.

32 Section 577 of the Criminal Code allows the attorney general to send a case directly to trial without a preliminary hearing or after an accused has been discharged at a preliminary hearing. It essentially permits the attorney general to override the preliminary-hearing process and compel an accused to go to trial. Sometimes referred to as a "preferred indictment," it appears to be used in cases where witnesses are ill or have been threatened.

33 Following the inquiry, Driskell instituted a lawsuit against the city, province, and several police officers, claiming $20 million in damages. In 2011 all parties agreed to settle the lawsuit with a lump-sum payment of $4 million to Driskell and $25,000 to his mother; the province paid $2.4 million and the city the balance (http://www.winnipegfreepress.com/breakingnews/Driskell-114196669.html).

34 Manitoba News Release, 15 Feb. 2007, "Driskell Inquiry Report Released. Implementation of Recommendations to Begin Immediately," http://news.gov.mb.ca/news/index.html?archive=&item=1221.

35 A number of the ideas in this section have been discussed in Campbell and Walker (2012).

36 C. 15, Amending the Coroners Act 1990, c. 37.

37 Previously, Ontario's forensic pathology services had been decentralized, operating in regional forensic-pathology units and hospitals where autopsies were carried out. See https://news.ontario.ca/mcscs/en/2013/08/ontario-strengthening-death-investigation-system.html.

38 https://news.ontario.ca/mcscs/en/2008/10/strengthening-ontarios-death-investigation-system.html.

39 https://news.ontario.ca/mcscs/en/2008/10/strengthening-ontarios-death-investigation-system.html.

40 http://www.novusenv.com/news/torontos-new-forensic-services-and-coroners-complex-opens.

41 http://www.cpso.on.ca/whatsnew/committeeschedule/default.aspx?id=1448&terms=Charles+Smith.

42 The recommendations discussed here represent only a brief overview. Each inquiry's recommendations contain much greater detail and can be accessed in Botting (2010).

43 Cf., for example, the Sophonow Inquiry (Wolson and London 2004, 690).

44 See chapter 6.

45 *R. v. Stinchcombe* [1991] 3 S.C.R. 326.

46 Gomery (2006, 794).

Chapter 11

1 http://www.theglobeandmail.com/news/national/the-life-and-death-of-donald-marshall-jr/article4283981/?page=2.

2 These factors were drawn the *Commission of Inquiry concerning Adequacy of the Compensation Paid to Donald Marshall, Jr, Report of the Commissioner* (Nova Scotia, 1990), which included suggestions from H.A. Kaiser.

3 The last point was added by Justice Cory in specific reference to Thomas Sophonow's experience (Cory, 2001).

4 Following the Sophonow Inquiry report, released in November 2001, Thomas Sophonow was to receive $2.6 million in compensation for his ordeal and for the forty-five months spent in prison for the murder of Barbara Stoppel. As noted in chapter 10, this amount was to be divided between the city of Winnipeg, the Manitoba government, and the federal government (Cory, 2001). While the federal and provincial governments paid Sophonow their shares (40 and 10 per cent, respectively) shortly after the inquiry report was released, it took another year before Sophonow received the full amount. It seems that the city of Winnipeg was reticent to pay out its portion of the compensation (50 per cent) since it believed that the Sophonow case was a provincial matter. See http://news.gov.mb.ca/news/?item=25458&posted=2001-11-05; https://www.theglobeandmail.com/news/national/manitoba-completes-sophonow-compensation/article22393493/.

5 Nevertheless, in a number of cases compensation has also been awarded to family members, particularly mothers, for example, the mothers of David Milgaard, Guy Paul Morin, and Donald Marshall, Jr.

6 The stigma of being a criminal, although incorrectly labelled as such, tends to follow the wrongly convicted even after exoneration. In Canada, the Canadian Police Information Centre (CPIC) database includes information about all Canadians who have been arrested, convicted, and imprisoned in Canada. Following exoneration from a wrongful conviction, there is an assumption that criminal-record information should be expunged, but it is not a straightforward process. There is no provision in the Criminal Records Act (CRA), R.S.C. 1985, c. C-47, for automatically expunging a record. Similarly, the CRA does not define a "record" or what it includes. In the case where a conviction is quashed (either a new trial is ordered by the minister or Court of Appeal or an acquittal is entered), the exonerated (or counsel) would need to make

a formal request to either the RCMP and/or the police force that laid the original charges to remove the conviction from his or her record. Further to that, the request must explicitly state that any photographs or fingerprints should be destroyed. In the United States, the FBI uses a National Crime Information Center which has a computerized index of criminal records, provided by the FBI and state, local, and foreign agencies. Information in this database can be accessed by federal, state, and local law-enforcement agencies and it serves to supplement state databases, since state offenders are not necessarily entered into the FBI database. If the person's name is on the Interstate Identification Index File, his or her name will be removed when they reach the age of eighty years. Each state has its own requirements or statutes for how to expunge state records, and in most states a petition must be filed requesting the sealing of records, which will be granted only if certain criteria, as required by law, are met.

7 The attorney general of each province and territory has the right to recommend compensation awards outside of this reference.

8 Paul St-Denis, from Graeme Hamilton, "Fighting 'Distinct Society of Injustice,'" *National Post*, 5 Oct. 2005.

9 Non-pecuniary losses include losses incurred as a result of incarceration, including the assorted indignities inherent in imprisonment, the loss of reputation, and the interruption of family or other relationship ties.

10 Pecuniary losses include livelihood, earnings, future earnings, and loss of property.

11 Section C of the Guidelines indicates that a judicial or administrative inquiry must be appointed to consider the issues surrounding compensation in a particular case, including apportioning financial responsibility between federal, provincial, and municipal governments.

12 Michel Dumont was wrongly convicted of sexual assault in June 1991 in the province of Quebec. He served thirty-four months in prison before he was released; his conviction was quashed in February 2001 by the Quebec Court of Appeal and he was acquitted. Dumont has sought compensation since that time from various authorities (including from the attorneys general of Quebec and Canada) and has been unsuccessful. In 2010 he brought a claim to the United Nations Human Rights Committee accusing Canada of being in violation of its obligation to compensate him under art. 14, para. 6 of the ICCPR, as per the Federal/Provincial/Territorial Guidelines (*Michel Dumont c. Canada*, UN International Covenant on Civil and Political Rights, Human Rights Committee, Ninety-Eighth Session, Communication No. 1467/2006, 8–26 March 2010). The state party (Canada) had a number of arguments against Dumont's claim – principal among them the fact that he had never been proven innocent of the crime in question and was thus not eligible for compensation. Yet the victim claimed to have some doubts as to whether or not Dumont was the perpetrator and the Court of Appeal concluded that the victim's statements gave rise to a reasonable doubt as to Dumont's guilt – hence he was acquitted, but the court did not rule on his innocence. While finding in Dumont's favour, the UN Human Rights Committee required the Canada to provide an effective remedy to Dumont in the form of adequate compensation – as well as ensuring that "similar violations do not occur in the future" (para. 25). Similarly, it required that Canada provide evidence about the measures taken within 180 days; however, no action has been taken at time of writing.

13 This is the case for a prosecutorial stay entered by the Crown; when a stay is entered by the court (judicial stay of proceedings), it is deemed to be an acquittal (*R. v. Jewitt*

[1985] 2 S.C.R. 128 at para. 56), as found in Roach, 2006, 17n.51. A judicial stay of proceedings is entered only in cases where there has been a Charter violation or an abuse of process (Roach, 2006, 17).

14 In Scotland, a unique verdict that can be handed down by the courts is that of "not proven," which falls between guilty and not guilty. Considered a middle ground for juries and controversial among victims' advocacy groups, this verdict has essentially the same consequences as a not-guilty verdict: the accused is free and cannot ever be retried for the same offence (Cunningham, 2006).

15 As stated, the attorney general of each province has the discretion to award compensation to the wrongly convicted beyond the current caps or when the circumstances of the case do not technically comply with the requirements of a ministerial review (cf. Roach, 2006, 50). As an example, in the case of Herman Kaglik, he was acquitted through the normal court process but still received compensation for a wrongful conviction of sexual assault after he was cleared by DNA evidence.

16 See chapter 10 for more details about the overall recommendations from this inquiry.

17 This differs from the thirty-two cases in appendix A that have received compensation, since Jason Dix is included here. Dix was not technically wrongly convicted, but wrongly accused, and served time in pre-trial custody and was compensated for malicious prosecution. Thus, Dix's case did not meet the criterion for inclusion in the appendix.

18 This table is not exhaustive but based on a legal document and Internet research. Therefore, some of the monetary figures provided here may be more estimative than definitive.

19 Public Broadcasting Service, Frontline: "The Burden of Innocence" (2003), http://www.pbs.org/wgbh/pages/frontline/shows/burden/.

20 Brenda Waudby received compensation prior to her child abuse conviction being overturned.

21 Ex-gratia payments as reported by: Teresa Boyle, "Man Wrongfully Convicted in Smith Case Gets $4.25 Million," *Toronto Star*, 22 Oct. 2010 (William-Mullins Johnson); Katz (2011, 87, 203) (Simon Marshall, Wilfred Truscott); Government of Ontario, https://www.attorneygeneral.jus.gov.on.ca/english/about/pubs/truscott/ (Donald Marshall, Jr, Kenneth Norman Warwick, Richard Norris, Linda Huffman, Guy Paul Morin, David Milgaard, Rejean Pepin, Thomas Sophonow, Steven Truscott); unidentified author, "N.L. Compensates Dalton for 8-Year Prison Wait," CBC, 26 Oct. 2007 (Ronald Dalton); Newfoundland and Labrador Department of Justice, http://www.releases.gov.nl.ca/releases/2006/just/1214n05.htm and http://www.releases.gov.nl.ca/releases/2005/just/0901n07.htm (Randy Druken, Gregory Parsons); Innocence Compensation Project, http://www.montrealgazette.com/James+Driskell+spent+years+jail+1990+murder+Winnipeg+conviction+eventually+quashed+received+million+compensation/10043209/story.html; (James Driskell); Roach (2012, 523) (Tammy Marquardt); ForeJustice, http://forejustice.org/db/Folland--Gordon-.html (Gordon Folland).

22 Payments obtained through civil actions as reported by: Borden Ladner Gervais, http://www.blg.com/en/newsandpublications/news_1322 (Rejean Hinse); Nova Scotia Department of Justice, http://novascotia.ca/news/release/?id=20040618007 (Clayton Johnson); unidentified author, "Wrongly Convicted, Man Awarded 2.2M," Canada.com, 4 Oct. 2006, https://www.pressreader.com/canada/edmonton-journal/20061005/282024732750188] (Steven Kaminski); Injusticebusters, http://

injusticebusters.org/index.htm/Dix.htm, http://injusticebusters.org/04/Frumusa_Peter.htm, and http://injusticebusters.org/index.htm/Benoit_Proulx.htm (Jason Dix, Peter Frumusa, and Benoit Proulx); Sheldon Gordon "University Affairs: Innocence Regained" (York University Innocence Project) (Gary Staples); unidentified author, "N.B. Settles Walsh Wrongful Conviction Lawsuit," CBC News, 16 Oct. 2009, http://www.cbc.ca/news/canada/new-brunswick/n-b-settles-walsh-wrongful-conviction-lawsuit-1.794182 (Erin Walsh).

23 http://www.innocenceproject.org/free-innocent/improve-the-law/fact-sheets/compensating-the-wrongly-convicted.

24 Wrongful Conviction Compensation Statutes, CNN.com, http://www.cnn.com/interactive/2012/03/us/table.wrongful.convictions/# (retrieved 2 July 2015).

25 Ibid.

26 Act of 30 Oct. 2004, Pub. L. No. 108–405; 118 Stat. 2260 (2004).

27 Act of 30 Oct. 2004, Pub. L. No. 108–405, § 301; 118 Stat. 2260 (2004).

28 Act of 30 Oct. 2004, Pub. L. No. 108–05, 18 U.S.C.S. § 3600–3600A (2004).

29 B. Rokus, "Time Doesn't Pay, Wrongfully Imprisoned Find," CNN Special Investigations, 29 March 2012, http://www.cnn.com/2012/03/25/justice/wrongful-conviction-payments/index.html.

30 A search of the Innocence project website (www.innocenceproject.org), which lists those individuals who have received compensation, does not mention anyone who received compensation under this act; most have received compensation through state legislation and/or through civil suits filed against the state or the federal government.

31 Stephanie Slifer, "How the Wrongfully Convicted Are Compensated for Years Lost," CBS News, 27 March 2014, http://www.cbsnews.com/news/how-the-wrongfully-convicted-are-compensated/.

32 "Wrongfully Convicted Man Awarded $25 Million," NBC News, 25 Jan. 2012, http://usnews.nbcnews.com/_news/2012/01/25/10233263-wrongfully-convicted-man-awarded-25-million.

33 Cf. R. (on the application of Mullen) v. Secretary of State for the Home Department [2007] EWHC 1495 (Admin); [2007] A.C.D. 75; [2008] EWCA Civ 755, and further R. (on the application of Clibery) v. Secretary of State for the Home Department [2007] EWHC 1855 (Admin), R. (on the application of Siddall) v. Secretary of State for Justice [2009] EWHC 482 (Admin); 2009 A.C.D. 35.

34 L. Smith, "Wrongly Jailed Men Lose 'Living Expenses' Case," The Guardian, 14 March 2007, http://www.theguardian.com/uk/2007/mar/14/prisonsandprobation.ukcrime.

35 "Victims Say Payment Caps Are Unjust," Guardian Unlimited, 26 April 2006, http://www.guardina.co.uk/crime/article/0,,1756737,00.html?gusrc=rss.

36 http://researchbriefings.parliament.uk/ResearchBriefing/Summary/SN02131.

37 R (Adams) v. Secretary of State for Justice [2011] UKSC 18, para. 9.

38 S. 1ZA, Criminal Justice Act, 1988.

39 Mark Hennessy, "UK Law: Renewed Bid to Make It Difficult for Those Wrongfully Convicted to Claim Compensation," Irish Times, 3 Feb. 2014, http://www.irishtimes.com/news/world/uk/uk-law-renewed-bid-to-make-it-difficult-for-those-wrongfully-convicted-to-claim-compensation-1.1677062.

40 "Crime Appeal Pay-Outs Cut by £5m," BBC News, 19 April 2006, http://news.bbc.co.uk/2/hi/uk_news/4921230.stm.

41 See chapter 1 for a discussion of conviction error rates.

42 Some of these ideas have been discussed in detail in Campbell (2005).

Chapter 12

1 I am grateful to Michael Lait for greatly clarifying Nobles and Schiff's work in this area.

2 Even the original conviction is interpreted differently by subsystems: the concern of the legal system rests solely with conviction or acquittal; the media interpret this more broadly to mean actual guilt or innocence, without questioning how a conviction is coded or the authority of the system itself (Nobles and Schiff, 2000, 98).

3 Courts have long struggled with balancing the rights of the press to cover a trial and the risk of that coverage compromising a fair trial (Walton, 2001, 408).

4 Presumably, when the press refers to victims as "innocent," they are stating that a victim was undeserving of his/her fate. According to media stereotypes, a more deserving or less "innocent" victim would doubtless be one who had a criminal record or who became victimized through some fault of his/her own.

5 With respect to accounts of crime and criminal activity, the United Kingdom tabloids are particularly virulent and play a unique role in terms of shaping public opinion, to an extent that is unrivalled in North America and elsewhere. In fact, Paul Farrelly, a Labour MP, has publicly referred to the "increasingly feral tabloid press" and noted that British politicians are thought to "fear their power and are generally loath to cross them" (Lyall and Arango, 2009).

6 Heather Mills, "Murder Trial Sisters Convicted by the Media: Court of Appeal Is Told That Police Concealed Evidence Which Might Have Pointed to Michelle and Lisa Taylor's Innocence, in a Case That Was Always Thin," *The Independent*, 12 June 1993, http://www.independent.co.uk/news/uk/. Particularly damning was an innocuous wedding photo showing Michelle Taylor embracing her lover at his wedding, under the headline "The 'Killer' Mistress Who Was at Lover's Wedding," with an arrow running from the word "killer" to Michelle Taylor's face on the cover (Stephens and Hill, 1999, 265). See also Shaw (1995).

7 *R. v. Taylor, R. v. Taylor* (1993) (1994) 98 Cr App Rep 361 at 368–9.

8 As discussed in greater detail in chapter 13, the Birmingham Six were six men wrongfully convicted of a series of pub bombings, in which 21 people died and over 180 were injured, in Birmingham, England, in 1975. Their convictions were overturned in 1991 and influenced the creation of the Criminal Cases Review Commission.

9 Now deceased, Myra Hindley was convicted, along with Ian Brady, of the Moors Murders in 1963–5 in Manchester, England. The victims were five children. Hindley was described by the UK press as "the most evil woman in Britain" and refused parole on a number of occasions prior to her death in prison in 2002. "Hindley: I Wish I'd Been Hanged," BBC News, World Edition, 29 Feb. 2000, retrieved online 29 Jan. 2016 (http://news.bbc.co.uk/2/hi/uk_news/661139.stm).

10 Factors that are taken into consideration in contempt citations include: how close in time the reporting is to the actual trial; whether the report explicitly links the accused to the crime or reveals a past criminal record or the fact the accused is known to the police; whether the report reveals a confession or other evidence not presented to the jury; whether it expresses opinions that could influence the outcome or otherwise "scandalize" the courts (CJC, 2007, 4–5).

11 This was clear in the case of Karla Homolka, who was charged in 1993 with the sexual slaying of two teenage girls in Ontario. While the court in Canada issued a publication ban excluding all media from the courtroom and prohibited pre-trial publicity, the U.S. media were able to publicize details of the case that were eventually heard in Canada (Evans, 1995; Huffman, 2002).

12 *R. v. The National Post*, 2008 ONCA 139, at 75.

13 *R. v. The National Post*, 2010 SCC 16.

14 120 D.L.R. (4th) 12 (S.C.C.) [*Dagenais*].

15 Ibid., 839.

16 Some statutory bans (some mandatory, others not) in criminal cases found in the Criminal Code include: ban on publication of the name or any information that could disclose the identity of an alleged victim of or witness to sex-related crimes (s. 486.4); ban on identifying "justice system participant" (s. 486.5); ban on the contents of an accused person's bail hearing (s. 517); ban on the evidence taken at a preliminary hearing (s. 539(1)); ban on any "admission or confession" presented by the prosecution at a preliminary hearing (s. 542(2)); ban on publishing information regarding any portion of the trial where the jury is not present before the jury retires to consider its verdict (s. 648(1)); ban on the publication of the contents of an application to introduce a complainant's sexual history in sexual-assault cases (s. 276.3(1)); ban on publication of the contents of an application to admit the private records of a complainant or witness (s. 278.9(1)); restrictions on interviewing and identifying jurors (ss. 649, 631(3.1), 631(6)); exclusion orders (ss. 486(1), 486(2), 537(1)(h)); disposition hearings for those declared not criminally responsible (ss. 672.5(6), 672.51(11)); bans on certain aspects of search warrants and related documents (ss. 487.2(1), 487.3(1), 487.3(4)); prohibition against identifying accused, tried, sentenced young persons, and youth witnesses and victims in youth criminal cases (Youth Criminal Justice Act, ss. 1 10(1), 111(1) – with exceptions in cases where an adult sentence is received or the youth requests that the ban be lifted) (CJC, 2007, 16–24).

17 See K. Campbell and M. Denov (2004).

18 http://www.cbc.ca/archives/entry/joyce-milgaard-snubbed-by-kim-campbell.

19 http://www.cbc.ca/news2/background/milgaard/.

20 http://www.publications.gov.sk.ca/freelaw/Publications_Centre/Justice/Milgaard/Milgaard.pdf.

21 See also J. Milgaard and Edwards (2000).

22 This story was in response to the suicide of a disgraced former Miami city commissioner who shot himself in the lobby of the offices of the *Miami Herald*.

23 The following discussion of independent lobby groups is in no way exhaustive; there may be other movements in existence that are not discussed here.

24 http://www.centurionministries.org/.

25 http://www.deathpenaltyinfo.org/innocence-and-death-penalty.

26 As noted earlier, one particularly problematic case was that of Cameron Todd Willingham, executed in Texas in 2004 for the arson murder of his three children. There are now serious questions as to the validity of the forensic science conclusions as to how the fire started that led to his conviction (Grann, 2009). See also http://www.newyorker.com/reporting/2009/09/07/090907fa_fact_grann?currentPage=2. Furthermore, Willingham's family has started a campaign to seek a posthumous pardon (https://prisonreformmovement.wordpress.com/2012/10/25/todd-willinghams-family-seeks-posthumous-pardon/).

27 http://www.deathpenaltyinfo.org/innocence-and-crisis-american-death-penalty.

28 The Justice for Guy Paul Morin Committee was created in 1992 and was comprised of a small group of concerned volunteers (Win Wahrer, Geeta Hobson, and Stephen Seymore) who believed in Morin's innocence. In 1993, once Morin was released on bail pending his appeal, the committee reconstituted itself with some new members and became AIDWYC.

29 http://www.aidwyc.org/cases/historical/.

30 As discussed in chapter 13, the CCRC functions as an independent lobby group, separate from the Ministry of Justice, to investigate possible cases of miscarriages of justice in England, Wales, and Northern Ireland; it assesses both convictions and sentences (http://www.ccrc.gov.uk/). There is also a Scottish CCRC (sccrc.org.uk).

31 One example of a successful justice campaign came about following the death of Stephen Lawrence in the United Kingdom in 1993. The incident was widely viewed as a racially motivated killing, and the mismanagement of the investigation by the police prompted Lawrence's family and supporters to lobby the government to the extent that in 1999 an inquiry (Macpherson Inquiry) was called. This inquiry resulted in sweeping recommendations regarding police investigations policy, police recruitment and training, police-community relationships, and police treatment of victims (Savage et al., 2007, 85).

32 http://www.mojoscotland.com/.

33 Some would argue that a country that has a Criminal Case Review Commission (CCRC) has no need for Innocence Projects, since the CCRC's mandate is to "investigate possible miscarriages of justice" and make decisions around referrals to the Court of Appeal. Yet several commentators have stressed that, despite the operation of the CCRC, Innocence Projects are still necessary to overturn wrongful convictions in the United Kingdom (McCartney, 2006b; Naughton, 2006; Roberts and Weathered, 2009, 59; for an opposing view see Quirk, 2007). Indeed, Naughton (2006) claims that "the CCRC has recently conceded that it is often unable to assist innocent victims of wrongful conviction and recognizes the contribution that could be made by Innocence Projects in the UK."

34 Most of the information contained in this table came from: http://www.law.wisc. edu/fjr/innocence/other_ips.htm, http://www.truthinjustice.org/ipcontacts.htm, and http://forejustice.org/wc/wrongful_conviction_websites.htm. The list is clearly not exhaustive and includes only those Innocence Projects affiliated with a university; many other organizations function in a number of jurisdictions to assist in exonerating the innocent and are affiliated with law firms and individual lawyers.

35 In the United Kingdom, INUK (Innocence Network UK) acted as a clearinghouse for its university members; it provided supports, contacts, training, and actual cases to its member Innocence Projects from 2004 to 2015. Up to thirty universities had innocence projects at one point; however, the system is now described as being in "disarray" as a result of infighting and many projects have disbanded. Altogether, the UK innocence projects have made twenty-five applications to the CCRC from six universities, with one successful appeal. See https://www.theguardian.com/law/2016/apr/27/university-innocence-projects-where-are-they-now.

36 http://www.innocenceproject.org.

37 http://www.osgoode.yorku.ca/programs/jd-program/clinics-intensives/innocence-project/.

38 The Center on Wrongful Convictions at Northwestern University School of Law is an exception to this, but Medwed (2003: 1106n.30) notes that it is still principally concerned with claims of actual innocence rather than wrongful convictions based on legal technicalities.

39 One example is the Kentucky Innocence Project, which consists of two law schools and one social-work graduate program operating in conjunction with the state's Department of Public Advocacy (Medwed 2003, 1100n.9).

40 McCartney (2006b) gives a concise summary of the typical operational process of innocence projects: "Once a case is accepted after preliminary screening, participants read trial transcripts and other documentation. Cases are then re-investigated by students, with new evidence or new arguments pursued through the courts by the students or staff, or taken up by legal professionals. Most often, it takes several years before an exoneration may be secured, but experience demonstrates that once the first exoneration is secured, it does not take so long for others to follow. Exonerations, while clearly welcome and indicative of an effective project as well as incredible motivation for staff and students (and fund-raisers), are not an evaluative tool for innocence projects. 'Success' is measured rather, in educational terms, with student experiences and learning outcomes being the true evaluative mechanism."

41 http://www.genexdiagnostics.com/service/dna-forensic-test. In Canada there are a number of private laboratories that do DNA forensic testing (with costs ranging from $100–$400 for a single sample); however, laboratories that are accredited through the Standards Council of Canada are more credible.

42 The same is true in Australia, where innocence projects have increased the opportunity for DNA testing as well as improved access to the appellate courts (Weathered 2003, 78).

43 Findley stresses fact finding and development as the key aspect of litigation practice taught by innocence projects; by requiring law students to examine case evidence and carry out the investigation themselves, innocence projects help them recognize the relationship between facts and law (Findley 2006, 243).

44 Journalism-based innocence projects include the Medill Justice Project (formerly the Medill Innocence project) at Northwestern University and the Innocence Institute of Western Pennsylvania at Point Part University (Buck 2005, 1). The Medill Innocence Project has helped exonerate eleven people – including five capital cases – since 1992 (Warden 2002, 845). The no-representation model used in such projects is also occasionally adopted by innocence projects based in law schools, for example, the Innocence Project at the Thomas M. Cooley Law School (Medwed 2003, 1100n.9).

45 http://www.chicagomag.com/Chicago-Magazine/February-2010/Anita-Alvarez-turns-up-the-heat-in-her-battle-with-Northwesterns-David-Protess-and-his-Medill-Innocence-Project/index.php?cparticle=4&siarticle=3#artanc.

46 http://articles.chicagotribune.com/2009-10-19/news/0910180592_1_wrongful-conviction-prosecutors-students-at-northwestern-university. See also S. Smith (2010).

47 *Reporter's Privilege* Chapter 735 Illinois Compiled Statutes Act 5 Article VIII Part 9 Sections 901–909 (735 ILCS 5/8-901 to -909).

48 In September 2011 Cook County Criminal Court Judge Diane Cannon found that journalism student reporting is protected under Illinois law but ruled that the students were acting as private investigators and not student journalists in the McKinney case (Davis, 2012). http://www.chicagoreader.com/Bleader/archives/2013/08/28/anthony-mckinney-dies-in-prison.

Chapter 13

1 For a detailed historical account of the Irish Troubles, see Hennessey (2005), Kennedy-Pipe (1997), and Ó Dochartaigh (2005).

2 They were Patrick Hill, Gerry Hunter, Richard McIlkenny, Billy Power, Johnny Walker, and Hughie Callaghan.

3 There were several other high-profile miscarriages of justice that occurred in England during the 1970s and 1980s which were later overturned, including the cases of Judith Ward (1974), the Guildford 4 (1975), the Maguire 7 (1976), and Stefan Kiszko (1976).

4 Equivalent to the Ministry of Justice (Home Office) and the minister of justice (home secretary) in Canada.

5 Nobles and Schiff have argued that, while the CCRC emerged partly in response to a number of high-profile miscarriages of justice that occurred in the 1970s and 1980s, they believe that alleged "loss of public confidence" in the wake of these cases was generated by and existed within the media (2001, 295). In their opinion, the initial success of the CCRC was not as a result of its effectiveness in addressing (or not) miscarriages of justice, but rather in the very fact of its inception. For them, within the context of a media-created crisis, the existence of the CCRC could be framed as the government actually doing something before it had carried out a single investigation (Nobles and Schiff, 2001).

6 Criminal Appeal Act, 1995, c. 35 § 8.

7 For this reason, INUK (Innocence Network UK) was established, comprised of Innocence Projects affiliated with different law schools throughout the United Kingdom, lobby groups such as MOJO (Miscarriages of Justice Organization), and committed solicitors. It functioned from 2004 to 2015 and served to educate the public about the existence of wrongful convictions and acted as a clearing house for referring alleged cases of wrongful convictions to its various members.

8 In fact, the English CCRC has posthumously exonerated a number of individuals, including Derek Bentley, Mahmoud Mattan, and George Kelly.

9 This time frame is considerably shorter than the wait for conviction review by the Criminal Conviction Review Group (CCRG) in Canada, as discussed in chapter 9, and a much larger number of cases are examined in a year by the CCRC, perhaps owing in part to a larger number of investigators and legally trained professionals working for the commission. These numbers are also indicative of the United Kngdom's much larger population relative to Canada's.

10 Figures are from https://ccrc.gov.uk/case-statistics/.

11 According to Bob Woffinden (journalist with the *Guardian*), the CCRC should have ultimately contained the seeds of its own destruction. Besides addressing individual cases of miscarriage of justice, the commission could have developed protocols for avoiding similar mistakes in the future and thus put itself out of business (Innocence Network United Kingdom Symposium, University of Bristol, England, 31 March 2007). Some of these criticisms were previously raised in Walker and Campbell (2010).

12 "Real possibility" is not defined in the act but has been taken to mean "more than an outside chance or a bare possibility, but which may be less than a probability or a likelihood or a racing certainty" (from *R. v. CCRC, Ex Parte Pearson*, [1999] 3 All E.R. 498 at 505, *per* Lord Bingham C.J., as found in James et al., 2000, 145).

13 Or "statutory straightjacket" as Naughton refers to it (2010, 4).

14 While the manner in which commissioners are appointed is not entirely apolitical, nor could it ever be, judicial appointments occur in a similar fashion and the impartiality of judges is rarely questioned.

15 In its defence, when determining an application that is founded on new evidence, the CCRC must, in fact, consider how the Court of Appeal is likely to view that evidence (Leigh, 2000, 367).

16 Roberts and Weathered (2009, 53) underscore the importance of differentiating lay perceptions from "legal" perceptions of the meaning of a quashed conviction. Borrowing from Nobles and Schiff's (2000) framework of autopoietic systems theory, they note how the media and political actors view a quashed conviction in lay terms as a declaration of innocence, when in fact courts of appeal reject notions of innocence and examine convictions for their "safety," where innocence plays no role.

17 *Scottish Criminal Cases Review Commission v. HM Advocate*, 2001 JC 36, 40; 2001 SLT 905, 908–9, at para. 9, as referenced in Leverick et al. (2010).

18 The commission's most famous referral was said to be its 2007 decision to refer Abdelbaset Ali al-Megrahi's conviction for the Lockerbie terrorist bombing back to the Court of Appeal, based on new evidence of eyewitness-identification frailties (Roach, 2010, 347). Ultimately al-Megrahi was released on compassionate grounds and returned to Libya in August 2009. While he died in 2012, his family has recently attempted to clear his name through a renewed application to the SCCRC (https:// www.theguardian.com/world/2017/apr/23/abdelbaset-al-megrahis-family-to-appeal-lockerbie-bombing-conviction-libyan).

19 http://www.sccrc.org.uk/case-statistics.

20 These include when an appeal was prevented as a result of threats to the applicant or his/her family; when only the commission can uncover the new evidence needed; and when previous attempts to seek legal advice from solicitors have been unsuccessful (http://www.sccrc.org.uk).

21 In its early days, the SCCRC received about 100 cases per year, of which it referred about 8 per cent, which is roughly double the rate of the English CCRC (Nobles and Schiff, 2010, 164n.7.)

22 A precognition involves a face-to-face meeting with a witness who may be called to give evidence at trial or proceedings, and it is done to evaluate the evidence to be given under oath at trial (http://www.scotland.police.uk/about-us/finance/service-fees-and-charges/146967/).

23 If successful, the case is then referred to another court for review; the previous system allowed the same court to retry its own cases (NCCRC, 2004). See also Stridbeck and Magnussen (2012).

24 http://www.gjenopptakelse.no/fileadmin/download/Aarsrapport_2015_eng.pdf.

25 Although what exactly "coercive measures" constitute is not articulated.

26 http://www.gjenopptakelse.no/fileadmin/download/Aarsrapport_2015_eng.pdf.

27 For a more detailed discussion of the risks of wrongful conviction in the inquisitorial system, see M. Killias, G. Gilliéron, and N. Dongois (2007).

28 They include the Royal Commission on the Donald Marshall, Jr Prosecution (1989a, 1989b), the Commission on Proceedings involving Guy Paul Morin (1998), the Inquiry regarding Thomas Sophonow (2001), the Lamer Commission of Inquiry pertaining to the Cases of: Ronald Dalton, Gregory Parsons, Randy Druken (2006), the Commission of Inquiry into Certain Aspects of the Trial and Conviction of James Driskell (2007),

and the Commission of Inquiry into the Wrongful Conviction of David Milgaard (2008), as well as the Goudge Commission of Inquiry that investigated the errors in paediatric forensic pathology made by Dr Charles Smith which resulted in numerous wrongful convictions (Goudge, 2008).

29 Most executions occur in the U.S. south; the state with the greatest number of prisoners on death row is California (743), followed by Florida (399) and Texas (263). While New Mexico no longer has the death penalty, there are currently two prisoners on death row in that state; some prisoners have also been sentenced to death in more than one state (Death Penalty Information Center, Facts about the Death Penalty, 9 Oct. 2012, https://deathpenaltyinfo.org/documents/FactSheet.pdf).

30 In 2016 Georgia had the greatest number of executions (nine), followed by Texas (seven) and Alabma (two); Florida and Missouri had one execution each. http://www.deathpenaltyinfo.org/execution-list-2016.

31 An Oklahoma law would make nitrogen asphyxiation the state's execution method if lethal injection is ruled unconstitutional or the necessary drugs are no longer available. Tennessee allows for the use of the electric chair. Utah allows the firing squad to be used if the state cannot obtain lethal injection drugs thirty days before an execution. See http://www.deathpenaltyinfo.org/state-lethal-injection.

32 543 U.S. 551 (2005).

33 536 U.S. 304 (2002).

34 Until 2009, most states used a three-drug combination for lethal injections: an anesthetic (usually sodium thiopental, until pentobarbital was introduced at the end of 2010), pancuronium bromide (a paralytic agent, also called Pavulon), and potassium chloride (stops the heart and causes death). Because of drug shortages, states have adopted new lethal-injection methods, using varying combinations of different drugs. See http://www.deathpenaltyinfo.org/state-lethal-injection.

35 No. 07–5439, April 2008.

36 *Glossip et al. v. Gross et al.* (2015) No. 14-7955 [*Glossip v. Gross*].

37 For example: Clayton Lockett (Oklahoma), Charles Warner (Oklahoma), Joseph Wood (Arizona), Dennis McGuire (Ohio).

38 All death sentences imposed between the years 1967 and 1976 were commuted to life imprisonment and in 1976 a legislative amendment to the Criminal Code abolished the death penalty for all but military offences, replacing it with mandatory life sentences for murder with parole eligibility at twenty-five years. All references to the death penalty were finally removed from the National Defence Act in 1998.

39 (2001) 1 S.C.R. 283. Under the Extradition Act, section 44(2), Canada may choose to refuse a request to extradite a prisoner to another country if the offence in question is punishable by death under the laws of that country. In the past, what this has traditionally meant is that extraditions from Canada to the United States or other countries would not take place without assurances that the death penalty would not be sought or imposed. In 2001 the Supreme Court case of *U.S. v. Burns and Rafay* supported this policy. More recently, in 2007, the then Conservative government clarified its position on extradition when it refused a request from U.S. authorities to hand over Ronald Allen Smith, a Canadian from Alberta, who had been sentenced to death for the shooting at point-blank range of two men in Montana in 1982. While the previous Liberal government in 1997 had arranged clemency for Smith and had planned on commuting his sentence to life, to be

served in Canada, the Harper government quashed this offer in November 2007. It reiterated that government's position that it would no longer seek clemency, extradition, or commute sentences for Canadians facing capital punishment in other "democratic" countries where the prisoner had been convicted in a fair process, contrary to long-standing historical tradition. Smith challenged this lack of support in federal court (*Smith v. Canada* [*Attorney General*]), and the Court determined that the government lacked a coherent policy in seeking clemency in death-penalty cases and it needed to apply the former policy to Smith's case. While clemency guidelines then existed (https://www.canada.ca/en/parole-board/services/clemency.html?_ga=2.102298241.1897260922.1499969614-897108078.1499969614), the Conservative government's policy was to assess each request "on a case-by-case basis, using criteria based on Canadian values and international standards" (41st Parliament, 1st Session, Hansard, No. 146, 17 Sept. 2012). Subsequently, Smith remained on death row, but Stéphane Dion, then foreign affairs minister of a new Liberal government, stated: "Canada opposes the death penalty and will ask for clemency in each and every case, no exceptions." See http://www.huffingtonpost.ca/2016/02/16/hope-springs-eternal-ronald-smith-lawyer-encouraged-by-stephane-dion-s-comments_n_9246804.html; http://www.ctvnews.ca/victim-s-son-wants-no-mercy-for-canadian-on-death-row-1.804175; "Canadian on Death Row Suing Tory Government, *Globe and Mail*, 28 Nov. 2007, A7; M. Edward and L. Waldman, "Death and Diplomacy: Ottawa's Disappointing Track Record," *Globe and Mail*, 18 Nov. 2007; Editorial, "Ottawa Turns Away," *Globe and Mail*, 3 Nov. 2007, A26; B. Graveland, "Ronald Smith on Death Row as Montana Execution Protocol Trial Scheduled," *Canadian Press*, 20 Oct. 2012. The Smith case is still pending.

40 Section 7 states: "Everyone has the right to life, liberty and security of the person and the right not to be deprived thereof except in accordance with the principles of fundamental justice."

41 The Justice for All Act of 2004 (H.R. 5107, Public Law No: 108–405).

42 Pub. L. No. 108–405 (codified at 18 U.S.C. § 3771 (2004)). The Justice for All Act also includes the Debbie Smith Act, which provides grants to local and state governments so that DNA samples from sexual-assault cases (and others without an identified suspect) can be analysed in a timely manner.

43 Act of 30 Oct. 2004, Pub. L. No. 108–405, § 301; 118 Stat. 2260 (2004).

44 Act of 30 Oct. 2004, Pub. L. No. 108–405, 18 U.S.C.S. § 3600–3600A (2004).

45 129 S. Ct. 2308 (2009) [*Osborne*].

46 Act of 30 Oct. 2004, Pub. L. No. 108–405; 118 Stat. 2260 (2004).

47 Innocence Project, North Carolina Actual Innocence Commission, Mission Statement, Objectives and Procedures, https://assets.documentcloud.org/documents/2179899/aic-mission-statement.pdf.

48 http://www.innocencecommission-nc.gov/stats.html, 4 March 2016. What is particularly interesting about this commission and the CCRC and the SCCRC is that all three reject the vast majority of applications that they receive (Roach, 2010, 96).

49 http://www.innocencecommission-nc.gov/cases.html.

50 *State v. Reeves*, File No. 99 CRS 65056.

51 *State v. Taylor*, 91 CRS 71728.

52 *State v. Kagonyera and Wilcoxson*, File Nos. 00CRS 65086; 00 CRS 65088.

53 *State v. Womble*, File No. 75 CRS 06128.

54 *State v. McCollum/Brown*, 91 CRS 40727, 92 CRS 241–2.

55 *State v. Grimes*, 87 CRS 13541/42/44.

56 *State v. Sledge* 78 CRS 2415–2416.

57 *State v. McInnis*, File No. 88-CRS-1422.

58 *State v. McNeil*, 00 CRS 57073–4.

59 *State v. Isbell, Mills, Williams*, 00 CRS 65084, 01 CRS 06334, 35.

60 *State v. Knolly Brown*, 08 CRS 50309.

61 https://www.law.umich.edu/special/exoneration/Pages/casedetail. aspx?caseid=5009.

62 http://www.innocencecommission-nc.gov/Forms/pdf/robert-bragg/nciic-hearing-transcript-state-v-robert-bragg.pdf.

63 California Commission on the Fair Administration of Justice (2008).

64 https://www.innocenceproject.org/criminal-justice-reform-commissions-case-studies/.

65 Report of the Advisory Commission on Wrongful Convictions, February 2009, http://www.jud.ct.gov/committees/wrongfulconviction/.

66 https://www.innocenceproject.org/criminal-justice-reform-commissions-case-studies/.

67 "The Oklahoma Justice Commission: A Commission Dedicated to the Enhancing the Reliability and Accuracy of Convictions," http://www.okbar.org/Portals/15/PDF/2013/Commission_Final_Report.pdf.

68 *Final Report of the New York State Bar Association's Task Force on Wrongful Convictions*, 4 April 2009, https://www.nysba.org/wcreport.

69 https://www.innocenceproject.org/criminal-justice-reform-commissions-case-studies/.

70 Steven Avery was the subject of a Netflix documentary film in 2016 that shed light on how this wrongful conviction occurred.

71 Assembly Bill 648, 2005 Wisconsin Act 60.

72 https://www.innocenceproject.org/criminal-justice-reform-commissions-case-studies/.

73 https://www.prisonlegalnews.org/media/publications/innocence%20commission%20of%20va%2C%20wrongful%20convictions%20report%2C%202005.pdf.

74 *Report of the Advisory Committee on Wrongful Convictions, Advisory Committee on Wrongful Convictions*, September 2011, https://www.prisonlegalnews.org/media/publications/innocence%20commission%20of%20va%2C%20wrongful%20convictions%20report%2C%202005.pdf.

75 http://www.txcourts.gov/cca/texas-criminal-justice-integrity-unit/.

76 *Timothy Cole Advisory Panel on Wrongful Convictions, Report to the Texas Task Force on Indigent Defense*, August 2010, http://www.txcourts.gov/tidc/pdf/FINALTCAPreport.pdf.

77 On Illinois' abolition of the death penalty, see http://www.npr.org/2011/03/09/134394946/illinois-abolishes-death-penalty.

78 While some states have grappled with the death penalty since its reinstatement by the Supreme Court in 1976, the state of Kansas stands out for having abolished and reinstated it three times. In 2010 the Kansas state government was one vote short of replacing the death penalty with life without parole for aggravated murder (http://www.deathpenaltyinfo.org/kansas-1).

Chapter 14

1 The six inquiries discussed in chapter 10 examined the cases of Donald Marshall, Jr, Guy Paul Morin, Thomas Sophonow, Greg Parsons, Ronald Dalton, Randy Druken, James Driskell, and David Milgaard.

2 Glenn Ford was released from Angola State Prison in Louisiana in March 2014 after serving thirty years for a crime he did not commit and was given a $20 debit card, a raise from the pre-2011 $10 prisoners normally receive (A. Cohen, 2014). Sadly, Ford died over a year later without having received any state compensation.

3 *R (Adams) v Secretary of State for Justice* [2011] UKSC 18, para 9.

4 I would like to thank Fernanda Prates for the development of this idea.

5 An Act to Amend the Criminal Code, S.C. 2011, c. 16.

6 This allows for earlier resolution and for the judge to exercise the powers that a trial judge has before the presentation of the evidence on the merits.

7 This allows for a preliminary issue pertaining to more than one accused or count to be adjudicated by one judge only, prior to the severance. The intention behind delaying the enforcement of a severance order is to ensure consistent decisions, along with preventing unnecessary duplication.

8 This in response to the increased amount of time required to hear mega-trials, as well as a recognition that jurors must feel safe and free from intimidation when serving on a jury.

9 *Auclair c. R.*, 2011 QCCS 2661.

10 Yves Boisvert, "Quebec vs. the Hells Angels: A Case of Justice Failing to Deliver," *Globe and Mail*, 16 Oct. 2015, http://www.theglobeandmail.com/opinion/quebec-vs-the-hells-angels-a-case-of-justice-failing-to-deliver/article26832799/.

11 P. Cherry, "Internal Investigation Launched into Operation SharQc Trial," *Gazette*, 16 Oct. 2015, http://montrealgazette.com/news/local-news/ruling-that-halted-operation-sharqc-trial-wont-be-appealed.

12 These are song lyrics written by the musical band the Tragically Hip in reference to David Milgaard's wrongful conviction.

Appendix A

1 There may be some names on this list that not all would agree constitute wrongful convictions. Clearly, the list is not exhaustive and a decision was made to include cases where an individual was convicted of a crime and the case was later overturned or cleared in some manner by the courts. It is restricted to Canadian cases and information on some cases is more complete than on others. All of the information was taken from online media sources, case-law materials, and the literature. The format for the appendix follows the example of Dioso-Villa (2015) in her repository of wrongful convictions in Australia.

2 Jennifer Pritchett, "Beaulieu Free at Last," *Northern New Service*, 12 May 1997, http://www.nnsl.com/frames/newspapers/1997-05/may12_97out.html.

3 Department of Justice (2005a), "Applications for Ministerial Review – Miscarriages of Justice" Annual Report 2005, at 19.

4 Injusticebusters, "Steven Richard Kaminski," http://injusticebusters.org/2003/Kaminski_Steven.htm; Forejustice, "Wrongly Convicted Database Record: Steven Kaminski," http://forejustice.org/db/Kaminski--Steven-R.-.html.

5 "Canadian Wrongful Convictions Timeline," AIDWYC, https://www.aidwyc.org/cases/wrongful-convictions-timeline/.

6 "RCMP Officer Acquitted," *Windspeaker*, 10, no. 16 (1992), http://www.ammsa.com/publications/windspeaker/rcmp-officer-acquitted.

7 http://www.cbc.ca/news/canada/calgary/connie-oakes-murder-charge-stayed-speaks-ceo-1.3558965.

8 Katz, *Justice Miscarried*.

9 http://publications.gc.ca/collections/Collection/J1-3-2005E.pdf.

10 http://www.cbc.ca/news/canada/british-columbia/ivan-henry-award-wrongful-imprisonment-1.3622588.

11 https://www.canlii.org/en/bc/bcca/doc/1995/1995canlii2079/1995canlii2079.html?autocompleteStr=Huffman&autocompletePos=1.

12 https://www.canlii.org/en/bc/bcca/doc/2003/2003bcca353/2003bcca353.html?autocompleteStr=R.%20v.%20Robinson&autocompletePos=1.

13 "Pardoned Man Refuses Compensation Offer," *Ottawa Citizen*, 26 Oct. 1984; "Canadian Wrongful Convictions Timeline," AIDWYC, https://www.aidwyc.org/cases/wrongful-convictions-timeline/.

14 https://www.aidwyc.org/cases/historical/james-driskell/.

15 "High Court Tosses out Dangerous Driving Conviction," *Winnipeg Free Press*, 21 Aug. 2007, http://www.winnipegfreepress.com/historic/32375979.html.

16 Katz, *Justice Miscarried*; Justice Peter Cory, "Commission of Inquiry regarding Thomas Sophonow" (Winnipeg, Manitoba: Government of Manitoba 2001).

17 "Kyle Unger Files $14.5M Wrongful-Conviction Lawsuit," CBC News Manitoba, 21 Sept. 2001, http://www.cbc.ca/news/canada/manitoba/story/2011/09/21/kyle-unger-wrongful-conviction-lawsuit.html; Farid Muttalib, "Justice Deferred: Why You Don't Want to be Wrongfully Convicted in Canada," *McGill Daily*, 6 Oct. 2011, http://www.mcgilldaily.com/2011/10/justice-deferred/; InjusticeBusters, "Kyle Unger," http://injusticebusters.org/04/Unger_Kyle.shtml.

18 P. Lee, "New Brunswick Man Ready to 'Start Life Over' after Crown's Case Collapses," *Ottawa* Citizen, 2 June 2001, http://injusticebusters.org/index.htm/Michaud.htm.

19 https://www.aidwyc.org/cases/historical/erin-walsh/.

20 http://www.cbc.ca/news/canada/newfoundland-labrador/compensation-doesn-t-buy-back-lost-years-dalton-1.651841.

21 http://www.cbc.ca/news/canada/newfoundland-labrador/n-l-man-awarded-2-million-for-wrongful-conviction-1.580738.

22 http://www.cbc.ca/news/canada/newfoundland-labrador/nelson-hart-accused-of-killing-twin-daughters-quietly-released-from-custody-1.2727564.

23 https://www.aidwyc.org/cases/historical/gregory-parsons/#_ftn15.

24 http://www.fact.on.ca/news/news0112/oc011219.htm.

25 http://www.nnsl.com/frames/newspapers/2001-06/jun27_01crt.html.

26 http://www.cbc.ca/news/canada/nova-scotia/gerald-barton-wrongly-convicted-of-rape-loses-compensation-bid-1.3032294.

27 https://www.aidwyc.org/cases/historical/clayton-johnson/; http://novascotia.ca/news/release/?id=20040618007.

28 Royal Commission on the Donald Marshall, Jr Prosecution (1989a), at 1; InjusticeBusters, "Donald Marshall Jr.: One of the Most Pivotal People in N.S. History," http://injusticebusters.org/index.htm/Donald_Marshall.htm.

29 "No Cash for Wrongfully Convicted Men: Ontario," CBC News Toronto, 13 Jan. 2010, http://www.cbc.ca/news/canada/toronto/story/2010/01/13/baltovich-compensation.html; https://www.aidwyc.org/cases/historical/robert-baltovich/.

30 "Richard Brant: Father Vindicated," *AIDWYC Quarterly*, 1 (2011); "Conviction Quashed in Case Involving Disgraced Pathologist Charles Smith," *Toronto Star*, 12 July 2013, http://www.thestar.com/news/ontario/2011/05/04/conviction_quashed_in_case_involving_disgraced_pathologist_charles_smith.html. Other questionable cases associated with Dr Charles Smith include those of: Oneil Blackett, William and Mary Colville, "Jane Doe," Lianne Gagnon, Maureen Laidley, Louise Reynolds, Maria Shepherd, and Marco and Anisa Trotta: "In Depth: 14 Cases Tainted by Charles Smith's Evidence," http://www.theglobeandmail.com/news/national/14-cases-tainted-by-charles-smiths-evidence/article562711/?page=all.

31 "Ontario's Top Court Set to Examine 26-Year-Old Toronto Homicide Case," http://www.thestar.com/news/crime/2011/03/14/ontarios_top_court_set_to_examine_26yearold_toronto_homicide_case.html; Dan Robson, "Conviction in 1985 Toronto Shooting Appealed for Second Time," *Toronto Star*, 17 March 2011, http://www.thestar.com/news/crime/2011/03/17/conviction_in_1985_toronto_shooting_appealed_for_second_time.html; "Court Dismisses Appeal from Man Convicted of Murder," CTV News Toronto, 14 April 2011, http://toronto.ctvnews.ca/court-dismisses-appeal-from-man-convicted-of-murder-1.631535.

32 "Wrongfully Convicted Murder Suspect Freed," CBC News Ottawa, 31 Oct. 2005, http://www.cbc.ca/news/canada/ottawa/story/2005/10/31/ot-dimitrov20051031.html.

33 http://forejustice.org/db/Folland--Gordon-.html.

34 InjusticeBusters, "Peter Frumusa," http://injusticebusters.org/04/Frumusa_Peter.htm.

35 Maidment MaDonna, *When Justice Is a Game: Unravelling Wrongful Conviction in Canada* (Black Point, NS: Fernwood, 2009); "Wrongly Convicted Man Sues Police, Lawyer," CBC News Toronto, 7 July 2010, http://www.cbc.ca/news/canada/toronto/story/2010/07/07/anthony-hanemaayer-suit-assault-bernardo.html; "No Cash for Wrongfully Convicted Men: Ontario," CBC News Toronto, 13 Jan. 2010, http://www.cbc.ca/news/canada/toronto/story/2010/01/13/baltovich-compensation.html.

36 Leighton Hay, Wrongfully Convicted of Murder in 2002, Walks Free," CBC News, 28 Nov. 2014, http://www.cbc.ca/news/canada/toronto/leighton-hay-wrongfully-convicted-of-murder-in-2002-walks-free-1.2853578.

37 Ontario Justice Education Network, "Landmark Case: Negligent Investigation, Malicious Prosecution, and Racial Profiling: *Hill v Hamilton-Wentworth Police*" (2009), Case Summary Prepared for the Ontario Justice Education Network. http://ojen.ca/en/resource/landmark-case-negligent-investigation-malicious-prosecution-and-racial-profiling-hill-v-hamilton-wentworth-police.

38 http://injusticebusters.org/index.htm/KARTHIRESU.htm.

39 "Man Acquitted in Baby Son's Death," *Globe and Mail*, 20 Jan. 2011, http://www.theglobeandmail.com/news/national/man-acquitted-in-baby-sons-death/article576987/; "Dinesh Kumar," AIDWYC Exonerations: Individual Cases, https://www.aidwyc.org/cases/historical/dinesh-kumar/.

40 Kirk Makin, "Sex-Assault Case Thrown out after Evidence Suppressed: Judge Assails Prosecutors and Police," *Globe and Mail*, 9 Feb. 1999, https://www.fact.on.ca/newpaper/gm990209.htm.

41 http://forejustice.org/db/Mallory-Richard-.html; "Charges Stayed in Epic Trial," *Ottawa Citizen*, 18 Jan. 2007, https://www.pressreader.com/canada/ottawa-citizen/20070113/282209416376970.

42 Win Wahrer, "Tammy Marquardt: Rest in Peace, Son," *AIDWYC Quarterly*, 1 (2011); "Conviction Quashed in Case Involving Disgraced Pathologist Charles Smith," *Toronto Star*, 12 July 2013, http://www.thestar.com/news/ontario/2011/05/04/conviction_quashed_in_case_involving_disgraced_pathologist_charles_smith.html; Kirk Makin, "Tammy Marquardt Faces Possible New Trial after Murder Conviction Overturned," *Globe and Mail*, 31 Jan. 2011, http://www.theglobeandmail.com/news/toronto/tammy-marquardt-faces-possible-new-trial-after-murder-conviction-overturned/article565782/; Allison Jones, "Murder Charge Withdrawn against Mother Who Spent 14 Years in Prison," *Globe and Mail*, 7 June 2011, http://www.theglobeandmail.com/news/national/murder-charge-withdrawn-against-mother-who-spent-14-years-in-prison/article1322378/.

43 InjusticeBusters, "Chris McCullough," http://injusticebusters.org/index.htm/chrismccullough.htm.

44 InjusticeBusters, "Michael McTaggart's Life," http://injusticebusters.org/index.htm/Subway_Elvis.htm; "Canadian Wrongful Convictions Timeline."

45 https://www.canlii.org/en/on/onca/doc/1996/1996canlii1268/1996canlii1268.html?autocompleteStr=Miapono&autocompletePos=1.

46 https://www.aidwyc.org/cases/historical/guy-paul-morin/.

47 https://www.aidwyc.org/cases/historical/william-mullins-johnson/.

48 http://www.theglobeandmail.com/news/national/canadas-prisoner-of-conscience/article762995/.

49 Katz, *Justice Miscarried.*

50 https://www.aidwyc.org/cases/historical/romeo-phillion/.

51 https://www.aidwyc.org/cases/historical/john-salmon/.

52 http://www.cbc.ca/news/canada/toronto/maria-shepherd-conviction-1.3468706.

53 https://www.aidwyc.org/cases/historical/sherry-sherrett-robinson/.

54 Katz, *Justice Miscarried*; InjusticeBusters, "Gary Staples," http://injusticebusters.org/index.htm/Staples.htm.

55 http://cnews.canoe.com/CNEWS/Canada/2007/01/12/3321426-sun.html; "Men Jailed 17 Years in Murder Trial Demand Public Inquiry," http://www.cbc.ca/news/canada/ottawa/story/2007/03/15/cumberland.html; http://netk.net.au/Canada/Trudel.asp.

56 "Steven Truscott: The Search for Justice," CBC News in Depth, 7 July 2008, http://www.cbc.ca/news2/background/truscott/; https://www.aidwyc.org/cases/historical/steven-truscott/.

57 Alyshah Hasham, "Brenda Waudby Officially Innocent of Child Abuse," *Toronto Star*, 27 July 2012, http://www.thestar.com/news/gta/2012/06/27/brenda_waudby_officially_innocent_of_child_abuse.html; Sarah Deeth "Judge Overturns Waudby's 1999 Child Abuse Conviction," *Peterborough Examiner*, 27 June 2012, http://www.thepeterboroughexaminer.com/2012/06/27/crown-apologies-to-brenda-waudby.

58 Kyle Rea "Webber Free after Being Wrongfully Accused," *St-Thomas Times Journal*, 14 Jan. 2010, http://www.stthomastimesjournal.com/2010/01/14/webber-free-after-

being-wrongfully-accused; https://news.ontario.ca/mag/en/2011/12/attorney-general-responds-to-wrongful-conviction.html.

59 "Jack White," AIDWYC Exonerations: Individual Cases, https://www.aidwyc. org/cases/historical/jack-white/; Roberta Bell, "Wrongfully Convicted Former HRC Worker Sees End of Case," *Barrie Examiner*, 18 Sept. 2012, http://www. thebarrieexaminer.com/2012/09/17/wrongfully-convicted-former-hrc-worker-sees-end-of-case.

60 http://www.cbc.ca/news/canada/prince-edward-island/former-soccer-coach-wins-appeal-in-sexual-exploitation-case-1.652485.

61 "Charlottetown Man Sues for Wrongful Conviction," CBC News Prince Edward Island, 7 March 2007, http://www.cbc.ca/news/canada/prince-edward-island/story/2007/03/07/cooper-lawsuit.html.

62 http://injusticebusters.org/2003/Duguay_Taillefer.htm. In 1999 the Poitras Commission investigating misconduct by the Sûreté du Québec found that important information had been withheld from the defence.

63 Ibid.

64 https://www.theglobeandmail.com/news/national/how-a-womans-love-corrected-an-injustice/article4145158/; http://www.cbc.ca/news/canada/montreal/no-damages-for-wrongfully-convicted-montreal-man-1.795518.

65 "Ottawa to Appeal $8.6M Wrongful Conviction Ruling," CBC News Montreal, 16 May 2011, http://www.cbc.ca/news/canada/montreal/story/2011/05/16/canadian-government-will-appeal-wrongful-conviction-settlement-for-rejean-hinse.html; Ingrid Peritz, "Quebec Man Wins Largest Award for Wrongful Conviction," *Globe and Mail*, 14 April 2011, http://www.theglobeandmail.com/news/national/quebec-man-wins-largest-award-for-wrongful-conviction/article576466/.

66 Katz, *Justice Miscarried*; https://www.theglobeandmail.com/news/national/mentally-handicapped-quebec-man-receives-millions-for-injustice/article20418207/.

67 Marshall had limited intelligence and borderline personality disorder, which led him to falsely confess to having committed the assaults.

68 https://www.pressreader.com/canada/national-post-latest-edition/20051005/281633890628928.

69 "Yves Plamondon Freed after 28 Years in Prison for Murder," CBC News Montreal, 14 March 2014, http://www.cbc.ca/news/canada/montreal/yves-plamondon-freed-after-28-years-in-prison-for-murder-1.2572451; Daniel Mallard, "Wrongfully Imprisoned Quebec Man Seeks $30M from the Province," *Sun News*, 10 May 2014, http://www.torontosun.com/2014/05/10/wrongfully-imprisoned-que-man-seeks-30m-from-province.

70 http://www.tvanouvelles.ca/2012/10/25/30-ans-plus-tard-le-meurtrier-court-toujours.

71 Department of Justice, "Annual Report 2010 Minister of Justice," http://www.justice. gc.ca/eng/rp-pr/cj-jp/ccr-rc/rep10-rap10/p3.html.

72 "David Milgaard," AIDWYC Exonerations: Individual Cases, https://www.aidwyc. org/cases/historical/david-milgaard/.

73 The cases considered in this section show evidence that could possibly exonerate the accused persons but has not been established by the courts.

74 Wiebe and Johnson, *Stolen Life*.

75 http://injusticebusters.org/index.htm/Joe_Warren.htm.

76 http://injusticebusters.org/05/Koehn_Darren.shtml.

77 "Ostrowski Freed on Bail after 23 Years," CTV News, 18 Dec. 2009, http://www.ctvnews.ca/ostrowski-free-on-bail-pending-review-after-23-years-in-jail-1.466187; http://www.cbc.ca/news/canada/manitoba/frank-ostrowski-court-of-appeal-1.3980710.

78 Robert Mailman and Walter Gillespie, "Witnesses Lied at Murder Trial. By Gary Dimmock," *Ottawa Citizen*, fall 1998, http://injusticebusters.org/index.htm/Gillespie.htm

79 http://truthinjustice.org/george-pitt.htm.

80 "Glenn Assoun Released from Prison Pending Federal Review of 1999 Murder Conviction," https://www.aidwyc.org/assoun-bail/; http://www.cbc.ca/news/canada/nova-scotia/glen-eugene-assoun-granted-bail-as-murder-conviction-reviewed-1.2846671.

81 https://www.thestar.com/news/canada/2016/07/03/woman-convicted-of-killing-child-in-1982-granted-day-parole.html.

82 http://www.cbc.ca/news/canada/sudbury/convicted-murderer-john-moore-appealing-for-clemency-again-1.2562166.

83 https://www.thestar.com/news/canada/2014/05/10/plea_bargain_haunts_quebec_man.html.

84 http://www.cbc.ca/news/canada/montreal/wilbert-coffin-execution-cda-1.3441076.

85 http://www.cbc.ca/news/canada/montreal/jacques-delisle-judge-bail-decision-1.3906910; http://www.cbc.ca/fifth/episodes/2014-2015/murder-and-the-judge.

86 http://leaderpost.com/news/crime/sask-man-convicted-of-murdering-estranged-wife-loses-bid-to-reopen-case.

Legislation and Case Citations

Legislation – Canada

Access to Information Act, R.S.C., 1985, c. A-1

Anti-Terrorism Act, S.C. 2001, c. 41

Bill C-13, An Act to Amend the Criminal Code, the DNA Identification Act and the National Defence Act, S.C. 2005, c. 25

Bill C-18, An Act to Amend Certain Acts in Relation to DNA Identification, S.C. 2007, c. 22

Bill C-104, An Act to Amend the Criminal Code and the Young Offenders Act, S.C. 1995, c. 27

Bill S-10, An Act to Amend the Criminal Code, the DNA Identification Act and the National Defence Act, S.C. 2005

Canadian Charter of Rights and Freedoms, Part I of The Constitution Act, 1982, Enacted as Schedule B to the Canada Act 1982, (UK) 1982, c. 11

Controlled Drugs and Substances Act, S.C. 1996, c.19

Coroners Amendment Act 2009, c. 15, Amending the Coroners Act 1990, c. 37

Criminal Code, R.S.C. 1985, c. C-46

Criminal Records Act, R.S.C. 1985, c. C-47

DNA Identification Act, 1998, c. 37

Extradition Act, S.C. 1999, c. 18

Fair and Efficient Criminal Trials Act, An Act to Amend the Criminal Code, S.C. 2011, c. 16

Human Rights Act, R.S.N.S. 1989, c. 214

Identification of Criminals Act, R.S.C. 1985, c. I-1

National Defence Act, R.S.C., 1985, c. N-5

Proceedings Against the Crown Act, R.S.O. 1990, c. P.27

Safe Streets and Communities Act, S.C. 2012, c. 1

Young Offenders Act, R.S.C. 1985, C.Y-1

Youth Criminal Justice Act, S.C. 2002, c. 1

Legislation – International

International Covenant on Civil and Political Rights – Adopted and opened for signature, ratification, and accession by General Assembly Resolution 2200A (XXI) of 16 Dec. 1966 – enters into force 23 March 1976, in accordance with Article 49

Criminal Procedure Act (CPA), 1981 – with subsequent amendments, the latest made by act of 30 June 2006 No. 53 (Norway)

Legislation – United Kingdom

Contempt of Court Act, 1981 (UK)
Criminal Appeal Act, 1968 (UK), 1968, c. 35, s. 2
Criminal Appeal Act, 1995 (UK), 1995, c. 35
Criminal Justice Act, 1988, c. 33
Criminal Procedure (Scotland) Act, 1995 (UK), 1995, c. 46
Prevention of Terrorism (Temporary Provisions) Act, 1974 (UK), 1974, c. 56

Legislation – United States

DNA Sexual Assault Justice Act, Act of 30 Oct. 2004, Pub. L. No. 108–405, § 301; 118 Stat.
    2260 (2004)
Innocence Protection Act, Act of Oct. 30, 2004, Pub. L. No. 108-405, 18 U.S.C.S.
    § 3600–3600A (2004)
Justice for All Act, 2004 (H.R. 5107, Public Law No: 108–405)
Reporter's Privilege, Chapter 735 Illinois Compiled Statutes Act 5 Article VIII Part 9
    Sections 901–9 (735 ILCS 5/8-901 to -909) (USA)
Scott Campbell, Stephanie Roper, Wendy Preston, Louarna Gillis, and Nila Lynn Crime
    Victims' Rights Act, Pub. L. No. 108–405 (codified at 18 U.S.C. § 3771 (2004))

Case Citations – Canada

In re. Acosta Andres, Azola Blanco and Veliz Garcia (No. 2), (Application for Review)
    Judgment No. 570, 20 December 1983. The Administrative Tribunal
Auclair v. R., 2011 QCCS 2661
Boucher v. The Queen, (1954), 110 C.C.C. 263 (S.C.C.)
Canada (Attorney General) v. Canada (Commissioner of the Inquiry on the Blood System), [1997]
    3 S.C.R. 440
Childs v. Desormeaux, [2006] 1 S.C.R. 643, 2006 SCC 18
Cooper v. Hobart, [2001] 3 S.C.R. 537, 2001 SCC 79
Dix v. Canada (Attorney General) [2002] A.J. No. 784
Dixon v. Hamilton (City) Police Services Board, [2011] O.J. No. 3836 (S.C.J.)
Henry v. British Columbia (Attorney General), 2015 SCC 24, [2015] 2 S.C.R. 214
Her Majesty the Queen v. Lindley Charles McArthur, et al. (Ontario) (Criminal) (By Leave),
    2012–12–03, 35695
Hill v. Hamilton-Wentworth Regional Police Service Board, 2007 SCC 41 [2007] 3 S.C.R. 129
Hinse c. Québec (Procureur général) [2011] J.Q. no 3760
Krieger v. Law Society of Alberta, [2002] 3 S.C.R. 372
Laflamme c. R., 2015 QCCA 1517 (CanLII)
McArthur v Ontario (Attorney General) 2013 ONCA 668
Miazga v. Kvello Estate, [2009] S.C.J. No. 51
Nelles v. Ontario [1989] 2 S.C.R. 170
Perreault c. R., 2015 QCCA 694 (CanLII)
Proulx v. Québec, [2001] 3 S.C.R. 9
R. v. A.(F.). (2004), 183 C.C.C. (3d) 518 (Ont. C.A.)

R. v. Abbey [2009] ONCA 624

R. v. Abdow [2011] A.J. No. 218

R. v. Ahmed [2002] O.J. No. 4597

R. v. Arcuri, [2001] 2 S.C.R. 828

R. v. Béland [1987] 2 S.C.R. 398

R. v. Belic [2011] ONCA 671

R. v. Bennett (2003) Ont CA 179 C.C.C. (3d) 244

R. v. B. (K.G.), [1993] 1 S.C.R. 740

R. v. Boissonneault (1986), 29 C.C.C. (3d) 345 (Ont. C.A.)

R. v. Bonisteel [2008] BCCA 344

R. v. Borden (1994) 3 S.C.R. 145

R. v. Brighteyes (1997) A.J. No. 363

R. v. Brooks [2000] 1 S.C.R. 237

R. v. Broyles [1991] 3 S.C.R. 595

R. v. Butorac [2010] B.C.J. No. 1518

R v. Burke, [1996] 1 S.C.R. 474

R. v. Chaplin [1995] 1 S.C.R. 727

R. v. Chapple 2012 ABPC 229

R. v. Charemski, [1998] 1 S.C.R. 679

R. v. C.K.R.S. [2005] B.C.J. No. 2917

R. v. Collins [2001] 160 C.C.C. (3d) 85 (Ont. C.A.)

R. v. Cooper, [1969] 53 Cr. App. R. 82

R. v. Copeland (1999) BCCA 744

R. v. Corbett [1988] 1 S.C.R. 670, 41 C.C.C. (3d) 385, 64 C.R. (3d) 1

R. v. Daunt [2007] Y.J. No. 63

R. v. D.(D.) [2000] 148 C.C.C. (3d)

R. v. Delisle, (1999) 133 C.C.C. (3d) 541 Que CA

R. v. Dhillon [2001] B.C.J. No. 1944416

R. v. Dimitrov [2003] O.J. No. 5243

R. v. Dougan [2008] O.J. No. 5292

R. v. E. (O.N.) [2000] B.C.J. No. 1922 (QL) (S.C.)

R. v. Farler (1837), 8 Car.

R. v. Fitzgerald [2009] B.C.J. No. 2333

R. v. Fry [2011] BCCA 381

R. v. G.D.B [2000] S.C.R. 520

R. v. Godron, (2008) NSCA 109

R. v. Grandinetti [2005] 191 C.C.C. (3d) 449

R. v. Hall [2004] O.J. No. 5007

R. v. Handy [2002] 2 S.C.R. 908

R. v. Hart, 2012 NLCA 61

R. v. Hart, 2014 SCC 52

R. v. Hathaway [2007] S.J. No. 245 (QL) (Q.B.)

R. v. Hebert [1990], 57 C.C.C. (3d) 1 (S.C.C.)

R. v. Henderson [2009] M.J. No. 145

R. v. Henry (2010) BCCA 462

R. v. Hibbert [2002], 163 C.C.C. (3d) 129 (S.C.C.)

R. v. Hinse [1997] S.C.J. No. 1.

R. v. Ho [1999] O.J. No. 4720 127 OAC 132

R. v. Hodgson [1998] 127 C.C.C. (3d) 449 (S.C.C.)

R. v. Huffman, [1995] 2079 (BCCA)

R. v. Hurley [2010] 1 S.C.R. 637

R. v. J.A.A. [2011] 1 S.C.R. 628

R. v. Jack (1992), 70 C.C.C. (3d) 67 (Man. C.A.)

R. v. Jeffrey (1989), 35 O.A.C. 321 (C.A.)

R. v. J.(L-J) [2000] 148 C.C.C. (3d)

R. v. Johnson, 2010 ONCA 646

R. v. Kehler, [2004] 1 S.C.R 328

R. v. Khela [2009] 1 S.C.R. 104

R. v. Khelawon, [2006] SCC 57

R. v. Kines (2012) MBCA 97

R. v. Koivisto [2011] O.J. No. 2794

R. v. Laurin [2012] O.J. No. 4357

R. v. Lavallée [1990] 1 S.C.R. 852

R. v. MacDonald [2002] O.J. No. 3315

R. v. Mack [2014] 3 S.C.R. 3

R. v. MacKenzie, (2007) NSCA 10

R. v. Marcoux [1976] 1 S.C.R. 763

R. v. McInnis, [1999] 44 O.R. (3d) 772

R. v. McIntosh (1997), 117 C.C.C. (3d) 385 (Ont. C.A.)

R. v. McIntrye [1999] 2 S.C.R. 480

R. v. Meer [2015] ABCA 141

R. v. Meer [2016] SCC 5

R. v. Melaragni [1992] O.J. No. 4176

R. v. Mentuck [2000] M.J. No. 447

R. v. Mezzo, [1986] 1 S.C.R. 802

R. v. M.J.S. [2000] A.J. No. 391

R. v. Mohan [1994] 2 S.C.R. 9

R. v. Monteleone, [1987] 2 S.C.R. 154

R. v. Moore-McFarlane [2001] O.J. No. 4646

R. v. Mullins-Johnson, 2007 ONCA 720

R. v. Myrie [2003] O.T.C. 219

R. v. Nasogaluak, 2010 SCC 6, [2010] 1 S.C.R. 206

R. v. The National Post, 2008 ONCA 139

R. v. The National Post, 2010 SCC 16

R. v. Nedelcu, 2012 SCC 59

R. v. Nelles (1982), 16 C.C.C. (3d) 97 (Ont. Prov. Ct.)

R. v. Oickle [2000] 2 S.C.R. 3

R. v. Osmar [2007] O.J. No. 244

R. v. Palmer, [1980] 1 S.C.R. 759

R. v. Parent (1988) 65 Alta L.R. (2d) 18 (Alta. Q.B.)

R. v. Pelletier, [2012] ONCA 566

R. v. Penner [2009] A.J. No. 447

R. v. R.C. (2005) S.C.J. No. 62

R. v. Rhodes [2002] B.C.J. No. 1113

R. v. Rodgers (2006) 1 S.C.R. 554

R. v. Roks, [2011] ONCA 526

R. v. Ross [1989] 1 S.C.R.

R. v. Rowbotham, [1993] 4 S.C.R. 834

R. v. S.A.B. (2003) 2 S.C.R. 678

R. v. Samuels [2005] O.J. No. 1873

R. v. Schofield, (1996) N.S.J. No. 69

R. v. Seaboyer, [1991] 2 S.C.R. 577, 66 C.C.C. (3d) 321, 7 C.R. (4th) 117

R. v. Sinclair, 2010 SCC 35

R. v. Singh [2007] S.C.J. No. 48

R. v. Smith [2007] O.J. No. 2172

R. v. Spence [2005] S.C.J. No. 74

R. v. S.(R.D.), [1997] 3 S.C.R. 484

R. v. Stillman (1997) 1 S.C.R. 607 (S.C.C.)

R. v. Stinchcombe, [1991] 3 S.C.R. 326

R. v. Sutton, [1970] 2 O.R. 358 (C.A.)

R. v. Tebo, [2003] O.J. No. 1853

R. v. Terceira (1999) S.C.J. No. 74

R. v. Trochym [2007] SCC 6

R. v. Trudel [2004] O.J. No. 248

R. v. Trudel (appeal by Sauvé) [2004] S.C.C.A. No. 246

R. v. Trudel [2007] O.J. No. 113

R. v. Truscott [2007] ONCA No. 575

R. v. Vetrovec (1982) 1 S.C.R. 811

R. v. Weagle, (2008) NSCA 122

R. v. White [2011] 1 S.C.R. 433

R. v. Whittle, [1994] S.C.J. No. 69

R. v. Willis [2008] O.J. No. 1875

R. v. Wood (2006) ABCA 343

R. v. Woodward (2009) 240 Man R (2d) 24 (Man. C.A.)

R. v. Wristen (1999), 141 C.C.C. (3d) 1 (Ont. C.A.)

Reference re Milgaard, [1992] 1 S.C.R. 866

Re. Louise Reynolds [2007] ONCA 375

Reynolds v. Kingston (City) Police Services Board [2007] ONCA 166

Rothman v. The Queen [1981] 1 S.C.R. 64

Ruffo c. Conseil de la magistrature, [1995] 4 R.C.S. 267

Smith v. Canada (Attorney General), 2009 FC 228 [2010] 1 FCR 3

United States of America v. Burns and Rafay, [2001] 1 S.C.R. 283

Ward v. Vancouver (City), [2010] 2 S.C.R. 28

Case Citations – United Kingdom

Donoghue v. Stevenson, [1932] A.C. 562 (H.L.)

R. (on the application of Clibery) v. Secretary of State for the Home Department [2007] EWHC
1855 (Admin)

R. (on the application of Mullen) v. Secretary of State for the Home Department [2007] EWHC
1495 (Admin); [2007] A.C.D. 75; [2008] EWCA Civ 755

R. (on the application of Siddall) v. Secretary of State for Justice [2009] EWHC 482 (Admin); 2009 A.C.D. 35

R. v. Cannings [2004] EWCA Crim 1

R. v. CCRC, Ex parte Pearson, [1999] 3 All E.R. 498

R. v. Clark [2003] EWCA Crim 1020

R. v. Harris [2005] EWCA Crim 1980

R v. Knights, The Times, 5 Oct.1995, cited in Stephens and Hill (1999)

R. v. McCann, Cullen and Shanahan (1991) 92 Cr.App.Rep. 239

R. v. Reade, cited in B. Naylor (1994)

R. v. Taylor, R. v. Taylor (1993) (1994) 98 Cr.App.Rep. 361

Case Citations – United Nations

Michel Dumont c. Canada, UN International Covenant on Civil and Political Rights, Human Rights Committee, Ninety-Eighth session, Communication No. 1467/2006, 8–26 March 2010

Case Citations – United States

Atkins v. Virginia, 536 US 304 (2002)

Baze et al. v. Rees, Commissioner, Kentucky Department of Corrections, No. 07–5439, (2008)

Brady v. Maryland, 373 US 83 (1963)

Connick v. Thompson, 563 US 51 (2011)

Daubert v. Merrel Dow Pharmaceuticals, Inc 113 S Ct. 2786 [1993]

Frye v. United States, 293 F. 1013 [DC Cir., 1923]

Gideon v. Wainwright, 372 US 335 (1963)

Giglio v. US, 405 (1972)

Glossip et al. v. Gross et al. (2015) No. 14–7955

Kansas v. Marsh, 548 US 163, 208 (2006)

Khumo Tire Company Ltd v. Patrick Carmichael 143 L. Ed (2d) 238 [1999] [U.S.S.C.]

Manson v. Braithwaite 432 US 98, 114 (1977)

In the Matter of an Investigation of the W.Va. State Police Crime Lab., Serology Div., 438 S.E.2d 501, 510–511 (W. Va. 1993)

McCarty v. State, 765 P.2d 1215, 1218 (Okla. Crim. App. 1988)

Neils v. Biggers 409 US 188, 198–9 (1972)

Peretz v. United States, 501 US 923 (1991)

Roper v. Simmons, 543 US 551 (2005)

State v. Grimes, General Court of Justice – Superior Court Division, 87 CRS 13541/42/44

State v. Isbell, Mills, Williams, General Court of Justice – Superior Court Division, 00 CRS 65084, 01 CRS 06334, 35

State v. Kagonyera and Wilcoxson, General Court of Justice – Superior Court Division, File Nos. 00CRS 65086; 00 CRS 65088

State v. Knolly Brown, Edgecombe County, 08 CRS 50309

State v. Lindsey, 621 So. 2d 618 (La. Ct. App. 1993)

State v. McCollum/Brown, County of Robeson, Superior Court Division, 91 CRS 40727, 92 CRS 241–2

State v. McInnis, County of Scotland, Criminal Court Division, File No. 88-CRS-1422

State v. McNeil, General Court of Justice – Superior Court Division, 00 CRS 57073–74

State v. Reeves, General Court of Justice – Superior Court Division, File No. 99 CRS 65056

State v. Robert Charles Bragg, 94 CRS 4929

State v. Sledge, Columbus County, 78 CRS 2415–2416

State v. Taylor, General Court of Justice – Superior Court Division, 91 CRS 71728

State v. Womble, Granville County, File No. 75 CRS 06128

Stovall v. Denno, 388 US 293, 301–02 (1967)

Strickland v. Washington, 466 US 668 (1984) (U.S.S.C.)

United States v. Cervantes-Pacheo, 826 F.2d 310, 315 (5th Cir 1897)

United States v. Garsson, 291 F. 646, 649 (S.D.N.Y. 1923)

United States v. Scheffer 523 US 303 [1998]

United States v. Shephard, [1977] 2 S.C.R. 1067

United States v. Sudikoff, 36 F.Supp. 2d 1196 (C.D. Cal. 1999)

United States v. Wade, 388 US 218, 235 (1967)

Washington v. Texas, 388 US 14, 87 S.Ct. 1920, 1925, 18 L.Ed.2d 1019 (1967)

Bibliography

Aboriginal Legal Services of Toronto (ALST). 2007. *Factum*. Retrieved 3 Oct. 2009 at: http://aboriginallegal.ca/docs/hill_factum.htm.

Ainsworth, P.B. 1998. *Psychology, Law and Eyewitness Testimony*. New York: John Wiley and Sons.

Alarcon, A.L., and P.M. Mitchell. 2011. "Executing the Will of Voters? A Roadmap to Mend or End the California Legislature's Multi-Billion Dollar Death Penalty Debacle." *Loyola of Los Angeles Law Review*, 44: S41–224.

Alexander, M. 2010. *The New Jim Crow: Mass Incarceration in the Age of Colourblindness*. New York: New Press.

Anderson, B., and D. Anderson. 1998. *Manufacturing Guilt: Wrongful Convictions in Canada*. Halifax: Fernwood Publishing.

Arson Review Committee. 2006. *Report on the Peer Review of the Expert Testimony in the Cases of: The State of Texas v. Cameron Todd Willingham and The State of Texas v. Ernest Ray Willis*. Retrieved at: https://www.innocenceproject.org/wp-content/uploads/2016/04/file.pdf.

Bala, N. 2005. "*R. v. D.(D.)*: The Supreme Court and Filtering of Social Science Knowledge about Children." *Criminal Reports*, 36, no. 5: 283–90.

Ballard, P. 2006. Potential Jurors Say They Want to See Scientific Evidence. *Miami Herald*. 23 May 2006. Retrieved at: http://www.herald-mail.com/.

Ballenden, N., K. Laster, and J. Lawrence. 1993. "Pathologist as Gatekeeper: Discretionary Decision-Making in Cases of Sudden Infant Death." *Australian Journal of Social Issues*, 28: 124–39.

Bandes, S. 2005–6. "Loyalty to One's Conviction: The Prosecutor and Tunnel Vision." *Howard Law Journal*, 49: 475–94.

– 2011. "The Lone Miscreant, the Self-Training Prosecutor, and Other Fictions: A Comment on *Connick v. Thompson*." *Fordham Law Review*, 80: 715–36.

Baxter, A. 2007. "Identification Evidence in Canada: Problems and a Potential Solution." *Criminal Law Quarterly* (Toronto), 52: 175–89.

Beatty, P.C., and G. Willis. 2007. "Research Synthesis: The Practice of Cognitive Interviewing." *Public Opinion Quarterly*, 71, no. 2: 286–311.

Beck, U. 1992. *Risk Society: Toward a New Modernity*. London: Sage.

Beecher-Monas, E. 2007. *Evaluating Scientific Evidence: An Interdisciplinary Framework for Intellectual Due Process*. New York: Cambridge University Press.

Bernhard, A. 1999. "When Justice Fails: Indemnification for Unjust Conviction." *University of Chicago Roundtable*, 6: 73–112.

– 2001. "Effective Assistance of Counsel." In S. Westervelt and J. Humphrey, eds., *Perspectives on Failed Justice*, 220–40. New Brunswick, NJ: Rutgers University Press.

– 2003. "Exonerations Change Judicial Views on Ineffective Assistance of Counsel." *Criminal Justice*, 18: 37–42.

– 2004. "Justice Still Fails: A Review of Recent Efforts to Compensate Individuals Who Have Been Unjustly Convicted and Later Exonerated." *Drake Law Review*, 52: 703–38.

Bird, S. 2010. "The Inadequacy of Legal Aid." In M. Naughton, ed., *The Criminal Cases Review Commission: Hope for the Innocent?* Hampshire, UK: Palgrave Macmillan. 134–47.

Blintiff, R.L. 1993. *Police Procedural: A Writer's Guide to Police and How They Work.* New York: Writers Digest Books.

Bloom, R.M. 2005. *A Historical Overview of Informants.* Legal Studies Research Paper Series, Research Paper No. 64, Boston College of Law.

Bloos, M., and M. Plaxton. 2000. "An Almost-Eulogy for the Preliminary Inquiry: We Hardly Knew Ye." *Criminal Law Quarterly* (Toronto), 43: 516–28.

Blume, J. 2005. "Killing the Willing: 'Volunteers,' Suicide and Competency." *Michigan Law Review*, 103: 939–1006.

Botting, G. 2010. *Wrongful Conviction in Canadian Law.* Toronto: Lexis Nexis Canada.

Boyd, N., and K. Rossmo. 1994. "David Milgaard, the Supreme Court and Section 690: A Wrongful Conviction Revisited." *Canadian Lawyer*, 28–32.

Boyle, C., and E. Cunliffe. 2012. "Right to Counsel during Custodial Interrogation in Canada: Not Keeping Up with the Common Law Joneses." In P. Roberts and J. Hunter, eds., *Criminal Evidence and Human Rights: Reimagining Common Law Procedural Traditions.* West Sussex, UK.: Hart Publishing. 79–102.

Bradfield, A.L., G.L. Wells, and E.A. Olson. 2002. "The Damaging Effect of Confirming Feedback on the Relation between Eyewitness Certainty and Identification Accuracy." *Journal of Applied Psychology*, 87: 112–20.

Braiden, P., and J. Brockman. 1999. "Remedying Wrongful Convictions through Applications to the Minister of Justice under Section 690 of the *Criminal Code*." *Windsor Yearbook of Access to Justice*, 17: 3–34.

Brewer, N., and M.A. Palmer. 2010. "Eyewitness Identification Tests." *Legal and Criminological Psychology*, 15, no. 1: 77–96.

Bright, S.B. 1994. "Counsel for the Poor: The Death Sentence Not for the Worst Crime but for the Worst Lawyer." *Yale Law Journal*, 103: 1835–83.

– 1997. "Neither Equal nor Just: The Rationing and Denial of Legal Services to the Poor When Life and Liberty Are at Stake." *Annual Survey of American Law*, 7: 783–836.

– 1999. "Death in Texas – Not even the Pretense of Fairness." *Champion* 23: 1–10.

Broeder. D. 1959. "The University of Chicago Jury Project." *Nebraska Law Review*, 38: 744–67.

Brookman, F., and J. Nolan. 2006. "The Dark Figure of Infanticide in England and Wales: Complexities of Diagnosis." *Journal of Interpersonal Violence*, 21: 869–89.

Brown, C.L., and R.E. Geiselman. 1990. "Eyewitness Testimony of the Mentally Retarded: Effect of the Cognitive Interview." *Journal of Police and Criminal Psychology*, 6: 14–22.

Buck, A. 2005. "Innocence Projects." *IRE Journal*, 28, no. 3: 18–21.

Burke, A.S. 2006. "Improving Prosecutorial Decision-Making: Some Lessons of Cognitive Science." *William and Mary Law Review*, 47: 1–44.

Burnett, C. 2002. "Constructing Innocence." *UMKC Law Review*, 70, no. 4: 971–82.

– 2005. "Restorative Justice and Wrongful Capital Convictions: A Simple Proposal." *Journal of Contemporary Criminal Justice*, 21, no. 3: 272–89.

Burtch, B. 1981. "Reflections on the Steven Truscott Case." *Canadian Criminology Forum*, 3: 131–45.

Caldero, M.A., and J.P. Crank. 2000. *Police Ethics: The Corruption of Noble Cause (1st Edition).* Cincinnati, OH: Matthew Bender and Company.

– 2004. *Police Ethics: The Corruption of Noble Cause (2nd Edition).* Cincinnati, OH: Matthew Bender and Company.

California Commission on the Fair Administration of Justice. 2008 *California Commission on the Fair Administration of Justice Final Report.* Northern California Innocence Project Publications, Book I. Retrieved at: http://digitalcommons.law.scu.edu/ncippubs/1.

Campbell, A. 2006. *Bernardo Investigation Review: Summary.* Retrieved at: https://www.attorneygeneral.jus.gov.on.ca/inquiries/cornwall/en/hearings/exhibits/Wendy_Leaver/pdf/10_Campbell_Summary.pdf.

Campbell, K. 2005. "Policy Responses to Wrongful Conviction in Canada: The Role of Conviction Review, Public Inquiries and Compensation." *Criminal Law Bulletin*, 41, no. 2: 145–68.

– 2008. "The Fallibility of Justice in Canada: A Critical Cxamination of Conviction Review." In M. Kilias and R. Huff, eds., *Wrongful Convictions: International Perspectives on Miscarriages of Justice.* Philadelphia, PA: Temple University Press. 117–36.

– 2011. "Expert Evidence from 'Social' Scientists: The Importance of Context and the Impact on Miscarriages of Justice." *Canadian Criminal Law Review*, 16, no. 1: 13–36.

– 2012. "Innocent but Presumed Guilty: The Wrongful Conviction of William Mullins-Johnson (Interview)." In J. Roberts and M. Grossman, eds., *Criminal Justice in Canada: A Reader*, 4th ed. Toronto: Harcourt Brace. 269–78.

– 2013. "The Changing Face of Miscarriages of Justice: Preventive Detention Strategies in Canada and the United States." In C. Ronald Huff and Martin Kilias, eds., *Wrongful Convictions and Miscarriages of Justice: Causes and Remedies in North American and European Criminal Justice Systems.* New York: Routledge.

Campbell, K. (forthcoming). "Exoneration and Compensation for the Wrongly Convicted: Enhancing Procedural Justice?" *Journal of Law and Society.*

Campbell, K., and C. Walker. 2007. *Medical Mistakes and Miscarriages of Justice: Perspectives on the Experiences in England and Wales. Paper for the Inquiry into Pediatric Forensic Pathology in Ontario,* chaired by Justice Stephen T. Goudge.

– 2012. "Pathological Error: Reacting to the Limits of Expertise in Legal Process." *Law and Justice Review*, 5: 16–38.

Campbell, K., and M. Denov. 2004. "The Burden of Innocence: Coping with a Wrongful Imprisonment." *Canadian Journal of Criminology and Criminal Justice*, 46, no. 2: 139–64.

Campbell, L.M. 2009. "Statutory Review of the DNA Identification Act." Appearance before the Standing Committee on Public Safety and National Security (SECU), 26 Feb. 2009. Retrieved at: https://www.priv.gc.ca/en/opc-actions-and-decisions/advice-to-parliament/2009/parl_090226_lc/.

Campobasso, C.P., and F. Introna. 2001. "The Forensic Entomologist in the Context of the Forensic Pathologist's Role." *Forensic Science International*, 120: 132–9.

Canada. 1973. *Final Report of the Commission of Inquiry into the Non-Medical Use of Drugs.* Ottawa: Information Canada. Gerald LeDain, chair.

– 1986. *Report of the Commission of Inquiry into the Hinton Train Collision.* R.P. Foisy, chair.

Canada Gazette. 2002. *Regulations Respecting Applications for Ministerial Review – Miscarriages of Justice*, pt. 1, vol. 136, no. 39, 28 Sept. 2002.

Canada, House of Commons, Standing Committee on Public Safety and National Security. 2009. *Statutory Review of the DNA Identification Act: Report on the Standing Committee on Public Safety and National Security.* Retrieved at: http://www.ourcommons.ca/Committees/en/SECU/StudyActivity?studyActivityId=2605846.

Canada, Senate, Standing Senate Committee on Legal and Constitutional Affairs. 2010. *Public Protection, Privacy and the Search for Balance: A Statutory Review of the DNA Identification Act: Final Report.* Retrieved at: http://publications.gc.ca/collections/collection_2011/sen/yc24-0/YC24-0-403-9-eng.pdf.

Canadian Judicial Counsel (CJC). 2007. *The Canadian Justice System and the Media.* CJC Ottawa. Retrieved at: http://www.cjc-ccm.gc.ca/cmslib/general/news_pub_other_cjsm_en.pdf.

Carvel, J. 1992. "Many Prisoners Could be Wrongly Jailed. *Guardian Weekly*, 5 April.

Castelle, G., and E. Loftus. 2001. "Misinformation and Wrongful Convictions." In S. Westervelt and J. Humphrey, eds., *Wrongly Convicted: Perspectives on Failed Justice.* New Brunswick, NJ: Rutgers University Press. 17–35.

Ceci, S.J., and M. Bruck. 1993. "Suggestibility of the Child Witness: A Historical Review and Synthesis." *Psychological Bulletin*, 113: 403–39.

Center for Prosecutorial Integrity. 2014. *Conviction Integrity Units: Vanguard of Criminal Justice Reform – White Paper.* Retrieved at: http://www.prosecutorintegrity.org/wp-content/uploads/2014/12/Conviction-Integrity-Units.pdf.

Chaklos, D.L., and M.N. Kuehner. 2007. "Firearm and Toolmark Identification." In C. Wecht and J. Rago, eds., *Forensic Science and Law: Investigative Applications in Criminal, Civil and Family Justice.* Boca Raton, FL: Taylor and Francis Group. 333–55.

Chalmers, J., and F. Leverick. 2010. "The Scottish Criminal Cases Review Commission and Its Referrals to the Appeal Court: The First Ten Years." *Criminal Law Review (London, England)*, 8: 608–22.

Chamberlain, E. 2008. "Negligent Investigation: A New Remedy for the Wrongly Accused: *Hill v. Hamilton Wentworth Regional Police Services Board.*" *Alberta Law Review*, 45: 1089–104.

– 2012. "Negligent Investigation: Faint Hope for the Wrongly Accused?" *Advocates Quarterly*, 39: 153–70.

Charney, R.E., and J. Hunter. 2011. "Tort lite? Vancouver (City) v. Ward and the Availability of Damages for Charter Infringements." *Supreme Court Review*, 54, no. 2: 393–425.

Chaubert, S., and C. Wyss. 2003. "Suicide in a Forest: Determining Post-Mortem Interval with Blowfly and Fleshfly Species." *Forensic Science International*, 136, no. 1: 388–91.

Chesen, J. 2007. "Canada's Use of Expert Witnesses and Scientific Evidence Admissibility." Unpublished paper. Retrieved at: www.ncstl.org/picture/129.

Cicchini, M.D., and J.G. Easton. 2010. "Reforming the Law on Show-up Identification." *Journal of Criminal Law & Criminology*, 100, no. 2: 381–413.

Clark, S.E., T.E. Marshall, and R. Rosenthal. 2009. "Lineup Administrator Influences on Eyewitness Identification Decisions." *Journal of Experimental Psychology: Applied*, 15, no. 1: 63–75.

Clark, S.E., M.B. Moreland, and S.D. Gronlund. 2014. "Evolution of the Empirical and Theoretical Foundations of Eyewitness Identification Reform." *Psychonomic Bulletin and Review*, 21, no. 2: 251–67.

Clements, N. 2007. "Flipping a Coin: A Solution for the Inherent Unreliability of Eyewitness Identification Testimony." *Indiana Law Review*, 40: 271–90.

Code of Professional Conduct, Law Society of Upper Canada. Retrieved 7 June 2010 at: http://www.lsuc.on.ca/lawyer-conduct-rules/.

Cohen, A. 2014. "Glenn Ford's First Days of Freedom after 30 Years on Death Row." *The Atlantic*, 14 March 2014. Retrieved at: http://www.theatlantic.com/national/archive/2014/03/glenn-fords-first-days-of-freedom-after-30-years-on-death-row/284396/.

Cohen, D., and J.C. Smith. 1986. "Entitlement and the Body Politic: Rethinking Negligence in Public Law." *Canadian Bar Review*, 64, no. 1: 1–57.

Cohen, S. 1986. *Visions of Social Control: Crime, Punishment and Classification*. Cambridge: Polity Press.

Cole, S.A. 2006. "Prevalence and Potential Causes of Wrongful Conviction by Fingerprint Evidence." *Golden Gate University Law Review, Golden Gate University, School of Law*, 31, no. 1: 39–105.

– 2008. "The 'Opinionization' of Fingerprint Evidence." *Biosocieties*, 3: 105–13.

Cole, S.A., and R. Dioso-Villa. 2007. "CSI and Its Effects: Media, Juries and the Burden of Proof." *New England Law Review*, 41, no. 3: 435–69.

Connors, E., T. Lundregan, N. Miller, and T. McEwan. 1996. *Convicted by Juries, Exonerated by Science: Case Studies of the Use of DNA Evidence to Establish Innocence after Trial*. Washington, DC: National Institute of Justice.

Conroy, J., and R. Warden. 2011. *The High Costs of Wrongful Conviction*. Retrieved at: http://www.bettergov.org/news/special-investigation-the-high-costs-of-wrongful-convictions.

Conway, R. 2006. "A Criminal Mind." *Law Times*, 8 May 2006.

Cory, P. 2001. *The Inquiry regarding Thomas Sophonow*. Manitoba Justice. Retrieved at: https://websites.godaddy.com/blob/6aaa6fc2-99d9-4af2-a3b4-51e9d74ea37a/downloads/Thomas%20Sophonow%20Inquiry.pdf?2bd500cf.

Cournoyer, G. 2001. "Saying 'No' to Interrogation: The Quebec Court of Appeal Asserts a Meaningful Right to Silence." *Criminal Reports*, 5th series.

Court of Appeal for Ontario. 2006. *Her Majesty the Queen and Steven Truscott: Appellant's Factum*. Vol. 5, pts. VI and VII – C42726.

Criminal Lawyers Association. 2000. "Submissions on Behalf of the Criminal Lawyers Association, Addressing Miscarriages of Justice: Reform Possibilities for Section 690 of the Criminal Code." [No longer available.]

Cromett, M., and S. Thurston-Myster. 2005. "Work of an Innocence Project: Forensic Science and Wrongful Conviction." *Forensic Magazine*, 21, no. 5: 8–12.

Cunningham, J. 2006. "Agony of 'Not Proven'" Verdict. *The Herald*, 21 April 2006. Retrieved at: http://www.heraldscotland.com/news/12401239.We_wouldn_apos_t_wish_the_agony_of_this_verdict_on_anyone_else_Joe_Duffy_lost_his_daughter__Amanda__and_cannot_find_peace__he_says__because_of_Scotland_apos_s_finding_of__apos_not_proven_apos___Now_the_home_secretary_is_considering_introducing_the_verdict/.

Cutler, B.L. 2004. "Overview of Estimator Variables: Findings from Research on the Effects of Witness, Crime and Perpetrator Characteristics on Eyewitness Accuracy." Presented at: Reforming Eyewitness Identification: Convicting the Guilty, Protecting the Innocent, 12–13 Sept. 2004, Benjamin N. Cardozo School of Law, Yeshiva University, New York.

– 2011. *Conviction of the Innocent: Lessons from Psychological Research*. Washington, DC: American Psychological Association Press.

Cutler, B.L., K. Findley, and D. Loney. 2014. "Expert Testimony on Interrogation and False Confession." *UMKC Law Review*, 82, no. 3: 589–622.

Cutler, B.L., and R. Leo. 2016. "Analyzing Videotaped Confessions and Interrogations." *University of San Francisco Law Research Paper* 14.

Cutler, B.L., and S.D. Penrod. 1995. *Mistaken Identification: The Eyewitness, Psychology, and the Law*. New York: Cambridge University Press.

Cutler, B.L., S.D. Penrod, and T.K. Martens. 1987. "The Reliability of Eyewitness Identification: The Role of System and Estimator Variables." *Law and Human Behavior*, 11: 233–58.

Dahlstrom, D., P. Latrunus, D. Wilkinson, and B. Yamashita. 2013. "Forensic Physical Sciences." In M. Pollanen, M.J. Bowes, S.L. VanLaerhoven, and J. Wallace, eds., *Forensic Science in Canada: A Report of Multidisciplinary Discussion*. University of Toronto: Centre for Forensic Science and Medicine. 61–71.

Dando, C., R. Wilcock, R. Milne, and L. Henry. 2009. "A Modified Cognitive Interview Procedure for Frontline Police Investigators." *Applied Cognitive Psychology*, 23, no. 5: 698–716.

Davis, A. 1998. "Prosecution and Race: The Power and Privilege of Discretion." *Fordham Law Review*, 67: 13–68.

Davis, K. 2012. "Journalism & Justice: Did Innocence Project Student Reporters Get Too Close to Lawyers?" *ABA Journal*. January. http://www.abajournal.com/magazine/article/journalism_justice_did_innocence_project_student_reporters_get_too_close.

Delisle, R.J. 1987. "Evidence – Tests for Sufficiency of Evidence: *Mezzo v. The Queen*." *Canadian Bar Review*, 66: 389–99.

Delisle, R.J., D. Stuart, and D. Tanovich. 2004. *Evidence: Principles and Problems*. 7th ed. Toronto: Carswell.

Delisle, R.J., D. Stuart, D. Tanovich, and L. Dufraimont. 2015. *Evidence: Principles and Problems*. 11th ed. Toronto: Carswell.

Denov, M., and K. Campbell. 2003. "Wrongful Conviction." In J. Roberts and M. Grossman, eds., *Criminal Justice: A Reader*. Toronto: Harcourt. 228–43.

– 2005. "Criminal Injustice: Understanding the Causes, Effects and Responses to Wrongful Conviction in Canada." *Journal of Contemporary Criminal Justice*, 21, no. 3: 1–26.

Department of Justice. 1998a. "Addressing Miscarriages of Justice: Reform Possibilities for Section 690 of the Criminal Code: A Consultation Paper."

– 1998b. "The Section 690 Application of Clayton Johnson." [No longer available.]

– 2003. *Applying for a Conviction Review: Minister of Justice, Communication Branch*. Ottawa: Department of Justice.

– 2005a. *Applications for Ministerial Review – Miscarriages of Justice: Annual Report 2005. Minister of Justice, Communication Branch*. Ottawa: Department of Justice.

– 2005b. *Report on the Prevention of Miscarriages of Justice*. Federal/Provincial/Territorial Heads of Prosecution Committee Working Group.

– 2011. *The Path to Justice: Preventing Wrongful Convictions*. Report of the Federal/Provincial/Territorial Heads of Prosecution, Sub-Committee on the Prevention of Wrongful Convictions.

Devlin, P. 1966. *Trial by Jury*. 3rd ed. London: Stevens and Sons.

Devlin, R.F. 1995. "We Can't Go on Together with Suspicious Minds: Judicial Bias and Racialized Perspective in *R. v. R.D.S.*" *Dalhousie Law Journal*, 18: 408–46.

Dew, M. 2006. "Ineffective Assistance of Counsel as a Contributing Cause of Wrongful Convictions." Retrieved 4 June 2010 at: http://www.legaltree.ca/node/643.

Dewart, S. 2009. "Supreme Court Pondering Malicious Prosecution, Again." *For the Defence: Ontario Criminal Lawyers' Association Newsletter*, 30, no. 2.

Dioso-Villo, R. 2015. "A Repository of Wrongful Convictions in Australia: First Steps toward Estimating Prevalene and Causal Contributing Factors." *Flinders Law Journal*, 17: 163–202.

Dixon, R.A., C.M. Frias, and L. Backman. 2001. "Characteristics of Self-Reported Memory Compensation in Older Adults." *Journal of Clinical and Experimental Neuropsychology*, 23: 650–61.

Dodson, J., and X. Schooler. 1997. "The Verbal Overshadowing Effect: Why Descriptions Impair Face Recognition." *Memory & Cognition*, 25, no. 2: 129–39.

Dorschner, J., and C. Hoag. 2005. "Tragedy Reveals Conflicts over Media's Watchdog Role." *Grand Forks Herald*. [No longer available.]

Douglas, B. 2009. "'That's What She Said': Why Limiting the Use of Uncorroborated Eyewitness Identification Testimony Could Prevent Wrongful Convictions in Texas." *Texas Tech Law Review*, 41, no. 2: 561–85.

Douglass, A.B., J.S. Neuschatz, J. Imrich, and M. Wilkinson. 2010. "Does Post-Identification Feedback Affect Evaluations of Eyewitness Testimony and Identification Procedures?" *Law and Human Behavior*, 34, no. 4: 282–94.

Doyle, J.M. 2005. *True Witness: Cops, Courts, Science and the Battle against Misidentification*. New York: Palgrave Macmillan.

Dripps, D.A. 1997. "Ineffective Assistance of Counsel: The Case for an Ex Ante Parity Standard." *Journal of Criminal Law & Criminology*, 88: 242–308.

Drizin, S., and R. Leo. 2004. "The Problem of False Confessions in the Post-DNA World." *North Carolina Law Review*, 82, no. 3: 891–1007.

Dror, I.E., and D. Charlton. 2006. "Why Experts Make Errors." *Journal of Forensic Identification*, 56, no. 4: 600–16.

Dufraimont, L. 2008a. "Evidence Law and the Jury: A Reassessment." *McGill Law Journal / Revue de Droit de McGill,* 53: 199–242.

– 2008b. "Regulating Unreliable Evidence: Can Evidence Rules Guide Juries and Prevent Wrongful Convictions?" *Queen's Law Journal*, 33: 261–326.

– 2008c. "The Common Law Confessions Rule in the Charter Era: Current Law and Future Directions." *Supreme Court Review*, 40: 249–69.

– 2012. "The Patchwork Principle against Self-Incrimination under the Charter." *Supreme Court Review*, 57: 241–62.

Dwyer, J., P. Neufeld, and B. Scheck. 2000. *Actual Innocence: Five Days to Execution and Other Dispatches from the Wrongly Convicted*. New York: Doubleday.

Edmond, G. 2002. "Construing Miscarriages of Justice: Misunderstanding Scientific Evidence in High Profile Criminal Appeals." *Oxford Journal of Legal Studies*, 22, no. 1: 53–89.

Evans, T.J. 1995. "Fair Trial vs. Free Speech: Canadian Publication Bans versus the United States Media." *Southwestern Journal of Law and Trade in the Americas*, 2: 203.

Feeley, M., and J. Simon. 1992. "The New Penology: Notes on the Emerging Strategy of Corrections and its Implications." *Criminology*, 30, no. 4: 449–74.

– 1994. "Actuarial Justice: The Emerging New Criminal Law." In D. Nelkin, ed., *The Futures of Criminology*. London: Sage. 173–202.

Feige, D. 2003. "The Dark Side of Innocence." *New York Times Magazine*, 15 June.

Findley, K. 2006. "The Pedagogy of Innocence: Reflections on the Role of Innocence Projects in Clinical Legal Education." *Clinical Law Review*, 13, no. 1: 231–78.

– 2009. "Toward a New Paradigm of Criminal Justice: How the Innocence Movement Merges Crime Control and Due Process." University of Wisconsin Law School, Legal Studies Research Paper Series Paper No. 1069. http://ssrn.com/abstract=1324660.

– 2013. "Judicial Gatekeeping of Suspect Evidence: Due Process and Evidentiary Rules in the Age of Innocence." *Georgia Law Review*, 47: 723–72.

– 2016. "Implementing the Lessons from Wrongful Convictions: An Empirical Analysis of Eyewitness Identification Reform Strategies." *Missouri Law Review*, 81: 377–451.

Findley, K., and M.S. Scott. 2006. "The Multiple Dimensions of Tunnel Vision in Criminal Cases." *Wisconsin Law Review*, 2: 291–397.

Findley, M., and J. Grix. 2003. "Challenging Forensic Evidence? Observations on the Use of DNA in Certain Criminal Trials." *Current Issues in Criminal Justice*, 14, no. 3: 269–82.

Finkle, D. 1998. *No Claim to Mercy: The Controversial Case for Murder against Robert Baltovich.* Toronto: Penguin Group Canada.

Fish, M.J. 1979. "Committal for Trial: 'Some' Evidence is *Not* 'Sufficient.'" *Revue du Barreau*, 39, no. 3: 607–34.

Fisher, R.P., and R.E. Geiselman. 1992. *Memory Enhancing Techniques for Investigative Interviewing: The Cognitive Interview.* Springfield, IL: Charles C. Thomas.

– 2010. "The Cognitive Interview Method of Conducting Police Interviews: Eliciting Extensive Information and Promoting Therapeutic Jurisprudence." *International Journal of Law and Psychiatry*, 33: 321–8.

Fisher, R.P., R.E. Geiselman, and M. Amador. 1989. "Field Test of the Cognitive Interview: Enhancing the Recollection of the Actual Victims and Witnesses of Crime." *Journal of Applied Psychology*, 74, no. 5: 722–7.

Fisher, S.Z. 1988. "In Search of the Virtuous Prosecutor: A Conceptual Framework." *American Journal of Criminal Law*, 15: 197–261.

Fleming, J.G. 1977. *The Law of Torts.* 5th ed. Sydney: Law Book.

Florida Innocence Commission. 2012. *Final Report to the Supreme Court of Florida.*

Forensicmag.com. https://www.forensicmag.com/article/2005/01/work-innocence-project.

Forst, B. 2004. *Errors of Justice: Nature, Sources, and Remedies.* Cambridge: Cambridge University Press.

Foucault, M. 1980. *Power/Knowledge: Selected Interviews and Other Writings 1972–1977.* Ed. C. Gordon. London: Harvester.

Fourney, R.M., J.C. Newman, S. Porter, and G. Yost. 2013. "Forensic Biology." In M. Pollanen et al., eds., *Forensic Science in Canada: A Report of Multidisciplinary Discussion.* University of Toronto: Centre for Forensic Science and Medicine. http://www.crime-scene-investigator.net/forensic-science-in-canada.pdf. 80–90.

Frank, J. 1957. *Not Guilty.* New York: Doubleday.

Fraser, N. 2007. "Police Reps Worry about SCC's New Tort." *Lawyers Weekly*, 27, no. 28.

Frater, R.J. 2002. "The Seven Deadly Prosecutorial Sins." *Canadian Criminal Law Review*, 7: 209–22.

Freund, J. 2008. "Police Civil Liability for Negligent Investigation: An Analysis of the Supreme Court of Canada Decision in *Hill v. Hamilton-Wentworth Regional Police Services Board.*" *Criminal Law Quarterly* (Toronto), 53: 469–89.

Frieberg, A. 2011. "Post-Adversarial and Post-Inquisitorial Justice: Transcending Traditional Penological Paradigms." *European Journal of Criminology*, 8: 82–101.

Frowd, C.D., et al. 2005. "A Forensically Valid Comparison of Facial Composite Systems." *Psychology, Crime & Law*, 11: 33–52.

Fugelsang, J., and K. Dunbar. 2004. "A Cognitive Neuroscience Framework for Understanding Causal Reasoning and the Law." *Philosophical Transactions of the Royal Society of London. Series B, Biological Sciences*, 359 (1451): 1749–54.

Furgiuele, A. 2007. "The Self-Limiting Appellate Courts and Section 686." *Criminal Law Quarterly* (Toronto), 52: 237–74.

Garland, D. 2001. *The Culture of Control: Crime and Social Order in Contemporary Society.* Chicago: University of Chicago Press.

– 2005. "Capital Punishment and American Culture." *Punishment & Society,* 7, no. 4: 347–76.

Garrett, B. 2008a. "Judging Innocence." *Columbia Law Review,* 108: 55–142.

– 2008b. "Claiming Innocence." *Minnesota Law Review,* 92: 1629–723.

– 2010a. "The Substance of False Confessions." *Stanford Law Review,* 62: 1051–119.

– 2010b. "DNA and Due Process." *Fordham Law Review,* 78: 101–41.

– 2011. *Convicting the Innocent: Where Criminal Prosecutions Go Wrong.* Cambridge, MA: Harvard University Press.

Garrett, B., and P.J. Neufeld. 2009. "Invalid Forensic Science Testimony and Wrongful Convictions." *Virginia Law Review,* 95, no. 1: 1–97.

Geiselman, R.E., et al. 1986. "Enhancement of Eyewitness Memory with the Cognitive Interview." *American Journal of Psychology,* 99: 385–401.

Genua, P. 2006. "Prison Informants: Learning the Lessons of the jailhouse Informant," http://www.justicebehindthewalls.net/resources/jailhouse_informants/informants.pdf.

Gerlach, N. 2004. *The Genetic Imaginary: DNA in the Canadian Criminal Justice System.* Toronto: University of Toronto Press.

Giannelli, P. 2010. "Scientific Fraud." *Criminal Law Bulletin,* 46 (6): 1313–33.

– 2013. "Junk Science and the Execution of an Innocent Man." *New York University Journal of Law & Liberty,* 7, no. 2.

Gilliéron, G. 2013. "The Risks of Summary Proceedings, Plea Bargains, and Penal Orders in Producing Wrongful Convictions in the U.S. and Europe." In C.R. Huff and M. Killias, eds., *Wrongful Convictions and Miscarriages of Justice: Causes and Remedies in North American and European Criminal Justice Systems.* New York: Routledge. 237–59.

Givelber, D. 1997. "Meaningless Acquittals, Meaningful Convictions: Do We Reliably Acquit the Innocent?" *Rutgers Law Review,* 49: 1317–96.

Godsey, M.A., and M. Alou. 2011. "She Blinded Me with Science: Wrongful Convictions and the 'Reverse CSI-Effect.'" *Texas Wesleyan Law Review,* 17: 481–98.

Goff, M.L. 2000. *A Fly for the Prosecution: How Insect Evidence Helps Solve Crimes.* Harvard University Press.

Goldsmith, A. 2005. "Police Reform and the Problem of Trust." *Theoretical Criminology,* 9, no. 4: 443–70.

Goldsmith, P. 2006. *The Review of Infant Death Cases: Addendum to Report, Shaken Baby Syndrome* (London, UK).

Gomery, John H. 2006. "The Pros and Cons of Commissions of Inquiry." *McGill Law Journal / Revue de Droit de McGill,* 51: 783–98.

Goodman, G.S., and R.S. Reed. 1986. "Age Differences in Eyewitness Testimony." *Law and Human Behavior,* 10: 317–32.

Goudge, S.T. 2008. *Inquiry into Pediatric Forensic Pathology in Ontario.* Retrieved at: https://www.attorneygeneral.jus.gov.on.ca/inquiries/goudge/report/index.html.

Gould, J. 2008. *The Innocence Commission: Preventing Wrongful Convictions and Restoring the Criminal Justice System.* New York: New York University Press.

Granhag, P., and L. Stromwell. 2004. *The Detection of Deception in Forensic Contexts.* Cambridge: Cambridge University Press.

Grann, D. 2009. "Trial by Fire: Did Texas Execute an Innocent Man?" *New Yorker*, 9 September.

Green, A. 2010. "Challenging the Refusal to Investigate Evidence Neglected by Trial Lawyers." In M. Naughton, ed., *The Criminal Cases Review Commission: Hope for the Innocent?* Hampshire, UK: Palgrave Macmillan. 46–58.

Green, M. 2005. "Crown Culture and Wrongful Convictions: A Beginning." *Criminal Reports*, 29, no. 6: 262–73.

Greer, S. 1994. "Miscarriages of Justice Reconsidered." *Modern Law Review*, 57, no. 1: 58–74.

Griffin, L. 2001. "The Correction of Wrongful Convictions: A Comparative Perspective." *American University International Law Review*, 16, no. 5: 1241–308.

Gronlund, S.D., et al. 2009. "Robustness of the Sequential Lineup Advantage." *Journal of Experimental Psychology*, 15, no. 2: 140–52.

Gronlund, S.D., J.T. Wixted, and L. Mickes. 2014. "Evaluating Eyewitness Identification Procedures Using ROC Analysis." *Current Directions in Psychological Science*, 23, no. 1: 3–10.

Gross, S. 2008. "Convicting the Innocent." *Annual Review of Law and Social Science*, 4: 173–92.

Gross, S., and B. O'Brien. 2008. "Frequency and Predictors of False Convictions: Why We Know So Little and New Data on Capital Cases." *Journal of Empirical Legal Studies*, 5: 927–62.

Gross, S., and M. Shaffer. 2012. "Exonerations in the United States, 1989–2012." University of Michigan Public Law Working Paper No. 277, 7th Annual Conference on Empirical Legal Studies Paper. Retrieved at: https://www.law.umich.edu/special/exoneration/Documents/exonerations_us_1989_2012_full_report.pdf.

Gross, S.R., et al. 2005. "Exonerations in the United States, 1989 through 2003." *Journal of Criminal Law & Criminology*, 95: 523–60.

Grounds, A. 2004. "Psychological Consequences of Wrongful Conviction." *Canadian Journal of Criminology and Criminal Justice*, 46, no. 2: 165–82.

Gudjonsson, G. 2002. *The Psychology of Interrogations and Confessions: A Handbook*. Chichester, UK: John Wiley and Sons.

Gudjonsson, G., and J. MacKeith. 1997. *Disputed Confessions and the Criminal Justice System*. Maudley Discussion Paper No. 2. London: Institute of Psychiatry.

Gudjonsson, G., and J. Sigurdsson. 2004. "The Relationship of Suggestibility and Compliance with Self-Deception and Other-Deception." *Psychology, Crime & Law*, 10, no. 4: 447–53.

Hageman, C., D. Prevett, and W. Murray. 2002. *DNA Handbook*. Markham, ON: Butterworths Canada.

Hamer, D. 2014. "Wrongful Conictions, Appeals and the Finality Principle: The Need for a Criminal Cases Review Commission." *University of New South Wales Law Journal*, 37, no. 1: 270–311.

Hannem, S. 2012. "Theorizing Stigma and the Politics of Resistance: Symbolic and Structural Stigma in Everyday Life." In S. Hannem and C. Bruckert, eds., *Stigma Revisited: Implications of the Mark*. Ottawa: University of Ottawa Press. 10–28.

Headley, M.R. 2002. "Long on Substance, Short on Process: An Appeal for Process Long Overdue in Eyewitness Lineup Procedures." *Hastings Law Journal*, 53: 681–703.

Hébert, J. 1958. *Coffin était innocent*. Beloeil, QC: les Editions de l'Homme.

– 1963. *J'accuse les assassins de Coffin*. Montreal: Les Éditions du Jour.

Hennessey, T. 2005. *Northern Ireland: The Origins of the Troubles*. Dublin: Gill and Macmillan.

Hickman, A.T. 2004. "Wrongful Convictions and Commissions of Inquiry." *Canadian Journal of Criminology and Criminal Justice*, 46, no. 2: 183–8.

Hill, C., A. Memon, and P. McGeorge. 2008. "The Role of Confirmation Bias in Suspect Interviews: A Systematic Evaluation." *Legal and Criminological Psychology*, 13, no. 2: 357–71.

Hillyard, P., et al. 2004. *Beyond Criminology: Taking Harm Seriously*. London: Pluto Press.

Hoffman, M. 2007. "The Myth of Factual Innocence." *Chicago-Kent Law Review*, 82, no. 2: 663–90.

Hoffmann, J. 2005. "Protecting the Innocent: The Massachusetts Governor's Council Report." *Journal of Criminal Law & Criminology*, 95, no. 2: 561–85.

Hogg, P. 2007. *Constitutional Law of Canada (Student Edition)*. Toronto: Thomson Canada Limited.

Howden, Peter H. 2002. "Judging Errors of Judgment: Accountability, Independence and Vulnerability in a Post-Appellate Conviction Review Process." *Windsor Yearbook of Access to Justice*, 21: 569–600.

Huff, R.C. 2004. "Wrongful Convictions: The American Experience." *Canadian Journal of Criminology and Criminal Justice*, 46, no. 2: 107–20.

Huff, R.C., A. Rattner, and E. Sagarin. 1986. "Guilty until Proven Innocent: Wrongful Conviction and Public Policy." *Crime and Delinquency*, 32, no. 4: 518–44.

– 1996. *Convicted but Innocent: Wrongful Conviction and Public Policy*. Newbury Park, CA: Sage Publications.

Huffman, C. 2002. "Has the Charter Freed the Press? A Comparison of the Effects of the United States and Canadian Constitutional Provisions on the Freedom of the Press to Attend and Cover Criminal Trials." *Michigan State University, Detroit College of Law's Journal of International Law*, 11: 141–73.

Humphrey, J., and S. Westervelt. 2001. "Introduction." In S. Westervelt and J. Humphrey, eds., *Wrongly Convicted: Perspectives on Failed Justice*. New Brunswick, NJ: Rutgers University Press. 1–16.

Inbau, F., et al. 2001. *Criminal Interrogations and Confession*. 4th ed. Boston, MA: Jones and Bartlett Publishers.

Innocence Project, n.d. https://www.innocenceproject.org/causes/eyewitness-misidentification/.

Innocence Project. 2009a. *Reevaluating Lineups: Why Witnesses Make Mistakes and How to Reduce the Chance of Misidentification*. An Innocence Project Report. Benjamin N. Cardozo School of Law, Yeshiva University. Retrieved 17 July 2009 at: https://www.innocenceproject.org/reevaluating-lineups-why-witnesses-make-mistakes-and-how-to-reduce-the-chance-of-a-misidentification/.

– 2009b. *Making up for Lost Time: What the Wrongfully Convicted Endure and How to Provide Fair Compensation*. Retrieved at: https://www.innocenceproject.org/executive-summary-making-up-for-lost-time-what-the-wrongfully-convicted-endure-and-how-to-provide-fair-compensation/.

INUK. 2007. Innocence Network United Kingdom Symposium, University of Bristol. Bristol, UK, 31 March.

Ives, D.E. 2003–4. "The 'Canadian' Approach to Ineffective Assistance of Counsel Claims." *Brandeis Law Journal*, 42: 239–65.

– 2007. "Preventing False Confessions: Is *Oickle* up to the Task?" *San Diego Law Review*, 44: 477–500.

Ives, D.E., and C. Sherrin. 2008. "*R v. Singh* – A Meaningless Right to Silence with Dangerous Consequences." *Criminal Law Review*, 6: 250.

James, A., N. Taylor, and C. Walker. 2000. "The Criminal Cases Review Commission: Economy, Effectiveness and Justice." *Criminal Law Review*, 140–53.

Johnson, D.T. 2002. *The Japanese Way of Justice: Prosecuting Crime in Japan*. Oxford: Oxford University Press.

Johnson, S.L. 1984. "Cross-Racial Identification Errors in Criminal Cases." *Cornell Law Review*, 69, no. 5: 934–87.

Joy, P. 2008. "*Brady* and Jailhouse Informants." Faculty Working Papers Series. No. 08–06–02. Washington University in St Louis, School of Law. Retrieved at: https://papers.ssrn.com/sol3/papers.cfm?abstract_id=1144344.

Joy, P.A. 2006. "The Relationship between Prosecutorial Misconduct and Wrongful Convictions: Shaping Remedies for a Broken System." *Wisconsin Law Review*, 2: 399–429.

Kahn-Fogel, N.A. 2015. "The Promises and Pitfalls of State Eyewitness Identification Reform." *Kentucky Law Journal*, 104, no. 1: 99–164.

Kaiser, H.A. 1989. "Wrongful Conviction and Imprisonment: Towards an End to the Compensatory Obstacle Course." *Windsor Yearbook of Access to Justice*, 9: 96–153.

Kanaki, K., J. Stiakakis, and E. Michalodimitrakis. 2003. "Forensic Entomology in Greece." *Forensic Science International*, 136, no. 1: 388–91.

Kassin, S. 1997. "The Psychology of Confession Evidence." *American Psychologist*, 52: 221–33.

– 2005. "On the Psychology of Confessions: *Does* Innocence *Put* Innocents *at Risk?*" *American Psychologist*, 60, no. 3: 215–28.

Kassin, S.M., et al. 2001. "On the 'General Acceptance' of Eyewitness Testimony Research." *American Psychologist*, 56, no. 5: 405–16.

Kassin, S., and L. Wrightsman. 1985. "Confession Evidence." In S. Kassin and L. Wrightsman, eds., *The Psychology of Evidence and Trial Procedure*. Beverly Hills, CA: Sage Publications. 67–94.

Kassin, S.M., and S.R. Sommers. 1997. "Inadmissible Testimony, Instructions to Disregard and the Jury: Substantive versus Procedural Considerations." *Personality and Social Psychology Bulletin*, 23, no. 10: 1046–54.

Katz, H. 2011. *Justice Miscarried: Inside Wrongful Convictions in Canada*. Toronto: Dundurn Press.

Kaufman, F. 1998a. *Commission on the Proceedings involving Guy Paul Morin: Executive Summary and Recommendations*. Toronto: Ontario Ministry of the Attorney General.

– 1998b. *The Commission on Proceedings Involving Guy Paul Morin*, vol. I. Toronto: Queen's Printer for Ontario, Publications Ontario.

– 1998c. *Commission on the Proceedings involving Guy Paul Morin*, vol. 2. Toronto: Ontario Ministry of the Attorney General.

Keegan, S. 1999. "The Criminal Cases Review Commission's Effectiveness in Handling Cases from Northern Ireland." *Fordham International Law Journal*, 22: 1776–821.

Keenan, K.T., and J. Brockman. 2010. *Mr. Big: Exposing Undercover Investigations in Canada*. Halifax: Fernwood Publishing.

Keirle, H. 2010. "Thoughts from a Victim Support Worker." In M. Naughton, ed., *The Criminal Cases Review Commission: Hope for the Innocent?* Hampshire, UK: Palgrave Macmillan. 41–5.

Kennedy-Pipe, C. 1997. *The Origins of the Present Troubles in Northern Ireland*. London: Longman.

Kerrigan, K. 2010. "Real Possibility or Fat Chance?" In M. Naughton, ed., *The Criminal Cases Review Commission: Hope for the Innocent?* Hampshire, UK: Palgrave Macmillan. 166–77.

Khoday, A. 2013. "Scrutinizing Mr. Big: Police Trickery, the Confessions Rule and the Need to Regulate Extra-Custodial Undercover Interrogations." *Criminal Law Quarterly* (Toronto), 60: 277–300.

Kidd-Hewitt, D. 1995. "Crime and the Media: A Criminological Perspective." In D. Kidd-Hewitt and R. Osborne, eds., *Crime and the Media: The Post-Modern Spectacle*. London: Pluto Press. 1–24.

Kiely, T.F. 2006. *Forensic Evidence: Science and the Criminal Law*. 2nd ed. Boca Raton, FL: Taylor and Francis.

Killias, M., G. Gilliéron, and N. Dongois. 2007. *Erreurs judiciaire en Suisse de 1995 à 2004: Report to the Swiss National Science Foundation*. Lausanne, Zurich: University of Lausanne and University of Zurich.

King, M., and A. Schutz. 1994. "The Ambitious Modesty of Niklas Luhmann." *Journal of Law and Society*, 21, no. 3: 261–87.

Kirwin, B. 1981. *Thomas D'Arcy McGee: Visionary of the Welfare State in Canada*. Alberta: Faculty of Social Welfare, University of Calgary.

Kleinig, J. 2002. "Rethinking Noble Cause Corruption." *International Journal of Police Science & Management*, 4, no. 4: 287–314.

Klockars, C.B. 1980. "The Dirty Harry Problem." *Annals of the American Academy of Political and Social Science*, 452: 33–47.

– 2005. "The Dirty Harry Problem." In T. Newburn, ed., *Policing: Key Readings*. Cullompton, UK: Willan Publishing. 581–95.

Kramer, T.H., R. Buckhout, and P. Eugenio. 1990. "Weapon Focus, Arousal and Eyewitness Memory." *Law and Human Behavior*, 14: 167–84.

Kyle, D. 2004. "Correcting Miscarriages of Justice: The Role of the Criminal Cases Review Commission." *Drake Law Review*, 52, no. 4: 657–76.

Lamer, A. 2006. *The Lamer Commission of Inquiry pertaining to the Cases of: Ronald Dalton, Gregory Parsons, and Randy Druken*. Ministry of Justice, Government of Newfoundland and Labrador. Retrieved at: http://www.justice.gov.nl.ca/just/publications/lamerreport.pdf.

Law Reform Commission of Canada. 1977. "Commissions of Inquiry." Working Paper 17: Administrative Law. Ottawa: Supply and Services Canada.

Lawrence, F. 2009. "Delcaring Innocence: Use of Declaratory Judgments to Vindicate the Wrongly Convicted." *Public Interest Law Journal*, 18: 391–401.

Layton, D., and M. Proulx. 2001. *Ethics and Canadian Criminal Law*. Toronto: Irwin Law.

Leigh, L.H. 2000. "Correcting Miscarriages of Justice: The Role of the Criminal Cases Review Commission." *Alberta Law Review*, 38, no. 2: 365–77.

Leippe, M.R. 1995. "The Case for Expert Testimony about Eyewitness Memory." *Psychology, Public Policy, and Law*, 1, no. 4: 909–59.

Leippe, M.R., and D. Eisenstadt. 2007. "Eyewitness Confidence and the Confidence-Accuracy Relationship in Memory for People." In R.C.L. Lindsay et al., eds., *Memory for People: The Handbook of Eyewitness Psychology*. Mahwah, NJ: Erlbaum. 377–425.

Leo, R. 1992. "From Coercion to Deception: The Changing Nature of Police Interrogation in America." *Crime, Law, and Social Change*, 18, no. 2: 35–59.

– 2001. "False Confessions: Causes, Consequences and Solutions." In S. Westervelt and J. Humphrey, eds., *Wrongly Convicted: Perspectives on Failed Justice*. New Brunswick, NJ: Rutgers University Press. 36–54.

– 2005. "Rethinking the Study of Miscarriages of Justice: Developing a Criminology of Wrongful Conviction." *Journal of Contemporary Criminal Justice*, 21, no. 3: 201–23.

Leo, R., and R. Ofshe. 1998. "The Consequences of False Confessions: Deprivations of Liberty and Miscarriages of Justice in the Age of Psychological Interrogation." *Journal of Criminal Law & Criminology*, 88, no. 2: 429–96.

LeSage, P. 2007. *Report of the Commission of Inquiry into Certain Aspects of the Trial and Conviction of James Driskell*. Winnipeg, MB: Attorney General for Manitoba.

Leverick, F. 2014. "Jury Directions." In J. Chalmers, F. Leverick, and A. Shaw, eds., *Post-Corroboration Safeguards Review: Report of the Academic Expert Group*. Edinburgh: Scottish Government. Retrieved at: http://www.gov.scot/Resource/0046/00460650.pdf. 101–17.

Leverick, F., et al. 2009. Scottish Criminal Cases Review Commission, 10th Anniversary Report. Retrieved at: http://eprints.gla.ac.uk/41609/.

– 2010. "Part of the Establishment? A Decade of the Scottish Criminal Cases Review Commission." *Scots Law Times*, 27: 147–51.

Leverick, F., K. Campbell, and I. Callander. 2017. "Post-Conviction Review: Questions of Innocence, Independence and Necessity." *Stetson Law Review*. Forthcoming.

Levine, M., L. Wallach, and D. Levine. 2007. *Psychological Problems, Social Issues and the Law*. 2nd ed. Boston, MA: Ally and Bacon.

Levinson, J. 2001. "Don't Let Sleeping Lawyers Lie: Raising the Standards for Effective Assistance of Counsel." *American Criminal Law Review*, 38: 147–78.

Lindsay, R.C., et al. 1994. "Using Mug Shots to Find Suspects." *Journal of Applied Psychology*, 79: 121–30.

Lindsay, R.C., and G.L. Wells. 1985. "Improving Eyewitness Identifications from Lineups: Simultaneous versus Sequential Lineup Presentation." *Journal of Applied Psychology*, 70, no. 3: 556–64.

Lipscombe, S., and J. Beard. 2015. "Miscarriages of Justice: Compensation Schemes." Home Affairs. http://researchbriefings.parliament.uk/ResearchBriefing/Summary/SN02131.

Litkowski, R. 2008. "Silencing the Right to Remain Silent." *Ontario Criminal Lawyers' Association Newsletter*, 29, no. 1: 1–4.

Lofquist, W. 2001. "Whodunit? An Examination of the Production of Wrongful Convictions." In S. Westervelt and J. Humphrey, eds., *Wrongly Convicted: Perspectives on Failed Justice*. Newark, NJ: Rutgers University Press. 174–98.

Loftus, E.F. 1979. *Eyewitness Testimony*. Cambridge, MA: Harvard University Press. (National Media Award, Distinguished Contribution, 1980; reissued with new Preface in 1996.)

– 2005. "Planting Misinformation in the Human Mind: A 30-Year Investigation of the Malleability of Memory." *Learning & Memory* (Cold Spring Harbor, NY), 12: 361–6.

Loftus, E.F., J.M. Doyle, and J. Dysert. 2008. *Eyewitness Testimony: Civil & Criminal*. 4th ed. Charlottesville, VA: Lexis Law Publishing.

Loftus, E.F., and K. Ketcham. 1991. *Witness for the Defense; The Accused, the Eyewitness, and the Expert Who Puts Memory on Trial*. New York: St Martin's Press.

Loftus, E.F., G.R. Loftus, and J. Messo. 1987. "Some Facts about 'Weapon focus.'" *Law and Human Behavior*, 11: 55–62.

Londono, O. 2013. "A Retributive Critique of Racial Bias and Arbitrariness in Capital Punishment." *Journal of Social Philosophy*, 44: 95–105.

Lonergan, J. 2008. "Protecting the Innocent: A Model for Comprehensive, Individualized Compensation of the Exonerated." *New York University Journal of Legislation and Public Policy*, 11: 405–52.

Lounsberry, E. 2007. "Arson Science – to the Rescue?" *Philadelphia Inquirer*, 23 January.

Lucas, D.M. 2006. *Report on Forensic Science Matters to the Commission of Inquiry re: James Driskell*. In P. Lesage, *Report on the Commission of Inquiry into certain aspects of the trial and conviction of James Driskell* (2007). Library and Archives Canada Cataloguing in Publication. Retrieved at: http://www.driskellinquiry.ca/pdf/final_report_jan2007.pdf.

Luhmann, N. 1995. *Social Systems*. Stanford, CA: Stanford University Press.

– 2004. *Law as a Social System*. Oxford: Oxford University Press.

Lussier, M. 1992. "Tailoring the Rules of Admissibility: Genes and the Canadian Criminal Law." *Canadian Bar Review*, 71, no. 2: 319–56.

Luther, G.E. 2002. "The Frayed and Tarnished Silver Thread: *Stinchcombe* and the Role of Crown Counsel in Alberta." *Alberta Law Review*, 40: 567–92.

Lutz, B.J., G.W. Ulmschneider, and J.M. Lutz. 2002. "The Trial of the Guildford Four: Government Error or Government Persecution." *Terrorism and Political Violence*, 14, no. 4: 113–30.

Luus, C.A.E., and G.L. Wells. 1994. "Eyewitness Identification Confidence." In D. Ross, J.D. Read, and M. Toglia, eds., *Adult Eyewitness Testimony: Current Trends and Developments*. Cambridge Cambridge University Press. 348–62.

Lyall, S., and T. Arango. 2009. "Britain Confronts Cloaked Journalism." *New York Times*. Retrieved at: http://www.nytimes.com/2009/07/11/world/europe/11britain.html.

MacCallum, E.P. 2006. *Commission of Inquiry into the Wrongful Conviction of David Milgaard*. Final Report. Retrieved at: http://www.publications.gov.sk.ca/freelaw/Publications_Centre/Justice/Milgaard/Milgaard.pdf.

MacDonald, C. 2009. "Wrong Man, Yet Again? The List of Alleged Wrongful Convictions Tied to Attorney Grows." *Maclean's*, 22 October. Retrieved 17 June 2010 at: http://www2.macleans.ca/tag/george-dangerfield/.

Macdonald, R.A. 2011. *An Analysis of the Forms and Functions of Independent Commissions of Inquiry (Royal Commissions) in Canada*. Center for Legal and Economic Studies. Retrieved at: https://www.mcgill.ca/roled/files/roled/roled_commissioninquiries_en_-roderick_macdonald.pdf.

MacDonnell, V.A. 2012. "*R v Sinclair*: Balancing Individual Rights and Societal Interests Outside of Section 1 of the *Charter*." *Queen's Law Journal*, 38, no. 1: 137–64.

MacFarlane, B. 2006. "Convicting the Innocent: A Triple Failure of the Justice System." *Manitoba Law Journal*, 31: 403–87.

– 2008. "Wrongful Convictions: The Effect of Tunnel Vision and Predisposing Circumstances in the Criminal Justice System." Paper prepared for the Goudge Commission of Inquiry into Pediatric Forensic Pathology in Ontario. Retrieved 21 June 2010 at: https://www.attorneygeneral.jus.gov.on.ca/inquiries/goudge/policy_research/pdf/Macfarlane_Wrongful-Convictions.pdf.

– 2012. "Wrongful Convictions: Is It Proper for the Crown to Root around, Looking for Miscarriages of Justice?" *Manitoba Law Journal*, 36, no. 1: 1–35.

MacKay, R. 2007. Bill C-18: An Act to Amend Certain Acts in relation to DNA Identification. Ottawa: Library of Parliament: Parliamentary Information and Research Service.

– 2011. *Legislative Summary of Bill C-2: Fair and Efficient Criminal Trials Act.* Library of Parliament Research Publications. Retrieved at: http://www.parl.gc.ca/About/Parliament/LegislativeSummaries/bills_ls.asp?Language=E&ls=c2&Parl=41&Ses=1&source=library_prb#fn7.

Maddocks, G., and G. Tan. 2010. "Applicant Solicitors: Friends or Foes?" In M. Naughton, ed., *The Criminal Cases Review Commission: Hope for the Innocent?* Hampshire, UK: Palgrave Macmillan. 118–33.

Magnussen, S., et al. 2010. "Beliefs about Factors Affecting the Reliability of Eyewitness Testimony: A Comparison of Judges, Jurors and the General Public." *Applied Cognitive Psychology*, 24, no. 1: 122–33.

Makin, K. "Gag Order Obscures Man's Innocence." *The Province*, 23 Oct. 2000, A3, D2.

Malavé, E.L., and Y. Barkai. 2014. "Conviction Integrity Units: Toward Prosecutorial Self-Regulation?" In M. Zalman and J. Carrano, eds., *Wrongful Conviction and Criminal Justice Reform: Making Justice.* New York: Routledge. 189–206.

Malleson, K. 1994. "Appeals against Conviction and the Principle of Finality." *Journal of Law and Society*, 21: 151–64.

– 1995. "The Criminal Cases Review Commission: How Will It Work?" *Criminal Law Review* (London, UK), 16, no. 2: 929–37.

Malone, C. 2010. "Only the Freshest Will Do." In M. Naughton, ed., *The Criminal Cases Review Commission: Hope for the Innocent?* Hampshire, UK: Palgrave Macmillan. 107–17.

Mandery, E.J. 2005. "Commentary: Efficiency Considerations of Compensating the Wrongfully Convicted." *Criminal Law Bulletin*, 41, no. 3: 492–506.

Manitoba. 2004. *Forensic Evidence Review Committee: Final Report.* Winnipeg.

– 2005. *Forensic Evidence Review Committee #2: Final Report.* Winnipeg.

Marcon, J.L., et al. 2010. "Perceptual Identification and the Cross-Race Effect." *Visual Cognition*, 18, no. 5: 767–79.

Marquis, J. 2005. "The Myth of Innocence." *Journal of Criminal Law & Criminology*, 95, no. 2: 501–21.

Marshall, L. 2002. "Do Exonerations Prove That 'the System Works?'" *Judicature*, 86, no. 2: 83–9.

Martin, D. 2001a. "The Police Role in Wrongful Convictions: An International Comparative Study." In S. Westervelt and J. Humphrey, eds., *Wrongly Convicted: Perspectives on Failed Justice.* Newark, NJ: Rutgers University Press. 77–98.

– 2001b. "Distorting the Prosecution Process: Informers, Mandatory Minimum Sentences and Wrongful Convictions." *Osgoode Hall Law Journal*, 39: 513–27.

McCartney, C. 2006a. *Forensic Identification and Criminal Justice: Forensic Science, Justice and Risk.* Devon, UK: Willan Publishing.

– 2006b. "Liberating Legal Education? Innocence Projects in the US and Australia." *Web Journal of Current Legal Issues*, 3. Retrieved at: http://www.bailii.org/uk/other/journals/WebJCLI/2006/issue3/mccartney3.html.

McLellan, M. 2012a. "Private, Public and Prerogative Remedies to Compensate the Wrongfully Convicted." Unpublished report.

– 2012b. "The Pursuit of Innocence Compensation in Canada." Unpublished report.

Medwed, D. 2003. Actual Innocents: Considerations in Selecting Cases for a New Innocence Project. *Nebraska Law Review*, 81, no. 3: 1097–151.

– 2004. "The Zeal Deal: Prosecutorial Resistance to Post-Conviction Claims of Innocence." *Boston University Law Review*, 84: 125–83.

– 2006. "Anatomy of a Wrongful Conviction: Theoretical Implications and Practical Solutions." *Villanova Law Review*, 51: 101–38.

– 2008. "Innocentrism." *University of Illinois Law Review*, 5: 1549–72.

– 2012. *Prosecution Complex: America's Race to Convict and Its Impact on the Innocent*. New York: New York University Press.

Meissner, C.A., and J.C. Brigham. 2001. "Thirty Years of Investigating the Own-Race Bias in Memory for Faces: A Meta-Analytic Review." *Psychology, Public Policy, and Law*, 7: 3–35.

Mello, M. 1995. "Death and His Lawyers: Why Joseph Spaziano Owes His Life to the Miami Herald – and Not to Any Defense Lawyer or Judge." *Vermont Law Review*, 20: 19–54.

Memon, A., C. Meissner, and J. Fraser. 2010. "The Cognitive Interview: A Meta-Analytic Review and Study Space Analysis of the Past 25 Years." *Psychology, Public Policy, and Law*, 16, no. 4: 340–72.

Memom, A., S. Mastroberardino, and J. Fraser. 2008. "Munsterberg's Legacy: What Does Eyewitness Research Tell Us about the Reliability of Eyewitness Testimony?" *Applied Cognitive Psychology*, 22: 841–51.

Messerschmidt, J. 1993. *Masculinities and Crime: Critique and Reconceptualization of Theory*. Baltimore, MD: Rowman and Littlefield.

Mickes, L., H.D. Flowe, and J.T. Wixted. 2012. "Receiver Operating Characteristic Analysis of Eyewitness Memory: Comparing the Diagnostic Accuracy of Simultaneous and Sequential Lineups." *Journal of Experimental Psychology: Applied*, 18, no. 4: 361–76.

Milgaard, J., and P. Edwards. 2000. *A Mother's Story: The Fight to Free My Son David*. Toronto: Random House Canada.

Millan, L.C. 2015a. "Mr. Big Stings Taking Another Hit in Quebec." *Lawyers Weekly*, 35, no. 22, 16 October.

– 2015b. "Convicted Murderer to Get New Trial in Quebec." *Lawyers Weekly*, 35, no. 3. May.

Mnookin, J.L. 2001. "Fingerprint Evidence in an Age of DNA Profiling." *Brooklyn Law Review*, 67, no. 1: 13–70.

– 2008. "The Validity of Latent Fingerprint Identification: Confessions of a Fingerprinting Moderate." *Law Probability and Risk*, 7: 127–41.

Moore, T. 2008. "The Right to Silence Offers the Only Real Protection during Interrogations." *Ontario Criminal Lawyers' Association Newsletter*, 29, no. 1: 2–4.

Moore, T., and L. Fitzsimmons. 2011. "Justice Imperilled: False Confessions and the Reid Technique." *Criminal Law Quarterly* (Toronto), 57, no. 4: 509–42.

Moore, T., P. Copeland, and R. Schuller. 2009. "Deceit, Betrayal and the Search for Truth: Legal and Psychological Perspectives on the 'Mr. Big' Strategy." *Criminal Law Quarterly* (Toronto), 55, no. 3: 348–404.

Mullin, C. 1991. *Royal Commission on Criminal Justice (Runciman Commission) Report (CM 2263)*. London: HMSO.

Mumma, C. 2004. "The North Carolina Actual Innocence Commission: Uncommon Perspectives Joined by a Common Cause." *Drake Law Review*, 52, no. 4: 647–56.

Munsterberg, H. 1908. *On the Witness Stand: Essays on Psychology and Crime*. New York: Doubleday, Page (1976 reprint of 1927 edition published by Boardman, New York).

National Academy of Sciences. 2009. *Strengthening Forensic Sciences in the United States: A Path Forward*. The National Academies Press, Washington, DC. Retrieved at: https://www.ncjrs.gov/pdffiles1/nij/grants/228091.pdf.

– 2014. *Identifying the Culprit: Assessing Eyewitness Identification.* Washington, DC: National Academies Press. Retrieved at: https://www.innocenceproject.org/wp-content/uploads/2016/02/NAS-Report-ID.pdf.

National DNA Data Bank of Canada. 2006. *Annual Report 2005–2006.* Ottawa: RCMP Forensic Science and Identification Service.

– 2014. *Annual Report 2013–2014.* Ottawa: RCMP Forensic Science and Identification Service. http://www.rcmp-grc.gc.ca/en/the-national-dna-data-bank-canada-annual-report-2014-2015?wbdisable=true.

– 2016. *Annual Report 2015–2016.* Ottawa RCMP Forensic Science and Identificaton Service. http://www.rcmp-grc.gc.ca/en/the-national-dna-data-bank-canada-annual-report-2015-2016#a2.

National Institute for Justice. 1999. *Eyewitness Evidence: A Guide for Law Enforcement.* Washington, DC: United States Department of Justice.

Naughton, M. 2004. "Re-orienting Miscarriages of Justice." In P. Hillyard et al., eds., *Beyond Criminology: Taking Harm Seriously.* London: Pluto Press. 1–12.

– 2005a. "Redefining Miscarriages of Justice: A Revived Human Rights Approach to Unearth Subjugated Discourses of Wrongful Criminal Conviction." *British Journal of Criminology,* 45: 165–82.

– 2005b. "Miscarriages of Justice and the Government of the Criminal Justice System: An Alternative Perspective on the Production and Deployment of Counter-Discourse." *Critical Criminology,* 13: 211–31.

– 2006. "Wrongful Convictions and Innocence Projects in the UK: Help, Hope and Education." *Web Journal of Current Legal Issues,* 3. Retrieved at: http://www.innocencenetwork.org.uk/wp-content/uploads/2014/09/wrongful-convictions-innocence-project.pdf.

– 2007. *Rethinking Miscarriages of Justice: Beyond the Tip of the Iceberg.* Hampshire, UK: Palgrave Macmillan.

– 2010. "The Importance of Innocence for the Criminal Justice System." In M. Naughton, ed., *The Criminal Cases Review Commission: Hope for the Innocent?* Hampshire, UK: Palgrave Macmillan. 17–38.

– 2013. *The Innocent and the Criminal Justice System: A Sociological Analysis of Miscarriages of Justice.* Hampshire, UK: Palgrave Macmillan.

Naylor, B. 1994. "Fair Trial or Free Press: Legal Responses to Media Reports of Criminal Trials." *Cambridge Law Journal,* 53, no. 3: 492–501.

NCCRC. 2004. "Annual Report for 2004: Norwegian Criminal Cases Review Commission." Retrieved at: http://www.gjenopptakelse.no/fileadmin/download/NCCRC_Annual2004r.pdf.

Neuschatz, J., et al. 2007. "The Effects of Accomplice Witnesses and Jailhouse Informants on Jury Decision Making. *Law and Human Behavior,* 32, no. 2: 137–49.

Newby, M. 2010. "Historical Abuse Cases: Why They Expose the Inadequacy of the Real Possibility Test." In M. Naughton, ed., *The Criminal Cases Review Commission: Hope for the Innocent?* Hampshire, UK: Palgrave Macmillan. 97–106.

Nicholson, K. 2009. "Expanding the Duties and Shifting Standards: *Hill v. Hamilton-Wentworth Regional Police Services Board* and the Tort of Negligent Investigation." *Field Files,* 1: 1–2, 4.

Nickerson, R.S. 1998. "Confirmation Bias: A Ubiquitous Phenomenon in Many Guises." *Review of General Psychology,* 2: 175–220.

Nobles, R., and D. Schiff. 2000. *Understanding Miscarriages of Justice: Law, the Media and the Inevitability of Crisis*. Oxford: Oxford University Press.

– 2001. "The Criminal Cases Review Commission: Reporting Success?" *Modern Law Review*, 64, no. 2: 280–99.

– 2010. "After Ten Years: An Investment in Justice?" In M. Naughton, ed., *The Criminal Cases Review Commission: Hope for the Innocent?* Hampshire, UK: Palgrave Macmillan. 151–65.

Nova Scotia. 1990. Commission of Inquiry concerning the Adequacy of Compensation Paid to Donald Marshall, Jr. *Report of the Commissioner*. Halifax: The Commissioner, Gregory T. Evans.

O'Connor, D. 2006a. *Commission of Inquiry into the Actions of Canadian Officials in Relation to Maher Arar*. Ottawa. Retrieved at: http://www.sirc-csars.gc.ca/pdfs/cm_arar_bgv1-eng.pdf.

– 2006b. *Report of the Events relating to Maher Arar, Factual Background, Volume 1, Commission of Inquiry into the Actions of Canadian Officials in Relation to Maher Arar. Dennis R. O'Connor, Commissioner*. Retrieved at: http://www.sirc-csars.gc.ca/pdfs/cm_arar_bgv1-eng.pdf.

Ó Dochartaigh, N. 2005. *From Civil Rights to Armalites: Derry and the Birth of Irish Troubles*. 2nd ed. New York: Palgrave Macmillan.

Office of the Chief Coroner. 2007. "Public Announcement of Review of Criminally Suspicious and Homicide Cases Where Dr. Charles Smith Conducted Autopsies or Provided Opinions." Backgrounder. Toronto.

Ofshe, R., and R. Leo. 1997a. "The Decision to Confess Falsely: Rational Choice and Irrational Action." *Denver University Law Review*, 74: 979–1122.

– 1997b. "The Social Psychology of Police Interrogation: The Theory and Classification of True and False Confessions." *Studies in Law, Politics, and Society*, 16: 189–251.

O'Malley, P. 2005. "Governing Risks." In A. Sarat, ed., *The Blackwell Companion to Law and Society*. Oxford: Blackwell. 292–308.

Ontario. 1984. *Report of the Royal Commission of Inquiry into Certain Deaths at the Hospital for Sick Children and Related Matters*. Toronto: Ministry of the Attorney General.

– 2005. "Crown Policy Manual, Ministry of Attorney General." Retrieved 1 June 2010 at: https://www.attorneygeneral.jus.gov.on.ca/english/crim/cpm/.

Oscapella, E. 2012. "Genetic Privacy and Discrimination: An Overview of Selected Major Issues." British Columbia Civil Liberties Association. Retrieved at: http://bccla.org/wp-content/uploads/2012/03/2012-BCCLA-Report-Genetic-Privacy.pdf.

Ottley, B. 2010. "Beyond the Crime Laboratory: The Admissibility of Unconfirmed Forensic Evidence in Arson Cases." *New England Journal on Criminal and Civil Confinement*, 36, no. 2: 263–88.

OVC (Office for Victims of Crime). 2006. "OVC Fact Sheet: The Justice for All Act." U.S. Department of Justice, Office for Victims of Crime. Retrieved at: https://www.ovc.gov/publications/factshts/justforall/welcome.html.

Paciocco, D. 2009. "Taking a 'Goudge' out of Bluster and Blarney: An 'Evidence-Based Approach' to Expert Testimony." *Canadian Criminal Law Review*, 13, no. 2: 135–58.

Paciocco, D.M. 1999. "Coping with Expert Evidence about Human Behaviour." *Queen's Law Journal*, 25, no. 2: 305–46.

Paciocco, D.M., and L. Stuesser. 2015. *The Law of Evidence*. 7th ed. Toronto: Irwin Law.

Packer, H. 1968. *The Limits of the Criminal Sanction*. Stanford, CA: Stanford University Press.

Parker, L., and M. Lynn. 2002. "What's Race Got to Do with It? Critical Race Theory's Conflicts with and Connections to Qualitative Research Methodology and Epistemology." *Qualitative Inquiry*, 8, no. 1: 7–22.

Pedzek, K. 2007. "Expert Testimony on Eyewitness Memory and Identification." In M. Costanzo, D. Krauss, and K. Pedzek, eds., *Expert Psychological Testimony for the Courts*. Mahwah, NJ: Lawrence Erlbaum Associates. 99–117.

Perreault, S. 2009. "The Incarceration of Aboriginal People in Adult Correctional Services." *Juristat*, 29, no. 3: 1–27.

Phillips, J.K. 2002–3. "The Rest of the Story of *R. v. Stinchcombe*: A Case Study in Disclosure Issues." *Alberta Law Review*, 40: 539–65.

Pickel, K.L. 2009. "The Weapon Focus Effect on Memory for Female versus Male Perpetrators." *Memory* (Hove, UK), 17, no. 6: 664–78.

Pickel, K.L., et al. 2008. "The Weapon Focus Effect in Child Eyewitnesses." *Psychology, Crime & Law*, 14, no. 1: 61–72.

Pollanen, M., et al. 2013. "Introduction." *Forensic Science in Canada: A Report of Multidisciplinary Discussion*. University of Toronto: Centre for Forensic Science and Medicine. Retrieved at: http://www.forensics.utoronto.ca/Assets/ LMPF+Digital+Assets/Forensic+Science+in+Canada.pdf.

Poloz, A. 2015. "Motive to Lie? A Critical Look at the 'Mr. Big' Investigative Technique." *Canadian Criminal Law Review*, 19: 231–51.

Post, L. 2005. "Innocence Projects Spark Debate." *National Law Journal*, 3 July 2005.

Pozzulo, J.D., et al. 2009. "Examining the Relation between Eyewitness Recall and Recognition for Children and Adults." *Psychology, Crime & Law*, 15, no. 5: 409–24.

Pretty, I.A. 2006. "The Barriers to Achieving an Evidence Base for Bitemark Analysis." *Forensic Science International*, 159S: 111–19.

Pretty, I.A., and D. Sweet. 2001. "A Look at Forensic Dentistry Part I: The Role of Teeth in the Determination of Human Identity." *British Dental Journal*, 190, no. 7: 359–66.

Public Prosecution Service. 2002. "Crown Halts Johnson Murder Prosecution," 18 February. Retrieved at: http://www.gov.ns.ca/news/details.asp?id=20020218002.

Quirk, H. 2007. "Identifying Miscarriages of Justice: Why Innocence in the UK Is Not the Answer." *Modern Law Review*, 70, no. 5: 759–77.

Raeder, M.S. 2007. "See No Evil: Wrongful Convictions and the Prosecutorial Ethics of Offering Testimony by Jailhouse Informants and Dishonest Experts." *Fordham Law Review*, 76: 1413–52.

Rapp, C.G. 2000. "DNA's Dark Side – Book Note." *Yale Law Journal*, 110, no. 1: 163–71.

Ratushny, E. 2009. *The Conduct of Public Inquiries: Law, Policy and Practice*. Toronto: Irwin Law.

Read, J.D. 2006. "Features of Eyewitness Testimony Evidence Implicated in Wrongful Convictions." *Manitoba Law Journal*, 31: 523–42.

Read, J.D., J.R. Vokey, and R. Hammersley. 1990. "Changing Photos of Faces: Effects of Exposure Duration and Photo Similarity on Recognition and the Accuracy-Confidence Relationship." *Journal of Experimental Psychology, Learning, Memory, and Cognition*, 16, no. 5: 870–82.

Reichs, K.J. 2007. "Forensic Anthropology." In C. Wecht and J. Rago, eds., *Forensic Science and Law: Investigative Applications in Criminal, Civil and Family Justice*. Boca Raton, FL: Taylor and Francis Group. 455–63.

Ritzer, G. 2010. *Contemporary Sociological Theory and Its Classical Roots: The Basics*. 3rd ed. St Louis, MO: McGraw-Hill.

Roach, K. 1994. "Public Inquiries, Prosecutions or Both?" *University of New Brunswick Law Journal*, 43: 415–26.

– 1995. "Canadian Public Inquiries and Accountability." In P.C. Stenning, ed., *Accountability for Criminal Justice: Selected Essays*. Toronto: University of Toronto Press. 268–93.

– 1999a. "Four Models of the Criminal Process." *Journal of Criminal Law & Criminology*, 89, no. 2: 671–716.

– 1999b. "Preserving Preliminary Inquiries." Editorial, *Criminal Law Quarterly* (Toronto), 42, nos. 2 and 3: 161–3.

– 2006. "Report relating to Paragraph 1(f) of the Order in Council for the Commission of Inquiry into Certain Aspects of the Trial and Conviction of James Driskell." Retrieved 23 January 2007 at: http://www.driskellinquiry.ca/pdf/roachreport.pdf.

– 2007. "Unreliable Evidence and Wrongful Convictions: The Case for Excluding Tainted Identification Evidence and Jailhouse and Coerced Confessions." *Criminal Law Quarterly* (Toronto), 52: 210–36.

– 2008. "Exonerating the Wrongfully Convicted: Do We Need Innocence Hearings?" In M.E. Beare, ed., *Honouring Social Justice*. Toronto: University of Toronto Press. 55–84.

– 2010. "The Role of Innocence Commissions: Error Discovery, Systemic Reform or Both?" *Chicago-Kent Law Review*, 85: 89–125.

– 2012. "Wrongful Conviction in Canada." *University of Cincinnati Law Review*, 80, no. 4: 1465–526.

– 2015. "The Wrongful Conviction of Indigenous People in Australia and Canada." *Flinders Law Journal*, 17: 203–62.

Roach, K., and G. Trotter. 2005. "Miscarriages of Justice in the War against Terror." *Penn State Law Review*, 109, no. 4: 967–1041.

Roberts, S., and L. Weathered. 2009. "Assisting the Factually Innocent: The Contradictions and Compatibility of Innocence Projects and the Criminal Cases Review Commission." *Oxford Journal of Legal Studies*, 29, no. 1: 43–70.

Robinson, G. 2002. "Exploring Risk Management in Probation Practice: Contemporary Developments in England and Wales." *Punishment & Society*, 4, no. 1: 5–25.

Rosen, P. 1992. *Wrongful Convictions in the Criminal Justice System*. Ottawa: Library of Parliament, Background Paper-285E. January.

Ross, R. 2007. "*R. v. Singh*: Addressing the Divide between the Section 7 Right to Silence and the Common Law Confessions Rule." *The Court*, 1, no. 4. https://www.thecourt.ca/r-v-singh-addressing-the-divide-between-the-section-7-right-to-silence-and-the-common-law-confessions-rule/.

Roth, J. 2016. "Informant Witnesses and the Risk of Wrongful Conviction." *American Criminal Law Review*, 53: 737–97.

Royal Canadian Mounted Police. 2010. "Operational Manual, 25.4 Sequential Photograph Packs."

Royal Commission on the Donald Marshall, Jr Prosecution. 1989a. *Digest of Findings and Recommendations, Vol. 1*. Halifax.

– 1989b. *Commissioners' Report: Digest of Findings and Recommendations*. Halifax.

Royal Commission on the Ocean Ranger Marine Disaster. 1984–5. *Report One [microform]: The Loss of the Semisubmersible Drill Rig Ocean Ranger and Its Crew*. St John's.

Rutledge, John P. 2001. "They All Look Alike: The Inaccuracy of Cross-Racial Identifications." *American Journal of Criminal Law*, 28: 207–28.

Ryan, K.J., and C.G. Ray. 2004. *Sherris Medical Microbiology: An Introduction to Infectious Diseases*. 4th ed. New York: McGraw Hill-Medical.

Saks, M., and D. Faigman. 2008. "Failed Forensics: How Forensic Science Lost Its Way and How It Might Yet Find It." *Annual Review of Law and Social Science*, 4: 149–71.

Salter, L. 1990. "The Two Contradictions in Public Inquiries." In A.P. Pross, I. Christie, and J.A. Yogis, eds., *Commissions of Inquiry*. Toronto: Carswell. 173.

Sangha, B., K. Roach, and R. Moles. 2010. *Forensic Investigations and Miscarriages of Justice: The Rhetoric Meets the Reality*. Toronto: Irwin Law.

Savage, S., J. Grieve, and S. Poyser. 2007. "Putting Wrongs to Right: Campaigns against Miscarriages of Justice." *Criminology & Criminal Justice*, 7, no. 1: 83–105.

SCCRC. 2006. "Annual Report and Accounts, 2005–2006, Scottish Criminal Cases Review Commission." Retrieved at: http://www.audit-scotland.gov.uk/docs/central/2006/fa_0506_criminal_cases_review.pdf.

Schacter, D.L. 2001. *The Seven Sins of Memory: How the Mind Forgets and Remembers*. New York: Houghton Mifflin Company.

Scheck, B., and P. Neufeld. 2002a. "DNA and Innocence Scholarship." In S. Westervelt and J. Humphrey, eds., *Wrongly Convicted: Perspectives on Failed Justice*. New York: Scholarly Book Services. 241–52.

– 2002b. "Toward the Formation of 'Innocence Commissions' in America." *Judicature*, 86, no. 2: 98–105.

Scheck, B., P. Neufeld, and J. Dwyer. 2000. *Actual Innocence: Five Days to Execution and Other Dispatches from the Wrongly Convicted*. New York: Random House.

Schehr, R. 2005. "The Criminal Cases Review Commission as a State Strategic Selection Mechanism." *American Criminal Law Review*, 42, no. 2: 1289–302.

Schermbrucker, D. 2004. "Eyewitness Evidence: The Role of Experts in the Criminal Courts." Paper presented to the Canadian Bar Association (Nova Scotia) Conference on Key Developments in the Law of Evidence, Halifax. Alan D. Gold Collection of Criminal Law Articles ADGN/RP-186, 23 April 2004.

Schmitz, C. 2000. "Supreme Court Splits on Handling of Jailhouse Informants." *Lawyers Weekly*, 19, no. 40: 1–4.

Schneider, E.M. 2000. *Battered Women and Feminist Lawmaking*. New Haven, CT: Yale University Press.

Schoenfeld, H. 2005. "Violated Trust: Conceptualizing Prosecutorial Misconduct." *Journal of Contemporary Criminal Justice*, 21, no. 3: 250–71.

Scott, D.W. 1990. "The Rights and Obligations of Those Subject to Inquiry and of Witnesses, in Commissions of Inquiry." In A.P. Pross, I. Christie, and J.A. Yogis, eds., *Commissions of Inquiry*. Toronto: Carswell. 133.

Sellar, W. 1947. "A Century of Commissions of Inquiry." *Canadian Bar Review*, 25, no. 1: 1–28.

Shaw, J.S., III. 1996. "Increases in Eyewitness Confidence Resulting from Post-Event Questioning." *Journal of Experimental Psychology: Applied*, 2: 126–46.

Shaw, J.S., III, and K.A. McClure. 1996. "Repeated Post-Event Questioning Can Lead to Elevated Levels of Eyewitness Confidence." *Law and Human Behavior*, 20: 629–53.

Shaw, T. 1995. "Murder Case Sisters Lose Fight against Tabloid Press." *Electronic Telegraph*. Retrieved at: http://www.innocent.org.uk/cases/mltaylor/index.html.

Sheehy, C. 1999. "Compensation for Wrongful Conviction in New Zealand." *Auckland University Law Review*, 8: 977–1000.

Shelton, D.E., Y.S. Kim, and G. Barak. 2006. "A Study of Juror Expectations and Demands concerning Scientific Evidence: Does the 'CSI Effect' Exist?" *Vanderbilt Journal of Entertainment & Technology Law*, 9: 331–68.

Sher, J. 2001. *"Until You Are Dead": Steven Truscott's Long Ride into History*. Toronto: Alfred A. Knopf Canada.

Sherrer, H. 2003. "The Complicity of Judges in the Generation of Wrongful Convictions." *Northern Kentucky Law Review*, 30, no. 3: 539–83.

Sherrin, C. 1997. "Jailhouse Informants, Part 1: Problems with Their Use." *Criminal Law Quarterly* (Toronto), 40: 106–22.

– 2005. "False Confessions and Admissions in Canadian Law." *Queen's Law Journal*, 30, no. 2: 601–59.

– 2007. "Comment on the Report on the Prevention of Miscarriages of Justice." *Criminal Law Quarterly* (Toronto), 52: 140–74.

– 2008. "The Charter and Protection against Wrongful Conviction: Good, Bad or Irrelevant?" *Supreme Court Review*, 40: 377–414.

– 2010. "Declarations of Innocence." *Queen's Law Journal*, 35: 438–92.

– 2011. "Guilty Pleas from the Innocent." *Windsor Review of Legal & Social Issues*, 30, no. 1: 1–35.

Shulgan, C. 2006. "Framed?" *Toro*. April. 79–85.

Siegel, A. 2005. "Moving down the Wedge of Injustice: A Proposal for a Third Generation of Wrongful Convictions Scholarship and Advocacy." *American Criminal Law Review*, 42: 1219–37.

Simon, D. 2006. "Are Wrongful Convictions Episodic or Epidemic?" Paper presented at the Annual Meeting of the Law and Society Association. July.

Singh, K., and G. Gudjonsson. 1992. "Interrogative Suggestibility among Adolescent Boys and Its Relationship with Intelligence, Memory, and Cognitive Set." *Journal of Adolescence*, 15: 155–61.

Skagerberg, E.M. 2007. "Co-Witness Feedback in Line-Ups." *Applied Cognitive Psychology*, 21: 489–97.

Skinner, M.F., et al. 2010. "Taking the Pulse of Forensic Anthropology in Canada." *Canadian Society of Forensic Science*, 43, no. 4: 191–203.

Skurka, S. 2002. "A Canadian Perspective on the Role of Cooperators and Informants." *Cardozo Law Review*, 23: 759–70.

Slapper, G., and D. Kelly, 1996. *Sourcebook on the English Legal System*. London: Routledge-Cavendish.

Slatterly, T.P. 1972. *"They Got to Find Me Guilty Yet."* Toronto: Doubleday and Company.

Smith, B. 2010. "The Professor and the Prosecutor: Anita Alvarez's Office Turns up the Heat on David Protess's Medill Innocence Project." *Chicago Magazine*. Retrieved at: http://www.chicagomag.com/Chicago-Magazine/February-2010/Anita-Alvarez-turns-up-the-heat-in-her-battle-with-Northwesterns-David-Protess-and-his-Medill-Innocence-Project/index.php?cparticle=4&siarticle=3#artanc.

Smith, S., V. Stinson, and M.W. Patry. 2009. "Using the "Mr. Big" Technique to Elicit Confessions: Successful Innovation or Dangerous Development in the Canadian Legal System?" *Psychology, Public Policy, and Law*, 15, no. 3: 168–93.

Solicitor General of Nova Scotia. 1992. *Marshall Update: Justice Reform Review.* Halifax: Province House.

Somji, S. 2012. "A Comparative Study of the Post-Conviction Review Process in Canada and the United Kingdom." *Criminal Law Quarterly* (Toronto), 58, no. 2: 137–90.

Sossin, L. 2014. "The Goudge Inquiry: Anatomy of Success for an Inquiry to Change Policy?" In G.J. Inwood and C.M. Johns, eds., *Commissions of Inquiry and Policy Change: A Comparative Analysis.* Toronto: University of Toronto Press. 244–60.

Spector, M., and J.I. Kitsuse. 1977. *Constructing Social Problems.* Hawthorne, NY: Aldine de Gruyter.

Spencer, J.R. 2010. "Compensation for Wrongful Imprisonment." *Criminal Law Review* (London, UK), 11: 803–22.

Spiegelman, C., and W. Tobin. 2013. "Analysis of Experiments in Forensic Firearms/Toolmarks Practice Offered as Support for Low Rates of Practice Error and Claims of Inferential Certainty." *Law Probability and Risk,* 12, no. 2: 115–33.

State of Connecticut. 2009. *Report of the Advisory Commission on Wrongful Convictions.* Pursuant to Public Act 08–143, an Act concerning the Compensation of Wrongfully Convicted and Incarcerated Persons, the Duties and Duration of the Sentencing Task Force and the Preparation of Racial and Ethnic Impact Statements. Retrieved at: http://www.jud.ct.gov/committees/wrongfulconviction/WrongfulConvictionComm_Report.pdf.

State of Illinois. 2002. *Report of the Governor's Commission on Capital Punishment.* Chicago. Retrieved at: http://illinoismurderindictments.law.northwestern.edu/docs/Illinois_Moratorium_Commission_complete-report.pdf.

State of New Jersey. 2007. *New Jersey Death Penalty Study Commission Report.* Trenton, NJ. Retrieved at: http://www.njleg.state.nj.us/committees/dpsc_final.pdf.

Steblay, N., et al. 2001. "Eyewitness Accuracy Rates in Sequential and Simultaneous Lineup Presentations: A Meta-Analytic Comparison." *Law and Human Behavior,* 25: 459–73.

Steblay, N.K., J. Dysart, and G.L. Wells. 2011. "Seventy-Two Tests of the Sequential Lineup Superiority Effect: A Meta-Analysis and Policy Discussion." *Psychology, Public Policy, and Law,* 17, no. 1: 99–139.

Steblay, N.M. 1992. "A Meta-Analytic Review of the Weapon Focus Effect." *Law and Human Behavior,* 16: 413–24.

Steiker, C., and J. Steiker. 2005. "Seduction of Innocence: The Attraction and Limitations of the Focus on Innocence in Capital Punishment Law and Advocacy." *Journal of Criminal Law & Criminology,* 95, no. 2: 587–624.

Stephens, M., and P. Hill. 1999. "The Role and Impact of Journalism." In C. Walker and K. Starmer, eds., *Miscarriages of Justice: A Review of Justice in Error.* London: Blackstone Press. 262–84.

Stiglitz, J., J. Brooks, and T. Shulman. 2002. "The Hurricane Meets the Paper Chase: Innocence Projects New Emerging Role in Clinical Legal Education." *California Western Law Review,* 38: 413–31.

Stoddart, J. 2005. *Standing Committee on Justice, Human Rights, Public Safety and Emergency Preparedness, with respect to Bill C-13, an Act to Amend the Criminal Code, the DNA Identification Act and the National Defence Act.* Retrieved at: https://www.priv.gc.ca/en/opc-actions-and-decisions/advice-to-parliament/2005/parl_050208/.

Stridbeck, U., and P.S. Magnussen. 2012. "Prevention of Wrongful Convictions: Norwegian Legal Safeguards and the Criminal Cases Review Commission." *University of Cincinnati Law Review*, 80, no. 4: 1373–90.

Stuesser, L. 2002. "The Accused's Right to Silence: No Doesn't Mean No." *Manitoba Law Journal*, 29, no. 2: 149–70.

– 2006. "Experts on Eyewitness Identification: I Just Don't See It." *Manitoba Law Journal*, 31: 543–53.

Stutz, J. 2008. "What Gets Done and Why: Implementing the Recommendations of Public Inquiries." *Canadian Public Administration*, 51, no. 3: 501–21.

Sullivan, T.P. 2004. *Police Experiences with Recording Custodial Interrogations*. Chicago: Center on Wrongful Convictions, Bluhm Legal Clinic.

Suni, E.Y. 2002. "Ethical Issues for Innocence Projects: An Initial Primer." *UKMC Law Review*, 70, no. 4: 921–69.

Surette, R. 1998. *Media, Crime and Criminal Justice: Images and Realities*. 2nd ed. Belmont, CA: Wadsworth Publishing Company.

Sutherland, K. 2007. "The Tort of Negligent Investigation: Hill v. Hamilton-Wentworth." *The Court*. 19 October. Retrieved 20 Oct. 2009 at: http://www.thecourt.ca/the-tort-of-negligent-investigation-hill-v-hamilton-wentworth.

Sweet, D., and B. Wood. 2013. "Forensic Odontology." In M. Pollanen et al., eds., *Forensic Science in Canada: A Report of Multidisciplinary Discussion*. University of Toronto: Centre for Forensic Science and Medicine. http://www.crime-scene-investigator.net/forensic-science-in-canada.pdf. 31–40.

Sweet, D., and J.A. DiZinno. 1996. "Personal Identification through Dental Evidence-Tooth Fragments to DNA." *Journal of the California Dental Association*, 24: 35–42.

Tanovich, D.M. 1994. "*Monteleone*'s Legacy: Confusing Sufficiency with Weight." *Criminal Reports*, 27, no. 4: 174–81.

Taylor, N.W. 2004. "Compensation for Miscarriage of Justice, Eligibility." *Journal of Criminal Law Review*, 68, no. 5: 380–2.

Teubner, G., R. Nobles, and D. Schiff. 2003. "The Autonomy of Law: An Introduction to Legal Autopoiesis." In D. Schiff and R. Nobles, eds., *Jurisprudence*. London: Butterworth. https://www.jura.uni-frankfurt.de/42852943/autonomy_of_law.pdf.

Thompson, S. 2011. "Judicial Gatekeeping of Police-Generated Witness Testimony." University of Houston Law Center, No. 2011-A-8. Retrieved at: https://papers.ssrn.com/sol3/papers.cfm?abstract_id=1911548.

Thompson-Cannino, J., R. Cotton, and E. Torneo. 2009. *Picking Cotton: Our Memoir of Injustice and Redemption*. New York: St Martin's Press.

Trott, S. 1996. "Words of Warning for Prosecutors Using Criminals as Witnesses." *Hastings Law Journal*, 47: 1381–432.

Trotter, G.T. 2001. "Justice, Politics and the Royal Prerogative of Mercy: Examining the Self-Defence Review." *Queen's Law Journal*, 26: 339–95.

– 2005. "False Confessions and Wrongful Convictions." *Ottawa Law Review*, 52: 181–210.

Tulving, E. 1984. "Precis of Elements of Episodic Memory." *Behavioral and Brain Sciences*, 7: 223–68.

Uphoff, R. 2006. "Convicting the Innocent: Aberration or Systemic Problem?" *Wisconsin Law Review*, 2: 739–842.

Van Harten, G. 2003. "Truth before Punishment: A Defence of Public Inquiries." *Queen's Law Journal*, 29: 242–57.

VanLaerhoven, S.L., and G.S. Anderson. 2013. "Forensic Entomology." In M. Pollanen et al., eds., *Forensic Science in Canada: A Report of Multidisciplinary Discussion.* University of Toronto: Centre for Forensic Science and Medicine. http://www.crime-scene-investigator.net/forensic-science-in-canada.pdf. 53–60.

Vick, D. 1995. "Poorhouse Justice: Underfunded Indigent Defence Services and Arbitrary Death Sentences." *Buffalo Law Review*, 43, no. 2: 329–460.

Vonn, M. 2011. "Can a DNA Dragnet Undermine an Investigation? A Case Study in Canada." *Genewatch*, 24, no. 5. Retrieved at http://www.councilforresponsiblegenetics. org/GeneWatch/GeneWatchPage.aspx?pageId=377.

Wagstaff, G.F., et al. 2003. "Can Laboratory Findings on Eyewitness Testimony Be Generalized to the Real World? An Archival Analysis of the Influence of Violence, Weapon Presence, and Age on Eyewitness Accuracy." *Journal of Psychology*, 137, no. 1: 17–28.

Walker, C. 1999a. "Miscarriages of Justice in Principle and Practice." In C. Walker and K. Starmer, eds., *Miscarriages of Justice: A Review of Justice in Error*. London: Blackstone Press. 31–55.

– 1999b. "Miscarriages of Justice in Scotland." In C. Walker and K. Starmer, eds., *Miscarriages of Justice: A Review of Justice in Error*. London: Blackstone Press. 323–53.

– 2002a. "Miscarriages of Justice." In M. McConville and G. Wilson, eds., *The Handbook of the Criminal Justice Process*. Oxford: Oxford University Press. 505–23.

– 2002b. "Miscarriages of Justice: An Inside Job." Centre for Criminal Justice Studies, University of Leeds, *Criminal Justice Review*, www.leeds.ac.uk/law/ccjs/an_ reps/13rep07f.doc.

Walker, C., and K. Campbell. 2010. "The CCRC as an Option for Canada: Forwards or Backwards?" In M. Naughton, ed., *The Criminal Cases Review Commission: Hope for the Innocent?* Hampshire, UK: Palgrave Macmillan. 191–204.

Walker, C., and R. Stockdale. 1999. "Forensic Evidence." In C. Walker and K. Starmer, eds., *Miscarriages of Justice: A Review of Justice in Error*. London: Blackstone Press. 119–50.

Walker, S. 2010. "The Subjective-Objective Dimension in *R. v. Singh*: Rethinking the Distinction between the Common Law Confessions Rule and the Charter Right to Silence." *Criminal Law Quarterly* (Toronto), 55: 405–28.

Walton, J.A. 2001. "Struck by the Falling Bullet: The Continuing Need for Definitive Standards in Media Coverage of Criminal Proceedings." *Cleveland State Law Review*, 49: 407–15.

Warden, R. 2002. "The Revolutionary Role of Journalism in Identifying and Rectifying Wrongful Convictions." *UKMC Law Review*, 70, no. 4: 803–46.

– 2006. *The Snitch System: How Snitch Testimony Sent Randy Steidl and Other Innocent Americans to Death Row.* Northwestern University School of Law. A Center on Wrongful Convictions Survey. Retrieved at: https://www.innocenceproject.org/wp-content/ uploads/2016/02/SnitchSystemBooklet.pdf.

Weathered, L. 2003. "Investigating Innocence: The Emerging Role of Innocence Projects in the Correction of Wrongful Conviction in Australia." *Griffith Law Review*, 12, no. 1: 64–90.

Wecht, C., and Rago, J., eds. 2007. *Forensic Science and Law: Investigative Applications in Criminal, Civil and Family Justice*. Boca Raton, FL: Taylor and Francis Group.

Wecht, C., and V. Weedn. 2007. "Forensic Pathology." In C. Wecht and J. Rago, eds., *Forensic Science and Law: Investigative Applications in Criminal, Civil and Family Justice.* Boca Raton, FL: Taylor and Francis Group. 387–400.

Weigand, H. 2009. "Rebuilding a Life: The Wrongfully Convicted and Exonerated." *Public Interest Law Journal*, 18: 427–37.

Weinper, F., and M. Sandler. 2003. *Criminal Procedure: Cases, Notes, and Materials*. 2nd ed. Toronto: Butterworths.

Weinstein, S. 2005. "Confessions: Are Undercover Officers Ever Persons in Authority?" *Ontario Criminal Lawyers' Association Newsletter*, 26, no. 2: 3.

Weisberg, R. 1995. "Who Defends Capital Defendants?" *Santa Clara Law Review*, 35: 535–46.

Weitzman, L.R., and K. Campbell. 2012. "The Admissibility of Confessions: A Review of Hebert, Oickle, Singh and Sinclair." *National Judicial Institute / Institut national de la magistrature*.

Wells, G.L. 1984. "The Psychology of Lineup Identifications." *Journal of Applied Social Psychology*, 89: 92–103.

– 2006. "Eyewitness Identification: Systemic Reforms." *Wisconsin Law Review*, 2: 615–43.

Wells, G.L., and A.L. Bradfield. 1998. "'Good, You Identified the Suspect': Feedback to Eyewitnesses Distorts Their Reports of the Witnessing Experience." *Journal of Applied Psychology*, 83, no. 3: 60–76.

Wells, G.L., and E.A. Olson. 2003. "Eyewitness Testimony." *Annual Review of Psychology*, 54: 277–95.

Wells, G.L., and E.F. Loftus. 2012. "Eyewitness Memory for People and Events." In A. Goldstein, ed., *Forensic Psychology*, 2nd ed., vol. 1, A. Goldstein. *Handbook of Psychology*. New York: John Wiley and Sons.

Wells, G.L., and L.E. Hasel. 2008. "Eyewitness Identification: Issues in Common Knowledge and Generalization." In E. Borgida and S.T. Fiske, eds., *Beyond Common Sense: Psychological Science in the Courtroom*. Malden, MA: Blackwell. 159–76.

Wells, G.L., et al. 1998. "Eyewitness Identification Procedures: Recommendations for Lineups and Photospreads." *Law and Human Behavior*, 22: 603–47.

– 2000. "From the Lab to the Police Station: A Successful Application of Eyewitness Research." *American Psychologist*, 55, no. 6: 581–98.

Westervelt, S., and K. Cook. 2012. *Life after Death Row: Exonerees' Search for Community and Identity*. New Brunswick, NJ: Rutgers University Press.

Whitman, J.Q. 2003. *Harsh Justice: Criminal Punishment and the Widening Divide between America and Europe*. New York: Oxford University Press.

Wiebe, Rudy, and Yvonne Johnson. 1999. *Stolen Life: The Journey of a Cree Woman*. Toronto: Alfred A. Knopf Canada.

Wildsmith, B.H. 1991. "Getting at Racism: The Marshall Inquiry." *Saskatchewan Law Review*, 55: 97–126.

Williams, P., and J. Dickinson. 1993. "Fear of Crime: Read All about It? The Relationship between Newspaper Crime Reporting and Fear of Crime." *British Journal of Criminology*, 33, no. 1: 33–56.

Wise, R.A., et al. 2009. "What US Prosecutors and Defence Attorneys Know and Believe about Eyewitness Testimony." *Applied Cognitive Psychology*, 23, no. 9: 1266–81.

Wise, R.A., K. Dauphinais, and M. Safer. 2007. "A Tripartite Solution to Eyewitness Error." *Journal of Criminal Law & Criminology*, 97, no. 3: 807–71.

Witelson, T. 2003. "Declaration of Independence: Examining the Independence of Federal Public Inquiries." In A. Manson and D. Mullan, eds., *Commissions of Inquiry: Praise or Reappraise*. Toronto: Irwin Law.

Witherspoon, P. 2014. "Policy Body Cameras in Missouri: Good or Bad Policy? An Academic Viewpoint Seen through the Lens of a Former Law Enforcement Official." *Missouri Policy Journal*, 2: 35–40.

Wolch, H., and J. McLean. 2004. *In the Matter of the Commission of Inquiry into the Wrongful Conviction of David Edgar Milgaard*. Submissions. http://www.publications.gov.sk.ca/freelaw/Publications_Centre/Justice/Milgaard/FinalSubmissions/341421.pdf.

Wolf, S., and D. Montgomery. 1977. "Effects of Inadmissible Evidence and Level of Judicial Admonishment to Disregard on the Judgments of Mock Jurors." *Journal of Applied Social Psychology*, 7: 205–16.

Wolson, R.J., and A.M. London. 2004. "The Structure, Operation, and Impact of Wrongful Conviction Inquiries: The Sophonow Inquiry as an Example of the Canadian Experience." *Drake Law Review*, 52: 677–93.

Woods, P.M. 2007. "Trace Evidence Examination." In C. Wecht and J. Rago, eds., *Forensic Science and Law: Investigative Applications in Criminal, Civil and Family Justice*. Boca Raton, FL: Taylor and Francis Group. 323–31.

Wright, R., and M. Miller. 2008. "Dead Wrong." *Utah Law Review*, 1: 89–106.

Zacks, R.T., and L. Hasher. 2006. "Aging and Long-Term Memory: Deficits are Not Inevitable." In E. Bialystok and F.I.M. Craik, eds., *Lifespan Cognition: Mechanisms of Change*. New York: Oxford University Press. 162–77.

Zalman, M. 2006. "Criminal Justice System Reform and Wrongful Conviction: A Research Agenda." *Criminal Justice Policy Review*, 17, no. 4: 468–92.

– 2012. "Qualitatively Estimating the Incidence of Wrongful Convictions." *Criminal Law Bulletin*, 48, no. 2: 221–79.

Zalman, M., B. Smith, and A. Kiger. 2008. "Officials' Estimates of the Incidence of 'Actual Innocence' Convictions." *Justice Quarterly*, 25: 72–100.

Zander, M., and P. Henderson. 1993. *Crown Court Study*. Royal Commission on Criminal Justice Research Study No. 19. London: HMSO 1993. 171.

Zehr, H. 2002. *The Little Book of Restorative Justice*. Intercourse, PA: Good Books.

Zellick, G. 2006. "Facing up to Miscarriages of Justice." *Manitoba Law Journal*, 31, no. 3: 555–64.

Zimmerman, C. 1994. "Toward a New Vision of Informants: A History of Abuses and Suggestions for Reform." *Hastings Constitutional Law Quarterly*, 22: 81–178.

Zimring, F. 2003. *The Contradictions of American Capital Punishment*. New York: Oxford University Press.

Index